D1710923

A Breviate of
Parliamentary Papers

SOUTHAMPTON UNIVERSITY STUDIES
IN PARLIAMENTARY PAPERS

A Breviate of

Parliamentary Papers

1900–1916

The Foundation of the Welfare State

P FORD

Professor Emeritus

and

G FORD

University of Southampton

SHANNON IRELAND

1969

First edition Basil Blackwell & Mott Limited Oxford 1957.
This IUP reprint is a revised edition of the original and has
been reproduced by photolithography.

© 1969

Irish University Press Shannon Ireland

Microforms

Microfilm, microfiche and other forms of micro-publishing
© *Irish University Microforms Shannon Ireland*

SBN 7165 0575 4

Irish University Press Shannon Ireland
DUBLIN CORK BELFAST LONDON NEW YORK
Captain TM MacGlinchey Publisher

PRINTED IN THE REPUBLIC OF IRELAND AT SHANNON
BY ROBERT HOGG PRINTER TO IRISH UNIVERSITY PRESS

PREFACE

THIS volume covers the years 1900 to 1916, and thus links up with the *Select List of British Parliamentary Papers 1833–1899* and the *Breviate of Parliamentary Papers 1917–1939*. We have included in a separate section papers relating to Ireland up to the date of the establishment of separate governments in that country, and in an appendix a select list of 'annuals' for the whole period 1900–1939. As a result of two world wars and the difficulties of the years between them, the papers of this exciting period have received less attention than they merit, so that the full extent of the fresh thinking which took place in many fields of public policy has been obscured. It is hoped that this volume will help to open out the great stores of material of historical and modern relevance which these papers contain.

We are grateful for the assistance we have been given by our librarian, Miss D. M. Marshallsay, B.A., A.L.A., and by our clerical staff, Mrs. P. Dunn and Mrs. J. Hunt.

We wish to thank the British Academy for showing their interest in this volume by giving financial assistance to its publication.

We would like to take this opportunity of thanking the Printer for the way he has dealt with the rather special problems involved in setting up this and the other volumes of this series on Parliamentary Papers.

NOTE

FOR an explanation of the principles of selection and methods used in this volume, readers should consult the Introduction to the *Breviate of Parliamentary Papers 1917–1939*, especially pp. xii, xiii. In order to make the story of a particular inquiry or line of investigation intelligible or complete, and to dovetail this volume with that for 1917–1939, we have necessarily sometimes gone outside the limiting dates of the period, and included papers issued before 1900 or after 1916.

INTRODUCTION

THE period of seventeen years from 1900 to 1916 was one of intense activity in Parliamentary investigation. The 1048 reports, etc., here dealt with were produced by over 600 investigating bodies and individuals, including 59 Royal and Vice-Regal Commissions. Some of the reports, with their documentation, are on a massive scale—the Commission on the *Poor Laws* produced 53, those on *Canals* and *Vivisection* 15 and 17 separately numbered papers. The Select Committee of 1906 on *Official Publications* felt that there had been some extravagance and lack of discrimination in printing, a point referred to again by the Committee of 1910 on the *Procedure of Royal Commissions*, which set out the constitutional doctrine of their purpose and procedure. Nevertheless, the papers contain invaluable historical introductions and memoranda by expert witnesses, those by Loch, Mrs. Webb and Smart on the history of the Poor Law (1910 Cd. 4983), by economists on the classification and incidence of taxes (1899 C. 9528) and a report on the history of valuation for rating (1899 C. 9141) being examples of the rich and varied material to be found in them.

What was all this activity about? What problems were they working at? Changed ethical standards led to the Report on *Divorce and Matrimonial Causes*, the demand of new classes to share the administration of justice to that on *The Selection of Justices of the Peace*. Society had to adjust itself to new inventions. Providing for the new motor transport involved learning how to carry petrol through the streets, how to construct and finance new kinds of roads; and a choice had to be made between competing systems of wireless. In the fields of intellectual activity, there were inquiries into the questions of copyright, the piracy of musical publications and the censorship of stage plays. But problems such as these may be regarded as the day-to-day work of a changing society.

As a review of the papers shows, the striking fact about the period is in how many fields of fundamental public policy a searching out of the facts and constructive thinking took place. Of this the subject list of papers included in this volume is evidence. Four groups of papers in particular—those on the machinery of government, the place of labour in society, on social security and on health—illustrate the vigour with which these problems were met.

While some of the inquiries on the machinery of government—those on proportional representation in Parliamentary and municipal elections, and on the reform of the House of Lords—were abortive in the sense that they had no immediate effect on our political structure, others were of great importance. First come the papers on the radical re-organization of the War Office and the administration of military affairs which followed the incompetent muddles of the Boer War. It was but ten years after they were issued that we had to embark on what was up to then the greatest struggle of our history. That defects remained, as the reports on the Dardanelles campaign showed, (see *Breviate 1917–39*, p. 18) is scarcely surprising, for it takes many years to re-organize, re-staff and re-train a great military organization; one wonders what our position would have been in 1914 had the criticisms made in the report been less radical than they were. Next, the Colonial Conferences turn into Imperial Conferences, and though a proposal for an Imperial Defence Council did not survive the objections as to the difficulties of making such a body effective in non-contiguous territories, a scheme of Imperial Federation based on 'Home Rule all round' was seen by some participants in the Irish Conference as one into which self-government for a united Ireland could be fitted. The experiment of the Irish Conference of all parties, called to work out an agreement on the Government of Ireland, eventually broke down, but a glance back at the records of its proceedings might lead some to feel how much, rather than how little progress towards agreement had been made. In the field of local government, the minority of the Royal Commission on *Local Taxation* (1896–1902) faced with the problem of the growing pressure of national services locally administered on the local authorities' exchequers, proposed the famous 'Balfour of Burleigh formula' for central grants to equalize local burdens. This was welcomed by the Poor Law Minority Commissioners, by the members of the Vice-Regal Commission on *Poor Law Reform in Ireland*, and by the Committee on *Local Taxation* (1914) and found final expression in revised form, in the scheme of reform of 1928 (1928 Cmd. 3134, xix.).

The inquiries in the second group were directed to working out the new position of labour in society. To begin with, between 1908 and 1913, an immense effort was made by the Board of Trade to establish the statistical facts about workers' conditions, in six great reports on the comparative cost of living in English, French, Belgian, German and American towns, and in eight reports on earnings and hours in various industries, following two reports on the conditions of agricultural workers. And the Committee on *Home Work*, in recommending experimental trades boards to fix minimum wages in sweated trades, accepted the view that an industry which could not pay its industrious workers a minimum income was parasitic and should not continue. But the centre of interest is, of course, the papers on trade unions and their position in society. They include the report of the Royal Commission, arising out of the Taff Vale judgment, on the liability of trade unions in trade disputes and the rights of picketing; information papers on conciliation and arbitration boards, on profit sharing and co-partnership, and on *Collective Agreements*. In a remarkable report on *Industrial Agreements* (1913) and the problems of securing their fulfilment and enforcement on persons not parties to them, which was in the main assented to by a considerable number of prominent employers and trade unionists, an attempt was made to set out a code of industrial conduct for workers' and employers' organizations. Difficulties the report discussed had already arisen in the railway dispute—(1911 Cd. 5923) and dock dispute (1912–13 Cd. 6367). And the discussion of the relation of the pay of State employees to that of workers in private trade and whether their claim to 'prior consultation' could be sustained in view of the Postmaster-General's responsibility to Parliament, surely foreshadowed problems to come.

Amongst the papers on social security, first place is naturally taken by the Reports of the Royal Commission on the *Poor Laws and the Relief of Distress*. There is no need to emphasize the contribution of the Minority to our thinking on the organization of the labour market, the principles of prevention and universal provision, the break up of the poor law, and the development of the health services. Nevertheless, the Reports are so lengthy and the volumes of evidence, etc. so massive, that, except for the Minority Report, they have suffered from some neglect. The Majority and Minority Reports on Scotland and Ireland show how each group wished to apply their principles, admittedly first worked out for English conditions, to the very different circumstances of those two countries, but the qualities of vision shown in the far-sighted report of the Vice-Regal Commission on *Poor Law Reform in Ireland*, issued only three years earlier, throws into relief both the dangers of such a process and the unimaginative quality of the Majority Report on that country. That as compared with the later Committee on *The Relief of the Casual Poor* (1929–30 Cmd. 3642, xvii) which discussed, not unsympathetically, the 'right to wander', both the Minority of 1909 and the earlier Committee on *Vagrancy* (1906) took a humane but unsentimental view of the vagrant, may no doubt be attributed in part to the fact that he did not fit well into a scientifically organized labour market. The Minority Commissioners' declaration that the qualifying age for the receipt of old age pensions should be reduced to 65 and eventually to 60 reads rather oddly now, when our problem is how to enable older people to go on working: they had not realized the full significance of the expected increase in the numbers of the aged pointed out by the Committee on the *Aged Deserving Poor* (1900). Similarly, some of the reports on the growing pains of the new social security services might have reminded us of the difficulties to expect in our experiments since 1945, e.g. that on excessive sickness claims in the paper on *Sickness Benefit Claims under the National Insurance Act* (1914–16).

There was a similar upsurge of constructive thinking on public health. As in the case of trade and labour conditions, the statistical facts are set out: the report on *Public Health and Social Conditions* (1909) gives many important statistical series extending from 1850–1908. It was from the report on *Physical Deterioration* (1904) that many of the services later established really derived: indeed, it may perhaps be regarded as a blue print of much future legislation. It included recommendations that the local authorities should prohibit overcrowding above a fixed standard of persons per room, should provide open spaces in some proportion to the density of population and preserve 'green belts', should tackle infant mortality by educating mothers and girls; and that the government should fix purity standards for all foods and drinks. Habitually underfed school children should be fed, school children should be periodically inspected medically, and given open-air organized games, and there should be an organized factory medical service. The detailed arrangements for carrying out some of these recommendations were taken up later by other committees of inquiry (e.g. *Medical Inspection and Feeding of School Children attending Elementary Schools*, 1906; *Education (Provision of Meals) Bill*, 1906). The new conception that education involved the care of physical health as well as class-room instruction had already been vigorously explained in *Physical Training (Scotland)* (1903) and necessary steps were set out in *Model Courses of Physical Exercises* (1904) and *Playgrounds of Public Elementary Schools* (1912–13). There were also inquiries into some of the great diseases and disorders, e.g. the *Relations of Human and Animal Tuberculosis, Tuberculosis, Infant and Child Mortality, Feeblemindedness, Venereal Disease*; into the creation of a proper nursing service in Poor Law institutions, and into proposals to register nurses and to increase the supply of qualified midwives in rural areas. Students searching for early versions of the *National Health Service* (1943–44 Cmd. 6502, viii) should go back further than the famous sections in the Minority Report of the Poor Law Commission to the Report of the Vice-Regal Commission *Poor Law Reform in Ireland* (1906) which showed that a salaried medical service was a natural development of Irish history and conditions. The proposal to extend to Ireland medical benefits under the National Insurance Act (1913) so cut across this historical development that the committee concluded that such a state salaried medical service was the only proper solution.

There was, however, one field of public policy in which there were no inquiries and no papers: monetary policy. There was no inquiry into the '*Depression in Trade*', as in 1884–86, or into *Finance and Industry*, as in 1930–31. To begin with, there had been no crises of the magnitude of that of 1873; from 1895 the economy was in a period of rapid growth, and the crises which occurred seemed to be getting weaker, the waves of boom and depression gentler. True, the crisis of 1907 was sharp and the subsequent unemployment deep, though fairly short lived. But from 1910 we were building up into a boom. Then there was no theory of trade cycles; they were thought to be due to causes, some traceable, some obscure, which would certainly continue to operate for a long time (e.g. Beveridge *Unemployment: a Problem of Industry*, 1909, p. 67; Nicholson,

Elements of Economics, 1909, pp. 309–10). The doctrine contained in the papers did not therefore concern monetary policy, but dealt with the other causes of unemployment as then seen, such as seasonal trades, casual labour, chronic under-employment. Attention was thus concentrated on organizing the labour market, e.g. by 'labour exchanges', by regulating demand (which meant public works in depression, not maintaining a high level of employment by monetary means) and by building up an unemployment insurance fund 'ready for the depression that must come in due course' (1913 Cd. 6965, para. 269). Even the depression after the first world war had at first been confused with pre-war cyclical employment and perhaps regarded as a 'delayed trade cycle'. (R. Com. on *Unemployment Insurance*, 1932. Evidence of Price, qq. 18, 23, 123, 138–9). The cure for this central weakness had to be worked out by the economists. It was not till 1913 that Wesley Mitchell showed that depression was bred in prosperity, until 1915 that Hawtrey in *Good and Bad Trade* emphasized the importance of monetary causes, nor till 1944 that the doctrine finally worked out was expounded in a Government White Paper.

As compared with those of the last decade of the nineteenth century, on many subjects the papers show not only the great change of opinion, but a capacity to find a solution where none had been found earlier. The difference between the Final Report of the Committee on *Sweating* (1890 (169) xvii) and that of the Committee on *Home Work* (1908), and between the Final Report of the Labour Commission, which said that 'many of the evils cannot be remedied by legislation, but we may look forward with confidence to their gradual amendment by natural forces now in operation, which tend to substitute a state of industrial peace for one of industrial conflict' (1894 Cd. 7421, xxxv), and those on *Trade Disputes* (1906) and *Industrial Agreements*, (1913), measured the distance thought had travelled.

The committees and commissions were manned by people from all walks of life and the reports record their reasoned answers to the specific questions put to them in their terms of reference. A full history of each reform would be necessary to determine in each case what was contributed by the practical politician, the political philosopher, the voluntary enthusiast, or the noisy malcontent. The 'new experts' also played a part. The civil servant, the medical officer, the education officer had become dynamic elements in society, ever led, irrespective of political philosophies, by their own expertise to enter new fields, to apply new knowledge, to think out how to deal with the new problems arising within their Departments' sphere of responsibility. They appear as members of official committees, as responsible for initiating enquiries, or as expert witnesses. The Committee on *Physical Deterioration* was composed entirely of civil servants, and a large number of the witnesses were 'experts'. It is surely no accident that so many of the great official investigations into labour conditions were undertaken during Llewellyn Smith's tenure of office at the Board of Trade, that Dr. Arthur Newsholme was an important witness before the Poor Law Commission, a member of the committee on *Tuberculosis*, and the author of official reports on *Infant and Child Mortality*. Nor is it irrelevant that some of them, such as Llewellyn Smith and Miss Collet, had had their sympathies and understanding enlarged by work on the Booth surveys, or, like Beveridge, by residence at Toynbee Hall. Then the reports give little indication of the political din going on outside the committee room: to understand that one must couple together the great statistical 'fiscal blue books' with the tariff reform campaign; the reports on the taxation of land values with the Liberal Land Song and Lloyd George's rejected Budget, that on the reform of the House of Lords with the virulent anti-peer cartoons in *Reynolds News* and the Peers' Shilling Defence Fund. Only in the proceedings of the Committee on the 'Marconi Scandals' do the political acerbities of the time show themselves. But the rise in number of trade unionists, only a million and a half in 1892, and still only two millions in 1900, to four millions and a half by 1916, and the election to Parliament in 1906 of 29 Labour and 26 'Lib-Lab' members constituted an inescapable demand for attention to 'the social question'.

The clashes of the party battalions do not fully explain the way the problems are approached, the kind of evidence demanded, the arguments regarded as cogent or the ethical values against which they are judged. For these one must turn to the intellectual history of the time. First, there was heightened awareness of the suffering, deprivation and uncertainty endured by a substantial part of the working population. It was but ten years before the period begins that the private enquiries of Booth and Rowntree and the public enquiries on *Sweating* and the *Aged Poor* had shown what life was like on '*Round About a Pound a Week*' (M. S. Reeves, 1913) and *Across the Bridges* (Paterson, 1911). The literature of social criticism—the novels of Wells and Galsworthy, the plays of Shaw—and the direct attack by Wells in *New Worlds for Old* (1908), emphasized the connection of these evils with social institutions. Next, it was characteristic that an endeavour should be made to establish the precise quantitative facts by large scale statistical investigations into the trade of Britain and her competitors, the resources of the Dominions, wages and earnings in the great industries, the cost of living in this and other countries, and into trends in public health. Thirdly, streams of thought from different sources converged to produce and strengthen an ethical quality in political thinking, a desire to see individual activity in harmony with social good. Religious bodies turned their attention to the problems of 'social righteousness', Peabody's *Jesus Christ and the Social Question* (1901), Rauschenbush's *Christianity and the Social Order* (1912) being typical examples of the endeavour to measure social arrangements by moral standards; Biblical scholarship had been looking anew at the minor prophets, Amos and Hosea, with their emphasis on justice and mercy rather than sacrifice. And a remarkable volume of essays on *Property: its Rights and Duties* (1913) by leading scholars (e.g. Gore, Hobhouse, Rashdall, Lindsay, A. J. Carlyle, H. G. Wood and others) directed attention to the fact that the Church had always regarded the right of property as conditional on the social good, and not as a means of exercising power over others. Fourthly, the spread of scientific economic studies, though not primarily concerned with ethical questions, worked in the same direction. Cannan stressed the importance of distribution according to need and showed that the greatest hindrance to equality was the inheritance of property and the cost of training for better paid occupations. Pigou found circumstances in which the statutory limitation of the hours of work, minimum wages in certain trades, and an increase in the share and stability of the national income received by the poorer classes had sound economic reasoning behind them. It could thus be concluded, e.g. by Hobhouse, that one duty of the State was to guarantee to each individual a share in the common stock, that economic justice implied that each function whether of work or enterprise must be rendered the amount needed to sustain that function, that inherited wealth had less claim to recognition than acquired wealth, and that socially created wealth should belong to the community. These doctrines help to explain the contrast between the Reports of the Select Committees on *Distress from Want of Employment* of 1895–6 and Part II of the Poor Law Minority Report; they appear explicitly in the reports on the taxation of land values and lie behind the distinction between earned and unearned income in that on *Income Tax* (1906 (365)).

The precise weight to be attached to these different influences varies from case to case; and sometimes, no doubt, ideas the members of the committee picked up from those in circulation at the time contributed to form their judgment on what were and what were not acceptable solutions. What the Papers show is groups of men and women of varied experience concentrating on practical tasks and working out the new institutions and practical expedients which carried us into what is known broadly, if not very accurately, as the Welfare State.

ABBREVIATIONS

The following abbreviations have been used:

Committee	Cttee.
Select Committee	Sel. Cttee.
Joint Select Committee	Jt. Sel. Cttee.
Select Committee of House of Lords	Sel. Cttee. HL.
Departmental Committee	Dept. Cttee.
Inter-Departmental Committee	Inter-Dept. Cttee.
Commission	Com.
Royal Commission	R. Com.
Board	Bd.
Report	Rep.
Proceedings	Proc.
Minutes of Evidence	Mins. of ev.
Appendix	App.
Chairman	Ch.
Lord	L.
Delete	del.
Appointed	apptd.
Signed	sgd.
Ordered to be Printed	o.p.
Presented	pres.
Local Government Board	L.G.B.
London County Council	L.C.C.

CONTENTS

SUBJECT CLASSIFICATION OF PAPERS

SUBJECT LIST OF PAPERS

I. MACHINERY OF GOVERNMENT

5. Organization of Departments

6. Civil Service

7. (a) Local Government

6. Coast Erosion, Land Reclamation

7. Commons

8. War Problems: Food Requirements, Production, Prices

V. TRADE AND INDUSTRY

VII. TRANSPORT

VIII. POST OFFICE, TELECOMMUNICATION

1. Post Office

2. Cables, Telephones, Wireless Telegraphy

IX. PATENTS, COPYRIGHT, TRADE MARKS

X. LABOUR

1. Factory and Industrial Regulation

2. Industrial Relations, Trade Disputes

7. Resettlement of Ex-Service Men, Land Settlement

8. Employment of Women

9. Juveniles

10. Migration, Employment, War Refugees

11. Professions

XI. SOCIAL SECURITY

1. Poor Law

2. Unemployment Insurance

3. Health Insurance

3. Particular Problems and Diseases

4. Food Purity, Drugs, Patent Medicines

3. Teachers' Salaries and Training

4. Universities, Scientific Institutions

5. Galleries, Museums, Public Records

XV. SOCIAL PROBLEMS

1. Children

2. Charities

A Breviate of
PARLIAMENTARY PAPERS, 1900-1916

I. MACHINERY OF GOVERNMENT

1. Crown, Peerage, etc.
2. Imperial Relations, Government of Isle of Man
3. Parliament
4. Ministers
5. Organization of Departments
6. Civil Service
7. (a) Local Government
   (b) Local Taxation and Financial Administration
8. London

1. CROWN, PEERAGE, Etc.

Osborne Estate

Committee appointed by The King. Rep. pp. 3. 1902

1902 *Cd.* 1384, *lxxxiii*, 717
sgd. Dec., 1902

L. Esher, Probyn, Hamilton, McDonnell, Ward, Laking, Treves, Tyrwhitt, Horner.

'*To consider the disposition of His Majesty's Osborne Estate in the Isle of Wight.*'

'We humbly recommend for Your Majesty's approval the following proposals:—(1) That the Osborne Estate should be transferred to the care partly of the Office of Woods, and partly to the Office of Works: the respective spheres of influence to be settled by the Departments concerned. (2) That the Park and Woods adjoining the Sea Front should not be treated as Land bearing Revenue Estate: that your Majesty's Government should be requested to take whatever steps may be necessary to secure this; and that the Office of Woods, and Office of Works, should arrange the Boundary of the Osborne Estate as apportioned in the Plan to the care of the Departments respectively. (3) That having heard representatives of the Navy and Army, and of the Medical Departments of these Services, we venture to recommend your Majesty to approve the appropriation of Osborne, with the exception of that portion of the House reserved by Your Majesty, to the uses of the Navy and Army, as a Convalescent Home for Officers, the details of the Scheme to be drawn up by Representatives of the Admiralty, the War Office and the Office of Works. (4) We further recommend that the Stables and Cricket Ground be utilized as a Gymnasium and Recreation Ground for the Naval Cadets of the Training Ship, in future to be stationed off the Isle of Wight. All of which we submit for Your Majesty's Gracious consideration.'

'I entirely approve of the recommendations of the Committee. (Signed) Edward R., 6th December 1902.'

Civil List

Sel. Cttee. Rep., proc., apps. pp. xx.
1910

1910 (211) *vi*, 315
apptd. June, o.p. July, 1910

The Prime Minister and twenty other members.

'*To consider His Majesty's most Gracious Message of the 14th June with regard to the Civil List and the provision to be made for the Members of the Royal Family.'*

The total provision made for the Royal Family at the death of Her late Majesty was £576,000; the provision for the present reign is £634,000. The increase is due to arrangements made in 1901 to provide for Queen Alexandra on the death of King Edward VII.

Titles, etc., held by Enemies Bill [H.L.]

Sel. Cttee. HL. Rep., proc. pp. v. 1917

1917 (HL. 44) v, 19
apptd. March, o.p. May, 1917

Lord Dunedin (*Ch.*), L. Camperdown, L. Bryce, L. Brodrick, L. Barrymore, L. Atkinson, L. Sanderson, L. Weardale, L. Stuart.

Enquiries based on historical research showed that '(1) a Peerage cannot be forfeited or affected except by Act of Parliament; (2) mere alienage is not inconsistent with the holding of a Peerage; (3) so long as a person is a Peer he has a right to demand a writ of Summons, even although when he presented himself he would not be allowed to sit if he refused to take the oath of allegiance; (4) there is precedent for Parliament dealing with the Peerage of a person espousing the cause of the King's enemies, irrespective of the question of whether such person could be convicted of Treason; (5) even in the case of Treason the Act 33 & 34 Vic., cap. 23, has provided that the descendants of the convicted Peer should not suffer.'

'As regards the title of Prince, . . . with the exception of the eldest son of the Sovereign who is in use to be created Prince of Wales by Letters Patent, and who is by birth Prince of Scotland, there is no title of Prince conferring any legal status as such. By long custom the children and grandchildren of the Sovereign have been known under this title. Further, the title has been recognized in various Royal Warrants and Letters Patent dealing with the question of precedence and appellation of Highness.'

Baronetage

Dept. Cttee. Rep., apps. pp. iii, 14. 1907

1907 Cd. 3445, *lxvii*, 79
apptd. Nov., 1905. *sgd. Dec.,* 1906

Lord Pembroke (*Ch.*), Maxwell, Harington, Temple, Cunynghame, Renshaw.

'To consider and report whether any, and if so what, steps should be taken to safeguard the status of the holders of Baronetcies, and to prevent the assumption of the title Baronet by persons who have no right thereto.'

A number of persons had assumed the title of baronet either wrongfully or on a doubtful basis. An official roll of baronets should be compiled and the machinery for settling peerage claims could be used. The Warrants of 1783, 1785 and 1789 should be cancelled but the registration of pedigree preserved.

2. IMPERIAL RELATIONS, GOVERNMENT OF ISLE OF MAN

Colonial and Imperial Conferences

The subjects discussed by the Colonial Conferences of 1902 and 1907, and the Imperial Conference of 1911 included consultation with the Dominions overseas before making treaties with foreign powers, an Imperial Defence Parliament, increased Dominion contributions to the Navy, Imperial preference and a state-owned chain of wireless stations.

The chief documents of the series are: 1902 Cd. 1299, lxvi.   1903 Cd. 1597, xliv.   1907 Cd. 3523, Cd. 3524, lv. 1911 Cd. 5745, Cd. 5746–1, Cd. 5746–2, liv.

Constitution, etc., of the Isle of Man

Dept. Cttee. Rep. pp. 31. 1911. Mins. of ev., apps., index. 1912

1911 Cd. 5950, *xxix* Pt. I, 631.   *Mins. of ev., etc.;* 1912–13 Cd. 6026, *xxxiv,* 585 *apptd. April, sgd. Aug.,* 1911

Lord MacDonnell (*Ch.*), Adkins, Byrne, Primrose, Wilkins.

'*To enquire into the petition of the House of Keys of the 27th February 1907, and into the representations made to His Majesty's Government respecting the constitution of the Isle of Man and the civil, judicial, and financial administration of the Island; and to report whether any, and if so what, alterations are desirable and practicable.*'

The Government of the Island consisted of a Crown-appointed Lieutenant-Governor, who possessed the power of veto, a Legislative Council, the House of Keys, and the Tynwald Court. The constitution had been revised in 1866 but members of the House of Keys were dissatisfied with it, in particular the unrepresentative character of the Legislative Council. A petition was presented in 1907. Recommendations are made affecting the Keys, Tynwald, and the administration of justice. The post of Lieutenant-Governor should be for a definite term of years; and four of the members of the Council should be elected by the Keys from among their members or from the body of electors.

If certain financial recommendations were carried out Tynwald should have sufficient funds to finance schemes of administrative and social improvement, without special Imperial aid. In a memorandum, W. R. Adkins disagreed with some of the conclusions on finance on the ground that the additional funds raised by further taxation and full expenditure of the year's revenue would fall short of the current needs for educational, economic, and social developments, and recommended an annual grant of £5,000 for eight years.

3. PARLIAMENT

The Presence of the Sovereign in Parliament

Jt. Sel. Cttee. Rep., proc., mins. of ev., app. pp. xx, 71. 1901

1901 (212) *vii*, 213
apptd. March, o.p. June, 1901

L. Spencer (*Ch.*), Akers-Douglas, Hart-Dyke, Gladstone, Holland, Lowther, L. Cholmondeley, L. Howe, L. Carrington, L. Rathmore.

'*To consider the accommodation available in the House of Lords when the Sovereign is personally present in Parliament, and the advisability of substituting Westminster Hall on such an occasion for the House of Lords.*'

The Committee began by examining Mr. Tritton, M.P., and Sir H. Fowler, M.P., who tried to follow the Speaker to the House of Lords when the King opened Parliament on 14th February, 1901. Neither succeeded in getting in and Mr. Tritton was severely injured owing to the overpowering rush of members.

With the exception of the Peers, Judges and Members of the House of Commons, no person can claim a right to be present at ceremonies in Parliament when the Sovereign is present. Suggestions were made to transfer the ceremony to Westminster Hall, but it was thought that before this was done a fair trial should be made of the accommodation in the House of Lords. Recommendations were made for removing furniture, etc., to make room for the number of people who would wish to follow the Speaker 'in dignity and comfort'.

Palace of Westminster

Sel. Cttee. HL.

Lord Stanmore (*Ch.*), L. Cholmondeley, L. Carlisle, L. Brownlow, L. Lytton, L. Plymouth, L. Denman.

'*To enquire and report with respect to the unfinished condition of the Rooms in the Palace of Westminster appropriated to the service of this House, and their Approaches.*'

The first Report is a formal presentation of the minutes of evidence, etc.; 1906 (HL. 256) ix, 317.

—— Second Report, proc., mins. of ev., app. pp. xx, 22. 1907

1907 (*HL.* 104) (104–*Ind.*) *vii*, 457
re-apptd. Feb., o.p. July, 1907

In 1841 a Royal Commission presided over by H.R.H. Prince Albert, recommended a scheme of decoration for the Palace of Westminster for the 'purpose of promoting and encouraging the Fine Arts in our United Kingdom . . .' (1841 (423) vi). The work was continued until 1861, the year of the death of the Prince Consort. So active and zealous had been the Prince that it was thought that the appointment of any one to take his place 'would be repugnant to the feelings of Her late Majesty', and the Commission was brought to an end. Since that date no similar decorations had been done. The general result of the Committee's investigations throughout the building is 'that of the 161 panels which it was intended to fill with painting, only 57 have been so filled. Of the statues, 23 have been executed and 27 have yet to be provided'. In the survey no account was taken of all the many hundreds of square feet which the Fine Arts Commission had intended to employ as surface for painting.

It was recommended that, in the main, the 1847 plan should be carried out; that a small Advisory Committee should be appointed to watch over the work and report progress and that an annual sum of £4,000 should be allocated for the work.

House of Lords

Sel. Cttee. HL. Rep., proc., apps.
pp. xlii. 1908

1908 (HL. 234) x, 111
apptd. Jan., o.p. Dec., 1908

Lord Rosebery (Ch.), L. Archbishop of Canterbury, L. Norfolk, L. Bedford, L. Devonshire, L. Northumberland, L. Landsdowne, L. Jersey, L. Lauderdale, L. Onslow, L. Cawdor, L. Camperdown, L. Lytton, L. Halsbury, L. Selby, L. St. Aldwyn, L. Clinton, L. Brodrick, L. Ribblesdale, L. Belper, L. Kenry, L. Newton, L. Curzon, L. Courtney, L. Collins.

'*Further to consider the suggestions which have from time to time been made for increasing the efficiency of the House of Lords in matters affecting legislation, and to report as to the desirability of adopting them either in their original or in some modified form.*'

The various proposals which have been made from time to time for increasing the efficiency of the House of Lords have been based on the assumption that it was advisable to modify its hereditary character. The three main grounds for the assumption were '(i) That the numbers of the House within recent years have increased so largely that some reduction for legislative purposes is expedient; (ii) That it is desirable to relieve from their Parliamentary duties Peers to whom such work is irksome and ill-suited, but to whom it has come inevitably by inheritance; and (iii) That it is necessary in the interests of the House itself to eliminate by a process of selection Peers whom it is inexpedient for various reasons to entrust with legislative responsibilities'.

Except in the case of Peers of the Blood Royal, the Committee thought it undesirable that the possession of a Peerage should of itself give the right to sit and vote in the House of Lords; in future the dignity of a Peer and the dignity of a Lord of Parliament should be separate and distinct, the latter carrying with it a right to sit and vote which the former would not. The Committee were divided into three different schools of thought; two of which thought the basis of reform should be direct election by hereditary Peers, with the addition of a limited number of life Peers, while the third thought the basis should be qualification by experience in affairs, with the inclusion of some delegates of the hereditary Peerage and of life Peers. The Committee accepted the principle of qualification, and made proposals for the representation of the hereditary Peerage and for life Peerages. All hereditary Peers should be formed into an electoral body for the purposes of electing from among them 200 Lords of Parliament to sit and vote during the life of a Parliament. The Episcopal representatives should number ten—two Archbishops and eight elected bishops. Qualified Peers should include Peers who have held high office at home or abroad, e.g. a Cabinet Minister; a Governor General of a Dominion; any Peer who has held a high Judicial Office or has succeeded to a Peerage after ten years in the House of Commons or has been created a Peer after twenty years in the House of Commons, etc., should be entitled to receive a writ of summons to the House of Lords.

The Crown should be empowered to summon annually as Lords of Parliament four Peers for life, three of whom should have held high office, but the total number of life Peerages existing at any one time should not exceed forty. Under such arrangements there would be 350 members: '3 Peers of the Blood Royal, 200 representatives elected by the hereditary Peers, 130 qualified hereditary Peers, 10 Spiritual Lords of Parliament, and 5 Lords of Appeal in Ordinary. To these must be added a possible annual increment of 4 Peers for life, up to the number of 40, thus bringing the total number of the House to something under 400'. A signed statement of willingness to sit should be required; absence without leave should cause the seat to be vacant, and a Lord of Parliament should be able to resign his seat. The party in power in the House of Commons should be able to count on a substantial following in the House of Lords. Flooding the House with permanent Peerages was no remedy nor was the summoning of Peers chosen because they supported the Government of the day. The Committee was divided on representation of County Councils and Municipal Corporations.

Redistribution of Seats at Parliamentary Elections

Cttee. Rep. and Supplementary Rep. pp. 41 [1906]

1906 (79) xcvi, 113
apptd. Aug., sgd. Oct., Nov., 1905

D. A. Johnston (Ch.), Glen, Thomas

'To inquire and report—(a) As to the changes of boundaries which would be necessary or advisable for the purpose of giving effect to the principles of a Scheme of Redistribution based on the general Rules set out in the Memorandum of the President of the Local Government Board, dated the 10th July, 1905; and (b) Whether any division or re-division of any County or Borough is necessary or advisable for that purpose or for the purpose of remedying any considerable disparity in the population of the divisions of that County or Borough.'

The chief rules set out in the President's Memorandum were that the total number of members should not be materially increased, that boroughs and urban districts should not be given separate representation unless they had a population of 65,000, while those with less than 18,500 should lose it. Counties and boroughs with more than one member should have their representation adjusted in relation to the rule of one member for each 65,000 population. The Parliamentary and administrative boundaries of counties and boroughs should as far as possible be co-terminous. No general revision of boundaries of divisions of counties and boroughs was intended, but only such alterations as were required to give effect to the rules or where there was a considerable disparity of population. The raising of the minimum population required for separate representation to 25,000 was to be investigated. The rules were not to be interpreted too rigidly. The Committee presented the results of one scheme (C) worked out in detail, together with a description of five other schemes, and a comparative statement of the effect of all of them.

Existence of Corrupt Practices at the last Election for the City of Worcester

R. Com. Vol. I. Rep. pp. iii, 7. 1906.
Vol. II. Mins. of ev. 1906

1906 *Cd.* 3268, *xcv*, 473.   *Mins. of ev.*;
1906 *Cd.* 3269, *xcv*, 485
apptd. July, sgd. Nov. 1906

E. T. Atkinson (*Ch.*), Avory, Mathews.

'*To inquire into the existence of corrupt practices at the last Parliamentary Election for the City of Worcester.*'

The election of January 1906 had been declared void, following a petition against the return of the Conservative candidate. A bribable class numbering about 500 existed and systematic corrupt practices had been committed in the January election. On that occasion it was the Conservative workers who engaged in bribery; there was no evidence that the Liberals had taken part in such proceedings. But corruption had taken place since 1883, and the abstention of the Liberals was dated from 1904.

See *Election Petition.* Notes of the Judgment and mins. of ev. taken at the trial; 1906 (198) xcv, 255.

Electoral Systems

R. Com. Rep., apps. pp. iv, 63. 1910
    Mins. of ev. 1910

1910 *Cd.* 5163, *xxvi*, 295. *Mins. of ev.*;
1910 *Cd.* 5352, *xxvi*, 363
apptd. Dec., 1908. *sgd.* —

R. F. Cavendish (*Ch.*), Lord Lochee, Montagu, Hopwood, Ilbert, Eliot, Reeves, Hills.

'*To examine the various schemes which have been adopted or proposed, in order to secure a fully representative character for popularly elected legislative bodies: and to consider whether, and how far, they, or any of them, are capable of application in this country in regard to the existing electorate.*'

The enquiry was confined to methods of actual election. At the time of the redistribution of seats in 1885 the principle of minority representation was rejected, but it was widely believed that the single member constituency would effect a close relation between the number of votes cast for a party and its representation in Parliament. This had not been the result and there was a demand for a review of the position. The proposals could be classified into three groups: those for redistribution on a basis of equal electoral districts, those for absolute majority systems, and those for proportional representation. On the first there was nothing to suggest that the varying size of constituencies accounted for exaggerated majorities; schemes for proportional representation, while giving mathematically more accurate results than the existing system, only partially achieved their ideal and were not suited to English conditions. The transferable vote was open to objection because of the size of the constituency, the difficulty of bye-elections and the undue effect of late preferences. Lochee disagreed with this conclusion on the transferable vote, which he maintained was the simplest and the best system.

Only two of the absolute majority systems were feasible, the second ballot and the alternative vote methods. The former involved no change in the practice of recording votes, and eliminated the possibility of the least popular candidate being elected, but the practical difficulties of having two successive elections, led the Committee to reject it. The defects of the alternative vote system were carefully considered, but it remained the best method of eliminating the return of minority candidates and its adoption in single member constituencies was recommended. Two member constituencies should be abolished as soon as possible. See Memoranda handed in during evidence by Mr. J. Humphreys, mins. of ev., pp. 33–43.

Electoral Reform

Conference. Letter from Mr. Speaker (J. W. Lowther) to the Prime Minister.
        pp. 8. 1917

1917–18 *Cd.* 8463, *xxv*, 385
Jan. 1917

'To examine, and, if possible, submit, agreed resolutions on the following matters: (a) Reform of the Franchise. (b) Basis for Redistribution of Seats. (c) Reform of the System of the Registration of Electors. (d) Method of elections and the manner in which the costs of elections should be borne.'

The desire for a conference had been expressed in a debate in the Commons in August 1916, and the Speaker convened the conference consisting of Members and Peers whom he selected as representative of the various shades of political opinion. The resolutions passed by the Conference included recommendations for a uniform franchise: every person of full age who, for a qualifying period of six months had resided in, or occupied for purposes of business, profession or trade, premises of the value of £10 or more p.a. could be registered. Seventy-thousand was to be taken as the standard unit of population for each member of the House of Commons, but the City and a modified University representation were to continue. A majority of the conference decided that woman suffrage should be granted to women on the Local Government Register who had reached the age of 30 or 35.

A Parliamentary borough which would be entitled on a basis of population to return three or more members should be a single constituency, in which elections should be based on proportional representation and each elector should have a transferable vote. When there were more than two candidates in a single member constituency the alternative vote system should be used. There were recommendations on candidates' deposits and expenses. The growing practice during an election of political and other organizations incurring expenditure to further the views of a particular candidate was a contravention of the spirit of the Corrupt and Illegal Practices Prevention Act. The law should be amended to make this a corrupt practice unless the expenditure were authorized and duly returned by the candidate.

Boundary Commission (England and Wales). (Representation of the People Bill, 1917. Redistribution of Seats)

Vol. I. Rep., apps. pp. 16. 1917.
Vol. II. Schedule (Pt. I). 1917.
Vol. III. Schedule (Pt. II). 1917.

1917–18 Cd. 8756, xiii, 1. Schedules; 1917–18 Cd. 8757, Cd. 8758, xiii, 17 apptd. May, sgd. Sept., 1917

The Speaker (J. W. Lowther, Ch.), Provis, Elliott, Close, Jerred.

'To determine, for the purposes of the Representation of the People Bill about to be introduced by His Majesty's Government, the number of members to be assigned to the several counties and boroughs in England and Wales and the boundaries of such counties and boroughs and divisions.'

The instructions (App. A.) to the Commissioners had been amended by a Resolution of the Commons (App. B). The amendments gave the Commissioners a degree of discretion in determining the boundaries and population of Parliamentary constituencies. This discretion was used sparingly since (a) the general rules were elastic in that the standard unit of 70,000 population per constituency was in some cases reduced to 50,000, (b) the number of M.P.s was to remain much the same, and (c) a wide departure from the rules would have increased the disparity between the populations of different constituencies. The latter were, as far as possible, to coincide with administrative areas, of which the urban and rural districts were chosen as the unit.

The general effect of the determinations was to increase the number of members for England and Wales from 490 to 520, the largest increase going to English boroughs outside London, and to reduce the average population per member from 73,613 to 71,078. While the average population per county member was reduced considerably in England, and to a less extent in Wales, that of Welsh boroughs and of English boroughs outside

London was enhanced. The average population per member of London boroughs was decreased.

Boundary Commission (Scotland). (Representation of the People Bill, 1917. Redistribution of Seats)

Rep., app. pp. 8. 1917

1917–18 *Cd.* 8759, *xiv*, 47
apptd. May, sgd. Sept., 1917

The Speaker (J. W. Lowther, *Ch.*), L. Dundas, MacDougall, Close, Jerred, Shennan.

'*To determine, for the purposes of the Representation of the People Bill, the number of members to be assigned to the several counties and burghs in Scotland and the boundaries of such counties and burghs and divisions thereof.*'

The instructions (App. A) to the Commissioners had been amended by a Resolution of the Commons (App. B). The discretion afforded by the amendments had enabled a fairer representation for the Highlands and Islands. The general effect of the determinations was to increase the number of members for Scotland from 70 to 71, and to reduce the average population per member from 68,013 to 66,862. The Parliamentary burghs gained two members, while the Parliamentary counties lost one seat. The average population per member of the burghs was increased, of the counties, decreased.

Vacation of Seat (Member Holding Contract).

Sel. Cttee. Special Rep. pp. 2. 1913.
Special Rep. pp. iii. 1913. Special Rep., proc., app. pp. xxxiii. 1913

1912–13 (379) (406) (452) *ix*, 451
apptd. Nov., o.p. Nov., Dec., 1912, *Jan.*, 1913

Prime Minister (*Ch.*), Butcher, Hohler, Lyttelton, Macdonald, MacNeill, Pollock, Solicitor-General, Wason.

'*To consider whether Sir Stuart Samuel has vacated his seat as a Member of this House in consequence of the firm of Samuel Montagu and Company, in which firm he is a partner, having entered into transactions with the Secretary of State for India in Council.*'

In a Special Report (379) of 27th November, the Committee asks leave of the House to hear Counsel to such extent as they think fit. A further Special Report (406) of 19th December, states that difficult questions of law arose, on some of which unanimity was impossible; the Committee asks if the House, whilst reserving the rights of ultimate decision, wished to refer the questions of law to the Judicial Committee of the Privy Council. Special Report (452) states that Sir Stuart Samuel, member of Tower Hamlets (Whitechapel), was at all material times a partner in the firm of Samuel Montagu and Company, which entered into a number of financial transactions with the Secretary of State for India.

Private Business

Sel. Cttee. Rep., proc., mins. of ev., apps., index. pp. xxii, 231. 1902

1902 (378) *vii*, 321
apptd. May, o.p. Nov., 1902

A. F. Jeffreys (*Ch.*), Brand, Flynn, Hobhouse, Jones, Renshaw, Worsley-Taylor.

'*To inquire whether, in view of the time at which Private Business is taken under the Resolution of 1st May 1902, any alterations in Standing Orders are desirable in the interests of economy, efficiency, and general convenience.*'

Standing Orders should be amended so as to reduce both loss of time and unnecessary expenditure. Petition for leave to introduce a Bill and the first reading stage should be dispensed with. Reduction of fees and the amalgamation of the two Private Bill Offices should be considered, General Public Health legislation brought up to date, the

Court of Referees reconstituted and given power to award costs, and other changes made in procedure. To ensure the proper examination of unopposed Bills the Deputy Chairman should be a salaried official of the House and with the aid of a panel of four members, be responsible for all Private Business.

Private Legislation Procedure (Wales) Bill

Sel. Cttee. Reps., proc., mins. of ev., apps. index. pp. xvi, 244. 1904

1904 (243) *vi*, 409
apptd. April, o.p. July, 1904

A. F. Jeffreys (*Ch.*), Cripps, Vaughan-Davies, Ellis, Hobhouse, Jones, Redmond, Smith, Wason, Worsley-Taylor, Wyndham-Quin.

'*To inquire and report upon the working in Scotland, under The Private Legislation Procedure (Scotland) Act*, 1899, *of the scheme proposed in the Bill, and upon the expediency of extending the provisions of the Bill, with or without modifications, to other parts of the United Kingdom.*'

The Private Legislation Procedure (Scotland) Act, 1899, had, on the whole, worked successfully, and this was largely due to the work of the Scottish Office. As Wales did not possess this machinery, the Scottish procedure should not be adopted there, but Welsh needs should be met by some adaptation of the principles of the Scottish Act, viz. local enquiry, and the devolution of powers to some competent tribunal. Any extension of the system of local enquiry would have to be accompanied by the effective control of Parliament, and the complete absence of personal interests or local prejudice on the part of those conducting the enquiry. The Bill was reported without amendment.

House of Commons (Procedure)

Sel. Cttee. 1st and 2nd Reps., proc., mins. of ev., apps., index. pp. xxii, 87. 1906

1906 (89) (181) *viii*, 429
apptd. Feb., o.p. March, May, 1906

H. Fowler (*Ch.*), Blake, Craig, Akers-Douglas, Ellis, Evans, Forster, Keir Hardie, Hardy, Leese, M'Crae, Redmond, Whitley, Wood, Woodhouse.

'*To consider the question of Procedure in the House of Commons, and to report as to the amendment of the existing Rules and upon any new Rules which they may consider desirable for the efficient despatch of business.*'

There should be single sittings beginning at 3 p.m. and ending at 11.30 p.m., except for Unopposed or certain Exempted Business. There should be an informal suspension ending at 8.30 p.m. and 12.30 a.m. should be substituted for 1 a.m. Sittings on Fridays should end at 5 p.m. Questions should commence immediately Private Business is disposed of, or in any case at 3.15 p.m. and end at 4 p.m. with certain exceptions. Postponed Private Business should commence at 8.30 p.m. The Chairman or Deputy Chairman of Ways and Means should be empowered to take the Chair as Deputy Speaker under Standing Order No. 1. Unofficial Members' Motions and Bills should be given precedence at 8.30 p.m. but no opposed Private Business other than that under consideration should be taken after 9.45 p.m. Mr. Speaker was the only witness.

—— Second Report

After the second reading any Bill other than a finance Bill or Bills confirming provisional orders should stand committed to one of the Standing Committees, of which there should be not less than four. The Bills should be distributed amongst the Committees by Mr. Speaker, and in all but one Standing Committee Government Bills should have precedence.

Procedure (Anticipatory Motions)

Sel. Cttee. Rep., proc., mins. of ev., app. pp. vi, 19. 1907

1907 (264) *vii*, 519
apptd. July, o.p. July, 1907

Chancellor of the Exchequer (*Ch.*), L. Robert Cecil, Ellis, Fenwick, Forster, Jones, O'Connor, Seely, Shackleton.

'*To consider and report upon the Procedure of the House in relation to Anticipatory Motions and Bills.*'

The 'rule against anticipation' 'rests for its authority, not upon any Standing Order, but upon usage and a body of decisions given from the Chair. It was originally intended to serve a useful purpose—namely, to prevent any Member from unfairly forestalling the discussion of a matter which another Member had already given notice of his intention to bring before the House by Motion or Bill. But it has, in practice, been developed in such a way as to have an almost exactly opposite effect—namely, to enable a Member, by giving such a Notice, to prevent any effective discussion of the matter at all.' It would be brought back to its original purpose 'if it were laid down that the discussion of a matter should not be ruled out of order on the ground of anticipation, unless there was, in the opinion of the Chair, a probability of the matter anticipated being brought before the House within a reasonable time.'

It was recommended that as the rule was supposed to be a safeguard against the abuse of the power of moving the adjournment, Standing Order 10 be amended by adding at the end: 'When a Motion so stands over the proceedings under discussion at a quarter-past eight may be resumed and proceeded with, though opposed, after the interruption of business.' A new Standing Order should be adopted to the following effect: 'In determining whether a discussion is out of order on the ground of anticipation, regard shall be had by Mr. Speaker to the probability of the matter anticipated being brought before the House within a reasonable time.' This history of the rule is given in a Memo. by Sir Courteney Ilbert, Clerk of the House.

Local Legislation

Sel. Cttee. Reps.

'*To whom were referred all Private Bills promoted by Municipal and other Local Authorities, by which it is proposed to create powers relating to Police, Sanitary or other Local Government Regulations in conflict with, deviation from or excess of the Provisions of the General Law.*'

1909 (260) *viii*, 249.   1910 (323) *vi*, 521.   1911 (260) *vii*, 477.   1912–13 (347) *vii*, 537.   1913 (267) *vii*, 41. 1914 (432) *viii*, 47.   1914–16 (342) *iv*, 161.   1916 (79) *iii*, 595.

A series of reports (1909–1916) on Private Bills promoted by local authorities which proposed to create powers in conflict with, deviating from or in excess of the provisions of the general law. Amongst the decisions of the Committee were: power to close unnecessary streets refused, as this should be obtainable under general law, whose provisions should be revised (1909 (260)); Keighley was granted powers to run trackless trolleys on roads outside its boundary on payment of one-third the cost of road widening, but was not required to contribute to the repair of roads (1912–13 (347)); but Sheffield obtained powers to run motor buses on roads outside its boundary, on a payment which included one-third the cost of upkeep of such roads; it was anomalous to make local authorities contribute to upkeep, but not private enterprise (1914 (432)). The Committee recommended that an authority should be constituted to decide which should be the main roads of the country and if their maintenance should be from taxes and not rates (1912–13 (347) 1914 (432)). The clauses of an L.C.C. Bill relating to cinematograph films, celluloid, etc., because of the danger from fire, were referred to another Select Committee, which approved them but recommended early general legislation (1914 (432)). A clause frequently allowed requiring means of escape from fire in case of buildings over a certain height, and applying to taverns, hotels, schools, boarding houses, etc., was also granted to apply to shop premises where sleeping accommodation for staff was provided. General legislation was desirable (1913 (267)). Liverpool was granted powers to 'cope with sectarian disturbances, to make byelaws respecting meetings and processions, and to prohibit weapons, emblems or inflammatory music (1912–13 (347)). East Ham applied by Bill for county borough powers after they had been refused by the L.G.B. after inquiry. The Committee also refused, but arranged that an appeal should be made to the House, which re-committed the Bill and the Committee re-inserted the clauses (1913 (267)). A local authority whose powers are scattered over many local acts should consolidate its legislation (1913 (267) 1914 (432)). The time had come for embodying in the general law a number of clauses on police and sanitary matters which have now become common form clauses (1914 (432)).

Police and Sanitary Committee
Sel. Cttee. Reports

'The Select Committee to whom were referred all Private Bills promoted by Municipal and other Local Authorities by which it is proposed to create powers relating to Police or Sanitary Regulations in conflict with, deviation from, or excess of the provisions of the general Law' issued 23 reports between the years 1882 and 1909.

Imprisonment of a Member
Sel. Cttee. Reps., procs., mins. of ev., app. pp. xvi, 35. 1902

1902 (309) *vi,* 5
apptd. June, o.p. July, 1902

A. J. Balfour (*Ch.*), Attorney General, Attorney General for Ireland, Atherley-Jones, Campbell-Bannerman, Cochrane, Dorington, Hart-Dyke, Halsey, Mac-Neill, Powell, Redmond (J.), Redmond (W.), Robertson, Walton, Wharton, Wodehouse.

'*For the purpose of inquiring into all the matters connected with the Proceedings referred to therein, and of reporting whether they demand the further attention of the House.*'

McHugh had been charged at Sligo under the Criminal Law and Procedure (Ireland) Act, 1887 and had insulted the Magistrates, who had imprisoned him for three months until he found surety for good behaviour. As McHugh was in gaol and unable to appear before the Committee, in a Special Report it recommended that the House should take the necessary steps to secure his attendance. The Committee reported that there was no distinction to be drawn between cases of criminal contempt and other indictable offences, and the privilege of Parliament did not extend to such cases.

Privileges
Cttee. Rep. pp. iii. 1909

1909 (281) *viii,* 349
o.p. Sept., 1909

'*To inquire into an alleged breach of privilege by the Duke of Norfolk.*'

It was alleged that the Duke of Norfolk had infringed the sessiona order relating to the interference of Peers and Prelates in Elections by writing to Mr. Profumo, a Parliamentary candidate for the High Peak Division of Derbyshire, wishing him success. In view of precedents, the letter was not such a breach of the order as called for further action on the part of the House.

—— Report, proc., mins. of ev., apps. pp. viii, 7. 1911

1911 (153) *vii,* 631
o.p. May, 1911

Prime Minister (*Ch.*), Attorney-General, Balfour, Lockwood, MacNeill, Parker, Wason.

'*To inquire into alleged breaches of privileges by the Earl of Roden and by the Earl of Aberdeen.*'

The Earl of Roden was under the impression that as his name was on the Register, he was entitled to vote. He did contravene a Sessional Resolution, but in view of his explanation, it was recommended that no action should be taken.

The Earl of Aberdeen, in the election of 1910, sent the following telegram to the candidate for the West Division of Aberdeen: 'On Home Rule for Ireland I repeat and emphasize the opinion of my former telegrams, especially regarding apprehension of religious intolerance. Numerous Protestant ministers in Roman Catholic parts of Ireland support me in this view.' He did not use his authority as Lord-Lieutenant of Aberdeenshire to influence the election and therefore did not commit a breach of the privileges of the House.

Procedure of Royal Commissions

Dept. Cttee. Rep. pp. 16.   1910

1910 *Cd.* 5235, lviii, 371
apptd. April, 1909. *sgd. June,* 1910

Lord Balfour of Burleigh (*Ch.*), L. Radnor, Byrne, Ashton, Hobhouse.

'*To consider what should be the procedure of Royal Commissions in regard to the arrangement of business, the selection and reception of evidence, the decision of questions arising on the terms of reference, and any other matters of order and procedure, with special reference to the duties and powers of the Chairman in regard thereto.*'

Royal Commissions are useful for elucidating difficult subjects in which there is insufficient accurate information, but should not be appointed when there is no prospect of early legislation. They are valuable in so far as they express the agreement of competent minds after full and impartial enquiry, and their reports are valuable in proportion to the extent to which their unanimous recommendations cover the whole field. The persons appointed should not be so deeply committed on the question as to render impartial enquiry and a unanimous report impossible. When these conditions are disregarded the Commissioners are apt to divide into parties. Minority reports should be confined to a statement of differences and to giving only such evidence as may be necessary to support the alternative conclusions. In addition to the Circular of Instructions already issued by the Treasury and the Home Office, the procedure of Commissioners should be guided by certain general principles which should be embodied in a circular sent to the Chairman and Commissioners simultaneously with the terms of reference. A draft circular and the report deal with the functions of the Chairman, oral evidence and other methods of investigation, the functions and appointment of the Secretary, the confidential character of the proceedings of the Commission, etc. A proposal for a permanent staff for Royal Commissions was rejected.

Publications and Debates

Sel. Cttee. Reports

In 1906 it was recommended 'that a Sessional Committee be appointed to supervise the amount of matter printed and the distribution of publications, and to assist Mr. Speaker'. From 1906 to 1916 these sessional reports deal mainly with the details of printing, cost, sales and distribution of Government documents, general questions of economy connected therewith, and the development of the Stationery Office's responsibilities in the whole field.

—— Report, proc., mins. of ev., apps. pp. xxxii, 141. Index.   1906
1906 (279) *xi*, 95

Mr. Crombie (*Ch.*), Cavendish, Cox, Devlin, Maddison, Bowles, Toulmin.

'*To inquire into the Number, Bulk, Cost, and Circulation of the Documents printed by Order of this House, or presented to it through Public Departments, and to report what Reductions, if any, can be made thereon.*'

'It is estimated that in 1905 2,670,000 copies of Parliamentary Papers . . . of these classes were printed; of which 1,460,000 were distributed to the Houses of Parliament and Public Departments, and 750,000 were sold; leaving 460,000 for reserve. Probably one-half of the latter number will be sold for waste paper. The Sessional Papers for 1904 contained 140,000 separate pages, and occupied seventeen feet of shelving.' Much overlapping and expense is caused by the number and various ways in which Papers are produced and printed. Messrs. Nichols have been for 140 years printers of Votes and Proceedings and it is estimated that the cost is some 25 per cent over what it would be if submitted to open contract. Officials of the House of Commons, none of whom necessarily have any technical knowledge of printing, are entirely responsible for the form in which the Votes and Proceedings and Journals are printed. Messrs. Eyre and Spottiswoode hold the contract for Bills and Acts of Parliament. It was not obtained in competition, but was granted to them as part of an arrangement by which they agreed to sell to the public at certain rates copies of the Acts which were their own private property. This contract expires in September 1907. Parliamentary Debates are reported and printed under contract with Messrs. Wyman, who receive a subsidy of £220 for each volume produced, and who sell copies to the Government at about 13s. a copy. The contract expires in December 1907. The Stationery Office arranges for the printing of House of Commons and Command Papers by contracts in groups. Certain contracts are at a much higher rate owing to their confidential nature. A copy of these Papers is generally sent direct to the printers by the Librarian of the House of Commons, an official in the Department concerned, or the Secretary of a Royal Commission. None of these possess any technical knowledge of printing: matter has been printed in a needlessly expensive form and the indexing of Royal Commissions and other publications is often clumsily done. Nobody upon a Royal Commission 'knows anything at all about printing or publishing, or the cost . . . —Everything not published in the report is thrown into the Appendix' (Wilson Fox q.1529). The conditions of Government contracts for printing are not always advantageous to the printer. The paper is supplied to him, stipulations are made as to rates of wages, performance of work, and the confidential or special nature of the work. Apart from the question of costs, there is difficulty in getting the work done quickly as there is a tendency of contractors to isolate Government work from the rest of their business. The Savings Bank Department induced the Treasury to sanction their doing their own printing and they have succeeded in doing it more economically than when it was contracted for.

The distribution of Papers is carried out by the Vote Office. Certain Papers are distributed to all members; the others are scheduled in the Pink Demand Papers, from which members select those they want. The Stationery Office distributes Papers according to a list drawn up by the Treasury. In the United Kingdom there are distributed 25 complete sets of Parliamentary Papers paged and bound, 106 complete sets of Command and 111 complete sets of House of Commons Papers, each of the Public Departments receiving one complete set of Command and House Papers, and some more than one. Where component parts of a Report are issued separately they may be duplicated in the bound set.

The sale of Parliamentary Papers is subject to a public contract which ends in 1914. Messrs. Wyman, who hold the contract for England and Wales assured the Committee that the contract did not pay them, but that they did it for advertisement. The amount sold is disappointing because of too much gratuitous distribution, publication of the most interesting Papers by the newspapers, and too little being done to advertise them. If the Stationery Office acted as its own agent it could extend the system of printing and circularising lists of publications for sale.

Amongst the recommendations were: '(1) The Controller of the Stationery Office to be appointed printer of the Votes and Proceedings and Journals. (2) The Controller to be consulted as to the form of all Parliamentary Printing. (3) A Sessional Committee to be appointed to supervise the amount of matter printed and the distribution of publications, and to assist Mr. Speaker. (4) Printing of the Votes and Proceedings, Journals, Bills and Acts to be submitted to contract. (5) Overlapping in contracts to be avoided. (6) "Copy" handed in at the Table to be in a more complete form. (7) Certain onerous conditions in contracts to be reconsidered before entering on new contracts. (8) Ordinary work not to be included in contracts for Confidential work. (9) Papers to be printed, as far as possible, in octavo and not reprinted in foolscap folio size. (10) The form of printing in which a Return is moved for to be submitted to the Controller of the Stationery Office, and the probable cost of Return to be stated to the House. (11) Indexing to be done by experts. (12) Royal Commissions to obtain Treasury sanction for the amount and nature of the matter proposed to be published with their Reports. (13) Matter in Appendices of Royal Commissions to be deposited for reference when publication is unnecessary. (14) Departments to apply for what publications they need, instead of receiving complete sets. (15) Gratuitous distribution of publications by Departments to be curtailed. (16) Duplicates not to be included in complete sets. (17) Certain publications to be omitted from the Vote Office Demand Schedule. (18) Progress of sales to be watched with a view to deciding whether contracting should be continued or not. (19) A Government printing department to be established for doing Confidential and urgent work.'

—— Report, proc., mins. of ev., apps., pp. xviii, 163. Index. 1907

1907 (239) and (239-*Ind.*) *vii*, 15

C. Allen (*Ch.*), Barran, Beach, Bowerman, Lehmann, Redmond, Toulmin, Taylor, Walrond.

'*To Inquire and Report as to the Cost and Method of Reporting and Publishing the Debates and Proceedings in Parliament.*'

The Select Committee on Parliamentary Debates (1893 (213) xiii) recommended 'that the Reports should be obtained by the Stationery Office by contract after tender; that the printing contract should be separated from the reporting contract' and the arrangements supervised by a Committee of the House. It recommended 'that a full Report', which it defined as a Report—'which, though not strictly verbatim, is substantially the verbatim Report with repetitions and redundancies omitted and with obvious mistakes corrected, but which, on the other hand, leaves out nothing that adds to the meaning of the speech or illustrates the argument'—should be given in the first person of all speeches alike. It recommended further 'that the Reports should be issued in the first instance in daily parts as before; that the daily parts should be available for Members asking for them at the Vote Office not later than 4 p.m. of the day following that to which they relate, and should be finally issued to Members desiring them on the morning following with Votes and Proceedings'. These recommendations were not fully carried out; reporting and printing contracts were not separated, and no Committee of Supervision was appointed. Contractors followed one another in quick succession, until in 1898 Messrs. Wyman took over the contract both for reporting and printing.

The system of obtaining Reports by contract could not be successful when it is to the interest of the contractor to lengthen or shorten his Reports or to limit the number of Reports, according to the terms he has received, and it is unfair to Members that a contractor should in any way be the judge as to the length at which speeches are reported, or that newspaper cuttings should be used as sources when there were not a sufficient number of reporters in the House. The House of Commons should have its own reporting staff, who should give full Reports, as defined by the Select Committee of 1893, in place of condensed versions. Better accommodation should be provided for the reporters. If a Government Printing Office were established as recommended by the Select Committee on Official Publications, the printing of Debates should be one of its first tasks. The Controller of the Stationery Department gave estimates of costs.

—— Report, proc., mins. of ev., pp. xii, 76. 1907

1907 (272) *vii*, 545

Mr. Crombie (*Ch.*), Cleland, Cox, Jones, MacVeagh, Maddison, Rickett, Roberts, Toulmin.

Unnecessary expense in the printing of Parliamentary Publications arises principally from printing necessary matter in an expensive form and from printing matter which is unnecessary. Examples of the first were marginal notes, parts of tables in red ink, printing in tabular form. There should be the closest co-operation between the Departments and the Stationery Office, to which manuscript should be submitted before printing and which should be consulted on the form of elaborate or extensive tables. Unnecessary matter included unnecessary and extensive appendices, summaries of statistics already found in other Papers, elaborate details of dietaries, etc.

—— Report, proc., mins. of ev., app. pp. xv, 115. 1908. Index. 1910

1908 (358) *and* (358-*Ind*) *x*, 849

Mr. Toulmin (*Ch.*), Bowerman, Cleland, Cox, Jones, Lehmann, MacVeagh, Maddison, Robertson.

As a result of the recommendations of the Committee of 1906 a special department of the Stationery Office was created for revising and advising on the printing of Departments. Departments will not secure the full advantage of expert assistance unless they utilize it before the 'copy' is prepared and not as has been done, after a Report is absolutely completed. It is in the preparation of Reports and returns that economies can be made, especially as the cost of a Department's publications falls not on its own but on the Stationery Office Vote.

—— Reports, proc., mins. of ev., pp. xii. Index. 1909

1909 (60) (285) *and* (285-*Ind*.) *viii*, 357

Mr. Toulmin (*Ch.*), Arkwright, Bowerman, Cleland, Cox, Jones, Lehmann, Maddison, MacVeagh, Pease, Redmond.

The arrangements made, beginning that Session, for the delivery of full reports of each day's Debate on the following morning, for the issue of Commons' Reports separately from those of the House of Lords, the issue of bound volumes of reports of Debates and the receipt of corrections of speeches for those volumes, were working well.

—— Report, proc., mins. of ev., app. pp. vi, 23. 1910

1910 (315) *vi*, 587

Mr. Toulmin (*Ch.*), Arkwright, Bathurst, Bowerman, Cleland, Jardine, Jones, Lehmann, MacVeagh, Redmond, Wheler.

Was concerned with details of administration.

—— Report, proc., mins. of ev., apps. pp. xii, 73. Index. 1911

1911 (259) *and* (259 *Ind*.) *vii*, 663

G. Toulmin (*Ch.*), Arkwright, Bathurst, Bowerman, Collins, Guest, Jardine, MacVeagh, Rea, Redmond, Wheler.

Since 1847-8, when a Select Committee recommended that the reports only of royal commissions should be printed, leaving the House to decide thereafter whether evidence and other papers should be printed, there has been recurring criticism of unnecessary printing of royal commissions' papers. The commission, through the chairman, should be made responsible for decisions in the matter; each commission should be given a credit at the Stationery Office, which should not be exceeded without Treasury sanction. A specific annual sum, to be administered by the Stationery Office, which may not be exceeded without Treasury sanction, should be allotted to each Department. In each Department a high official should be responsible for all requisitions from the Stationery Office, and a staff clerk in charge of storage and distribution. An official of the Stationery Office should examine each Department's methods of storage and distribution and make recommendations.

—— Report, proc., mins. of ev., apps. pp. xiv, 69. Index. 1912

1912–13 (283) (283 Ind.) ix, 225

G. Toulmin (Ch.), Arkwright, Bathurst, Bowerman, Collins, Guest, MacVeagh, Rea, Redmond, Wheler, MacMaster.

The termination of the printing contracts at the end of 1913 affords an opportunity for considering the establishment of an auxiliary printing department under the control of the Stationery Office. The Committee will investigate the feasibility of this. Before the printing contracts were last allotted, an Inter-Departmental Committee of 1907 (*Report not published*) inquired whether it would be desirable for the Government to execute the whole or part of the printing required for public Departments without the intervention of contractors; but a scheme for a central printing office, proposed by Mr. Rowland Bailey, the Controller of the Stationery Office, was rejected and the Committee answered in the negative. The public service has to rely upon too limited a number of printing firms, and

this is due to elements of risk and uncertainty over which the Stationery Office has no control. These arise from Departments sending bad copy, delay in returning proofs, extravagant corrections in proof, etc.

—— Report, proc., mins. of ev., app. pp. ix, 40. Index. 1913

1913 (224) *and* (224 *Ind.*) *xiii*, 569

G. Toulmin (*Ch.*), Bathurst, Bowerman, Collins, Guest, Locker-Lampson, MacMaster, MacVeagh, Rea, Redmond, Wheler.

The recommendation of 1907 and 1908 that Departments should consult the Stationery Office *before* the 'copy' is prepared has not been completely adopted; a department of the L.G.B. had never been informed of the existence of the Treasury Circular.

Concerning the expense caused by printing matter in more than one form, Sir Courtenay Ilbert, Clerk of the House stated in evidence that the 'duplication of records appeared to him to lead to duplication of labour, and consequent waste of labour and time and money . . . If he wished to find a precedent in the form of a ruling by the Speaker, the Journal of the House would only aid him to the extent of giving the form of the Order made consequent on the ruling; and that in order to find the ruling itself it would be necessary to search the official report of Debates'. He advocated the adoption of a system which would 'combine the official report of things said with the official report of things done,' but explained that there were certain difficulties to be surmounted, and that he was only indicating the general outline of what in his opinion the Committee should work up to. 'Your Committee are in agreement with these views, and they recognize that the method and the steps by which this end should be accomplished require careful consideration.'

The expense of printing Written Answers to Questions in duplicate both with Votes and Proceedings and in the

Official Daily Report, was not less than £1,000 a Session and is increasing, and this duplication was unnecessary.

See the Speaker's letter in the Rep.; 1916 (112) iii, 601.

—— Report, proc., mins. of ev., apps. pp. xiv, 68. Index. 1914

1914 (401) (401 *Ind.*) x, 249

G. Toulmin (*Ch.*), Bathurst, Bowerman, Collins, Guest, Locker-Lampson, MacVeagh, Rea, Redmond, Wheler, Malcolm.

The chief advantages of a Government Printing Department were administrative. 'At the present moment—beyond the regular fixed work in a few Government printing offices,—all Government work must be given out.' The essence of the success in the Inland Revenue Department in its recent contracts was that the 'contractors knew that if they did not come forward with satisfactory prices the Inland Revenue would step in and do the work themselves'. With a printing department, the Stationery Office would be in that favourable position with all its contracts as they came round. In evidence the Controller, Mr. Atterbury, made a plea for a printing office based on the cultivation of the technical skill of his Department. He said that clever young printers who are recruited by examination, cease to have any practical touch with their trade from the moment they enter the Stationery Office. The comprehensive scheme involving £280,000 and employing 2,100 workers proposed by Sir Rowland Bailey in 1907 was not pursued, especially as many of the difficulties which he hoped to overcome by it had been removed by the vigorous administration of Sir Rowland Bailey himself. A more limited undertaking with a capital outlay of £20,000 'to be added to gradually as experience suggests,' was recommended.

—— Report, proc., mins. of ev., apps. pp. xx, 94. Index. 1915

1914–16 (321) *and* (321. *Ind.*) iv, 655

G. Toulmin (*Ch.*), Agg-Gardner, Bowerman, Collins, Fletcher, Guest, Ingleby, MacVeagh, Partington, Redmond, Wheler.

The expiration in December 1916 of the contract of Messrs. Wyman and Sons for the sale of Government Publications necessitates a consideration of the policy in connection with their sale. The Select Committee of 1874 recommended direct sale. The present system of appointing a contractor by competitive tender, to act as agent first came into operation in 1887. On this the Controller, Mr. Atterbury, said that to pass State documents through the Stationery Office and then through the warehouse of one central agent on the way to the bookseller is merely to add one more turnover to each parcel. Recommended that the sale of Government Publications be entrusted to the Stationery Office.

—— —— Second Report, proc., mins. of ev., apps., pp. xii, 42. 1915. Index. 1916

1914–16 (398) (398 *Ind.*) iv, 781

add Doris, Grant, Lloyd, Roch, Scott, del. Collins, Guest, Ingleby, Redmond, Wheler.

'*To inquire into and report on the position, duties, and remuneration of the Shorthand Writer to this House and of his staff.*'

The report reviews the history of the office since the first appointment of Mr. W. B. Gurney in 1813, the duties being performed by three members of the family until 1912. The remuneration was entirely by fee. 'There was a concensus of opinion amongst the witnesses that the position of Shorthand Writer should be held by a person responsible to the House.' Recommended that the Shorthand Writer shall be paid an adequate salary and that a minimum staff of notetakers shall be engaged by him at a guaranteed minimum remuneration.

—— Report, proc., mins. of ev., apps.
    pp. x, 68. Index. 1916

1916 (112) *and* (112-*Ind.*), *iii,* 601

G. ˏToulmin (*Ch.*), Agg-Gardner,
Bowerman, Doris, Fletcher, Grant,
Lloyd, MacVeagh, Partington, Roch,
Scott.

Owing to the war the Committee
were concerned with the curtailment
of reports dealing with the routine
activities of the Departments. A list
of suspended publications is given in
Appendix No. 1.

An inquiry was contemplated into
the preparation and printing of the
Journal of the House of Commons, but
in consequence of Mr. Speaker's reply
to a letter from the Treasury suggesting
the amalgamation of the Journal with
the Official Report of the Debates, the
Committee were of the opinion 'that
without impairing its value as part of a
continuous record, the archaic and
formal language might be abbreviated
and the labour of compilation reduced.'

Mr. Speaker's reply, in App. 2, states
that the purpose and value of the
Journal as the record of what was done
and decided by Parliament was entirely
different from the purpose and value of
the Official Report, which was mainly
a record of words spoken; any attempt
to combine them would make them
both difficult to use as works of reference and more costly. It would break
the continuity of a record which had
been maintained since 1547, whilst
in their present form the Journals were
a ready instrument in the hands of
those whose duty it might be to
search for precedents in procedure. Sir
Courtenay Ilbert, Clerk to the House
said that the Journal is 'an elaborate
translation of twentieth-century facts
into eighteenth-century fiction', is an
unsafe guide to anyone not familiar
with its conventional language, that
the index was unsuitable, and that he
was sceptical of its value in its existing
form. *Official Publications.* Sel. Cttee.
Rep. qq. 520-563; 1906 (279) xi, 95.

House of Commons (Admission of Strangers)

Sel. Cttee. Report, proc., mins. of ev.
    pp. x, 24. 1908

1908 (371) *ix,* 1
apptd. Dec., *o.p.* Dec., 1908

Mr. Buchanan (*Ch.*), Fenwick, Redmond, Shackleton, Stuart, Valentia,
Stuart-Wortley.

'*To inquire into the Rules and Regulations under which Strangers are admitted
to this House and its precincts, and to
Report whether any alterations in the same
are expedient.*'

The rules and regulations needed
improvement, both to prevent disorder and for the convenience of the
members and the public. It should be
made clear to visitors that admission
was subject to an obligation of good
conduct, and serious disturbance in
the galleries during the sitting of the
House should be made a criminal
offence. All orders for admission
should be issued under the authority
of the Serjeant-at-Arms.

House of Commons (Ventilation)

Sel. Cttee. Rep., proc., mins. of ev.,
    apps. pp. viii, 97. 1903

1903 (227) *v,* 635
apptd. April, 1902. *o.p.* June, 1903

A. Akers - Douglas (*Ch.*), Dillon,
Farquharson, Foster, Goddard, Penn,
Tuke

'*To inquire into the ventilation of the
House.*'

Chemical and bacteriological tests to
atmosphere had been made, but no
conclusions had been arrived at.

—— Report. mins. of ev., app., index.
    pp. xxii, 56. 1903

1903 (283) *v,* 741
apptd. June, *o.p.* July, 1903

M. Foster (*Ch.*), Dillon, Farquharson,
Goddard, Tuke, Smith, Cavendish.

When the Chamber was half full of
Members, the air contained slightly less

than five volumes per 10,000 volumes of carbonic acid. As the air of cities ordinarily contained about 4 volumes, it was thought that the air of the Chamber was unusually good. 'But this objective test was not confirmed by the subjective test of the Members' own feelings.'

Eight recommendations were made for improving the present system, including more frequent removal of the matting for cleaning, and the placement of cleaning arrangements under one authority. There should be further inquiries into the unsolved problems of ventilation.

Other Reps.: 1902 (327) v, 797.   1905 Cd. 2404, lxii, 321.   1906 Cd. 3035, Cd. 3068, xciv, 561.

4. MINISTERS

Marconi's Wireless Telegraph Company, Limited, Agreement

Sel. Cttee. Rep., proc., mins. of ev., apps. pp. xxviii, 977. Index. 1913

1912–13 (351, 430, 515) (515–I Ind.) viii, 1

apptd. Oct., o.p. Oct., 1912, Jan., Feb., 1913

A. Spicer (Ch.), Amery, Booth, L. Robert Cecil, Faber, Falconer, Harvey, Macmaster, Mooney, Parker, Primrose, Redmond, Roberts, Smith, Terrell.

'To investigate the circumstances connected with the negotiation and completion of the Agreement between Marconi's Wireless Telegraph Company, Limited, Commendatore Guglielmo Marconi, and the Postmaster-General, with regard to the establishment of a chain of Imperial wireless stations, and to report thereupon.'

Special Report, 28th Oct., 1912. The Committee proposed to retain the conduct of the enquiry entirely in their own hands, but if the House gave leave, would accept the help of Counsel, if they thought it necessary, and invited any person in possession of evidence to communicate with them.

Special Report, 14th Jan., 1913. It was a matter of urgency that a chain of Imperial Wireless Stations should be established, and that whatever system was finally adopted and whether or not the Agreement was modified or confirmed, the first six stations should be in the places named in the second article of the Agreement. The Government should be free to accept or reject any system of wireless telegraphy from time to time; it should appoint a highly qualified scientific Committee to report on existing systems of wireless telegraphy, within three months. See *Wireless Telegraphy*. Below, p. 180.

Special Report, 12th Feb., 1913. Mr. L. Maxse, a witness, refused to give information in his possession and to produce letters asked for by the Committee, which in their opinion should be laid before them. The Chairman was instructed to report the circumstance to the House.

Report.—Formal Report, presenting minutes and suggesting re-appointment.

—— Report, proc., apps. pp. lxv. 1913. Mins. of ev., apps. Vol. I. Index. 1913

1913 (152) and (152 Ind.) vii, 95. Mins. of ev., etc.; 1913 (152) vii, 161 apptd. March, o.p. June, 1913

add Banbury, Butcher, Essex. del. Primrose, Smith, Terrell.

Part I.—The charges or suggestions which reflected on the conduct of several Ministers of the Crown (Sir Rufus Isaacs, Attorney General; Mr. D. Lloyd George, Chancellor of the Exchequer and Mr. H. Samuel, Postmaster General) were that: (1) a member or members of the Government, in disregard of public interests, had exercised undue influence on the negotiations to procure a Government contract for the English Marconi Company; and (2) a member or members of the Government, knowing that an agreement of value to the company would be completed, during the negotiations purchased shares with a view to reselling them later at a profit. No evidence had been forthcoming or disclosed in the Committee to support either of these suggestions and the persons who made the charges had no reason to believe them to be true. The Postmaster General did not press unduly for the approval of the agreement before the rising of the House on 7th Aug., 1912, since the Committee of Imperial Defence had declared that the constitution of an Imperial Wireless chain was a matter of extreme urgency, and the Admiralty and War Office had supported this view.

Part II.—The Committee investigated the circumstances relating to purchases by the Attorney General from his brother of shares in the 'American' Marconi Wireless Company, and of the purchase of shares by the Chancellor of the Exchequer and Lord Murray of Elibank. Before he made the purchases the Attorney General made special enquiry and was satisfied that the American Company had no interest in the contract between the English Company and the Postmaster General, and there was no ground of objection to purchase by a British Minister. The other Ministers were so informed and acted *bona fide*. The American Company was registered and formed in the United States, its organization and business were confined to that country, and it had no interest direct or indirect in the proposed agreements. The English Company was not party to these transactions, or interested in them, nor did the Ministers concerned receive any favour or advantage from the English Company.

Part III.—All the Ministers concerned have acted throughout in the sincere belief that there was nothing in their action which would in any way conflict with their duty as Ministers of the Crown.

The Proceedings show that three draft reports (printed in full) were presented to the Committee, one being by the Chairman, the second by Sir Robert Cecil, and the third by Mr. Falconer. Comparisons with the Special Report as adopted show that considerable sections of it were in the terms of Mr. Falconer's draft or later amendments.

—— Report, proc., mins. of ev., apps. pp. viii. 1913

1913 (185) *vii*, 805
o.p. July 1913

The Postmaster-General, Mr. H. Samuel, M.P., made a statement to the Committee that the Government did not propose to take legal proceedings to enforce the agreement (qq. 10,829–10,834 and 10,844). In consequence, the Committee's Report was as follows: 'That the Committee, having been informed that the Marconi's Wireless Telegraph Company, Limited, have repudiated the Agreement entered into between the Marconi's Wireless Telegraph Company, Limited, Commendatore Guglielmo Marconi and the Postmaster-General, and having heard from the Postmaster-General that he is not prepared to enforce the Agreement, are of opinion that as the Agreement which formed the subject matter of the reference to them is not to be enforced, it is unnecessary for them further to pursue their enquiry, and they so report to the House.'

See *Agreement between Marconi's Wireless Co. Ltd. and the Postmaster-General;* 1913 (217) li, 625. *Return of Patents in respect of Royalties;* 1913 (302) li, 689.

Charges against Lord Murray of Elibank

Sel. Cttee. HL. Rep., proc., mins. of ev., apps. pp. xii, 166. 1914

1914 (*HL.66*) *ix*, 253
apptd. Feb., o.p. April, 1914

Lord Halsbury (*Ch.*), L. Loreburn, L. Sanderson, L. Desart, L. Charnwood.

'To *inquire into certain charges and allegations made in the public Press against a member of this House, namely, the Lord Murray of Elibank, and into all matters relating thereto.'*

The principal charge was that Lord Murray had purchased 1,000 shares in Marconi's Wireless Telegraph Company of America from Sir Rufus Isaacs at £2 a share on 17th April, 1912, that the transaction was of a speculative character and that he possessed private information concerning them which was kept from the public. It is now recognized by Lord Murray that he ought not to have bought the shares because as Chief Whip he had to procure the ratification of the contract between the British Government and the English Company, which would favourably affect the value of the Marconi shares. The purchase of the shares was a speculative transaction and a grave error, but he was acquitted of dishonourable conduct. Another of the accusations was that as Chief Whip and sole manager of the Liberal Party Funds he had used trust funds to secure shares for the Party, and had not disclosed the facts to the right people, hoping to keep the matter secret until the Marconi affair had been cleared up. Meanwhile Lord Murray's broker, Mr. Fenner, was in difficulties and he had been loaned £2,300. Mr. Fenner, however, went bankrupt and the Party Fund lost about £39,000. Lord Murray has repaid losses amounting to £40,000.

Lord Murray committed grave errors, but was acquitted of dishonourable conduct. The Committee concluded that 'we think it is within our province to express our strong opinion that there should be henceforth an inflexible rule to preclude those who hold any public office from entering upon any speculative transactions in stocks or shares in any circumstances whatsoever, and that this rule should be by them inculcated on their subordinates both by precept and example. The evils that may arise from a violation of this principle are incalculable.'

5. ORGANIZATION OF DEPARTMENTS

War Office Contracts

Sel. Cttee. Rep. proc., pp. xxx. 1900. Index and Digest of ev. 1900

1900 (313) (313 *Ind.*) ix, 1
apptd. May, o.p. Aug. 1900

Mr. Jackson (*Ch.*), Denny, Donelan, Elliot, Firbank, Howell, Lewis, Lockwood, Loyd, McKenna, O'Brien, Paulton, Rasch, Reid, Mellor.

'*To consider and report upon Allegations of Fraud and Irregularity in connection with War Office Contracts during the last Twelve Months.*'

With a view to obtaining evidence, the Committee resolved that it would recommend that any person coming forward and making a full disclosure should not have any punishment or disability placed upon him in respect of any irregularity he might admit, and regretted that merchants, etc., were not publicly invited by proclamation to give evidence and that no indemnity was definitely promised to witnesses.

The Committee considered a number of cases of firms placed on the ineligible list, and also cordite contracts. The Committee had received evidence of some cases in which bribes had been offered and of a few in which bribes had been accepted. In view of the prevalence of secret commissions in private commerce, they doubted whether the system of inspection gave complete security against it. It should be an inflexible rule that any firm offering the slightest gratuity to any officer in connection with a Government contract should be struck off the list. The Public Bodies Corrupt Practices Act, 1889, should be extended to the Government Service, and if adequate evidence were secured prosecution should invariably follow. The discovery of frauds and secret commissions by the methods of committee examination was extremely difficult. It was undesirable that negotiations for contracts should be conducted personally between Members of Parliament and Departmental officials.

War Office Organization

Cttee. Rep. pp. 25. 1901. Mins. of ev., apps., index. 1901

1901 *Cd.* 580, *xl*, 179. *Mins. of ev., etc.;*
1901 *Cd.* 581, *xl*, 207
apptd. Dec., 1900. *sgd. May*, 1901

C. E. Dawkins (*Ch.*), Beckett, Clarke, Gibb, Mather, Miles, Welby.

'To consider—1. *Whether the present method of conducting the administrative and financial business of the War Office, and its distribution as between the civil and military departments, is satisfactory.* 2. *Whether the detailed financial audit as conducted in the War Office is required by the public interest; and whether the existing financial checks on the War Office hinder the efficient transaction of its business.* 3. *Whether the office of the Director of Contracts should deal with all the business now transacted there, or whether the making of contracts could be in whole or part transferred to the military districts, or to the military departments of the War Office.* 4. *Whether (with or without a transfer of staff) any of the administrative and financial business now transacted in the War Office could be delegated to the military districts.* 5. *Whether any change in the numbers, status, and pay of the clerical staff is desirable.* 6. *Whether military Officers and military clerks should be substituted in any degree for the present trained civilian staff; and to report any other amendments of procedure in connection with the afore-mentioned subjects which would bring the work of the War Office more into harmony with that of large business undertakings.*'

'The general structure of the War Office organization has been built up piecemeal as the result of constant changes and compromises. Principles of administration and of business have been too frequently subordinated to temporary exigencies, or to personal and political considerations. Thus, in place of becoming a compact machine working smoothly upon lines well conceived and thoroughly understood, the constitution of the War Office has been subjected to so many modifications, large and small, that the relations of the various parts have been shifting and indeterminate. What has been so perpetually changed and refashioned, not infrequently without reference to any ascertainable principle, is necessarily wanting in the element of permanence. Definitions of the duties of departments have, therefore, been wavering and uncertain . . . there is a disposition on the part of energetic heads of departments to draw power to themselves, and to enlarge the area of their activities beyond all reason and expediency. Great confusion is thereby introduced, and individual responsibility cannot be assigned.'

'These evils are enormously augmented owing to the government of the Army by the War Office being mainly carried on by a vast system of minute regulations, which tend to destroy the responsibility of General Officers, and to suppress individuality and initiative in all ranks. The complexity of regulations is now so great that their interpretation alone leads to a mass of useless correspondence. This state of affairs constitutes a grave detriment to the public service. The practice of making endless references to obtain authority, and reluctance to take direct action, are inevitable consequences. . . . It follows that the mass of unnecessary routine work within the War Office is so great as to absorb the energies of the staff, which is generally overworked, and that high officials engrossed in routine have not sufficient time to devote to questions of real importance. Matters of policy are, therefore, not adequately considered. The necessary sense of proportion is lost, and the training and preparation of the Army for war must inevitably suffer. An unfortunate suspicion also exists in the Army that technical military questions are sometimes decided by permanent civilian officials. All these unsatisfactory conditions necessarily promote distrust of the

War Office on the part of the Army and of the public.'

'The following principles are particularly applicable to the War Office, and are conspicuously absent from it: 1. The division of the work of the War Office into well-defined sections. 2. Distinct definition of duties and responsibilities of individuals, accompanied by an adequate delegation of powers. 3. A clear adjustment of the relations between the Civil and Military Departments. 4. Adequate provision for dealing with questions of policy and military preparation, unhampered by administrative routine work. 5. The substitution of an effective system of inspection for elaborate returns and minute regulations in the government of the Army by the War Office. 6. Decentralization, meaning a large and real delegation of authority and responsibility to General Officers Commanding districts. 7. Adequate machinery for co-ordinating work of all kinds, Civil and Military, and for securing effective supreme control and management of the business of the War Office as a whole under the authority of the Secretary of State.'

The recommendations were based on these principles and were designed to abolish the present system of ruling the Army by minute regulations and elaborate reports; to simplify regulations which could not be dispensed with; to create effective inspection; to define the powers and duties of heads of departments; to place a branch of the Accountant-General's Department in touch with each spending department, to simplify Company pay lists, and to increase the financial power of the Secretary of State and of General Officers Commanding by providing an annual sum to cover small items of unforeseen expenditure. Other recommendations dealt with unexpended balances, audit, Contract and Supply branches, staffing and the decentralization of routine work, etc.

The most important recommendation of the Committee, and one on which the practical success of its proposed reforms

depended, was for the creation of a new War Office Board. In central control and direction the methods of the War Office were out of harmony with the best business practice. The co-ordination of military and civilian business required a central authority, a permanent War Office Board formally constituted and placed on an authoritative basis as an integral part of the War Office. It would supersede the War Office Council and the Army Board, and would consist of the heads of the military and civil departments, under the chairmanship of the Secretary of State. It should supervise and control the working and management of the War Office, consider annual estimates and allocate the moneys. Members of the Board should be empowered to bring to it any important matters affecting their Departments for the Board to consider and decide. The Board's recommendations would go direct to the Secretary of State. Heads of Departments would be responsible to the Secretary of State for the executive working of the Departments and render him annual reports.

See *Decentralization of the War Office.* Rep.; 1898 C. 8934, xiii, 123. *War Office Establishments* 1898–99. (Unpublished. War Office Library.)

War Office (Reconstitution)

Cttee. Rep., Part I. pp. 15. 1904

1904 *Cd.* 1932, *viii*, 101
apptd. — sgd. Jan., 1904

L. Esher, Fisher, Clarke.

'To *make recommendations for the reconstitution of the War Office.*'

I. *Defence Committee.* For many years the War Office has been administered from the point of view of peace, so that it is necessary to make a complete break with the past and constitute it with a single eye to the effective training and preparation of the Forces for war. The Cabinet in 1899 had no adequate means of obtaining reasoned opinions on which to base a war policy. Such advice must embrace the policy not only of the War Office but of the Admiralty, etc. The Defence Committee of the Cabinet as now reconstituted contains no permanent nucleus, is composed of political and professional members pre-occupied with administrative duties and cannot deal adequately with the complex problems of Imperial Defence. Although we are a great naval, Indian and Colonial power, there are no means of co-ordinating defence problems. The Committee should have a permanent nucleus, consisting of a Permanent Secretary, appointed for five years, and two naval, two military and one colonial officer, each appointed for two years, which should consider all questions of Imperial Defence, collect information from the various services, and prepare documents for the Prime Minister and the Committee, and furnish advice on problems involving more than one department.

II. *Army Council.* The terms of reference directed that the Admiralty system of higher administration should be taken as the basis of action: it conforms closely to arrangements under which the largest businesses are conducted, and is absolutely sound in principle. This cannot be said of the War Office. Since the partial re-organization after the complete breakdown of the complex systems which prevailed during the Crimean War, there has been no organic change of the War Office system, although no department has been so frequently examined or so scathingly criticized. In 1890 the Hartington Commission urged drastic re-organization, but nothing was done. The South African campaign shows that the system was not adapted to the preparation for or conduct of war. The centralization of a vast number of incongruous functions in the Commander-in-Chief results in the neglect of matters of primary importance. The War Office has no thinking department, the branches are not sufficiently in touch with the Secretary of State, the duties and relations of military heads are ill-defined.

The Secretary of State should be on the same footing as the First Lord of the Admiralty and all submissions to the Crown should be made by him alone. There should be set up an Army Council of four military and three civil members, with the Permanent Under-Secretary as Secretary. The high office of Commander-in-Chief is inconsistent with the principle of administration by the Secretary of State and a Board or Council. Attempts to combine the administrative and executive functions have led to confusion, duplication, expense, dual control, divided responsibility and ultimately to the conditions of the South African War. The office of Commander-in-Chief should be abolished, administration divorced from executive command, and the latter decentralized. In appointing members of the Army Council no consideration save that of special fitness for the duties should arise; the question of military rank can remain in abeyance amongst members.

Independent inspection is the corollary of effective decentralization, and the Commander-in-Chief, though theoretically the inspecting officer, did not perform the duty. An Inspector-General should be appointed to be the eyes and ears of the Secretary of State, and should hold office for five years.

A Selection Board, composed of General Officers Commanding-in-Chief, should be established to make recommendations to the Secretary of State and Army Council, for all promotions and appointments of officers above the rank of captain, except officers of the General Staff.

—— Report. Part II. pp. 29. 1904
1904 *Cd.* 1968, *viii*, 121
sgd. Feb., 1904

The proposals already made in Part I having been approved and the Army Council constituted by Patent, Section I of this Report lays down the principles by which the proceedings of the Council should be governed. But unless the proposals in Sections II. and III are accepted, the reforms already carried out will bear no fruit.

Section II. Decentralization. No reconstitution of the War Office can lead to a permanent improvement unless there is a large and real measure of decentralization. The result of an inordinately centralized system has been the destruction of initiative throughout the Army. The Army is bound and tied in the toils of complex and minute regulations drawn up without any reference to the requirements of modern war. Decentralization to General Officers Commanding-in-Chief on the basis of the Army Corps system would involve them in a mass of routine business and divert their attention from their first and undivided duty, that of preparing the Forces for war. And the despatch of an expeditionary force would destroy the administrative machine. This course is rejected: instead the country should be divided into eight Administrative Districts under 'Major-Generals'.

Section III. Military Finance. The present arrangements for financial administration are to the last degree unsatisfactory; they do not promote economy in peace, they produce waste in war and at all times foster the maximum of friction with the minimum of efficiency. The Department of the Accountant General has become a large and costly machine which uses regulations to aggrandise its power over the military branches. A proper Army Finance Branch should be created, responsible to the Finance member of the Army Council. The Military Officers must have financial powers and responsibilities, and to aid them there should be a specially trained and homogeneous body, instead of the two at present existing. The Finance Branch of the Accountant-General and the Army Pay Department should be amalgamated. There must be a change of personnel, to make a complete

change of system: nothing else will fully convince the rank and file of the Finance Branch that the old system must be abandoned and completely new habits formed.

Section IV. The Chief of the General Staff. The lack of trained General Staff gravely imperilled the operations in South Africa. Such a staff should be constituted with defined functions in peace and war, educated for its special duties, drawing on the pick of the brains of the army and working continuously to improve the training of the troops and their preparation for war. It should be recruited mainly from the Staff College, entry to which should be by competitive examination. As this process will take several years delay, which already cost the nation heavy sacrifices, would be dangerous.

Section V. Promotion and Selection of Officers. The Selection Board should be reconstituted, and some of the functions of the Military Secretary transferred to the General Officers Commanding-in-Chief. There should be a Military Secretary to the Secretary of State, and he should act as Secretary to the Selection Board.

—— Report. Part III. pp. 31. 1904
1904 *Cd.* 2002, *viii*, 157
sgd. March, 1904

This Part deals with the duties of the several branches of the War Office. The duty of remedying the state of affairs revealed by the War Commission, 'we have endeavoured to fulfil in such a manner as to uproot a system which had been scathingly condemned by the Hartington Commission in 1890'.

See *Civil and Professional Administration of the Naval and Military Departments and the Relation of those Departments to each other and to the Treasury.* R. Com. (Hartington). Further Rep., *The Internal Administration of the War Office.* pp. xix-xxv. Also App. VI; 1890 C.5979, xix, 1.

Staff and Organization of the Education Department and the Science and Art Department

Dept. Cttee. Three Interim and a Final Rep.

unpublished

appt. July, 1899. *sgd. March*, 1900

H. Walpole (*Ch.*).

'*To consider and report what changes in staff and organization of the Education Department and the Science and Art Department were necessary in order to carry into effect the Minute of 29th June, 1899, and to bring those Departments into closer relation to each other.*' Added Nov., 1899—'*To have regard, in their recommendations, to the provisions of the Board of Education Act relating to Secondary Schools, and the undertaking of the Government to establish a third banch of the Education Office to deal therewith.*' Added Feb., 1900—'*To consider those provisions of the Board of Education Act which relate to the powers of the Board of Agriculture.*'

See Bd. of Education. Ann. Rep.; 1900 Cd. 328, xix, 1.

The Administration by the Meteorological Council of the Existing Parliamentary Grant

Cttee. Vol. I. Rep., pp. 20. 1904. Vol. II. Mins. of ev., apps. 1904

1904 *Cd.* 2123, *xviii*, 823. *Mins. of ev., etc.*; 1904 *Cd.* 2124, *xviii*, 843 *apptd. Dec.*, 1902. *sgd. May*, 1904

H. Maxwell (*Ch.*), Dewar, Abney, Hopwood, Elliott, Heath, Glazebrook, Larmor.

'*To inquire and report as to the administration by the Meteorological Council of the existing Parliamentary grant, and as to whether any changes in its apportionment are desirable in the interests of meteorological science and to make any further recommendations which may occur to them with a view to increasing the utility of that grant.*'

On the advice of the Royal Society, the Meteorological Office was started as a department of the Board of Trade, but in 1867 was put under the control of the Royal Society which, in return for an annual grant of £10,000, appointed a committee, later called the Meteorological Council, for the purpose. The Council was turned into a limited liability company with five directors paid out of a Parliamentary grant but appointed by the Society, to which an annual report was made. The Directors were bound by the Articles of Association to observe the directions of the Treasury. The Council had done its routine work with energy, but funds had not permitted it to undertake adequate research.

The Meteorological Office should now become a department under the control of the Ministry of Agriculture and Fisheries, to whose vote the grant of £15,000 should be transferred. The Post Office should arrange for earlier transmission of daily telegraphic reports from the 27 reporting stations. The efficacy of wireless telegraphy in transmitting advance news of Atlantic weather should be tested.

Constitution of the Consular Service

Cttee. Rep. pp. 5. 1903

1903 *Cd.* 1634, *lv*, 253 *apptd.* — *pres. July*, 1903

W. H. Walrond (*Ch.*), L. Cranborne, Mackay, Law.

'*To enquire (a) Whether the present limits of age for candidates, viz., 25 to 50, should be altered, and whether service in the capacity of Vice-Consul for a certain period should be required to qualify for promotion to the rank of Consul. (b) Whether any changes are desirable in the regulations governing entrance into the Consular Service and in the character of the examination, and in particular whether the subjects of examination should be extended, more especially with a view to encourage the acquisition of knowledge connected with commercial matters. (c) Whether the salaries should be, so far as possible, equalized, and a system of local allowances adopted, in order to remedy the present inequalities in the matter of pensions. The question of dividing the Service into distinct grades could be considered at the same time. (d) Whether means could be adopted to give Consular officers opportunities of increasing their personal knowledge of commercial matters, and to bring them more into personal contact with the commercial community.'*

The general Consular Service was unattractive to capable young men, as it was not a properly graded service; it offered no definite prospects of promotion since new entrants to the Service might be given promotion over those who had been in it for years. The present system of nomination should be abolished, and with few exceptions admission should be by limited competition and the age limits 22 to 27. This would encourage men with both a University and commercial training, who should be given preference, to enter, especially if the Service were reconstituted as recommended. The Secretary of State should have a reserved power to appoint any person to one of the higher posts for which special qualifications may be required, but such appointments should be exceptional. The Committee drew up recommended salary scales.

Board of Trade and the Local Government Board

Cttee. Rep. pp. vi. 1904

1904 *Cd.* 2121, *lxxviii*, 439
apptd. July, 1903. *sgd. May*, 1904

Lord Jersey (*Ch.*), Mackay, Ryan, Ryder, Emmott.

'To consider the position and duties of the Board of Trade and the Local Government Board, and to report whether any, and if so what, alterations should be made in the constitution and status of those Offices: also whether in the interests of administrative efficiency any rearrangement of duties between those and other Government Departments is desirable.'

The constitution of the Board of Trade was obsolete and should be abolished. It was important that relations between the commercial classes and the Board, whose responsibilities had greatly increased, should be amicable, and the view of those classes that the President of the Board should rank with the Secretaries of State was endorsed. No change in the constitution of the L.G.B. was necessary, and no transfer of duties was recommended.

Commercial Intelligence

Advisory Cttee. Rep., apps. pp. 43. 1904

1904 *Cd.* 2044, *xxiii*, 495
apptd. May, 1900. *sgd. March*, 1904

A. E. Bateman (*Ch.*), Smith, L. Avebury, L. Strathcona, Brittain, Craig-Brown, Dunstan, Harris, Hickman, Holderness, Holland, Law, Rollit, Wolff.

'For the purpose of advising the Board on the work of the Commercial Intelligence Branch of the Commercial, Labour, and Statistical Department for five years from this date.'

The Intelligence Branch of the Commercial, Labour and Statistical Department was created in 1900 as a result of the recommendations of the Committee on *The Dissemination of Commercial Information* (1898 C. 8962, xxxiii). The report gives an account of the four years' work of the Committee in aiding the Intelligence Branch, and calls attention to the publication of the Board of Trade Journal, and the expenditure of a grant of £1,000 in promoting a commercial mission to Siberia and in securing information through other commercial missions. The Appendices contain reports on *German Tariff* and *The new Russian and proposed new Austro-Hungarian Customs Tariffs.*

Further Reports. 1905–09; 1909 Cd. 4917, lxxxix, 307. 1910–13; 1913 Cd. 6779, lxvii, 383. 1913–17; 1917–18 Cd. 8815, xviii, 687.

British Trade After the War. Commercial Intelligence with Respect to Measures for Securing the Position, after the War, of Certain Branches of British Industry

Advisory Cttee. Rep.

1916 *Cd.* 8181. See *Trade*, p. 116.

Future Organization of Commercial Intelligence

Bd. of Trade and Foreign Office. Memo., apps. pp. 33. 1917

1917–18 *Cd.* 8715, *xxix*, 683

In view of the plans for developing commercial intelligence by both the Board of Trade and the Foreign Office, some difficulties had arisen in defining and adjusting the limits of responsibilities between them.   Under the existing system the Department of Commercial Intelligence of the Board of Trade has been the centre for the collation and dissemination of commercial intelligence, whether received from H.M. Trade Commissioners and Trade Correspondents within the Empire, or from H.M. Diplomatic and Consular Officers in foreign countries, but as the latter were under the Foreign Office, inconvenience had been caused by the duality of direction involved.   The Memo. contains the reports of the two Committees set up by the Secretary of State for Foreign Affairs and the President of the Board of Trade to consider the future relationship of the two Departments in these matters. There was agreement concerning the control of Commercial Attaches by the Foreign Office, but not on matters concerning the control of the collation and distribution of commercial intelligence by the Board of Trade.   The Memo. sets out the scheme agreed to by the two Departments in the light of the two Reports.   There 'will be created an enlarged Commercial Intelligence Department with a new Parliamentary Secretary who will act as an additional Parliamentary secretary at the Board of Trade and an additional Parliamentary

under-secretary for Foreign Affairs. All instructions issued to Commercial Attaches, etc., will come from the Secretary for Foreign Affairs; on all other matters the responsibility will lie with the Board of Trade.

Re-Organization of the Board of Trade

Memo., apps. pp. 7.   1918

1917–18 *Cd.* 8912, *xxix*, 675 *sgd. Jan.*, 1918

'After the War much greater demands than heretofore will be made upon the Board of Trade by the business interests of the country, and it is essential that steps should be taken forthwith to strengthen and improve the organization of the Department with a view to affording the assistance required for the maintenance of our commercial and industrial position.'

There will be two main departments: Commerce and Industry, and Public Services Administration. The former will include the following sections: Commerce Relations and Treaties, Industries and Manufacture, Industrial Property, Industrial Power and Transport, Statistics, a General Economic Department and a joint department with the Foreign Office, the Department of Overseas Trade. The Department of Public Services Administration will include the Marine Department, the Railway Department, the Public Utilities and Harbours Department, the Companies Department and the Bankruptcy Department. Attached to the Commerce and Industry Department there will be a strong Advisory Council with representative trade committees.

Organization of the Crown Agents' Office

Cttee. Rep. pp. xxiii. 1909. Mins. of ev., apps., index. 1909

1909 *Cd.* 4473, *xvi*, 377. *Mins. of ev., etc.*; 1909 *Cd.* 4474, *xvi*, 403 *apptd. May, sgd. Dec.*, 1908

J. E. B. Seely (*Ch.*), Mowatt, Spicer, Moor, Gibson, Bailey, Leathes, Harris.

'*To report upon the best method of selecting the clerical and technical staff for the Office of the Crown Agents for the Colonies, and particularly to consider the conditions of tenure, the scale of payment of salaries and pensions, and how far arrangements in that Office are in accord, or can be brought into harmony, with the principles governing the Civil Service.*'

A number of questions had been asked in Parliament and there had been agitation on the method of selecting and paying the staff. The Crown Agents are selected by the Secretary of State and hold office during the pleasure of the Crown, though the staffs are appointed by the Agents. The expenses of the office are met by fixed annual contributions and commissions fixed roughly in accordance with the amount of work done for each Colonial Administration. They are the agents of the Colonial Governments and are bound to carry out their instructions, though distance and their knowledge of markets means that considerable discretion must be given to them. It is incorrect to regard it as of the nature of a private mercantile firm doing work for the government. But no one Colony can claim an effective voice in the organization of the office, which must remain in the hands of the Secretary of State. The office as a general agency for the Colonies transacts miscellaneous financial business, including work connected with loans; selects and makes agreements with candidates for Colonial appointments; arranges for the carriage of indentured Indian labourers to the West Indies; buys and ships stores, etc.

It should be organized like a Department of the Home Civil Service, with a proper establishment and a definite scale of salaries based on those of the Home Civil Service. Appointment by open competitive examination should be in future applied to all the clerical staff. The work of shipping stores, now entrusted to an outside firm,

Messrs. Freelands, is unduly expensive, and does not provide for close supervision of the progress of contracts: it should be transferred to the Department of Crown Agents.

See *Functions of the Crown Agents for the Colonies.* Papers; 1881 C. 3075, lxiv, 589.

Remuneration of the Ordnance Survey Staff

Dept. Cttee. Rep. pp. 28. 1911. Mins. of ev., apps., index, analysis of ev. 1911

1911 *Cd.* 5825, *xxxvii*, 625. *Mins. of ev., etc.*; 1911 *Cd.* 5826, *xxxvii*, 653 *apptd. June*, 1910. *sgd. July*, 1911

Lord Ilkeston (*Ch.*), Barstow, Greig, Kelley, Rogers.

'*To enquire into the pay and classification of the Civil Assistants, Temporary Civil Assistants and Labourers employed on the Ordnance Survey, and to report whether, having regard to the conditions of their employment and to the rates current in analogous occupations, their remuneration is adequate.*'

The Ordnance Survey had been established over 100 years for the purpose of producing military maps for the War Office; but its function had changed over time, so that its activities now covered the needs of other government departments. Similarly the constitution of its staff had changed from a purely military personnel to a combination of military and civilian staff; in 1910 the civilian staff numbered 1,800 and the soldiers about 330. The control of civilian employees by military officials differentiated the Ordnance Survey from other branches of the public service and this was, in some degree, responsible for the complaints amongst civilian employees about conditions of service. A large number of complaints were examined, the chief of which concerned the new classification of Civil Assistants, which introduced a newly constituted third-class grade and also limited numbers coming under the first class to one-sixth of total numbers, and matters relating to periods of service qualifying for maximum and minimum pay, allowances, etc. No general alterations in the minimum and maximum rates of pay were recommended, but the age at which employees should become entitled to minimum rates should be 22 years instead of 24, and final maximum pay should be obtained after 30 years instead of 35 years' service. The third-class classification should be abolished and a new second-class grade substituted for it, and the existing second class subject to new scales of pay. Promotion to the first-class grade should generally be by seniority and the numbers in this class should remain at one-sixth of total numbers, but the Director-General should have discretionary powers to alter this proportion. The position of Superintendents was more clearly defined and promotion should be solely by merit. Other recommendations concerned sick leave, allowances and rates for various trades.

Coast Guard
Rep.

1908 *Cd.* 4091. See *Sea Transport.* p. 171.

Amalgamation of the Customs and Excise Departments

Cttee. Rep. pp. 24. 1911. Mins. of ev. 1911

1911 *Cd.* 5830, *xv*, 287. *Mins. of ev.*; 1911 *Cd.* 5834, *xv*, 313 *apptd. March*, 1909. *sgd. Aug.*, 1911

C. E. H. Hobhouse (*Ch.*), Parry, Meers, Holt, Ramsay.

'*To consider the conditions under which the amalgamation of the Customs and Excise Departments, rendered necessary by the Finance Act of* 1908, *can best be carried out, with regard to the particular classes of officers affected by such amalgamation.*'

The most difficult problems which would have to be solved if the two departments were united arose from scales of salaries, grades and promotion prospects, all of which were the subject of detailed recommendations. Seniority and the promotion open to the lower staff of both services were especially complex questions: it was recommended that there be only one class of subordinate officers, with a uniform scale of remuneration and promotion. There should be one entrance examination for the whole service, both indoor and outdoor, and candidates should be between 19 and 21 years.

Customs Waterguard Service and the Customs Watchers

Cttee. Rep., apps. pp. 23. 1912. Mins. of ev. 1912

1912–13 *Cd.* 6290, *xvii*, 647. *Mins. of ev.*; 1912–13 *Cd.* 6299, *xvii*, 671 *apptd. Oct.*, 1911. *sgd. May*, 1912

J. W. Cawston (*Ch.*), Lewis, Armitage-Smith.

'*To inquire into the organization, pay, and conditions of employment, etc., of the Customs Waterguard Service and the Customs Watchers.*'

The Customs Waterguard is primarily a preventive force charged with the duty of protecting the revenue and preventing frauds thereon. Certain duties relating to public health have also been performed for many years. The present organization of the service dates from 1891, but since that date there has been an addition of various non-revenue duties performed for other departments, such as those under the Merchant Shipping Acts of 1894 and 1906, the Aliens Act of 1905, and the Diseases of Animals Acts, etc. There has also been a large increase in revenue duties proper, owing to the large increase in passenger traffic.

The contention was that promises held out to the staff in the Minute of 1891 had been broken. The Committee did not agree that there was any valid argument based on retrospective grievances, but they examined the various ranks of the service upon their merits and made recommendations as to recruitment, pay, promotion, etc., and on general questions such as night work, superannuation, etc., which affected the whole service.

See Customs. Ann. Rep.; 1890–91 C. 6538, xxvi, 179. Treasury Minute; 1890–91 (161) lxiii, 401.

The Architects and Surveyors' and Engineering Divisions of H.M. Office of Works, London

Cttee. Rep. pp. 32. 1914

1914 *Cd.* 7416, *xlix*, 835
apptd. Feb., sgd. Oct., 1913

G. C. V. Holmes (*Ch.*), Robinson, Millar.

'*To inquire into and report upon the organization of the Architects and Surveyors' and the Engineering Divisions of the Office of Works.*'

The Principal Architect and Surveyor is responsible to the Board (the First Commissioners, the Secretary, the Assistant Secretary) for the general supervision and control at headquarters of the work of the whole staff. The Principal Architect and Surveyor for Scotland is responsible for all the Board's architectural interests in Scotland. There are eleven architects and surveyors and the division of work between them is by services, each having charge of a particular type of building. This system tends to narrow their experience and involves additional time and expense in travelling; and headquarters' architects are apt to act independently of one another in the same area, thus giving rise to confusion and loss of public money. The system should be retained, especially as two-thirds of provincial expenditure is on post offices, but assistant architects should be moved from branch to branch before being specialized. The pressure of administrative work leaves little time for the more important work

of design and supervision of new buildings, etc.

Recommendations were made for bringing the staff at headquarters in London together in one building; for regularizing the work not included in contracts already sanctioned; for centralizing the books and records containing the same facts but now kept in separate divisions; and for the establishment of a contract branch for all invitations and acceptances. There were also recommendations on architectural work for the diplomatic and consular services, on the employment of outside architects and on the appointment and conditions of service of the various branches of the architects, surveyors, and engineering divisions.

Special Work of the Local Government Board Arising out of the War

Rep., app. pp. 42. 1915

1914–16 *Cd.* 7763, *xxv*, 299
pres. Dec., 1914

H. C. Munro.

There were six reports on the special work of the various departments. 1. *Steps taken for the prevention and relief of distress* and 2. *Special Work of the Poor Law Division* by A. V. Symonds. 3. *Reception and Accommodation of War Refugees* by E. H. Rhodes. 4. *Steps taken to secure Co-operation between Civil and Military Authorities in regard to sanitary matters* by Dr. Newsholme and F. J. Willis. 5. *Colonial Gifts in kind received in the country, and on a scheme for supplying the poor in London with coal*, and *The Christmas Ship from the United States* by N. T. Kershaw. See *State of Employment in the United Kingdom*. Reps. p. 238.

Public Offices (Sites) Bill

Sel. Cttee. Rep., proc., mins of ev. pp. vi, 41. 1912

1912–13 (204), *ix*, 175
apptd. April, o.p. July, 1912.

W. Benn (*Ch.*), Murray, Ormsby-Gore, Radford, L. Thynne.

The Bill was introduced on behalf of the Office of Works for the acquisition first of certain premises in Whitehall Gardens for the purpose of enabling new offices to be built for the Board of Trade; secondly, of certain premises at Took's Court adjoining the Patent Office, for the extension of the Patent Office; and, thirdly, of certain land and premises adjoining the Record Office, for the extension of the Record Office and its protection from fire.

See 1912–13 2 & 3 Geo. 5. c. cx.

6. CIVIL SERVICE

Superannuation in the Civil Service

R. Com. Rep. pp. xviii. 1903. Mins. of ev., apps., index. 1903

1903 *Cd.* 1744, *xxxiii,* 209. *Mins. of ev., etc.*; 1903 *Cd.* 1745, *xxxiii,* 227 *apptd. Nov.,* 1902. *sgd. Aug.,* 1903

Lord Courtney (*Ch.*), Henderson, Gurdon, Moulton, Dickinson, Morton, Bunn, Knox, Brabrook.

'To inquire whether it is possible so to amend the existing system of superannuation of persons in the Civil Service of the State as to confer greater and more uniform advantages upon those to whom it applies without increasing the burden which it imposes on the taxpayer.'

The conditions of service whereby each servant was assured a definite remuneration during service, and of a pension upon retirement was satisfactory. The Commissioners rejected the argument that the difference between current remuneration and the higher salary which would have had to be paid had there been no pension was more than was necessary to provide for a pension. But some provision, which could be financed by a reduction in the amount of the pension, should be made for the representatives of a servant who died either in the Service or before a certain amount had been paid out to him, after retirement. This should apply to all classes of pensionable servants except women, unless their

omission would be administratively inconvenient. Henderson and Moulton disagreed with the recommendation that the new system should be obligatory on new entrants. In a Minority Report Knox and Brabrook maintained that short of increasing the cost to the taxpayer, no more advantageous system of superannuation than the existing one could be devised.

Civil Service

R. Com.

apptd. March, 1912

Lord MacDonnell (*Ch.*), Duke of Devonshire, Bishop of Southwark, Mackenzie, Primrose, MacAlister, Granet, Baker, Booth, Boutwood, Clynes, Hoare, Holt, Matheson, Shipley, Snowden, Wallas, Haldane (Miss E. S.), Streatfeild (Mrs. L. A. E.).

'To inquire into and report on the methods of making appointments to and promotions in the Civil Service, including the Diplomatic and Consular Services, and the legal departments; to investigate the working and efficiency of the system of competitive examination for such appointments, and to make recommendations for any alterations or improvements in that system which may appear to be advisable; and to consider whether the existing scheme of organization meets the requirements of the Public Service, and to suggest any modifications which may be needed therein.'

The first three Reports are formal presentations of the following volumes of minutes of evidence: 1912–13 Cd. 6210, Cd. 6535, xv, 113.   1913 Cd. 6740, xviii, 279

—— Fourth Report. pp. v, 157. 1914. App. 1914. Mins. of ev. 1914

1914 *Cd.* 7338, *xvi,* 1. *Mins. of ev., etc.* 1914 *Cd.* 7339, *Cd.* 7340, *xvi,* 165 *sgd. April,* 1914.

add Beck, del. Baker

Majority Report. Lord MacDonnell, Duke of Devonshire, Bishop of Southwark, Mackenzie, MacAlister, Beck, Boutwood, Clynes, Hoare, Holt, Matheson, Shipley, Snowden, Wallas, Haldane (Miss E. S.), Streatfeild (Mrs. L. A. E.).—Manual workers, and post office servants, etc., whose conditions were being investigated by other bodies being excluded, the number covered by the enquiry was 65,000, of whom 35,000 are permanent. A review of the development of the method of appointment from patronage, to limited and finally to open competition, which regulates entry to the administrative and clerical classes and a large number of departmental posts, shows that there are still many posts open only to limited competition, to qualifying examination without competition, and to patronage. Of the 65,000, 20,000 are selected by open competition, 2,000 by limited competition between persons having prescribed qualifications and 8,500 persons needing physical strength, integrity, etc., by nomination followed by a qualifying examination (e.g. prison officers); 250 permanent heads of departments, etc., are appointed directly by the Crown. There are also 1,200 professional officers (e.g. lawyers, accountants, scientists) and 25,000 temporary civil servants (3,000 clerical, 2,000 semi-technical, the remainder unskilled and subordinate).

(1) General Civil Service.—Administrative and Clerical. The duties range from simple routine duties to those requiring high intellectual effort; the increasing complexity of administration requires division of labour as a fundamental principle. Recruitment should be organized to fit the stages of the educational system—at 16, at the completion of secondary education at 18, and at 22–24, the end of the University stage and the competitive examinations should be framed accordingly. The educational system should be organized so that passage from one stage to the next is open to suitable candidates. The competitive examination is the best method of recruiting this group. (a) Boy clerks are recruited between 15 and 16, and discharged at 18. The service is temporary, it is not an apprenticeship, and the age limit does not correspond with either the primary or secondary school course. This class should be abolished and merged with the assistant clerks to form a new Junior Clerical Class, recruited at 16, with one year's probation, at a salary of £50, rising to £200, with an efficiency bar at £130. (b) The Second Division consists of 4,000 clerks of varied capacity and training performing a great variety of duties, a quarter of them being boy clerks promoted by passing the Second Division Examination, others holding a university degree. The age of recruitment, 17–20, does not correspond to the end of the secondary school course, 18; one-third of the work could be assigned to a lower class. This class and the intermediate class should be merged into a new Senior Clerical Class, recruited at the end of the secondary school course at 18. Salary should be £85–£350 with an efficiency bar at £290. Within the class there should be a number of staff posts of special responsibility, with salaries of £450–£500. There should be an immediate downgrading of work which could be done by a lower class. (c) The Administrative Class consists of 450 persons. The best education taken in conjunction with the training and influences of university life produces the best type of public servant. It is not by lowering the standard of entry, but by enabling the sons of poor parents to get university education that the interests of democracy and the public service can best be reconciled. The suggestion that the written examination should be accompanied by a *viva voce* conducted by three experienced examiners is made, as well as the appointment of a specially qualified committee to examine the syllabus, etc., to see if the examination gave undue bias in favour of the older universities and particular studies.

(2) Appointments held directly from the Crown should include all permanent headships of great departments, but certain offices now so held should

be ranked as professional. It is undesirable that any of these should be made by patronage; appointments made from outside the Civil Service should be notified to Parliament. (3) Departmental Civil Servants recruited for service in particular departments.—The number of different examinations should be reduced and brought into harmony with the educational system; and the remaining cases of personal selection by Minister or official abolished. (4) Professional and Technical.—Where possible qualified persons under 27 should be recruited by competitive examinations, others by public advertisement and scrutiny of the most suitable by the Civil Service Commission. (5) Temporary employment.—Temporary employees should be engaged for definite periods. Where the situation proved likely to become permanent, those who are satisfactory should be established and others discharged. The rule that promotion should be by merit should be made universal.

The opportunities for promotion to the Administrative Class have been adequate, but it should take place early, the period of qualifying service being reduced to six years. Efficiency bars should be strictly enforced. All officers of the administrative and clerical classes should be liable to be transferred. A large number of specific recommendations are made regarding individual departments.

General Control.—A third member should be added to the Civil Service Commission. General discipline should remain under the control of the Departmental Head. Defects in the organization and recruitment of the Service could have been obviated if Treasury control had been more informed and effective; a new Section of the Treasury should be created for this purpose.

Employment of Women. — The governing principle should be to employ women where the public interest will be promoted; in so far as the character and condition of work approximate to those of men, women's pay should approximate to that of men; where the efficiency of men is higher, their pay should be higher. The Treasury should hold an inquiry to see what positions should be filled by women. Termination of service on marriage should continue.

Civil Service and Citizenship.— Claims to full political rights are rejected, as conflicts between public duty and private interest would arise, and the Civil Service would lose public confidence. Members of the general Departmental and Professional Service should be placed under an obligation by Order in Council or Departmental Regulation, to observe reticence in speech and writing on political questions; as it is undesirable that they should run the risk of being mixed up in local politics, uniform regulations should be made by the Treasury with respect to candidatures for local bodies. For subordinate officers it would be sufficient if they were prohibited from using their official position to influence elections. The rules have imposed restrictions on the political action of individuals and left associations unfettered, but the difficulty arises only because of the desire of associations to affiliate with political parties. A special inquiry should be made into the question of recognition of associations, their trade union functions, the right to strike, and rights of affiliation to political bodies.

There are a number of reservations. Minority Report. Primrose, Granet, Booth.—The organization must have regard not only to the service as a whole, but to the departments of which it is composed. The existing five classes should be replaced by three, selected by separate examinations, at 16, 18 and 22-24. Promotion must be on a Departmental, not a Service basis, and there should not be systematic transfers between departments. Women's employment should be extended, mainly in classes of work in which they are now engaged. Civil Servants should be allowed to vote, but not to be candidates for Parliament or local bodies. Associations of Civil Servants for the promotion of Service interests should not be allowed to affiliate to outside bodies.

—— Fifth Report. pp. iv, 47. 1914. Mins. of ev., apps., index. 1914

1914–16 Cd. 7748, *xi*, 673. *Mins. of ev., etc.*; 1914–16 Cd. 7749, *xi*, 725 *sgd. Dec.*, 1914

del. Granet

I. The Diplomatic Corps and the Foreign Office.—Candidates for admission to the Diplomatic Corps and Diplomatic Establishment first had to obtain permission of the Secretary of State, as persons suitable for a diplomatic career and as having the prescribed income, to appear before a Board of Selection, after which they took an examination. This was unsatisfactory. The income qualification and the Secretary of State's initial inquiry should be abolished. The Board of Selection was too departmental in membership and should be widened. Acceptance of candidates, who should be able to present themselves at any time before the age of 19, would depend on their being passed by the Board before sitting for the examination. In a reservation Beck, Holt, Clynes, Wallas and Mrs. Streatfeild, said that this would limit the area of selection to schoolboys who had a uniform social background. Selection should be at 24 after the examination, when candidates of varied educational careers would be available.

Amongst the numerous recommendations on the organization of the Service were that the Diplomatic Corps and Diplomatic Establishment should be amalgamated into a single foreign service, that there should be a Promotions Committee to advise the Secretary of State, and that the principle of transfer should be applied to the Foreign Office. The number of Commercial Attachés should be increased and their functions should be advisory. Proposals were made on salaries, etc., living allowances, etc.

Primrose and Booth objected to the amalgamation of the two branches of the service, Boutwood to the abolition of the property qualification and to any assimilation of the Diplomatic Service to clerical services outside the Foreign Office. Hare dissented from the report because the Foreign Service differs from the Home Service in essentials and should not have imposed on it the uniformity of recruitment and organization suitable for the latter, because it is at present efficiently administered and is the best in the world.

II. The Consular Service.—From an early date the service has consisted of three divisions, the General, the Levant and the Far Eastern, each of which had a distinct history and organization, based on the languages, government and customs of the countries concerned. Much would be lost by any attempt at amalgamation. The attempt, following the Walrond Committee (1903) to recruit from candidates possessing commercial experience had failed. They should be recruited from the open market at any age corresponding to a definite stage in the educational system, and then trained for the work. For the General and Levant divisions this should be at the completion of secondary education and the proposed Senior Clerical Examination should be passed, followed by two years at a university and an extended period as probationers with the Foreign Office and the Board of Trade. For the Far Eastern Service recruitment should be by the Class I examination, followed by a study of Oriental languages in a university and the countries concerned. Salary scales are proposed, as well as a Promotions Committee.

—— Sixth Report. pp. vi, 84. 1915. Mins. of ev., apps., index. 1915

1914–16 Cd. 7832, *xii*, 1. *Mins. of ev., etc.*; 1914–16 Cd. 8130, *xii*, 91 *sgd. Nov.*, 1915

add H. B. Smith (*Ch.*), L. Mersey, L. Dundas, Paul, Coward, Kempe, Hewett.

del. Lord MacDonnell (*Ch.*), Duke of Devonshire, Primrose, Mackenzie, Beck, Booth.

This Report concerned the English and Scottish Legal Departments, but there was no enquiry into those not maintained from Parliamentary funds nor into the position of judges. Certain reforms were urgently required. (1) England. With few exceptions all appointments were by nomination, subject in certain higher offices to a statutory qualification and in the case of clerical staff to an elementary examination. No public announcement is made, and in England influence is exerted to obtain posts for relatives and friends; in the case of clerks the educational standard is unduly low. In England the Lord Chancellor should control all legal departments and appointments to them. He should be assisted by an Advisory Committee, promotions should be by merit, and there should be transfers between departments. As far as possible selection of clerical staff should be by open competition, based on the examination for the Senior Clerical Class. The work of different classes of clerks should be clearly defined, routine work assigned to subordinate officers and Civil Service rules of promotion, sick leave, etc., should be adopted. The officers should be liable to attend seven hours a day and attendance books should be kept at all offices. (ii) Scotland. Nominations to the more important legal offices were in the hands of the Lord Advocate and were political. The system was indefensible and should be ended. Where selection by open competitive examination could not be applied, the appointing authority (Lord Advocate or Secretary for Scotland) should be assisted by an Advisory Committee as recommended for Civil Service Professional Appointments. Entrants to certain offices should have passed a legal or a qualifying Civil Service examination, with an age limit to entry of 35. There should be regular

systems of promotion, Civil Service conditions should be applied to all departments, and the retirement age fixed at 65. Recommendations are made on the organization of the legal departments.

Seven members disagreed with the exception to open competition proposed for certain English appointments, four thought that the abolition of political appointments in Scotland required a change in the system of appointment, and disagreed with the proposal to transfer certain appointments from the Secretary for Scotland to the Lord Advocate. Dundas was not in favour of altering the existing system of appointment by the Lord Advocate.

Formal Reps. not cited. Mins. of ev.; 1912–13 Cd. 6210, Cd. 6535, xv, 113. 1913 Cd. 6740, xviii, 279.   4th Rep. Mins. of ev.; 1914 Cd. 7338, Cd. 7339, Cd. 7340, xvi, 1.   5th Rep. Mins. of ev.; 1914–16 Cd. 7748, Cd. 7749, xi, 673.   6th Rep. Mins. of ev.; 1914–16 Cd. 7832, Cd. 8130, xii, 1.

Employment of Conscientious Objectors

Cttee. Rules. pp. 4. 1917. 1918

1917–18 *Cd.* 8550, *Cd.* 8627, *Cd.* 8884, *xix*, 685

The papers give the rules made by the Committee governing its employment of conscientious objectors. The rules deal with their allocation to work, their lodging, food and other allowances, the hours at which they should be in their quarters, and also prohibiting them from undertaking public propaganda, making public speeches, etc.

Cd. 8884 gives additional rules under which after twelve months good conduct, they might qualify for employment by private employers at full wages, subject to satisfactory monthly reports by the employers.

Civil Service—Class I. Examination

Cttee. Rep., apps. pp. 32. 1917

1917–18 *Cd.* 8657, *viii*, 119
apptd. Nov., 1916. *sgd. June*, 1917

S. Leathes (*Ch.*), Ewing, Miers, Hadow, Adams.

'*To consider and report upon the existing scheme of examination for Class I of the Home Civil Service: To submit for the consideration of the Lords Commissioners of His Majesty's Treasury a revised scheme such as they may judge to be best adapted for the selection of the type of officer required for that class of the Civil Service, and at the same time most advantageous to the higher education of this country: And in framing such a scheme, to take into account, so far as possible, the various other purposes which the scheme in question has hitherto served, and to consult the India Office, the Foreign Office, and the Colonial Office as to their requirements, in so far as they differ from those of the Home Civil Service.*'

The Civil Service Commissioners had decided that although literary subjects were, on the whole, the best preparation for the Higher Civil Service, effect should be given to the recommendation of the Royal Commission of 1912 (4th Rep., recommendation 22) that a Committee should consider a new scheme for the examination. Macaulay's theory underlying selection by open competitive examination was based upon conditions which no longer existed; a great number of subjects had been added to the syllabus of universities, and classification was taking the place of strict order of merit. The examination system had been condemned on various grounds, such as laying too much emphasis on the classics and giving excessive preference to Oxford and Cambridge, and while these views were not endorsed by the Committee, they proposed that the system should be adapted to the chief varieties of university education. The main schools of learning were to be put on an equal footing in the new scheme, complete details of which were given.

7 (*a*). LOCAL GOVERNMENT

Fire Brigades

Sel. Cttee. Rep., proc. pp. lxiv. 1900

1900 (278) *vi*, 943
apptd. Feb., *o.p.*, *July*, 1900

J. Collings (*Ch.*), Bowles, Cameron, Duncombe, Fardell, Farrell, Heath, Howell, Jones, Malcolm, Palmer, Pym, Reckitt, Richardson, Wyndham-Quin.

'*To inquire and report as to the existing arrangements for the provision of Fire Brigades (including both staff and appliances) in England and Wales excepting the Metropolitan Fire Brigade; the adequacy of such arrangements for the due protection of life and property from destruction or injury from fire, and the Amendments, if any, which are necessary or desirable in the law on the subject.*'

The systems for dealing with fire vary considerably throughout the country. Some of them are established under the general law, or what is understood to be the general law, and others under special or local Acts of Parliament. In the large cities and towns the arrangements are generally adequate, but in the smaller places they are often inadequate, whilst in very many places there are no arrangements at all. Where there is a volunteer fire brigade, there is no guarantee that they possess adequate knowledge for the job. All previous Acts should be repealed. Local Authorities should be constituted fire authorities. Professional fire brigades should be on an established superannuation scheme. Licences for public building should be conditional upon the provision of suitable fire appliances. Records of loss of life and property should be forwarded to the Government Department. Fire Insurance Companies should be required to contribute some portion of the expenses connected with fire estimates.

Municipal Trading

Jt. Sel. Cttee. Rep., proc., mins. of ev.,
    apps. pp. x, 513. Index. 1900

1900 (305) and (305-*Ind.*), *vii*, 183
apptd. April, o.p. July, 1900

Lord Crewe (*Ch.*), L. Rothschild, L.
Peel, L. Hampden, L. Windsor,
Lawson, Hobhouse, Fry, Foster, Dunn.

'To *consider and report as to the principles
which should govern powers given by Bills
and Provisional Orders to municipal and
other local authorities for industrial enterprise within or without the area of their
jurisdiction.*'

The report is a formal presentation
of the minutes of evidence with a
recommendation that the Committee
should be re-appointed in the next
Session. Although the terms of reference are specific on the point that
guidance is asked on the principles
which should govern the powers given
in Bills, the Committee had investigated
a much wider field. This was due to the
public discussion as expressed in the
resolution passed by the London
Chamber of Commerce in 1899 to the
effect 'that the scope and sphere of
municipal enterprise in opposition to
private enterprise should be defined'
(q. 762) and in the debate in the House
of Commons on 29th March, 1900 on
the discrepancies which could arise in
the treatment of individual Bills where
there was not sufficient direction given
by Parliament to the Departments
concerning new developments, in e.g.
the conditions of purchase of individual
companies; the demand of authorities
to operate outside their areas, or to
operate in new fields of trading.

Sir Courtenay Boyle, Permanent
Secretary, Board of Trade, stated in
evidence that many proposals had been
made by municipalities for novel powers,
either to carry on within their own
boundaries new forms of trading, such
as pawnbroking, accepting money on
deposit, selling internal gas and
electric fittings, providing bathing huts,

recreational equipment, etc., or to
extend their undertakings beyond their
boundaries. The Department needed
guidance from Parliament on treatment;
these should be given in Provisional
Orders, but should not be required
to call the attention of Parliament to
every novel power outlined in every
private Bill.

Much of the evidence was on the
difficulty of setting the limits to novel
powers, which were often an out-
growth of existing services, and on the
pros and cons of municipal trading in
general and in particular services.
Lord Avebury argued against it 'from
the old school of political economists'
(Mill, Fawcett) on the grounds of
probable loss, and checking of individual enterprise, the excessive demands
on the time of councillors, and the
development of municipal labour
problems. Other evidence was that
municipal trading should be confined
to things which are beyond the powers
of an individual to supply (q. 764);
municipalities should not be allowed
to make profits or use profits for rate
relief (q. 2798). Electrical development
had been hindered by municipalities
protecting their gas undertakings, and
by slackness in electrifying trams
(Swinton qq. 1304-5: Garcké q. 1186).
The use of the Fair Wages clause and
of direct labour were also criticized.
Municipal works departments were
unable to establish proper relations
between master and workman (Shepherd qq. 3538-9) and were unfair in
competition with retailers and other
private traders.

Officers and representatives of local
authorities gave evidence on the
municipal trading in relation to local
circumstances (e.g. Birmingham, Manchester, Liverpool, Leeds, Glasgow),
pointing out that other motives for
municipal trading were better service
and reduced costs; it was justified where
the service was a necessity, was a
monopoly, or required the use of the
streets (qq. 2765, 3047-53).

Municipal Trading

Jt. Sel. Cttee. Rep., proc., mins. of ev., app., index. pp. xviii, 462. 1903

1903 (270) *vii*, 1
apptd. June, o.p. July, 1903

Lord Crewe (*Ch.*), L. Zouche, L. Barnard, L. Brougham and Vaux, L. Aberdare, L. Lamington, L. Rothschild, Bartley, Fenwick, Joyce, Platt-Higgins, Powell - Williams, Stirling - Maxwell, Woodhouse.

'*To consider and Report as to the principles which should govern powers given by Bills and Provisional Orders to Municipal and other Local Authorities for Industrial Enterprise within or without the Area of their Jurisdiction.*'

The Committee decided not to discuss the general question of municipal trading dealt with by the former Committee, but to confine its attention to the form of municipal accounts, their audit and the ratepayers' right of access to them. Wherever municipal trading exists, 'ratepayers should be not less fully and continuously informed of the success or failure of each undertaking than if they were shareholders in an ordinary trading company. In a large number of cases this is undoubtedly done, but there is in some instances evidence to a contrary effect, and in view of the ever-increasing number and magnitude of municipal undertakings, it is most desirable that a high and uniform standard of account-keeping should prevail throughout the country.' As it was doubtful in view of the different local conditions, whether a standard form of keeping accounts could be prescribed, the professional bodies should be asked to confer with the local government departments on the matter.

As regards Audit, the 'Municipal Corporations in England and Wales, with a few exceptions, are subject only to the provisions of the Municipal Corporations Act, 1882, by which one auditor who must be a member of the Town Council, is nominated by the Mayor, and two, who cannot be members of the Town Council, are elected by the ratepayers. The evidence shows that no effective system of audit is thus supplied. The elective auditors are poorly paid, or are unpaid altogether, little interest is taken in their election, and although in some cases they are able to lay a finger on a particular irregularity, it is not clear that they could not make the same discovery in the capacity of active ratepayers. No complete or continuous audit is ever attempted by them. All county councils, the London borough councils, the urban district councils are subject to the L.G.B. audit. This audit is carried out by District Auditors, who as a rule are not accountants, and are not, in the opinion of the Committee, properly qualified to discharge the duties which should devolve upon them. The duties of the auditors seem to be practically confined to certification of figures, and to the noting of illegal items of expenditure.'

A uniform system of audit should be applied to all the major local authorities. The auditor should have right of access to all material necessary and be entitled to require from officers of the authority such information and explanations as may be necessary for his duty. He should certify that separate accounts of all trading undertakings have been kept, and that every charge which each ought to bear has been duly debited, that in his opinion the accounts issued present a true and correct view of the transactions and results of trading and that due provision has been made out of the Revenue for the repayment of loans, that items of receipts and expenditure and all known liabilities have been brought into account, and that the value of all assets has in all cases been fairly stated. He should also be required to express an opinion upon the adequacy of the amounts set aside to meet depreciation and obsolescence of plant in addition to the statutory sinking funds, etc. In view of these proposals, powers of surcharge and disallowance could be dispensed with, but the local authority should forward detailed accounts and the auditor's report to the L.G.B.

Mr. T. B. Cockerton, and some witnesses who appeared before the 1900 Committee, including Mr. Floyd, elected auditor and Mr. Orford Smith, City Clerk, of Birmingham, gave evidence on methods of audit, and the duties and discretion of auditors.

Public Health Acts (Amendment) Bill [H.L.]

Sel. Cttee. HL. Rep., proc., mins. of ev., index. pp. x, 118, 22. 1905

1905 (343) vii, 573
apptd. June, o.p. Aug., 1905

Lord Allerton (Ch.), L. Zouche, L. Digby, L. Kenyon, L. Stanley, L. Hylton, L. Burghclere.

The Bill was devised to confer upon the L.G.B. the power to extend the Public Health (Amendment) Act, 1890 to rural areas. The clauses relate chiefly to streets, buildings, sewers, sanitary provisions, etc. Reported with some amendments.

Municipal Representation Bill [H.L.]

Sel. Cttee. HL. Rep., proc., mins. of ev., apps. pp. xviii, 171. 1907

1907 (HL. 132), vii, 123
apptd. April, o.p. July, 1907

Lord Belper (Ch.), L. Hardwicke, L. Cathcart, L. Beauchamp, L. Colchester, L. Monteagle, L. Ampthill, L. Avebury, L. Haversham, L. Courtney, L. Allendale, L. Bishop of Bristol.

Dissatisfaction was felt with the triennial elections in some metropolitan boroughs where the minority did not get a single seat. The Committee stated that it was not surprising that where this happens the minority should 'turn its attention to some system of election which would ensure a fair representation of minorities'. In boroughs outside London, where a third of the councillors are elected each year, there had been no discussion on alternative

methods of conducting elections and no witness from them was empowered to speak for their Authority on the matter.

The system of proportional representation was explained by Mr. Fischer Williams, who drafted the Bill, and by Mr. Humphreys, the secretary of the Proportional Representation Society. The Committee saw no difficulties from the administrative point of view, but doubted 'whether the ordinary voter, ... even if he carried out accurately the instructions ... would get the result he desired'.

The Bill would provide for a more adequate representation of minorities, and should be amended so as to enable any council to make an experiment for three years, if it decided to do so by a three-fifths majority, to extend the period, or to revert to the existing mode of election.

Highway Authorities and Administration in England and Wales

Rep.

1904 Cd. 1793. See Transport. p. 154.

Question of Devolution by County Education Authorities

Rep.

1908 Cd. 3952. See Education. p. 309.

7 (b). LOCAL TAXATION AND FINANCIAL ADMINISTRATION

Local Taxation

R. Com.

apptd. Aug., 1896

Lord Balfour of Burleigh (Ch.), L. Cawdor, L. Blair Balfour, Hibbert, Wortley, Hamilton, Murray, Dalton, Cripps, Clare, Elliott, O'Connor, Smith, Stuart, Wharton.

'To inquire into the present system under which taxation is raised for local purposes, and to report whether all kinds of real and personal property contribute equitably to *such taxation, and, if not, what alterations in the law are desirable in order to secure that result.'*

—— First Report, *Valuation for and Collection of Local Rates*, apps. pp. 62. 1899

1899 C. 9141, *xxxv*, 733
sgd. Dec., 1898

An alteration of the law for the purpose of obtaining a uniform basis of valuation is a necessary preliminary to any revision of the system of local taxation, and is independent of any recommendations ultimately made on the general questions in the terms of reference.

The Acts of 1597 and 1601 made a poor rate compulsory, but left open many questions as to who was liable and on what basis the rates should be levied, and gave no directions on the method of assessment. In 1589 Jeffrey's case decided that an occupier as well as an inhabitant was liable, while the Act of 1597 and a conference of judges laid down as the basis of ability the annual benefit of specified properties. Anthony Earby's case, 1633, laid it down that taxable capacity was to be measured by the visible properties, both real and personal, of the inhabitants within and only within, the parish. Wages, profits from labour and investment, and furniture were exempt. There was a long legal controversy as to whether stock-in-trade was rateable, and, in spite of legal decisions favouring this course, in practice it was not generally rated, except in the south and west centres of woollen and cloth manufacture. The difficulties of rating by ability were increased as manufacture and commerce increased and as capital could migrate. In 1840 the rating of stock-in-trade was prohibited. The Parochial Assessments Act, 1836, gave a definition of net annual value, but laid down no scale of deductions from gross value, and provided no means of compelling new valuations, although some valuations had been used for 100 years.

A review of the current systems of valuation and collection of the poor rate, borough rate and rates in the County of London shows that they lacked uniformity, equality and simplicity. Outside London there could be five independent valuations in the same area, the number of valuation authorities was over 1,000, there was no uniform system of deductions, no necessary time at which a valuation list had to be made, nor any guarantee that the Union Assessment Committees were fairly representative of the interests within their areas. Frequently collections were made in the same area at different times by different collectors appointed by different authorities. Many attempts to improve the assessment had been abortive.

There should be only one valuation authority in each county and its valuation list should be the basis of all rates. Counties and County Boroughs might agree to one such authority for the geographical county. District Committees should be appointed. The valuation list should be prepared by professional surveyors, every property valued at least once every five years and a maximum scale of deductions laid down. Special properties, such as railways, mines, telephones and electricity works should be valued by an appointed valuer, with a right of appeal. Collections of all rates in boroughs should be made by borough councils and in urban districts by the Guardians; and the rate should be levied on one demand note.

In a separate memo. T. H. Elliott objects to the proposal to give the work of valuation to counties and county boroughs and prefers the use of smaller areas and of the surveyors of taxes.

—— Second Report, *Valuation and Rating in Respect of Tithe Rentcharge.* pp. 39. 1899

1899 C. 9142, *xxxv*, 795
sgd. Jan., 1899

After reviewing the history of the statutory liability of the incumbent to be assessed to the poor rate and of the ambiguity arising from the Act of 1601 as to whether he was to be rated as an occupier or as an inhabitant, the Commission conclude that the owners of tithes not severed from the benefice have shown that the rate burden is unduly onerous, insufficient allowance having been made for the fact that they are under an obligation to perform duties in return for them and that in practice the existing law places them in a much less favourable position than other owners who are occupiers. Since 1836 tithe rent-charge has decreased in value by 30 per cent, the incumbents have been deprived by the Courts of deductions which used to be made, many new rates have been placed upon tithes and the Agricultural Rates Act, 1896, has had the effect of adding to their burdens. For no other class of owners does assessment result in the contribution of so large a proportion of income to local taxation. They are entitled to some special relief pending the Commission's final recommendations. Blair Balfour dissents from any proposal for special treatment pending final recommendation; Cripps, Hibbert and Murray proposed further deductions on gross values, O'Connor an extension to tithe rent-charge of the Agricultural Rates Act, 1896.

—— Final Report, England Wales. pp. viii, 184. 1901

1901 Cd. 638, xxiv, 413 sgd. May, 1901

Majority Report—L. Balfour of Burleigh, L. Cawdor, L. Blair Balfour, Hibbert, Wortley, Dalton, Cripps, Clare, Elliott, Smith, Stuart, Wharton.

The chief grievances were that ratepayers in general had to bear too much of the cost of national services, that the burden was heavier in some districts than others, that too large a share of local taxation fell on rateable property and on owners of businesses which made large use of such property, that urban ratepayers received no relief

corresponding to that given to agricultural property, and that owners of land were not rated, although they benefited from expenditure on improvements. To secure fair play all round, a distinction must be made between services national in character, in which the State insisted on a certain standard of efficiency and which were onerous to ratepayers, and services local in character, preponderantly beneficial to local inhabitants. The national services were the poor law, police and criminal prosecutions, education and main roads. The funds for them ought to be raised in accordance with the principle of ability, but local rates complied with this condition less exactly than national taxes. This could not be done by transferring their whole cost to the national funds, like that of the armed forces, since local self-government implied local taxation. The defect could not be remedied by a local income tax, on account of the difficulty of deciding whether incomes should be taxed in the place from which they are derived or in the place in which they are enjoyed, and because persons with large incomes often congregate in areas in which little relief was needed. A special rate on inhabited houses was also rejected. Meeting the cost of national services on the basis of ability therefore required an extension of State aid by grant or by assigned revenues.

In 1888 Mr. Goschen replaced grants-in-aid by assigning the proceeds of certain taxes, which were paid into the Local Taxation Account and distributed to the authorities. The Commission rejected the view that as it was a matter of indifference to the taxpayer whether the proceeds were granted or assigned, this operation was fictitious. It concluded that the principles should be adhered to, the separation of imperial and local taxes carried out and the 'local' revenues extended and diversified. The central authority must continue to collect the revenues and must have some control over expenditure. Trading and establishment licences should be increased and the inhabited house duty transferred. The proposals included additional grants-in-aid of local expenditure on police (up to half the cost) on pauper lunatics, imbeciles, etc., on asylums, poor law children, the sick and infirm, on the residue of poor law expenditure, and on main roads. These grants, amounting £9,700,000, should be paid out of the Local Taxation Account, into which should be paid the existing assigned revenues of £7,145,000 and the proceeds of the additional taxes indicated above. Proposals for a Poor Law block grant based on calculations of rateable value, population and expenditure in each union were rejected.

The full value of agricultural land was excessive as a measure either of ability or of benefits received, and after reviewing the evidence taken before earlier inquiries, the Commission concluded that agricultural land should be rated at one-half its annual value for onerous burdens and for highways, and at one-fourth for other local burdens, the deficiencies being made good by a grant from the Estate Duty on personalty. Proposals to rate land values and alternatively to rate sites and buildings separately were rejected. Though machinery had not been rateable *per se* since 1840, legal decisions had led to uncertainty. Movable machinery should not, but plant for power, heating and lighting factories should be rated.

Separate Recommendations by L. Balfour of Burleigh.—Balfour of Burleigh and Blair Balfour accept the principle that the cost of national and onerous services should be raised in accordance with ability and that therefore State aid was necessary, but they disagreed with the majority on the way State grants should be made. The object of the assigned revenue system was to separate imperial and local finance, to give local authorities revenues which would grow with their requirements and to secure for local purposes contributions from personalty.

But the separation had not been carried out nor would it be desirable, the assigned revenues did not secure a special contribution from personalty, since all taxes were ultimately derived from a common purse, and their proceeds were allocated neither according to the needs of the national services nor the requirements of the localities. It would be more economical and convenient to pay a fixed sum into the Local Taxation Account and to distribute it amongst the local authorities in relation to the cost of national services and in a way which would promote equity and local efficiency.

The pressure of rates for these services was very unequal, the expenditure in some unions being twelve times greater than in others, while there were wide differences in the capacity to meet it as tested by rateable value per head. The total grant should not exceed one-half the cost of national services, but the proportion should vary between different services and different districts. Block grants should be given for each service as a whole, in such a way as to equalize as far as possible the local burden remaining. Regard should be paid to the ability to raise local funds and to the necessity for the expenditure, larger grants being given to those whose ability was high and expenditure low. Ability was best measured by assessable value, the necessity by the ratio between population and expenditure in the more economical districts. For the Poor Law grants this minimum expenditure should be fixed at 3s. 6d. per head of population; all unions should be required to raise a rate of 4d. in the £, which would meet one-third of the expenditure in the more economical poor unions. The grant would then consist of (i) the difference between the minimum expenditure and the product of the minimum rate, in those areas where the rate yield did not meet the minimum, and (ii) one-third of expenditure in excess of the minimum. These arrangements would not only help to equalize burdens, but would give an inducement to prudent administration. Police and asylums grants should be distributed on similar principles.

Central grants should be accompanied by central powers to ensure uniformity, efficiency and economy; these are not given either by the system of assigned revenues, or by stereotyped grants towards particular items of expenditure, but only by conditional block grants of the kind proposed. The scheme involves a uniform valuation system on the lines proposed in the main report.

Minority Report. Hamilton, Murray. —The main proposals in this report are broadly similar to those in Lord Balfour of Burleigh's separate recommendations. It is persons not properties on whom taxation really falls and the legal distinctions between reality and personalty and between rateable and non-rateable properties are not applicable. It is not possible to decide if taxes are equitably distributed unless it is known where the burden rests, and that involves problems of incidence between owners, occupiers and other persons which are particularly obscure in the case of local rates.

The complaint of ratepayers, e.g., that local rates operate unfairly as between those whose income is derived mainly from fixed, and those whose income is derived from immovable, property has been alleviated but not removed by the system of assigned revenues, which aimed at placing personalty under some direct contribution to local taxation. For it makes little or no difference to the ratepayer in what way he is assisted by the taxpayer; the procedure is complicated and the money is distributed on no uniform or equitable principle. Further transfer of local services to the State or of central taxes to local authorities is impracticable, as is any proposal to rate industrial undertakings according to profits. Graduated rates on dwelling houses would be a rough income tax, but it is now impracticable to limit rating to dwelling houses.

The State should not contribute to local and beneficial services, but should contribute to national and onerous services. The assigned revenues should be replaced by a grant, fixed for ten years, limited to one-half local authorities' expenditure on national services. The proceeds should be distributed according to the needs and ability of the districts, and for Guardians should consist of a primary grant of the difference between a standard minimum of expenditure of 3s. 6d. per head and the product of a 4d. rate, and a secondary grant of one-third of expenditure in excess of the standard expenditure. Reform of the system of valuation is essential.

Separate Report on Urban Rating and Site Values.—Lord Balfour of Burleigh, Lord Blair Balfour, Hamilton, Murray, Stuart. The signatories are unable to concur in the conclusions of the majority on the rating of site values. The value of the site as well as of the structure is at present assessed to rates, and whilst site value is enhanced by extraneous causes, it may also be increased by local expenditure. Site value and structure value differ essentially in character and should be separately valued. When so separated, site value is capable of bearing somewhat heavier taxation and should be taxed by a separate site value rate, payable in part by deduction from rent. The amount raised by such a tax will not be large; the tax is not primarily a redistribution between the parties interested in an hereditament, but is a local redistribution between districts. The proceeds should go to relieve local taxation. It might be expedient to apply 'local option' and to limit its immediate introduction to places of given size and density.

Report by O'Connor.—The Commissioners were directed to inquire into the equity of existing local taxation in respect of real and personal property. The sense intended in this context by these legal terms is better conveyed by 'immovable' and 'movable' property, though the only property really immovable is the land, which cannot be produced or destroyed. While the separate occupation of land is essential for its development, there are few owners and an immense number of non-owners. The value of land and the price which has to be paid for it by non-owners increases with the size of population. Structure value is due to individual action, site value to the action of the community. Houses and machinery should not be rated for local purposes, but the cost of local services should be defrayed from the increasing value received by the landlords. Unoccupied land should be rated according to its value. O'Connor agrees with the principle of the separate report on Urban Rating and Site Values, but not to the limitation of site rating to urban land. The valuation of site as distinct from structure is practicable. If the levy is first made from the occupier, with the right of deduction for each lessee in respect of superior interests, the charge will be equitably distributed in proportions corresponding with the different interests in the land. Land, and land only, should be rated for local services.

———— Scotland. pp. vi, 111. 1902
1902 *Cd.* 1067, *xxxix*, 57
sgd. April, 1902

Scottish rates are now levied on the annual value of lands and heritages, but there are certain differences from the English system. In Scotland, for some rates the owner is liable, for others the occupier, but the majority are divided between occupiers and their immediate landlords. Notwithstanding this, the final incidence is thought not to be different from that of English rates. And for many rates the basis is the gross value, derived from the rent actually paid or, where this is not applicable (e.g. where the owner occupies) on an estimate of rent or 'contractor's rent'. As in England, since 1888 assigned revenues have been paid into the Local Taxation Account and these are paid out to local authorities in twenty-two separate grants, eighteen of which are fixed annual sums.

Relief to rates in Scotland should be dealt with on lines uniform with the relief proposed for England. The share of assigned revenues allocated to Scotland is 11 per cent as compared with 80 per cent for England and Wales, and though division on the basis of population would be better, the result would be roughly the same. As in England, further Imperial revenues should be appropriated to local purposes. A block grant for poor law is rejected; instead, there should be a system of grants for specific services, similar to those suggested for England, plus a sum to burgh and county councils in aid of general expenditure. All rates should be levied on net annual value and a maximum scale of deductions be fixed by statute; the existing division of rates between occupiers and landlords should continue, as all parties are accustomed to it. The rateable value of railways, which equals about $16\frac{1}{2}$ per cent of their total receipts, should be allocated to the areas through which they run not on line mileage, as heretofore, but on train mileage.

Separate Recommendations on the Distribution of Exchequer Contributions and on the Valuation of Railways and Corporation Water Works.—Lord Balfour of Burleigh and Lord Blair Balfour. I. — Scottish subventions should be distributed on the same broad principles as proposed for English grants; they should be confined to expenditure on national services locally administered, should not exceed one-half of that expenditure, should be fixed for a period of years and be distributed amongst local authorities in accordance with their needs and ability. This should be done for poor relief grants by the use of a scale of percentages, by which the grant decreases as the assessable value per inhabitant rises and increases with each addition to expenditure per head. II. — The principle that total railway valuation should be allocated on the basis of train mileage is accepted, but there should be periodical re-valuation of working stock and plant and changes in the deductions. Although corporation water works are not usually allowed by statute to make profits, they are valued on what is called a profits basis; gross revenue is a wrong starting point.

Hamilton and Murray accept these recommendations on the distribution of grants.

Report on Urban Rate and Site Values. — Lord Balfour of Burleigh, Lord Blair Balfour, Hamilton, Murray and Stuart. Subject to differences on points of detail arising from Scottish law and custom regarding the tenure of land, the conclusions of the report on rating urban and site values in England and Wales should be applied to Scotland.

O'Connor.—As in England, local public services should be paid out of the fund represented by the value of the land of the locality.

———— Ireland. pp. 48. 1902

1902 Cd. 1068, xxxix, 9
sgd. April, 1902

Since 1898 there have been two rates, the new Poor Rate, now payable by the occupier, and Municipal Rates, which exhibit a great variety of arrangements. Belfast has a system of graduated rates. The Irish system of local taxation does not differ materially from the English system and the changes suggested for England should as far as possible be applied to Ireland. In Ireland primary education and police are administered nationally and no charge falls on the rates. As in England, in order to diversify the sources of revenue for local purposes, further Imperial revenues should be assigned but the amounts should not be determined on the basis of population as suggested for Scotland but, because Ireland is poorer and more services are centrally administered, on the amount the State should be called upon to contribute. The Irish share of Beer

and Spirit Duties should be raised from 9 per cent to 11 per cent.

Separate Recommendations by Lord Balfour of Burleigh and Lord Blair Balfour. — The central subventions are large in amount, but owing to the poverty of the country the pressure of local taxation is severe and very unequal as between rural districts, some of the Congested Districts bearing a burden which has no parallel in England. The total effect of the method of distributing the grants is that the poorest and neediest unions get least and have to raise the largest rate, and the richer unions get more and raise a lower rate. The rating question in the West of Ireland is grave and urgent. Systematic and orderly help is better than wasteful doles of public money in periods of distress. The Local Taxation Account should be increased by £125,000 to £1,550,000, £150,000 should be provided for technical and secondary education, and all other grants from the Local Taxation Account should cease. The whole of the available balance in the account should be distributed on the principle of necessity and ability, the grants for each service being fixed for a term of years. Hamilton and Murray concur, stating that the State contribution to the Account should be a fixed sum charged to the Consolidated Fund.

O'Connor.—The cost of local services should be paid out of the fund represented by the value of the land. For general public services there should be paid from the Imperial Revenues whatever sum is necessary to bring them up to the same level of completeness and efficiency as in England and Scotland. For a hundred years there has not been spent in Ireland from the Imperial Exchequer a single pound sterling which has not been drawn from it by taxation.

Report on Urban Rating and Site Values. — Lord Balfour of Burleigh, Lord Blair Balfour, Hamilton, Murray, Stuart.—The system by which rates were divided between occupier and owner was abolished in 1898, except that a county borough rate under a local Act could be so divided if a majority of two-thirds of the council so resolved. Advantage should be taken of this to enable these councils to levy a limited site value rate on the lines suggested in the English report.

—— Report, *Valuation in Ireland.* pp. 5. 1902

1902 *Cd.* 973, *xxxix*, 1.
sgd. Feb., 1902

The work of valuation in Ireland is performed entirely by a Government Department, the basis being net annual value. Land was, however, separately valued from the buildings, but the total valuation of land and buildings was not to exceed fair letting value to a solvent tenant. The general revision provided for by the Act of 1852 was never made because no funds were made available for it; and the annual revision is incomplete because the value of uncovered land cannot be increased, despite the many reclamation and drainage schemes which have raised its value, and because alterations in the value of the structures are not brought to official notice except when they have decreased. There is also under-valuation in Dublin and other areas. A general re-valuation is necessary and practicable, despite the difficulties due to the fact that in Ireland farms are not now let at a competitive rent and that judicial rents are unsuitable as a basis. Transfer of valuation from the central to the local authority is undesirable, though the introduction of some local element in the process might be considered.

Classification and Incidence of Imperial and Local Taxes

Memoranda. pp. 250. 1899

1899 *C.* 9528, *xxxvi*, 673

This important volume contains: (1) a Memorandum (sgd. July, 1897) on Imperial Relief of Local Burdens and on the System of Imperial and Local Taxation, prepared by Sir E. Hamilton in his capacity of Assistant Secretary to the Treasury. His conclusion is that a mere classification of taxes cannot represent their primary incidence, that the local rates which have increased are mostly beneficial, that however central assistance is given it must come from persons in the proportions in which they contribute to Imperial taxation generally. The answer to the terms of reference can be given only by first probing the question of the true incidence of rates and taxes. (2) Memoranda containing the answers by economic and financial experts, including Giffen, Farrer, Marshall, Edgeworth, Cannan, Bastable, Gonner and Price to fifteen questions on these points. The questionnaire was sent to the recipients in the autumn of 1897. Farrar's reply is dated Jan., 1898. This volume was published in 1899 and the date of the signatures of the Final Report on England and Wales is May, 1901.

Hospitals (Exemption from Rates)

Sel. Cttee. Rep., proc., mins. of ev., apps., index. pp. xii, 144. 1900

1900 (273) *vii*, 1
apptd. May, *o.p.* July, 1900

T. W. Russell (*Ch.*), Bonsor, Farquharson, Fisher, Gull, Maclure, McCrae, Pickersgill, Round, Tomlinson, Walton, Warr, Woodhouse.

'*To consider the operation of the law by which hospitals and other institutions for the care and treatment of the sick and of those afflicted in mind or body, are liable to Local Rates, and to report under any and what conditions, it is for the public interest that such hospitals and institutions, or any of them, should be exempted wholly or in part from such liability in the future.*'

Hospitals and other charitable institutions become rateable for Poor Rate after a decision in 1865 in the case of Jones and others *v.* the Mersey Docks and Harbour Board which held that properties producing no profit to the owners were, under Statute 43 Elizabeth c.2. rateable to the relief of the poor. Numerous anomalies in the rating of hospitals appeared after this, different authorities taking different views as to the rating obligation of hospitals. Recommended that all voluntary hospitals should be relieved of rates.

Burden of the Existing Rates and the General Financial Position of the Outer Hebrides

Reps., apps. pp. lxvii, 24. 1906

1906 Cd. 3014, *civ*, 689
apptd. Sept., 1905

Parishes of Barra, North Uist, South Uist, and Harris. Rep.
sgd. Jan. 1906

J. A. Fleming (*Sheriff*).

'To inquire *into and report on the facts, figures, and statistics, raised and set forth in the minutes of meeting and petitions forwarded to the Board from the parishes of Barra, Harris, and South Uist, and generally into the poor law administration and pressure of local rates in these parishes and in the parish of North Uist*.'

The increases in rates between 1895–6 and 1905–6 were as follows: Harris 65.4 per cent, North Uist 78.9 per cent, South Uist 97.8 per cent, and Barra 170.4 per cent. Much of this increase was due to a reduction in assessable rental under the Agricultural Rates Act; and the proportion which such Government grants as are allocated according to expenditure bears to total expenditure has decreased. The balance of normal expenditure after deducting grants has not materially increased, except in Harris. Any increase in actual cash paid by ratepayers is due to an increase in the total number of the poor, exceptional causes and faulty collection of rates. The statement that the inhabitants of these islands are unable to pay rates would be true if they depended on the islands themselves for a livelihood. But as a considerable amount of money is earned outside, e.g. herring-gutting by the women, failure to pay rates is due more to unwillingness than inability. 'The true remedy in theory is in the widening of the area which is to be called upon to support its own burden of pauperism.'

The Lews Parishes. Rep.
sgd. May, 1906

Mr. Millar, Mr. Maxwell.

To inquire '*into the causes of the high rates in the Island of Lewis, and with reference to the ability of the ratepayers to bear their local burdens*'.

The higher rates are due primarily to the low rentals per family fixed by the Crofters Commission. This is in part due to the fact that the houses of the cottars and squatters are not included in the Valuation Roll, and in respect of which neither rents nor rates are paid. The cottars, whose houses are frequently newer and better than those occupied by the crofters, receive the full benefits of education and poor relief, yet have no share in the local burdens. Whilst the rate per £ is high, the assessable rental of the croft is so low that the rates do not form an unduly heavy burden upon that class of the population. The great bulk of the rates, nearly one half in 1904–5 is borne by the Matheson Estate. The Memorandum by Mr. Maxwell gives a statistical analysis of the rate increases and expenditures over a number of years for each parish in the Lews. See below, p. 76.

Education Rates

Dept. Cttee. Rep., apps. pp. vi, 208.
1907

1907 Cd. 3313, *xxi*, 521
apptd. Oct., 1905.   sgd. Aug., 1906

H. W. Primrose (*Ch.*), Blain, Pitts, Bromley, Sheppard, Tripp.

'To inquire into the *expenditure on public education in England and Wales from*

Exchequer grants, local rates, and other sources, with a view to ascertaining the various causes for the existing diversity in the amount of rate levied for education by local authorities, and the varying relation which this amount bears to the total local rates in each area.'

As the conditions arising from the operation of the Education Act, 1902, were nowhere fully developed, and Parliament was considering great changes in the Act, the enquiry was discontinued on the representation of the Committee. There is a memorandum, together with statistical tables, on the causes of divergencies in the burden of education rates.

Land Values Taxation, etc. (Scotland) Bill

Sel. Cttee. Reps., proc., mins. of ev., apps. pp. lxviii, 810. 1906. Index and digest of ev. 1907

1906 (379) (379–*Ind.*) x, 55
apptd. April, o.p. Dec., 1906

Mr. Solicitor-General for Scotland (*Ch.*), Barrie, Dewar, Findlay, Henderson, M'Killop, Mitchell-Thomson, O'Hare, Remnant, Richards, Sutherland, Trevelyan, White, Wood, Younger.

The contribution of each ratepayer to burgh expenditure is based on the yearly value of the land he owns or occupies, that is, the rent at which the land, with the buildings on it, might in its actual state be reasonably expected to let. Contribution to rates is made partly by owners and partly by occupiers, but 26.6 per cent of burgh assessments are on owners and 73.4 per cent on occupiers. The object of the Bill is to levy a new additional rate on owners of land in burghs according to the yearly value (calculated at 4 per cent on capital) of land apart from the buildings and erections on it. Every owner of land is to have the right to seek relief from any one to whom he pays feu duty of a part of the rate proportional to the amount of the feu duty. The rate which might be levied

was not more than 10 per cent of the value on this new standard. The Bill does not give complete effect to the new rating standard, for the rating of occupiers is to proceed as at present, on land and buildings, and of owners partly on the old and partly on the new standard; it is confined in operation to burghs, and the additional rate is to be on an arbitrary basis of 10 per cent, which no one justified. The Bill ought not to be proceeded with in its present form.

But the Committee deemed it its duty to report on the principle underlying this class of legislation, that rates should be levied not upon buildings and improvements, but solely on the value of the land, which is not created or maintained by the owner, but by the energy and expenditure of the community. The adoption of this principle would effect a redistribution of rating, owners and occupiers thus paying rates in very different proportion from those in which they are now paying them. The Bill does not tax site value twice; it is individuals, not things, which are taxed; the tax-burdens are re-allocated. The precise extent of redistribution of burden could not be estimated until a proper valuation on the new basis has been made.

The Committee reject the contention that it is not practicable to separate site value from the value of the buildings, since expert valuators do this in practice, and the experience of other countries shows that it can be done. If expenditure has been incurred on preparing a site, or reclaiming land from the sea, it should be properly allowed. In valuing the land allowance should be made for every restriction placed on it and legally valid at the date of valuation. Controversy had arisen on the question whether occupiers or owners of feu duties should have to contribute to the new rates in proportion to their share of the yearly value. The Committee reject the claim that owners of feu duties should be exempt; they are owners with an interest in the land, the new duties did not exist at the time the contract was made, but would be new in character and should not rest wholly upon the feuar. The desirability of making land the basis of valuation does not, however, rest solely on the distribution of the burden between the parties. Its advantages are that houses, industrial and other improvements will be encouraged by relief from rating, and that land on the outskirts of large towns will become ripe for building sooner than at present, thus assisting in the solution of the housing problem. A new measure should be introduced making provision for a valuation of land in the burghs and counties of Scotland apart from the buildings and improvements upon it, and no assessment should be determined upon until the amount of that valuation is known, and considered.

The Proceedings of the Committee show that beside the chairman's draft, two others, by Henderson and Remnant respectively, were presented to the Committee for discussion. Henderson's draft stated that the weight of evidence was against the Bill, and that several members of the Committee were pledged to the principle of taxing land values before the sitting of the Committee began.

Taxation of Land, etc.

Papers bearing on Land Taxes and on Income Tax, etc., in certain Foreign Countries, and on the Working of Taxation of Site Values in certain Cities of the United States and in British Colonies, together with Extracts relative to Land Taxation and Land Valuation from Reports of Royal Commissions and Parliamentary Committees. pp. 327. [1909]
1909 Cd. 4750, lxxi, 365

—— Second Series of Memoranda and Extracts relating to Land Taxation and Land Valuation prepared for the Chancellor of the Exchequer. pp. 79. [1909]
1909 Cd. 4845, lxxi, 693

Includes extracts from memos. on the separate rating of land values by economic and financial experts, including Giffen, Sidgwick, Marshall, Edgeworth, Cannan, Bastable and Gonner.

Local Taxation
Dept. Cttee.
apptd. — 1911.

J. A. Kempe (*Ch.*), Robinson, Struthers, Monro, Barstow, Beard, Harper, Hughes, Murison, Murray, O'Neill, Rogers, Stevenson.

'To inquire into the changes which have taken place in the relations between Imperial and Local Taxation since the Report of the Royal Commission on Local Taxation in 1901; to examine the several proposals made in the Reports of that Commission, and to make recommendations on the subject for the consideration of His Majesty's Government, with a view to the introduction of legislation at an early date.'

The First Report is a formal presentation of the following volumes of minutes of evidence, etc.; 1912–13 Cd. 6303–I, Cd. 6303–II, xxxviii, 5.

—— Final Report. England and Wales. pp. vi, 120. 1914. Mins. of ev., etc. 1914
1914 Cd. 7315, xl, 537. Mins. of ev., etc.; 1914 Cd. 7316, xl, 663
sgd. March, 1914

Additional terms: 'The question of valuation and problems presented by the inequalities of local government rating areas.'

Since the Report of the Royal Commission of 1901, the system of assigned revenues has been modified by the substitution of stereotyped fixed sums, additional taxes have been laid on real property, education has been reorganized, old age pensions, health and unemployment insurance established and a central Road Fund created. And there has been a great increase in local expenditure on national services, while proposals for a local income tax have been affected by the greater mobility of the population.

The proportion which the State contributes to the cost of semi-national services, i.e. those locally administered services whose efficiency the State may justly claim to supervise, has fallen below that of 1888 and 1901, while the great increase in local expenditure has emphasized the inequalities between persons and districts. Assigned revenues should be abolished, central aid restricted to semi-national services and paid direct to the administering authorities. The Committee makes its recommendations in the light of a discussion of the alternative systems of grants allocated to specific branches of a service and block grants, and of whether they should be calculated per unit of service or as a proportion of expenditure. Powers should be given to the Government Departments to reduce grants to the extent needed to secure effective supervision. To remedy the inequalities of net burdens of elementary education a block grant on the 'Balfour of Burleigh' principles should be paid, on the basis of a standard expenditure of 60s. per child, a standard rate of 7d. and a State contribution of two-fifths of excess expenditure. Although block grants on similar principles had been recommended for Poor Law by Balfour of Burleigh (1901) and for health by the Minority of the Commissioners on Poor Law, both were rejected, the first in favour of specific grants based on the 'facts of pauperism', the second in favour of a grant per head of the population.

Proposals to substitute a system of rating on site values alone, or alongside the existing system (as suggested in 1901) were rejected, as were proposals for a local income tax and for the transfer of the Inhabitants House Duty to local authorities.

The valuation for rating purposes should be prepared by the Land Valuation Office, all rates should be collected on one demand note and rate collection handed to urban and district councils.

Landlords should be compelled to provide weekly and other tenants with a rent book which showed the rates levied in respect of the house.

Differences of rating between areas were not necessarily inequalities; these should be reduced by the system of grants proposed, by making the counties and county boroughs the areas of administration and rating for semi-national services, and by facilitating boundary extensions. Grouping of areas for rating purposes only presented no less difficulties than boundary adjustments.

Three members thought the proposed grants too high, three dissented from the proposed grants for small schools, one favoured the grouping of areas for rating in cases where the machinery for securing boundary extensions had failed. In a separate report Struthers, Barstow, Harper, Hughes, Morrison and Stevenson recommended a relief of rates on buildings and improvements, the deficiency to be made up by a separate rate on site values.

Repayment of Loans by Local Authorities

Sel. Cttee. Rep., proc., mins. of ev., apps., index. pp. xlviii, 461. 1902

1902 (239) viii, 1
    apptd. March, o.p. June, 1902

G. Lawson (Ch.), Bill, Brigg, Donelan, Jones, Hutton, Johnstone, Law, Loyd, M'Crae, Murray, Nannetti, Rollit, Runciman, Wodehouse.

'To inquire and report as to the Statutory and other conditions limiting the periods for Repayment of Loans raised by Local Authorities in England and Wales; whether any relaxation of such conditions is desirable, and whether uniformity of practice can be secured in this matter; with an Instruction from the House that they have power to extend the scope of their inquiry to all parts of the United Kingdom.'

The maximum periods for the repayment of loans specified in Acts applicable to England and Wales vary from

10 to 60 years. Many of these Acts deal with a considerable number of subjects for loans, but there is no attempt to distinguish between these subjects. Under the Public Health Act, 1875, money may be borrowed for purposes widely different in permanence, such as ambulances and the purchase of land and in both cases the general maximum period for repayment is 60 years. This has led to wide discretion being exercised by the L.G.B. In fixing the period of repayment, it takes into account both the probable future condition of the localities in regard to debt and, aided by the advice of inspectors, also the probable useful life of each part of the work concerned. When the loan covers works with different terms of life, the period is the weighted average (App. I, p. 261), except where the sums for each item are large and the local authority prefers separate loans. One anomaly is that under the Municipal Corporations Act, 1882, the maximum period is 30 years, whilst under the Public Health Act, 1875, it is 60 years. Town Halls erected by town councils under the Municipal Corporations Act cannot be considered less substantial than offices built by urban district councils under the Public Health Act. There is a want of uniformity between the periods sanctioned under statutes and those granted in local Acts, owing to the conditions in which the Committees to which such Bills are referred have to do their work. Local authorities often prefer to proceed by Private Bill in order to obtain longer loan periods, even when their powers under statute are ample.

The chief recommendations were that the maximum period for repayment under the Municipal Corporations Act, 1882, the Local Government Act, 1888, and the Municipal Corporations (Ireland) Act, 1843, should be 60 years; for rehousing operations under Parts I and II, and the purchase of land under Part III of the Housing of the Working Classes Act, 1890, should be 80 years. The sanctioning authority should be empowered to fix the method of repayment in all cases. Standing Orders of the House should be amended to prohibit the use of Private Bill procedure to obtain loans for longer periods than provided by statute where there is no legal necessity; and where Private Bill Committees make no detailed enquiry, the exact period of repayment should be determined by a Government Department.

Application of Sinking Funds in the Exercise of Borrowing Powers

Sel. Cttee. Rep., proc., mins. of ev., app. pp. v, 75. 1909. Rep., proc., mins. of ev., apps. pp. xxxvi, 111. Index. 1909

1908 (372) vi, 653. 1909 (193) (193-Ind.) vi, 437
apptd. Nov., o.p. Dec., 1908. re-apptd. Feb., o.p. June, 1909

Mr. Masterman (*Ch.*), Ashton, Fenwick, Harmood-Banner, Nicholson.

'To inquire and report as to the powers conferred on Local Authorities by Local Acts, Provisional Orders, Stock Regulations, or otherwise, of utilizing for purposes for which such authorities have Borrowing Powers, Sinking Funds (including loan funds and redemption funds) set aside by them for the repayment of redemption of loans raised by the issue of stock or by any other method; as to the expediency or otherwise of such powers being conferred; and as to any conditions which it is desirable to attach to the granting or use of such powers.'

When local authorities borrow by an issue of stock the Regulations require that a Sinking Fund shall be created to make adequate provision for the redemption of the stock within the prescribed period for the borrowing powers exercised. The 'prescribed periods' vary with the nature of the capital works and may be for shorter or longer periods than that for which the stock is issued. Stock may be cancelled at any time out of this fund. So long as the provision is made, the stock need not be actually repaid. There are thus considerable sums in these funds, and they need not be idle, but may be invested in certain securities. For many years it was considered inadvisable for a local authority to invest these funds in their own securities; some witnesses argued that it was a breach of contract and that if it were generally known that it was the practice of corporations to use their Sinking Funds for these purposes, their credit would suffer. The power to use Sinking Funds in that way was obtained in various local acts. In 1889 Lord Goschen (Chancellor of the Exchequer) stated that although he had been against it two years earlier, he was now in favour of it 'as being more economical and the soundest course to adopt, inasmuch as it would check the growth of loans, and do away with the necessity of creating stock on the one hand and investing largely in securities on the other'. Mr. Haward, Comptroller of the L.C.C. said that 'we treat each use of the Sinking Fund money for capital purposes as if it were a loan to ourselves and charge ourselves . . . the current rate of interest'. The Committee concluded that 'the principle of utilizing Sinking Funds (including loans funds and redemption funds) for purposes for which local authorities have borrowing powers is, if properly safeguarded, financially unobjectionable; and the power is undoubtedly a great advantage, inasmuch as it affords a convenient and economical method of exercising new borrowing powers'. Certain operations should require the consent of the L.G.B., which should review all the local authority's transactions of this kind.

Accounts of Local Authorities

Dept. Cttee. Vol. I. Rep., apps. pp. 101, xxv. 1907. Vol. II. Mins. of ev., apps., digest of ev., index. 1907

1907 Cd. 3614, xxxvii, 577. Mins. of ev., etc.; 1907 Cd. 3615, xxxvii, 711 apptd. Jan., 1906. sgd. July, 1907

W. Runciman (Ch.), Bromley, Pitts, Barrow, Burd, Burnley, Gane, Merrifield.

'To inquire and report with regard to (1) The systems on which the accounts of Local Authorities in England and Wales are at present kept; (2) Generally as to the system on which the accounts of the various Local Authorities in England and Wales should be kept, and in particular whether such accounts should be prepared on a system requiring the entries of receipts and payments to be confined as far as possible to actual receipts and payments of money or not; and (3) The regulations which should be made on the subject, regard being had to the necessity for showing accurately the amounts raised by local taxation and the purposes for which they are applied.'

There was no uniform system of account-keeping and often the different branches of the accounts of the same authority were kept in different ways. The chief causes of the lack of uniformity were the increasing realization of the inadequacy of the purely cash system, which was used by many of the smaller, and by some of the larger authorities, and the absence of precise regulations and definitions. The systems of accounting for all local authorities should be prescribed by one central authority. There is little uniformity in the form in which the abstracts of accounts are presented to the ratepayers. The power of regulation should be wide enough to secure sound and uniform principles. Most of the larger authorities used the more or less comprehensive system of income and expenditure, which was the most efficient method of accounting and which should be extended; the system should be adopted in all cases where statements of profit and loss were required. All authorities of sufficient importance should be required by statute to appoint finance committees, and account keeping should be in the hands of officers not responsible for pecuniary transactions or administrative duties.

App. I gives a Return from local authorities respecting the systems of their accounts. App. II is a Statement as to the regulations in force respecting the forms of accounts of local authorities.

Local Government Acts, 1888 and 1894, and the Local Government (Scotland) Acts, 1889 and 1894 (Financial Adjustments)

Jt. Sel. Cttee. Rep., proc., mins. of ev., apps. pp. xxviii, 408. 1911. Index. 1912

1911 (246) *vii*, 1
apptd. March, o.p. Aug., 1911

Duke of Devonshire (*Ch.*), L. Welby, L. Newlands, L. MacDonnell, L. Mersey, Arkwright, Bagot, Price, Nicholson, White.

'*To inquire into the application of the provisions contained in the Local Government Acts, 1888 and 1894 and the Local Government (Scotland) Acts, 1889 and 1894, relating to financial adjustments consequent on the alteration of the boundaries of a Local Government area or on an alteration in the constitution or status of the governing body of a Local Government area.*'

Provision had been made for the creation of 10 county boroughs and 61 other boroughs in the Local Government Act, 1888, and very full authority had been given to the Commissioners appointed under the Act. The general principles of the equitable adjustment of the financial relations between the counties and the county boroughs had been laid down by the Commissioners (p. iv and App. aa), but certain difficulties had arisen and legal decisions making a distinction between compensation and adjustment had made necessary a different practice from that followed by the Commissioners. It would be difficult to extend boroughs unless some principles were enunciated for the guidance of an arbitrator in determining settlements under the Act of 1888. Compensation should not be given for the loss of rateable area unless it could be proved that alteration meant an increased burden on one administration. A maximum amount should be fixed, which the arbitrator

should not exceed. After the satisfaction of priority payments and one half the cost of main roads, the surplus of Exchequer contributions should be distributed on the basis of rateable, not assessable, value. The Acts in question should be amended in accordance with these and other recommendations.

8. LONDON

Port of London. Reps.

See *Transport.* p.171

Water Supply Within the Limits of the Metropolitan Water Companies

R. Com. 1st Rep., app. pp. ii, 19. 1898

1899 *C.* 9122, *xli*, 491
apptd. May, 1897. *sgd. Dec.,* 1898

Lord Llandaff (*Ch.*), Mellor, Dorington, Bruce, Porter, Scott, Cripps, Lewis.

'*To inquire* (1) *Whether having regard to financial considerations and to present and prospective requirements as regards Water Supply in the Districts within the limits of supply of the Metropolitan Water Companies, it is desirable in the interests of the Ratepayers and Water Consumers in those Districts that the undertakings of the Water Companies should be acquired and managed either—*(a) *by one Authority; or* (b) *by several Authorities, and, if so, what should be such Authority or Authorities. To what extent physical severance of the works and other property and sources of supply of the several Companies, and the division thereof between different Local Authorities within the limits of supply, are practicable and desirable; and what are the legal powers necessary to give effect to any such arrangements.* (2) *If the undertakings are not so acquired, whether additional powers of control should be exercised by Local or other Authorities; and, if so, what those powers should be.* (3) *Whether it is practicable to connect any two or more of the different systems of supply now administered by the eight Metropolitan Companies; and, if so, by whom, and in what proportion, should the cost of connecting them be borne, and what are the legal powers necessary to give effect to any such arrangement.'*

This report was on No. 3 of the terms of reference. The failure of the East London Company's supply in the summer of 1898 had given urgency to the question of interconnexion of the various water companies. If this connexion were to be of use, the margin between the ordinary demand during the height of summer and the capacity of the companies would have to be increased. The margin of five of them, the Chelsea, Grand Junction, Kent, Lambeth and West Middlesex Companies, was very small. The New River, and the Southwark and Vauxhall Companies had, however, been able to transfer considerable quantities to the East London Company, and until the latter had extended its resources, co-operation between the companies could ensure a constant supply in the East London district.

Inter-communication would still be necessary in case of emergency, even though each company had, as it should have, surplus capacity. The companies had approved inter-communication and since they regarded it as beneficial to all, the cost involved should be shared in proportion to their water rentals. Where any company actually receives water, it should pay such proportion of the interest as should be agreed or decided by arbitration. Certain statutory difficulties would have to be removed and a Bill should be passed as soon as possible. No rigid scheme of connexion should be laid down, but the L.G.B. should have power to order any necessary works to be undertaken.

—— Final Report, index, pp. 89. 1899
1900 Cd. 25, *xxxviii* Pt. I, 1
sgd. Dec., 1899

del. Scott, Cripps.

Since 1891 periods of severe drought had occurred. It would be much more costly and difficult to obtain the necessary supplies from the Thames and Lea Basins than had previously been sup-

posed, but it would be possible to meet from these sources the future needs of London up to 1941. The Water Companies had, on the whole, performed their duties to the public satisfactorily, but in view of the magnitude of London's future requirements, they should be acquired and managed by a public authority. As the Commission had been directed to enquire into the expediency, on financial grounds, of purchase in the interests of ratepayers and water consumers, there is a detailed examination of the conflicting principles put forward on which an arbitrator should determine the purchase price. The Commission concluded that it should be on the value of present net and prospective income, without any allowance for compulsory purchase. The shareholders would neither gain nor lose, but there was a possibility of increased charges being necessary if a sinking fund had to be established. Public control should prevent waste and ensure economical distribution and purity of the water. Further, a public authority would find it easier to raise the funds necessary for large storage works, especially as expenditure would probably become unremunerative.

For various reasons the L.C.C. would not be a suitable authority, the most important of which was its pledge to give the other county councils concerned control over their water supplies if it acquired the companies. This division of the works and sources of supply of the companies would be very difficult and was undesirable. A permanent Water Board should be established, consisting of not more than 30 members who were to be appointed by the Conservators of the River Thames, the County Councils of London, Middlesex, Surrey, Hertford and Kent, the Lea Conservancy Board, the Common Council of the Borough of West Ham, and the L.G.B. The Board, whose proceedings should be under the control of Parliament, should acquire the eight water companies and issue 3 per cent stock to cover the purchase. In the event of there being no public purchase various measures of control, such as extended supervision by the Water Examiner, should be adopted, but no additional powers should be granted to the local authorities. Even though the companies were purchased, these controls should still be imposed. See *Statistics and Estimates put before the Commission.* Col. Rathborne. Rep. App. Z. 13.

1st Rep.; 1899 C. 9122, xli, 491.   Final Rep.; 1900 Cd. 25, xxxviii Pt. I, 1. Mins. of ev., Vols. I, II; 1900 Cd. 45, xxxviii, Pt. I, 95. 1900 Cd. 198, xxxviii, Pt. II, 1.   Apps., Maps; 1900 Cd. 108, Cd. 267, xxxix, 1.

London Water Bill

Jt. Sel. Cttee. Reps. proc., mins. of ev., index. pp. xxvi, 686.   1902

1902 (222) *vi*, 259
apptd. March, o.p. June, 1902

Lord Balfour of Burleigh (*Ch.*), L. Crewe, L. De Mauley, L. Llandaff, L. Ludlow, Arrol, Houldsworth, Kitson, M'Crae, Vincent.

The object of the Bill was to define the constitution of the Metropolitan Water Board and the transfer to that Board of the undertakings of eight Metropolitan Water Companies. The Bill having been read a second time, the Committee were concerned with what the constitution of the authority should be, and the terms of dealing between that authority and the companies. Mr. Fitzgerald, for the L.G.B., presented the historical and contemporary case for the changes outlined in the Bill. (Mins. of ev., pp. 9–33). The Bill was amended by the Committee, who agreed to a Special Report to the effect that on the question being put 'that the Third Schedule be disagreed to', there was equal division. The Chairman ruled that the Schedule had to stand part of the Bill, on the principle that no amendment to a Bill which had been referred after its second reading in the Commons could be made unless there were a majority in favour of it.

London Underground Railways

Jt. Sel. Cttee. Rep., proc., mins. of ev., apps., index. pp. xxiv, 435.   1901

1901 (279) *vi*, 427
apptd. March, o.p. July, 1901

Lord Windsor (*Ch.*), Arrol, Ashton, Cawley, Foster, Dickson-Poynder, L. Lauderdale, L. Rosse, L. Knutsford, L. Herries.

'*To consider and report:* 1. *Whether the lines of route for underground railways in and near London, proposed by Bills which have been or may be introduced during the present Session, are best calculated to afford facilities for present and probable future traffic; and, if not, what modifications of those lines of route are desirable;* 2. *What special provisions, if any, should be made for the protection of the owners, lessees, and occupiers of properties adjacent to underground railways from possible damage and annoyance;* 3. *What special terms and conditions, if any, as to construction and working should be imposed upon the promoters;* 4. *Whether any, and which, of the schemes proposed by the said Bills should not be proceeded with during the present Session.*'

The difficulty of suggesting the best route was increased by the fact that a number of lines had already been authorized and some were already constructed.   Underground railways are the best means of dealing with London's present and future traffic, and should run from well-recognized centres of traffic to other such centres and to districts from which large numbers of people must be carried to work. As the effect of lines being in abeyance had been to prevent other companies from coming forward, applications for extension of time should be closely scrutinized. Interchange stations and connecting subways are recommended. The damage to owners and occupiers of adjacent properties might occur through subsidence or vibration. The former question must be decided on the circumstances in each case. The second was under discussion by Lord Rayleigh's Committee. A clause should be inserted in every bill binding the company to give effect to whatever recommendation that Committee might make in its final report.

As the lines were in various hands, the Committee could not make specific suggestions regarding uniformity of fares or through fares, but the Board of Trade should report to Parliament every five or ten years on the reasonableness of the fares and their relation to one another, and these would have a moral effect. The Committee made recommendations on the routes proposed by the ten bills before them. It also agreed that there should be a central authority, such as a Department of the Board of Trade, an independent Commission, or a Joint Committee of both Houses, to control and supervise all underground railway projects affecting traffic in or near London; the City Council and the L.C.C. should be enabled to construct or aid in the construction of underground railways. An early enquiry should be made by the Board of Trade into systems of underground locomotion by subways or shallow tunnels immediately under the surface of the roadways, as developed on the Continent and in America.

Central London Railway (Vibration)

Cttee. Rep. pp. 9. 1902. Apps. pp. 19. 1902

1902 *Cd. 951, xxiii*, 495. *Apps.*; 1902 *Cd. 975, xxiii*, 505
apptd. Jan., 1901. sgd. Jan., 1902

Lord Rayleigh (*Ch.*), Barry, Ewing.

'To *consider and Report to what extent the working of the traffic on the Central London Railway produces Vibration in the adjacent Buildings, and what alterations in the conditions of such working or in structure can be devised to remedy the same.*'

There were two main sources of vibration, the uneven surfaces of the rails and the unspring-borne weight of the locomotives. This weight was subject to vertical accelerations as it passed over the rails. Where there were suitable springs the pressure on

the rails remained nearly uniform. Experiments with new types of locomotives had been carried out and in view of the results of these, the Committee recommended that locomotives with a minimum unspring-borne load should be used. The motor-car type, in which motors were carried in the passenger cars and in which the load on the axles was for the most part spring-borne, was the most efficient in reducing vibration.

See *Paris Metropolitan Railways.* Reps.; 1902 Cd. 977, xxiii, 479.

London Traffic

R. Com. Vol. I. Rep., index. pp. ix, 147. 1905. Vols. II–VIII. Mins. of ev., apps., Special Reps. 1905–6

1905 *Cd.* 2597, *xxx*, 533. *Mins. of ev., etc.*; 1906 *Cd.* 2751, *xl*, 1. 1906 *Cd.* 2752, *xli*, 1. 1906 *Cd.* 2987, *xlii*, 1. 1906 *Cd.* 2798, *xliii*, 1. 1906 *Cd.* 2799, *xliv*, 1. 1906 *Cd.* 2743, *xlv*, 1. 1906 *Cd.* 2744, *xlvi*, 1.
apptd. Feb., 1903. sgd. June, 1905

D. Barbour (*Ch.*), L. Cobham, L. Ribblesdale, Dimsdale, Dickson-Poynder, Reid, Wolfe-Barry, Hopwood, Gibb, Murdoch, Schuster, Bartley.

'To *inquire into the means of locomotion and transport in London, and to report:* (a) *As to the measures which the Commission deem most effectual for the improvement of the same by the development and interconnexion of Railways and Tramways on, or below, the surface; by increasing the facilities for other forms of mechanical locomotion; by better provision for the organization and regulation of vehicular and pedestrian traffic, or otherwise.* (b) *As to the desirability of establishing some authority or tribunal to which all schemes of Railway or Tramway construction of a local character should be referred, and the powers which it would be advisable to confer on such a body.*'

The Commission appointed an Advisory Board of Engineers, presided over by one of its members, Wolfe-

Barry, and adopted many of its recommendations, contained in Vols. VII and VIII.

The inadequate transport facilities had caused overcrowding in the central area of London, and the high price of land made it impossible to re-house the working classes, but in the suburbs the price was low enough to admit of housing at economic rents. It had been estimated that the population of Greater London would be eleven millions by 1931, and it was necessary to evolve a comprehensive plan to solve the transport problems caused by the daily movement from and to the suburbs. The fundamental obstacles to improved facilities were the narrowness of the streets and the high cost of their improvement. The two main avenues running north-south and east-west through the City, recommended by the Advisory Board of Engineers, were desirable since they would relieve the already serious congestion and also would bring a complete system of railway and tramway lines through the City and the central area.

Railway facilities should be improved by a new underground line from Victoria to Marble Arch, and by better facilities between the north east and the centre, and between east and west. One of the main road avenues should have four railway tracks underneath it. For financial reasons, new central area railways should be of the shallow subway, not the 'tube' type. The tramways system is disconnected and insufficient, and should be immediately extended wherever the width of the streets permit this; and the power of veto on the construction of tramways possessed by the various administrative authorities of London should be abolished. A new central authority, The Traffic Board, should be appointed to consider Private Bills dealing with transport, to report on them to Parliament, to suggest improvements and investigate special problems and to perform various other duties which were defined.

Both Dimsdale and Bartley disagreed with the recommendations to extend the tramways. Dimsdale pointed out the dangers of further congestion, which would be caused by tramways, criticized the adoption of the Advisory Board's recommendations and pressed for the retention by the local authorities of their veto. Bartley, who did not sign the report, maintained that to increase tramway facilities without immediate street improvements would increase, not diminish congestion; new broad thoroughfares and widened streets, which could be financially practicable, were the solution. Further, the future of motor omnibuses was not certain, and it would be unwise to extend tramways until more experience of omnibuses had been gained.

Note. The London-Traffic Branch of the Board of Trade was formed in Aug. 1907 and issued annual reports from 1908 to 1916. See *London Traffic.* 1920. *Breviate 1917-39,* p. 58.

Cabs and Omnibuses (Metropolis) Bill

Sel. Cttee. Rep., proc., mins. of ev., apps., index. pp. xliv, 295. 1906

1906 (295) *vii*, 581
apptd. March, o.p. July, 1906

Mr. Norman (*Ch.*), Armitage, Baker, Bowerman, Cullinan, Gibbs, Harmsworth, Keswick, Lambton, McKillop, Partington, Scott, Stanger, Steadman, Wiles.

'To inquire into the means to be adopted to prevent the use of drivers' and conductors' badges and licences by unlicensed persons, and the fees charged for those badges and licences; the restriction imposed on cabs when not carrying passengers; the restriction imposed by railway companies on the admission of cabs to their premises; the structural requirements to be enforced with regard to cabs and omnibuses driven by mechanical power; the scale of cab fares, and particularly the extension of the four mile radius, and modification (if any) to be

*made in the case of cabs carrying taxi-
meters'*.

1. Licences and badges. There exists
a well-known class of men known as
'bucks' who buy, borrow or hire
badges, and are thus enabled to drive
cabs without police permission, and
are almost free of identification in the
case of misbehaviour. Recommended
that cabmen should have a photograph
attached to a licence, and that there
should be three sets of badges of
different colours issued in rotation
every third year.

2. Fees. An annual fee of 5*s.* is
charged separately for horse-drawn
cabs, horse-drawn omnibuses, motor
cabs and motor omnibuses. Recommended, there should be one licence of
5*s.* held by a driver qualified to drive
horse-drawn and motor vehicles.
Drivers' and conductors' licence and
plate licence fees should go to defray
the extra expenses of the police, but as
the public derive so much benefit from
the extra police expenditure, the plate
licence should be substantially reduced
from £2.

3. Cabs not carrying passengers.
Crawling cabs cause serious congestion,
but much inconvenience would be
caused if all empty cabs were confined
to stands. The position of the law is
that a cabman who solicits a fare by a
sign or by saying 'Cab, sir?' as he
passes in the street commits an offence.
The police wanted a crawling cab to
be deemed 'plying for hire'. Recommended that there should be no change
in the police system of controlling traffic
in view of street widening which was
taking place.

4. Privileged cabs. The matter of
privileged cabs in railway stations has
been the subject of vehement discussions and industrial strife for many
years. The system of privileged cabmen was organized by the railway
company to secure adequate cabs at all
times of the day and night, but disputes
have continually arisen because privileged cabmen picked up passengers
outside the stations whilst other cab-

men were not allowed in the railway
stations. The contention of the cab
drivers' trade union was that cab drivers
knew the time of arrival of trains as
well as the companies, and that if all
stations were thrown open there would
be cabs wherever there were fares.
Recommended, the abolition of the
privilege system without further delay.

5. Motor vehicles. Matters concerning motor vehicles present an entirely
novel series of questions both as regards
the advantages conferred by self-
propelled vehicles and the injuries and
annoyances they inflict. When the first
motor omnibuses appeared, the Commissioner of Police conferred with
interested parties and drew up a code
of regulations for inspection and licensing; these were elastic to meet the
experimental situation. The Committee
agreed that this period was now over
and that more severe standards should
be enforced: for instance, a holder of a
Metropolitan Police drivers' licence
should not drive a motor omnibus outside the area. The structural requirements demanded by the police are
correct, brightly illuminated omnibuses
need not carry side lamps or red tail
lamps; the speed limit of 12 miles an
hour is sufficient. Other problems
from complaints, by the public, e.g.
vibration, noise, exhaust, oil on road,
were commented upon.

The Metropolitan Cab Area (enclosed within a circle described with a
radius of four miles from Charing
Cross) was established in 1853. A
demand had been made, chiefly by cab
proprietors, that it should be extended.
An extension to six miles would create
intolerable irregularities and discrepancies, and a readjustment of fares would
remove dissatisfaction. Recommended,
the legalization of a tariff commencing
with a sixpenny fare for a short distance
combined with a taximeter working
on the hour-mile system; for horse-
drawn hackney carriages with a taximeter 6*d.* for ¼ mile advancing by
units of 1*d.* for each extra one-sixth of a
mile, this tariff to be doubled outside
the circle.

Taxi-Cab Fares

Dept. Cttee. Rep. pp. 14. 1911. Vol.
    II. Mins. of ev., index.   1911

*1911 Cd. 5782, xli, 547. Mins. of ev.,
etc.; 1911 Cd. 5875, xli, 561
apptd. April, sgd. June, 1911*

A. Williamson (*Ch.*), Hyde, Edwards.

'*To enquire and report whether any
alteration is desirable in the scale of fares
for taximeter cabs in London fixed by the
Home Secretary's Order of 30th December,
1907, and whether they recommend any
modification of the arrangements made
between the proprietors and drivers for the
remuneration of drivers.*'

The London taxi-cab trade was still
in an experimental stage, and the
extent of the public demand, which was
seasonal, was not definitely known.
The decline in average takings per
cab was due mainly to the increasing
number of cabs, and therefore the
Committee could not recommend an
increase in fares which would probably
keep, or increase, an excessive number
in use. The remuneration of the drivers
should be a percentage of the takings
(20 per cent for the first £1 and 25 per
cent thereafter) and they should keep
any extras. But the best resolution of
many of the disagreements between
owners and drivers would be effected
by the introduction of the mileage
system under which drivers would pay
a certain amount per mile recorded,
whether waste or engaged, and guarantee a minimum mileage to the owners,
and in return keep the takings entirely.
The report contains estimates of the
number of cabs, capital employed,
takings, mileage, etc.

Motor Traffic

Sel. Cttee. Rep., proc. pp. xcii. 1913.
Mins. of ev., apps. Vols. I, II.   1913.
    Index.   1914

*1913 (278) viii, 1. Mins. of ev., etc.;
1913 (278) viii, 93. 1913 (278) (278 Ind.)
ix, 1
apptd. March, o.p. Aug., 1913*

G. Toulmin (*Ch.*), Baker, Benn, Boyle,
Goldsmith, Guiness, Harris, Kellaway,
L. Kerry, Morison, Munro, Nolan,
Thorne, L. Thynne.

'*To inquire into the circumstances which
have led to the large and increasing number
of fatal accidents in the Metropolis, due to
Motor Omnibuses and other forms of power-
driven vehicles, and to make recommendations as to the measures to be taken to
secure greater safety in the streets.*'

It was difficult if not impossible to
consider safety separately from the
general problem of traffic in London.
The Royal Commission 1903-5 had
considered improvement of means of
locomotion rather than the safety of the
pedestrian, but many of their recommendations would have increased
safety if they had been carried out.
The problem has become urgent since
1905 because of the changed conditions
due to the development of mechanical
traction. These include not only the
increase in the number of mechanical
vehicles of all kinds, but in the number
of journeys per head of the population
—now 228, a rise of 51 per cent in
seven years—and the number of injuries
and fatal road accidents arising therefrom. These increases are 'stupendous',
and the problems involved become
'month by month more intractable.'
    The outstanding feature of the
control of traffic in London is the
necessity for simplification and more
direct action in every direction. Three
methods of securing powers to construct tramways are open to promoters,
with advantages for one or other
purpose attending each. Three Government Departments are concerned with
the regulation of matters connected
with street traffic in London, yet none
of them nor all of them together, are
responsible for the whole of it. There
are three types of Municipal Government in the Administrative County and
one hundred and forty-two in the Outer
Ring; and the Metropolitan Police,
under the Home Secretary, is separated
from any municipal control, which
itself is a significant fact making the

traffic conditions of London different from those of any other populous area in the United Kingdom.

The Committee rejected the proposal of the Royal Commission to set up a Traffic Board, on the grounds that it would involve interference with the functions of elected municipal bodies, and that the possession of advisory powers only would make it ineffective. The origination of traffic schemes and regulation was a municipal duty. Co-ordination should be secured under the advice of a new Traffic Branch of the Board of Trade. This should be small, have expert advice, and absorb the London Traffic Branch of the Board of Trade. It should examine and report upon all schemes relating to London traffic, and no other Department should report to Parliament except through it. The veto of borough councils in regard to tramway schemes should be replaced by a full hearing before the new Traffic Branch, which should report to Parliament; the county councils in the Metropolitan area should have the widest possible bye-law making powers, subject to confirmation by the Traffic Branch. County and county borough byelaws regarding the numbers of stage carriages, routes, time-tables, etc., should be subject to its confirmation. Licensing should be the duty of the County Councils, subject to a right of appeal to the Traffic Branch. Special speed limits for motor buses, omnibuses and other heavy motor traffic should be imposed where conditions are especially dangerous. Closer control should be exercised by the Police, more traffic points where a constable is stationed and more refuges provided. As soon as practicable, means should be taken to remove the congestion caused by dead ends of tramways, street markets and road obstructions; and the measures taken to warn children and parents as to street dangers should be continued. The rules of the road should be revised and codified, points of road etiquette and standardized arm signals established.

Protection of Life from Fire

Sel. Cttee. Rep., proc. pp. iv. 1905

1905 (254) *vii*, 567
apptd. June, o.p. July 1905

M. Ferguson (*Ch.*), Arkwright, Bailey, Brigg, Kennedy, Lawson, Norman, Ridley, Soames, Tuff, Pym.

'*To inquire as to the provision of means of Escape from Fire in Factories, Work-shops, Laundries, Offices, Shops, Hotels, and other Buildings where persons work or live in large numbers, and to report what changes in the Law are necessary for the Protection of Life, having special regard to the case of buildings in the occupation of more than one occupier.*'

Pending the decisions on the London Building Acts (Amendment) Bill, which was being promoted by the L.C.C., and which dealt with the means of escape from buildings within the County of London, the Committee felt they could not usefully take evidence during the present Session. They requested the Home Office to prepare a precis of the evidence given before the Committees of both Houses of Parliament on the Bill.

London Building Acts (Amendment) Act 1905

Select Committees of both Houses of Parliament. Précis of ev. pp. 74. 1906

1906 Cd. 3041, *xcviii*, 559

The attention of the L.C.C. had been called to the need for acquiring fresh powers after the Queen Victoria Street fire in June 1902, when ten girls, working on the 4th and 5th floors had lost their lives as a result of a fire breaking out on the 3rd floor. The L.C.C., as the existing fire authority for the whole of the London area, claimed that their powers were insufficient. Sections of the London Building Act, 1894, providing for safety measures against fire could easily be evaded, or were not adequate in the case of buildings under 60 feet in height, or for buildings erected before

1894, which were subject only to the Act of 1855. Provisions under the Factory and Workshop Acts were also inadequate. A definition of 'more than 40 persons' made no provision, as in the Queen Victoria Street fire, for '20 or 22 persons' employed.

The opponents of the Bill did not deny the need for fresh legislation, but amongst the many objections to the Bill, fear was expressed regarding the use of new powers by the L.C.C., the costs involved in the provisions, and the relationship of the legislation in London to the country as a whole. The Bill is printed in App. I.

See *Local Legislation*. Sel. Cttee. Rep.; 1913 (267) vii, 41.

Ambulance Service in the Metropolis

Dept. Cttee. Vol. I. Rep., apps. pp. iv, 125. 1909. Vol. II. Mins. of ev., index. 1909

1909 *Cd.* 4563, *xxxi*, 1. *Mins. of. ev., etc.*; 1909 *Cd.* 4564, *xxxi*, 131 *apptd. Dec.,* 1906. *sgd. March,* 1909

K. E. Digby (*Ch.*), L. Stamford, Collins.

'*To inquire as to the provision made for dealing with cases of accident and sudden illness occurring in streets and public places within the Metropolis, and to report whether any, and if so what, improvements in ambulance provision are necessary or desirable, and how they could be best effected with due regard to efficiency and economy.*'

There were voluntary organizations, such as the St. John and the Metropolitan Street Ambulance Associations, but the London hospitals had not felt themselves in a position to establish or maintain an ambulance service generally available to the public. This had made it necessary for the police to deal with street cases. The system was 'gravely defective' and unsuitable vehicles were used to carry serious cases to hospital. But consideration of costs prevented the Committee from recommending the complete supersession of the wheeled litters by 'rapid' (horse or motor)

ambulances. A sufficient number of these rapid ambulances should be introduced 'tentatively and experimentally', to deal with all serious street cases. The Metropolitan Asylums Board should be empowered to establist and maintain this non-infectious ambulance service. No payment should be required for their use by persons suffering from accident or sudden illness in streets or public places.

In a Memorandum Collins pointed out that the superiority of the 'rapid' ambulance was generally recognized and recommended that it should be widely used and not merely regarded as experimental. The establishment and use of telephone call boxes should also be more boldly advocated. The expenditure for such a necessary municipal service should be faced. The L.C.C. was a more appropriate ambulance authority than the Metropolitan Asylums Board.

Tree Pruning, Royal Parks and Gardens

Rep. p. 7. 1911

1911 *Cd.* 5823, *lxiii*, 731 *sgd. April,* 1911

I. B. Balfour.

The art of pruning takes into account all the characters 'in each individual tree in relation to the conditions both below ground and above ground in which it grows, and I say without qualification that the trees in the Mall are a picture of the correct art of pruning in relation to environment. . . . In contrast with, and emphasizing the excellence of, the method pursued in the Mall and the parks, the young plane trees in Piccadilly, opposite Hamilton Place, show mutilation by unscientific pruning.'

Mall Approach Improvement Bill

Sel. Cttee. Rep., proc., mins. of ev. pp. vi, 50. 1914

1914 (237) *viii*, 607 *apptd. April, o.p. May,* 1914

W. Benn (*Ch.*), Bird, Morton, Essex, Boyton.

The Bill was promoted by the Office of Works in co-operation with the L.C.C. for carrying out improvements with a view to enhancing the dignity of the approach to the Mall from Charing Cross and the east, and for acquiring lands for that purpose. Petitions were heard from the interests affected by the proposed changes. The Bill was reported back with a new clause for protection of Canadian Pacific Railway Company.

See: 4 & 5 Geo. 5. c. 28.

London Electricity

See *Fuel and Power*, p. 142.

II. NATIONAL FINANCE

Finance Act, 1894

Cttee. Rep. pp. 7. 1900

1900 Cd. 89, *xlvii*, 189
apptd. Oct., 1899. *sgd. Feb.*, 1900

R. B. Finlay (*Ch.*), Reid, Haldane, Pretyman, Primrose.

'*To examine into the operation of Section 4 of the Finance Act, 1894, and to report whether and to what extent it might be properly amended so as, without unduly impairing the general principle of aggregation, to provide for its equitable incidence and to investigate and advise upon the present practice of the Inland Revenue Department under Section 17 of the Finance Act, 1896, in connection with the allowance of margins in the assessment of estates to the Estate Duty.*'

(1) By the proviso of Section 4 of the Finance Act, 1894, it is enacted that property passing on the death of the deceased, in which he never had an interest, or which passes under a disposition not made by him, to some person other than the wife or husband or persons lineally connected with the deceased, shall be treated as an estate by itself, for determining the rate of duty. This provision was to protect the family of the deceased from having to pay on the property passing to them at a rate enhanced by the fact that other property passes on the death of the deceased to persons outside the family. The rest of the proviso is so worded as to result in conferring on collaterals or strangers the same exemption from aggregation. The practical grievance arises from the fact that in the case of settlements made before the Act the duty may be taken and, therefore, the aggregation may take effect on the death of the life tenant instead of on the death of the settler. The proviso should be repealed, except in so far as it relates to property in which the deceased never had an interest, and there should be an abatement or return in the case of settlements before the Act in 1894.

(2) The allowance margins of £100 were introduced to avoid delay. As the duty is taken without a minute examination of the statement of property, minor corrections would have to be made on a corrective Affidavit, and the margins were intended as an administrative convenience to allow taxpayers to disregard small errors. But with the introduction of aggregation of property under separate accounts, each separate account practically gets the £100 margin, and the difficulties now outweigh the advantages. The margin of £100 should be abolished, and the duty paid on the exact amount of the property, but the Commissioners should be allowed to accept a simple statement of correction.

National Expenditure

Sel. Cttee. Rep:., proc., mins. of ev., apps., index. pp. 262. 1902

1902 (387) *vii*, 15
apptd. May, o.p. July, 1902

J. Fergusson (*Ch.*), Foster, Trevelyan, Lough, Wason, M'Iver, Churchill, Law, Vincent, Smith, Dorington, Mowbray, Chamberlain.

'To inquire whether any plan can be advantageously adopted for enabling the House, by Select Committee or otherwise, more effectively to make an examination, not involving criticisms of policy, into the details of National Expenditure.'

The Committee had taken sufficient evidence, but suggested its reappointment for the purpose of presenting a final report. The witnesses included W. Blain and R. Chalmers (Treasury), D. C. Richmond (Comptroller and Auditor General), Sir G. H. Murray (sometime Chairman, Board of Inland Revenue), Sir E. W. Hamilton (Permanent Secretary, Treasury), and Lord Welby (retired Permanent Secretary, Treasury). The appendices include the following papers: *Annual Estimates. Functions of Accounting Officers in the Supply Services. The Comptroller and Auditor General's Office.* Blain. Apps. 1, 6 and 7; *Treasury Control over the War Office and Admiralty.* R. Chalmers. App. 3; *Functions of the Accountant General of the Navy.* R. Awdry. App. 8; *Intercepted Revenue, Appropriation in Aid and Grants-in-Aid.* Gibson Bowles. App. 8; *Bowles' Memorandum.* Sir E. W. Hamilton. *Control of the House of Commons over Public Expenditure.* Lord Welby.

—— Sel. Cttee. Rep., proc., mins. of
        ev. pp. xxiv, 15. 1903

1903 (242) *vii*, 485
apptd. *April, o.p. July*, 1903

Expenditure must depend mainly on policy elaborated and proposed by the Government of the day, and accepted by Parliament. Nevertheless there is a large field for the vigilance of the Commons in combining the most efficient with the most economical methods. All control of expenditure from the preparation to the final audit, is either (i) departmental or (ii) extra-departmental.   (i) Departmental. — Each department has one or more accounting officers whose duty it is to see that money is spent properly and that obsolete expenditure is stopped, though the Minister can overrule the accounting officer. (ii) Extra-departmental control comes from the action of the Treasury, the Comptroller and Auditor-General and the Commons through the Public Accounts Committee and the Committee of Supply of the whole House. The control by the Treasury makes for economy and efficiency. Accounts should be submitted early for scrutiny. The Comptroller considered that his duties went beyond audit; he was a Parliamentary officer who had a free hand to report to Parliament things he thought Parliament should know. He should scrutinize and criticize improper expenditure and should indicate where censure was required. The Public Accounts Committee checks wasteful expenditure, and the minutes on their report written by the Treasury are valuable. Present Parliamentary rules give no opportunity for the House to discuss the reports regularly. This omission should be promptly rectified and the House given one day for the consideration of them. This would also allow it to indicate which Vote required vigilant examination. The examination of estimates by the whole House leaves much to be desired. Members of Parliament do not discuss with knowledge of the details and the discussions are unavoidably partisan. More details, especially of new expenditure, should be supplied to the House. At the beginning of each Session an Estimates Committee should be appointed in the same way as the Public Accounts Committee, to examine a branch of estimates for the current year, not exceeding one fourth of the whole. In order to unify the machinery of financial control, a proportion of Members should be appointed to both committees.

Rates of Drawback on Tobacco

Inter-Dept. Cttee. Rep., mins. of ev.,
        apps., index. pp. xxxvi, 91. 1904

1904 *Cd.* 2133, *xxxix*, 1
apptd. *July*, 1903. sgd. *March*, 1904

J. Fleming (*Ch.*), Leah, Helm.

'To inquire into the charges which the Drawback on Tobacco ought to cover and what those charges amount to.'

By the Finance Act, 1896, drawback was granted on all manufactured tobacco on a simple moisture content reckoned at 14 per cent, and authority was given to the Commissioner to relax the 18 per cent limitation on the content of inorganic matter. The composition of imported tobacco has changed since this Act and the moisture content, quantity of sand, other inorganic matter and offal varies with the different usage of the tobacco. Cigar and cigarette-makers use whole-leaf and cannot utilize the stalk, which contains more moisture and inorganic matter than the leaf. Offal must be ground before drawback can be claimed and grinding involves cost. An examination of samples showed that the permitted moisture content of 14 per cent was fair, but that the content of inorganic matter was 4 per cent higher than the 18 per cent assumed hitherto. Stalks and shorts which would not pass through the official sieve should be allowed drawback on a moisture basis and dried tobacco should be allowed 22 per cent of inorganic matter. The charges proposed varied from 3s. 2d. for snuff to 3s. 5d. for cigars.

Income Tax

Dept. Cttee. Rep. pp. xxv. 1905. Mins. of ev., apps., index. 1905

1905 *Cd.* 2575, *xliv,* 219. *Mins. of ev., etc.;* 1905 *Cd.* 2576, *xliv,* 245 *apptd.* — *sgd. June,* 1905

C. T. Ritchie (*Ch.*), Primrose, Buxton, Bonsor, Murray, Gayler.

'To inquire into and report whether it is desirable to effect any alteration in the System of the Income Tax, as at present prescribed and administered, under the following heads: (a) The prevention of fraud and evasion; (b) The treatment of income derived from copyrights, patent rights, and terminable annuities; (c) The allowances made in respect of the depreciation of assets charged to capital account; (d) The system of computing profits assessable under Schedule D on the average of the profits actually realized in the three years preceding the year of assessment. (e) The rules and regulations governing the recovery by taxpayers of over-payments of Income Tax.' Additional terms added during the inquiry: 'Whether the Co-operative Societies enjoy under the present law any undue exemption from liability to Income Tax.'

At the commencement of each financial year the local assessor for each parish prepares a list of all persons who in his opinion are liable or probably liable to assessment under Schedule D, and issues to each a form of Return. The tax had, on the whole, been levied efficiently. About four - fifths were assessed at source, or subjected to other satisfactory methods. There was, however, considerable evasion by self-assessors. The existing powers to remedy this evasion were inadequate and the Committee therefor recommended that, among other things, the completion and return of income-tax forms be made obligatory.

Generally, the procedure for assessing tax on income derived from such sources as copyright, and for making allowances on depreciation of capital was satisfactory, but some minor recommendations were made. The Committee would have preferred a system of levying tax on the income of the previous year, but the existing practice of basing it on the average of the three previous years had caused little complaint. But Section 133 of the Act of 1842, and Section 6, of the Act of 1865, giving concessions when actual profits in the year of assessment were less than the average had created anomalies and should be repealed. Suggestions were made to facilitate repayments and the granting of exemptions, but it was recommended that no person outside the United Kingdom should obtain exemption on grounds of smallness of income. The Committee did not accept the suggestion (made by

Traders' Associations) that Co-operative Societies' dividends should be
considered taxable profits. But the
position of those Societies also registered under the Industrial and
Provident Societies Act, which carried
on substantial business with non-
members, was perhaps worth investigating.

The Appendices include memoranda
by officers of the Board of Inland
Revenue on subjects in the terms of
reference, in particular on the average
system and taxation of Co-operative
Societies' dividends.

Income Tax

Sel. Cttee. Rep., proc., mins. of ev.,
apps., index. pp. l, 261. Index. 1906

1906 (365) *ix*, 659
apptd. May, o.p. Nov., 1906

C. Dilke (*Ch.*), Beach, Brace, Bridge-
man, Cavendish, Evans, Faber, Hardie,
Hayden, Holland, King, McCrae,
McKenna, Redmond, Rose, Trevelyan,
Whittaker.

'*To inquire into and report upon the
practicability of graduating the Income Tax
and of differentiating, for the purpose of
the Tax, between Permanent and Precarious
incomes.*'

Questions of the desirability or
equity of various proposals on general
grounds of public policy were outside
the scope of the Committee, which
confined itself to considering their
practicability. The income tax is already
graduated by abatement in the case of
incomes not exceeding £700. It would
be easy to extend graduation according
to the total net income of the individual
if the tax were collected on the basis of
personal declaration, but two-thirds is
collected at the source, and it was
extremely undesirable that this system
should be abandoned. It would be
practicable to graduate by extending
the existing system of abatements.
The revenue so lost would have to be
compensated for by raising the tax rate
on the higher levels of income; the

limit would be reached when this
required a large increase in the normal
or foundation rate of tax, and the total
amount of tax collected in excess of
what was ultimately retained, i.e. the
returnable tax, was so large as to cause
inconvenience to taxpayers and commerce. This difficulty would not arise
if the limit of abatement were extended
to £1,000. Graduation by super-tax
was practicable, but would have to be
based on personal declaration.

For the distinction between 'permanent' and 'precarious' the Committee
substituted that between 'earned' and
'unearned incomes'; differentiation
between these categories was practicable, provided it was limited to
incomes not exceeding £3,000, and was
made by charging earned incomes at
rates below the foundation rates. The
Committee endorsed the recommendation of the Committee of 1905 that
personal declaration of total net income
should be compulsory.

The witnesses included Sir Henry
Primrose, Chairman, and Bernard
Mallet, member, of the Board of Inland
Revenue; Sir L. G. Chiozza Money and
A. L. Bowley on statistical questions.

Mode of Issuing the Dollar in the East

Cttee. Vol. I. Rep. pp. 10. 1913.
Vol. II. Mins. of ev., index. 1913

1913 Cd. 6973, *lxvii*, 183. *Mins. of ev.,
etc.;* 1913 Cd. 6974, *lxvii*, 193
apptd. Feb., sgd. July, 1913

R. Balfour (*Ch.*), Elliott, Mitchell-
Thomson, Goschen, Blackett.

'*To consider the arrangements in force
under the Treasury Minute of 22nd
November* 1888 *as to the mode of issuing
the dollar in the East in order to secure
the equivalent of sterling in local currency,
and to report what changes, if any, should be
made therein.*'

The Minute of 1888 laid down the
rules observed in the Far East for
converting into dollars salaries fixed in
sterling. The silver value of the dollar

—in sterling—was obtained by averaging the price of silver in London over a period of three months. The mode of conversion had resulted in substantial losses to the Treasury, the main cause of which was the time lag between the determination of the official value of the dollar and the raising of money at the market rate. Whenever the market rate was favourable to the Treasury the unrestricted power of the payee to choose payment in local currency or in sterling cancelled the gain. Arrangements for conversion should be as flexible as possible. It was recommended that the official rate be fixed at the monthly average of the exchange rate for telegraphic transfers, and that steps be taken to ensure a more advantageous method of raising money for the Treasury Chest in Hong Kong.

Retrenchment in the Public Expenditure

Cttee. 1st Rep. pp. 6. 1915

1914–16 *Cd.* 8068, *xxxiii*, 369
apptd. July, sgd. Sept., 1915

R. McKenna (*Ch.*), Montagu, L. Midleton, Baker, Money, Mason, Cecil, Thomas, Claughton, Farrer, Cox.

'*To inquire and report what savings in public expenditure, in view of the necessities created by the war, can be effected in the Civil Departments without detriment to the interests of the State.*'

Many departments had reduced expenditure and many had economies under consideration. Although postal services had been curtailed, the rates for services which were unremunerative at present rates and were therefore a subvention to particular users, should be increased. Activities of the Road Board should be suspended and the surplus £3 mn. should be retained by the Exchequer. Pressure from the centre which stimulates local spending should be relaxed. The cost of printing Papers Presented to Parliament is £40,000 a year, besides the expenses of

compilation. The sales are usually negligible, and in some cases the original demand for information supplied has now ceased and the publications could be dispensed with. Goverment Departments should review all publications hitherto presented to Parliament or published, with a view to the permanent discontinuance of those which do not justify the expenditure, and the temporary discontinuance of those necessary in normal times. The expenses for shorthand writers for commissions and committees should receive the personal attention of the chairman and similar arrangements should be adopted for Parliamentary Committees.

—— Second Report. p. 1. 1915

1914–16 *Cd.* 8139, *xxxiii*, 375
sgd. Dec., 1915

add A. Birrell (*Ch.*), Lonsdale, Kavanagh. del. R. McKenna (*Ch.*), Montagu, Claughton.

The legislation needed for economies in Ireland was likely to be contentious. The matter was therefore left to be dealt with by the Irish Government and the Treasury.

—— Third Report. pp. 4. 1916

1916 *Cd.* 8180, *xv*, 177
sgd. Jan., 1916

add E. S. Montagu (*Ch.*), Acland. del. Lonsdale, Kavanagh.

Excluding the cost of maintenance, the estimates for the upkeep of museums and picture galleries in 1915–16 was £300,000. Attendances and receipts have already fallen, some of the best exhibits having been withdrawn from view. All museums and galleries should be closed, and placed at the disposal of the Government, except for the British Museum Reading Room, where a small charge should be made to the readers.

—— Final Report. pp. 26.   1916

1916 *Cd.* 8200, *xv*, 181
sgd. Feb., 1916

add R. McKenna (*Ch.*), Claughton.

The scope of the inquiry was necessarily restricted as questions of expenditure on the Army, Navy and the Merchant Services could not be dealt with, and it was not possible to introduce controversial legislation affecting the civil departments during the war. Moreover, whilst many departments had introduced economies, many of these were counterbalanced by increases of expenditure due to expansion of direct or indirect war work.

The problem of economy was presented by the increase of civil expenditure from £32 mn. in 1895 to £90 mn. in 1916, largely as the result of legislation or parliamentary policy. If any wholesale reduction were desired it could be effected only by a general restriction of State activities. The general recommendations included (*a*) an eight-hour day for the Civil Service, (*b*) restriction of inspection, (*c*) revision of subsistence allowances, and (*d*) suppression of statutory offices where they could be dispensed with. The detailed recommendations on the separate departments included a reorganization of the sub-departments of the Board of Trade; and the continuance of some of the smaller departments, e.g. the London Traffic Branch, the Light Railways Commission, and the Exhibitions Branch should be reconsidered. In local government, 'Returns' and other forms required by Government departments from local authorities should be revised so as to reduce to a minimum the work of compilation both for the period of the war and permanently. The recommendations of the Royal Commission on the Civil Service regarding the Legal Department should be carried out as soon as possible. Consideration should be given to raising the school entry age to six.

War Loans for the Small Investor

Cttee. Interim Rep. pp. 2.   1915

1914–16 *Cd.* 8146, *xxxvii*, 473
apptd. —— *sgd.* Dec., 1915

E. S. Montagu (*Ch.*), L. Cunliffe, Bradbury, Baldwin, Bell, Burn, Cargill, Goldstone, Harmsworth, Holmes, Le Bas, Mackinder, May, Needham, Wilson.

'The existing restrictions which limit the amounts deposited by any one depositor in the Post Office and Trustee Savings Banks to £50 in any one year, and £200 in all, should be removed for the period of the war and six months thereafter. An immediate issue should be made of Exchequer Bonds of the denominations of £5, £20, and £50, on the same terms as the existing issue of £100 Bonds. They should be on sale at all post offices, facilities should be offered for depositing them at the post offices, and books should be given to the depositor in which the deposit of the Bonds could be recorded.' The Chancellor recommended that both proposals should be carried out forthwith.

—— Report. pp. 10.   1916

1916 *Cd.* 8179, *xv*, 649
sgd. Jan., 1916

The problems the Committee set itself to solve were: to obtain for the State a certain amount of money for the prosecution of the war, and to reduce the general level of consumption and so lower the high price level. The small investor looks for security of his capital against depreciation, wants to be able to withdraw it at short notice, and to have as high a return as the large investor. Saving in every item of expenditure not necessary for efficiency and health of the individual was essential, as well as drastic taxation calculated to curtail all unnecessary expenditure. Some of the things needed from abroad could be obtained from people outside the Empire who were either willing to lend us money or buy part of our capital possessions.

The Committee repeated the recommendations of the Interim Report, and added a scheme, set out in the appendix, for saving small sums by instalments. Voluntary savings associations should be organized on an extensive scale. To aid 'investment associations' whose task would be to collect from members and invest in Government securities held by the Society, a strong central committee of experts should advise the societies, and Treasury bills of smaller denominations than £1,000 should be issued to them only.

In a reservation Goldstone and May regretted that there was not a more remunerative scheme to attract the savings of the small investor. The State could well afford to support a scheme under which 5 per cent would be paid on all deposits withdrawable at three months notice, and 10 per cent of which would be withdrawable at seven days notice without diminution of interest.

See *National War Savings*. Cttee. 1st Annual Rep.; 1917–18 Cd. 8516, xviii, 703; *Scottish War Savings*. Cttee. 1st Ann. Rep.; 1917–18 Cd. 8799, xviii, 721. Also succeeding Ann. Reps.

III. BANKING, FINANCIAL INSTITUTIONS

Savings Banks Funds

Sel. Cttee. Rep., proc., mins. of ev., apps., index. pp. xxiv, 257. 1902

1902 (282) *ix*, 1
apptd. March, o.p. July, 1902

Chancellor of the Exchequer (*Ch.*), Agnew, Banbury, Bartley, Campbell, Faber, Garfit, Gurdon, Holland, Pease, O'Shaughnessy, Rollit, Warr, Woodhouse, Hartland, Wilson, Morton.

'*To inquire into the general condition of both Savings Banks Funds in respect of their capital and income accounts, and the authorized investments thereof, with special reference to the loss of income which will be incurred by the reduction of the rate of interest on Consols in* 1903; *and to report whether any administrative reforms are required in either class of Savings Banks.*'

The net charge on the taxpayers, since the Act of 1877, for the benefit of depositors in savings banks, had amounted to over £617,000. The Act had provided that any deficiency of the Trustee Savings Banks' annual income should be met by parliamentary vote. With the intended reduction in the rate of interest on consols, in which the banks' funds were largely invested, the deficits were expected to increase.

The National Debt Commissioners held £154 mn. on behalf of the Savings Banks, of which £84 mn. was invested in Consols. The yield on consols was falling, but the Committee rejected a suggestion that the Commissioners' powers of investment should be enlarged. But by means of a reduction in the rate of interest paid on deposits, and certain economies suggested, the anticipated deficits could be turned into small surpluses. The latter could be devoted to strengthening the capital assets of the banks and to securing a reserve fund for meeting possible future deficits. The Committee were satisfied that a reduction of 1/8th per cent in the rate of interest would not adversely affect the inducements to deposit. Various alterations in the administration of the Trustee Savings Banks were recommended.

Thrift and Credit Banks Bill [H.L.]

Sel. Cttee. HL. Rep., proc., mins. of ev. pp. viii, 67. 1910

1910 (HL. 96) *ix*, 171
apptd. April, o.p. July, 1910

Lord Mersey (*Ch.*), L. Shaftesbury, L. Cromer, L. Herschell, L. Welby, L. Northcote, L. MacDonnell.

Some hundreds of Thrift and Credit Banks already existed. They served as loan societies and as savings banks and were of great use to farmers and others in their vicinity. They have been registered under the Friendly Societies Act, 1896, which fixes no limitation on the liability of the members. The Committee thought that whilst unlimited liability created confidence, secured careful discrimination and gave assurance that money would be used for the purpose for which it was borrowed, such registration limited the functions of banking. There would be advantages if co-operative trading could be added to the activities, but in this case registration would come under the Industrial and Provident Societies Acts and would limit the liability of the members.

Recommended that registration under the Friendly Societies Acts should empower banks to carry on jointly with their banking business a co-operative trading business. Trading should be confined to members, and accounts should be kept separate from the accounts of the banking business; banks should be limited geographically to enable a bank to know its members; certificate of registration should be made to enable the banks to sue and be sued; banks should be empowered to combine to form a central bank.

Financial Facilities for Trade

Cttee. Rep. pp. 8. 1916

1916 *Cd.* 8346, *xv*, 583.
apptd. July, sgd. Aug., 1916

Lord Faringdon (*Ch.*), Beckett, Blackett, Clark, Docker, Goschen, Jackson, Leaf, Wills, Simpson, Vassar-Smith.

'*To consider the best means of meeting the needs of British firms after the War as regards financial facilities for trade, particularly with reference to the financing of large overseas contracts, and to prepare a detailed scheme for that purpose.*'

Banking facilities in the British sense were defined by the Committee as 'properly limited to those which can be provided without a "lock-up" such as would impair the liquidity of funds and deposits at call and short notice. For this reason the usual practice of bankers here is to confine their advances as a rule to a currency not exceeding a few months. Financial facilities, generally speaking, are those which involve a longer currency than this.

The machinery and facilities for the finance of home trade and large overseas contracts already existed to a considerable extent, but more co-ordination was required. Further, British industry often needed financial aid of a kind which British Joint Stock Banks could not prudently provide, and an Institution called the 'British Trade Bank' should be created to fill the gap. It should be willing to make advances for the extension of existing plant and take a leading part in the inception of transactions and in overseas business. It should have an Information Department to examine industrial projects and overseas branches and agencies, making large use of existing banks for this purpose. It would be able to grant longer credits to younger men and should be the centre of syndicates for developing business of magnitude. The Bank should be constituted under Royal Charter, with a capital of £10 mn.; it should not accept deposits at call or short notice, or open current accounts save for parties proposing to make use of its facilities.

Enemy Banks (London Agencies)

Rep. to the Chancellor of the Exchequer, app. pp. 32. 1917

1916 *Cd.* 8430, *v*, 1
sgd. Dec., 1916

Sir W. Plender.

The five British branches of German and Austrian banks operating in London discontinued business after the outbreak of war, but licences were granted to them under which they were permitted, subject to the supervision of Sir William Plender as Controller, to undertake such operations as were necessary for making their realizable assets available for meeting liabilities to British, Allied and Neutral creditors arising out of transactions entered into with the London Branches before the outbreak of war, and to discharge these liabilities as far as possible. It was provided that upon

completion of these transactions any surplus assets which remained and were not required to fulfil the objects of the licences should be deposited with the Bank of England to the order of the Treasury, and so held pending a decision as to their ultimate disposal. The report describes the steps taken to collect the banks' assets and the vesting of any surpluses in the Custodian of Enemy Property.

IV. AGRICULTURE AND FOOD SUPPLY

1. GENERAL—OUTPUT, SMALL HOLDINGS, CROFTS

Decline in the Agricultural Population of Great Britain, 1881-1906

Rep. pp. 143. 1906

1906 Cd. 3273, xcvi, 583

R. H. Rew.

The geographical diversity of the United Kingdom made generalizations about agriculture difficult, yet for the years 1881-1901 there had been a decline in the numbers of farmers and graziers of 1,432, and of labourers and servants of 29,467; and the decline in unrecorded casual labour was thought to be proportionately greater. There was probably a surplus of labour prior to 1870, but the continued decline of perhaps 20 per cent per decennium was a serious economic and social fact. The conversion of some arable land to pastoral had reduced demand, but perhaps the chief factor was the extended use of labour-saving machinery. The attraction of high wages and the greater amenities of the towns had been accentuated by the effect of the Education Acts in reducing family

earnings. Agricultural cottages were unsatisfactory, whilst the poor opportunities for advancement offered few incentives. The number of small-holdings was insufficient in many districts and the costs of equipment too high. The report concluded that the general picture was gloomy, but that the spread of dairy, fruit and market-gardening was proof of adaptation. The report includes a summary of replies to questions sent out through the Board of Agriculture's Correspondents, and statistical tables.

The Agricultural Output of Great Britain (Census of Production Act, 1906)

Rep., memo, tables. pp. 62. 1912

1912-13 Cd. 6277, x, 529

R. H. Rew.

For purposes of the census of production of the agricultural and stock-raising industries, the Board of Trade asked the Board of Agriculture and Fisheries for co-operation in the collection of the requisite particulars. In the case of agriculture there was the longstanding system of annual returns of crops and live stock which, to a considerable extent, provided the information required. The additional information needed was collected with the voluntary assistance of the farmers. The occupiers of the 508,629 agricultural holdings exceeding one acre in extent were asked, in addition to their usual annual return for Inland Revenue, for information on breeds of live stock and poultry kept and sold, dairy produce produced and sold, lbs. of wool clipped in 1907, labour employed on the farm, and motive power on the farm. The total output is represented by the value of the products sold off the farms for consumption. In 1908 this output of farm crops was about one-third of total production, which included crops converted at the farms into another form of marketable product or used to maintain fertility. The 'materials used' included also about £26 mn. of purchased feeding stuffs. The total 'sales' output of Great Britain amounted to £150,800,000, of which £46,600,000, £61,400,000 and £30 mn. were the 'sales' of farm crops, animals and dairy produce respectively. The total labour permanently employed (excluding occupiers) was 1,173,000; and mechanical power of 213,525 h.p. was used.

Small Holdings in Great Britain

Dept. Cttee. Rep. pp. iii, 61. 1906. Mins. of ev., apps., index. 1906

1906 Cd. 3277, lv, 411. Mins. of ev., etc.; 1906 Cd. 3278, lv, 477 apptd. April, 1905. sgd. Dec., 1906

Lord Onslow (Ch.), Anstruther, Craigie, Bidwell, Brown, Channing, Long, Bund, Yerburgh, Ferguson, Collings.

'To enquire into the administration and working of the Small Holdings Act, 1892; to examine the various arrangements made by landowners in recent years for the provision of smaller agricultural holdings; and to report as to the conditions under which such holdings are most likely to be attended with success, and as to the measures which may most advantageously be taken, either by legislation, co-operative association, or otherwise, to secure the increase of their number.'

The Act of 1892 gave County Councils the power to create small holdings; the State could provide capital at low rates of interest, and the intending small holder could purchase on an instalment system provided he made a deposit of 1/5 of the purchase price. If he could not put down this sum, the County Council could rent him a holding at no more than £15 per annum. The Act had not been as effective as had been expected, only 652 acres having been acquired over a period of 10 years. The principal reasons given by County Councils for this failure included the difficulty of obtaining suitable land and insufficient demand. The Committee regarded these reasons as inadequate. Some Councils had been inactive, and had taken a strained view of the way the Act should be operated. In three counties, Worcestershire, Norfolk and Lincolnshire, enthusiasm and public spirit had led to successful experiments. There was evidence of a desire in the country for the creation of small holdings. To be successful, they must originate in a genuine demand by suitable tenants, the land must be good and the system of cultivation appropriate. There was some division of opinion amongst witnesses as to whether holders preferred ownership or tenancy. Some argued that the purchase money could be more profitably used in stocking a larger, rented farm, but the Committee concluded that the advantages of ownership had not been fully presented, and that a smaller deposit, together with an arrangement of interest and instalments so that they did not exceed rent, might develop the desire for ownership. In addition to the machinery provided by the Act of 1892, the Board of Agriculture should conduct experiments in the creation of small holdings, with the assistance of grants and by the use, where necessary, of powers of compulsory purchase. The Act should be amended by reducing the deposit from 1/5 to 1/8 of the purchase price, and by making state loans available to landowners for adaptation and equipment of voluntarily-provided small holdings. There should be further facilities for agricultural instruction and an annual grant should be made to the Agricultural Organization Society.

In a minority report Mr. Jesse Collings said that he wished to see the restoration of peasant proprietorship. County Councils should be empowered to advance the whole of the purchase money, so that poverty should be no bar to sensible men becoming owners of the land they tilled, and substantial sums should be placed at the disposal of the Board of Agriculture for this purpose. He disagreed with the proposal to make loans to landlords to provide and equip tenancies. In a supplementary report Channing emphasized the necessity of placing the purchase of land, selection of men, and methods of working on a strictly economic basis; of co-operative action in equipping holdings, and of agricultural education. Reservations by Anstruther, Ferguson and Long.

Allotments and Small Holdings

Memo. of evidence contained in Parliamentary Papers as to the demand for allotments and small holdings and as to the difficulty of obtaining land for those purposes. pp. 15. 1907

1907 Cd. 3468, lxvii, 1

Extracts from evidence given in five inquiries in the period 1890–1906.

Duration of Buildings for Small Holdings

Dept. Cttee. Rep. apps. pp. 21. 1912

1912–13 Cd. 6536, xlvi, 907
apptd. Feb., sgd. Nov., 1912

E. G. Strutt (Ch.), Baines, Barker, Law, Ralston.

'To inquire and report as to the probable duration of the various classes and descriptions of buildings and other works required for the equipment and adaptation of land for small holdings in the various districts of England and Wales.'

The Committee examined buildings, fencing, water supply, roads and land drainage in Yorkshire, Sussex, Warwickshire, Wiltshire, Devonshire, Essex, Flintshire and Denbighshire, which were considered as representative of conditions in other parts of England and Wales. Detailed tables are given in the Appendices showing the age, condition, state of repair and cost of maintenance of these works together with a statement of the terms allowed by the L.G.B. for the repayments of loans for the adaptation and equipment of small holdings.

Buildings for Small Holdings in England and Wales

Dept. Cttee. Rep., mins. of ev., apps., index. pp. 122. 1913

1913 Cd. 6708, xv, 561
apptd. Feb., 1912. sgd. March, 1913

C. Turnor (Ch.), Campbell, Cheney, Cochrane (Miss C.), Newman, Harmsworth, Hunt, Law, Tate, Unwin.

'1. To inquire and report as to the nature and character of the buildings which should be provided for use in connection with small agricultural holdings in England and Wales, regard being had—(a) to the convenience and requirements of the occupiers; (b) to considerations of economy, and also the possibility of the reduction of cost by the use of materials and methods of construction different from those ordinarily employed at present; (c) to the special agricultural and building conditions of the different parts of the country; and (d) to the various requirements of the Public Health Acts, and any Orders or Regulations made thereunder. 2. To submit a series of plans and specifications likely to be of assistance to *local authorities and landowners for the purpose.'*

The possibility of providing small holdings at an economic rent depends largely on the price of land and the cost of equipment. The buildings for a small holding should be suitable and sufficient, but not in excess of practical requirements. Erection of houses in pairs and groups may effect some saving. No house should contain accommodation less than a living room of 180 sq. ft., a scullery of 80 sq. ft., and pantry of 24 sq. ft., with additional space for other purposes, to give a combined floor space of at least 315 sq. ft. for three bedrooms. Not less than 500 cub. ft. per adult and 250 cub. ft. per child should be allowed in the bedrooms. There is an abstract of evidence, plans and specifications. A sub-committee consisting of Turnor, Campbell, Hunt, Law, Tate and Unwin visited Sweden to examine the methods by which small holdings had been encouraged there. Two important conclusions they reached were that the creation of 'colonies' or groups of small holdings was sounder in principle than a system of isolated holdings, and that in the early years the small holders' financial burdens should be as light as possible.

Land Settlement for Sailors and Soldiers

Dept. Cttee. Final Rep. Pt. I. pp. 30.
  1916 (Interim Rep. not printed)

1916 *Cd.* 8182, *xii*, 1.
apptd. July 1915. *sgd. Jan.,* 1916

H. C. W. Verney (*Ch.*), L. Northbrook, Hobhouse, Crutchley, Nash, Mager, Padwick, Roberts, Scott.

'To consider and report what steps can be taken to promote the settlement and employment on the land in England and Wales of sailors and soldiers, whether disabled or otherwise, on discharge from the Navy or Army.'

Part I of the report deals with the settlement of men in holdings of their own, whether as proprietors or tenants. A scheme for attracting a large population to the land is urgently required at the present time not only in view of the obligation of the State to the ex-Service men, but in the highest interests of the nation as a whole. The defensive power of a country is strengthened by its capacity to produce food for its inhabitants, and the developments of modern warfare have emphasized the danger of an undue dependence on foreign sources of food supply. Further, the stability and physical strength of a nation depend largely on those classes who have either been born and brought up in the country or have had the advantages of country life. It is certain that the physique of those portions of our nation who live in crowded streets rapidly deteriorates, and would deteriorate still further if they were not to some extent reinforced by men from the country districts. 'One of the best means of attaining the objects we have in view is by promoting a policy of closer land settlement.' 'The duty of carrying out a scheme of land settlement for ex-Service men must, in the main, be undertaken by the State.' The existing machinery of the Small Holdings Act will not be sufficient, as this was devised for 'men who had the necessary experience and capital' and as experience has shown, the united efforts of all the county councils in England and Wales has succeeded in providing land directly only for about 15,000 applicants in seven years.

As a large quantity of land comes into the market every year, there should be powers to acquire by purchase or by lease. Settlement should be on a 'colony system' and the 'ideal size would be a village community of 100 families.' 'Speaking generally, the minimum acreage to be taken for a fruit farm and market garden settlement should be 1,000 acres, and for a settlement on dairying or mixed holdings 2,000 acres.' Small mixed holdings were favoured. Amongst the other recommendations were: No men without experience should be allowed to take up holdings of their own; men without such experience should be offered employment at wages in the first instance; any small holdings established should be on a basis of tenancy rather than ownership; 'colonies' should be laid out so that more land can be added to each holding in due course; the War Office should hand over to the Board, free of cost, any of the military hutments which are not required for military purposes after the war; expert guidance should be provided for the settlers in each colony by the appointment of a resident director and an agricultural or horticultural instructor. Steps should be taken to encourage co-operation in all directions; a depôt should be established in each colony for the collection and disposal of produce, and a store for the sale of requirements; part of each colony should be retained as a central farm, from which horses, implements, etc., can be let out on hire to the settlers; a co-operative credit society should be established in connection with each colony, the State taking up share capital to the extent of 5s. for each acre. All possible social amenities, including women's institutes and clubs, should be provided in the colonies; the rents of the small holdings should be sufficient to recoup the capital outlay and the cost of management, except the salaries of the resident staff and the cost of preliminary training, but no sinking fund for the repayment of the purchase price of the land should be charged. Immediate steps should be taken by the Board to acquire and equip land for three pioneer colonies, comprising 5,000 acres in all, and additional land should be acquired for the establishment of further colonies; in the first instance a sum of £2 mn. should be placed at the disposal of the Board for the purposes of land settlement, and also such further sums as may be needed should be provided; the County Council should provide for ex-Service men who do not want to go into colonies, and the State should provide adequate funds for training disabled men who wish to settle on the land.

—— Final Report. Pt. II, app. pp. 39. 1916. Mins. of ev., index. 1916

1916 *Cd.* 8277, *xii*, 33. *Mins. of ev., etc.*; 1916 *Cd.* 8347, *xii*, 73

sgd. June, 1916

add H. Hobhouse (*Ch.*), White, Strutt. del. H. C. W. Verney (*Ch.*), Nash.

Employment, dealt with in Part II of the report means 'employment at wages, with or without bonus or share in profits, upon the farm or holding of another person'.

(1) Some 320,000 men had left the land since the beginning of the war. This deficiency had been met by an increase in the employment of women and children and by the introduction of machinery, and it was thought that the post-war shortage would in some measure be filled in the same way. But in order to get men to the land employment would have to be made more attractive. There would have to be an adequate number of houses built by the local authorities, more social amenities and a reasonable prospect of men being able to improve their position through the provision of allotments, small holdings, co-operation and agricultural credit. Wages had gone up during the war, and the Committee saw no reason to suppose that these would be reduced. (2) The serious unemployment which might occur on demobilization should be met by schemes for land reclamation and afforestation. (3) It was not possible so to change national policy regarding the production of home-grown food as to have ready, in time for demobilization, schemes which could absorb large numbers of men, many of whom had no knowledge of the land. Some employment could be found in the development of agricultural industry, e.g. sugar beet. The only way to increase the home production of food in a manner likely to absorb large

numbers of men would be to bring under the plough land now pasture and this might involve a guaranteed price for wheat, a bonus for grass land brought under the plough, and import duties. This problem was outside the terms of reference. In a note, the Chairman strongly urged that one million acres, or one-third of the land which had been allowed to go down to grass during the last thirty years, should be brought under the plough.

In a Minority Report, Roberts, Scott and Strutt said that the majority proposals failed in two essentials: conditions on the land should be good enough to attract the ex-Service man and the policy must be carried out in time. They proposed a minimum wage for agriculture and that all the necessary legislation for expanding agricultural production and employment, including guaranteed prices, bonus and import duties if necessary, should be passed through Parliament as emergency legislation before the end of the war. Each million acres broken up for arable would provide employment for 40,000. The Appendix contains a Memo. on the Reclamation of Land by A. D. Hall.

Social Condition of the People of Lewis in 1901, as Compared with Twenty Years Ago

Crofters   Commission.   Rep.,   apps.
        pp. civ, 65. 1902

1902 *Cd. 1327, lxxxiii,* 287
sgd. March, 1902

D. Brand (*Ch.*), Hosack, Macintyre.

'*To prepare an exhaustive Report on the social condition of the people of Lewis at present as compared with about* 20 *years ago.*'

The report is a factual one dealing with the progress of the island, with special reference to 'the last twenty years', the topics including population, land distribution, education, the poor,

public works, etc. The population had increased from 9,168 in 1801 to 28,949 in 1901, the increase between 1881 and 1901 being 3,462. Marriages were early and the average size of family, though declining, larger than on the mainland. Fishing and farming were the two main industries. The former employed 3,617 men and boys, about 300 less than in 1898, the value of the catch being £84,000, a little less than in 1891. White fishing was confined mainly to the islanders, but the herring catch, which was the more important, did not wholly benefit them, since a large majority of the boats for summer fishing came from other quarters and carried away the proceeds with them. Five-eighths of the land was occupied by crofters, or tenants of the crofting class, the remainder being deer forests and farms. The pressure of increased population was seen by the increased sub-division of crofts, and the number of cottars and squatters who had no title and paid no rent. Despite the progress made, the condition of the crofters was still far behind those of the better class of crofters in most parts of the Highlands. The Crofters Act gave more security of tenure and a means of obtaining fair rents, but did nothing to enlarge holdings or make more land available. The cottars would say 'Break down the remaining farms and take certain of the low lying parts of the deer forests; divide these into individual holdings with an assigned area of common pasture for each township, and many of us will have sufficient house room.' This course might be adopted with advantage to a reasonable extent, but it would be a temporary palliative and would not lead to a permanent adjustment. There should be a more vigorous enforcement of the Crofters Act against the sub-division and sub-letting of holdings; technical instruction for teaching trades and handicrafts and the elements of scientific vocation should be established and fostered.

Live Stock and Agriculture in the Congested Districts of Scotland

Dept. Cttee. Rep. pp. 16. 1910. Mins. of ev., index. 1911

1910 Cd. 5457, *xxi*, 225. *Mins. of ev., etc.;* 1911 Cd. 5509, *xiii*, 507 *apptd. Aug.,* 1909. *sgd. Nov.,* 1910

J. N. Forsyth (*Ch.*), Cameron, Dunlop, MacDiarmid, Esslemont, Gordon.

'*To inquire and report upon the work of the Board for the Improvement of Agriculture and Live Stock and its further development, with special regard to the quality of the stock reared upon the crofters' holdings.*'

The Congested Districts Board had promoted agricultural shows and somewhat advanced the breeds of cattle, horses and ponies by supplying stud bulls and stallions. Corn and potato seeds had been supplied at low cost, but this scheme, like the plan of providing potato spraying machines, was not a success. In many parts primitive and backward systems of agriculture still prevailed, crofts being too small and fencing often non-existent. The Board had been unable to give financial assistance to Co-operative Societies.

The Board should further extend and encourage the schemes for using good bulls and, in certain areas, more emphasis should be laid upon dairy cattle. A more vigorous policy of selective sheep breeding should be followed and over-stocking definitely prevented. A stud farm and breeding centre was absolutely necessary to the Board. Drainpipes and spraying machines should be sold at reduced prices and loans granted for the purchase of fencing. £10,000 should be used for furthering education schemes and steps taken to extend co-operative organizations.

Tenant Farmers and Sales of Estates

Dept. Cttee. Rep., apps. pp. 42. 1912. Vol. II. Mins. of ev., apps., index. 1912

1912–13 Cd. 6030, *xlvii*, 337. *Mins. of ev., etc.;* 1912–13 Cd. 6031, *xlvii*, 379 *apptd. March,* 1911. *sgd. Jan.,* 1912

Lord Haversham (*Ch.*), L. Clinton, Cawley, Rose, Holden, Campbell, Davies, Frank, Nicholls, Smith, Weigall, Parker, Eve.

'*To inquire into the position of tenant farmers in England and Wales, on the occasion of any change in the ownership of their holdings, whether by reason of the death of the landlord, the sale of the land or otherwise, and to consider whether any legislation on the subject is desirable.*'

Abnormal numbers of estates were being broken up, the value of land sold in 1911 exceeding £2 mn. Much land is let at rents below economic values, and landlords sell as an alternative to increasing them; land heavily mortgaged can at present be sold at prices which will enable the vendor to pay the mortgages off and retain an income in excess of that which he received as landowner. There is no evidence of a general desire on the part of the tenants to become owners. Though the percentage of cases in which a tenant is dispossessed is small, he is affected by uncertainty of tenure, the risk of loss of subsidiary business, and the possibility of being rented on his improvement. No alteration of Section 11 of the Agricultural Holdings Act, 1908, should be made by which compensation should be granted to tenants who are given notice merely for purpose of sale; the period of notice of intention to claim for disturbance should be extended. In the absence of agreement two years' notice should be required to determine the tenancy. Sir Edward Holden's scheme for State-Aided purchase of land for tenants, which provided for a Land Bank which could advance up to four-fifths of the purchase price, and provide for repayment over a period up to seventy-five years in order to make the annual repayments no more or little greater than rent, satisfied the Committee's criteria of a successful scheme. As only a small proportion of farmers would wish to use it, it should be supplemented by a scheme of State purchase of land to be let to sitting tenants.

In a reservation Davies, Nicholls and Parker urged that tenants should be given compensation for improvements and Parker opposed the proposals both for State-aided purchase and occupying ownership. Frank and Weigall opposed the recommendation that farmers might claim extension of notice in the event of sale, on the grounds that such a contingency was already provided for in the Committee's other recommendations. L. Clinton, Campbell, Frank, Smith and Weigall opposed State purchase and management of estates as it foreshadowed the nationalization of land. In a minority report, Trustram Eve rejected State purchase and State-aided purchase by existing tenants, because they would place undue burdens on the purchaser and because the 20 per cent deposit would deprive them of working capital. Instead, all sitting tenants should be able to buy their holdings, without deposit, by reducible mortgages arranged by the State.

Existing Methods of Collecting and Recording the Prices of Agricultural Products in Scotland

Dept. Cttee. Rep. pp. xxi. 1901. Mins. of ev., apps., index. 1901

1902 *Cd.* 805, *xxi*, 1. *Mins. of ev.;* 1902 *Cd.* 828, *xxi*, 23
apptd. *March*, 1900. *sgd. Aug.*, 1901

Lord Mansfield (*Ch.*), Cheyne, Bateman, Craigie, Glendinning.

'To inquire into the existing methods by which the prices of agricultural products are collected and recorded in Scotland, and to report as to the measures, if any, which can with advantage be taken for their improvement.'

An Act of 1723 required Sheriffs to call Fiars courts at which a jury of 15 competent men was to ascertain from expert witnesses the just and fair price of corn. Much dissatisfaction was expressed with this system, which is described in detail. The juries were often unsatisfactory, they weighted data incorrectly and used inadequate

evidence. The considered price might be a market or a farm price and there could be little uniformity. Nevertheless the Fiars system was used in the computation of tithes, grain rents, feu-duties and other valuations and seemed superior to other existing systems of price-fixing. The Edinburgh Corn Market is required by the Corporation to record quantities and prices, whilst for livestock the Board of Agriculture has an official system which calls for returns from all market authorities. The Committee recommended that the Board of Agriculture should obtain weekly returns from grain buyers at the principal corn markets and that the livestock system be extended to more places. Market correspondents should be appointed by the Board to specific markets and sales. Finally, if ministers' stipends were to be dependent upon Fiars Prices, then the courts' procedure must be made more uniform.

R. H. Rew, the Secretary to the Committee, gave evidence on the collection of agricultural prices in England.

Fiars Prices in Scotland

Dept. Cttee. Rep. pp. 12. 1911. Mins. of ev., apps., index. 1911

1911 *Cd.* 5763, *xxiv*, 1. *Mins. of ev., etc.;* 1911 *Cd.* 5764, *xxiv*, 13
apptd. *June*, 1910. *sgd. May*, 1911

D. Crawford (*Ch.*), Johnston, Aikman, Davidson, M'Micking, Rew, Conacher.

'To inquire into the present system of Striking Fiars Prices in Scotland and to report whether the procedure of Fiars Courts can be amended so as to ensure that the annual value of corn and other produce shall be ascertained on a more uniform basis and with greater accuracy, and if so, what are the best means of attaining that object.'

The Act of Sederunt 1723 established that Fiars Courts should consist of 15 knowledgeable men appointed by the Sheriff to consider and fix certain agricultural prices. The Teinds Act 1808 tied Ministers' stipends to Fiars prices. Both religious and agricultural interests have criticized the Fiars Court system and the composition of the jury. The evidence used was rarely comprehensive and the weighting of different elements was statistically unsound. Lack of uniformity between areas was aggravated by the acceptance of some prices which included transport costs. Nevertheless the Fiars Courts should not be abolished, but reformed. The Sheriff should be aided by 8–12 assessors and 3–5 of the assessors should examine the schedules of witnesses, and receive remuneration. The schedules should be completed by grain merchants, etc., who would thus acquaint the Court with current market information. A payment of 3s. should be paid to the witness for each return, but R. H. Rew saw serious objection to paying for returns required by statute.

2. PARTICULAR PRODUCTS AND REQUIREMENTS

Milk and Cream Regulations. Butter Regulations

Reps. 1901–1906

See *Food Purity.* p. 299.

Agricultural Seeds

Dept. Cttee. Rep. pp. xv. 1901. Mins. of ev., apps., index. 1901

1901 *Cd.* 489, *ix*, 1. *Mins. of ev. etc.;* 1901 *Cd.* 493, *ix*, 17
apptd. May, *sgd.* Oct., 1900

Lord Onslow (*Ch.*), Thiselton-Dyer, Wilson (J.), Anderson, Stratton, Sutton, Watt, Wilson (D.).

'To inquire into the conditions under which agricultural seeds are at present sold, and to report whether any further measures can with advantage be taken to secure the maintenance of adequate standards of purity and germinating power.'

The Committee found no widespread complaint. There had been an improvement in the last twenty years, due partly to the work of agricultural

societies, and to the Adulteration of Seeds Act. Farmers of 'education and position' had no difficulty, but inferior seeds found their way to N. and S. Ireland, because the poor, small farmer was content with a cheap article. Farmers who were members of agricultural societies could have their seeds tested, but merchant seedsmen did not have this facility. Seedsmen should be advised to sell, and farmers to buy only seeds subject to guarantee. To reduce the difficulties of this practice, a Central Seed Testing Station should be set up under Government auspices. In reservations, Thiselton-Dyer disagrees with the establishment of a Government Seed Testing Station and Sutton objects to the recommendation that seeds should be sold on guarantee because this will induce farmers to rely upon the guarantee instead of consulting the testing station.

Fertilizers and Feeding Stuffs Act, 1893

Dept. Cttee. Rep. pp. iii, 38. 1905. Mins. of ev., apps., index. 1905

1905 *Cd.* 2372, *xx*, 259. *Mins of ev., etc.;* 1905 *Cd.* 2386, *xx*, 301
apptd. July, 1903. *sgd.* Jan., 1905

Lord Burghclere (*Ch.*), Thorpe, Loyd, Clark, Burnard, Gordon, Pearson, Spear.

'To enquire into the working in Great Britain of the Fertilizers and Feeding Stuffs Act, 1893, the various methods in which it has been administered, and the results which have attended its operation; and to report whether any, and if so, what, further measures can, with advantage, be taken for the better protection of vendors and purchasers of the articles to which the Act applies.'

The Act of 1893 had been generally successful in protecting the farming class from fraud and carelessness in the preparation of fertilizers and feeding stuffs. The deficiencies of the Act arose mainly from the fact that claims against manufacturers and sellers had

to be initiated by the farmers themselves and in this respect apathy
and lack of information, the relation
between buyer and seller, the expense and general inconvenience of
the regulations tended to reduce the
number of cases in which proceedings
were taken. The work of detecting
fraud should be placed in the main
upon local authorities, under the control of the Board of Agriculture, and
public funds should be available for the
purposes of the Act. Local Authorities
should appoint well-qualified official
samplers who should be authorized to
take samples when requested to do
so by purchasers. Sellers should be
required to give, within reasonable
limits, the actual constituents of fertilizers and feeding stuffs, and to
guarantee the oil and albumen oils in
manufactured feeding stuffs. The onus
of discriminating between culpable and
unavoidable variation from the guarantee should be placed on the District
Agricultural Analyst. In any determination of the value of basic slag,
regard should be had to the proportion
of phosphoric acid which is soluble
in a 2 per cent solution of citric acid.
Poultry food should be brought within
the scope of the Act. No prosecution
should be instituted except with the
approval of the Board of Agriculture.

Sales for Agricultural Purposes Bill [H.L.]

Sel. Cttee. HL. Rep., proc., mins. of
ev., apps. pp. xviii, 183. 1912

1911 (HL. 237) x, 25
apptd. May, o.p. Dec., 1911

Lord Clinton (Ch.), L. Leven, L.
Chichester, L. Saye, L. Clifford, L.
Saltoun.

The Act of 1906 has had much
success, but full advantage had not
been taken of it because of the apathy
of farmers and of inherent faults in
the Act. Whilst small farmers show
want of understanding in appreciating
the chemical content of commodities

purchased, large farmers show an
increasing interest in them. But the
administration of the Act should be the
responsibility of the county councils.
They should take the initiative in
sampling and should be allowed 21
instead of 10 days to do this. It would
be an advantage if civil proceedings
could be developed so as to allow
county councils to assist in pressing for
damages and so limit criminal proceedings to dishonest trading.

Agricultural Seeds.—Under this Bill
control of agricultural seeds is the
subject of legislation for the first time
since the Adulteration of Seeds Act,
1869. Seedsmen now send seeds abroad
to be tested. It was suggested that a
testing station should be set up similar
to those in Germany and Switzerland,
but the Committee thought the cost
too great and recommended instead a
Government seed tester. Further provision was made for a statement of the
carbohydrate content of feeding stuffs
and suggestions put forward for
protection against adulteration.

Cider-Making

Results of Investigations. Rep., index.
pp. xii, 145. 1903

1904 Cd. 1868, xvi, 219

F. J. Lloyd.

Investigations into the manufacture
of cider carried out between 1893 and
1902 had strikingly revealed the possibilities of further improvements in
English cider and other orchard products. The experiments had stimulated
interest in the West and South-West of
England and had led to the formation of
the National Fruit and Cider Institute.

Fruit Industry of Great Britain

Dept. Cttee. Rep. pp. iii, 39. 1905.
Mins. of ev., apps., index. 1905

1905 Cd. 2589, xx, 541. Mins. of ev., etc.;
1906 Cd. 2719, xxiv, 1
apptd. Dec., 1903. sgd. June, 1905

A. G. Boscawen (*Ch.*), Radcliffe-Cooke, Hodge, Long, Monro, Pickering, Somerville, Vinson, Wilks.

'*To inquire into and report upon the present position of Fruit Culture in Great Britain, and to consider whether any further measures might with advantage be taken for its promotion and encouragement.*'

In 1904 the total acreage under orchards was 243,008, three-fifths of which was in six counties, viz. Kent, Hampshire, Devonshire, Somerset, Worcestershire and Gloucestershire. In the same year the small fruit acreage was 77,947, Kent, Middlesex, Worcestershire, Cambridge, Norfolk, Hampshire and Essex being the most important growing areas. It is the only form of agriculture which has exhibited any signs of progress in recent years, and the expansion is due to an increase in the taste for and consumption of fresh fruit, jam and preserved fruit and cider. The industry is capable of further expansion, but is hindered by an insufficiency of knowledge of the techniques involved in planting, tending, and packing fruit, difficulties due to land tenure and to the cost of transport, foreign competition, etc.

Under the Market Gardeners' Compensation Acts, a tenant who is allowed to plant trees and erect buildings without the consent of the landlord may claim compensation. The value of the land is increased by his improvements, which he should not lose. But this arrangement means that the landlord might be called upon to provide a large sum in compensation when he had no ready money available, and he often suffered from unfair valuations. Section 4 of the Act should be made retrospective so as to cover improvements made before the Act, but the tenant should be entitled to claim compensation only if he presented the landlord with a successor willing to take the holding at the same rent. The compensation should, after the manner of the Evesham custom, be paid direct to the outgoing by the incoming tenant,

at a fair valuation. The State should be prepared to lend to landlords to help them pay compensation State - aided purchase of holdings, on the lines of Mr. Jesse Collings' Bill, would be an advantage. A special sub-Department of the Board of Agriculture should be established to deal with matters connected with the fruit industry, including the dissemination of information, establishing an experimental fruit farm, and the control of diseases and pests. Other recommendations concerned rural education, school gardens, rail transport at company's risk rates, half-time release from school at picking seasons, grading of fruit, co-operative selling, etc.

Hop Industry

Sel. Cttee. Rep., proc., mins. of ev., apps. pp. liv, 597. 1908. Index. 1909

1908 (213) (213-*Ind.*) viii, 285
apptd. Feb., o.p. July, 1908

W. Collins (*Ch.*), Arkwright, Barker, Courthope, Gretton, Mallet, Napier, Rowlands, Strauss, Verney, White.

'*To inquire into the past and present condition of. the Hop Industry.*'

Between 1878 and 1907 the acreage under hops had fallen by 37 per cent in England generally, by 40 per cent in Kent and 36 per cent in Sussex, but owing to increased yields, production had remained steady. The demand for hops had fallen, partly because of the reduced consumption of beer and the smaller proportion of hops used in brewing. Public taste had changed towards a lighter, brighter, less heavily hopped beer than formerly—and this was said to have been aided by the substitution of glass for pewter vessels in the retail trade. Brewing for quick consumption had made it less necessary to use hops for their preservative qualities. The use of cold storage during the last fifteen years had meant that in a good season hops could be stored and put on the market later. The brewer could buy fresh hops all the year round. Complaints were made that the home grower had to pay higher railway rates for his small loads than were charged for the bulk assignments of the foreign merchant. Considerable attention was paid to the world's supply of and international trade in hops, and the effect of foreign competition on home production. The hop growers of the country did not have at their disposal recent information which would give them the world view essential to a prudent grower. Information for their farming communities was collected by the Governments of U.S.A. and Denmark, and the Committee endorsed the recommendations of the Royal Commission on *Agricultural Depression* (1897 C.8540, xv), that the same should be done for ours.

Poultry Breeding in Scotland

Dept. Cttee. Rep. pp. iv, 18. 1909.
    Mins. of ev., apps., index. 1909

1909 *Cd.* 4616, *xxxvi*, 409. *Mins. of ev., etc.*; 1909 *Cd.* 4617, *xxxvi*, 431 *apptd.* — *sgd. April*, 1909

J. Murray (*Ch.*), Wright, Smith, Prain, Hope.

'*To inquire into and report upon the methods commonly followed in the Highlands and Islands of Scotland in the Breeding and Keeping of Poultry and the Sale of Poultry and Eggs, and especially into the results of the efforts of the Congested Districts Board to promote this industry, and to suggest how these may be developed and improved.*' Inquiry extended to '*the Lowland Districts of Scotland*'.

For the thirty years prior to 1908 the demand for poultry and eggs in Great Britain had been greater than domestic supply, and unlike other agricultural prices, that for eggs had steadily increased. In Scotland annual consumption was valued at £3,092,017, of which £1,914,017 represented imports and £1,178,000 Scottish produce. The general trend of increased consumption had induced some develop-

ment in the Scottish poultry industry, but not to the same extent as in England and Ireland. Efforts to improve and increase products had been only sporadic and intermittent, and despite the general suitability of the Scottish climate for poultry breeding, methods employed were antiquated and unsatisfactory. The stock was very poor and often diseased, housing was very bad and the principles of feeding, hatching and rearing almost unknown. The practice of preserving eggs was not general and no regular system of marketing eggs or poultry existed. Delays were very frequent and tests for freshness too few. The farmers were apathetic in their attitude towards further development and improvement.

An extension of the poultry industry throughout Scotland would be generally beneficial, especially for small farmers, crofters and cottars, where the small expenditure of capital required and favourable market conditions would combine to keep people on the land and prevent rural depopulation. This could be achieved only by continuous central action, together with local education and organization. A large number of detailed recommendations were made to increase interest and provide instruction in the practice of poultry keeping through the medium of schools, lectures and a system of scholarships through which suitable students might receive specialized training. Production of eggs and table fowls could be increased by creating subsidized breeding centres, each keeping only one breed of fowl or-duck. Scottish methods of egg marketing were very unsatisfactory; detailed recommendations were made to secure more rapid collection of eggs, to increase their size, to increase winter production and to ensure efficient testing, grading and packing in order to compete more effectively with the better qualities of foreign produce. Subsidized fatting stations should be established to increase the production and quality of table fowl. Transport facilities (postal, railway, shipping), should be the subject of inquiry with a view to their improvement, and the collection and dissemination of market information to producers should be extended and developed by the central authority. To ensure the success of any scheme there should be efficient supervision and inspection, exercised through an expert Commissioner, to cover activities all over Scotland.

See *Eggs and Poultry for Scotland. Breviate 1917–39*, p. 114.

Combinations in the Meat Trade

Dept. Cttee. Rep., apps. pp. 27. 1909. Mins. of ev., apps., index. 1909

1909 Cd. 4643, *xv*, 1. *Mins. of ev., etc.*; 1909 Cd. 4661, *xv*, 33 *apptd. July*, 1908. *sgd. April*, 1909

Lord Cecil (*Ch.*), Bowerman, Elliott, Field, Fountain, Ward, Weddel.

'*To inquire how far and in what manner the general supply, distribution and price of meat in the United Kingdom are controlled or affected by any combination of firms or companies.*'

The terms of the inquiry limited it to ascertaining the facts regarding combinations in the meat trade and did not ask for any assessment of their effect, or for any proposals for action. No combination controlled or attempted to control the Home Grown meat trade, or that of New Zealand or Australia, but there was an American combination known as the United States Beef Trust, which included the firms of Armour, Swift, Morris and the National Packing Company, and was alleged to have a black list, to divide the country into non-competitive districts allocated to one or other of the firms, and to have opened retail shops to drive out competition by undercutting. It was difficult to obtain evidence to substantiate these and other criticisms. Though a degree of combination existed, the Beef Trust did not appear to be sufficiently powerful to be a serious danger to the beef trade as a whole, especially as three-fifths of

the whole supply of beef and veal came from home grown supplies, and an increasing proportion was imported from New Zealand and Australia. The American concerns have acquired two of the largest Argentinean companies, and further purchase of interests in the Argentine would place almost the whole of the imported live cattle and chilled and frozen beef under its control and might even enable it to exercise a determining influence on prices at Smithfield.

See *Breviate 1917–39*, pp. 117–18, 209.

Meat Export Trade of Australia

R. Com. (Australian). Rep., apps. pp. 50. 1915

1914–16 Cd. 7896, *xlvi*, 1 *apptd. June, sgd. Nov.*, 1914

Mr. Justice Street.

'*To inquire into and report as to the operations of any person, combination, or trust tending to create any restraint of trade or monopoly in connexion with the export of meat from Australia.*'

This report is a document of the Commonwealth of Australia, transmitted to the Secretary of State for the Colonies and presented to the United Kingdom Parliament. The inquiry was confined to reporting the facts relating to the existence of any combination or monopoly in the Australian meat export trade and was not concerned with proposing legislation. The inquiry owed its origin to the entry of companies of the American Beef Trust into the export trade in meat from Australia, and the belief that these companies intended to gain control of the trade, menace its healthy development, and control prices to the detriment of the community. No evidence could be found to prove this, but between 1908 and 1913 the United States had virtually disappeared as a source of United Kingdom supply, leaving the Argentine and Australia as the main suppliers. The American companies were not blind to the necessity of securing supplies outside the United States of America. The Beef Trust had come to control one-half of the beef exported to the United Kingdom from the Argentine, its activities in Australia should be very closely followed, and the Governments of the United Kingdom, Australia, and the Argentine should keep in touch with a view to concerted action should a detrimental monopoly appear likely. There were minor and unimportant instances of combination amongst Australian firms engaged in the meat trade, but there was no evidence of any combination amongst exporting firms for the purpose of suppressing competition or fixing and regulating prices.

3. HORSES, CATTLE, DISEASES

Horse Breeding

R. Com. Rep., app. pp. ix. 1888

1888 C. 5419, *xlviii*, 1
apptd. Dec., sgd. Dec., 1887

Duke of Portland (*Ch.*), L. Coventry, L. Ribblesdale, Chaplin, Ravenhill, Wilson, Gilmour, Bowen-Jones.

'*To consider the regulations under which your Royal Bounty, and also any moneys which Parliament may grant, may best be expended, for the purpose of encouraging the breed and maintenance of a race of sound horses.*'

The reports of the Royal Commission issued during this period can be understood only in relation to the first report, presented in 1888. This stated that 'there can be little doubt that for a considerable period the Royal Bounty, as expended in Queen's Plates, has failed effectively to fulfil the purpose for which it was originally intended. But it is only within recent years that any further necessity for encouraging the breed of horses, apart from the influence of private enterprise, has arisen. Private enterprise was formerly sufficient to produce and to maintain a breed of horses in this country, which was unrivalled in the world; and that pre-eminence was successfully maintained until the Governments of foreign countries became alive to the importance of acquiring an equal advantage for themselves. The foreign Haras, which were established for this purpose in various countries on the continent, created a most serious drain upon our resources in this country. There is no record, unfortunately, contained in any of the official statistics of the number of stallions which have been annually exported from the country, but it is a matter of common notoriety that year after year the United Kingdom has been swept by the agents of foreign Governments for the stallions and the mares best suited to their purpose, and they have been bought with public money, and taken from the country, frequently at prices with which it was impossible for private enterprise successfully to compete. The consequence of this has been that, with the exception of the highest class of stallions and of mares, for the breeding of race horses, this country has been left, for the most part, with the inferior and often unsound animals, which the foreign agent has rejected, and the result has been a gradual but marked deterioration in the general breed, for which England, at one time, was famous.'

The Commission recommended that there should be premiums, called the Queen's Premiums, given at the Shows for thorough-bred stallions suitable for getting half-bred horses of general utility and that statistics should be collected of imported and exported stallions, mares and geldings. By the terms of the Royal Warrant of Appointment Her Majesty indicated her intention of bestowing any moneys hitherto expended in the Bounty, together with any further moneys provided by Parliament, in accordance with the recommendations of the Commission. Between the years 1888 and 1911 fourteen reports were issued by the

Commission giving account of the spending of the £5,000 yearly sum and of the success of the scheme in raising the standards in breeding, in work in connexion with hereditary disease, and in the collection of statistics. In 1910 the grant was increased and an extended scheme was approved of by the Development Commission. The Appendices to the reports give statistical details of the stallions exhibited at the various shows.

See 2nd–14th Reps.: 1888 C. 5595, xlviii, 11. 1890 C. 6034, xxvii, 319. 1893–94 C. 6897, xxxi, 897. 1895 C. 7811, xxxv, 365. 1897 C. 8593, xxxiv, 233. 1899 C. 9487, xxxiii, 1029. 1901 Cd. 712, xxiv, 1. 1903 Cd. 1678, xxiii, 667. 1905 Cd. 2646, xxx, 515. 1907 Cd. 3712, xxxvii, 29. 1908 Cd. 4039, xlvii, 299. 1910 Cd. 5307, xxxvi, 769. 1911 Cd. 5936, xxix, Pt. I, 1.

See *Supply of Horses for Military Purposes (England and Wales)*; 1914–16 Cd. 8134, xxxix, 477.

The Improvement of Mountain and Moorland Breeds of Ponies

Cttee. Rep. pp. 41. 1912

1912 *Non-Parl. Bd. of Agric. and Fish.*

Lord Cecil (*Ch.*), Dale, Marden, Northey, Rogers.

'*To advise as to the measures to be adopted for the improvement of mountain and moorland breeds of ponies.*'

Ponies bred in the open are the natural reservoirs from which all our national breeds of light horses derive; they re-invigorate many with their characteristics of temperament, courage, intelligence and resource. To preserve the quality of the breeds and to improve and maintain their admirable qualities there should be compulsory registration in recognized stud books, encouragement of a pony association in each district and the exercise of the Commons Act, 1908. (8 Edw. 7. c. 44).

British Export Trade in Live Stock with the Colonies and other Countries

Dept. Cttee. Rep. pp. 47. 1911. Mins. of ev., apps., index. 1912

1911 *Cd. 5947, xxii, 359. Mins. of ev., etc.*; 1912–13 *Cd. 6032, xxv, 335 apptd. March, 1910. sgd. Sept., 1911*

E. Strachey (*Ch.*), Cooper, Adeane, Carr, Davies, Fraser, Gordon, Roy-Lewis, Middleton, Spencer, Stericker.

'*To enquire and report as to the character and extent of the British Export trade in Live Stock (including horses and poultry) with the Colonies and other countries, and to consider whether any steps can with advantage be taken by the Board of Agriculture and Fisheries, or otherwise, with a view to its development.*'

The Committee made a detailed analysis of the various markets to which British livestock is exported and the particular breeds each demands. The export of inferior or unsuitable pedigree stock should be discouraged, and persons guilty of falsification of pedigrees and certificates of registration punished. The system of milk reports should be officially encouraged and assisted. Where difficulties exist in the importing countries over the tuberculin test they should be invited to appoint an officer here to test the cattle before export or failing that a Government Testing Station should be established. Other recommendations were that the Board of Agriculture should provide a Bureau of Information to deal specially with the export of pedigree stock; research into the contagious diseases of animals should be assisted and, if necessary, official action taken against shipping combines where the deferred rebate system hindered livestock exports.

Glanders

Dept. Cttee. Rep. pp. 22. 1902

1903 *Cd. 1396, xxiii, 645 apptd. Jan., 1901. sgd. Dec., 1902*

A. C. Cope (*Ch.*), Hunting, McFadyean, McCall.

'(1) *To ascertain whether an apparently healthy horse which reacts to mallein (a "reactor") is capable of spreading the infection of glanders under ordinary circumstances.* (2) *To ascertain whether an apparently healthy horse that has first reacted to mallein and subsequently ceased to react (a "ceased reactor") is capable of spreading the infection of glanders.'*

The experiments included the testing of the originally healthy horses with mallein after a period of exposure to infection in the experimental stable, and ultimately a post-mortem examination of all the horses, coupled with the application of cultural and inoculation tests to any lesions thus discovered, except those that were obviously not of a glanderous nature. In the experiments with 'reactors' fourteen horses (six reactors and eight healthy on admission) were used. A reactor which becomes clinically glandered may be capable of spreading glanders to healthy horses in the same stable, but is unlikely to do so whilst at work. The experiments with 'ceased reactors' indicated that a horse that has ceased to react to mallein is incapable of spreading the infection.

Louping-Ill and Braxy

Dept. Cttee. Pt. I. *General Rep.* pp. 36. 1906. Pt. II. *Details of Investigation.* pp. 342. 1906. Pt. III. *Summary of Suggestions.* pp. 13. 1906

1906 Cd. 2932, Cd. 2933, Cd. 2934, xxiv, 519

D. J. Hamilton (*Ch.*), McCall, Wheler.

'(*a*) *To report as to the aetiology, pathology, and morbid anatomy of the diseases of sheep known as Louping-ill and Braxy; (b) To make experimental investigations as to the bacteriology and life history of these diseases, and as to their communicability, either directly or indirectly from animal to animal; (c) To bring together the results, if any, of the work of investigation at home or abroad;*

and (d) To indicate the directions in which preventive or remedial measures are likely to be successful.'

Louping-ill, Braxy and the collateral diseases belong to a class having certain features in common. They are all anaërobes, they have an extreme tendency to spore, and their natural habitat is the alimentary canal. The disease breaks out in the spring because then the blood of sheep possesses less bactericidal or protective influence than at any other time. The pathology and prevention of this class of disease is intricate, and as the subject is almost untouched, it requires lengthy inquiry, although such experiments as have been made point in the direction of immunization to several diseases at the same time.

Epizootic Abortion

Dept. Cttee. Rep. Pt. I. *Epizootic Abortion in Cattle.* Rep. pp. 24. [1909.] App., index. 1909

1909 Cd. 4742, xvi, 889. *App., etc.;* 1909 Cd. 4863, xvi, 915
apptd. April, 1905. *sgd.* —

J. McFadyean (*Ch.*), Strachey, Gillespie, Hunting, Nuttall, Stockman.

'*To inquire, by means of experimental investigation and otherwise, into the pathology and etiology of Epizootic Abortion, and to consider whether any, and if so, what, preventive and remedial measures may with advantage be adopted with respect to that disease.'*

In the absence of orders requiring the disease to be reported, its exact incidence was not known, though the Committee concluded that it was 'very prevalent', and that at least 99 per cent of the cases were due to infection by the bacillus of cattle abortion. The Report is a review of the scientific evidence on the pathology and etiology of the disease, of experiments conducted for the Committee by J. McFadyean and S. Stockman, and of the natural methods of infection (by the mouth and by the vagina); and examines critically the methods of prevention and eradication relied upon in the past, which 'either singly or collectively have not brought about any material improvement in the general condition of our herds'.

The isolation of animals immediately they showed signs of abortion; the destruction of virulent material; and the disinfection of everything contaminated with it was of greatest importance. No animal should be sold for three months after it has aborted. There was sufficient evidence to show that non-pregnant heifers and cows could be treated for immunity and it was suggested that experiments should be made in herds which were already infected. McFadyean's and Stockman's experiments are described in the Appendix.

—— Part II. *Epizootic Abortion in Cattle*. Rep., mins. of ev., apps., index. pp. 118. 1910

1910 *Cd.* 5279, *xxii*, 423
sgd. June, 1910

add Duke of Devonshire, Anstruther, Alison, Fox.

Extended terms of reference. *'An inquiry as to the administrative measures which in view of the results of the investigation made by the Committee should now be taken to deal with cases of the disease and to prevent the spread of infection.'*

Private effort at preventing the spread of the disease was a failure because of the movement of cattle by purchase; witnesses generally agreed with compulsory notification and restriction of the movement of infected cows. Public or State intervention was justified because (1) it is recognized that private or individual effort as a means of combating the disease is from the nature of the case inadequate; (2) knowledge has reached such a point that it is possible to devise regulations which are likely to prove effectual if enforced by law; (3) the weight of opinion amongst those whose interests are affected is in favour of State control; (4) the loss

occasioned when the disease is uncontrolled exceeds the probable cost of the measures required to counteract it. As a preliminary measure an Order of the Board of Agriculture and Fisheries should require (1) compulsory notification of suspected cases of the disease; (2) veterinary inquiry to establish the existence of disease on any particular premises; and (3) temporary isolation and restrictions on the movement of any cow that has recently aborted.

—— Part III. *Abortion in Sheep*. Rep. pp. iii, 12. 1913. App., index. 1913

1914 *Cd.* 7156, *xii*, 85. *App.*, etc.; 1914 *Cd.* 7157, *xii*, 101
sgd. Oct., 1913

del. Gillespie.

The microbe—a vibrio—is the cause of sheep abortion. The bacillus of cattle abortion is not found in sheep abortion, but experiments have shown that it is possible to infect cattle with vibrionic abortion. Two natural outbreaks of vibrionic abortion in cattle have been reported; one in Ireland, and one in Wales. The seasonal nature of sheep breeding isolates an outbreak of the disease to a particular flock, which allows the use of preventive measures easy to operate. As in cattle, the most common method of infection is by the mouth and therefore the preventive measures should be similar in both cases. As soon as a case appears in a flock, the ewe should be isolated, all infected material destroyed, everything contaminated should be disinfected, and the flock put to clean pasture. Having regard to the conditions in which sheep breeding is carried on, legislative measures are not applicable to this disease in sheep. The Appendix is a report describing the experiment carried out by J. McFadyean and S. Stockman.

Swine Fever

Dept. Cttee. Pt. I. Interim Rep. pp. 16. 1911. Pt. II. Mins. of ev., apps., index. 1911

1911 *Cd.* 5671, *ix*, 497. *Mins. of ev.,*
etc.; 1911 *Cd.* 5680, *ix*, 513
apptd. April, 1910. *sgd. May*, 1911

G. L. Courthope (*Ch.*), White, Anstruther, Blake, Douglas, Garnett, Long-
more, Penberthy, Stockman.

'*To inquire into the cause of the continued*
prevalence of Swine Fever in Great Britain,
and to report whether it is practicable to
adopt any further measures with a view
to secure its speedy extirpation.'

An historical review is given in the
Report on *Swine Fever* (1893–94 C.6999,
xxiii). The Board of Agriculture com-
menced operations against the disease
in that year, and between then and 1910
its policy had alternated between
general slaughter where the disease
existed, the slaughter only of suspected
pigs, closing infected areas, compulsory
cleansing of dealers' carts and premises,
the operation of model orders, and the
regulation of movement of pigs, etc.
The general beneficial results of this
activity can be seen in the fall of the
prevalence of the disease. For the three
years 1894–96 there was an average of
5,718 confirmed outbreaks, whilst the
average for the three years 1908–10
was 1,571. In between these years the
highest figure was 3,140 for 1901 and
the lowest 817 for 1905. There was
however a general feeling that 'much
ignorance and misconception exists as
to the nature of and procedure employed in the attempts to eradicate
the disease'. After considering the
present position of scientific knowledge
the Committee decided to investigate
(*a*) To what extent it is possible for
contagion to spread, by infective excre-
tions being carried mechanically by
attendants and animals other than swine?
(*b*) Whether external parasites, such as
certain lice, carry the disease from sick
to healthy swine? (*c*) Whether pigs
which have, to all appearance, recovered
from swine fever remain long infective
to other swine? (*d*) Whether apparently
healthy pigs which have been exposed
to infection are capable of transmitting
the disease as carriers? (*e*) For what

period it would be safe to consider
swine, which have recovered from
swine fever, to be immune against a
further attack? (*f*) What use, if any,
could be made of artificial methods of
immunization to expedite the eradication of swine fever? (*g*) Whether any
of the methods, which have lately
come into use in connection with other
diseases, could be employed in the
diagnosis of non-typical cases of swine
fever? To enable experimental observations to be carried out the Treasury
gave a grant of £1,000 for styes,
apparatus, etc.

There was much divergence in the
views expressed by witnesses on
compulsory veterinary inspection at
markets, general disinfection of all
carts at markets, licensing of dealers,
and problems of slaughter; there was
also criticism on the details of administration which caused delays, hardships
and concealments. Some argued for
centralization of administration whilst
others argued for decentralization. But
the Committee was satisfied that control
must remain with the Board, restriction
of movement must remain, present
scales of compensation be maintained,
and the size of infected areas kept as
small as possible. It recommended the
slaughter of all suspected cases, with
compensation to the owners, and the
control of the movement of swine from
markets by licence requiring subsequent isolation, as well as stricter
licensing, inspection and disinfection.
A completely uniform procedure
should be adopted by all local authorities.

—— Part III. Second Interim Rep.,
    mins. of ev., app. pp. 38. 1914

1914 *Cd.* 7247, *xii*, 199
sgd. Jan., 1914

No evidence was obtained to show
that effective immunization by artificial
methods can safely be employed, except
in conjunction with isolation and restriction on movement. The Committee
formed the opinion that (*a*) inoculation
with serum alone affords too brief

immunity to be of practical value; (b) every known method of vaccination, or simultaneous inoculation with serum and virus, exposes the inoculated animal to risk and renders it infective to others; (c) existing methods of inoculation do not promise assistance in the eradication of swine fever, though they might be serviceably employed in connection with a policy of control; (d) further experiment is necessary with a view to finding a form of vaccination which will give active immunity to the inoculated animal, without risk of further loss and dissemination of the disease.

—— Part I.V. Final Rep., mins. of ev., apps. pp. xvi, 63. 1915

1914–16 Cd. 8045, xxxv, 761
sgd. Aug., 1915

The Committee took evidence from W. S. Douglas and A. H. Pryce, Inspectors of the Board, regarding the operation of the Special Procedure Areas Orders, considered the report on experiments by Sir S. Stockman, and arrived at the following conclusions. Pig manure is infective, but fourteen days may be regarded as sufficient to bring about disinfection through natural causes; rats and external parasites are not carriers; while persons, vehicles and animals may carry infective material mechanically (subject to a time limit), all wide dissemination is due to the movement of infective pigs. A pig may become infective in three days after it has contracted infection and before it has exhibited clinical symptoms and may be infective for a variable period, the extent of which has not yet been fully ascertained. The possibility of healthy pigs acting as carriers should not be lost sight of.

The continuance of swine fever seems to be due principally to its highly contagious character and the difficulty of its recognition by the pig owner in its early stages and in its milder form. To these causes must be added the difficulty of tracing the place of origin and the movement of pigs.

Extirpation of the disease was possible only by drastic slaughtering measures involving prohibitive outlay and by such severe restrictions on movement as would be fatal to the industry. Attempts to extirpate the disease by general slaughtering should therefore be abandoned for the present, the use of protective serum in infected herds without avoidable delay should be encouraged and the production of immune herds by simultaneous administration of serum and virus under careful supervision should be undertaken where pig owners so desire. In a reservation Professor Penberthy stated that further experiments would have to be made before administrative measures could be based on the assumption that pig manure was rendered non-infective by natural causes in a period of fourteen days. App. I (pp. 57), contains the Report by Sir Stewart Stockman on the experiments made for the Committee.

Foot-and-Mouth Disease

Dept. Cttee. Rep. pp. 12. 1912. Mins. of ev., apps., index. 1912

1912–13 Cd. 6222, xxix, 1. Mins. of ev., etc.; 1912–13 Cd. 6244, xxix, 13 apptd. Nov., 1911. sgd. May, 1912

A. Fellowes (Ch.), Rose, Verney, Bowen-Jones, Bathurst, Field, Hinds, Lane-Fox, Carr, Dunne, Morrison, Nunneley.

'To inquire into the circumstances of the recent outbreaks of Foot-and-Mouth Disease and to consider whether any further measures can be adopted to prevent their recurrence.'

Very little is known about the causes of the outbreaks, but evidence points in one direction, that it is brought into the country by mediate contagion. At the date of the first recorded outbreak in this country, 1839, the landing of animals was entirely prohibited, and outbreaks have continued since the Act of 1896. Denmark has its visitations of the disease, although there is a prohibition on the import of animals. The things cited in the report as carriers are hay and straw; milk and milk products; hides and skins; heads and feet; carcases of calves in skins; vaccine seed lymph, hoofs, horns, bones and other animal offal, persons and their clothing, but no mention is made of the possibility of air-borne carriers. This was brought out in the evidence of Professor Bang of Denmark, who felt there was strong evidence for assuming that the infection was carried by birds, insects, and the wind, but more particularly by the birds (pp. 239–47, esp. qq. 6709–15). Professor Bang, in App. II, states that 'the virus is not known, but it has been proved to exist . . . that it passes through the pores of the filter . . . is smaller than the smallest bacteria visible under the microscope'. In answer to a question on research work, he said that Denmark had considered it too dangerous. Herr Loeffler, who was experimenting in Germany, had removed his research station from Greifswald to an isolated island, because it had been thought that infection had spread from his station (q. 6741). The Committee did not approve of an experiment station being set up in this country, but welcomed the appointment of a scientific committee to study in India.

Evidence had been given to show that immunization had been successfully carried out, but it was felt that any experimental work or any immunization attempted should be done under conditions which would satisfy the Board of Agriculture and Fisheries. The Committee drew attention to the training of veterinary inspectors and recommended that local authorities should appoint inspectors in accordance with uniform rules relating to qualifications, which should be laid down by the Board of Agriculture and Fisheries. Every local authority or group of local authorities should have the services of a chief veterinary officer of special qualifications. They also made suggestions for the tightening up of preventive methods of notification, cleansing and disinfection, etc.

Foot-and-Mouth Disease

Dept. Cttee. Rep. pp. 32. 1914

1914 Cd. 7270, xii, 139
apptd. June, 1912. sgd. Sept., 1914

S. Stockman (Ch.), McFadyean, Mettam.

'To make further investigations as to the characteristics of Foot - and - Mouth Disease, and the manner in which it is contracted and spread.'

In the six months which was allowed for investigations in India it was not possible to make exhaustive experiments, but it was hoped that fresh knowledge regarding various points of practical importance might be gained. A record of the experiments is given. The Committee concluded that the Plains cattle, sheep and swine of India were absolutely unsuitable for the purpose of experiments with regard to foot-and-mouth disease, owing to their exceptionally high degree of natural insusceptibility to the disease, and that further investigations in India were inadvisable. Great Britain should collaborate with Germany and France. Joint international investigation should be undertaken in Europe, but not on a mainland; research stations in France and Germany had to be closed on account of the spread of the disease. A station on an island near to a mainland was desirable, but the Committee stated that it was *not* suggested that a station should be established off the coast of Great Britain.

See *The Outbreak of Foot-and-Mouth Disease at Birkenhead*. Conference Rep.; 1914 Cd. 7326, xii, 171.

Humane Slaughtering of Animals

Cttee. Rep., apps. pp. 26. 1904. Mins. of ev. 1904

1904 Cd. 2150, xxiv, 469. *Mins. of ev.*; 1904 Cd. 2151, xxiv, 505
apptd. Jan., sgd. July, 1904

A. H. Lee (*Ch.*), Clayton, Cope, Game, Miller, Murphy, Yorke.

'To ascertain the most humane and practicable methods of slaughtering animals for human food, and to investigate and report upon the existing slaughter-house system.' (The word 'animals' to include only the following: cattle, calves, sheep, lambs and pigs.)

The object of the inquiry was humanitarian and was concerned solely with the act of slaughter itself and the conditions precedent thereto. The methods employed in this country were capable of considerable improvement. All animals should be stunned before blood was drawn, and as far as possible animals awaiting slaughter should be spared contact with the sights and smells of the slaughter-house, whose design should be modified to this end and should include provision for waiting pens and screening facilities. Private slaughter - houses should be gradually replaced by public abattoirs, and in both types uniform methods of killing should be adopted, subject to an efficient system of inspection and supervision. All slaughtermen and those employed in or about slaughter-houses should be licensed by local authorities. Recommendations were made concerning the disposal of blood, hides, etc., and plans for a model slaughter-house were printed as an appendix. Details of methods of killing for cattle, calves, sheep, lambs and pigs were also given.

Tuberculosis (Animals) Compensation Bill

Sel. Cttee. Reps., proc., mins. of ev., apps., index. pp. xiv, 151. 1904

1904 (272) *vii*, 429
apptd. April, o.p. July, 1904

G. Lawson (*Ch.*), Ellice, Farquharson, Field, Gray, Hutchinson, Jessel, Kilbride, Loyd, Price, Spear, Storling-Maxwell, Strachey, Stewart, Taylor.

No serious pecuniary loss is inflicted upon butchers who deal in high class meat, as the vast majority of carcases seized are old dairy cows. The loss in respect of such cows is considerable, but the butcher who deals in them takes the probability of that loss into consideration in fixing the price he gives for them. With regard to home-bred pigs there is serious loss. Witnesses complained that the recommendation of the Royal Commission on Tuberculosis 'that the presence of tubercular deposit in any degree should involve the destruction of the whole carcase' is too stringent, especially as detection in imported pigs is difficult because they are imported without head and neck glands.

Mutual insurance by butchers against loss is difficult because of the variety of practice with regard to the amount of tubercular deposit in a carcase held to justify the total condemnation, a matter on which the central authority should enforce uniformity. But it would not entirely meet the butchers' loss, since it is not possible to make any regulation which might not involve the destruction of some meat which might with impunity have been used for human food. Compensation should be paid from public funds, provided that the meat was bought in good faith and the local authority notified immediately of tubercular symptoms. No assistance should be given in the case of foreign meat.

The Relations of Human and Animal Tuberculosis (Bovine Tuberculosis)

R. Com. Reps. 1904–11

See *Health.* p. 289

The Nature and Cause of Grouse Disease

Dept. Cttee. Rep., app. pp. 12. 1911

1911 *Cd.* 5871, *xxvi*, 599
apptd. April, 1905. *sgd. Aug.,* 1911

Lord Lovat (*Ch.*), Drummond, Munro-Ferguson, Mackintosh of Mackintosh, Middleton, L. Ripon, Scott, Somerville, L. Tullibardine, Rimington-Wilson.

'*To inquire into the nature and cause of "Grouse Disease", and to report whether any, and if so what, preventive or remedial measures can with advantage be taken with respect to it.*'

The terms of appointment marked a departure from the usual procedure in that no further funds were provided for the inquiry, which was to be financed at the expense either of the members of the Committee or private subsidies. It did not cost more than £4,366 during the six years, and this was due to voluntary work and the fact that the scientific staff worked unremunerated or remunerated on an inadequate scale. The report gives a brief summary of the work of the Committee and the table of contents of the scientific inquiry, which was published in two volumes entitled *The Grouse in Health and Disease.*

Public Veterinary Services

Rep.

1912–13 *Cd.* 6575. See *Labour.* p. 241

4. FORESTRY

New Forest (Sale of Lands for Public Purposes) Bill

Sel. Cttee. Rep., proc., mins. of ev. pp. 6. 1902

1902 (265) *vii*, 287
apptd. May, o.p. July, 1902

A. Chamberlain (*Ch.*), Fuller, Scott-Montagu, L. Balcarres, Soanes.

The object of the Bill was to enable the Commissioner of Woods and Forests to sell or let land for a necessary term for the purpose of any local sanitary requirement. For example, Lyndhurst had grown rapidly and needed forest land for drainage. The problem had been growing for some years and had finally attracted the attention of the sanitary authority because of the recent outbreak of typhoid fever. Government legislation was necessary, as there was no urban sanitary authority at Lyndhurst able to initiate it (q. 1). Bill reported to the House with certain amendments.

British Forestry

Dept. Cttee. Rep. pp. iii, 10. 1902. Mins. of ev., apps., index. 1903

1902 *Cd.* 1319, *xx*, 1203. *Mins. of ev.,* etc.; 1903 *Cd.* 1565, *xvii*, 717
apptd. Feb., sgd. Nov., 1902

R. C. Munro-Ferguson (*Ch.*), Rolleston, Howard, Schlich, Bailey, Campbell, Lewis, Marshall, Somerville.

'*To inquire into and report as to the present position and future prospects of Forestry, and the planting and management of Woodlands in Great Britain, and to consider whether any measures might with advantage be taken, either by the provision of further educational facilities, or otherwise, for their promotion and encouragement.*'

The Committee's inquiry starts at much the same point as that of the Select Committee 1885. There are 21 million acres of waste, heather, rough pasture, or land out of cultivation, a large proportion of which could be used for forestry. There have been a few scattered efforts at methodical treatment, but there has probably been a further reduction of the already inadequate stock of timber. European red and white wood, which we import in large quantities, are yielded from Scots spruce and pine, two of the most common trees of English woodlands. Foreign grown timber was preferred not because our soil and climate were unsuitable, but because of our neglect of sylvicultural principles.

Two demonstration areas should be started, one in England and the other in Scotland. Oxford and Cambridge should each appoint a lecturer in Forestry, which should be an integral part of the curriculum of all Colleges giving instruction in agriculture. Provision should be made for the education of foresters and woodmen by employing students to work in the demonstration areas. The Board of Agriculture inquiries concerning the area of woodlands should be repeated. App. I is a digest of the Reports and Evidence of the Select Committees on Forestry; 1884–85 (287) viii, 799. 1886 Sess. 1 (202) ix, 689. 1887 (246) ix, 537.

Dean Forest Bill

Sel. Cttee. Rep., proc., mins. of ev.
    pp. vii, 16. 1904

1904 (233) vi, 39
apptd. June, o.p. June, 1904

D. A. Thomas (Ch.), Renwick, Seely.

A Bill to facilitate the opening and working of certain of the lower series of coal seams in His Majesty's Forest of Dean and in the Hundred of St. Briavels in the county of Gloucestershire, and for certain other purposes connected with the mines in the said Forest and Hundred. The Committee report the Bill with amendments. See 4 Edw. 7. c. clvi.

Dean Forest Bill, 1906

Sel. Cttee. Rep., proc., mins. of ev.
    pp. vi, 4. 1906

1906 (160) viii, 37
apptd. April, o.p. May, 1906

G. Kekewich (Ch.), White, Butcher, Stanley, Agnew.

To amend the Act of 1904; to give the Commissioners of Woods power to exchange parcels of the waste land and to improve the small holdings which fall into the Commission's hands from time to time. The Committee report the Bill without amendment. See 6 Edw. 7. c. cxix.

Afforestation

2nd Rep. R. Com. on *Coast Erosion*

1909 *Cd.* 4460. See p. 103

Forestry in Scotland

Dept. Cttee. Rep., mins. of ev.,
    apps. pp. 95. 1912

1912–13 *Cd.* 6085, *xxix*, 355
apptd. — sgd. Dec., 1911

J. S. Maxwell (*Ch.*), L. Lovat, Ferguson, Sutherland, Fleming, Wallace, Sellar.

'*To report as to the selection of a suitable location for a Demonstration Forest Area in Scotland; the uses, present and prospective, to which such Area may be put (including the use that may be made of it by the various Forestry teaching centres in Scotland); the staff and equipment required for successful working; the probable cost; and the most suitable form of management. To report as to any further steps, following upon the acquisition of the said Area, which in the opinion of the Committee it is desirable should be taken with a view to promoting sylviculture in Scotland, due regard being had to the interests of other rural industries.*'

Of the 860,000 acres of woodlands in Scotland, none, except for the estate recently purchased at Interliever, was owned by the State and much of it was understocked and badly managed. The Demonstration Forest Area in Scotland should consist of at least 4,000 acres, including 2,000 acres already wooded; it should contain variety in elevation, aspect and soil and should be reasonably accessible from the main teaching centres and all parts of Scotland. Its purpose was to demonstrate the growth and utilization of timber from the seed to the saw mill, on strictly commercial and scientific lines, with control vested in the Department of Forestry of the proposed Scottish Board of Agriculture. The Forest should be adequately staffed and equipped to accommodate staff and students; small holdings should be provided for workmen periodically employed there, and these should form an integral part of any State schemes for afforestation. If possible the Forest should be supplemented by a lowland, and east and west coast areas so as to encompass general geographical and climatic conditions representative of Scotland as a whole.

Completely new buildings would cost £15,000 and the annual expenditure, other than the wages of labourers and apprentices and the general expenses of forest management, would be £2,400. There was an insufficient supply of forest officers. There should be two grades of foresters, forest officers and foresters, the distinction being analagous to that between officers and non-commissioned officers in the Army. Besides lecturers, one or more advisory officers for private woods, and one officer for every 4,000 acres of state or assisted forest is required. They should be trained at a university centre, with work in the Demonstration Forest. Working foresters should be trained in an Apprentices' School in the Demonstration Forest, and the output should be 10 per year; which would, after 30 years, maintain a total of 300 foresters. State Trial Forests should be established, and an extension of private woodlands encouraged by loans at a reasonable rate of deferred interest and alleviation of burdens of death duties.

Supplies of Home-Grown Pit-Wood in England and Wales

Rep. pp. 13. 1914

1914-16 Cd. 7729, xxvii, 617
sgd. Nov., 1914

'About half of the total amount of pit-wood imported into the United Kingdom comes from Baltic ports and, as a result of the outbreak of war and the action of Germany in declaring pit-wood contraband, the supplies from this source have been very seriously curtailed. It became necessary, therefore, to ascertain the extent of home resources (from which only a fraction of the total supplies of pit-wood consumed in this country is normally drawn), and the means by which home supplies could, if necessary, be stimulated in order to compensate for the possible deficiency in foreign supplies.'

The annual consumption of pit-wood amounts to about 1·7 per cent of the weight of coal raised. The report and statistical analysis show that 'extraordinary' fellings in anticipating three to five years' fellings, would provide a year's supply of pit-wood in England and Wales, and that the United Kingdom holds 1½ years' supply.

Supply of Imported Pit-Timber with special reference to the Resources of Newfoundland and the Maritime Provinces of Eastern Canada

Rep. pp. 20. 1914

1914-16 Cd. 7728, xxvii, 597
sgd. Dec., 1914

Total annual consumption of pit-wood was about 4,500,000 tons, of which all but 700,000 to 800,000 tons was imported, mainly from Baltic sources from which we might be completely cut off. Stocks were about 1 mn. tons. Imports since 1st September, 1914, were, with home supplies, just sufficient for consumption in the period, so that stocks had not fallen. Increased supplies have come from Norway, Spain and Portugal and more could come from France. Ample supplies were available in Canada and Newfoundland and could be marketed at a reasonable price.

5. FISHING

Sea Fisheries Bill

Sel. Cttee. Reps., proc., mins. of ev., apps., index. pp. xvi, 180. 1900

1900 (287) viii, 371
apptd. May, o.p. July, 1900

Mr. Ritchie (*Ch.*), Vaughan-Davies, Doughty, Foster, Goldsworthy, Gull, Gurdon, Seal-Hayne, Murray, Pretyman, Redmond, Rothschild, Sinclair.

It was proved beyond doubt that there was a serious diminution, owing to the destruction of immature fish, of the supply of certain kinds of flat fish, particularly in the North Sea.

Vast quantities of such fish are thrown away as unfit for any market. The evil was a growing one, and in default of a remedy it would lead to disastrous consequences. It was thought to be established that there were certain well-known areas in the North Sea where small and young fish congregated. To prevent fishing in these areas would be of great value, but it would not be expedient to pass a Bill without further inquiry, especially as to the effects of the prohibition of the sale of fish below the limits as proposed in the Bill. The precise position of foreign law in regard to restrictive legislation should also be ascertained.

Collecting Fishery Statistics in England and Wales

Inter-Dept. Cttee. Rep., mins. of ev., apps., index. pp. xiii, 74. 1902

1902 *Cd.* 1063, *xv*, 1
apptd. Aug., 1900. *sgd. April*, 1901

T. H. W. Pelham (*Ch.*), Archer, Bence-Jones, Smith, Spring-Rice, Towse.

'*To inquire into the present system of collecting Fishery Statistics in England and Wales, and to report how the system could be improved and extended, and what additional cost (if any) would be entailed thereby, having special regard to the opinion expressed by the Select Committee of the House of Commons on Sea Fisheries, 1893, and the proposals of the Stockholm Conference, 1899.*'

The Board of Trade began the systematic collection of fishery statistics in 1885 (excluding salmon and freshwater fish), and by 1902 these comprised monthly returns by 157 part-time collectors from about 161 places in respect of the amount and value of all fish landed. The value of fishery statistics was widely recognized. The existing system of collection should be continued in an improved and extended form. For this purpose the remuneration of collectors should be increased to enable them to devote more time to their work, which should be subject to supervision and inspection by Board of Trade officials in order to secure uniformity and accuracy. Separate returns should be made for the catches in various fishing grounds, the different types, and where practicable sizes of fish landed being distinguished. Information should also be obtained as to the number and class of vessels engaged on each method of fishing; the types of fishing gear used; the quantities of fish caught by each type of gear; and the number and duration of voyages of different boats.

Fisheries of Great Britain and Ireland (Ichthyological Research)

Cttee. Rep., mins. of ev., apps., index. pp. xxv, 168. 1902

1902 *Cd.* 1312, *xv*, 215
apptd. Aug., 1901. *sgd. Sept.*, 1902

C. S. Moncrieff (*Ch.*), Archer, Crawford, Green, Herdman, Pelham, Thomson.

'*To inquire and report as to the best means by which the State or Local Authorities can assist scientific research as applied to problems affecting the Fisheries of Great Britain and Ireland; and, in particular, whether the object in view would best be attained by the creation of one central Body or Department acting for England, Scotland and Ireland, or by means of separate Departments or Agencies in each of the three countries.*'

The Central Fishery Authority for England and Wales was the Board of Trade, which collected statistics but did not directly undertake scientific research work. This was carried out for local purposes by a few of the Sea Fisheries Committees, by one or two official scientific committees, and by the Marine Biological Association, which was established in 1888 with the aid of a Treasury Grant. In both Scotland and Ireland research was carried out by the Central Fishery Authority. The most pressing problem was to estimate the increase or decrease of yields from the fisheries, to determine whether any decreases were due to natural causes or to man's operations, in which localities they took place, and how fishing could best be regulated to protect food fish. Detailed statistics should be collected at the main fishing ports as to the quantity and types of fish landed, and the places where they were caught. Three new research boats should supplement those possessed by the Central Authority for Ireland and the Marine Biological Association. Their function should be to study definite sea areas, in conjunction with land-based biological laboratories which should be established for this purpose. To control and correlate the work of existing research organizations, the functions of the Fishery and Harbour Department of the Board of Trade should be considerably enlarged, and a Departmental Fishery Council for England and Wales should be established to formulate schemes for investigation, to allocate Government Grants, to report on the findings of research, and generally to control investigations. No alteration in the Central Authority responsible for research in Scotland and Ireland is suggested, but a Conference consisting of representatives of the three Central Authorities should be held to prevent overlapping of areas of research. The Committee also recommended the establishment of a National Fishery Museum at one of the principal fishing ports, e.g. Grimsby.

To carry out the Committee's recommendations the State should provide funds for the collection and examination of statistics, the provision of assistants at marine laboratories, the provision and maintenance of the three research vessels, and for putting the staff of the Central Fishery Authorities for Scotland and Ireland on a permanent basis.

Pollution of Tidal Waters with special reference to Contamination of Shell-Fish

4th Rep. R. Com. on *Sewage Disposal*

1904 *Cd.* 1883. See *Health*. p. 284

Herring Fishery in the Firth of Clyde

Rep. pp. 12.   1903

1903 *Cd.* 1674, *xiv*, 819

apptd. Oct., sgd. Dec., 1902

L. Milloy, D. W. Thompson.

'*To inquire and report as to whether or not it would be in the interests of the herring fishing (a) to enforce in Loch Fyne and the territorial waters of the Firth of Clyde the close time for herring fishing on the West Coasts of Scotland established by the Act 28 and 29 Vict., cap. 22, Section 2, and restricted to the territorial waters through the operation of the Act 31 and 32 Vict., cap. 45 (Sections 6 and 71, and relative Convention, Article X); and (b) to amend the regulations for the purchase and sale of fresh herrings made by the Board on 28th February, 1898, under the powers conferred by the Act 52 and 53 Vict., cap. 23 (Section 4), or to recommend any amendment of that statutory provision.*'

There was a long history of protest against and disregard of the law setting a close time for herring fishing. Witnesses from Lochgilphead, Ardrishaig, Upper Loch Fyne, Rothesay and Arran, and the great majority of Glasgow herring-buyers and salesmen were in favour of a close time, but could not agree upon the dates. They argued that early fishing on the Ballantrae Banks destroyed the spawn, dispersed shoals and that the herring caught were too immature. The principal opposition to a close time came from Campbeltown, Carradale and Ayrshire fishermen and two important fish-buyers of Glasgow. The close time would not improve Loch Fyne summer fishing, they claimed, but it would rob fishermen of a living and deprive Glasgow poor of cheap food. In view of these very diverse opinions the Committee could not recommend any action, except the investigation of migration and spawning grounds of herring in the Loch Fyne and Clyde areas. The law prohibiting daylight fishing in certain periods had been disregarded and should be enforced and extended. The illegal use of different measures by the trade had caused trouble, as had various practices of filling the measures. The use of the quarter-cran basket should not be interfered with, but the 'Glasgow Box' should be the recognized measure and be legalized. A member of the crew should supervise the packing and counting.

See *State of the Markets for Scottish Cured Herrings on the Continent and in the United States of America.* Reps.; 1900 Cd. 247, xiii, Part I. 869.

Sea Fisheries Bill [H.L.]

Sel. Cttee. HL. Rep., proc., mins. of ev., apps. pp. xvi, 192. Index. 1904

1904 (356) and (356-*Ind.*) *vii*, 13 *apptd.* Feb., *o.p. Aug.*, 1904

Lord Onslow (*Ch.*), Duke of Abercorn, L. Yarborough, L. Meldrum, L. Tweedmouth, L. Northbourne, L. Heneage.

The Select Committee of 1900 found proved beyond doubt that there was a serious diminution in the supply of certain kinds of flat fish, particularly in the North Sea, but the present Committee had some difficulty in arriving at any conclusion as to the extent of any decline, since the substitution of steam for sailing trawlers, new types of trawl and the discovery of extensive grounds off Iceland and the Faroe Islands meant that the statistics were not strictly comparable. The figures afford strong grounds for believing that the imposition of a size limit would make it unremunerative to fish in the shallow grounds in the eastern side of the North Sea, but would not interfere with fishing operations in deeper waters. Instead of a fixed limit below which fish should not be *sold*, the present Bill proposed to enable the Board of Agriculture and Fisheries to make orders prohibiting the *landing* of fish below a size limit fixed from time to time. While some hardship might

be caused to line fishermen and small coastal trawlers if the sale of undersized fish were entirely prohibited, orders could be so framed which would make it not worth while for large steam trawlers to frequent the eastern grounds where undersized fish are most abundant. Such orders should be laid on the table of each House for 30 days. The ideal manner of protecting feeding grounds most frequented at certain seasons by young and immature fish was by international agreement, and this would be assisted by the passage of the Bill.

Whaling and Whale-Curing in the North of Scotland

Dept. Cttee. Vol. I. Rep. pp. 11. 1904. Vol. II. Notes of ev., apps. 1904

1904 Cd. 2138, *xlii*, 449. Notes of ev., etc.; 1904 Cd. 2153, *xlii*, 461 *apptd.* — *sgd.* —

D. Crawford (*Ch.*), Haldane, Leask.

'*To inquire into the new whaling and whale-curing industry as pursued or proposed to be pursued at stations on the coast of Scotland and in the adjacent waters, and to report generally thereon, and specifically as to the allegation that other forms of the fishing industry are injuriously affected thereby.*'

In compliance with demands of fishermen, who thought that whaling damaged herring fishing, in 1903 Norway passed a Bill prohibiting the whaling industry from operating in certain Norwegian waters for ten years. Since then Norwegian whale factories have been established in the Shetlands and Scottish fishermen have now put forward complaints regarding damage to the herring fishing. In addition, there are complaints that the stations are a danger to public health. There is much evidence that the industry is a great nuisance in the district, but this was largely due to the fact that the number of whales brought in is too great for the factories to handle efficiently and that putrid waste had been left about. Unrestricted whaling might not only be a danger to the herring industry, but might lead to over-fishing and the virtual disappearance of the industry, with a consequent loss of local employment.

The industry should be permitted to continue under limitations and regulations, the chief of which was that all persons and companies undertaking whaling should be licensed, that each company should not possess more than one boat, that there should be a close season from 1st November to 31st March, and that during the summer herring season whale fishing should be prohibited within forty miles from the coast. Some sanitary regulations were also proposed.

Sea Fisheries of Sutherland and Caithness

Dept. Cttee. Vol. I. Rep. pp. 16. 1905. Vol. II. Mins. of ev., apps. 1905

1905 *Cd. 2557, xiii, 735. Mins. of ev., etc.*; 1905 *Cd. 2608, xiii, 751 apptd. Dec., 1904. sgd. June, 1905*

Lord Mansfield (*Ch.*), Thompson, Anstruther, Sinclair.

'*To inquire into the causes of the recent decrease in the prosperity of the Sea Fisheries in parts of the Counties of Sutherland and Caithness referred to in two Petitions presented to the Secretary for Scotland in October 1904, and to report generally thereon, and especially whether any steps can be taken which would tend to restore that prosperity, or to assist the fishermen in the prosecution of their calling.*'

The Committee was appointed as a result of the following petition to the Congested Districts Board: 'That the industry by which we gain our living along our coasts has, during the last few years, been disastrously affected, and that we as fishermen, or as workpeople connected with the fishing industry, have been reduced to extreme poverty. Our means of livelihood is in serious jeopardy from a variety of circumstances, and unless some strong steps are taken in the immediate future

to assist us, we fear the very worst results to our families and to ourselves.'

The unanimous opinion was that the trawlers were wholly to blame. 'British trawlers were said to be in the habit of fishing, by day and night, on seven days a week within the closed area. The effect of this continual disturbance was, according to the evidence, to clear the spawning beds, to destroy immature fish of all kinds, and to break up the shoals of herring and harry them from their accustomed haunts.' The remedies proposed by the fishermen were (*a*) a close time for herring on the East Coast; (*b*) the provision by the Government of larger and more modern boats. The close time seemed to be suggested more for the protection of the market than for the protection of the fish. It is said that large quantities of small immature fish are caught on the East Coast during June and July, that the market is glutted, and that later on there is no price when the better herring is caught. A close time on the East Coast involved technical and economic questions more in the province of the Fishery Board. The Committee did not think that the institution of a close time would help the local fishing population. To be a staple means of livelihood, herring fishing must be conducted on a large scale; a suitable boat giving employment to six or seven men requires a harbour with not less than 8 feet at low water and costs little less than £1,000. A limited number of loans should be made to experienced men and the boat should remain the property of and be inspected by the Fishery Board until the loan is redeemed. But the disadvantages of remoteness and of sparseness of population are such as no governmental interference and no remedial measures can soon remove. It is not possible by artificial aid to create there such an industry as that on which the large East Coast ports depend. It is on the combination of small industries, such as lobster and haddock fishing, engagements for the season at the herring fishing, and the cultivation of the land, that the support of the people must continue in the main to depend. Such a mode of life, whatever may be its disadvantages from the larger economic point of view, is that for which most of the people are fitted by nature and long habit and by which they are able and content to live. Occupancy of a croft, unless it be so small as to be practically useless, makes a vast difference to these people's comfort and welfare, and should be considered as a hopeful method of alleviating poverty.

The Scientific and Statistical Investigations into the Fishing Industry of the United Kingdom

Cttee. Rep. pp. xx. 1908. Mins. of ev., apps., index. 1908

1908 *Cd. 4268, xiii, 515. Mins. of ev., etc.*; 1908 *Cd. 4304, xiii, 535 apptd. Sept., 1907. sgd. —*

H. J. Tennant (*Ch.*), L. Nunburnholme, Macleod, Helme, Williamson, Mitchell, Gardiner, Green, Rew, Hewby.

'*To enquire into the Scientific and Statistical Investigations now being carried on in relation to the Fishing Industry of the United Kingdom by the Fishery Departments of the Government, the Sea Fisheries Committees, the International Council for the Exploration of the North Sea, and the Marine Biological Association; and to report what work of this character is required in the interests of the Fishing Industry, and by what methods or agencies it can be most usefully and economically carried out in future.*'

The Committee traced the development and powers of the existing fishery authorities of the United Kingdom and of a number of separate national and international agencies. Valuable research work has been done, but it suffers from diversity of aim and lack of co-ordination. Urgent practical questions relate to the movements of migratory fish, the intensity of fishing and depletion of fishing areas, the taking of immature fish, improvements

of supply by hatcheries or transplantation, etc. The scientific investigation can yield practical results only when co-ordinated with statistical investigations of the widest scope. There should be established a Central Fisheries Council for the United Kingdom, including representation of the three Central Fishery Authorities, which should control further funds for fishery investigations. The Board of Agriculture's position as the Central Fishery Authority for England and Wales should be strengthened, adequate financial provision to the Fishery Board for Scotland for the encouragement of local work, British participation in the International Council should be continued. Provision and maintenance of research steamers is required. The grant of £1,000 to the Marine Biological Association should be continued.

The Devon and Cornwall Local Fisheries Committees

Cttee. Rep., apps. pp. 49. 1913

1913 *Cd. 6752, xxiv, 283 apptd. Nov., 1912. sgd. —*

C. Harmsworth (*Ch.*), Fremantle, Reynolds.

'*To consider the applications of the Devon and Cornwall Sea Fisheries Committees, respectively, for grants of £10,000 each for the purpose of assisting the fishermen of those counties to install motor power in their boats, and to advise the Board whether such installation is desirable, and whether for this or other purposes connected with the development of the fisheries of those counties it is necessary to make advances out of public funds, or whether the same can be adequately secured by alternative measures.*'

The following resolution had been passed at meetings of fishermen: 'That the Cornish Sea Fisheries Committee urgently requests that the Cornish Members of Parliament should join with the Members of Parliament from Devon, and such Scotch Members as were interested in the fishery, to form a deputation to the Development Commissioners, calling upon them at the earliest possible moment to place in the hands of the various Sea Fisheries Committees in England and Wales, and other local authorities in Scotland, all available moneys in their possession for the purpose of forming credit banks to assist fishermen to obtain the most modern equipment, whereby they might be able to successfully prosecute the industry'. Each county applied for a grant of £10,000. 'No shadow of doubt' was left in the minds of the Committee about the honesty of the 'proper fisherman' and his value to the nation as a community.

In the case of Devon, a sum of £3,000 by way of loan should be afforded for a system of credit banking and £2,000 for making approved experiments with motor power in fishing boats. Cornwall had already experimented with motor power; £3,000 should be allocated for a system of credit banking, to be loaned for installing and repairing motor power to fishing boats, and a further sum of £4,000 may be allocated among the declining fisheries of Mounts Bay ports and St. Ives. A *Note on the Organization of Credit for the Inshore Fisheries* sets out the principles and details on which these co-operative credit arrangements would work. The Fisheries Department of the Board of Agriculture should form an Inshore Fisheries Sub-Department, and an Inshore Fisheries Association should be established, to do work analogous to that of the Agricultural Organization Society. In a Minority Note, Stephen Reynolds criticized the system of credit banks. He suggested a loan of £4,000 free of interest for 12 years to the Cornish Committee.

Fishery Research

Advisory Cttee. Rep., apps. pp. 19. 1913

1914 *Cd.* 7200, *xxx*, 929
apptd. Jan., sgd. Sept., 1913

H. G. Maurice (*Ch.*), Allen, Bourne, Dendy, Fowler, Gardiner, Harmer, Hepworth, Herdman, Hoyle, MacBride, Meek, Ogilvie, Shipley, Schuster.

'*To advise the Board of Agriculture and Fisheries on questions relating to the elucidation through scientific research of problems affecting fisheries.*'

The questions raised in Fishery Research were entrusted to three sub-committees: *Plankton and Hydrography*—Professors Herdman, Gardiner, MacBride, Doctors Fowler, Allen, Harmer, Hoyle and Captain Hepworth. *Shellfish*—Professors Gardiner, Herdman, Dendy, Bourne and Doctors Shipley and Fowler. *Statistics*—Professor Meek and Doctors Ogilvie, Allen and Schuster. *Fishery*—Professors Herdman, Gardiner, McBride and Doctors Ogilvie, Allen.

Each sub-committee made proposals, set out in the Appendices, for the conduct of research, which it regarded as absolutely necessary. Three research vessels would be required. While fully sensible of the useful marine research work hitherto carried out by the Board with imperfect machinery, they disapprove of the existing arrangements for conducting research work on a purely temporary basis and with temporary staff. The time has arrived when the Department should have a properly equipped permanent scientific staff, without which a programme of intensive research over a continuous sequence of years cannot be carried out.

North Sea Fishing Industry

Scottish Dept. Cttee. Vol. I. Rep., apps. pp. v, 225. 1914. Vol. II. Mins. of ev., index. 1914

1914 *Cd.* 7221, *xxxi*, 533. *Mins. of ev.*, etc.; 1914 *Cd.* 7462, *xxxi*, 773 *apptd. Sept.,* 1911. *sgd. Jan.,* 1914

A. Sutherland (*Ch.*), Sutherland (J. E.), Conacher, Fulton, Moffat.

'To inquire and report upon the character and national importance of the inshore and deep-sea fisheries of Norway and other countries engaged in the North Sea fisheries, and the efforts made for the development of the fishing and fish-curing industry in all its branches, including—(1) The system of fishery administration, including the constitution and function of the local committees formed for this purpose in Norway and of any similar organizations in the other countries; (2) The facilities provided for research and for educating and training those engaged in these industries, by the establishment of technical schools, museums, laboratories, classes, or other special facilities; (3) The nature of the various means of capture employed and the methods (including any use of State credit) by which fishermen obtain the necessary capital to maintain the efficiency of their vessels and equipment: and to report in regard to each of the foregoing matters whether it would be advisable for similar action to be taken, with or without modification, in the case of the Scottish fishing industry, and, if so, what means should be adopted.'

The Committee surveyed the Norwegian, Swedish, Danish and German Fisheries and Administrations and the methods of research and educational facilities in those countries. In one or other of these countries, the fishing industry was touched by State activity in: the regulation of fishing rights; marine police; collection of statistics and the dissemination of information; scientific research; the provision of special transport facilities; educational facilities for fishermen; the provision of funds for the purchase of boats and gear; the building and maintenance of fishing harbours; and the insurance of men, vessels and gear. The Committee decided that the form of the Fishery Board should be assimilated to that of other public departments, possessing a permanent head, responsible to Parliament through the Secretary of State for Scotland. A Statistical and Intelligence Department should be formed and a fund of £10,000 per annum placed at its disposal for the development of fishing. Attention should be paid to the diffusion of scientific knowledge by lectures, practical demonstrations and publications. Recommendations were made to improve the educational facilities open to persons employed in the Fishing Industry, including continuation classes in navigation, mechanical propulsion and the treatment of fish.

In the late nineteenth century the herring fishery was carried on by sail boats owned by fishermen who relied mainly on local fishing grounds. But the size of boat has increased and steam engines have been fitted. The number of sailing boats fell from 2,228 in 1900 to 1,486 in 1912, when the steam drifter fleet numbered 800, its value being about £200,000 as compared with £500,000 for the sail fleet. The great cost of the drifters placed them out of the reach of most fishermen, more and more of whom ceased to own boats and gear and hired themselves out as wage earners. Boat and gear owners were much dissatisfied with the terms on which they could secure advances to enable them to enlarge and modernize boats and fleets, but the Committee did not recommend a State loan to enable fishermen to own steam drifters or to add oil engines to sail boats. Fish salesmen and merchants help to provide the cost of drifters, but are said to insist on the fishermen dealing exclusively through them, and to follow other practices disadvantageous to the fishermen. The Committee suggested an alteration in the existing division of the proceeds equally between boat, nets and crew.

A Minority Report, signed by H. M. Conacher and I. Moffat, agreed that there should be no State intervention to assist fishermen to obtain an interest in a steam drifter but, after a technical survey, concluded that Inshore Fishermen should be aided to acquire new boats with oil engines or to install oil engines in existing boats.

Inshore Fisheries

Dept. Cttee. Vol. I. Rep., apps. pp. xxxviii, 49. 1914. Vol. II. Mins. of ev., index. 1914

1914 *Cd.* 7373, *xxx*, 481. *Mins. of ev., etc.*; 1914 *Cd.* 7374, *xxx*, 569

apptd. Jan., 1913. *sgd. April,* 1914

E. S. Howard (*Ch.*), Pelham, Anderson, Helme, Fay, Harmsworth, Brace, Pease, Bostock, Hellyer, Lane, Reynolds.

'To inquire into the present condition of the Inshore Fisheries of England and Wales, and to advise the Board as to the steps which could with advantage be taken for their preservation and development.'

In addition to making their obvious contribution to food production, inshore fishermen were a valuable national asset performing many rescue functions and providing many recruits for the Naval Reserves. Of late, the condition of many inshore fisheries had declined owing to both external factors and the inability of fishermen to meet changing conditions. Witnesses complained of the operations of steam trawlers, of the decline in the numbers of fish, of excessive transport charges, poor landing facilities and of the discharge of sewage into the fishing grounds.

The main recommendations were that the powers of the Central Department be greatly increased, that four or five fishery districts, each with a resident local inspector, be considered and that it be adequately supplied by Parliament with funds for fishery development. It should have power to make and amend byelaws, have sufficient vessels to enforce regulations and sufficient local inspectors to keep in close touch with the fishermen. Local Authorities and others should increase the facilities for the technical instruction of fishermen. Local Fisheries Committees must be reorganized as advisory bodies. Sales of undersized fish should be prohibited. Loans to encourage the installation of motors should be made through Fishermen's Co-operative Societies and a Fisheries Organization Society to promote co-operation. The territorial limit should be extended in bays.

Salmon Fisheries

R. Com. Pt. I. Rep. pp. 64. 1902. Pt. II. Mins of ev., indexes. 1902. Pt. III. Apps. Sections I and II. 1902

1902 *Cd.* 1188, *xiii*, 1. *Mins. of ev., etc.*; 1902 *Cd.* 1269, *xiii*, 75. 1902 *Cd.* 1280, *Cd.* 1281, *xiv*, 1.

apptd. March, 1900. *sgd. July,* 1902

Lord Elgin (*Ch.*), L. Bedford, L. Moray, Paton, Fell, Archer, Burn, Travers.

'(1) To consider the causes affecting the yield of the Salmon Fisheries in England, Wales and Scotland; (2) The operation and influence of the present method of fishing; (3) The extent to which fish have access to the upper waters; (4) The protection of spawning fish and fry, and the cultivation and protection of stock; and (5) To report whether any change of the law is desirable in the several interests concerned.'

Much research has to be done before there can be certainty regarding the causes affecting increase and decrease in the number of salmon. Experience shows that in spite of artificial hatching, the maintenance of natural conditions is the best safeguard. The primitive character of the river and the natural habitat for fish are affected where rivers pass through densely populated areas and manufacturing districts where the water is used for artificial purposes, and the river bed is dredged and levelled. In England the Boards of Conservation are inefficient and cumbersome, being composed of ex-officio members, nominees of the County Councils and representatives of the licensees. One board had 335 members, and another 100. They are too poor to be effective, the income being derived from the fees paid by the licensees. There should be a Central Authority in charge of all fishery matters, and failing the establishment of Watershed Boards to deal with both fouling and pollution, there should be local Fishery Boards. These should be financed by assessment or special rate. Detailed recommendations are made regarding uniform close seasons, pollution, netting, protection of the volume of water in rivers. Maps show the areas of pollution.

6. COAST EROSION, LAND RECLAMATION

Coast Erosion and the Reclamation of Tidal Lands in the United Kingdom

R. Com.

apptd. July, 1906

I. C. Guest (*Ch.*), Ffolkes, Lyell, Matthews, Beale, Frederick, Haggard, Jehu, Lever, Nicholson, O'Brien, Summerbell, Wilson.

'*To inquire and report: (a) As to the encroachment of the sea on various parts of the Coast of the United Kingdom, and the damage which has been or is likely to be caused thereby; and what measures are desirable for the prevention of such damage; (b) Whether any further powers should be conferred upon Local Authorities and owners of property with a view to the adoption of effective and systematic schemes for the protection of the Coast and the banks of tidal rivers; (c) Whether any alteration of the law is desirable as regards the management and control of the foreshore; (d) Whether further facilities should be given for the reclamation of tidal lands.*'

The First Report is a formal presentation of the following volume of minutes of evidence, etc.; 1907 Cd. 3684, xxxiv, 7.

—— Vol. II. Second Report, *Afforestation.* Pt. I. Rep. pp. x, 48. 1909. Part II. Mins. of ev., apps., index. 1909 1909 *Cd.* 4460, *xiv,* 125. *Mins. of ev., etc.;* 1909 *Cd.* 4461, *xiv,* 185 *sgd. Jan.,* 1909

add Howard, Monro, Galvin, Somerville, Story, Ward.

Reference added '(*e*) *Whether in connection with reclaimed lands or otherwise, it is desirable to make an experiment in afforestation as a means of increasing employment during periods of depression in the labour market, and if so by what authority and under what conditions such experiment should be conducted.*'

Although natural conditions in the United Kingdom favour the growth of trees and there are particular examples of successful forest operations, many woodland areas do not furnish high class timber and the financial returns are unsatisfactory. This is due to the excessive openness of our woods, i.e. an insufficiency of trees upon the ground. Approximately $8\frac{1}{2}$ million acres in Great Britain and 500,000 acres in Ireland are available without material encroachment on agricultural land. The best rotation to secure sustained yield requires 150,000 acres annually. Any scheme of natural afforestation should be on an economic basis. Forests take time to reach maturity and afforestation requires well thought-out schemes of operation, with continuity of management. While the co-operation of private owners should be encouraged, a large scheme of national afforestation administered by a central authority was necessary. The scheme, which would require £2 mn. per annum, should be financed by loan. The deficit would rise to £3,131,000 in the fortieth year, but the scheme would then become self-supporting, and at existing prices, in 80 years the net revenue would rise to £$17\frac{1}{2}$ mn. The central authority should have powers of compulsory acquisition. Permanent employment would be given to one man per 100 acres, and would rise to 90,000, temporary employment to 18,000 during the winter months, with an equal number for subsidiary occupations.

A. S. Wilson in a Reservation, expresses general agreement with the findings of the Commission, but thinks the expectations are too optimistic; in particular, afforestation ought to stand on its own merits, quite apart from the question of using unemployed labour.

—— Vol. III. Third and Final Report. Part. I. Rep. pp. xi, 177. 1911. Part II. Mins of ev., apps., index. 1911

1911 Cd. 5708, xiv, 1. Mins. of ev., etc.; 1911 Cd. 5709, xiv, 203 sgd. May, 1911

add St. Ledgers, del. Guest, Howard, Monro, Story, Summerbell.

The rate of erosion varies with the geological formation of the coast, but is most marked along the east and south coasts of England. On the other hand there have been considerable gains, particularly in the mouth of the Humber and the Wash. Natural protection is afforded to the coast by the foreshore and beach material produced by erosion and it is essential that such material should not be removed. In some places erosion has been aggravated by the erection of defences of the wrong type. The Central Authority, aided by scientific experts, should make systematic observations of coastal changes. In late years the gains had generally outweighed losses, but this took no account of the value of the property, especially as many accretions were below high-water level. There had been some serious losses calling for effective measures of prevention. The cost of protecting purely agricultural land will usually exceed the value of the land and such works should be undertaken only when they preserve a considerable area of lowlying land.

There were many local authorities responsible for the coasts. The Board of Trade should be made the Central Sea-Defence Authority for the United Kingdom, with powers (a) to control the removal of materials and the construction of works, and (b) to supervise and assist existing authorities concerned with coast protection, and to create where necessary new authorities representing the affected interests in particular areas. Removal of materials

without the consent of the Board of Trade should be prohibited. A clear right of passage on foot upon all the foreshores of the United Kingdom, whether the property of the Crown or not, should be conferred on the public, in addition to existing rights of navigation and fishing. The Board of Trade should be empowered by order, after public enquiry, to define and limit other rights, e.g. bathing, riding, collecting seaweed, etc., and local authorities should be able with consent of the Board of Trade, to make bye-laws. Public Works Loan Commissioners should be empowered to make loans to local authorities, on the security of the rates, for sea defence purposes. With regard to reclamations of tidal lands, there is a difference between industrial and agricultural reclamation. In the former, where growth of population and prosperity demand them, they will be undertaken by those who benefit from them. There exist areas of possible agricultural reclamation which might not be profitable from a financial point of view, but which could be reclaimed with benefit to the community, and at the same time could give opportunity for the use of the unemployed. The Board of Trade should be charged with the duty of initiating schemes of reclamation. Part VI of the Report includes an analysis of the legal arguments as to whether by Common and Statute Law the responsibility for sea defence rests on the nation at large. The Committee did not find this proved and did not recommend grants from public funds for this purpose, though incidental assistance might be given to some poor communities. Nicholson dissented from the view that there was no legal obligation on the Crown; Wilson and Ffolkes thought that the Board of Trade's power to prohibit the removal of materials should be limited to cases where it would injure the public interest; Jehu wished to have the 'limits of foreshore' legally defined.

Formal Rep. not cited. Mins. of ev.; 1907 Cd. 3684, xxxiv, 7. 2nd Rep. Mins. of ev.; 1909 Cd. 4460, Cd. 4461, xiv, 125. Final Rep. Mins. of ev.; 1911 Cd. 5708, Cd. 5709, xiv, 1.

7. COMMONS

Commons
Sel. Cttee. Rep., proc., mins. of ev. pp. vi, 23. 1901

1901 (152) *v*, 659
apptd. Feb., o.p. May, 1901

Mr. Jeffreys (*Ch.*), Crombie, Thomas, Johnstone, Jones, Loyd, Montagu, More, Roche, Wingfield-Digby, Wilson, Bagot.

'*To consider every Report made by the Board of Agriculture certifying the expediency of any Provisional Order for the enclosure or regulation of a Common.*'

Sutton
The enclosure of the open fields and the heath and wastes in the parish of Sutton, Northamptonshire, was proposed by Mr. Hopkinson the local landowner, who had promised to make a road across the heath, at his own expense, to connect neighbouring villages, and to fence the fields to protect the crops.
'The same ought to be confirmed by Parliament without modification.'

Skipwith, East Riding, Yorkshire
The proposal was to end the rights of a scattered strip system and divide it in such a way as to allow for modern methods of cultivation and to reserve about 5½ acres for a recreation ground.
'The same ought to be confirmed by Parliament without modification.'

—— Select Committee. Proc., mins. of ev., apps. pp. vi, 14. 1902

1902 (237) *v*, 759.
apptd. May, o.p. June, 1902

Chipping Sodbury Common. The Commons lend themselves to abuses which only regulation can correct.

They are in a dilapidated state, overrun with bushes and rubbish tips. Mangy cattle with infectious sores damage good store cattle. It was the unanimous proposal of the Parish Council to sell the rights of pieces of land—Grant's Field and Mill-Acre—and use the money so raised for the preservation and regulation of the Commons.
'The Provisional Orders ought to be confirmed by Parliament.'

—— Select Committee. Rep., proc., mins. of ev. pp. vi, 17. 1904

1904 (137) *vi*, 1
apptd. March, o.p. April, 1904

add Campbell, Burns, Nicholson, del. Roche, More, Montagu.

Oxshott Heath, Cobham, Surrey. Merry Down, Surrey. Owing to increasing facilities of access from the Metropolis large numbers of the public—schools and other people—came out for holiday. Great damage to the trees, heather, and the surface sand has been caused. The residents proposed to raise voluntary subscriptions and appoint conservators to regulate and preserve the local beauty spot.
'The Provisional Orders ought to be confirmed by Parliament.'

—— Select Committee. Reps., proc., mins. of ev. pp. vi, 36. 1908

1908 (217), *vi*, 865

W. Foster (*Ch.*), Hills, Gomme, Lardner, Hicks Beach, Davis, Harmsworth, Keir Hardie, Cowan, Winfrey, Johnson, Arkwright.

Towyn Trewan Common, Anglesey. From time to time the ownership and rights of the Common had been challenged in the courts, with the result that parts of the Common fell under different ownerships with varying rights. The Commoners wanted preservation and regulation 'for all time', and said this should include the privilege of playing games, including golf, and the setting aside of 10 acres for supplying sand, gorse, rushes, etc., to the inhabitants. Agreed that the Regulation should be confirmed by Parliament without modification.

The procedure under the Commons Enclosure Acts should be referred to a Select Committee.

York (Micklegate Strays) Bill [H.L.]

Sel. Cttee. Rep., proc. pp. vi.   1907

1907 (320) *viii*, 821
apptd. Aug., o.p. Aug., 1907

J. Leese (*Ch.*), Corbett, Nicholls, O'Connor, Parker, L. Ronaldshay, Waterlow.

A Bill to enable the Lord Mayor, Aldermen and citizens of the City of York to acquire the rights of the freemen and others in or in respect of certain lands and strays known as the Micklegate Strays and to make provision for the management thereof and for other purposes. 7 Edw. 7. c. clxxvi.

Commons

Sel. Cttee. Reps., proc., mins. of ev., apps. pp. xii, 73.   1911

1911 (222) *vi*, 639
apptd. Feb., o.p. April, May, July, 1911

Brunner (*Ch.*), Beach, Bentham, Buxton, Cautley, Lardner, Mount, Cowan, Hardie, Bathurst, Eyres-Monsell, Davies.

'*To consider every Report made by the Board of Agriculture and Fisheries certifying the expediency of any Provisional Order for the enclosure or regulation of a Common, and presented to the House during the last or present Sessions, before a Bill be brought in for the confirmation of such Order.*'

Winton and Kaber Commons, Westmorland. The area involved consisted of 6,199 acres. Complaints were made to the effect that owners of the upland farms, close to the moor, turned on to the Commons more stock than they were entitled to turn on, and that when the farmers occupying farms at a distance turn their sheep on to the

Commons, the upland farmers set their dogs on them or worry them (q 106). The attitude of the upland farmer was based on a dispute over customary and legal rights of certain parts of the Common (Dawson, qq. 405-412; Clark, q. 252).

The Provisional Orders should not be confirmed unless modified. The chief modifications were that no dog should be allowed unless on leash, and that for the election of Conservators one vote and no more should be given to each individual entitled to exercise right of common.

Burrington Commons, Somerset. The area involved consisted of 1,060 acres. The chief complaints were that the late Lord of the Manor had allowed rabbits to increase and so poison the pasturage that only a much smaller stock of sheep could be grazed (Leach, q. 916). It was increasingly the practice of people from adjoining parishes to take fern, furze and soil, and Bristol hauliers contracted with individuals to have their horses grazed there (Wood, q. 1010). The Provisional Order should be confirmed.

—— Second Special Report

'The experience of your Committee has convinced them that the usefulness of the Committee's work is greatly restricted by the limited powers granted them under the Commons Act, 1876, and they recommend that the whole procedure under the Commons Inclosure Acts should be referred to a Select Committee of the House to consider what legislation (if any) is needed for improving the same.'

—— Select Committee. Rep., proc., mins. of ev. (Elmstone Hardwicke Common Fields Inclosure) and (Gosford Green Regulations). pp. vi, 30.
1913

1913 (221, 225) *vi*, 233

Mr. Brunner (*Ch.*), Bentham, Cowan, Gibbs, Lardner, Lloyd, Peel, Davies, Outhwaite, Keir Hardie, Mount, Bathurst.

Elmstone Hardwicke Common Fields. The Common Fields are under strip cultivation—the same owner will own various but not contiguous strips in the same field and in order to plough he will sometimes have to trespass over his neighbour's strips. This wasteful common field system has continued because of the life leases let out by the Ecclesiastical Commissioners. Now that the last of those lives has dropped out the way is clear for united action in the parish to get Enclosure (D. Lewis, q. 168). In view of modifications inserted therein, the Committee could not with advantage proceed with the order and adjourned consideration of it *sine die.*

Gosford Green, Coventry. Nineteen acres of common land with rights of over 3,000 freemen, who were willing to relinquish what had become valueless rights in favour of the City of Coventry whose intention it was to lay out the land as a recreation ground. 'The Provisional Orders ought to be confirmed by Parliament.'

—— Select Committee. Reps., proc., mins. of ev. pp. iv, 4. 1914

1914 (179) *vii*, 55
apptd. March, o.p. April, 1914

add White, del. Lardner.

Arising out of a point of order the Committee re-considered an amendment put by Mr. Keir Hardie, and heard further evidence from Mr. Rew. The main report states that the 'Order ought to be confirmed without modification'. The Special Report states 'that there should be inserted in the Award of the valuer provisions that the grazing of the allotment or allotments should be carried out in such a manner as not to interfere unduly with its or their use for the purposes of recreation'.

Commons (Inclosure and Regulation)

Sel. Cttee. Rep., proc., mins. of ev., apps. pp. xxii, 154. Index. 1913

1913 (85) (85-*Ind.*) vi, 35
apptd. June, 1912. *re-apptd. March, o.p. April,* 1913

Mr. Brunner (*Ch.*), Beach, Beck, Davies, Anstruther - Gray, Hamersley, Keir Hardie, Lardner, Lawson, Perkins, Wiles.

'*To inquire into the existing requirements of the Law as to the procedure prescribed in connection with the Inclosure and Regulation of Commons and to Report whether any alterations are desirable.*'

The Act of 1876 was intended to discourage inclosure and introduce regulation, but the procedure involves much difficulty and complication. Inclosures are now practically obsolete (R. H. Rew, q.10) but the regulation of Commons is beneficial. It is everywhere needed because of the dangers caused by fires, the insanitary habits, etc., of gypsies, the depositing of refuse on Commons, the increased use of Commons for golf playing, the over-stocking of the pasturage, illegal enclosures and encroachments, etc.

Recommended that a new Act be passed complete in itself for dealing with regulation, and containing the following provisions: 'no change should be permitted in the legal estate of any interested party; the method of applying for regulation should be simplified; the procedure of the Act of 1899 should be adopted with the necessary modifications; the absolute veto of any person or group of persons upon a scheme of regulation should be abolished; where agreement between interested parties, including the local authorities, can be arrived at, recourse should not be had to Parliament; where no agreement can be arrived at the usual procedure of a Provisional Order Bill should be adopted with the modification that the Select Committee on Commons should be substituted for the Provisional Order Bill Committee; increased regard should be given to the rights or privileges of the "labouring poor", and to the rights exercised by the neighbouring public over Commons which are not part of manors; where no one can prove a title to a village green, this should be vested in the Parish Council; the present provisions as to the confirmation of byelaws should be altered'.

8. WAR PROBLEMS: FOOD REQUIREMENTS, PRODUCTION, PRICES

Supply of Food and Raw Material in Time of War

R. Com. Vol. I. Rep., apps. pp. xii, 204. 1905. Vols. II, III. Mins. of ev., apps. 1905

1905 *Cd.* 2643, *xxxix*, 1. *Mins. of ev.*, *etc.*; 1905 *Cd.* 2644, *xxxix*, 217.   1905 *Cd.* 2645, *xl*, 1

apptd. April, 1904. *sgd.* —

Lord Balfour of Burleigh (*Ch.*), H.R.H. the Prince of Wales, Duke of Sutherland, L. Burghclere, Chaplin, Wharton, Colomb, Bateman, Seton-Karr, Cunynghame, Robertson, Holland, Emmott, Montgomery, Street, Wilson, Bosanquet.

'*To inquire into the conditions affecting the importation of food and raw material into the United Kingdom of Great Britain and Ireland in time of war, and into the amount of the reserves of such supplies existing in the Country at any given period; and to advise whether it is desirable to adopt any measures, in addition to the maintenance of a strong Fleet, by which such supplies can be better secured and violent fluctuations avoided.*'

The stocks of raw materials and food in the country, in terms of the time they would last at the current rate of consumption, varied from 7 months' supply in the case of cotton, 6 months for home grown and 2 to 3 months for foreign and colonial wool, 1 to 2 months for iron ore, 2 to 8 months for softwood, 1 to 2 months for rubber and 2 years for tobacco. For tea, coffee and sugar the usual stocks amounted to 6, 25 and 3 months' supply respectively. Stocks of perishable foodstuffs were obviously small, that of cheese varying from 1 to 2½ months and

butter from 7 to 10 days' supply. Forty-five per cent of meat was imported. Wheat and flour presented the most serious problem, as 80 per cent of the supply was imported. Stocks usually amounted to 17 weeks' supply in September and rarely fell below 7 weeks' supply, except possibly in August. In addition, there were afloat for the United Kingdom 3 to 7 weeks' supply, of which 20 per cent was within a week's sailing.

We should not allow the safety of our supplies to depend too largely on the observance of the rules of international law by a hostile power. There is unlikely to be a total cessation of supplies through hostile naval action, so that there is no question of the stocks indicating the limit of the country's power of resistance. The chief concern was the effect of war on prices and on the condition and consumption of the poorer classes. Shortages and expected shortages could bring about panic rises of price, and because of the importance of bread as an article of diet (Booth, evidence q. 6192) a rise of price would cause a substitution of bread for other commodities. Various schemes designed to steady prices by increasing the holding of wheat and flour in the country were examined. The storage of Government wheat in Government granaries would not only expose the Government to risk of loss, but the existence of the stock might discourage importers. Subsidies to merchants and millers to keep stocks in excess of normal were also objectionable. The offer of free storage for private stocks might merely divert stocks from existing stores. An experiment to test this would be worth considering, but might cost £100,000 per annum. The cost of schemes put forward to induce farmers to increase their production of wheat and keep the grain in rick for a longer period was out of proportion to any results likely to be obtained. In order to minimize the effect of war risks in raising prices, two schemes had been proposed; national insurance, by which the cost of war risk insurance should be reimbursed to shipowners or merchants by the Government; and national indemnity, by which the Government would make good to shipowners and shippers all or part of their war losses. The Committee preferred a scheme of national indemnity; a small expert Committee should be appointed to investigate the subject and prepare a scheme after consultation with underwriters and other shipping interests.

The Report was subject to a number of reservations from all the members of the Commission, with the exception of the Prince of Wales, L. Balfour of Burleigh and Bosanquet. The most important of these was a Supplementary Report signed by the Duke of Sutherland, Chaplin, Wharton, Seton-Karr and Cunynghame which recommended the adoption of a system of free storage for increasing stocks of grain, and a memorandum signed by the same members, with the addition of Holland, which disagreed with the conclusions set out in Annex B on shipping requirements, and the paras. in the Report based upon it, on the grounds that the problem had been misconceived, the shipping potential available for carrying wheat had been overestimated, and that British Steam Tonnage required to carry total imports of wheat and flour had been underestimated. Other reservations were made by Emmott, Holland, Robertson and Wilson.

Vol. III, Appendices, consists of many tables showing imports, production, stocks and consumption of a large number of materials and foodstuffs; on the cost and consumption of food by workers' families (H. Llewellyn Smith) and of families of workers on strike (J. Burnett); on the rules of international law as bearing on the problem of the Commission (Holland, Westlake); and Food Values, by Dr. Hutchinson; on war risk, insurance, storage, etc.

See *National Guarantee for the War Risks of Shipping*. p. 158.

Natural Resources, Trade and Legislation of Certain Portions of His Majesty's Dominions

R. Com. Reps.

1912–17. See *Trade*. p.112.

Food and Raw Material Requirements of the United Kingdom

Memo. R. Com. on Natural Resources

1914–16 *Cd*. 8123. See *Trade*. p. 115.

Production of Food in England, Wales, Scotland

Reps.

1915–17. See *Breviate 1917–39*, pp. 92–5.

Increase of Prices of Commodities since the Beginning of the War

Dept. Cttee. Interim Rep., *Meat, Milk and Bacon*, apps. pp. 20. 1916

1916 *Cd*. 8358, xiv, 731.
apptd. June, sgd. Sept., 1916

J. M. Robertson (*Ch.*), Anderson, Ashley, Boland, Brodrick, Claughton, Clynes, Fraser, Prothero, Reeves, Shaw, Slaughter.

'*To investigate the principal causes which have led to the increase of prices of commodities of general consumption since the beginning of the War, and to recommend such steps, if any, with a view to ameliorating the situation as appear practicable and expedient having regard to the necessity of maintaining adequate supplies.*'

By September 1916 the increase of the cost of living of the working classes was about 45 per cent. Increases of rates of wages were generally below the rise in the price of food and other necessaries, but owing to increased earnings and transfers to more highly paid employments, there was less total distress in the country than in a normal year of peace. Certain classes whose earnings had not increased were hard pressed. Any practicable method of checking the rise of prices should be considered. Following a detailed review of meat, milk and bacon prices, the Committee recommended a speed-up of the construction of merchant ships, reduction of dock congestion by increasing the number of workers, restriction of the import of less necessary goods, development of new sources of meat supply by Government bulk purchase, restrictions on retail meat prices, voluntary meatless days, increased use of women on dairy farms, grant of powers to local authorities to open municipal food shops where traders make excessive profits, the opening of maternity clinics and nurseries for the provision of milk and meals. The Government should see that all women in Controlled Establishments received adequate wages and employers should review their pay-roll to improve the position of those lower paid workers who have not adequately benefited from the rise in wages. Seven members propose in addition the public control of the prices of home produced meat, bacon and milk.

—— Second and Third Reports, *Increase of the Price of Commodities*, app. pp. 22.   1917

1917–18 *Cd.* 8483, *xviii*, 39
sgd. Nov., Dec., 1916

del. from the Third Report Claughton, Slaughter, Prothero.

Between the outbreak of war and November 1916 the price of bread had increased by 65 per cent, and nearly the whole of this was due to the rise in price of flour of 76 per cent. This latter rise was accounted for largely by the increase in the price of wheat, itself the consequence of increased military consumption and reduced supplies, and of the diversion of shipping from commercial uses and the rise of freight rates.

The Committee recommended that the Government should fix a maximum producer's price for home grown wheat, farmers should grow wheat and oats for the Government at fixed and published prices, the import of maize should be controlled, and steps taken to induce native growers in India and Egypt to grow more wheat on the basis of a guaranteed price. Control of shipping and freight rates should be extended. Five members added that as the exportable wheat surplus had declined, the normal consumption of bread had to be reduced, unless the supply of bread flour were increased; this could be done by closer milling, which would add 10 per cent to the recovered flour, and by the addition of 10 per cent of maize.

The third and final report examines in detail the rise in price of potatoes, tea, sugar and, in particular, practices arising out of speculative buying at tea auctions, and the powers over distribution exercised by the Sugar Commission.

Sugar Supply

R. Com. 1st (Interim) Report. pp. 8. 1917

1917–18 *Cd.* 8728, *xviii*, 633
apptd. Aug., 1914. sgd. Dec., 1916

R. McKenna (*Ch.*), Primrose, Lyle, Slaughter, Fountain.

'*To enquire into the supply of sugar in the United Kingdom; to purchase, sell and control the delivery of sugar on behalf of the Government, and generally to take such steps as may seem desirable for maintaining the supply.*'

By 1916, the reduction of supplies became appreciable, but the disturbance in the public mind was greater than the facts warranted, since a reduction of domestic consumption to ¾ lb. per week per head, requiring 14,000 tons, would cause no hardship, and the supplies distributed were 24,000 tons. The problem was thus one of even distribution. Raw sugars were disposed of to refiners at prices which gave limited profits. Although the Commission held a virtual monopoly, it had fixed prices to yield only a revenue which would cover costs.

See *Distribution of Sugar—July to Dec., 1916*. R. Com. Memo.; 1916 Cd. 8395, xxiv, 537. *Financing the Purchase of Sugar and Meat Abroad on behalf of H.M. Government.* Treasury Minute of 20th July; 1916 Cd. 8326, xxiv, 533.

Further Treasury Minutes; 1916 Cd. 8407, xxiv, 535. 1917–18 Cd. 8645, Cd. 8806, xxix, 767. 1919 Cmd. 38, xxxii, 537. 2nd Rep. of Commission; 1921 Cmd. 1300, xviii, 709. See *Breviate 1917–39*, p. 134.

V. TRADE AND INDUSTRY

1. General Trade Policy, Natural Resources
2. Particular Industries and Trades
3. Company and Commercial Law and Practice
4. Trade Combinations, Trusts
5. Weights and Measures

1. GENERAL TRADE POLICY, NATURAL RESOURCES

British and Foreign Trade and Industry

Memoranda and Statistical tables

1903 *Cd.* 1761, *lxvii. Second Series*; 1905 *Cd.* 2337, *lxxxiv. Third Series*, 1854–1908; 1909 *Cd.* 4954, *cii*

Invaluable detailed memoranda, statistical tables and charts on population, migration, foreign trade, shipping, railway traffic, finance and the money market, output of staple articles, production and consumption of foodstuffs, prices; together with comparisons with the United States, France and Germany. There are also tables on wages, employment and pauperism in the United Kingdom.

Trade Records

Dept. Cttee. Rep. pp. viii. 1908. Mins. of ev., apps., index. 1908

1908 *Cd.* 4345, *xxv*, 1041. *Mins. of ev., etc.*; 1908 *Cd.* 4346, *xxv*, 1049 *apptd. April, sgd. July*, 1908

R. Giffen (*Ch.*), Birchenough, Crawford, Hooper, Stanley.

'*To consider and report how far any change is desirable in the form in which the Trade Accounts of the United Kingdom are published as regards the countries from which imports are received and to which exports are sent.*'

The existing practice in trade returns of recording the imports according to the countries from which they happened to be shipped, and exports according to the countries to which they are shipped in the first instance were not convenient to traders, who wished to know the countries from which goods were procured and in which they were actually marketed. The mere knowledge of stages in the route by which goods reached this country or by which they go to the countries of destination was of less value to them. For example, the statistics based on shipment greatly exaggerated the apparent trade with Holland and understated that with Germany. (See evidence of Wood, including Appendix II, A. L. Bowley, Sauerbeck and Broomhall.) The Committee recommended that from the beginning of 1909 statistics should be on the consignment basis, that legislation should give powers to require returns from traders on that basis, and that for purposes of comparison a supplementary volume of figures of shipments should be published for six years.

Fiscal Policy of International Trade

Memo. pp. 29. 1908

1908 (321) *cvii*, 23
o.p. Nov., 1908

Alfred Marshall.

Part I discusses the incidence of import duties. Part II considers English fiscal policy with reference to the economic changes of 'the last sixty years' and especially the direct and indirect effects of various systems of import duties.

Natural Resources, Trade, and Legislation of certain portions of His Majesty's Dominions

R. Com.

apptd. April, 1912

E. Vincent (*Ch.*), Haggard, Garnett, Lorimer, Tatlow, Bateman, Foster, Campbell, Sinclair, Solomon, Bowring.

'*To enquire into and report upon the natural resources of . . . Canada, . . . Australia, New Zealand, South Africa and Newfoundland; upon the development of such resources; . . . the facilities for the production, manufacture and distribution of all articles of commerce in those parts of the Empire: upon the requirements of each such part and of the United Kingdom in the matter of food and raw materials; upon the trade of each such part with the other parts, with the United Kingdom, and with the rest of the world: upon the extent, if any, to which the mutual trade of the several parts has been or is being affected beneficially or otherwise by the laws now in force, other than fiscal laws: and, generally, to suggest any methods, consistent always with the existing fiscal policy of each part of the Empire, by which the trade of each part with the others and with the United Kingdom may be improved and extended.*

—— First Interim Report. pp. 3. 1912. Mins. of ev., apps., index. Pt. I. *Migration.* 1912. Pt. II. *Natural Resources, Trade and Legislation.* 1912

The First Report is a formal presentation of the following volumes of minutes of evidence, etc.; 1912-13 Cd. 6516, Cd. 6517, xvi, 95.

—— Second Interim Report, *Australia and New Zealand,* apps., index. pp. iv, 68 + maps. 1914. Mins. of ev. taken in New Zealand, apps., index. 1913. Mins. of ev. taken in Australia, apps., index. Pts. I–II. 1913. Mins. of ev. taken in London, Nov. 1913, papers, index. 1914

1914 *Cd.* 7210, *xviii,* 137. *Mins. of ev., etc.;* 1914 *Cd.* 7170, *Cd.* 7171, *Cd.* 7172, *xvii,* 101. 1914 *Cd.* 7173, *xviii,* 1 *sgd. Jan.,* 1914

del. Solomon.

The Report examines the trade of Australia and New Zealand and the United Kingdom's share in it, the need for and methods of selecting and settling immigrants; mail routes, cables, shipping and natural resources, etc. Amongst the conclusions and recommendations are: male emigrants to Australia need youth and adaptability and these are to be found in the towns as well as the country districts of Britain, provided there is proper selection and training. Women are also needed, but there is no evidence of a surplus of suitable women in this country. Methods of recruitment, transport and reception are antiquated or defective. First class harbours should provide a depth of 40 feet. Cable rates are too high. The speed of mail steamers should be increased or the subsidy saved, and the contract with a single privileged shipping line reviewed. The freight discrimination by shipping lines against British as distinct from Continental shippers is thoroughly unsatisfactory.

—— Third Interim Report, *South Africa,* index, pp. iv, 60. 1914. Mins. of ev. taken in South Africa, apps., index. Pts. I–II. 1914

1914 *Cd.* 7505, *xviii,* 447. *Mins. of ev., etc.;* 1914–16 *Cd.* 7706, *Cd.* 7707, *xiii,* 279 *sgd. June,* 1914

add Langerman.

The trade of South Africa, and the share of the United Kingdom therein is examined. The most immediate problem of South Africa was that of developing its mineral resources with a maximum of efficiency. The Union Government drew 45 per cent of its revenue from the Rand, and the mining royalties of four-fifths of the undeveloped areas of the Witwatersrand were vested in the State. While great technical progress had been made, the management had not succeeded in obtaining adequate efficiency and economy in the use of either white or coloured labour. The white labour force was discontented, unstable and of low technical skill, and for this the methods of engagement, pay and discharge were partly responsible. The method of recruitment of native labour was both undesirable and costly, and the methods of pay did not improve or encourage efficiency. The open compound should be replaced by the closed compound, or by locations in which native workers could live with their families. Free engagement of labour should be encouraged and the illicit drink traffic reformed. Lack of cohesion in the industry hindered reforms from within; amalgamations were desirable and should be encouraged. If reform were not undertaken, the natural asset of the gold mines was in danger of being wasted through inefficiency and want of co-ordination, industrial strife and parasitic growths.

—— Fourth Interim Report, *Newfoundland*, index, pp. v, 20. 1915. Mins. of ev. taken in Newfoundland, apps., index. 1915

1914–16 *Cd.* 7711, *xiv*, 1. *Mins. of ev., etc.*; 1914–16 *Cd.* 7898, *xiv*, 29 *sgd. Dec.*, 1914

The largest part of the Colony's production in fishing, mining and forestry is exported and its local production of some foodstuffs, e.g. cereals, is insufficient to meet home demands; its total external trade per head is therefore nearly as great as that of Canada, and three times that of the United States. In the classes of trade in which it can compete, e.g. manufactures, the United Kingdom supplies

45 to 50 per cent of Newfoundland's imports, but the United States is a severe competitor and British manufacturers do not study the needs of the market sufficiently. The solution of the international problems connected with the fishing industry had not led to a corresponding activity in development on the part of the Newfoundland Government. Scientific research should be carried out by the Newfoundland and Canadian Governments jointly, and a survey of the Labrador grounds made with assistance from the Imperial Government. Measures should be taken to regulate the cutting of timber. The hematite ores of Bell Island are of great importance to the iron and steel industry of Britain and Canada. Improvements in steamship services to the United Kingdom are required.

—— Fifth Interim Report, *Canada*, index. pp. vi, 61. 1917. Mins. of ev. taken in the Maritime Provinces of Canada, app., index. 1915. Mins. of ev. taken in the Central and Western Provinces of Canada, apps., index. Pts. I–II. 1917

1917–18 *Cd.* 8457, *viii*, 159. *Mins. of ev., etc.*; 1914–16 *Cd.* 7971, *xiv*, 173. 1917–18 *Cd.* 8458, *viii*, 229. 1917–18 *Cd.* 8459, *ix*, 1 *sgd. Jan.*, 1917 del. Campbell.

The external trade of Canada has developed with great rapidity, the increase between 1891 and 1900 being 79 per cent, between 1901 and 1913 190 per cent. But the trade with the United Kingdom has not kept pace, its share of Canada's exports being 20 per cent and of imports 46 per cent. Part of the large investment of British capital in Canada appears to have reached it in the form of foreign goods, and efforts should be made, through the proposed British Trade Bank, recommended by the Committee on *Financial Facilities for Trade* (see p. 70), to stipulate that orders in connection with undertakings it finances in Canada should be placed with British manufacturers. Immigrants from Britain, while forming 37 per cent of the arrivals, were only 27 per cent of those who took up homesteads in the Prairie Provinces, but there is room for another 145,000 homesteads north of latitude 54°, and unlimited land north of that latitude, but south of the northern limit of the wheat belt. Further aid should be given to settlers by the supply of capital, on easy terms, on the security of improvements and by the establishment of training farms. Child immigration should include both sexes in approximately equal numbers. Too large a proportion of Canadian exports have passed through United States' ports: complaint is made of the effect of high marine insurance rates to Canadian eastern ports, of the arbitrary spread of freight rates between grain and flour, and of discriminatory high rates on some goods to British ports. The provision of through communication between tide water and the head of the Great Lakes to admit vessels of great draught is important, but faces many difficulties. Canada contains a large proportion of the world's supply of nickel and asbestos. Adequate markets should be found for British Columbian timber, the export of Canadian pulp and paper to places within the Empire encouraged, and to this end companies granted leases of Crown lands should be required to install plant capable of producing the dry pulp required in the United Kingdom.

—— Final Report, apps., index. pp. ix, 199. 1917. Mins. of ev. taken in London, Jan. 1914, apps., index. 1914. Mins of ev. taken in London, June, July 1914, index. 1915. Papers laid before the Commission, 1914–17. 1917 1917–18 Cd. 8462, x, 1. Mins. of ev., etc.; 1914 Cd. 7351, xviii, 213. 1914–16 Cd. 7710, xiii, 865. 1917–18 Cd. 8460, ix, 475 sgd. Feb., 1917

This Report draws together and develops from an Imperial standpoint the arguments and conclusions set out in the previous Reports on the separate Dominions. *Scientific Developments of Natural Resources.*—A review of the leading characteristics of the resources, production and trade of the Dominions leads to the conclusion that the Empire should be placed in a position to resist pressure in peace or war from any foreign power or group of foreign powers by virtue of a control of raw materials or essential commodities. A complete survey should be made of the production and requirement of those materials and commodities, showing those (i) of which the world's requirements are produced mainly in the Empire (e.g. nickel, jute, asbestos), (ii) of which Empire production equals Empire requirements (wheat, butter, cheese, wool), and (iii) which are produced mainly outside the Empire (cotton, petroleum, nitrate, potash), and in respect of which the development of new sources or of substitutes within the Empire should be explored. The Dominions should develop their own research institutes. *Migration.* — The statistics of migration are very imperfect and must be improved if the problem of inter-Imperial migration after the war is to be dealt with scientifically. A far greater control must be exercised over the agencies involved in the selection of emigrants, including passage brokers and charitable societies, and for this purpose a Central Emigration Authority should be established, aided by a Consultative Board on which the Dominions should be represented. Greater attention should be paid to the emigration of women and their proper distribution throughout the country districts as well as the towns. *Communications.* — Cheap and efficient transport between all parts of the Empire required vessels of great length and draught. Harbours must be deepened to 33 feet on the Suez route to Australia, to 34 feet on the route from Canada to New Zealand and Australia, and to 38 feet on the route to East Canada, to Australia and New Zealand via South Africa, and via Halifax, Jamaica and Panama. The expenditure would not exceed that of constructing a few hundred miles of railway. In 1922 mail contracts should be revised, and harbours deepened, to provide for speedier service at reasonable cost. Australia, New Zealand and South Africa pay on goods as much freight as customs duties. A reduction of freight is required and for this some control over steamship companies is necessary, since the combination of shipping companies is strong enough to limit the freedom of the shippers and to grant more favourable freight rates on foreign goods than on British. Boards should be set up in the United Kingdom and the Dominions to deal with any cases where the interests of the shippers have been adversely affected by the shipping companies and conferences. Further reductions of cable rates are a necessity, and the control of the Postmaster General over the cable companies is not effective for this purpose. Public opinion in the Dominions favours a policy of state control of telegraph communication between the United Kingdom and Australia and New Zealand through Canada, and this the Commission regards as essential for the reduction of rates. The State should acquire, as soon as possible, a cable across the Atlantic. Existing organizations are inadequate for dealing with these problems and recommendations, and a permanent Imperial Board, representative of the United Kingdom and the Dominions and other parts of the Empire, should be set up. In its initial stage it should be advisory.

—— Memo. and Tables, *Food and Raw Material Requirements of the United Kingdom*, index. pp. iv, 123. 1915
1914–16 *Cd.* 8123, *xiv*, 371
sgd. Nov., 1915

While some statistical publications dealt with imports and exports, and others with home production, no attempt has hitherto been made, on any considerable scale, to correlate the two sets of figures in order to ascertain what the real requirements of the United Kingdom are. The tables and notes have been compiled to meet this deficiency, so far as the materials available permit, and in particular to indicate the share of the food and raw material needed for the United Kingdom which the Dominions and the rest of the Empire provide. The tables so far as possible cover the period 1901–1914.

'In the case of the more important articles the average consumption per head of the population has been calculated, so far as the materials available allow of this being done. Summary tables have been added, showing the value of the imports of food and raw materials, etc., in each year since 1901 (not including 1914), in order to supplement the information given in the detailed tables which is, in the main, quantitative.'

—— Memo. and Tables, *Trade Statistics and Trade of the Self-Governing Dominions.*
pp. vi, 241. 1916
1914–16 *Cd.* 8156, *xiv*, 499
sgd. Dec., 1915

The materials for the Commission's enquiry into the trade of the self-governing Dominions with one another and with the rest of the world were not easily accessible. There were divergencies of practice on the statistical year taken as basis, on whether the returns for imports were based on countries of shipment or of origin, and for exports on countries of arrival or of ultimate destination; on the classification of articles and groups of articles, and the methods of valuation used. Detailed tables for each of the Dominions accompany the memorandum.

—— Memo. and Tables, *Chief Harbours of the British Empire and certain Foreign Countries and as to the Suez and Panama Canals*, index. pp. xliv, 151. 1917
1917–18 *Cd.* 8461, *ix*, 523
sgd. Nov., 1917

The final Report proposed a policy of scientific and co-ordinated development of the harbours of the Empire as an urgent measure. The memorandum describes the main sea routes and sets out diagrammatically and in tabular form details relating to high water and low water, depth of channels, etc., wharf dimensions of all the principal harbours.

Financial Facilities for Trade
Rep.

1916 *Cd.* 8346. See *Banking, Financial Institutions.* p. 70.

Commercial Intelligence
Rep.

1904 *Cd.* 2044. See *Government.* p. 27.

British Trade After the War

Commercial Intelligence with Respect to Measures for Securing the Position, after the War, of Certain Branches of British Industry. Advisory Cttee. Sub-Cttee. Rep., app. pp. 18. 1916. Summaries of ev. 1916

1916 *Cd.* 8181, *xv*, 591. *Summaries of ev.*; 1916 *Cd.* 8275, *xv*, 611 *apptd. July*, 1915. *sgd. Jan.*, 1916

Firth, Hobson, Machin, Parkes, Spicer.

'To prepare and submit a Report showing what steps should be taken to secure the position, after the war, of firms who have undertaken industries in consequence of the Exchange Meetings leading up to the British Industries Fair held under the auspices of the Board of Trade.'

Inquiries were made into the following branches of industry: paper manufacture, printing trade, stationery trade, jewellers' and silver smiths' trade, cutlery, fancy leather goods, glassware, china and earthenware, toys, electrical apparatus, brush, etc., trade, hardware and the magneto industry. The total value of imported goods covered by the inquiry was £16 mn. of which £7,700,000 were of German origin and £500,000 of Austro-Hungarian origin.

A review of the evidence led to many recommendations, amongst which were: the new Committee on Industrial Research should be given larger funds; copyright law should be brought into line with that of the United States, the law regarding the compulsory working of patents more rigorously enforced, and information on German and Austrian patents given to British manufacturers. An impartial tribunal should secure that no preference should be given to foreign traders by British shipowners or railways. As German and Austrian manufacturers received readier and greater assistance from banks than their British competitors, and modern joint stock banks were said to be less inclined than the old proprietary banks to give credit to small local manufacturers, the joint stock banks should be asked to give more assistance. Public authorities should be under an obligation to buy British goods and finance houses issuing foreign loans should try to secure preferential treatment for British contractors.

All these questions were regarded as of secondary importance to the possibility of tariff protection after the war, for which nearly all firms and associations asked. There was a fear that Germany and Austria would undersell us after the war, partly because of railway preferences on export, the low export prices charged by German industrial combinations, and low wages. After examining the rates of duty and schemes of tariff suggested, to enable British manufacturers to continue to produce goods vital to national safety or essential to industry which before the war had been imported, the Committee recommended protection, and for other industries 'Imperial' and 'Allied' preference. In a reservation Spicer says that this would lead to a piecemeal protection of subsidiary industries, where a general tariff policy based on a review of the British industry as a whole was required. The Minister, in deciding to publish the report for information, notes that many of the recommendations were of wider scope than the particular group of industries to which the Committee's inquiries were confined.

See *Commercial Intelligence*. p. 27.

Commercial and Industrial Policy. Imperial Preference

Cttee. Resolutions and letter to Prime Minister on Imperial Preference. pp. 4.
1917
1917–18 *Cd.* 8482, *xiii*, 315
sgd. Feb., 1917

Lord Balfour of Burleigh (*Ch.*), Balfour (A.), Birchenough, Booth, L. Faringdon, Gosling, Hewins, Hyde, McCormick, McDowell, Muntz, Nimmo, Parsons, Pease, Smith (G. S.), Wardle, Smith (F. H.), O'Neill, Hazleton.

Although the Committee desired to wait until the reports of Committees on the great staple industries had been issued, the announcement of an Imperial Conference at an early date made it desirable to express their opinions on this topic. In view of war experience, in the interests of the safety and welfare of the Empire as a whole the production of food stuffs, raw materials and manufactured goods within the Empire should be stimulated; the Government should declare its adherence to the principle of giving tariff preference to the products and manufactures of the overseas dominions; consideration should be given to the establishment of a wider range of customs duties, which should be remitted or reduced for Empire products and form the basis of commercial treaties with Allied countries. O'Neill and Hazleton in a memo state that the necessity of conforming to a fiscal system suited to English industrial conditions has been a disadvantage to Ireland, which is an agricultural country. Ireland should have separate treatment and be given the same fiscal liberty enjoyed by the self-governing dominions.

See *Breviate 1917–39*, pp. 152–4.

Participation of Great Britain in Great International Exhibitions

Cttee. Rep., apps. pp. iv, 65. 1907.
Mins of ev., apps., index. 1907
1908 *Cd.* 3772, *xlix*, 1. *Mins. of ev.*, *etc.*; 1908 *Cd.* 3773, *xlix*, 71
apptd. Oct., 1906. *sgd. Aug.* 1907
A. E. Bateman (*Ch.*), L. Airedale, Fox, Harris, Law, Ramsay, Smith, Spielmann, Waring.

'*To enquire and report as to the nature and extent of the benefit accruing to British Arts, Industries and Trade, from the participation of this country in Great International Exhibitions, whether the results have been such as to warrant His Majesty's Government in giving financial support to similar exhibitions in future; and, if so, what steps, if any, are desirable in order to secure the maximum advantage from any public money expended on this object.*'

The increasing reluctance of manufacturers to exhibit at international exhibitions had been attributed to many causes, such as the growth of advertising, the decreasing value of awards, cost and the dangers of having exhibits copied. The direct effect of exhibitions on sales varied from trade to trade, but the indirect effects of advertising were considerable, though these depended on the representation of British industry being effective and complete. The representation had not been complete owing to the lack of permanent machinery for securing it. In large exhibitions the British Section should as heretofore be managed by a Royal Commission, but there should be a permanent officer of the Board of Trade to deal with all exhibition business and to act as Secretary to the Commission.

2. PARTICULAR INDUSTRIES AND TRADES

Workmen's Co-operative Societies in the United Kingdom

Rep., apps. pp. xlviii, 252. 1901
1901 *Cd.* 698, *lxxiv*, 463
J. J. Dent.

This is the first volume issued by the Board of Trade dealing exclusively with Co-operative Societies. The report describes the characteristics of the various classes of co-operative societies. From 1874 to 1899, the membership of all societies rose from 403,010 to 1,681,342, i.e. 1·2 per cent to 4·1 per cent of the total population. Total volume of transactions (exclusive of banking transactions) rose from 15 millions sterling to 68 millions. Retail societies account for nine-tenths of the membership and two-thirds of the volume of transactions, and co-operative production was valued at 11 millions sterling in 1899.

Industrial and Agricultural Co-operative Societies in the United Kingdom

Rep., apps. pp. lv, 273. 1912

1912-13 Cd. 6045, lxxv, 441
apptd. — sgd. Feb., 1912

This report revises and extends Cd. 698. The period covered by the report was 1899-1909, and as far as possible, 1910. Progress during the decade was remarkable both in the scale of activities and in the opening of new fields. Membership rose by 55 per cent to nearly 2,600,000, and sales by distributive societies reached £70 mn., an increase of £25 mn. Of particular note were the growth of agricultural co-operatives, whose combined sales reached £3,600,000, and of collective insurance, by which societies paid premiums to insure individual members for sums varying with their annual purchases from the societies. There are charts and tables covering every aspect of the societies' activities and figures of membership and sales for every individual society.

Industrial Alcohol

Dept. Cttee. Rep. pp. 27. 1905. Mins. of ev., apps., index. 1905

1905 Cd. 2472, lxiv, 1. Mins. of ev., etc.; 1905 Cd. 2477, lxiv, 29
apptd. Aug., 1904. sgd. March, 1905

H. W. Primrose (Ch.), Crookes, Holland, Montagu, Nicholson, Somerville, Thorpe, Tyrer.

'To inquire into the existing facilities for the use, without payment of duty, of spirits in arts and manufactures, and in particular into the operation of Section 8 of the Finance Act, 1902, and to report whether the powers conferred upon the Commissioners of Inland Revenue by this section permit of adequate facilities being given for the use of spirits in manufactures and in the production of motive power, or whether further facilities are required; and if it should appear to the Committee that the present facilities are inadequate, to advise the further measures to be adopted, without prejudice to the safety of the revenue derived from spirits, and with due regard to the interests of the producers of spirits in the United Kingdom.'

The existing law was laid down by the Spirits Act of 1880 and the amendments to it in 1890 and 1902. The duty on spirit used as a beverage in the United Kingdom was very heavy and restraints had to be placed on the manufacture of spirits to prevent any evasion of the duty. These restraints (listed in App. I) increased the cost of production by 3d. per proof gallon; moreover, to enable the home producer to compete, import duties and export allowances on spirits had been fixed. The effect of all this was to increase the price paid by the industrial consumer by about 8½d. per bulk gallon. In order to prevent any adverse effects on British industry caused by this artificially increased price, the Committee recommended that an allowance equivalent to the increased cost of production be granted. A similar allowance should be paid on spirit of foreign origin. No great increase in demand was anticipated if this and their other recommendations were put into effect. A sub-committee reported their investigation into spirits in Germany.

Bond Investment Companies

Dept. Cttee. Rep. pp. v, 13. 1905.
Mins. of ev., apps., index. 1905

1906 Cd. 2769, xcvii, 1. Mins. of ev., etc.;
1906 Cd. 2770, xcvii, 21
apptd. May, sgd. Oct., 1905

J. G. Butcher (Ch.), Cockburn, Sim, Barnes.

'To enquire as to the operation of Companies (not being Life Assurance Companies) which collect periodical payments from the industrial classes in return for benefits promised in the future, and whether it is desirable that there should be any restrictions imposed on such Companies or any Government supervision of their transactions, and to report to the Board of Trade.'

There had been a large increase in the number of companies, the more modern type of which in return for monthly subscriptions usually issued bonds or certificates payable at the end of 10 or 12 years. One group offered a lump sum equivalent to the subscriptions plus a low rate of compound interest, the other a lump sum in excess of subscriptions plus compound interest, at 3 or even 4 or 5 per cent. The expenses of management were large, especially at the beginning when business was being procured; in many cases they exceeded the amount of subscriptions. To prevent the formation of bubble companies it was recommended that every new company should deposit in court not less than £10,000, which was to be repaid when a fund amounting to double the sum deposited was secured for the bondholders.

The class of companies which contracted to pay out a larger sum than the combined amount of subscriptions, together with compound interest, seemed to rely for solvency on lapses of payment of subscriptions and on the surrender of bonds on which only a percentage of the subscriptions was returned. In view of the uncertainty of the numbers of lapses and surrenders which would occur, the Committee did not consider these companies to have a sound or desirable basis of finance. Not one company considered enabled bondholders to inspect the accounts. It was therefore recommended that annual statements of revenue account and balance sheets should be sent to every shareholder and bondholder; and that any company should be wound up on the application of bondholders (where claims were to be protected) once the insolvency of the company had been proved.

Life Insurance Companies

Sel. Cttee. HL. Reps., proc., mins. of ev., apps. pp. xii, 79. 1906

1906 (HL. 194) ix, 207
apptd. May, o.p. July, 1906

Lord Beauchamp (Ch.), L. Stanley, L. St. Oswald, L. Burghclere, L. Hutchinson.

'To enquire and report what steps should be taken, by deposit of funds or otherwise, to provide adequate security for British policy-holders in Life Insurance Companies which have their chief office outside the United Kingdom, but which carry on business in this country.'

There was an almost unanimous opinion amongst British Actuaries and Life Insurance Managers against compelling foreign Life Insurance Companies doing business in this country to deposit funds as security for their British policy-holders. The Committee accepted this view, but thought that such companies should be placed as far as possible in the same position as the English companies with which they compete, and as far as possible be made to comply with the Life Assurance Companies Act, 1870. This Act had given general satisfaction, because it ensured a full measure of publicity in the accounts of all British Insurance Companies. But the increase in business had made certain amendments desirable. Under the Act each company had to deposit £20,000, which could be withdrawn when premiums reached £40,000. The

£20,000 should be deposited as long as policies continued outstanding. In the case of Foreign and Colonial Companies, the appointment of British Trustees was highly desirable. Further, British Companies were required to give their full revenue accounts, their valuations, liabilities and assets, but foreign companies were required to give an account only of all their business all over the world (q. 546). The Board of Trade should require full accounts, valuation statements, and expenses of management of all companies. The Board should have powers to vary the form of questions and returns and to insist upon the complete and accurate answers. Foreign companies should make clear how far their funds are subject to preferential claims in any country and the business transacted in this country should be given separately. All companies should state the market value of securities held by them.

Post Office (Life Insurance)

Rep.

1908 (311). See *Post Office*. p. 174.

Government War Risks Insurance Scheme

Rep.

1914–16 *Cd.* 7997. See *War Losses*. p. 386.

Celluloid

Rep.

1914 *Cd.* 7158. See *Labour*. p. 197.

Government Factories and Workshops

Cttee. Rep. pp. v, 21. 1907

1907 *Cd.* 3626, x, 413

G. H. Murray (*Ch.*), Mackay, Wilson, Smith, Wilmot.

'(1) *To enquire into the effect which the concentration of Government Manufactories and Workshops in London and the Metropolitan Area has upon the rate of wages, the cost of living, including rent, the economy of production in time of peace, and power of expansion in time of war; and to enquire what change, if any, is desirable in the present distribution through the country of such Manufactories and Workshops. (2) To suggest principles on which work should be distributed among two or more Government Manufactories capable of producing similar articles. (3) To enquire whether Government production can be advantageously replaced by private enterprise, and, if so, to what extent and on what terms.*'

'If Government were considering *de novo* the best way to supply its needs for munitions of war three alternatives would present themselves. On the one hand, it might assume the responsibility of satisfying its requirements entirely by means of its own resources. This was the system which, in fact, prevailed in this country up to 1859, prior to which year the Arsenal at Woolwich was the sole source from which the Government obtained its warlike stores; it was this system also which prevailed in France prior to the Franco-Prussian War. On the other hand, Government might rely exclusively upon the resources of the private enterprise of the country, without itself possessing any facilities for manufacture—a system which prevails to a large extent in Germany at the present time. Again, there is a third alternative, viz. that of obtaining the munitions of war required partly from private enterprise and partly from factories under direct Government control. This is the system which has prevailed in this country for nearly half a century, and which was adopted in France after the war of 1870.'

The system of relying on the combined results of Government and private manufacture has become firmly established in this country and is not likely to be abandoned. The ultimate productive power of private industry is greater than that possessed by the Government establishments. But as the trade takes time to adapt itself to increased demand, the Arsenal must be adequately equipped for tiding over the first few months of a critical period. Therefore the proper establishment for the factories is a 'minimum' number of fully employed workmen which should form the nucleus army of labour. The precise number to be fixed by a special inquiry. No recommendation was made for decentralization.

Importation of Plumage Prohibition Bill [H.L.]

Sel. Cttee. HL. Rep., proc., mins. of ev., apps. pp. x, 47. 1908

1908 (HL. 137) x, 163
apptd. May, o.p. July, 1908

Lord Avebury (Ch.), L. Bedford, L. Rutland, L. Bristol, L. O'Hagan.

Birds are in their finest plumage during the nesting season. Evidence showed that they were slaughtered recklessly and that the methods employed, especially in the case of egrets, involved the destruction of young birds and eggs. The Drapers' section of the London Chamber of Commerce opposed the Bill on the grounds that the imported feathers of egrets were moulted plumes, but the Committee stated that this was not the case. The Bill was approved. It would be useful in rendering more effective similar legislation of India, of Australia and of the United States.

Whiskey and other Potable Spirits

R. Com. Interim Rep. pp. 4. 1908

1908 Cd. 4180, lviii, 415
apptd. Feb., sgd. June, 1908

Lord Hereford (Ch.), Guillemard, Adeney, Bradford, Brown, Buchanan (G. S.), Buchanan (J. Y.), Cushny.

'To inquire and report:—1. Whether, in the general interest of the consumer, or in the interest of the public health, or otherwise, it is desirable—(a) To place restric-tions upon the materials or the processes which may be used in the manufacture or preparation in the United Kingdom of Scotch Whiskey, Irish Whiskey, or any spirit to which the term whiskey may be applied as a trade description; (b) To require declarations to be made as to the materials, processes of manufacture or preparation, or age of any such spirit; (c) To require a minimum period during which any such spirit should be matured in bond; and (d) To extend any requirements of the kind mentioned in the two sub-divisions immediately preceding to any such spirit imported into the United Kingdom. 2. By what means, if it be found desirable that any such restrictions, declarations or period should be prescribed, a uniform practice in this respect may be satisfactorily secured: and to make the like inquiry and report as regards other kinds of potable spirits which are manufactured in or imported into the United Kingdom.'

While the work of the Commission had not been finished, the following conclusions had been arrived at: (1) No restrictions should be placed upon the processes of, or apparatus used in, the distillation of any spirit to which the term 'whiskey' might be applied as a trade description. (2) The term 'whiskey' having been recognized in the past as applicable to a potable spirit manufactured from (1) malt, or (2) malt and unmalted barley or other cereals, the application of the term 'whiskey' should not be denied to the product manufactured from such materials.

—— Final Report. pp. iii, 47. 1909.
1909 Cd. 4796, xlix, 451
sgd. July, 1909

The Commission originated from prosecutions and convictions at Islington in 1905, under the Sale of Food and Drugs Act, 1875. One defendant was prosecuted for selling as Irish whiskey something which was not Irish whiskey, and another for selling as Scotch whiskey something which was not Scotch whiskey. The magistrates decided that what the defendants sold was a 'patent still' spirit made largely from maize, to which had been added a dash, not 10 per cent, of genuine whiskey. Each had to be made in its own country, in Ireland from a barley malt up to 75 per cent, the rest being barley, wheat, oats and rye; in Scotland wholly from barley malt. 'Patent still' spirit alone was not whiskey.

The Commissioners decided that the term 'whiskey' should be applied to a product of malt and grain, including maize, and that there was no evidence that the form of still bore any necessary relation to the qualities of the spirit produced. The terms Scotch and Irish should be restricted to spirits distilled in the respective countries. Declarations of materials and processes used were neither desirable nor practicable, nor was it desirable to require a minimum period for maturing in bond. Consideration should be given to legislation enabling a magistrate to have two assessors to sit with him while dealing with prosecutions, and for a Committee to advise on technical questions arising out of the administration of the Acts.

Interim Rep.; 1908 Cd. 4180, lviii, 415. Final Rep.; 1909 Cd. 4796, xlix, 451. Mins. of ev., apps. Vol. I; 1908 Cd. 4181, lviii, 421. Vol. II; 1909 Cd. 4797, xlix, 503. Index and Digests of ev.; 1909 Cd. 4876, xlix, 785.

Home Industries in the Highlands and Islands

Rep., app. pp. ix, 207. 1914

1914 Cd. 7564, xxxii, 43
apptd. — 1911. sgd. Oct., 1913

W. R. Scott.

'To investigate and report upon Home Industries in the congested districts of Scotland, and in particular on the relation of these industries to the life of the people of the Highlands and Islands.'

This report is a detailed and penetrating analysis of the development from the sixteenth century of the various home industries of Scotland—linen, wool, kelp, tweeds, strawplaiting, hosiery, lace, etc. In 1911, the value of tweeds of the Islands, Shetland hosiery and rugs, Fair Isle hosiery, Tarbert lace, and all straw and basket work, sold in the open market was not less than £121,000 (excluding that used in the homes). The organization, changes of technique, merchanting, finance, markets and sales of the industries are reviewed, and their position in 1912-13 and probable future are assessed. Bearing in mind the warnings given by the falsification of previous optimistic forecasts, there nevertheless seemed a growing future for the seaweed, tweed and hosiery trades, and reason to look forward to a prosperous rural population dividing its time between agriculture and small industries.

Where crofts are small or poor, and where there is a large cottar population, the extension of home industries will have a material effect in raising the standard of comfort. They have, however, been based on women's labour. The people have a gift for artistic craftsmanship. Agriculture, the main occupation of the men, leaves them much spare time, and for this the remedy is to organize home industries suitable for males and to extend rural industries which are not home industries. There is room for the use of the streams to develop small mechanical power units. The Board of Agriculture for Scotland, as part of the general duty of promoting rural industries, should develop the production of the necessary raw materials, provide instructors for those districts which could claim technical teaching, provide economic, technological and chemical advice and research, inspect work done by instructors, and organize and assist schemes not of an educational nature, e.g. Shetland Hosiery marking. Local committees, constituted so as to include members capable of representing the local interests concerned in any industry, should be established and used for administering grants and supervising technical instruction. Truck, though diminishing, has deep roots in some of the rural industries. The Truck Acts are not well adapted to the crofting counties, since the worker is in many cases not an employed person but a small producer with no working capital. The person who makes a web of Harris Tweed must buy wool, etc., at £2 per piece of average length, and spinning takes a month to six weeks. The merchant advances goods in return for a lien on the tweed when finished. Co-operative credit societies offer great possibilities for rural industries, provided they are not pressed forward prematurely.

Royal Aircraft Factory

Cttee. Rep., apps. pp. 9. 1916

1916 Cd. 8191, iv, 761
apptd. March, sgd. May, July, 1916

R. Burbidge (Ch.), Parsons, Donaldson.

'To enquire and report whether, within the resources placed by the War Office at the disposal of the Royal Aircraft Factory and the limits imposed by War Office orders, the organization and management of the factory are efficient, and to give the Army Council the benefit of their suggestions on any points of the interior administration of the factory which seem to them capable of improvement.'

'From articles and letters in the Press it seems to be considered that British aviators, as compared with enemy aviators, suffer from want of speed in aeroplanes.' The Committee reported that in parts of the organization and management improvements were possible, and recommendations were made on the composition of a Board of Management, the qualifications of a Director, a Controller of Supplies, etc. The Report on the Royal Aircraft Factory, signed by Curzon of Kedleston, contains the points of difference between the Air Board and the Committee appointed by the Army Council.

The Chemical Trade

Cttee. Rep. pp. 4. 1917

1917–18 Cd. 8882, xviii, 381
apptd. — sgd. Nov., 1917

K. W. Price (Ch.), Anderson, Brunner, Carpenter, Lawn, Pearce, Quinan, Wilson, Smallwood.

'(i) To advise as to the procedure which should be adopted by the Minister of Reconstruction for dealing with the Chemical Trade. (ii) To consider and report upon any matters affecting the Chemical Trade which could be more effectively dealt with by the formation of special organizations for the purpose, and to make suggestions in regard to the constitution and functions of any such organization.'

To deal effectively with the difficult problems which were likely to arise in the Chemical Trade during the Reconstruction Period, there should be the closest possible collaboration between the Ministry and its representatives. The Association of British Chemical Manufacturers should be considered representative of the trade as a whole with the exception of certain branches. A Standing Committee should be appointed as a permanent link between the Ministry of Reconstruction and the trade. A Departmental organization, under a scientific man of good standing, should be set up in the Ministry to deal with all chemical questions.

3. COMPANY AND COMMERCIAL LAW AND PRACTICE

Company Law Amendment

Cttee. Rep. pp. v, 44. 1906. App. 1906

1906 Cd. 3052, xcvii, 199. App; 1906 Cd. 3053, xcvii, 249
apptd. Feb., 1905. sgd. June, 1906

C. M. Warmington (Ch.), Budd, Faber, Gore-Browne, Hichens, Holland, Palmer, Schuster, Speyer, Waterhouse, Worthington Evans, Barnes.

'To enquire what amendments are necessary in the Acts relating to Joint Stock Companies, and to report to the Board of Trade.'

The reference had been framed in wide terms, but the attention of the Committee was particularly directed to the growing practice of issuing companies without a prospectus, the registration abroad of companies doing business in England, the extension of the provisions of the Companies Act, 1900, with regard to the registration of certain mortgages and charges, and the Amendments of Table A in the First Schedule of the Act of 1862.

An increasing proportion of companies did not publish any prospectus; all companies not filing a prospectus before starting business should be compelled to file a preliminary statement containing information similar to that required by Section 10 of the Companies Act, 1900. A detailed revision of Section 10 is given. It would not be an advantage to require foreign companies trading here to comply with the requirements of the Companies Act, 1900, as to prospectuses or to make deposits here with a view to securing British creditors, but every such company should be required to file in England a verified translation of its charter, memorandum or articles, names of directors, etc., and a verified copy of its annual balance sheet, and if using the word 'Limited', to put its name and place of origin on its premises. For the protection of creditors, who should be able to find out how far the company's assets are mortgaged or charged, there should be revision of the law relating to the registration of mortgages and charges affecting the property of the company. The requirement of registration should be extended both to mortgages and charges created before the Act of 1901, and to charges on landed property and book debts. The demand for the abolition of floating charges on the undertaking and on the assets, present and future, of a company was rejected

as such charges were an important source of business capital. A legal decision in 1875 laid it down that the powers of a company were limited to the objects specified in its memorandum of association and this led to an over-elaborate statement of subsidiary objects; this could be simplified if a statutory schedule embodied these implied objects. A company might adopt any or all of the regulations of Table A, and if its memorandum were not accompanied by articles, these regulations were deemed to be regulations of the company. But Table A had been unaltered for forty years, and a revised Table A is set out in full on pages 33 to 34.

Gore-Brown, Faber and Holland, in a Minority Report, state that companies' unrestricted power to create charges on their property had sometimes been abused at the expense of trade creditors, and they should not be capable of charging after-acquired chattels, future book debts and other property not in existence at the time of the creation of the charge. Speyer argued that growth of guinea-pig and ornamental directors and other reasons rendered it necessary that the personal liability of directors for negligence should be made of general and compulsory application. Worthington Evans wished to legalize the formation of companies of two or more persons, instead of seven, as suggested by the majority.

Companies (Consolidation) Bill [H.L.], Post Office Consolidation Bill [H.L.], and the Statute Law Revision Bill [H.L.]

Jt. Sel. Cttee. Reps., proc., mins. of ev. pp. xviii, 49. 1908

1908 (343) x, 1023
apptd. — o.p. Dec., 1908

Lord Chancellor (Ch.), L. Halsbury, L. Granard, L. Stanley, L. James, L. Balfour, L. Faber, Beale, Cave, Herbert, Hills, Kavanagh, Solicitor - General, Stewart-Smith.

Evidence was taken on the three Bills, which were reported with amendments.

Bankruptcy Law and its Administration

Dept. Cttee. Vol. I. Rep. pp. iv, 43. 1908. Vol. II. Mins. of ev., apps., index. 1908

1908 *Cd.* 4068, *xxxiv*, 1. *Mins. of ev., etc.*; 1908 *Cd.* 4069, *xxxiv*, 49 *apptd. April*, 1906. *sgd. April*, 1908

M. M. Mackenzie (*Ch.*), Addison, Chamberlin, Evans, Fithian, Peat, Richardson, Smith, Barker.

'*To enquire into and report upon the effect of the provisions of the laws at present in force in the United Kingdom in relation to bankruptcy, deeds of arrangement and compositions by insolvent debtors with their creditors, and the prevention and punishment of frauds by debtors on their creditors, and the points and matters in which those laws and the procedure and administration under them require amendment with special reference to*' (nine subjects listed on pp. iii, iv).

The main features of the law and procedure did not cause any dissatisfaction, and there had been a large reduction in insolvency since the existing system came into force. The complaints related to special incidents of the law and its administration. Pages 36 to 43 set out in concise form the recommendations, particularly on the nine subjects specially referred to them. Amongst the chief recommendations were: To meet the complaint that the procedure for prosecuting debtors who have committed specified offences was dilatory and expensive, and that effective punishment was rare, the law should provide that they should be punishable in Courts of Summary Jurisdiction. Failure to keep proper books within two years preceding bankruptcy should, with certain limitations, be punishable on summary conviction by imprisonment. It should be an offence if a debtor has contributed to his bankruptcy by gambling, unjustifiable speculation or fails to supply a reasonable explanation of the loss of any substantial part of his estate within the year preceding his bankruptcy, or obtains credit without disclosing his bankruptcy or trades under an assumed name. Changes of procedure on the discharge of a bankrupt, and further protection for persons who have honestly become creditors of the bankrupt or have taken mortgages, etc., on after acquired property are recommended. A married woman who trades on her own account should be liable to the bankruptcy laws in the same way as if she were single. Detailed proposals are made for the regulation of voluntary arrangements between insolvents and their creditors.

Bankruptcy Law of Scotland and its Administration

Dept. Cttee. Vol. I. Rep. pp. 16. 1910. Vol. II. Mins of ev., app., index. 1910

1910 *Cd.* 5201, *ix*, 607. *Mins. of ev., etc.*; 1910 *Cd.* 5202, *ix*, 625. *apptd. Oct.*, 1908. *sgd. June*, 1910

W. J. Cullen (*Ch.*), Fyfe, Jameson, Morison Milligan, Campbell, McLintock.

'*To enquire into and report upon the effects of the provisions of the laws at present in force in Scotland in relation to bankruptcy, compositions, and arrangements by insolvent debtors with their creditors, and the prevention and punishment of frauds by debtors on their creditors, and the points and matters in which those laws and the procedure and administration under them require amendment.*'

The framework of the Bankruptcy (Scotland) Act, 1856, should be followed in consolidating it, with subsequent legislation, into a new statute. Sequestration, as the main process for winding up bankrupt estates, has proved its worth; recommendations are made (in an attached Schedule) for simplifying and reducing the cost of procedure. The process of cessio has not operated satisfactorily and the provisions relating to it in the Debtors (Scotland) Act, 1880, should be repealed. Statutory provision should be made for dealing with small estates by a simpler procedure. Winding up by trust deed, although it has defects, has been adopted to a much greater extent than sequestration; the only improvement recommended is statutory provision for the auditing of trustee's accounts, and the fixing of his remuneration by the Accountant of Court. Recommendations are made for making certain changes in clauses in the Debtors (Scotland) Act, 1880, relating to fraud, and for increasing the penalties which may be imposed by a Sheriff in summary jurisdiction.

Laws in force in the principal foreign countries to prevent the sale or importation of goods bearing a false indication of origin

Rep., app. pp. 204. 1911

1911 *Cd.* 5531, *lxxxvi*, 739

H.M. Representatives Abroad.

Complaints had been made to the Board of Trade that foreign goods sold abroad bore false marks of British origin. In order to determine whether the laws of foreign countries provided remedies, as did the 'Merchandise Marks' lists of the United Kingdom, H.M. Representatives in certain foreign countries were asked to furnish information on the laws in force to prevent the sale or importation of goods bearing a false indication of origin. The volume contains the reports, together with the text of three relevant international agreements on the Protection of Industrial Property.

Registration of Firms Bill [H.L.]
Sel. Cttee. HL. Rep., proc., mins. of ev. pp. vi, 42. 1916

1916 (*HL*. 68) *iv*, 15
apptd. March, o.p. July, 1916
Lord Muir-Mackenzie (*Ch.*), L. Peel, L. Southwark, L. Rotherham, L.

Sydenham, L. Wrenbury, L. Rathcreedan.

The object of the Bill being to include only those partnerships where their style conceals the identity of the traders, the most convenient limit would be expressed by requiring registration by all those who do not use their true surnames to designate their business. Anyone coming under the Act who did not register should be disabled from sueing on a contract whilst in default, the Court having power to give relief from this disability. Events have shown how desirable it was that the identity of those concerned with trade should be known at the beginning of the war, and it is generally accepted that it will be important in the future. The title of the Bill should be 'Registration of Business Names' as it covers Professional Partnerships as well as Trading Firms.

Enforcement of British Arbitration Awards. Legislation Abroad

Reps. pp. 74. 1912

1912-13 *Cd.* 6126, *xciii*, 213

H.M. Representatives Abroad.

The report contains the answers from the governments of the British Self-Governing Dominions and from H. M. Representatives in foreign countries to two questions: was an agreement in writing to refer to arbitration in the United Kingdom disputes arising out of commercial contracts valid and enforceable in the country in question, and could an arbitration award made in the United Kingdom be enforced in the country in question, and if so, by what means?

4. TRADE COMBINATIONS, TRUSTS

Anti-Trust Legislation in the British Self-Governing Dominions

Rep. pp. 25. 1912

1912-13 *Cd.* 6439, *lx*, 299
sgd. Sept., 1912

G. J. Stanley.

The report contains details of all the legislative measures enacted in the self-governing Dominions 'with the object of protecting their consumers from artificial high prices due to the manipulations of either the American, or home trusts or combines'. In Canada the Combines Investigation Act, 1910, provided for the appointment of Boards to investigate 'Combines, Monopolies, Trusts and Mergers', and for procedure leading up to pecuniary penalties, the import of goods free of duty, revocation of patents, etc. The Australian Industries Preservation Act, 1906-1910, imposes penalties on any person entering into any contract or combination in restraint of trade or combination injuring Australian industry by unfair competition, and prohibits rebates or refunds for exclusive dealing. The interpretation of this Act was in some doubt owing to certain decisions of the High Court. Details are also given of measures in New Brunswick, New Zealand and the Union of South Africa.

Shipping Rings and Deferred Rebates
Reps.
1909. See *Sea Transport*. p. 159.

Railway Agreements and Amalgamations
Rep.
1911 *Cd.* 5631. See *Transport*. p. 152.

Combinations in the Meat Trade
Rep.
1909 *Cd.* 4643. See *Agriculture*. p. 83.

Meat Export Trade (Australia)
Rep.
1914-16 *Cd.* 7896. See p. 83.

Meat Supplies of the United Kingdom
Rep.
1919 *Cmd.* 456. See *Breviate 1917-39*, p. 118-19.
M

Meat (Trusts)
Rep.
1920 *Cmd.* 1057. See *Breviate 1917-39*, p. 209.

5. WEIGHTS AND MEASURES

Weights and Measures (Metric System) Bill [H.L.]
Sel. Cttee. HL. Rep., proc., mins. of ev., app. pp. xii, 68. 1904
1904 (355) *vii*, 605
apptd. Feb., o.p. Aug., 1904
Lord Belhaven (*Ch.*), L. Colchester, L. Wolverton, L. Kelvin, L. Farrer, L. Addington.

There was a consensus of opinion that there should be some simplification of the system, but there were differences of opinion on details. For example, the farmers were more concerned with uniformity in weights, and the sale of corn by weight rather than measure (q. 822). The Director General of the Ordnance Survey viewed with dismay any attempt to alter land measurement to the metric system (q. 452). The Chairman of the Weights and Measures Committee, Hereford, was concerned with the cost (q. 867) and the Departments affected with the time needed for a change over. The amendments made by the Committee related chiefly to Provisional Orders. The Bill was dropped at the Second Reading.

Short Weight
Sel. Cttee. Rep., proc., mins. of ev., apps. pp. xvi, 168. 1914
1914 (359) *x*, 337
apptd. March, o.p. July, 1914.
A. Williamson (*Ch.*), Agg-Gardner, Barlow, Bentham, Cotton, Du Cros, Field, Hamilton, Hinds, Lawson, Parker, Radford, Rowntree, Weston, Wills.

'*To enquire whether any, and if so what steps should be taken to protect purchasers of goods sold in packages, and of bread from short weight or measure.*'

Except in the case of coal and bread, there was no general obligation to sell goods by weight or measure and consequently it was not an offence to sell short weight. There was general dissatisfaction amongst those officials operating the Weights and Measures Acts whose duty it was to see that weights and measures were correct, but who had no power to prevent short weight being given (qq. 678, 686). The growing tendency to increase the weight of wrappings, and to vary the size of packet, made it increasingly difficult for a customer to know the exact weights of the goods bought. The representative of the Co-operative Wholesale Society stated that they would gain £107,800 a year if they sold their packet tea by gross weight (q. 2619). The representatives of the Association of Municipal Corporations expressed the general dissatisfaction at the antiquated Bread Acts, the procedure of which was so difficult that some authorities did not attempt to administer them (q. 2894). The Bread Act (1822) required bakers to carry weights and scales in the Metropolitan Area 'in a cart or other carriage drawn by horse, mule or ass' (q. 294).

This had little meaning with modern methods of transport, and was easily evaded by selling bread to customers at the door.

Purchasers in the wholesale trade should be able to look after their own interests, and unnecessary interference in the customs of trade should be avoided, unless for exceptional reasons; these existed in the case of retail purchases by poor persons who are without the usual means of checking weights and measures. The Committee rejected the suggestions that all goods should be sold by net weight and that goods usually sold by weight should be sold by weight only. Short weight and measure should be a statutory offence; vendors who sell by gross weight should be compelled to state and prove that the weight of the wrapper is reasonable. Tea, coffee, cocoa, should be sold by net weight only, except in the case of 1 oz. packets. Vendors charged with an offence should be able to plead unavoidable loss by evaporation, bona fide accident, and fraud of a servant. The Bread Acts should be replaced by a law applicable to the whole of England and Wales that bread should be sold by weight only.

VI. COAL, FUEL AND POWER, WATER

1. **Coal**   2. **Petroleum**   3. **Gas**   4. **Electricity**   5. **Water**

1. COAL

Coal Supplies

R. Com. 1st Rep. Vol. I. Rep. pp. viii. 1903. Vol. II. Mins. of ev., apps., index. 1903. Vol. III. Plans. 1903

1903 Cd. 1724, xvi, 1. Mins. of ev., etc.; 1903 Cd. 1725, Cd. 1726, xvi, 9 apptd. Dec., 1901. sgd. Aug., 1903

Lord Allerton (Ch.), Lewis, Armytage, Briggs, Hull, Wood, Teall, Bell, Lapworth, Dixon (J. S.), Maclay, Dixon (H. B.), Sopwith, Brace, Young.

'To inquire into: The extent and available resources of the coalfields of the United Kingdom; the rate of exhaustion which

may be anticipated, having regard to possible economies in use by the substitution of other fuel or the adoption of other kinds of power; the effect of our exports of coal on the home supply, and the time for which that supply, especially of the more valuable kinds of coal, will probably be available to British consumers, including the Royal Navy, at a cost which would not be detrimental to the general welfare; the possibility of a reduction in that cost, by cheaper transport, or by the avoidance of unnecessary waste in working through the adoption of better methods and improved appliances, or through a change in the customary term and provisions of mineral leases; and whether the mining industry of this country, under *existing conditions, is maintaining its competitive power with the coalfields of other countries.'*

For the purpose of ascertaining the available coal resources of the United Kingdom, the known coalfields were grouped into seven districts and one or more members of the Commission were placed in charge of each district. Mining engineers were employed to examine the known coalfields, their enquiries being limited in the first instance to seams 12 inches thick or upwards lying at depths not exceeding 4,000 feet from the surface. These limits of depths and thickness were laid down by the Commission of 1866–1871 and a comparison of its estimates with those of the new enquiry could be made. The evidence presented bears entirely on the limits of the depth in mining; the minimum thickness of seams of coal, and waste in working. The appendices include reports on *Coal Mining in Westphalia*, by Herr Schultz-Briesen, *Temperatures Found in the Simplon Tunnel*, by Prof. Hein, and *Underground Temperatures*, by R. A. Thomas.

—— Second Report. Vol. I. Rep. pp. v. 1904. Vol. II. Mins. of ev., apps., index. 1904. Vol. III. Plans. 1904

1904 *Cd.* 1990 *xxiii*, 1. *Mins. of ev., etc.;*
1904 *Cd.* 1991, *Cd.* 1992, *xxiii*, 7
sgd. Feb., 1904

add Foster, Strahan, del. Lapworth.

The Report is a formal presentation of minutes of evidence, principally on possible economies and improvements in connection with the working, preparation, transport, and use of coal, and on the possibility of substituting other kinds of fuel, and of using power derived from other sources. The Appendices contain *An Analysis of the Natural Gas at Heathfield, Sussex,* Prof. Dixon, Dr. Bone; Memo on the *Use of Blast Furnace Gas*; Report on the *Cost of Running Producer Gas Plant at Messrs. Cadbury's Works, Bourneville.*

—— Final Report. Part I. General Rep. pp. vi, 38. 1905. Pt. X. Mins. of ev., index. 1905. Part XI. Apps. 1905. Pt. XII. Plans. 1905

1905 *Cd.* 2353, *xvi*, 1. *Mins. of ev., etc.;*
1905 *Cd.* 2362, *Cd.* 2363, *Cd.* 2364, *xvi*, 237
sgd. Jan., 1905

add Lapworth, del. Foster, Young.

Following the precedent of the Coal Commission of 1871, 4,000 feet was adopted as the limit of practicable depth in working and one foot as the minimum workable thickness. On this basis it was estimated that the available quantity of coal in the Proved Coalfields of the United Kingdom was 100,914 million tons, of which 79·3 per cent was contained in seams of two feet thick and upwards, and 91·6 per cent in seams of 18 inches and upwards. Although since the 1st January, 1870, and 31st December, 1903, 5,695 million tons of coal have been raised, the present estimates are 10,707 million tons in excess of those of the previous Commission. This excess was accounted for, partly by the difference in the areas regarded as productive by the two Commissions, and partly by discoveries due to recent borings, sinkings and workings, and more accurate knowledge of the coal seams. In addition, it is estimated that there are a further 5,239 million tons lying at greater depths in the proved coalfields.

The Geological Committee, appointed to enquire into the productive measures known or believed to exist outside the areas dealt with by the District Commissioners, estimated that some 39,483 million tons might be expected to be available in the concealed or unproved coalfields at depths less than 4,000 feet. Coal in undersea areas between 5 and 12 miles beyond high water mark was estimated at 1,237 million tons.

Temperatures and cost of working were the two factors influencing working at greater depths. It was not easy to determine the maximum temperature which was consistent with the healthy exercise of human labour, but there seemed to be no difficulty in working at upwards of ninety degrees, provided the ventilation were brisk and the air dry. There was no evidence to show that any collieries had stopped by reason of cost of working due to depth. No colliery in this country went down to 4,000 feet, which the Commission took as the limit of practicable working. The deepest was 3,483 feet at Pendleton Colliery. Experts on the Continent regard 4,900 feet as the working limit. In 1900 over 17 per cent of the output was obtained from seams of less than three feet thick. The calculations of resources were based on coal being worked from seams of a minimum thickness of one foot, and on the assumption that the existing methods of production, with their accompanying wastage of coal, were used. A greater amount of coal would be available if improved methods and appliances were used to save wastage. Evidence also showed that by methods of washing, sorting, coking and briquetting the coal, much small coal now left behind could be brought into use.

The probable duration of our coal resources turned on the annual output, which was 230 million tons. The annual increase in output for the last 30 years had been 2½ per cent per annum, and that of export (including bunkers) 4½ per cent per annum. It was highly improbable that the rate of future increase would continue long, as some districts had already attained a maximum. But increases would be influenced for some years by the output of the newer coalfields. 'We look forward to a time, not far distant, when the rate of increase of output will be slower, to be followed by a period of stationary output, and then by a gradual decline.'

Out of an annual consumption of from 143 to 168 million tons there was a possible saving of from 40 to 60 million tons a year. It was estimated that 52 million tons of coal were annually converted into steam power at mines and factories and that 'con-sumption of coal per indicated horse power per hour was on the average about 5 lbs.'. Waste and extravagance were shown by the fact that 'it should not exceed 2 lbs. or even less'. Though much had been done in the last 25 years, there were still immense economies capable of realization in connection with the raising of steam. Blast furnace gas and coke oven gas were further examples of waste: if utilized for power purpose these would save 2-3 million tons of coal annually.

Coal, it was maintained, was our only reliable source of power—one witness did not see how it would be possible to import oil in bulk at a price sufficiently low to compete with coal (q. 15079). But 'vast as our resources are, a large percentage of them are inferior in quality, and the cost of mining them will increase... These are the factors which will bring home to us the advantage of using coal with greater care.'

The maintenance of a large coal export was of supreme importance to the country and essential to the prosperity of the coal producing districts. It enabled the general and fixed charges to be spread over a larger tonnage, so that the average cost of working, and consequently the selling price to the British consumer, could be kept lower than would be the case if the collieries were worked for home consumption only. Any diminution of our coal export must cause a rise in the import rate on freights. Evidence showed that a large quantity of the coal exported abroad to foreign countries was destined for the use of British ships coaling abroad.

The consumption of coal by the Navy had rapidly increased during the last sixteen years, and was now about one-sixteenth of the output of the special class required. Experiments have shown that oil fuel could be used for auxiliary purposes, but that under existing conditions the Navy had to coal the ships with the best steam coal. The available resources of first-class Welsh steam coal were approximately

3,937 million tons, the annual output 18 million tons.

While large increases in output have been taking place in foreign coalfields, in the United Kingdom the cost of working has steadily increased thus adversely affecting our competitive power. Improved appliances and methods of working have enabled the colliery owners to some extent to keep down their costs, but they have steadily increased for various reasons, such as the necessity of working thinner and deeper seams, increased labour costs due to shorter hours and higher wages, and additional expenditure due to local taxation and to Government and Parliamentary requirements. The coal export duty which came into force in 1901 would affect our competitive power and our export of coal. Since the imposition of the tax, while the volume of exports excluding bunker coal had increased, the rate of increase of previous years has not been maintained.

Three tables show, for the several coalfields, the total available resources of the proved coalfields exceeding 4,000 feet in depth, and of the concealed and unproved coalfields.

Parts II–VIII of the Final Report give the estimates of coal resources in the seven districts of enquiry; Part IX is an important report on the resources of the concealed and unproved coalfields. These are all bound in the same sessional volume with the general Final Report.

1st. Rep., mins. of ev., etc.; 1903 Cd. 1724, Cd. 1725, Cd. 1726, xvi, 1.   2nd Rep., mins. of ev., etc.; 1904 Cd. 1990, Cd. 1991, Cd. 1992, xxiii, 1. Final Rep., Pt. I; 1905 Cd. 2353, xvi, 1. Other Reps., mins. of ev., etc., Pts. II to XIII; 1905 Cd. 2354 to Cd. 2365, xvi, 45.

Electricity in Mines

Dept. Cttee. Rep. pp. 29. 1904. Mins. of ev. 1904

1904 *Cd.* 1916, *xxiv,* 1. Mins. of ev.; 1904 *Cd.* 1917, *xxiv,* 31.
apptd. Oct., 1902. *sgd. Jan.,* 1904

H. H. S. Cunynghame, (*Ch.*), Fenwick, Hood, Patchell, Atkinson, Stokes.

'*To enquire into the use of Electricity in Coal and Metalliferous Mines, and the dangers attending it; and to report what measures should be adopted in the interests of safety by the establishment of Special Rules or otherwise.*'

The increasing use of electricity in mines was not regarded as more dangerous than the use of explosives or steam pressure, but it should be subject to careful regulation. Electric plant should always be treated as a source of potential danger, should be good in quality, designed to insure immunity from danger by shock or fire, and periodically tested for its efficiency. It should be under the charge of competent persons, and should be enclosed where there is any danger arising from the presence of gas. Detailed recommendations are made on generating stations, cables, stationary and portable motors, shot firing, electric lighting, etc., and a complete set of proposed rules is given.

Miners' Eight Hour Day
Dept. Cttee.

apptd. July, 1906

R. Rea (*Ch.*), Agnew, Cox, Crombie, Giffen, L. Glantawe, Redmayne.

'*To enquire into the probable economic effect of a limit of eight hours to the working day of coal miners, both when calculated from bank to.bank, and when otherwise calculated, upon (1) production; (2) wages; (3) employment; (4) the export trade; (5) other British industries which might be affected thereby; regard being had to the different conditions obtaining in different districts, seams, and collieries; and also into the probable effect of such a limit upon the health of the miners: and, if they think necessary, to extend their enquiry to metalliferous mines.*'

The First Report is a formal presentation of the following volumes of minutes of evidence, etc.; 1907 Cd. 3427, xiv, 529. 1907 Cd. 3428, xv, 1.

—— Final Report. Pt. I. Rep., apps.
pp. 87. 1907. Pt. II. Mins. of ev., apps.,
index. 1907

*1907 Cd. 3505, xv, 261. Mins. of ev.,
etc.; 1907 Cd. 3506, xv, 349
sgd. May, 1907*

Since the broad principle of limiting
the hours of adult workers for the first
time in this country was outside the
terms of reference, the most important
question left was the probable effect
of an eight hour day on production.
The average day of underground
workers was 9 hours 3 minutes or,
making allowances for customary stops
and idle days, 49 hours 53 minutes per
week. Assuming these customary short
and idle days to continue, an eight hour
day would reduce this time by 10·27
per cent and coal output by nearly
26 mn. tons. The Committee did not,
however, accept the view of most
colliery managers and owners that
there would be an exactly proportional
reduction of output, for through voluntary absenteeism and other causes
the hours actually worked averaged
only 7¼ hours a day. Voluntary absenteeism would decrease, labour efficiency would improve, and mechanical
methods could be extended. The
adoption of the multiple shift system,
though at present limited by union
opposition and the shortage of labour,
would not only be advantageous, but
a necessity in some mines. The difficulty of obtaining more labour was
exaggerated by the employers, since
shorter hours would stimulate an
increased flow of labour to the collieries. There would be a temporary
loss of production, varying from district
to district, the duration of which would
depend on the degree of co-operation
between the employers and employed.
The permanent effects could not be
foreseen, though an immediate advance
of wages and prices to an extent
dependent on the co-operation between
the parties appears to be certain. The
reduction of output need not be at
the expense of exports, though a
considerable part of the export trade

was in acute competition with foreign
coal and immediately felt any special
handicap. Germany and America, our
two most effective competitors, did
not limit hours by law, though the
hours worked were shorter than those
in Britain, but longer than they would
be under an eight hour day. A rise
of coal costs would be generally felt,
and the Government should retain
powers of suspension, regulation and
exception in administering any Act
providing for an eight hour day.

Mines

R. Com. 1st Rep., apps. pp. 52. 1907

*1907 Cd. 3548, xiv, 1
apptd. June, 1906. sgd. May, 1907*

Lord Monkswell (*Ch.*), Wood, Cunynghame, Abraham, Davis, Edwards, Ellis,
Haldane, Smillie.

'*To enquire into certain questions relating
to the health and safety of miners, and the
administration of the Mines Acts.*'

This report was restricted to the use
of breathing appliances, which enabled
persons to remain in a poisonous
atmosphere after an explosion or a fire.
Little attention had been paid to
the problem until after 1900, when several serious explosions had occurred
in France, England and Germany.
Breathing appliances were compulsory
in Austria and France, and much had
been done voluntarily in Germany; in
England there were four types of
appliances in use, which were great
improvements on earlier types, but still
had serious defects. The Commissioners felt that until further advances
had been made, it could not recommend any particular type or the compulsory provision of appliances. They
did, however, consider that the best
method of training men in the use of
appliances was by the establishment of
Central Rescue Stations from which
trained men could be obtained in time of
emergency. The appendices contain
reports from the South Yorkshire
Coalowners' Association, on *Colliery*

Fires and Rescue Apparatus; the Fife and Clackmannan Coalowners on *Rescue Apparatus*, and the French Commission on *Breathing Apparatus*, as well as Dr. Boycott's tests of breathing appliances, carried out on behalf of the Commission.

—— Second Report, apps. pp. viii, 297. 1909

1909 *Cd.* 4820, *xxxiv*, 599

sgd. July, 1909

There had been a remarkable reduction in the death rate in mines, particularly in deaths caused by explosions, but in spite of this, disasters on a large scale could, and did, occur. The inspection of mines should be made more efficient and more underground inspections undertaken, by reducing the number of inspection districts to six or seven based on the natural divisions of the principal coalfields, by increasing the number of inspectors and creating a new class of assistants and inspectors with lower qualifications and a more restricted field of duties. The responsibility of owner and agent for the observance of the Acts should be made clear. The Secretary of State should have power to limit the number of mines which a manager and under-manager might control. The standard of discipline of the men regarding the observance of rules was low in some districts. Recommendations were made regarding standards of ventilation. An examination of the sources and methods of dealing with coal dust led the Commission to set up a Committee consisting of some of its members, together with outside experts, who reported that large-scale experiments were necessary. Pending the results, the Commission limited its proposals to methods of preventing and dealing with accumulations. Other recommendations deal with the testing and use of safety lamps, shot-firing, the establishment of a Central Board for examining managers' and under-managers' certificates, the revision of Special Rules, and

the power of the Secretary of State to propose rules for individual mines or classes of mines.

Three Commissioners object to any lowering of qualifications required for the proposed new grade of inspectors, three considered that all firemen and engine-winders should possess a certificate of competence, two (Cunynghame and J. S. Haldane) dissented from the recommendation that owners and workers should be enabled to propose rules independently of the Secretary of State, on the ground that the aim of securing better rules on a more uniform basis would be frustrated by encouraging a multiplicity of independent codes. The appendices contain technical reports on coal dust, safety lamps, etc.

—— Third Report, apps. pp. iv, 17. 1911

1911 *Cd.* 5561, *xxxvi*, 465

sgd. Feb., 1911

Lord Monkswell (*Ch.*), deceased, add H. H. S. Cunynghame (*Ch.*).

The ventilation of coals mines was of the greatest importance since it was by ventilation that firedamp was removed. No men should work or pass in places, except those whose business it was to ensure safety, where there was more than $2\frac{1}{2}$ per cent of gas in the air; in naked light mines the percentage should be $1\frac{1}{4}$. This precaution was in *addition* to the existing duties of adequately ventilating the mines, reporting gas and withdrawing men when places were dangerous.

Pit ponies were employed in the majority of Great Britain's coal mines. There were rules governing their treatment, but whether or not they had been observed had been questioned. No widespread cruelty to the ponies had been proved; on the contrary the majority were well treated. But ill-treatment did occur and the recommendations of the Commission governing their care, prevention of overwork, sufficiency of food and water, tests for glanders, etc., should be embodied in an Act. It was not practicable to prohibit the use of ponies altogether. The Inspector of Mines should be responsible for the observation of the rules.

The appendices contain a memo by H. Cunynghame on how far and in what cases it is practicable to introduce a rule in mines regulating the percentage of firedamp in which it shall be permissible for the men to travel or work.

—— *Ventilation of Coal Mines and the Methods of Examining for Firedamp.* Rep., app. pp. ii, 112. 1909. Made on behalf of the R. Com.
1909 *Cd.* 4551, *xxxiv*, 913
J. Cadman, E. B. Whalley.

Contains the reports on technical investigations and statistical material which were used in the preparation of the Second Report and its recommendations on ventilation and firedamp.

—— *Causes of and Means of Preventing Accidents from Falls of Ground, Underground Haulage, and in Shafts.* Cttee. apptd. by the R. Com. Reps., apps. pp. vii, 181. 1909
1909 *Cd.* 4821, *xxxiv*, 1111

The Committee was composed of mining engineers. It made detailed technical recommendations, some of which were contained in the Second Report of the Royal Commission.

1st Rep.; 1907 Cd. 3548, xiv, 1. 2nd Rep.; 1909 Cd. 4820, xxxiv, 599. 3rd Rep.; 1911 Cd. 5561, xxxvi, 465. Reps.; 1909 Cd. 4551, Cd. 4821, xxxiv, 913. Mins. of ev.: Vol. I; 1907 Cd. 3549, xiv, 65. Vol. II, Vol. III; 1908 Cd. 3873, Cd. 4349, xx, 1. Vol. IV; 1909 Cd. 4667, xxxiv, 1. Vol. V; 1911 Cd. 5642, xxxvi, 487.

Electricity in Mines
Dept. Cttee. Rep., apps. pp. 45. 1911. Mins. of ev., index. 1911
1911 *Cd.* 5498, *xxxvii*, 1. *Mins. of ev., etc.*; 1911 *Cd.* 5533, *xxxvii*, 47
apptd. *Oct.*, 1909. sgd. *Dec.*, 1910

R. A. S. Redmayne (*Ch.*), Merz, Nelson.

'*To inquire into the working of the existing Special Rules for the use of Electricity in Mines, and to consider whether any, and if so what, amendments are required.*'

The existing code of rules was drawn up in 1902 (see *Electricity in Mines*, p. 131) and had been in practical operation for five years. Revised rules were needed to meet the remarkable extensions in the use of electricity which had occurred. The early applications of electricity to mines were restricted chiefly to lighting and small motors, but now it was applied to every operation requiring mechanical power. The most important development was the change from direct to alternating current. The proposed new rules should apply to metalliferous, as well as to coal mines. The revised rules, given in App. A, prohibit the use of electricity where on account of the risk of explosion its use would be dangerous, provide that inflammable material shall not be used in the construction of motor rooms, regulate the earthing of apparatus, require the better construction of gear and apparatus, and provide for competent supervision. There were parts of some mines in which electricity should not be used, and any intended introduction should be approved by H.M. Inspector of Mines.

Rescue and Aid in the Case of Accidents in Mines
Dept. Cttee. Rep. pp. 5. 1911
1911 *Cd.* 5550, *xxxvii*, 267
apptd. *Oct.*, 1910. sgd. *Feb.*, 1911
C. F. G. Masterman (*Ch.*), Redmayne, Atkinson, Hann, Blackett, Wilson, Wadsworth.

'*To consider the organization for rescue and aid in the case of accidents in mines, and to frame proposals for the making of an Order or Orders under the Mines Accidents (Rescue and Aid) Act, 1910.*'

Requirements for rescue and aid were outlined in a draft order to be made under the Miners' Accidents (Rescue and Aid) Act, 1910. It prescribes the number of rescue brigades to be kept in each mine according to the number of miners employed, the size of the brigades, their knowledge and training, and equipment, including sets of portable breathing apparatus.

Testing of Miners' Safety Lamps

Dept. Cttee. Rep. pp. 6. 1912

1912–13 *Cd.* 6387, *xlvii*, 625
apptd. — *sgd. Aug.*, 1912

Redmayne, Atkinson, Desborough.

After the erection of a safety lamp testing station at Eskmeals, near Barrow-in-Furness, and the carrying out of preliminary tests, the Committee were able to recommend that safety lamps should be subjected to mechanical and photometric tests, and tests in an explosive mixture. While the testing of every lamp was not possible, every lamp should conform in all particulars with a specification which was the outcome of the official tests. Each manufacturer of lamps should possess a certificate from the Home Office, stating that the 'make' of his product had passed the official tests.

Hours of Employment of Winding Enginemen. Draft Regulations. Coal Mines Act, 1911

Rep. pp. 6. 1913

1913 *Cd.* 6710, *xxxv*, 613

A. H. Ruegg.

The principal objection to the Regulation was raised by the Mining Association of Great Britian. They proposed that 'where the coal wound at any shaft does not exceed an average of 450 tons per 24 hours, a winding engineman may be employed for a period not exceeding 12 hours in any one day'. As the intention of the Act was that winding enginemen should work 8 hours per day and no more, and the proposal would make the restriction the exception and not the

rule, their point was not conceded. Adjustments were made on many points where objections and doubts had been raised.

Squibs for the Purpose of Firing Shots in Naked Light Mines

Dept. Cttee. Rep. pp. 8. 1913. Mins. of ev., apps. 1913

1913 *Cd.* 6721, *xxxiv*, 695. *Mins. of ev., etc.*; 1913 *Cd.* 6732, *xxxiv*, 703 *apptd. Nov.*, 1912. *sgd. March*, 1913

H. Johnstone (*Ch.*), Lamb, Walsh.

'To make inquiry and report with regard to the use of squibs for the purpose of firing shots in naked light mines, and particularly as to whether their use is attended with such special danger as to make it desirable that this method of firing shots should be prohibited, and if not, whether any special conditions in regard to the manufacture and use of squibs should be laid down.'

The original squibs, or 'straws' (ordinary oat straws were used), had at one time been charged by the miners themselves either in their homes or in the mine. The Explosives Act had prohibited charging in any place other than an establishment licensed for that purpose, and the straws had become obsolete. The modern squibs were manufactured in factories and workshops. The Committee did not consider that the use of properly constructed squibs was a specially dangerous method of firing shots and recommended regulations for their use. It should be an offence for any person to use a type of squib not approved by the Secretary of State.

Washing and Drying Accommodation at Mines

Dept. Cttee. Rep., app. pp. 11. 1913.

1913 *Cd.* 6724, *xxxiv*, 771 *apptd. May*, 1912. *sgd. March*, 1913

W. Walker (*Ch.*), Brain, Smillie.

'(1) *What should be regarded as sufficient and suitable accommodation and facilities?* (2) *Are different requirements necessary in respect of different classes and descriptions of mines, and, if so, what?* (3) *What should be the composition and procedure, powers and duties of the Committee of Management of the accommodation and facilities provided?*'

The Committee put forward detailed recommendations on the structure, fittings, ventilation and temperature, etc., of washing and drying facilities provided in those mines at which the employees wished to take advantage of the provisions of the Coal Mines Act, 1911. It was not necessary to prescribe different requirements for different classes of mines, but on joint representation of owners and workmen the Regulations could be varied by the Inspector of Mines of the Division. 'Baths Committees' of three representatives of the owner and three of the workers should be set up to manage the accommodation and facilities provided; their duties and powers were specified.

Explosions in Mines

Dept. Cttee. 1st Rep., app. pp. 17.
1912

1912–13 *Cd. 6307, xxv,* 245
apptd. May, 1911. *sgd.* June, 1912

Committee of inquiry: H. Cunynghame (*Ch.*), Redmayne, Desborough, Dixon, Blackett.

Consultative Committee in connection with the experimental inquiry: H. Cunynghame (*Ch.*), Abraham, Wood, Davis, Edwards, Ellis, Haldane, Smillie, Garforth, Pilkington, Forgie, Hood.

'*To inquire into the causes and means of prevention of coal dust explosions in mines.*'

The Committee was set up to carry out large-scale experiments, as recommended by the Royal Commission on Mines. It was established beyond all doubt that coal dust suspended in air is capable of being ignited without the presence of inflammable gas, and of propagating an explosion through the dusty galleries of mines. While further experiments were necessary before any final recommendation could be made, the liability of dry coal dust to ignite was largely reduced by air and an admixture of fine stone dust. Shale dust was recommended as being no more injurious to the lungs than fine coal dust. The Appendix contains Prof. J. M. Beattie's report on the *Effect Produced on the Lungs by the Inhalation of Coal Dust.*

—— Second Report, apps. pp. 43.
1912

1912–13 *Cd. 6431, xxv,* 281
sgd. ——

The great difference found in the inflammability of different coal dusts, and the importance of establishing some standard of measurement led to further experiments. These are summarized on page 17 of the report: 'A method is described by which the relative inflammability of different dusts can be ascertained by measuring the temperature of a platinum coil which just ignites a uniform cloud of dust and air projected across the coil fixed in a glass tube. It is shown that the relative inflammability does not depend upon the "total volatile matter", but on the relative ease with which inflammable gases are evolved. The order of inflammability so obtained corresponds in a remarkable degree with the percentage of inflammable matter extracted from the same coals by pyridine. We are of opinion that these two methods form a valuable means of discriminating between different coals in regard to the sensitiveness of their dusts to ignition. It must, however, be borne in mind that these tests have been made with dusts artificially ground and sieved to an equal degree of fineness, and since coals differ considerably in their power of resistance to pulverization, the friability of a coal must be taken into account.'

Appendix I gives extracts from papers by R. V. Wheeler and M. J. Burgess on *The Volatile Constituents of Coal.*

—— Third Report, apps. pp. 49. 1913
1913 *Cd. 6704, xxxv*, 529
sgd. March, 1913

Experiments were made to test Abel's conclusions on the danger of incombustible dusts in promoting the inflammation of otherwise uninflammable mixtures of firedamp and air. The conclusions drawn were that the presence of suspended incombustible dust would, as heat-absorbing material, render gaseous mixtures less explosive, and that the introduction of incombustible dust into a mine would not introduce a source of danger not already there.

—— Fourth Report. pp. 17. 1913
1913 *Cd. 6791, xxxv*, 585
sgd. April, 1913

Having found that inert dust had a retarding effect on the ignition of mixtures of gas and air, in this report the Committee gives the preliminary observations on the progressive development of a coal dust explosion as it travels along a gallery, and on the effects due to its obstruction.

—— Fifth Report, app. pp. 35. 1913
1914 *Cd. 7132, xxix*, 477
sgd. Oct., 1913

After further experiments it was suggested that stone dust should be mixed with the coal dust in dry and dusty mines in the proportion of one to one, or any higher proportion. The Consultative Committee did not feel able to express an opinion without further time to consider the matter and without consulting other persons.

—— Sixth Report. pp. 17. 1914
1914–16 *Cd. 7638, xxi*, 165
sgd. Sept., 1914
add Delevingne, del. Dixon, Blackett.

Having shown in the Fifth Report that equal proportions by weight of coal and incombustible dust is incombustible, further experiments were made to see what proportion of combustible gas would, if present in the air, render the mixture ignitable. It was concluded that the presence of firedamp in the air facilitated the inflammation of pure coal dust, but it did not diminish to any appreciable extent the protective effect of incombustible dust, and that a mixture of incombustible dust and coal dust could not be ignited by the flame of a fairly violent firedamp explosion. It was also established that the maintenance of 30 per cent of water in a state of intimate mixture with the dust throughout the roads or a combination of incombustible dust and water would be effective.

—— Seventh Report. *Effects of Inhaling Dusts Applicable for Stone-Dusting in Mines*, app. pp. 22. 1915
1914–16 *Cd. 8122, xxi*, 183
sgd. ——
Dr. Haldane.

In view of the recommendation for the use of shale dust, the Committee asked J. S. Haldane to experiment and report. He fully confirmed the conclusion of Professor Beattie that the dust of argillaceous shale, although it contains silica, is not dangerous to health. But he suspected that the use of flue dust was dangerous and should be discontinued.

Spontaneous Combustion of Coal in Mines
Reps.
1914 *Cd.* 7218. See *Breviate 1917–39*, p. 218.

Supplies of Home-Grown Pit-Wood in England and Wales
Rep.
1914–16 *Cd.* 7729. See *Forestry*, p. 94.

First Aid Certificates
Dept. Cttee. Rep., app. pp. 5. 1914
1914–16 *Cd. 7647, xxvii*, 591
apptd. May, 1913. *sgd. July*, 1914

W. N. Atkinson (*Ch.*), Richards, Lewis.

'To *consider and report what, if any, First Aid Certificates, besides those of the St. John and St. Andrew's Associations, should be recognized by the Home Office for the purpose of the grant of mine managers' certificates and other purposes under the Coal Mines Act, and on what conditions.*'

Glamorgan County Council, the British Red Cross Society, and Heriot-Watt College, Edinburgh, asked that their first aid certificates should be approved by the Secretary of State, for the purposes of the Coal Mines Act. The St. John's and St. Andrew's Association opposed the approval of the certificates of other societies or bodies. Ambulance certificates granted by responsible public authorities or institutions should be recognized on conditions to be laid down by the Home Office. The Appendix sets out the subjects to be added to the St. John's and St. Andrew's courses for the certificate for the purposes of the Coal Mines Act.

Retail Coal Prices

Dept. Cttee. Rep. pp. 11. 1915. Mins. of ev., apps., index. 1915

1914–16 *Cd.* 7866, *xxix*, 1. *Mins. of ev., etc.*; 1914–16 *Cd.* 7923, *xxix*, 13

apptd. Feb., sgd. March, 1915

V. Nash (*Ch.*), Ashley, Boyton, Crooks, Dent, Flux, Machin, Rowlands.

'To *inquire into the causes of the present rise in the retail price of coal sold for domestic use, especially to the poorer classes of consumers in London and other centres.*'

Prices had not risen in the North and Midlands to any extent comparable to the rise in London and the South. The initial cause of the rise was the deficiency of supply; demand had increased abnormally, while additional supplies had not been forthcoming. This deficiency was primarily due to a reduction in the output of 12 per cent consequent upon the enlistment of over 130,000 miners in the armed forces, but it could not by itself have caused the abnormal prices in London, other contributing causes being the lack of shipping, congestion on the railways caused by military requirements, and inadequate storage accommodation. While the high prices were not attributable to the existence of definitely constituted 'rings', there were obviously opportunities on the London Coal Exchange for concerted action on prices. This action was rendered possible by the sliding-scale contract system which, by linking the prices paid to the colliery with 'published prices' fixed by leading merchants, protected the merchants from outside competitors, who obtained no reduction of colliery prices if they reduced their retail price. There was no doubt that the rise in prices was considerably above that warranted by the increase in costs of production and distribution. Even if the estimated increase in costs of 3*s*. per ton were accepted—and this figure was probably too high—there was a great discrepancy between that and the increase in prices above the normal winter prices of from 7*s*. to 11*s*. Increased supplies were arriving regularly in London, and there seemed to be no legitimate reason for high prices being maintained. The Committee recommended the restriction of exports to neutrals while the scarcity lasted, various improvements in transport facilities, and the accumulation of stocks at London. Although maximum prices were not practicable, the Government should take control of coal output if prices did not fall to a reasonable level. The question of output was being dealt with by a Home Office Committee.

Conditions Prevailing in the Coal Industry Due to the War

Dept. Cttee. Pt. I. Rep., apps. pp. 54. 1915. Pt. II. Mins of ev., index. 1915

1914–16 *Cd.* 7939, *xxviii*, 1. *Mins. of ev., etc.*; 1914–16 *Cd.* 8009, *xxviii*, 55 *apptd. Feb., sgd. May*, 1915

R. A. S. Redmayne (*Ch.*), Nimmo, Hartshorn, Pease, Rhodes, Smillie, Walsh.

'*To inquire into the conditions prevailing in the coal-mining industry with a view to promoting such organization of work and such co-operation between employers and workmen as having regard to the large numbers of miners who are enlisting for naval and military service, will secure the necessary production of coal during the War.*'

The Committee's investigations covered 89 per cent of the industry. There had been a *net* reduction of 134,186 miners (or 13½ per cent) between July 1914 and February 1915. At the outset the exodus was due to the fact that for some weeks the mines were working short time, especially in Northumberland, where they were dependent on exports. But the main cause was enlistment in the armed forces. Output had fallen quite regularly by about 3 million tons per month, and in seven months the loss in production had amounted to over 21 million tons. But continued withdrawal of miners would mean an increased deficiency and whether or not miners should be encouraged to enlist should be seriously considered. An appeal should be made to the miners to reduce avoidable absenteeism, which amounted to about 4·8 per cent; if this ended, production could be increased by almost 14 million tons. On the limitation of exports, there could be no definite conclusion without further investigation. The probable reduction for the year 1914–15 was estimated at about 24 million tons, which could be set against a probable reduction in output of 36 million tons. The adoption wherever possible of more efficient methods in the mines was advocated and it was suggested that owners and workers confer on the extent to which the Eight Hours Act should be suspended in individual districts.

—— Second General Report, apps. pp. 33. 1916

1914–16 Cd. 8147, *xxviii*, 307 sgd. Dec., 1915

The effect of the war for a full year was that compared with 1913–14, there had been a decrease in production of about 30 million tons (11 per cent) instead of the expected decrease of 36 million tons. The average loss per month for the last five months of 1914–15 had been far below that for the first seven and was almost entirely due to the shortage of labour, the number of miners having fallen by 160,510 net. The elimination of voluntary absenteeism, which had been maintained at 4·9 per cent, would increase production by 13 to 14 million tons per annum. There had been no suspension of the Eight Hours Act, but much had been done in concentrating on the easily-worked sections of mines, and in curtailing time-off. The decline in exports had compensated for the decline in production, so far as the home market was concerned, but Admiralty demands were far in excess of normal. To solve transport problems the Railway Executive should prepare a scheme for pooling railway wagons, and an enquiry should be made into the possibility of restricting the movements of ships between foreign ports, in the interests of the industry.

—— Third General Report, apps. pp. 17. 1916

1916 Cd. 8345, *vi*, 471 sgd. Sept., 1916

There had been a continued improvement in production up to March 1916, but by June 16th the position had become so serious that the enlistment of miners was stopped. There were 165,000 fewer miners than in July 1914. There had been no improvement in avoidable absenteeism and various local committees had been set up in the mining districts to cope with the problem. Holidays had been reduced by 50 per cent, and the number of days worked at collieries had increased substantially in early 1916. There had, however, been no co-operation from private wagon owners in forming general pooling schemes such as had been accomplished by the railways. Steps had been taken to increase the supply and use of home grown timber. Local committees of coalowners, and a central committee presided over by the President of the Board of Trade, had been set up to control the internal distribution of coal, and the Committee emphasized the need for economies if necessary demands were to be fulfilled.

Bobbinite

Dept. Cttee. Rep., apps. pp. v, 67. 1907. Mins. of ev. 1907

1907 Cd. 3423, xxxii, 491. Mins. of ev.; 1907 Cd. 3465, xxxii, 589 apptd. April, 1906. sgd. March, 1907 H. H. Cunynghame (Ch.), Brain, Dixon, Richards, Thomson.

'To enquire into certain ignitions of gas by the explosive Bobbinite, and to report whether the continued use in coal mines of Bobbinite and explosives of a kindred nature is desirable.'

The non-detonating mechanical mixture explosives, of which bobbinite was the most important, were generally more suitable for coal-getting, but were also more likely to ignite gas and dust when insufficiently confined in a shot-hole. Their use should be confined to those mines which conformed to certain specifications and in which the danger of widespread explosion was slight. Two classes of explosives should be distinguished, those passing the Woolwich tests only, and those passing both the Woolwich and certain other tests. The former class, which would include bobbinite, should be excluded from mines to which the Explosives in Coal Mines Order applied, but permitted for the exclusive purpose of coal-getting in mines or seams naturally wet or artificially watered.

Manufacture of Patent Fuel

Rep., apps. pp. 12. 1911

1911 Cd. 5878, xxii, 697 sgd. Aug., 1911

A. H. Lush.

'On the Draft Regulations proposed to be made for the Manufacture of Patent Fuel (Briquettes) with Addition of Pitch.'

In 1910 the manufacture of patent fuel (briquettes) with addition of pitch had been certified as dangerous. Draft regulations had been issued and objections to the rules had led to this enquiry. The industry was not particularly unhealthy, but the pitch was dangerous to the skin and eyes. Adjournment of the enquiry to carry out certain experiments was recommended.

—— Second Report, apps. pp. 13. 1913

1914 Cd. 7051, xliv, 69 sgd. Aug., 1913

Washing accommodation and facilities had been provided in some factories, and efforts had been made to reduce the amount of dust. But to compel men to use the facilities was impracticable and it was therefore unreasonable to require employers to incur the expense involved by the Draft Regulations. An arrangement satisfactory to all had been decided upon and the Regulations should therefore be withdrawn.

2. PETROLEUM

Petroleum Spirit

Dept. Cttee. 1st Rep., apps. pp. iii, 41. [1910.] Mins. of ev., index. Vol. I. [1910]

1910 Cd. 5175, xliv, 609. Mins. of ev., etc.; 1910 Cd. 5176, xliv, 653 apptd. Feb., 1909. sgd. May, 1910

H. Cunynghame (Ch.), Redwood, Cooper-Key, Ollis, Boyle.

'To inquire into the sufficiency of the existing regulations relating to the storage,

*use and conveyance of petroleum spirit; and
to report what further precautions, if any,
are in their opinion desirable as tending to
diminish the dangers attendant thereon.'*

The regulations governing storage,
use and conveyance were laid down
by the Acts of 1871, and 1881, which
had either become out of date or were
'a dead letter', as one witness contended (Major, p. 140). Since 1871 the
use of petroleum spirit had increased
tremendously. For example, at Barrow-
in-Furness, before 1905 the amount
imported was nil; in 1908 it was over
8 mn. gallons. For the year 1909
21½ mn. were imported into London
from the Asiatic Petroleum Company.
In q. 2 of the minutes of evidence a
member of the Committee referred to
the danger of large quantities of petroleum spirit being brought up the
Thames in licensed barges in foggy
weather. In his statement and evidence
(pp. 172-7) A. H. Bodkin discusses
the 'great facility with which petrol
can be obtained and used on human
beings for hair-dressing purposes,
under circumstances in which no skill
in its use or knowledge of its dangerous
properties was necessarily possessed by
employees'.

There was no provision for Government control and supervision of the
working of the Acts. Administration
was excessively decentralized and in the
hands of district committees. There
was no obligation on the local
authorities to enforce the law or
to appoint officers and any officers
appointed had inadequate powers of
inspection. There was no proper
restriction on the conveyance of petroleum spirit, railways had no powers
to make byelaws as to its conveyance,
nor were the manufacture and use of
the spirit governed by the Acts.

Among many recommendations were
the following: that the central authority
should be able to issue rules guarding
against any dangers arising from the
handling of the spirit, and to appoint
officers to supervise the working of the
Petroleum Acts; local authorities should

be obliged to appoint officers, whose
powers should be enlarged, to enforce
the law. Detailed amendments to the
Act of 1871, the repeal of the Petroleum
(Hawkers) Act, 1881, and certain
restrictions on the domestic and trade
use of petrol were recommended.

—— Final Report. pp. 8. 1913. Mins.
    of ev., apps. Vol. II. 1913

*1912–13 Cd. 6565, xlii, 791. Mins. of
ev., etc.; 1912–13 Cd. 6644, xlii, 799
sgd. Feb., 1913*

This report dealt with the power of
harbour authorities to make byelaws
under the Petroleum Acts, and with the
conveyance of petroleum spirit by road
in motor-tank wagons. In their first
Report the Committee had already
recommended that all road tank wagons
should conform to a specification issued
by a central authority, and that they
should be horse-drawn only. After
considering further evidence on the
subject, and in view of the increasing
number of motor-lorries, the Committee had decided that the motor-tank
wagon could be safe in practice if it
were made to conform to an official
specification.

The definition of a 'harbour' and a
'harbour authority' should conform to
those of the Explosives Act, 1875. The
authority should have power to pass
byelaws enforcing proper precautions
in the handling of petroleum spirit.

The recommendations made in the
first Report were repeated, in particular
those relating to direct control through
a central authority.

3. GAS

Gas Testing in the Metropolis

Dept. Cttee. Rep. pp. 10. 1904. Pt. II.
    Mins. of ev., apps., index. 1904

*1904 Cd. 2118, xxiv, 567. Mins. of ev.,
etc.; 1904 Cd. 2203, xxiv, 577
apptd. Jan., sgd. May, 1904*

Lord Rayleigh (*Ch.*), Abney, Farquharson, King, Moulton.

'*To inquire and report as to the Statutory requirements relating to the illuminating power and purity of gas supplied by the Metropolitan Gas Companies, and as to the methods now adopted for testing the same, and whether any alteration is desirable in such requirements or methods, and, if so, whether any consequential alteration should be made in the standard price of gas.*'

It was important to define the quality of gas without ambiguity as a considerable proportion of it was used with flat flame burners (as distinct from incandescent mantles). There should be standard tests of the illuminating power of the product of all companies, and since gas was being increasingly used for heating, similar standard tests of its calorific power. The statutory requirement that gas should be wholly free from sulphuretted hydrogen was in fact impracticable; it should be modified and in future the test should not be more severe than that required by the Gasworks Clauses Act, 1871.

Gas Authorities (Residual Products)

Jt. Sel. Cttee. Rep., proc., mins. of ev., apps. pp. xi, 201. Index. 1913

1912–13 (392) *and* (392-*Ind.*), *vii*, 253
apptd. Aug., o.p. Dec., 1912

J. Hills (*Ch.*), Lardner, Rea, Roberts, Thorne, L. Craven, L. Braye, L. Howard de Walden, L. Plunket, L. Inchcape.

'*To consider and report whether any and, if any, what restrictions should be imposed on gas authorities with respect to the purchase and manufacture of the residual products resulting from the manufacture of gas by other gas authorities, or of other chemicals.*'

The chemical trade had objected to the manufacture and sale of chemical products by gas undertakings, which were their main source of supply of materials. The manufacture of gas necessarily involved the production of by-products which could be either sold to chemical manufacturers or converted

by the gas companies themselves. Though often permitted by their particular statutes, the purchase by gas undertakings of the residuals of other gas undertakings for the purpose of conversion was not general, but had recently been subject to a prohibitory clause inserted in gas companies' private bills; and this clause could be applied to previously established undertakings which asked for further legislation. The companies should be allowed to purchase the residuals of other gas undertakings, but they should not be permitted to manufacture chemicals exclusively from raw materials obtained from any source other than gas companies.

4. ELECTRICITY

Supply of Electricity Bill [H.L.]

Sel. Cttee. HL. Rep., proc., mins. of ev. pp. x, 115. Index. 1904

1904 (354) *and* (354-*Ind.*), *vii*, 287
apptd. May, o.p. Aug., 1904

Lord Wolverton (*Ch.*), L. Bath, L. Ellesmere, L. Colchester, L. Stanley.

The Committee reported the Bill, with amendments. In evidence, it was stated on behalf of the Board of Trade by T. W. W. Pelham, that under the Electric Lighting Acts, 1882, 1888, the Board of Trade have power to make Provisional Orders enabling local authorities, companies or persons to supply electricity for public or private purposes, but have no power to enable a local authority to purchase land compulsorily, or to supply energy in bulk; nor can they authorize two or more local authorities to carry out a scheme jointly. The object of the Bill was to enable promoters to proceed by Provisional Order, rather than by Bill and so save expense.

Electric Lighting (London) Bill

Sel. Cttee. Rep., proc., mins. of ev., app. pp. viii, 48. 1904

1904 (220) *vi*, 65
apptd. March, o.p. June, 1904

Mr. Bousfield (*Ch.*), Slack, Hayden, Hare, Younger.

The statement in evidence on behalf of the Board of Trade was that inconveniences arose from the divergencies between the old electricity areas and the areas of the new boroughs, for which the remedy was to transfer areas. Some of the difficulties of such compulsory transfers were that areas owning electricity works, or rights to supply electricity, would lose to other areas, and sometimes this involved transfers between companies and local authorities, or complications due to the differences between alternating and continuous currents, etc. There were fourteen local authorities supplying electricity in London: three of them, Islington, Southwark and Bermondsey, petitioned against the Bill. The Bill was reported, subject to three amendments.

London County Council (Electric Supply) Bill, 1906

Sel. Cttee. Rep., proc. pp. 30. 1906

1906 (219) *xi*, 1
apptd. March, o.p. June, 1906

L. White (*Ch.*), Chance, Nolan, Parker, Rutherford, Lowe, Norman, Bell, Duncan.

'*To whom the London County Council (Electric Supply) Bill was referred, and who were instructed by the House on 2nd April to consider, with special reference to the terms of the Bill, the best means of providing for the Supply of Electrical Energy in bulk and for power and motive purposes.*'

The main object of the Bill was to enable the London County Council to supply electricity (1) in bulk to authorized distributors within the administrative County of London and certain adjoining boroughs and districts in the Counties of Essex, Kent, Surrey and Middlesex; (2) to supply energy direct to railways, docks, tramways and various other undertakings; (3) to transform, distribute and use electrical energy in various buildings, works or

undertakings belonging to or maintained by them, etc.

The supply of electricity in the County of London and adjoining districts was in the hands of 16 local authorities and 13 companies, most of the latter being open to purchase by the local authorities in 1931. The Electric Lighting Acts had provided that there should be a separate undertaking in the area of each local authority. The Committee agreed that there should be one large and inclusive scheme extending over the County of London, the adjoining boroughs and districts, and that the L.C.C. should be the authority. But the Bill was merely permissive; the L.C.C. should be under an obligation to supply and authorized distributors have the right to require a supply. This change would alter the scope of the Bill and further consideration should be given to other improvements. The provision of cheap electric power for London was so pressing that the L.C.C. was urged to make a decision, so as to allow other Bills to be presented in the following session. The Committee reported to the House that the Preamble was not proved.

London Electric Supply Bill

Sel. Cttee. Rep., proc., mins. of ev. pp. iv, 1. 1910

1910 (221) *vi*, 559
apptd. —, o.p. July, 1910

Mr. Brunner (*Ch.*), Parker, Hickman, Marks, Archer-Shee.

Under the London Electric Supply Act, 1908, the L.C.C. was made the purchasing authority in respect of the undertakings of nine out of fourteen companies who supply electricity to London. The present Bill gives powers to purchase the rest.

Electric Mains Explosions

Dept. Cttee. Rep., apps. pp. 25. 1914

1914 *Cd.* 7481, *xxix*, 451
apptd. Dec., 1913. *sgd. May*, 1914

T. E. Thorpe (*Ch.*), Nelson, Slingo, Swinburne, Trotter.

'*To consider the causes of explosions which have occurred in connection with the use of bitumen in laying cable-mains at Nottingham, Hebburn, and elsewhere, and to report as to any steps which should be taken to prevent explosions in future from the use of this or similar substances.*'

In recent years a number of explosions had been caused by the ignition of vapour generated by short circuits between underground electric cables. Although the explosions had been produced by continuous current cables insulated mostly with vulcanized bitumen and laid in solid bitumen, in view of the small number of serious accidents compared with the large extent to which this method was used, the Committee could not recommend the Board of Trade to discontinue approval of this system. Specific proposals concerning insulation and methods of laying cables were made.

5. WATER

Water Supplies (Protection) Bill [H.L.]

Jt. Sel. Cttee. Rep., proc., mins of ev., apps. pp. xviii, 279. 1910. Index. 1911

1910 (226) *vi*, 653
apptd. March, o.p. July, 1910

Lord Liverpool (*Ch.*), L. Verulam, L. Clinton, L. Desborough, L. Mac-Donnell, L. Bentinck, Crossley, Holt, Lewis, Rolleston.

The Bill was reported to the House without amendment. It proposed to restrict the powers of authorized water undertakings (i) by requiring specific Parliamentary authorization for obtaining new supplies. Parliament should possess all information about any scheme, but in view of the imperfect state of knowledge about underground water, control could best be effected by considering each scheme on its merits rather than by imposing any general law. (ii) By making the undertakings liable for injury to private supplies caused by their works. Serious damage had been done to private property by pumping operations; the law, which as it stood did not recognize private property in underground water unless it flowed in a definite channel, should be revised in view of the altered circumstances. But enquiry should be made into this subject, which gave rise to many complications, before any legislative action was taken. (iii) By providing that where water was taken from one district to another, the local authorities of the districts from and through which the water was taken, should have the right to demand a supply on terms to be agreed or fixed by the L.G.B. The claim for water supply should be restricted to those local authorities which would normally have had recourse to the appropriated supply. Local authorities should be encouraged to make full use of local sources of supply, and this might not be done if other authorities than those referred to could claim a right to tap the mains of the great undertakings.

In order that the resources of the country should be efficiently utilized, a Central Administrative Authority should be established to enquire into the whole question of surface and underground water supplies, to supervise the future allocation of water, and to advise Parliament on schemes. The country should be divided into water-shed areas, in which there should be formed local Representative Boards under the guidance of the Central Authority. No action has been taken on the repeated recommendations of previous enquiries on this question, and the Committee strongly recommend that they should be carried out.

London Water

Reps.

See *London.* p. 54.

VII. TRANSPORT

1. Inland Waterways
2. Railways

3. Roads and Road Traffic
4. Sea Transport

1. INLAND WATERWAYS

Canals and Waterways
R. Com.

apptd. March, 1906

Lord Shuttleworth (*Ch.*), L. Brassey, L. Farrer, Dorington, Brunner, Rea, Wilson, Crossley, Hopwood, Snowden, Vivian, Waldron, Griffith, Herbertson, Killick, Minch, Remnant, Davison, Inglis, L. Kenyon.

'*To enquire into the Canals and Inland Navigations of the United Kingdom and to Report on:* (1) *their present condition and financial position;* (2) *the causes which have operated to prevent the carrying out of improvements by private enterprise, and whether such causes are removable by legislation;* (3) *facilities, improvements, and extensions desirable in order to complete a system of through communication by water between centres of commercial, industrial, or agricultural importance, and between such centres and the sea;* (4) *the prospect of benefit to the trade of the country compatible with a reasonable return on the probable cost; and* (5) *the expediency of canals being made or acquired by public bodies or trusts, and the methods by which funds for the purpose could be obtained and secured; and what should be the system of control and management of such bodies or trusts.*'

The First, Second and Third Reports are formal only presenting minutes of evidence. For the full citation of the documents see App., p. 448.

—— Fourth and Final Report, app. pp. xiv, 237. Index. 1909

1910 *Cd.* 4979, *xii*, 1.
sgd. Dec., 1909

del. L. Kenyon.

Present condition and financial position.—There had been no considerable extension of canal mileage since about 1830; the mileage of canals and navigations in use was about 4,670 of which 3,639 were in England and Wales, one-third of which (1,360) were owned and controlled by railways. The impediments to through traffic included differences in sectional areas, size of locks, depth of channel and divided ownership. The headway afforded by bridges and tunnels varied and this, with the breaks of gauge, meant that the size of barge which could be used was limited by the lowest bridge and narrowest gauge, unless there were transhipments.

In 1905 the amount of traffic conveyed in all canals in England and Wales, excluding the seaborne traffic of the Manchester Ship Canal, was 37 mn. tons, the net revenue being £537,000 or nearly 74 per cent of expenditure, though the figures included an element of double counting. Over half the traffic was carried by 984 miles of canal. Much of this was short-distance traffic, the average for a number of canals being 17½ miles; one of the reasons for the decline of long-distance traffic was the competition of sea coasting vessels, which did not exist when the canals were built. Although canals did not carry one per cent of the total coal moved by rail and sea, this traffic was 45 per cent of their total tonnage. Between 1888 and 1905 independent waterways showed a rise in revenue from tolls and from freight as carriers, whilst the railways' canals showed a decline from tolls and a barely stationary revenue from freight as carriers. Most of the main independent waterways in operation yield a small net profit or nominal returns, those showing a positive loss being half-abandoned navigations or small and unimportant ones.

Causes which have operated to prevent

*the carrying out of improvements by private
enterprise.* — The independent canal
companies did not have the means of
making large improvements, and the
returns were not sufficient to enable
them to attract new capital to invest
in improvements. This was due to
the haphazard system by which canals
were constructed, without uniformity
of gauge or locks; to the multiplicity of
ownership, which made it useless for
one company alone to improve the
section of a through route, and made
the quotation of through rates difficult;
and to the transfer of important
sections of the waterways to the railway
companies, who were said to have
discouraged through traffic by canal and
waterways. But some disadvantages
had arisen from errors in legislation
and neglect by Government and Parliament. The multiplicity of authorities
could have been remedied by amalgamation, but this was impossible because
of railway ownership of vital links.
The disorganization and want of unity
of canals made effective competition
impossible and discouraged improvements.

*The improvements and extensions desir-
able.*—Trade would increase on the
main routes if they were under a
uniform administration, were improved
to allow of mechanical traction and if
there were regular services and better
terminal facilities. These reforms could
be made by minor improvements in
the law. The waterways system must
be so improved and reconstructed as to
allow larger cargoes to be conveyed by
less labour and in shorter time, and to
permit the full use of · mechanical
improvements.

These considerations did not apply
to all waterways, but only to those
which conveyed bulky goods to and
from centres of production to great
consuming and other centres of industry. The waterways system was
centred in the Midland district round
Birmingham, and rested upon four
estuaries, the Thames, the Severn, the
Mersey and the Humber. The first
step would be to amalgamate and bring
into working order the four main
routes of this system, known as the
'Cross'. A review of the general policy
and results of waterway improvement
in France, Belgium and Germany led
to the conclusion that with modifications required by the different geographical and other circumstances, the
same policy could be applied in Britain.
A technical examination of the merits
and cost of improvements on the basis
of barges of 600 tons, 300 tons and
100 tons, aided by estimates prepared
by Mr. John Wolfe Barry and Partners,
led to a proposal to improve the four
main routes of the 'Cross' up to the
100-ton standard for parts of them,
and to greater widths for other parts.

*The benefit to trade and prospect of
financial return.*—The total mileage of
the four routes and necessary branches
would be 943, of which 792 required
improvements; these carried 9,888,000
tons in 1905 and had a net revenue of
£147,000. The cost of the improvements would be about £15¼ mn., or
£28,546 per mile. The annual charges
due to the improvements would be
£767,000 or £1,438 per mile. The
annual revenue of £568,000 in 1905
would have to be raised to £965,000.
The carrying capacity of the new 100-
ton stretches of the route would be
five times that of the old barge canals,
and the use of trains of barges of 200–
260 tons would make a reduction of
costs and charges possible. Any State
aid for the acquisition of canals should
take the form of free grant or advances
with deferred repayments. Exact forecasts of the probable traffic were not
possible, some·Commissioners thinking that it would, others that it would
not give an adequate direct return on
the capital outlay. But the indirect
benefits of stimulating industry and
trade would be great. And this is the
only return looked for in those counties
where improved canals and waterways
are free of toll.

*Ownership and Control. A new Water-
way Authority.*—As the improved canals
required amalgamation and unified
management, the Commission rejected

construction by local authorities after the model of the Light Railways Act, concessions to companies, reconstitution and amalgamation of existing companies, and regional public trusts. There should be a Central Waterway Board, in whom the main routes and subsidiaries should be vested, whether or not the larger improvements could be immediately undertaken. The amalgamation and unification of the routes should be undertaken immediately. The Board should then review the whole position and promote improvement schemes for submission to Parliament. The purchase of railway-owned canals should be included in the earlier schemes. The procedure for purchase of the routes should follow that of the Port of London Authority, i.e. fixed interest stock should be issued to the existing shareholders. The stock and loans issued for improvements should be guaranteed by the State; the stock issued for the purchase of the canals should take the form of a free grant or loan from the State with deferred interest and repayment.

Recommendations were made for the gradual transfer to the authority of feeder canals, for the continued independence of other canals, for the abandonment of other disused canals, and for a special enquiry to deal with waterways in the eastern counties to prevent floods, ensure drainage, etc. The Caledonian and Crinan canals should be transferred to the Board. The business interests affected should consider whether funds could be raised for a Forth-Clyde canal, and the Government what aid should be given on account of its strategic value.

Reservations. — Farrer, Wilson, Waldron and Killick stated that the report was based on the assumption that improved waterways would provide cheap transit compared with the railways. Carriage by sea was cheap because the waterway was ample and natural and involved no charge, and the cost of traction was low as compared with other methods, but those benefits held only where conditions were similar to this. They were similar in a great natural inland waterway, like the Rhine, but less so in costly, artificial canals. In England there was no prospect of reasonable return on the cost of acquisition and improvement. Cost of acquisition should not be borne by the State. Farrer dissents from State intervention, Russell Rea from the proposal to improve parts of the Severn and Trent to take sea-going vessels of 600 and 750 tons. In separate reports Remnant, Davison and Inglis stated that canals were less efficient than railways and were an obsolete form of transport, in that there was little prospect of sufficient traffic or reasonable return on cost. Remnant disagreed with the proposals for a central board, or for any State aid other than from the Development Commission for special improvements.

See *Inland Waterways. Breviate 1917-39*, pp. 257, 258.

—— Final Report, *Ireland*, index. pp. xii, 91. 1911

1911 *Cd.* 5626, *xiii*, 19
sgd. March, 1911

There were 837 miles of canals and waterways in Ireland of which 430 were canals, 268 inland navigations, the remainder being waterways without locks. Of the total, 165 miles were State-owned, 212 miles were owned by local authorities and trusts, 95 miles by railways, the rest belonging to independent companies. The total tonnage carried in 1905 was 1,070,000, only 25,000 tons being carried by railway-owned canals. Traffic per mile was thus much lighter in Ireland than in England. Ireland had 19 per cent of the total mileage, but only 3 per cent of the tonnage carried and 6 per cent of the gross revenue. In England there was a great bulk of inland traffic by rail and water, in Ireland but little. The inland districts were sparsely populated and without large industrial centres, and there was little mineral or other heavy traffic. The possibility of a large increase of waterborne traffic was therefore small and a large expenditure on improvements would not be justified. There were two connected systems of comparatively small extent— the Grand, the Shannon and Royal Canals, and the northern waterways. In contrast to English conditions, agricultural traffic had increased, and a moderate expenditure to promote uniformity of dimensions might be wise. In Ireland there was a conflict of interest between the claims of navigation and the interests, vital in that country, of drainage and prevention of floods, water power and fisheries. As a result State policy had been halting and vacillating, work begun had not been properly completed. Much of this failure arose from the attempt to deal with these problems separately.

There should be established a Water Board, consisting of 3 or 5 commissioners, one being a paid, full-time officer; it should be a branch of the Department of Agriculture and Technical Instruction. The Board should take over those waterways which were already publicly owned, and such other waterways as were important for drainage and navigation.

Farrer did not sign the report as he disagreed with recommendations to make administrative changes involving public expenditure until there was an Irish elected authority willing to pay for it.

2. RAILWAYS

Accidents to Railway Servants

R. Com. Pt. I. Rep. pp. 14. 1900. Pt. II. Mins. of ev., apps., index. 1900

1900 Cd. 41, *xxvii*, 1. *Mins. of ev., etc.*; 1900 Cd. 42, *xxvii*, 15 *apptd. May, 1899. sgd.* —

Lord Hereford (*Ch.*), L. Hampden, Fellowes, Paget, Molesworth, Scotter, Hickman, Hutchinson, Cunynghame, Acworth, Ellis, Elliott, Fenwick, Hudson.

'*To enquire into the causes of the accidents, fatal and non-fatal, to servants of railway companies and of truck owners, and to report on the possibility of adopting means to reduce the number of such accidents, having regard to the working of railways, the rules and regulations made, and the safety appliances used by railway companies.*'

'The operations carried on by goods-guards and brakesmen, permanent-way men and shunters, represent a far more dangerous trade than any trade or process subject to State control, except merchant shipping.' The chief causes for the high percentage of accidents were: the nature of the coupling gear, which called for hand methods in the use of the shunting pole in limited space between the rail tracks; inadequate lighting in the sidings, obstacles such as wires and lever rods over which men fell, and a disregard of safety owing to pressure of work.

There should be uniformity in the application of methods of securing safety. The Board of Trade should be empowered to appoint a Departmental Committee on automatic couplings to make experiments, with a warning that should changes in the system of coupling be made obligatory, the transition period should be sufficient to avoid dislocation of traffic. A time limit of 10 years should be set for the replacement of the 'dead' by the 'spring' buffer. The Board of Trade should be given powers of inspection and regulation and of making general rules and specific orders in the interests of safety, with the Railways and Canals Commission as the Appeals Tribunal.

See *Railway Employment (Prevention of Accidents) Act*, 1900. 63 & 64 Vict. c. 27.

Steel Rails

Cttee. Rep., apps. pp. 124. 1900

1900 Cd. 174, *lxxvi*, Pt. I, 553 *apptd. May, 1896. sgd..March*, 1900

Lord Blythswood (*Ch.*), Baker, Bell, Dunstand, Kennedy, Marindin, Martin,

Richards, Roberts - Austen, Thorpe, Unwin.

'*To enquire what extent of loss of strength in Steel Rails is produced by their prolonged use on Railways under varying conditions, and what steps can be taken to prevent the risk of Accidents arising through such loss of strength.*'

A summary of the technical investigations made by the Committee. There are twelve appendices which are reports on results of experiments made by individuals for the Committee.

Railway Employment Safety Appliances

Cttee. 1st, 2nd Reps., apps. pp. 13. 1907. 3rd, 4th Reps., apps. pp. 11. 1908. 5th, 6th, 7th, 8th Reps. pp. 7. 1910

1907 *Cd.* 3638, *lxxiv*, 823. 1908 *Cd.* 4213, *xcv*, 349. 1910 *Cd.* 5359, *lxxix*, 473

H. A. Yorke (*Ch.*), Bell, Turnbull.

'(1) *To examine, and if necessary to test, appliances designed to diminish danger to men employed in railway service; (2) To make, with the co-operation of the railway companies, such experiments as the Committee think expedient for the purpose under Section 15 of the Railway Employment (Prevention of Accidents) Act, 1900; (3) To report to the Board of Trade—(a) At intervals of not more than six months what appliances have been considered and dealt with, and with what results, and (b) From time to time whether, in the opinion of the Committee, rules should be made under the Act of 1900 either (1) prescribing or (2) prohibiting the use of appliances of a specified type, and if so, what interval, if any, might reasonably be allowed before such rules come into operation.*'

The reports are mainly concerned with brakes and automatic couplings. A rule should be made under the Railway Employment (Prevention of Accidents) Act, 1900, prescribing the period within which new and existing wagons should be fitted with the improvements specified. The third report includes a memorandum by the Chairman arguing that until means are found of financing the large capital outlay which the change-over to automatic coupling by railway companies and private wagon owners would involve, it was useless to make it compulsory or to initiate costly experiments.

London Underground Railways
Rep.

1901 (279). See *London*. p. 56.

Visit to America. (Steam and Electric Railways)
Rep., index. pp. 48. 1903

1903 *Cd.* 1466, *lx*, 843 *pres. Dec.,* 1902

H. A. Yorke.

The report is concerned chiefly with steam railways, railroads, surface lines or tramways, subways and elevated railways and high speed electric interurban railways.

Workmen's Trains
Sel. Cttee.

'*To enquire into the Working and Administration of the Cheap Trains Act, 1883, and to report whether any, and, if so, what, Amendments are reasonable and necessary to improve the service of Workmen's Trains in the Metropolis and elsewhere, and to secure the provision of the accommodation required by Workmen by all Railway Companies.*'

The Reports for 1903 and 1904 are formal presentations of the minutes of evidence; 1903 (297) viii, 591. 1904 (305) vii, 699.

—— Report, proc., mins. of ev., app. pp. xxxii, 58. 1905

1905 (270) *viii*, 501 *re-apptd. April, o.p. July,* 1905

Col. Bowles (*Ch.*), Bell, Fardell, Fison, Galloway, Harris, Lough, Lockwood,

Nannetti, Norton, O'Connor, Peel, Samuel, Ure, Wrightson.

The Cheap Trains Act, 1883, assumed that railways would run workmen's trains; it did not make it a duty, but provided a penalty, viz. the withdrawal of the remission of passenger duty granted by the Act, if a company did not provide or refused to provide such trains. The Board of Trade was entitled to take the initiative and institute an enquiry, but had never done so. Considerable divergencies existed in the practices of companies in the matter.

Applicants for facilities should have an equal right with the railway companies to request the Board of Trade to refer matters in controversy to the Railway and Canal Commission and to appeal to the Commission against any order of the Board of Trade. Where districts were only in process of development and there were not yet enough workmen to warrant a workmen's train, workmen's tickets for use on selected trains should be issued, if the statutory tribunal so directed. The statutory limits of the time of running workmen's trains, after 6.0 p.m. and before 8.0 a.m., had been criticized as compelling workmen to waste time in travelling earlier than was necessary, though the companies argued that trains later than 8.0 a.m. would tap a different class of person. The Committee decided not to define 'workman', but that the time limits should be removed and the Tribunal given discretion to determine the hours of arrival and departure. Other recommendations were that the Tribunal should be given power to control the conditions of issue of tickets; separate compartments for women should be provided in crowded workmen's trains; individual sailors should be given the same facilities as were given to parties of five from the port of discharge to home. The proceedings of the Committee contain alternative draft reports.

Railway Rates (Preferential Treatment)

Dept. Cttee. Rep. pp. iv, 41. 1906. Mins. of ev., apps., index. 1906

1906 Cd. 2959, lv, 1. *Mins. of ev., etc.*; 1906 Cd. 2960, lv, 47 *apptd. April*, 1904. *sgd. April*, 1906

Lord Jersey (*Ch.*), Kenyon-Slaney, Mackay, Jekyll, Owens, Gooday, Brown.

'*To inquire as to the Rates Charged by Railway Companies in Great Britain in respect of the Carriage of Foreign and Colonial Farm, Dairy, and Market Garden Produce from the Ports of Shipment, or of arrival, to the principal Urban Centres, and to report whether there is any evidence to show that preferential treatment is accorded to such produce as compared with home produce, and if so what further steps should be taken either by legislation or otherwise to secure the better enforcement of the law in the matter.*'

The majority of the Committee interpreted 'preferential treatment' as meaning preference beyond what was sanctioned by law, i.e. 'undue preference'. The complaints about preferential treatment had dealt mainly with the discrepancies between rates charged on foreign agricultural produce and those charged on home produce. There was prima facie preference in that rates on the former were often lower even though the distances covered were greater. The companies had, however, justified this by the greater bulk, more regular supply and better packing of the foreign consignments, and the necessity of quoting rates to meet competition by water, whether by canal or sea. Further, Parliament had explicitly recognized the legitimacy of charging lower rates on long hauls and large quantities. There was no proof of undue preference being granted to shipments of foreign produce, and therefore no further legislation was considered necessary. There had not been any extensive use of existing remedies; traders could make formal complaints to the Board of Trade or the Railway and Canal Commission.

In a dissenting report Mr. Haygarth Brown understood the term preferential treatment to mean differing charges for a service in proportion to the cost of that service. He was satisfied that, in this sense, preferential treatment to foreign produce existed, but whether it amounted to undue or illegal preference was outside the terms of reference. Owing to the complex way in which rates were calculated agriculturists had no way of determining whether preference was being given. The Board of Agriculture should obtain particulars of rates and their composition, assist the presentation of complaints to the Board of Trade, and meet either the whole or part of any expenses incurred by complainants. Appendix 10 is a Memorandum by Sir Francis Hopwood, Board of Trade, on *Undue Preference*.

See *Railway Rates and Facilities*. Correspondence between Bd. of Agric. and Fish., and Railway Companies; 1904 Cd. 2045, lxxxiv, 871.

Railway Conference

Rep., apps. pp. 174. 1909

1909 *Cd.* 4677, *lxxvii*, 135
apptd. Feb., 1908. *sgd. May*, 1909

Adam, Askwith, Beasley, Burton, Butterworth, Ellis, Fay, Granet, Inglis, F. H. Jackson, W. F. Jackson, Johnson, Lewis, Mitchell, Mond, Moon, Owens, Siemens, Smith, Spender.

'To review some of the more important questions that from time to time have been raised between the railway companies on the one hand and the traders and general public on the other.'

Questions which had arisen between the railway companies and the general public were considered. Detailed recommendations were made regarding increases of rates and charges, owner's risk rates, goods carried in merchandise trains, perishable merchandise carried in passenger trains and dangerous goods; an agreed code of regulations regarding the use and working of private owner's wagons was submitted. There were recommendations for the simplification and cheapening of procedure for the acquisition of and compensation for land. It was agreed that for settling disputes the procedure under the Railway and Canal Commission Court was formal and costly and therefore the preliminary procedure should be before the Registrar to the Commissioners, who, if desired, might receive the assistance of assessors, whose decisions should be final if so agreed. Such a cheap and informal way would follow the practice of the Commercial Court. A Railway Advisory Committee should be established.

A Committee of the Conference considered the conditions and procedure for working agreements, combinations and amalgamations of railways, and had before them memoranda on the subject by railways' and traders' representatives (App. II), an historical Memo. on the attitude of the State towards working agreements and combinations (App. V) and a Memo. on the Existing Powers of Railway Companies to make arrangements with each other (App. VI), both prepared by the Board of Trade. On the question of whether further regulation of such arrangements was necessary, the Committee agreed that where under any special Act incorporating Part III of the Railway Clauses Act, 1863, two or more companies are authorized to make a working agreement subject to the approval of the Railway and Canal Commission, the Commission should have power to insert protective conditions with the right to enforce the order to any person affected by it. The Committee did not carry its investigations further.

See App. IV. *Railways in Germany.* Rep. *Railways in Austria and Hungary.* Rep.; 1909 Cd. 4878, lxxvii, 309. *Railways in Belgium, France and Italy.* Rep.; 1910 Cd. 5106, lvii, 137.

Railway Agreements and Amalgamations

Dept. Cttee. Rep., app. pp. 49. 1911.
Mins. of ev., apps., index. 1911

1911 *Cd. 5631, xxix*, Pt. II, 1. *Mins. of ev., etc.*; 1911 *Cd. 5927, xxix*, Pt. II, 51 apptd. *June*, 1909. *sgd. April*, 1911

R. Rea (*Ch.*), Beale, Franks, L. Hamilton, Levy, Moon, L. Newton, Roberts, Russell, Siemens.

'*To consider and report as soon as practicable what changes, if any, are expedient in the law relating to agreements among railway companies, and what, if any, general provisions ought to be embodied for the purpose of safeguarding the various interests affected in future Acts of Parliament authorizing railway amalgamations or working unions.*'

Railway transportation is a service which can be supplied by a limited number of undertakings between which combination is easily accomplished and the out-of-pocket expenses attributable to a particular consignment are small. The second element both affects the results of competition and provides the motives for regulating it. The efforts of the companies to avoid competition have been successful and the era of competition is passing away. Such competition as exists has helped to produce the equalization of rates on the basis of the shorter route, the equalization as between competing ports and an inland centre and between competing ports and different inland centres. It has also operated to keep down the charges for subsidiary services and to maintain the facilities offered. But many of these rates and conditions were already the subject of agreement between the companies. The combination between the companies might take the form of amalgamation, working unions, leases or working agreements for the pooling and division of receipts and for uniformity of rates and charges. With these uniformities the public gets less benefit from competition and none of the advantages of complete combination.

The effects of the limited degree of competition still existing are not necessarily to the public advantage, but legislation cannot prevent companies from coming to an understanding or from ceasing active competition. Continued co-operation and a more complete elimination of competition are inevitable and can be beneficial to the public provided there are safeguards.

The Committee rejected as impracticable a proposal that all agreements should require sanction and preferred general legislation designed to protect the public against any changes to its disadvantage, whether these were the result of formal agreements or not. Amongst the detailed recommendations made for this purpose were that railways should have to justify the diminution or withdrawal of a service or a charge made for a service hitherto rendered gratuitously, and that these conditions should apply also to passenger fares. Changes in the conditions of owners' risk rates, more decentralization of machinery for dealing with complaints, and publicity for rates were also suggested. Working and pooling agreements should be published and the constitution and functions of conferences made public. When companies extend working agreements, etc., the systems should be deemed one system and maximum rates reckoned continuously. When companies extend into statutory unions, the maximum charges should generally be assimilated to the lower level. Where acts provided for amalgamation, they should contain clauses protecting railway servants from undue dismissal, providing compensation and protecting pension rights and funds.

Electrification of Railways

Advisory Cttee. Interim Rep. pp. 5. 1920

1920 *Non-Parl. Min. of Transport* apptd. *March*, sgd. *July*, 1920

A. B. S. Kennedy (*Ch.*), Aspinall, Cooper, Dawson, Cribb, Merz, Nash, Simpson, Smith, Snell, Thornton.

'(i) *Whether any regulation should be made for the purpose of ensuring that the future electrification of railways in this country is carried out to the best advantage in regard to interchange of electric locomotives and rolling stock, uniformity of equipment and for other matters; (ii) if any such regulations are desirable, what matters should be dealt with, and what regulations should be made; (iii) how far it is desirable, if at all, that strips or sections of railways already electrified, should be altered so that they may form parts of a unified system.'*

For future electrification of railways there should be certain general regulations directed to ensure standardization of methods and appliances. Details are given as to standard pressure of direct currents, etc., exceptions being made for the Brighton line which has extensions actually under construction.

—— Final Report. pp. 9. 1921

1921 Non-Parl.
sgd. June, 1921

Further consideration was given to the interchangeability of equipment and stock on the various railway systems, especially in relation to live wires, etc.

Railway Accounts and Statistical Returns

Dept. Cttee. Rep., apps. pp. iv, 65. 1909. Mins. of ev., index. 1910

1909 Cd. 4697, lxxvi, 705. *Mins. of ev., etc.;* 1910 *Cd. 5052, lvi,* 357
apptd. June, 1906. *sgd. May,* 1909

A. C. Cole (*Ch.*), Acworth, Bailey, Barnes, Fountain, Owens, Paish, Peel, Whitelaw.

'*To consider and report what changes, if any, are desirable in the form and scope of the Accounts and Statistical Returns (Capital, Traffic, Receipts and Expenditure) rendered by Railway Companies under the Railway Regulation Acts.*'

A close study of the form of accounts and statistical returns led to the following recommendations: Annual accounts and a uniform financial year for all companies should be adopted. A Standing Committee, on which the companies should be represented, should be set up to ensure uniformity of practice in the preparation of accounts and returns. Revised forms of the latter, presented by the Committee, should be adopted as the statutory forms. The statistical returns were meagre, they were not framed on any definite system, and the information they contained was very incomplete. The form of returns contained in Appendix I should be adopted as the statutory form.

There had been much controversy over the usefulness of ton-mile and passenger-mile statistics. These figures were compiled by nearly all foreign railways, but English companies in general did not use them. Apparently goods rates and passenger rates were declining and the separation of the two chief factors influencing earnings per mile, changes in average train load and in average charges, was possible with ton-mileage and passenger-mileage statistics. While such statistics would be of considerable value, a large part of their usefulness would no doubt be lost if compilation were compulsory and since there was no great demand for the statistics, the Committee merely recommended that the companies seriously consider the question. Acworth, Paish and Peel disagreed with this conclusion, declaring that ton-mileage and passenger-mileage statistics should be made statutory, in a form they suggested in Appendix II.

Railway Superannuation Funds

Dept. Cttce. Rep., apps. pp. iv, 98. 1910. Mins. of ev., apps., index. 1911

1910 Cd. 5349, lvii, 35. *Mins. of ev., etc.;* 1911 *Cd. 5484, xxix,* Pt. I, 687
apptd. May, 1908. *sgd. Aug.,* 1910

Lord Southwark (*Ch.*), Bayley, Fraser, Fry, Hall, Selbie, Wardle.

'*To inquire into the constitution, rules, administration and financial position of the Superannuation and similar Funds of Railway Companies; and to report whether it is desirable that all such Funds should be organized on a uniform basis as regards contributions and benefits, or whether any other changes should be recommended.'*

The contributions to the Superannuation Funds were made by both the company and the employee. The benefits for salaried employees had been based on one or a combination of three systems: the 'average salary', the 'last seven years' average salary' and the 'money value' systems. The first was in greatest use and was considered to be the most financially sound and best suited for the objects of a Fund. The Pensions Funds for the wages staff were not based on contributions of a fixed percentage of salary, as were the Superannuation Funds, but on fixed weekly payments. To prevent these Funds drifting into insolvency, as they had in the past, it was recommended that periodic valuations by actuaries be made.

Uniformity of contributions and benefits was impracticable. Schemes for new Funds should be prepared on the advice of actuaries and the Committees, to which Bills dealing with the Funds would be referred, should obtain special reports on them.

3. ROADS AND ROAD TRAFFIC

Highway Authorities and Administration in England and Wales

Dept. Cttee. Pt. I. Rep. pp. xvi. 1903. Pt. II. Mins of ev., apps., index. 1903

1904 Cd. 1793, *xxiv*, 279. *Mins. of ev., etc.*; 1904 Cd. 1794, *xxiv*, 295 *apptd. March, sgd. Aug.,* 1903

J. G. Lawson (*Ch.*), Dorington, Stanley, Scott-Montagu, Bull, Pickmere, Kent, Woodbridge, Challenor.

'To inquire into the general condition and sufficiency of the roads in England and Wales, and to report whether any, and if so what, amendment of the law relating to these matters or its administration is *desirable in view of the various purposes for which the roads now are or shortly may be utilized, and particularly whether any change of the authorities who have control over the roads or of their powers is required.'*

The enquiry was undertaken largely as a result of representations made to the President of the L.G.B. by the Road Improvements Association.

The total number of Highway Authorities in England and Wales (excluding the Administrative County of London) was 1,855. The Great North Road from London to Edinburgh was divided for administrative purposes amongst 72 authorities, whilst another road 18 miles in length, passed through 12 different Highway Authorities. Complaints were directed against want of uniformity, the excessive cost of repairs carried out by the U.D.C.s, and the friction which arose between the authorities over costs, materials and standards of maintenance. One witness, Jeffreys, stated that whilst there was nothing to prevent authorities promoting a bill for a joint scheme to make a new road, it was never done because of existing legal and administrative complications. In some counties nearly every road of importance has been declared a main road, in others there has been a strong disinclination to take over roads as main roads.

County Highway Boards, composed of representatives of counties and county boroughs, should be created to define main roads and to be completely responsible for them. As new forms of traction for long-distance traffic were making the maintenance and efficiency of trunk roads a national concern, some of them should be selected as National Roads and should be given State assistance. A central department, which might be a department of the L.G.B., should be set up to report to Parliament upon the condition of the roads under its supervision, to act as an advisory body to other Highway Authorities, and to approve the appointment of surveyors. There are numerous recommendations on changes in the law relating to highways, including the powers of counties regarding light bridges, the acquisition of land, widening and alternative routes.

Motor Cars

Dept. Cttee. Pt. I. Rep. pp. 15. 1904. Pt. II. Mins of ev., apps., index. 1904

1904 Cd. 2069, *lxxix*, 159. *Mins. of ev., etc.*; 1904 Cd. 2070, *lxxix*, 175 *apptd. Jan., sgd. April*, 1904

H. Hobhouse (*Ch.*), Arrol, Monro, Law, Deacon, Harris.

'*To inquire and report with regard to any regulations which should be made under section 6 of the Locomotives on Highways Act, 1896, and section 12 of the Motor Car Act, 1903, as respects any class of vehicle, for the purpose of increasing the maximum weights of three tons and four tons mentioned in section 1 of the former Act, and with regard to any conditions as to the use and construction of the vehicles which should be made by any such regulations.*'

The development of the heavier types of motor traffic was unduly restricted by Section 14 of the Highways Act, 1896. The maximum weights should be increased to five and six and a half tons, and cars over two tons unladen weight should be marked with both unladen and gross weight. Maximum speeds for cars with various types of metal tyres are suggested.

Motor Cars

R. Com. Vol. I. Rep. pp. iv, 82. 1906. Vol. II. Mins. of ev., apps., index. 1906

1906 Cd. 3080, *xlviii*, 1. *Mins. of ev., etc.*; 1906 Cd. 3081, *xlviii*, 89 *apptd. Sept.* 1905. *sgd.* —

Lord Selby (*Ch.*), L. Winchester, Harrel, Forwood, Henry, Mure, Monro.

'*To enquire and report as to* (1) *The working of the Motor Car Acts, 1896 and 1903, and of the Regulations under them;* (2) *The law and practice in relation to motor cars in the principal Foreign Countries;* (3) *What amendments, if any, should* be made in the Motor Car Acts and the Regulations under them; (4) *The injury to the roads alleged to be caused by motor cars; and* (5) *Whether any, and if so what, additional charges should be imposed in respect of motor cars, and how any money thus raised should be applied.*'

After the Locomotives and Highways Act, 1896, which had imposed much less stringent regulations, the use of motor cars had grown rapidly. This development had, however, led to further demands for relaxation, and also to complaints from the general users of the highway. The Motor Car Act, 1903, which raised the maximum speed limit from 14 to 20 miles an hour, but also imposed penalties for driving negligently, recklessly and at a speed or in a manner dangerous to the public, required drivers to have a licence, and to stop in case of accident, and provided for registration and identification numbers, etc. During the effective life of the Act the number of motor cars had increased by over 80 per cent and many witnesses had complained of dust, noise, smoke, etc.

Any general Motor Car Act should deal with tractor engines as well as cars. Speed should not be punished as speed, but when it was dangerous. The general speed limit of 20 miles per hour should be abolished and reliance placed on the prohibition of negligent or dangerous driving, speed being a possible element of danger. Local authorities should have power to reduce the limit to 12 miles an hour in towns and villages, dangerous corners, steep hills, etc. The maximum speed of heavy cars from 2 to 3 tons and with non-resilient tyres should be reduced to 5 miles an hour. Local authorities should be empowered to remove obstructions to the public view on rural highways. Cars should be registered annually and a registration card carried in the car.

The chief remedy for the great increase of dust due to fast-travelling motor cars was in the improved construction and maintenance of roads.

In most parts of the country improved construction would be an economy. The best type of macadam was most suitable; experiments with tar, tar macadam, etc., had not been on large enough scale to afford satisfactory proof of their success and cost. The taxes on motor cars should be consolidated and increased to the scale suggested, and the proceeds devoted to the improvement of roads. These taxes should not be passed through the Local Taxation Account; if they were the sums might not be used for or have any relation to the amount expended on road improvements. They should be administered by a central department, which should allocate them in part payment of costs incurred by local authorities not in ordinary and customary repairs, but on work intended to provide more durable and less dusty roads, and the removal of danger to traffic, etc. Henry and Monroe dissented from the proposal to abolish the general speed limit, which had not been uniformly enforced. It should remain, so that it could be applied when required.

The Horse-Power Rating of Motor Cars

Cttee. Rep. pp. 8. 1912. Mins. of ev., apps., index. 1912

1912–13 *Cd.* 6414, *xlii*, 229. *Mins. of ev., etc.*; 1912–13 *Cd.* 6415, *xlii*, 237
apptd. Dec., 1911. sgd. —

B. Hopkinson (*Ch.*), Beaumont, Clerk, Hicks, O'Gorman.

'To consider the Provisional Regulations which have been made under Section 86 (2) of the Finance (1909–10) Act for determining the horse-power of motor cars, and to report whether any amendments are desirable, with special reference to the equitable treatment of steam cars and electric cars.'

The horse-power of an engine depends on the conditions under which it is measured; racing power, touring power and power developed where the

car was free of traffic restrictions, for example, all giving different results. The basis of rating should be the average power which an engine could develop in regular use on the road, if there were no restrictions on speed other than those imposed by the car itself. No absolute measure of horse-power was possible, but a common standard would make possible a scale of relatively correct measures; this was sufficient for taxation purposes. Detailed technical amendments to Regulations giving effect to this were recommended.

Licensing of Partially Disabled Men as Drivers of Public Motor Vehicles

Cttee. Rep., apps. pp. 34. 1916

1916 *Cd.* 8314, *xxii*, 557
apptd. Jan., sgd. July, 1916

F. L. D. Elliott (*Ch.*), Bowerman, Craig, Eve, Orde, Simpson, Smith, Stanley.

'To consider and report whether, having regard to the normal conditions of traffic in the Metropolis, licences to drive motor cabs, motor omnibuses or tramway cars should be granted to men who suffer from some partial physical disability by loss of a limb or other similar cause, and, if so, within what limitations.'

As there had been an increase in the number of serious accidents the Committee could not recommend the admission of less efficient drivers to public vehicles; the safety of the public was the first consideration. Licences should not be given to men who had lost an arm, hand, leg, foot or eye. Cases of minor disabilities should continue to be judged individually at the discretion of the Commissioner of Police, with power of reference to a special medical referee.

—— Report. pp. 4. Mins. of ev. 1919

1919 *Cmd.* 312, *xxv*, 737. *Mins. of ev.*; 1919 *Cmd.* 333, *xxv*, 741

add Blain, Waring, del. Stanley, Eve.

'To review the conclusions arrived at by the Committee on the Licensing of Partially Disabled Men as Drivers of Public Motor Vehicles which reported on July, 1916, and to report whether those conclusions should be re-affirmed or modified.'

The Committee re-affirmed the recommendations of the 1916 Committee so far as they related to the loss of hand, arm, foot or leg, and to minor disabilities, but those relating to eyesight should be modified. As a result of the Report of 1916 some licensed men who had been driving public vehicles for years were deprived of their licences through failure to come up to the standard laid down. No man with only one eye should be allowed to drive a public vehicle, and for all other men regular standards of ocular efficiency should be introduced. There should be two standards of vision—the high (1916) standard to be applied to all new entrants, and a lower standard to be applied to men who had been continually licensed for three years and whose disability could be deemed to be balanced by experience. New entrants and those licensed under the lower standard of vision should be tested every five years.

London Traffic

Reps.

See *London.* p. 57.

4. SEA TRANSPORT

Steamship Subsidies

Sel. Cttee.

'To inquire into the Subsidies to Steamship Companies and Sailing Vessels under Foreign Governments, and the effect thereby produced on British Trade.'

The first Report is a formal presentation of the minutes of evidence; 1901 (300) viii, 271

—— Report, proc., mins of ev., apps., index. pp. xxvi, 311. 1902.

1902 (385) *ix*, 297
re-apptd. May, o.p. Dec., 1902

E. Cecil (*Ch.*), Cayzer, Cust, Denny, Duke, Joyce, Lawrence, Norman, Nussey, Price, Redmond, Ropner, Sassoon, Thomas, Vincent.

A review of the subsidies of various kinds paid by foreign governments to their shipping lines shows that amongst the conditions on which they are paid are a requirement as to speed in the case of mail subsidies, compliance with Admiralty requirements, restriction on the sale of subsidized vessels to foreigners, nationality of the crews, and some control over freight rates. The Committee thought that a speed condition should be attached to every subsidy; subsidies by the Admiralty are justified only for securing speed in a limited number of vessels; as a retaining fee for mercantile vessels they have little use, since in war the Admiralty can commandeer on the basis of payment of fair value. No subsidy should be granted except on the condition that the whole or partial sale or hire of a subsidized vessel required Government permission. On subsidized vessels a proportion of the officers and crew should be British subjects; a majority of the directors of subsidized companies should be British.

It is impossible to prove precisely how much effect foreign ship subsidies have on British trade as compared with the contributing effect of other causes. Orders have been placed with foreign instead of with British manufacturers on account of lower freights; transfer of ships to foreign ownership is due to a number of causes, of which the desire to secure foreign subsidies is one. Other causes include the enforcement against British ships of Board of Trade regulations which cannot be enforced on foreign ships, the reservation of the coasting trade by foreign countries, and imposition of light dues, from which foreign shipping is usually free. But shipping subsidies are the minor factor in the development of foreign shipping, industry and commercial skill being the major. On the whole, despite the subsidies, British steam shipping has held its own and can continue to do so under fair conditions. The general system of subsidies other than for services rendered is costly and inexpedient. Special cases may occur where imperial considerations require fast direct communication; a case exists in East Africa, where there is no direct British service.

Merchant Shipping Legislation

Report of a Conference between representatives of the United Kingdom, the Commonwealth of Australia, and New Zealand. pp. viii, 177. 1907

1907 Cd. 3567, liv, 541

In his opening address the chairman, the Rt. Hon. David Lloyd George (President of the Board of Trade), said that questions had arisen in the working of the New Zealand Shipping and Seamen's Act, 1904, and the Australian Navigation and Shipping Bill in relation to Imperial Legislation. There was apprehension amongst British shipowners lest there should be imposed on British ships in Colonial ports restrictions and requirements inconsistent with those imposed by Imperial Legislation. Understanding and uniformity was therefore required. A statement of the conclusions arrived at is given in the form of the resolutions passed at the Conference on a wide variety of topics, e.g. scale of provisions, coasting trade, encouragement of British seamen, eyesight tests, load line, payment of wages.

See *Navigation Bill of the Australian Commonwealth*. R. Com. Rep.; 1906 Cd. 3023, lxxvii, 149.

National Guarantee for the War Risks of Shipping

Cttee. Rep. pp. 50. 1908. Vol. II. Mins. of ev., apps. 1908

1908 Cd. 4161, lviii, 1. *Mins. of ev., etc.*; 1908 Cd. 4162, lviii, 53 apptd. — sgd. —

A. Chamberlain (*Ch.*), Finlay, Glen-Coats, Mackay, Murray, Smith, Ottley, Beauchamp, Gladstone, Jackson, Lindley.

'To consider and report (a) Whether it is desirable that the State should undertake to make good to shipowners and traders losses incurred through the capture of shipping by the enemy in time of war. (b) If so, whether such indemnity should be granted gratuitously or should be coupled with the payment of premiums calculated to recoup the State—either wholly or in part—for the cost to be incurred. (c) What conditions should be attached to the grant of the indemnity, and what arrangements should be made for the proper working of the scheme.'

The Royal Commission on the Supply of Food and Raw Materials in Time of War 1905 (paras. 266-9) recommended the appointment of a Committee to investigate the possibility of a national indemnity against war shipping losses. Although the evidence was conflicting, the Committee could not recommend that the State should make good to owners and traders the losses which might be incurred in wartime. Many shipowners and traders had argued that the absence of a 'National Guarantee' would either cause shipping to be laid up or transferred to neutral flags and that prohibitive insurance costs would raise the price of imports. These fears were exaggerated. Various schemes of contribution by shipping were examined and declared impracticable. The alternative, a free indemnity, would be administratively expensive, subject to many fraudulent claims and was not merited by the anticipated losses. The fact that the merchant or shipowner was compensated for losses would not ensure the nation its supplies, which depended on the safe arrival of cargoes. The only guarantee of that was the maintenance of a strong navy.

In a Note on the Draft Report, Sir George Clarke considered that an indemnity scheme based on fixed rates (as given in his memorandum) would meet most requirements, and that the Report had not adequately examined this scheme. He also thought that war would cause a grave disturbance in the insurance market and that a contributory indemnity scheme would allay early panic.

Insurance of British Shipping in Time of War

Cttee. of Imperial Defence. Sub-Cttee. Rep. pp. 20. 1914

1914 *Cd.* 7560, *lxx*, 121
apptd. May, 1913. *sgd. April*, 1914

F. H. Jackson (*Ch.*), L. Inchcape, Hill, Beck, Lindley.

'*To consider, without prejudice to the question of policy, whether an administratively practicable scheme can be devised for submission to His Majesty's Government, which will secure that, in case of war, British steamships shall not be generally laid up, and that oversea commerce shall not be interrupted by reason of inability to cover the war risks of ships and cargoes by insurance, and which will also secure that the insurance rates shall not be so high as to cause an excessive rise of prices.*'

Any scheme should be on the basis of reasonable contributions by owners of ships and cargoes, should aim not at a profit but at keeping trade going, while the State should be protected against incalculable losses. The insurance of hulls against war risks had passed from underwriters to clubs and mutual insurance associations, with which were insured £87 mn. out of £127 mn. of British shipping. Most of the remainder was uninsured. The mutual cover was limited to first arrival at a safe port after the outbreak of war, and was not extended to voyages started afterwards. Nearly 70 per cent of the ships in foreign trade would therefore be found in a safe port and would remain there until fresh insurances were effected. Existing clubs and associations should extend their policies for current voyages up to arrival at the final port of the voyage,

and issue policies to cover new voyages. The State should re-insure 80 per cent of these risks, and receive 80 per cent of the premium for voyages started after the outbreak.

Cargo-owners were not a distinct body like ship-owners; there was no combination for purposes of insurance, which was effected in the open market. But much cargo, especially grain, wool and cotton, was not insured against war risks. No arrangements should be made for the insurance of cargoes afloat at the outbreak of war. Immediately after it, a State insurance office should be opened for new voyages, the premium charged being between 5 per cent and 1 per cent.

On an estimate of 5 per cent of losses, the total loss on hulls would be £6,134,000, of which the State's share would be £4,907,000. On the same basis the cargo losses would be covered by a premium of 1 per cent.

Shipping Rings and Deferred Rebates

R. Com. Vol. I. Rep. pp. iv, 120. 1909. Vol. II. Apps. 1909. Vols. III–IV. Mins of ev., index. 1909. Vol. V. Sub-Com. Rep., mins. of ev., apps., *South Africa.* 1909

1909 *Cd.* 4668, *xlvii*, 1. *Mins. of ev., etc.*; 1909 *Cd.* 4669, *Cd.* 4670, *xlvii*, 127. 1909 *Cd.* 4685, *xlviii*, 1. *Sub-Commission. Report, etc.*; 1909 *Cd.* 4686, *xlviii*, 393
apptd. Nov., 1906. *sgd. May*, 1909

A. Cohen (*Ch.*), L. Inverclyde, Lawrence, Bell, Lewis, Bateman, Gonner, Maddison, Mitchell, Philipps, Sanderson, Barbour, Macdonell, Collins, Birchenough, Barry.

'*To inquire into the operation of Shipping "Rings" or Conferences generally, and more especially into the system of deferred rebates, and to report whether such operations have caused, or are likely to cause injury to British or Colonial trade, and, if so, what remedial action, if any, should be taken by legislation or otherwise.*'

Majority Report. Cohen, L. Inverclyde, Lawrence, Bell, Lewis, Bateman, Gonner, Maddison, Mitchell, Philipps, Sanderson.—The substitution of steamships for sailing ships and the development of telegraphic facilities made possible organized and regular services of vessels sailing and arriving at fixed dates. The tramp, which is a self-contained unit not attached continuously to any route, but transferring from one route to another in accordance with the demands of trade, came to be used for goods of rough character shipped in bulk. In the decade before and after the opening of the Suez Canal, British steamer tonnage increased five-fold, and this was followed by bitter competition and a fall of freight rates. As a result, Conferences of shipping lines were established to maintain rates and regulate competition. The practice of making contracts with individual shippers for exclusive custom was already known, but as the number of shippers and of the classes of goods dealt with increased, these were replaced by a 'tie', the deferred rebate. This was granted to a shipper who confined his custom to a Line, on condition that if during any period he ceased to do so he lost the rebate both for that and for the previous period. This system was in due course applied to most of the outward trades. It could, however, not be applied (1) where there was no need for regular or fixed sailings; (2) where there was a lack of balance between the inward and outward traffic. For example, in the R. Plate, Australian and Indian trades, the homeward cargoes exceeded the outward cargoes, so that the shipping of the Conference Lines sent outwards could not carry all the homeward cargoes, and the Lines could not enforce on shippers an obligation to offer cargo which they could not convey; (3) where there was a large quantity of goods suitable for carriage by tramps; (4) nor could it be applied in the coasting trade, which was exposed to rail competition, or in the North Atlantic trade, where the regular service of large fast passenger boats for passenger traffic provided an excess of space for cargo.

As far as the carriage of general merchandise was concerned, a Shipping Conference using the system of deferred rebates possessed a monopoly, but this monopoly was subject to important limitations. Outside a Conference there was often shipping ready to compete. Where bulk cargoes suitable for tramps were plentiful or where the routes were near the major highways of trade and ships could be diverted to them, the Conference was more exposed to competition. There was also competition between the Lines of a Conference in the provision of facilities. But the chief limitation was not so much the actual existence of alternative transport as the possibility that it would come into existence, or that there might be common and retaliatory action by shippers.

Some of the advantages of the Conference system were due to the organization it implied: regular sailings covering many ports and taking place throughout the year, arrangements of sailings to avoid clashing, stable rates and goods classification, etc. Other advantages arose from practices or understandings which had grown up with the system, such as equal rates for all shippers, protection of shippers during rate wars, etc. The system had established itself where an organized and regular service was required, and most shippers agreed that in such cases a Conference system, fortified by a 'tie' such as that provided by the deferred rebate, was necessary. The majority of the Commission accepted that view.

But monopoly could be abused and complaints had been made that rates had been maintained at a higher level than they would have been without the system. (i) The Conferences had powers of charging which might be used to get rates in excess of those required to maintain the organized system of sailings or which enabled the Lines to maintain on the routes a number and size of ships in excess of those required by the trade. (ii) Although the system had maintained rates from the United Kingdom at the same level as rates from the Continent, rates in the open freight market of the United States were lower owing to the laws against combinations. In consequence, in the South African and Australian trades there had been some diversion of orders to the United States and there was a possibility of a permanent diversion of orders to that country. Some means of checking this abuse should be found. (iii) Objections had been made to the conditions of the rebate, e.g. the amount of rebate, the length of period, etc., and to the unrestricted power of the Conferences to determine the ports of sailing. These sources of abuse could be checked by negotiation between merchants and the Conferences in accordance with the recommendations. (iv) There were complaints of arbitrary action by the Conferences, especially in raising rates without notice, in not publishing tariffs and goods classifications, and in other arbitrary acts. While in practice the first had caused no serious disability, the grounds for the Conferences' refusal to publish rates were quite insufficient, and the complaints of arbitrary action by the South African Conference were well-founded. (v) Complaints that some of the implied obligations had not been carried out were well-founded in the case of the South African Conference.

The Commission rejected the proposal to abolish the rebate system by law, since it was a necessary means for maintaining an organized service, and only a minority of shippers wished it to be prohibited altogether. But the abuses required some check. It was undesirable that a Board of Control like the Railway Commission, representing all the interests, including those of Colonial Governments, should be given powers to fix rates and classifications, for it would be difficult to do this without making the Conferences statutory monopolies or guaranteeing

their profits. The use of government powers through mail contracts and contracts to carry government cargo was an inadequate remedy. Modification of rebate conditions by legislation was also rejected. The main proposal of the Majority was the establishment of counter-combinations of shippers to deal with the Conferences by collective bargaining. Associations of shippers and merchants should be formed for areas of the Conferences and be registered by the Board of Trade. They should be able to negotiate on rates and classifications, dates and ports of sailing, and rebate conditions, including the implied obligation of shipowners. Where Conferences and Associations failed to reach agreement the Board of Trade should be empowered, on appeal, to promote settlement by conciliation or to appoint arbitrators. When it appeared to the Board of Trade that there were good grounds for believing that important national or imperial interests were affected, it should have power to appoint persons to enquire and report to them. Associations of this kind already existed in Australia and South Africa. That in Australia had secured some concessions, but the South African Association was ineffective because it was not representative; suggestions were made for its improvement. Any Conference using deferred rebates should be required to deposit confidentially with the Board of Trade all Conference agreements and understandings, all rebate circulars and any agreement with a registered shippers' association. They should also be required to publish their tariffs and classifications of goods.

In a reservation Lord Inverclyde objected to the publication of tariffs, etc., and did not agree with supervision by the Board of Trade. Without the Conference and rebate system it was doubtful if as much capital would be invested in shipping. Maddison did not agree that Conferences were necessary to or in the interests of trade, but the results, though undesirable, were not great enough to warrant State interference.

Minority Report. Barbour, Macdonell, Collins, Birchenough, Barry.— The Conference system with the deferred rebate had created on almost all the chief ocean routes a monopoly, the limitations to which were often either illusory or declining. They had been successful in maintaining or raising the rates and the public had had to pay higher rates than they would have done in the open market. The system had been injurious to tramps. It had led to Conference Lines carrying a larger share of traffic than they would have done in free competition, and had shut out tramps who could carry goods at lower freights; the tramps were involved in waste because they were hampered in their efforts to obtain cargoes to carry from port to port. Under the Conference system the trade was not under one monopoly, but was divided into sections each the subject of a monopoly, and the maintenance of higher rates inflated the tonnage of ships provided. The maintenance of equal rates from the United Kingdom and the Continent was not an advantage, as the Majority Report had suggested, for owing to British strength in ships, tramps and trade, and the accumulation of ships in British ports because of the excess of imports, in a free market the rates from Britain might be lower than those from the Continent. The United States, where the system is illegal, had the advantage of a free market over Great Britain.

The system should be subject to control. Legislation short of a law on the lines of the Sherman Act would not be effective; but before declaring the deferred rebate illegal, an attempt should be made to give effect to a system of conciliation and supervision by the Board of Trade. There should be facilities for bringing serious abuses to the notice of Parliament and associations of shippers should deal on equal terms with Conferences of shipowners. The limitations on these associations suggested by the Majority Report would greatly reduce their efficacy. To ensure a fair trial, the Board of Trade should be free to recognize any association which was adequately representative; it should have power to direct a full enquiry where it appeared that important public interests, including those of consumers and producers, were affected or when Colonial Governments represented that enquiry was expedient. The reports and enquiries should be presented to Parliament. An annual return should be made to Parliament of all shipping conferences, conference agreements, terms of deferred rebates, ports of sailing, etc. The Minority agreed with the Majority proposal as to publication of tariffs and classifications.

Barbour, in a reservation to the Minority Report, stated that if deferred rates were made illegal the rings and monopolies would disappear. If satisfactory legislation for this purpose were difficult, legislation on the lines of the Sherman Act would be simpler and could be limited to shipping rings. The proposal for collective bargaining by associations of shippers failed because in the last resort the shipowners possessed a monopoly and the shippers could not meet them on equal terms. The nominal power of check given to the Board of Trade in the Majority Report would be ineffective.

Two members, Pember Reeves and Taylor, were unable to sign as they had been prevented from attending meetings.

Vol. V (Cd. 4686) consists of a report, together with appendices and evidence, of a Sub-Commission appointed to take evidence in South Africa. The Report, by Bateman and Macdonell, does not state conclusions or make recommendations, but draws attention to the most important points in the evidence.

Arrears of Shipbuilding

Cttee. Rep., apps. pp. 78. 1902

1902 Cd. 1055, lxi, 1

apptd. Jan., 1901. sgd. Feb., 1902

H. O. Arnold-Forster (*Ch.*), Sutherland, Evans, White.

'*To enquire and report on: Part I, the exact amount of arrears outstanding in delivery of hulls, armour, armament, gun mountings and machinery, cause of delays, and remedies to be applied; Part II, what steps should be taken to prevent arrears in the future, including simplification of Admiralty forms of contract, etc.*'

The report deals with ten specific topics relating to the extent of arrears, methods of contracting and inspection and the use of commercial shipbuilding resources.

Mercantile Cruisers

Cttee. Rep. pp. v. 1902

1902 *Cd.* 1379, *xcii*, 267
apptd. April, sgd. July, 1902

Lord Camperdown (*Ch.*), Fitzgerald, Biles, Forman, Chalmers.

'*To take evidence, consider, and report in what manner and at what cost vessels can be secured which (a) Shall combine greater speed with a large radius of action. No subsidy to be given for a lower speed than 20 knots; (b) Shall be capable of carrying an armament of at least 4·7-inch guns; (c) Shall be subdivided as under the present system; (d) Shall possess a steering gear below the water-line if this does not entail too great a cost; (e) When once subsidized shall not be transferred to a Foreign flag without the consent of the Board of Admiralty.*'

The Admiralty desired Shipping Firms to produce Mercantile Cruisers, possessing 4·7-in. guns, capable of speeds over 20 knots and conforming to other specifications. These ships would be of size, length and draught which would exclude them from trading by the Suez Canal route.

Construction costs rise rapidly with increases in speed and there might be a loss in running them in peace time. These costs could be provided either by (i) the Admiralty guaranteeing the first cost of the ships, thus enabling

the shipowner to raise capital at 3 per cent; (ii) the contribution of a lump sum or (iii) an annual payment on a period of years. To prevent the transfer of subsidized vessels to a foreign flag, the Admiralty should be the registered owner of more than half the vessel, the management and profits being left to the company.

Light Load Line

Sel. Cttee. HL. Rep., proc., mins. of ev., apps., index. pp. xiv, 374, 3. 1903

1903 (356) *vi*, 139
apptd. Feb., o.p. Aug., 1903

L. Spencer, L. Ridley, L. Muskerry, L. Wolverton, L. Brassey, L. Inverclyde.

'*To enquire and report (1) whether and to what extent British Ships are sent to sea in an unseaworthy condition by reason of their being insufficiently or improperly ballasted; (2) whether any amendment or application of the present law is desirable in connection therewith; (3) if so, to what extent any such alteration of the law could be made equally applicable to Foreign Vessels.*'

Many British ships are sent to sea in ballast, and many shipmasters and engineers consider that some are unseaworthy because insufficiently ballasted. The opinion of the Merchant Service Guild, a body of captains and officers of the merchant service, as well as that of engineers, was that the dangers would be removed by a definition of what constituted insufficient ballast, i.e. by a compulsory light load line. This was supported for the National Seamen's Federation by Mr. Clement, who stated that penalties were imposed if a ship were submerged below the Plimsoll load line, and that the same thing should happen in reverse if the light load line were adopted (q. 745). The reason for the danger arising in its present form, according to Captain Wood, Nautical Assessor to the Board of

Trade, was the change over from private ownership, where the master as the largest owner had an interest in the safety of the ship and therefore a free hand with ballast, to ownership by joint stock companies, from which the master took his instructions and asked no questions (q. 282). Instances were given of the practice of ordering masters to clear the ship of ballast before entering a port in order to save loading time; this invited the risk of a ship riding light and getting out of control. Mr. Howell from the Board of Trade produced figures to show that there had been no serious loss of life on ships in ballast.

A light load line could be fixed for vessels, but it would have to vary with their type, length of voyage and character of the trade. It would afford no protection against improper loading. The Board of Trade was opposed to any legislation at the present time. Whilst further improvement was possible, the evil was being removed. The Board of Trade had powers to detain any British or foreign vessel attempting to leave in an unsafe condition, and the Committee was confident that the Board would exercise its powers and apply for more if it considered it necessary to do so.

See *Papers showing the action taken by the Board of Trade*; 1903 Cd. 1708, lxiii, 109.

Foreign Ships (Application of Statutory Requirements)

Sel. Cttee.

'*To inquire to what extent the Statutory Requirements applying to British Ships trading to and from Ports in the United Kingdom should be made applicable to Foreign Vessels trading to and from such Ports.*'

The first Report is a formal presentation of the minutes of evidence; 1904 (299) vi, 121.

—— Report, proc., mins. of ev., apps. pp. viii, 26. 1905.

1905 (269) *vii*, 37
re-apptd. June, o.p. July, 1905

A. Bonar Law (*Ch.*), Cecil, Crean, Devlin, Doxford, Ferguson, Harris, Johnson, McArthur, McKenna, Morgan, Rollit, Runciman, Wolff, Woodhouse.

The statutory requirements to which special attention has been drawn are those for preventing overloading and unseaworthiness; those relating to passenger and emigrant ships; the provision of proper storage of grain cargoes, and rules as to life-saving appliances. Except for emigrant ships for which no recommendation was made, the Committee saw no reason why foreign ships, trading to and from ports of the United Kingdom, should not be subject to the regulations as applied to British ships.

Life-Saving Appliances

Merchant Shipping Advisory Cttee. Rep., apps. pp. 16. 1909

1909 Cd. 4552, *lxxviii*, 63
apptd. —— sgd. Dec., 1908

S. Cross (*Ch.*), Barrie, Shearer, Trenery, Wilson.

'*Line-Throwing Appliances for communicating between the ship and the shore, and between ship and ship, in cases of shipwreck or distress at sea.*'

The Report of a Sub-Committee on this subject was unanimously adopted. It was essential that vessels carry effective line-throwing apparatus for communication with the shore in times of distress. Carriage of such an appliance should be compulsory. Kites, balloons and buoys were dismissed as inadequate, rocket projectiles were preferable to guns, as their flight was easily visible and the strain on the line less. Provision should be made for sending ashore a strong rope with a properly secured breeches lifebuoy attached. Appendix II describes various appliances.

Boats and Davits

Dept. Cttee. Interim Rep. pp. 18. 1913

1912–13 Cd. 6558, *xxxviii*, 845
apptd. Aug., sgd. Dec., 1912

J. H. Biles (*Ch.*), Gough-Calthorpe, Charles, Flint, Joyce, Maxton, Morison, Stephen, Wortley.

'*To advise the Board of Trade, in the interests of safety of life—*(1) *as to what are the most efficient arrangements for stowing boats on steamships of all classes, for launching them in an emergency, and for embarking the passengers and crew;* (2) *as to whether, and if so to what extent, mechanical propulsion can with advantage be adopted either in addition to, or in substitution for propulsion by oars and sails;* (3) *as to the question of rafts, and, in particular, whether, if, of approved character, they should be allowed in substitution for boats; and if so, to what extent and under what conditions;* (4) *whether, independently of the foregoing, the Committee desire to make any recommendations with reference to the above-mentioned matters which would, in their opinion, contribute to the safety of life at sea.*'

The report is a technical discussion, with recommendations of the types of boats, etc., and in particular, of the methods of stowage.

—— Report, app. pp. 33. 1913

1913 Cd. 6846, *xviii*, 1
sgd. May, 1913

add Bearcroft, del. Gough-Calthorpe.

The report consists of a technical discussion of the form, capacity and stability of ships boats, both open and decked; their storage, and transfer across deck; types of pontoon rafts and other buoyant apparatus, and appliances for launching boats; and the fitting of motors and other engines in ships boats of the size and type in use. There are also recommendations as to embarking of passengers in the boats, etc.

Derelicts

Dept. Cttee. Rep., mins. of ev., apps., index. pp. 93. 1913

1913 Cd. 6699, *xix*, 593
apptd. July, 1912. *sgd. Jan.,* 1913

A. Williamson (*Ch.*), Benn, Bolton, Hoare, Mackay, Malan, Parry, Pelham, Samman, Wilson.

'*To inquire and report as to the measures at present taken to protect shipping from the dangers of floating derelicts and sunken obstructions, and as to what changes, if any, are desirable.*'

The General Lighthouse Authorities and Harbour or Conservancy Authorities had dealt adequately with floating derelicts and sunken obstructions on or near the coasts of the United Kingdom. The danger from derelicts on the high seas was small and was chiefly confined to the western portion of the North Atlantic.

Lloyds should be the central body for the reception and dissemination of information. The requisite charts from the Meteorological Office should be issued free to all masters. Masters of wireless-equipped vessels should be obliged to send reports of dangerous derelicts to Coast Stations and other ships. The United States' provision of cruisers to destroy wrecks on the western side of the North Atlantic was absolutely necessary, and should be continued even if it were to involve the co-operation of other nations. It was not essential to provide a vessel for destroying or removing wrecks to the eastward of the area patrolled by American cruisers. In a Reservation, Captain Mackay thought a special Naval vessel should be stationed at Halifax to search for derelicts when reported.

Sub-Division of Merchant Ships. (Bulkheads and Watertight Compartments)

Dept. Cttee. 1st Rep., *Foreign-Going Passenger Steamers.* Vol. I. Rep., apps. pp. 58. 1914. Vol. II. Diagrams. 1915

1914–16 Cd. 7743, *xxvii*, 273. *Diagrams*; 1914–16 Cd. 7809, *xxvii*, 343
apptd. May, 1912. *sgd. Nov.,* 1914

A. Denny (*Ch.*), Bain, Buchanan, Champness, Hunter (G. B.), Hunter (S.), King, Laing, Luke, Welch.

'*To advise the Board of Trade in the interests of safety of life.* (1) *As to what, in their opinion, would constitute efficient sub-division with regard to each of the classes of vessels included in the Rules for Life-Saving Appliances made by the Board of Trade under Section 427 of the Merchant Shipping Act, 1894, having due regard to the nature of the service in which they are respectively engaged.* (2) *Whether independently of the foregoing the Committee desire to make any recommendations with reference to the sub-division of vessels already built, or of new vessels, which would, in their opinion, contribute to the safety of life at sea.*'

The Report is a technical investigation covering: (*a*) the number and disposition of transverse watertight bulkheads to be recommended for each class of vessel under consideration, and the fitting of double bottoms, watertight decks, double skins, and longitudinal bulkheads; (*b*) the scantlings and arrangements necessary for securing the adequate strength of watertight partitions; (*c*) whether openings may be permitted in watertight bulkheads below the level of the bulkhead deck, and, if so, what means of closing the openings should be provided; (*d*) whether openings may be permitted in the sides of ships below the level of the bulkhead deck, and, if so, what means of closing the openings should be provided; and (*e*) the provision of pumping plant to deal either with flooded compartments or with adjacent compartments into which water may pass by leakage.

On the spacing of transverse bulkheads the International Conference on Safety of Life at Sea, 1913, considered three systems. (1) The German system in use for the last three years: (*a*) increasing the number of compartments assumed to be flooded without sinking the vessel; (*b*) increasing the assumed permeability of the spaces in the one- and two-compartment vessels as the

length of the vessel increased in each of these two classes. (2) Proposed French system. Though not fully worked out, the essential feature was the factorial treatment of floodable length. (3) The proposed British system, in common with the German system, increased the safety by increasing the number of compartments floodable; but within the one- and two-compartment standards, it increased the safety by fixing margin lines so arranged that as the length of the vessel increased, the surplus buoyancy after flooding was also increased. Fixed permeabilities were used and the margins were visible instead of being obscured by variable permeability as in the German system, or by the factor of sub-division, as in the French system. The system adopted by the Convention was a mixture of all three. The Committee found itself in substantial agreement with the Convention. Certain provisions would have to be modified, and other provisions supplemented by rules giving details of how the principles should be applied in practice. The Report is mainly concerned with the technical details, on this and the other problems named above. In drawing up these suggestions, 'regard has been had to the fact that all foreign-going passenger steamers are surveyed while building and periodically thereafter by the Board of Trade surveyors'.

See *Circumstances attending the foundering on 15th April, 1912, of the British Steamship 'Titanic', of Liverpool . . . whereby loss of life ensued.* Rep.; 1912–13 Cd. 6352, lxxvi, 541.

—— Second Report, *Home Trade Passenger Steamers. Cargo Steamers.* pp. 16. 1915

1914–16 *Cd.* 8080, *xxvii*, 409

The Report deals with passenger steamers plying within the home trade limits; plying on short excursions along the coast; plying within partially smooth water limits; plying in smooth water limits, and cargo steamers, either foreign-going or home-trade. Subject to reservations, to exceptions and modifications, the recommendations of the First Report should apply to the above four classes of passenger steamers. With regard to new cargo steamers, bulkheads constructed should have equivalent efficiency to those built in accordance with the recommendations of the First Report.

Load Lines of Merchant Ships and the Carriage of Deck Cargoes of Wood Goods

Cttee. Rep., apps. pp. 58. 1916

1916 Cd. 8204, xiii, 623
apptd. April, 1913. sgd. Dec., 1915

P. Watts (Ch.), Abell, Archer, Denny, Gravell, King, Mares, Smith, Young.

'To advise as to the attitude which should be adopted by the British representatives at the forthcoming International Conference on Load Line, and for that purpose to inquire and report whether, and if so in what respects, the Tables of Freeboard revised by the Board of Trade in 1906 need further revision in the light of the experience gained since that date of their practical working and effect.' 'To consider the question of deck cargoes of wood goods and to advise as to the regulations for the carriage of such cargoes which might properly be adopted by International Agreement.'

On 29th February, 1912, the North Briton left Sunderland with a cargo of coal to her winter load line under the revised Tables of Freeboard. She encountered a gale and after her starboard ventilator of No. 3 hold had been carried away and No. 3 hatch lifted, she foundered with the loss of 20 lives. The Court of Inquiry said that the primary cause of loss was 'insufficient freeboard'. In the case of the loss of the Walter Gervase in August 1912, the Court of Inquiry was of opinion that the freeboard was 'dangerously small'. Both cases were examined and the Committee found that the loss of the North Briton was due to the failure to unship the ventilator, and

in the loss of the Walter Gervase there was no evidence to justify the opinion respecting the freeboard. All available information was examined regarding losses for seven years before the revision of the Tables of Freeboard in 1906 and seven years after the revision and nothing was found to indicate that freeboard was the dominant factor, or that the revision of the Tables had caused increased loss. But an examination of the existing rules showed preferential treatment for certain types of vessels and anomalies in respect of the allowances to be given to certain deck superstructure. New rules were outlined for the 'Conditions of Assignment of Freeboard'. Compliance with the new rules should be required not only on the first assignment, but through the whole life of a vessel. There should also be an annual survey to ensure that various fittings and appliances are maintained in proper condition, and the Freeboard Certificate should be endorsed each year.

Examination was made of the specific condition contained in the Load Line Rules of the Netherlands, Norway and Russia under which the deeper immersion is permitted, but it was not thought desirable to make any provision in the rules for the assignment of a special timber load line. Regulations are necessary for the carriage of deck cargoes of wood goods. Vessels were inspected particularly in regard to the stowage of the wood on deck and the arrangements for securing against shifting. The rules and regulations are set out in the appendices.

Measurement of Tonnage of Steam Ships

Cttee. I. Report. pp. iii, 9. 1906. II. Mins. of ev., apps., index. 1906

1906 Cd. 3045, cix, 1. Mins. of ev., etc.; 1906 Cd. 3046, cix, 15
apptd. Feb., 1905. sgd. May, 1906

A. Bonar Law (Ch.), Blake, Denny, Emmott, L. Inverclyde, Milburn, Scott, White, Wilson, Biles, Chalmers, Lewis, Lyster.

'To inquire into the operation of Section 78 of the Merchant Shipping Act, 1894, whether or not it tends to produce in any class of ship a disproportionately low Register Tonnage in comparison with the Gross Tonnage and, if so, to report what amendments may be required by way of fixing a limit to the deduction for propelling power which shall be reasonable and equitable. Also whether it is desirable to amend Section 87 of the Act for the purpose of securing a uniformity of basis upon which rates are to be levied by the various bodies dealt with in that Section 87 and, if so, what amendments may be required in that Section.'

In assessing the register tonnage of a ship, allowance is made for propelling power space. It was alleged the existing allowance produced a low register tonnage in the case of coasting and cross Channel steamers, and swift ocean-going passenger steamers. One effect of an unduly low register was to give an inadequate return to dock and harbour authorities. Since the Board of Trade's revision of its instructions in 1901, only a very small percentage of British shipping was affected. Though not free from objection, the existing tonnage law had favoured free expansion in the manner most suited to particular trades and vessels and had encouraged ample provision for the crew and working machinery. There was no reason for the alteration of a system of measurement which had been adopted by principal maritime powers. Messrs. Biles, Chalmers, Lewis and Lyster dissented because the deduction for propelling power space was inequitable between ships and affected the revenue of certain ports—even prejudicing the dock accommodation afforded. They concluded that the deduction for propelling power should be limited to 32 per cent of the gross tonnage.

H. Tennant (Ch.), Brodie, Hills, Joyce, Walters, Cecil, Jenkins, Raphael, Partington.

'The Bill is a measure promoted by the Board of Trade to limit the deduction for propelling power in the case of screw-steamers to 35 per cent of the space which remains after deducting from the gross tonnage the deductions allowed for crew and navigation spaces. This figure had been arrived at by representatives of the Board of Trade, of the large shipowners, of the principal dock authorities, and a representative of the pilots of the Bristol Channel. . . . From this finding the representatives of the principal ports of South Wales and the representative of the pilots dissented.'

The dockowners and pilots maintained that the register tonnage, upon which they received dock and pilotage dues, is unduly low. The figure of 55 per cent in the Bill should be 35 per cent. The dockowners asserted that the relation between the gross tonnage for which the dockowners have provided by their expenditure, and the register tonnage on which their charges are based, had been altered by the present system of measurement regulations entirely to the disadvantage of the dockowner.

The figure of 55 per cent was maintained because the proposed deduction for propelling power would give a minimum figure for register tonnage of 40 per cent of the gross tonnage, a figure already prescribed by Parliament in numerous Private Acts. The opponents of the Bill admitted that only a small proportion of their trade, ranging from 5 to 14 per cent, was affected by the Bill.

Merchant Shipping (Tonnage Deduction for Propelling Power) Bill

Sel. Cttee. Reps., proc., mins. of ev., apps., index. pp. xviii, 388. 1907

1907 (256) vi, 507
apptd. May, o.p. July, 1907

Merchant Shipping Acts Amendment Bill [H.L.]

Sel. Cttee. HL. Rep., proc., mins. of ev. pp. viii, 28. 1907. Index. 1907

1907 (HL. 130) (HL. 130-Ind.) vii, 11
apptd. June, o.p. July, 1907

Lord Ampthill (*Ch.*), L. Muskerry, L. Ellenborough, L. Montagu, L. Joicey, L. Stanley.

The Committee reported the Bill, with amendments.

The Bill, promoted by the Association of Master Lightermen and Barge-owners of the Port of London, was intended to limit the liability of barge owners on the Thames. Collision with steamers had involved them in sums of money (q. 99), greatly in excess of the amounts which would have been payable if their liability had been limited by registration under the Merchant Shipping Act. Harry Gosling, secretary of the Amalgamated Society of Watermen, Lightermen and Watchmen of the River Thames, stated that the attitude of the union was that the employers' risks should not be limited without proper regulations for manning and for proper gearing of the craft. Barges were increasing in size rapidly. Each barge should have a minimum of a pair of oars, a rope and a boat hook, and should be periodically inspected (qq. 148–233). The employers agreed that further regulations should accompany limited liability.

Light Dues Exemption

Cttee. I. Rep. pp. 12. 1900. II. Apps., proc., index. 1901

1900 *Cd.* 413, *lxxvii*, 87. *Apps., etc.*; 1901 *Cd.* 446, *lxviii*, 143
apptd. March, sgd. Oct., 1900

C. Monkhouse (*Ch.*), Pelham, Murton, Vyvyan, Kent.

'*To examine the claims and suggestions received by the Board of Trade and the Trinity House for exemption from Light Dues, or for alteration of the existing scale or rules under the Merchant Shipping (Mercantile Marine Fund) Act*, 1898, *and to report thereon.*'

Before the Merchant Shipping Act of 1898, every vessel was charged a separate due for each lighthouse from which it might be assumed to derive benefit during the course of a voyage. The new system abolished payment by 'use' and substituted payment by voyage. This new method gave rise to claims for exemption in respect of certain voyages on the ground that none of the lights were of use to vessels on that voyage, and to partial exemption on the ground that the dues were heavier under the present than under the old system, e.g. in the Baltic, North German, Australian and Irish trades. No dues should be levied for voyages performed in waters neither lit nor marked by the General Lighthouse Authorities at the expense of the General Lighthouse Fund, and the home-trade scale should be extended to voyages to ports between the Elbe and the north bank of the Eider inclusive.

Lighthouse Administration

R. Com. Vol. I. Rep. pp. iv, 36. 1908. Vol. II. Mins. of ev., apps., index. 1908

1908 *Cd.* 3923, *xlix*, 457. *Mins. of ev., etc.*; 1908 *Cd.* 3937, *xlix*, 499
apptd. Aug., 1906. sgd. Jan., 1908

G. W. Balfour (*Ch.*), Adam, Herbert, Henderson, Ennis.

'*To inquire into the existing system of management of the Lights, Buoys, and Beacons on the coast of the United Kingdom by the three General Lighthouse Authorities, and as to the constitution and working of these Authorities, and to report what changes, if any, are desirable in the present arrangements.*'

The history and constitutions of Trinity House, the Commissioners of Northern Lighthouses and the Commissioners of Irish Lights were reviewed and reference made to the many local Lighthouse Authorities. There were no 'crying abuses' and the system had worked efficiently—charges of extravagance being unfounded. The recommendations were chiefly constitutional. There should be a system of retirement for the Acting Elder Brethren of Trinity House. An Elder Brother of Trinity House should act as assessor to the Scottish and to the Irish Boards respectively, but the statutory control exercised by Trinity House over the Commissioners of Northern Lighthouses and Commissioners of Irish Lights should cease. There should be a new Lighthouse Committee for the United Kingdom, with wider scope and composed of representatives of the Board of Trade, the Admiralty, the three General Lighthouse Authorities, shipowners, underwriters and cargo-owners. The Blackwall Works Establishment should receive a detailed examination as to its location and efficiency, and the accounts of each of the three General Lighthouse Authorities should be prepared in a form which would make their expenditure comparable.

In a Reservation, Ennis could not agree that the British system could not attain greater efficiency; French lighting was superior to that of the United Kingdom. France had three times more lights per mile of coast than Scotland. Proposals were made for reconstructing the constitution of the Lighthouse Authorities.

Pilotage

Dept. Cttee. Rep. pp. x, 113. 1911.
    Mins. of ev., apps., index. 1911

1911 *Cd.* 5571, *xxxviii*, 89. *Mins. of ev., etc.*; 1911 *Cd.* 5572, *xxxviii*, 213
apptd. July, 1909. *sgd. March*, 1911

K. E. Digby (*Ch.*), Brightman, Cole, Marshall, Marston, Pelham, Trenery.

'*To inquire and report as to the present state of the Law and its administration with respect to Pilotage in the United Kingdom, and as to what changes, if any, are desirable.*'

In 1911 there were in the United Kingdom 116 Pilotage Authorities divided into four main groups: Trinity Houses, Harbour Authorities, Municipal Corporations, and Pilot Boards, Trusts or Commissions. In each group there were innumerable differences in constitutions and in the manner in which

pilotage jurisdiction was exercised. Statute law relating to pilotage was contained partly in general acts and partly in local acts, and the absence of or disregard for any definite principle governing pilotage legislation had led to a 'chaotic' condition of the law and a consequent uncertainty in its administration. The most striking instance of the confusion arose from the fact that the present law recognizes in different localities opposite and inconsistent principles in regard to compulsory pilotage. In some ports it is compulsory to employ a pilot, in some compulsory to pay pilotage fees whether a pilot is used or not, in others it is 'free', i.e. there is no compulsion. A most important effect of compulsory pilotage, resulting from section 633 of the Merchant Shipping Act, 1894, was that an owner or master of a ship was not answerable for loss or damage whilst the ship was under compulsory pilotage. This has proved to be a doubtful benefit to the shipowner, enormous hardship to individuals, and a position of responsibility difficult to define or prove between master and pilot in circumstances leading to accidents, etc.

There should be a complete repeal of all local acts, charters or customs relating to pilotage, and the substitution of (i) a general act of Parliament laying down principles of pilotage; (ii) orders of a Central Authority defining the constitution and limits of jurisdiction of each Pilotage Authority; and (iii) byelaws of local Pilotage Authorities applying the general principles to the needs of the particular districts under their control. The Board of Trade should appoint Pilotage Commissioners, with powers to make orders, subject to confirmation by the Board of Trade, regarding the constitution of pilotage authorities and the limits of pilotage districts; and the examination of local pilotage byelaws. Immunity from liability of the shipowner or master for loss or damage occasioned by the fault of the pilot should be abolished; a master should at all times be legally responsible for the steering and safe conduct of his ship, and the pilot, whether he actually handles the ship or not should be his expert assistant. All ships, unless they are piloted by a duly qualified master or mate, should be obliged to employ the services of a licensed pilot when resorting to or quitting a port for which pilots are licensed or when entering a pilotage district and making use of a port within that district. Ships under 100 tons, ships passing through, and His Majesty's Ships should be exempt. Ships shifting moorings should be subject to byelaws.

Brightman and Pelham in a Reservation argue that the ideal system would be free pilotage for all ports, but as there would be difficulties in abolishing compulsory pilotage where it already existed, they are prepared to support its continuance in those districts. Marston makes a reservation regarding proceedings against pilots, and Cole a reservation on this and other matters.

Coast Guard

Inter-Dept. Conference. Rep., apps. pp. 152. 1908

1908 Cd. 4091, xcvi, 143
sgd. 1907

R. F. H. Henderson (*Ch.*), Harrel, MacLeod, Parry, Henderson (*R.*), Heron-Maxwell, Greene.

'*To consider the Naval Views on the general question of the Coast Guard Force, the effect of the policy and the arrangements which would be necessary for carrying it out.*'

Since 1856, the Admiralty had controlled the Coast Guard and now proposed (Admiralty Letter, 18th June, 1906) to reduce the service and transfer its men, other than those required for war signal or wireless telegraphy stations, to service afloat. Many Coast Guards performed Revenue services which were the concern of the Board of Customs; lifeboat and other services could be provided by various local

and other authorities, and so it seemed undesirable for the Admiralty to retain control of the Coast Guard. The existing Coast Guard Force of 4,000 was in excess of the 1,171 officers and men which the Customs would need for revenue protection (see App. B). The Coast Guard Force ashore should be reduced to Naval requirements and the Board of Customs given sole responsibility for Revenue protection. Responsibility for life-saving should be transferred to the Board of Trade and other miscellaneous functions could be managed by local authorities. Recommendations were made to effect the reduction and transfers without hardship to the personnel. Part of the Navy's costs of maintaining Revenue Protection afloat should be borne by the Board of Customs.

Port of London

R. Com. Rep., apps. pp. 192. 1902. Mins. of ev., index. 1902. Apps. 1902

1902 *Cd.* 1151, *xliii*, 1. *Mins. of ev., etc.;* 1902 *Cd.* 1152, *xliii*, 201. 1902 *Cd.* 1153, *xliv*, 1.
apptd. June, 1901. sgd. June, 1902

Lord Revelstoke (*Ch.*), Peel, Lyttleton, Giffen, Barry, Hext, Ellis.

'*To inquire into the present administration of the Port of London and the water approaches thereto; the adequacy of the accommodation provided for vessels, and the loading and unloading thereof; the system of charge for such accommodation, and the arrangements for warehousing dutiable goods; and to report whether any change or improvement in regard to any of the above matters is necessary for the promotion of trade of the port and the public interest.*'

The Port of London was in danger of losing part of its trade, not through any physical decline, but because the greater tonnage of modern vessels called for larger docks, more modern facilities and deeper river channels than it was providing. It was in danger of losing its re-export trade to the modernized Continental ports and might even cease to be the greatest distributor to the coasts of Britain. Owing to the multiplicity of authorities and the financial position of some of them, there had been little improvement to meet the new shipping requirements. The Thames Conservancy had the old duty of maintaining the river channels, but did not possess the revenue, and had not attempted to obtain the financial and other power necessary to undertake the necessary works for the permanent improvement of the river, nor was its condition such that it should be given the responsibility. Trinity House shared some buoying and lighting functions with the Conservancy, while the exclusive right of navigating lighters was in the possession of an ancient harbour guild whose monopoly had caused widespread complaint. The London and India Dock Company was unable to raise funds to construct new docks unless it were given power of levying dues which would cause keen resentment. The Millwall Dock Company was in an unfavourable financial position and the Surrey Commercial Dock Company prospered for special reasons. Even if the Dock Companies had been in a position to raise money and carry out improvements, the interdependence of proposals to deepen and improve the river and of those to improve the docks made it desirable that these two elements of the Port should be controlled by one authority.

All the powers and property of the Thames Conservancy below Teddington, and of the Dock Companies should be transferred to the new authority. This transfer should include the warehouses, but the new authority should have power to sell or lease such warehouses as it did not wish to retain for the enlargement of quays or transit sheds. The limits of the Port were defined. The Port authority should issue Port Stock to the owners so that the proprietors would be neither better nor worse off. In the next ten years, not less than £2½ mn. should be spent

upon improving channels and £4½ mn. upon modernizing docks. It was suggested that the first of these sums, i.e. that for improving the river, should be provided jointly by the City Council and the L.C.C. These two authorities should also guarantee the interest on the Port Stock. The new authority should take over the powers of the Thames Conservancy and of the Dock Companies to charge tonnage dues on shipping; its main source of additional revenue would be dues for goods.

On the assumption that the City Council and the L.C.C. accepted the financial responsibilities suggested, the constitution of the new authority should be as follows: L.C.C. 11; City Corporation 3; London Chamber of Commerce 2; Bank of England 5; and one each for the Admiralty, Board of Trade, Trinity House, Kent County Council, Essex County Council. The 'elected members' should be elected by different groups of voters, viz.: oversea (or ocean) trading shipowners 5; short-sea trading shipowners 2; wharfingers and owners of private warehouses on the river 3; owners of lighters, barges, etc., 2; railway companies connecting with docks 2. The electing persons, firms and companies should be given votes proportionate to the amount of dues they paid on goods or shipping. Other recommendations concerned the reconstitution of the Thames Conservancy for the inland river pilotage; and Custom House arrangements and the transfer of those powers of the Watermen's Company which related to the river.

See *Southampton Harbour Commission.* Rep.; 1912-13 Cd. 6347, xlvii, 1.

Port of London Bill

Jt. Sel. Cttee. Rep., proc., mins of ev., index. pp. xxii, 495. 1903

1903 (288) *viii*, 1
apptd. May, o.p. July, 1903

Lord Cross (*Ch.*), L. Wolverton, L. Brassey, L. Hawkesbury, L. Ludlow, Baldwin, Hardy, Renshaw, Mellor, Rea.

The report is a formal one to the effect that the Committee had gone through the Bill and made amendments. Some of the amendments are indicated in the Proceedings. The character and principles of the Bill were explained by J. D. Fitzgerald, K.C., Counsel for the promotion of the Bill, by the evidence of Mr. A. Bonar Law, M.P., Parliamentary Secretary to the Board of Trade, and Hon. N. M. Farrer, an officer of the Board of Trade.

—— Jt. Sel. Cttee. Rep., proc., mins. of ev., apps. pp. xxviii, 686. Index. 1908

1908 (288) x, 1
apptd. May, o.p. July, 1908

R. Rea (Ch.), L. Milner, L. Clinton, L. Hamilton, L. Dawnay, L. Ritchie, Bull Spicer, Williamson, L. Castlereagh.

The Bill examined by the Select Committee of 1903 did not advance to law. The report of this Committee on the Bill is a formal one, stating that it was expedient to proceed with it. Certain amendments are indicated in the Proceedings. The principles and character of the Bill were explained by J. D. Fitzgerald, K.C., Counsel for the promoters of the Bill, and in the evidence of Mr. H. E. Kearley, M.P., Parliamentary Secretary to the Board of Trade, and Mr. H. Llewellyn Smith, Permanent Secretary of the Board of Trade. Mr. Kearley points out some of the differences between this Bill and the previous one, and between the

Bill and some recommendations of the Royal Commission.

Schedule of Maximum Port Rates on Goods submitted to the Board of Trade by the Port of London Authority and the draft Provisional Order embodying the Schedule

Rep. pp. 14 [1910]

1910 Cd. 5156, xl, 863
sgd. April, 1910

Lord St. Aldwyn.

The Schedule was estimated to produce about £550,000 a year from maximum rates on oversea imports and £200,000 from maximum rates on exports. At the inquiry no objections to the enactment of any port rates were entertained, as Parliament had laid down the general principle that import and export rates should be levied on coastwise and oversea goods, and that the levy should commence as soon as it could be legalized. The questions discussed in the report are: definition of transhipment; rates on coastwise goods; rates or rebates on exports and re-exports; rates or rebates on raw materials; rates on the river trade; short sea trade; rates on particular goods, e.g. coal; systems of collection. Adjustments were made to the Schedule to meet objections and to assist Parliament in introducing a system of rates for the Port of London.

VIII. POST OFFICE, TELECOMMUNICATION

1. Post Office   2. Cables, Telephones, Wireless Telegraphy

1. POST OFFICE

Eastern Mail Service

Inter-Dept. Cttee. Rep., apps. pp. 11. 1904

1904 Cd. 2082, xxiii, 539
apptd. May, 1903. sgd. Jan., 1904

E. Cecil (Ch.), Forman, Anderson, Holiday, Doran, Graff, Smith, Blomefield.

'To consider the best means of providing for the conveyance of the Mails to and from the East and Australasia on the expiration of the existing contracts with the Peninsular and Oriental Steam Navigation Company and the Orient Steam Navigation Company.'

After a consideration of the conditions of speed, cost, competition, route, new places of call, etc., and the decision of the Australian Government against coloured labour, the Committee recommended that when the present contracts expire in 1905, sectional and through tenders for mail services, to commence in 1908, should be asked for. The Peninsular and Oriental Company contract should be extended for three years with 24 hours acceleration and an annual subsidy increased by £10,000, to give shipowners and companies opportunity to offer tenders and to build ships if required.

Universal Postal Union

Rep. of the British Delegates at the Sixth Congress of the Universal Postal Union, held at Rome in 1906. pp. 19. [1906]

1906 (356) *cxxi*, 687
o.p. Nov., 1906

Smith, Walkley, Davies.

The Universal Penny Postage was not practical politics. The first unit was to remain at 2½d., but succeeding units were reduced to 1½d. Other questions considered related to better facilities for pre-paid replies, etc., postcards, sample post, printed matter, etc.

Post Office (Life Insurance)

Dept. Cttee. Rep., mins. of ev., index. pp. xii, 88. 1908

1908 (311) *xxv*, 275
apptd. March, 1907. *sgd. May*, 1908

Lord Farrer (*Ch.*), Brown, Cochrane, Davies, Denman, Hewby, Turpin.

'*To consider whether it is practicable, and, if practicable, whether it is desirable, for the Post Office to provide facilities for the insurance of employers in respect of their liabilities under the Workmen's Compensation Acts, either generally or subject to limitations. And further, to consider whether it is desirable that steps should be taken to encourage the use of the present life insurance system of the Post Office; and, if so, what steps.*'

Only the second part of the terms of reference are dealt with in the Report. The Post Office life insurance system had not prospered and its extension should be encouraged. The removal of certain restrictions, together with greater publicity, would attract more business. The maximum amount of insurance should be increased to £300 and to suit the convenience of the wage-earning classes premiums should be collected more or less weekly, e.g. by a development of the stamp slip system used in connection with savings banks. As a general principle any surpluses ought to be used to benefit insurants. The funds should be invested not only in Consols, but in the most remunerative Parliamentary securities. The control of the system by the National Debt Commissioners should be confined to that of investment of funds and other matters of general finance. To ensure adequate supervision a separate annual report on the system should be made to the Postmaster General. Denman recommended that the maximum amount of insurance remain at £100, and that the commissions given to Post Office officials for obtaining contracts be increased.

Post Office Factories

Dept. Cttee. Rep. pp. ii, 42. 1912

1912–13 *Cd*. 6027, *xliii*, 303
apptd. March, 1910. *sgd. Oct.*, 1911

C. Norton (*Ch.*), Allen, Carey, Ferens, MacLean, Noble.

'*To consider and report—(1) Upon the steps to be taken to make the operation of the Post Office Factories more economical and efficient; (2) Upon the scale on which these Factories should be maintained, with special reference to the desirability of keeping the number of persons employed in them as constant as possible; and (3) Upon the policy to be pursued with regard to the manufacture and repair of telephone apparatus after the transfer to the Post Office of the National Telephone Company's undertaking.*'

At the transfer of the telegraphs to the Post Office in 1870, two factories were taken over, one from the Electrical and International Telegraph Company, and one from the Magnetic Company. Originally their function was repair work, with only a certain amount of constructional work, but since that date they have performed both functions according to the expansion and the technical developments in the Post Office services. This fluctuation, and the expansion and contraction of the work, led to difficulties in finding employment for the factory staff.

Competitive construction brings the factories into rivalry with private enterprise—a number of foreign governments maintain repair factories, but do not undertake construction work in bulk—so that the authority responsible for placing contracts is also competing for the contract. And if, as has happened, contracts are placed with the factories in order to keep the staff employed, even though the contract price may be higher than that of an outside contractor, he is unfairly penalized to the extent of cost of his estimate and tender. Save for certain special items, construction should be abandoned as the growth of repair work, or the normal wastage of staff renders this possible. The factories should no longer constitute an independent department but should be placed under the control of the Stores Department.

Post Office (London) Railway Bill

Sel. Cttee. Reps., proc., mins. of ev. pp. x, 206. 1913. Index. 1914

1913 (218) and (218-Ind.) x, 57
apptd. June, o.p. July, 1913

G. Baring (Ch.), Outhwaite, Peto, Barran, Willoughby.

The object of the Bill, presented to Parliament by the Postmaster General, was to enable the Post Office to cope more satisfactorily with the increasing volume of mails in London by the construction of certain underground railways and other works. The Bill affected private property and there were many petitions against it. The Committee's concern was that works involv-

ing so much expenditure should be as free as possible from the risk of becoming obsolete; they urged that within the powers granted by the Bill care should be given to the engineering details of the scheme.

Post Office Servants

See *Labour*. p. 217.

2. CABLES, TELEPHONES, WIRELESS TELEGRAPHY

Cable Communications

Inter-Dept. Cttee. Reps., apps. pp. iii, 84. 1902. Mins. of ev., apps., index. 1902. (Also 1st Rep. printed separately. Cd. 958)

1902 Cd. 1056, xi, 199. *Mins. of ev., etc.*; 1902 Cd. 1118, xi, 291
apptd. Nov., 1900. sgd. Aug., 1901, March, 1902

Lord Balfour of Burleigh (Ch.), L. Londonderry, Hanbury, L. Hardwicke, L. Onslow, Ardagh, Custance.

'To inquire into the present system of telegraphic communication between different parts of the Empire, and to consider in what respects it requires to be supplemented. To investigate the relations between private cable companies and the Imperial and Colonial Governments (including the Government of India), the amount of control at present exercised by these Governments, and the policy which should be pursued by them in future, especially when new concessions are sought. To examine existing rates, to report how far they are fair and reasonable; and, if not, how any reduction should be effected.'

In May 1900 a statement was made in the House of Commons on behalf of the India Office that it was practically arranged that there should be a reduction in the rates from 4s. to 2s. 6d., and then to 2s. a word. It was found later that although the Eastern Telegraph Company had a complete independent system of submarine cables from London to Bombay, the power of veto was possessed by Russia and

Germany under a Joint Purse Agreement with the Companies owning the land lines, and by Russia under the International Telegraph Convention, especially Regulation XXVII. The history of the pooling arrangements was tied up with the extension of cables, the growth of the cable companies and the development of an International Convention with its accompanying regulations.

The existing Joint Purse Agreement should be terminated, and if renewed in revised form, made subject to renewal over a moderate period. The clauses of the Convention should be amended, so that any country with a direct cable to a colony or dependence, should be allowed to fix its tariff between such places. Germany and Russia should be urged to withdraw the veto, but in case they should not do so, we should press for the withdrawal of the Regulation XXVII, as 'an arrangement which enables any foreign power possessing a fraction of a competing line to veto reductions on British lines constitutes an extreme anomaly'.

—— Second Report

The Committee was convinced that there was no widespread feeling of dissatisfaction with the present state of British cable enterprise and that such dissatisfaction as did exist was of a somewhat vague and unpractical character. Public opinion had tended to over-rate the importance of all-British routes. In view of the probability of cable cutting, a variety of alternative routes should be provided in case of war. Appreciable, although not paramount value should be attached to the provision of all-British routes and every important colony or naval base should be linked with this country by cables touching only British territory and that of friendly neutrals. 'After this, there should be as many alternative cables as possible', following commercial routes. The construction of two cables and one land line is recommended. The control exercised

by the state over cable companies included (i) conditions inserted in subsidy agreements, such as transmission speed, approved landing places, the right to take over in time of war, etc.; (ii) the power to construct competing lines; (iii) the granting or withholding of general facilities; (iv) withholding Government and unrouted messages; (v) the power to grant or withhold landing rights. Subsidies were usually given for strategic reasons, but a guarantee of a minimum revenue instead should be considered. 'Free trade in cables', i.e. permitting the landing of commercial cables, should be the normal policy and State purchase, mentioned in evidence by Sassoon, was strongly opposed. Rates were not excessive, except in the Gold Coast and Nigeria. Deferred rates should be introduced where the time required for postal communication was considerable, where the cables were not fully occupied with ordinary messages, but were sufficiently occupied to admit of real distinction between ordinary and deferred messages.

Injuries to Submarine Cables

Inter-Dept. Cttee. Rep., mins. of ev., apps., index. pp. xxv, 135. 1908

1908 Cd. 4331, xxv, 875
apptd. — sgd. Sept., 1908

J. C. Lamb (Ch.), Culley, Frederick, Fryer, Green, Marston.

'To enquire whether injury is caused to submarine cables by the operations of trawlers; and, if so, to consider and report what steps it is desirable and practicable to take to prevent such injury.'

The Board of Trade and the Post Office had received representations from Chambers of Commerce and other bodies on the complaints, which began about the year 1890, of the damage done to telegraph cables, more particularly with respect to the Transatlantic Cables in the neighbourhood of the South-West coast of Ireland. There is a strong probability, amounting practically to certainty, that injury to submarine cables is sometimes caused by trawlers. On steam trawlers the old form of trawl fitted with a beam has gone out of use and these vessels now invariably carry nets fitted with otter boards. There can be little doubt that certain types of otter boards, and boards out of repair, are capable of injuring cables. There would be little risk of injury from trawls if they were suitably constructed and in good condition. There should be a system of Government inspection which should aim at levelling up the trawling practices and gear generally to that which may be regarded as the best, and eventually an International Conference might be necessary to settle the terms of a Convention on the subject.

See *Report of the Proceedings of the Board of Agriculture and Fisheries*; 1914 Cd. 7091, xlviii, 579. *International Conference*; 1914 Cd. 7079, lxxi, 839.

Post Office (Telephone Agreement)

Sel. Cttee. Rep., proc., mins. of ev., app., index. pp. lxi, 388. 1905

1905 (271) *vii*, 113
apptd. May, o.p. July, 1905

Mr. Stuart-Wortley (*Ch.*), Benn, L. Bingham, Davies, Hardie, Helme, Holland, Lambton, Morrison, Nolan, Renshaw, Royds.

'*To consider the Agreement of the 2nd day of February* 1905 *between the Post-master General and the National Telephone Company, and to report as to any recommendations thereon whether it is desirable in the public interest that the Agreement should become binding, with or without modifications, and also whether the interests of the employees of the National Telephone Company have been duly considered.*'

In anticipation of the expiration in 1911 of the licence held by the National Telephone Company (which conducted 90 per cent of the telephone business of the country), an agreement was entered into by the Postmaster General and the Company for the taking over of the whole concern. This extended some of the principles of the London agreement (1901), which provided for the purchase of the plant of the Company in the London Exchange area in 1911. No payment was to be made for goodwill, past or future profits, or compulsory purchase. The Committee endorsed the agreement with certain modifications. They suggested that the wording of the Tramway Act, 1870, 'the then value' should be used instead of 'fair market value at time of purchase', as a legal decision had made it clear that the former phrase did exclude these elements and fixed the value of the property at the sum it would cost to construct and establish it, less depreciation. The agreement should not become operative until a pledge was given to the House that the future ownership and management of the local telephone installations (as distinct from trunk lines) now owned by Hull, Glasgow, Swansea, Brighton and Portsmouth, should not be prejudiced. No servant taken over should suffer by the transfer.

The Appendices contain 48 Papers handed in to the Committee. Amongst the witnesses giving evidence are representatives of the municipalities owning telephones.

Telegraph and Telephone Accounts

Dept. Cttee. Rep., apps. pp. 31. 1909

1909 Cd. 4520, *xxxvi*, 377
apptd. Oct., sgd. Dec., 1907, *Feb., Oct.,* 1908

C. A. King (*Ch.*), Blain, Bromley, Peat.

'*To consider the various accounts and returns presented to Parliament in connection with the Telegraph and Telephone services, and to report in what manner those Accounts and Returns can be modified or supplemented so as to show more clearly the financial results of those services.*'

In the Preliminary and Second Report proposals were submitted for re-casting the Parliamentary Estimate of Post Office Expenditure and the annual account of the Post Office Revenue, so as to distinguish telephone expenditure and receipts from telegraph expenditure and receipts. The Final Report dealt with the Annual Statutory Account and the various returns included in the Annual Report of the Postmaster General, and recommended the following series of accounts: For the telegraphs, a Revenue Account, and a Deficiency Account, including expenditure in the nature of capital and interest on the capital stock. For the telephones (I) A Revenue Account, showing income and working expenses, but not provision for depreciation; the balance to be carried to—(II) Net Revenue Account, showing surplus of income over working expenses, plus income from extraneous sources, and its application. (III) Capital Account, showing the loans raised, the expenditure thereout and the balance unexpended. (IV) Statement of balances. Specimens of accounts suggested are given in the Appendices.

Telegraph (Construction) Bill

Sel. Cttee. Rep., proc., mins. of ev. pp. vi, 60.   1911

1911 (241) *vii*, 925
apptd. Feb., o.p. Aug., 1911

H. Samuel (*Ch.*), Harmood-Banner, Norman, Dixon, Priestley.

The Committee found the case proved and reported it to the House. In his opening statement Sir Robert Hunter, Solicitor to the Post Office, said that the Telegraph Act, 1863, gave the old telegraph companies the right to put their telegraphs not only on the roads, but also upon the railways of the country, but it was qualified by the obligation to obtain the consent of the directors of the companies. At the time of the transfer in 1870, out of 88,000 lines of public telegraphs, 40,000 were constructed on railways. When the State took over the telegraphs further arrangements were made in which some railways did, and some did not, surrender rights previously held.

The main object of the Bill was to enable the Postmaster General to carry his telephones which were on roads across railways where they intersected the roads.

The Glasgow and South Western, the Caledonian, and the Great North of Scotland railway companies petitioned against the Bill, but the Committee ruled that their case had not been established.

High-Speed Telegraphy

Cttee. Rep., apps. pp. 29.   1917

1916 *Cd.* 8413, *xiv*, 699
apptd. Dec., 1913. *sgd. Jan.*, 1916

C. Norton (*Ch.*), Gavey, Lee, Mordey, Ogilvie, Slingo, Walkley.

'*To enquire into systems of High-Speed Telegraphy and to report thereon.*'

'The primary object in introducing high-speed apparatus is to effect economies by increasing the output of a telegraph wire. Except in the case of very short wires, the additional cost of providing and maintaining such apparatus is less than the cost of providing additional wires to be worked with low-speed apparatus.' In 30 years the Post Office had conducted experiments in some 31 types of apparatus designed to improve the service. The Committee instituted its tests on the following principles: '(i) The employment of equally expert operating staff at each instrument under test; (ii) the evaluation of attendant factors such as idle time due to absence of traffic, apparatus faults and line faults; (iii) the relation of theoretic speed to actual output; (iv) the comparative assessment of first costs, maintenance costs, and depreciation costs; (v) the flexibility of the apparatus in relation to fluctuations of traffic and atmospheric conditions.' The outbreak of war cut short these tests, but enough information had been obtained to enable the Committee to make recommendations. Systems on the multiplex principle were definitely superior to the automatic high-speed system for ordinary inland commercial telegraph work. Of the multiplex systems, the Western Electric had given the best results; a number of quadruple duplex installations should be ordered. The Western Electric Company's page printing on a continuous roll of paper cut off after each message was quite satisfactory, though it should not be adopted to the exclusion of tape printing. The five unit alphabet as a code for printing telegraphy was better than the morse code, news traffic and submarine cable communications being left out of account. The application of type keyboard signalling instruments to the present Baudot circuits was desirable. Creed receiving apparatus would most profitably be used in the Post Office service for news work. The application of printing methods to the less important circuits should be kept steadily in view, and early trials of the one-way and two-way installations of the Western Electric and of the light line printer of the Automatic Telephone Manufacturing Company should be made.

Radiotelegraphic Convention

Sel. Cttee. Rep., proc., mins. of ev., apps. pp. lvi, 334. 1907

1907 (246) *viii*, 1
apptd. March, o.p. July, 1907

J. Dickson-Poynder (*Ch.*), Adkins, Buxton, Edwards, Gwynn, Holland, Lambert, Lee, Macpherson, Parker, Sassoon.

'*To consider the Radiotelegraphic Convention, signed at Berlin on the 3rd day of November 1906, and to report what, from the point of view of national and public interests, would in their opinion be the effect of the adhesion or non-adhesion of this Country to the Convention.*'

The development of wireless telegraphy is shown by the fact that in the year 1899 the Marconi system had reached a stage where the Admiralty thought it desirable to obtain sets of apparatus for experiments. In 1901 an agreement of a limited character was entered into, and in 1903 a further agreement lasting until 1914 was made. In 1901 Lloyds made an agreement with Marconi which included an undertaking not to communicate with ships using any other system. By the year 1903 it was evident that the increasing use of wireless telegraphy for marine purposes had made international agreements a necessity. A conference met in Berlin in 1903 and Great Britain was represented by delegates from the Admiralty, the War Office and the Post Office. The chief proposal at the conference was that there should be 'universal compulsory intercommunication', which meant that no ship or shore station should be at liberty to refuse communication from another station on the ground that the system of wireless telegraphy employed was a different one. All the Great Powers, with the exception of Great Britain and Italy, agreed to this. Great Britain was, at that time, in the position of having no law which could enforce the provisions of the Convention. The Wireless Telegraph Act, 1904, gave the Postmaster General control over licences outside the territorial belt and the British delegates were able to sign the documents at the Second Convention held in Berlin in 1906.

The primary object of this Convention was to 'facilitate ship and shore communication', and its main provisions included: (i) the acceptance and transmission of telegrams; (ii) the adoption of uniform rules of working; (iii) the provision of the means of collecting charges and settling accounts between the different countries; (iv) arrangements for the publication of all information necessary for intercommunication; (v) rules to prevent interference and confusion in working, with adequate provisions for their enforcement; (vi) provision that, with certain exceptions, intercommunication must not be refused on account of differences in the systems of wireless telegraphy employed.

The Marconi Company was the only opponent of the Convention appearing before the Committee. They had secured something approaching a monopoly in respect of Great Britain, Italy and Canada, and they maintained that under the Convention their patent rights would be prejudiced in Great Britain. The Committee, however, advised ratification of the Convention, but suggested that provided the Marconi Company loyally co-operated, they should be compensated, if after proper conditions of audit it was found that their business had diminished.

See *Berlin Conferences*; 1904 Cd. 1832, cxi, 121.   1906 (368) cxxxvii, 825. *British Ratification*; 1909 Cd. 4559, cv, 207.

Marconi's Wireless Telegraphy Coy. Ltd. Agreement

1912–13. See *Government*. p.19

Wireless Telegraphy

Advisory Cttee. Rep. pp. 9. 1913

1913 *Cd.* 6781, *xxxiii*, 725 *apptd. Jan., sgd. April*, 1913

Lord Parker (*Ch.*), Duddell, Glazebrook, Kennedy, Swinburne.

'*To consider and report on the merits of the existing systems of long distance wireless telegraphy and in particular as to their capacity for continuous communication over the distances required by the Imperial chain.*'

The Committee was appointed on the recommendation of the Select Committee on the Marconi Wireless Telegraphy Company Agreement. There were five systems in existence—the Marconi, Telefunken, Poulsen, Goldsmidt and Galletti. From its enquiries and experiments the Committee concluded that the Marconi system was the only one capable of fulfilling the requirements for the Imperial chain, but this did not imply that the Company should be employed as contractors for all the work required. It might be better for the Government themselves to undertake the work, with scientific advice, using contractors, though the Marconi Company alone had practical experience of putting down stations and organizing traffic, etc.

In view of the rapid developments taking place the Post Office should not pledge itself to the continued use of any existing apparatus or be subject to any penalty for the disuse of apparatus installed. Two stations should be used also for experimental work. As existing patents might hinder development by preventing the combination of the best devices, the Committee laid stress on the fact that the Government was not fettered by considerations arising out of patent rights, but could use any patent on fair terms under section 29 of the Patents and Designs Act, 1907. The Post Office should have a special staff to test new inventions.

Wireless Telegraphy Research

Cttee. Rep. pp. 11. 1914

1914 *Cd.* 7428, *xliv*, 903 *apptd. — sgd. —*

Lord Parker (*Ch.*), Larmor, Norman, Glazebrook, Duddell, Wilkins, Charlton, Im Thurn, King, Slingo, Loring, Guest, Fowler.

'*To consider and report how far and by what methods the State should make provision for research work in the science of wireless telegraphy, and whether any organization which may be established should include problems connected with ordinary telegraphy and telephony.*'

The Engineering Department of the General Post Office conducted research, but it was confined to matters arising out of immediate service problems. Insufficiency of funds hampered research on the principles which underlay wireless telegraphy on its scientific side. Research by the Admiralty and the War Office was concerned with the practical requirements of these Services. In Germany and the U.S.A. liberal and extensive provision is made by the

State for research and experimental work.

Recommended, a National Committee for Telegraphic Research, a National Research Laboratory at Teddington to work under its direction, and a special scientific staff. Three members recommended that the new Committee should be provided with a fixed annual grant, but the majority thought that its primary task was to recommend to the Treasury the research which should be undertaken, and to provide annual estimates.

IX. PATENTS, COPYRIGHT, TRADE MARKS

Benefits afforded by the Patent Office to Inventors

Dept. Cttee. Rep., app. pp. 15. 1900

1900 Cd. 210, xxvi, 821
apptd. Nov., 1899. sgd. April, 1900

F. J. S. Hopwood (Ch.), Carpmael, Dalton, Kempe, Spring-Rice.

'To consider various suggestions which have been made for developing the benefits afforded by the Patent Office to Inventors.'

Classified illustrated abridgments of all specifications from 1617–1883 should be made. No action should be taken as regards the issue of reminders for repayment of patent renewal fees. To assist parties who live at a distance and those interested in a particular class of inventions, a system of deposit accounts for Patent Office publications should be experimentally adopted. The Comptroller General should be empowered to reprint specifications of expired patents. The financial provision for the Library, and the staff of the Patent Office should be increased.

Working of the Patents Acts

Cttee. Rep. pp. 12. 1901. Mins. of ev., apps. 1901

1901 Cd. 506, xxiii, 599. Mins. of ev., etc.; 1901 Cd. 530, xxiii, 611
apptd. May, 1900. sgd. Jan., 1901

E. Fry (Ch.), L. Alverstone, Houldsworth, Hopwood, Spring-Rice, Moulton, Harding, Carpmael, Hughes.

'To inquire into the working of the Patents Acts with reference to the following questions: (1) Whether any, and, if so, what additional powers should be given to the Patent Office to—(a) control; (b) impose conditions on; or (c) otherwise limit the issue of Letters Patent in respect of inventions which are obviously old, or which have been previously protected by Letters Patent in this country. (2) Whether any, and, if so, what amendments are necessary in the provisions of Section 22 of the Patents, etc., Act, 1883, and (3) Whether the period of seven months priority allowed by Section 103 of that Act to applicants for Letters Patent under the International Convention may properly be extended, and, if so, on what conditions.'

(1) The Patent Office investigated many applications which were old or had been previously protected by Letters Patent and of these 42 per cent had been anticipated in whole or in part. It was essential therefore that, in addition to existing enquiries, an examination should be made at the Patent Office into the question whether any invention claimed in a deposited specification had been claimed in the 50 years prior to the date of application. Measures were suggested to make this recommendation effective. (2) The 22nd Section of the Act of 1883 should be repealed. It contained no provision for costs, in the case of a foreign patentee was difficult to enforce, and jurisdiction depended on events following the failure of a patentee to grant licences on reasonable terms. The right of applying should be confined, as at present, to the person interested, and jurisdiction should arise when the reasonable requirements of the public have not been satisfied as a result of the patentee's neglect or refusal to work

or grant licences on reasonable terms. Jurisdiction should be transferred to the High Court and therefore accompanied by the power of awarding costs. (3) The period of seven months' priority allowed by Section 103 of the Act of 1883 might be extended to 12 months.

See Note by the Solicitor General on the Report; 1902 Cd. 1030, lxxxiii, 729.

Patent Office Extension Bill

Sel. Cttee. Rep., proc., mins. of ev. pp. vi, 2. 1903

1903 (308) *vii*, 523
apptd. June, o.p. Aug., 1903

V. Cavendish (*Ch.*), L. Balcarres, Rattigan, Trevelyan, White.

The Committee agreed to report the Bill to the House. See 3 Edw. 7. c. 41.

Copyright Bill [H.L.] and Copyright (Artistic) Bill [H.L.]

Cttee. HL. Rep., proc., mins. of ev., apps. pp. xiii, 103. 1900. Index. 1902

1900 (377) (377-*Ind.*) *vi*, 621
apptd. March, o.p. Aug., 1900

Lord Monkswell (*Ch.*), the Lord Chancellor, L. Selborne, L. Knutsford, L. Balfour, L. Hatherton, L. Thring, L. Farrer, L. Welby, L. Davey, L. Avebury.

Literary copyright covers (1) copyright properly so called, i.e. the right of multiplying copies of books; (2) performing rights, i.e. the rights of performing dramatic or musical works; (3) lecturing rights. The law is different in each case and is sometimes 'most puzzling'. The Bill proposes to give the same protection to the three types; copyright in a book is to last for the author's life and 30 years after he dies. Special provisions are proposed for certain works, e.g. posthumous works, where 42 years is substituted for 30 years, and 'news' is given protection.

The Copyright (Artistic) Bill assimulates the law for artistic work to that for literary work. In the case of pictures copyright should be vested in the author unless he assigned it in writing, but he should not exercise the right without the consent of the owner. In evidence S. Clemens (Mark Twain) argued for perpetual copyright in books on the ground that there was perpetual ownership of land. (See preambles to Bills 1900 (HL. 18), (HL. 19) iv, 203.) Other witnesses included John Murray, Edward Arnold, Thomas Brock, R.A. The Committee reported both Bills with amendments.

For previous Papers see *Select List*, p. 63.

Piracy of Musical Publications

Dept. Cttee. Rep., mins. of ev., app. pp. 85. 1904

1904 *Cd.* 1960, *lxxix*, 277
apptd. Dec., 1903. *sgd. Feb.*, 1904

E. N. F. Fenwick (*Ch.*), Galloway, Murray, Scrutton, Caldwell.

'To inquire into the complaints of Music Publishers as to the sale, especially in the streets, of pirated copies of their publications, and to report whether any, and, if so, what, amendment of the law is necessary.'

The sale of pirated music was, generally speaking, carried out in three ways; selling in the street, house to house canvass and by soliciting orders through the post. The printer usually had no fixed abode and did not put his name on the printed copy. He used lithography or some other cheap process. In 1901, 47 copyrights were infringed and in 1904, 231 piratical editions were on the market. In 15 months 1902–3, 460,000 pirated copies were seized by the police in London. Criminal proceedings under the Newspaper Act, 1869, where a printer did not print his name, usually meant that a successful prosecution did not recover costs. The Copyright Act, 1842, could not successfully restrain a person of no fixed abode who had no means to pay damages and who, if restrained, got a friend to carry on, whilst the Act of 1902 failed because there was no power of search.

The Committee recommended legislation which would give a summary power of inflicting penalties on printers and sellers of piratical works; power of arrest and power of search. The witnesses included A. Boosey and Lionel Monckton.

Law of Copyright

Cttee. Rep. pp. 48. 1909. Mins. of ev.,
    app., index. 1910

1910 Cd. 4976, *xxi*, 241. *Mins. of ev.*, etc.; 1910 Cd. 5051, *xxi*, 289 *apptd. March, sgd. Dec.*, 1909

Lord Gorell (*Ch.*), Alma-Tadema, Askwith, Granville-Barker, Boosey, Bowerman, Clayton, Cust, Cutler, Hawkins, Joynson-Hicks, Law, MacMillan, Raleigh, Scrutton, Williams.

'To *examine the various points in which the revised International Copyright Convention signed at Berlin on 13th November, 1908, is not in accordance with the law of the United Kingdom, including those points which are expressly left to the internal legislation of each country, and to consider in each case whether that law should be altered so as to enable His Majesty's Government to give effect to the Revised Convention.*'

The International Copyright Convention proposed a Union of Contracting States for the purpose of protecting the rights of authors of literary and artistic works throughout the Union. The works protected were defined to include not only books, pamphlets, etc., but choreographic works and pantomimes the acting form of which was fixed in writing, sculpture, painting, architecture, and to give composers an exclusive right over the mechanical reproduction of their works. The period of protection extended to 50 years after the death of the author.

Each article of the Convention was examined and the necessary changes in English law suggested. Three members dissented from the proposal to protect architecture, three from the proposal to extend the period of protection to include the life of the author, and from the proposals regarding the rights of a composer over the mechanical reproduction of his work. The witnesses included A. Boosey, W. Wallace, G. Bernard Shaw, Lionel Monckton, W. Heinemann and John Murray.

Trade Marks Bill

Sel. Cttee. Reps., proc., mins. of ev.,
    apps. pp. xvi, 180. 1905

1905 (231) *viii*, 257
apptd. March, o.p. July, 1905

Mr. Cripps (*Ch.*), Blake, Butcher, Eve, Fison, Moulton, Palmer, Renshaw, Tillett.

The present organization of the Patent Office should be maintained with a Comptroller of the whole office responsible to the Board of Trade. Further latitude was required in the definition of a trade mark and parties interested should have the option of appeal either to the Court or to the Board of Trade. If there has been no *bona-fide* trade user of a trade mark for a period of five years, it may be removed from the register on the application of any person aggrieved, but after seven years it should no longer be open to attack the validity of the original registration. The present powers of the Board of Trade to make general rules for the classification of goods should not be altered. There should be further protection of persons holding a Royal Warrant and, finally, statutory recognition should be given to the practice of dealing with cotton marks in the Manchester branch of the Trade Marks Registry Office.

See *Trade Marks Laws and Regulations*. H.M. Representatives Abroad. Reps; 1900 Cd. 104, Cd. 358, xc, 269.

X. LABOUR

1. FACTORY AND INDUSTRIAL REGULATION

Boilers, Registration and Inspection

Sel. Cttee. Rep., proc., mins. of ev., app., index. pp. v, 267. 1900

1900 (294) *vi*, 285
apptd. March, o.p. July, 1900

Mr. Penn (*Ch.*), Anol, Crombie, Emmott, Fenwick, Fortescue, Gallaway, Gourlay, Hazell, Heath, Hickman, Holdsworth, McGhee, Pilkington, Renshaw.

'*To inquire and report on the advisability of legislation to insure the systematic and regular inspection of boilers, with the object of reducing the risk to life and property arising from boiler explosions.*

Attention was confined mainly to boilers used for generating steam, fired either internally or externally. Some explosions occur through mistakes or the incapacity of the user and these could not be prevented by inspection. The responsibility should fall on the user, who should be subject to penalties if it is proved that an explosion has occurred through lack of care, the conditions of which are outlined. The Factory Acts should be extended to allow factory inspectors to satisfy themselves that the conditions of care and attention are being carried out.

Acetylene Generators

Dept. Cttee. Rep., apps. pp. 36. 1902

1902 *Cd.* 952, *x*, 25
apptd. Dec., 1900. *sgd. Oct.,* 1901

J. H. Thomson (*Ch.*), Boys, Jones, Lewes, Redwood, Spencer, Swinburne.

'*To advise as to the conditions of safety to which acetylene generators should conform, and to carry out tests of generators now in the market, in order to ascertain how far these conform with such conditions.*'

In view of the rapidly increasing use of acetylene generators the Committee laid down the conditions which a generator should fulfil before it could be considered safe.

Notification of Industrial Accidents

Dept. Cttee. Rep., app. pp. iv, 24. 1902

1902 *Cd.* 998, *x*, 1.
apptd. Nov., 1901. *sgd. Dec.,* 1902

H. Cunynghame (*Ch.*), Troup, Smith.

'*To consider and report upon the present system of notification of Industrial Accidents, and whether any and what legislative and administrative changes are desirable.*'

Notification of accidents serves an administrative and a statistical purpose, the one indicating how far the Factory Acts are being enforced and the other showing the causes and relative importance of accidents. The chief defects of the present system of notification of non-fatal accidents is the lack of elasticity in adapting the Acts to changing situations; the difficulty of defining serious accidents, and the enormous labour caused by the notification of trivial accidents in factories under the clause 'all other accidents'.

A uniform time limit of two weeks away from work would have simplified administration, but this was not found practicable as it would have concealed the class of special cause accidents which must and should continue to be reported, 'if on any one of the three working days after the accident the injured person is disabled from working at least five hours at his ordinary work'.

There should be three reportable classes. (1) Fatal. (2) Accidents from special causes, these to be defined for each class of industry. (3) Accidents causing more than two weeks' disablement. The effect of these changes would be that in mines there would be a complete and uniform system of reporting non-fatal accidents, and that in factories there would be a clear standard of reportable accidents and reports of trivial accidents of an unpreventable character would be excluded.

Causation and Prevention of Accidents at Docks, Warehouses, and Quays. Rep. Factory and Workshops. Ann. Rep. App. 12; 1900 Cd. 223, xi, 249.

Ventilation of Factories and Workshops

Dept. Cttee. 1st Rep., apps. pp. 122. 1902

1902 *Cd.* 1302, *xii*, 467
apptd. July, 1900. *sgd. August,* 1902

J. S. Haldane, E. H. Osborn.

'*To inquire into and report upon (a) the means of ventilation in factories and workshops, with especial reference to the use of fans; (b) the use and construction of respirators for the protection of workpeople exposed to dust or dangerous fumes.*'

Air in factories can be kept pure (a) by renewing it from the outside and (b) by removing impurities locally. Section 7 of the Factory and Workshops Act, 1901, requires that sufficient means of ventilation shall be provided, and gives the Secretary of State the power to prescribe a standard of 'sufficient' ventilation. The Committee recommends the standard of 12 volumes of carbonic acid per 10,000 of air, and also the steps needed to secure its enforcement.

—— Second Report. Pt. I. Report. pp. 12. 1907. Pt. II. Apps. 1907

1907 *Cd.* 3552, *x*, 449. *Apps*; 1907 *Cd.* 3553, *x*, 463
sgd. May, 1907

add Ritchie.

Experience has shown that serious mistakes are frequently made in the design of fan ventilation. The Report gives general guidance as to the application of fans to the ventilation of factories and workshops. The Appendix contains a large number of detailed illustrations and descriptions, together with results of experiments on the proper arrangement of branch ducts.

Outbreak of Ankylostomiasis in a Cornish Mine

Rep. pp. 8. 1902

1902 *Cd.* 1318, *xvii*, 827
sgd. Nov., 1902

J. S. Haldane.

Ankylostomiasis is due to the presence in the upper part of the small intestines of a species of nematode worm. The embryo develops in polluted soil into a sexually complete rhabdite form existing outside the body, and the infection is probably conveyed by eating dirt containing these worms, or by their passing through the skin. This was the disease diagnosed amongst the Cornish miners and was the first recorded outbreak, except among Lascars on vessels from India, in this country. The spread of the disease could be entirely checked by preventing the pollution of mines by human excrement, and unless this is effected, it will probably spread gradually throughout the mines of the country. Pails and disinfectants were introduced into the mines and strict orders made for the prevention of pollution of the mine by excrement.

See *Ankylostomiasis in Westphalian Collieries*. J. S. Haldane. Rep.; 1904 Cd. 1843, xiii, 817, and *The Diagnosis of Ankylostma Infection*. A. E. Boycott. Rep.; 1904 Cd. 2066, xiii, 805.

Health of Cornish Miners

Rep., apps. pp. 107. 1904

1904 *Cd.* 2091, *xiii*, 693

J. S. Haldane, J. S. Martin, R. A. Thomas.

'To enquire into and report upon the health of the miners employed in mines in Cornwall, with special reference to the injurious effects alleged to be produced by the state of ventilation in the mines, the dust arising from the use of rock-drills, and the introduction of impurities into the working-places through the use of compressed air.'

The Cornish mines are chiefly devoted to the production of tin, although copper, arsenic, wolfram, silver and other minerals are also obtained. The health of the tin, lead and copper miners has long been un-satisfactory as compared with that of men employed in other industries. Cornish mining is a healthy occupation, apart from the excessive mortality due to lung diseases, for which the death rate is, for men between 25 and 45, eight to ten times that for coal or ironstone miners. The recent rise in the death rate was due to the men who worked rock-drills. Stone-dust appears to be the chief cause of ill health and the recommendations provided 'that the use of percussion rock-drills in hard stone without satisfactory pre-cautions such as a small water-jet, for preventing the dust being inhaled by the men, be prohibited in all mines'. Special Rules should be established (1) 'for the carrying on of work in such a manner as to reduce to a mini-mum the inhalation of dust by the various classes of men employed in the mine' and (2) to render it a contravention of the Act to pollute unnecessarily any part of the mine with human faeces.

Flax and Linen Mills as Affecting the Health of the Operatives Employed Therein

Rep., apps. pp. 24. 1904

1904 *Cd.* 1997, *x*, 465 *apptd. — sgd. Dec.*, 1903

H. P. Smith.

In 1892 an exhaustive Report was presented on the Conditions of Work in the Belfast Flax Mills and Linen Factories, and the mortality of operatives (1893–4 C. 7287, xvii); in 1896 processes were declared dangerous, and Special Rules were published by the Home Office. These Rules should be amended and converted into Regulations under Section 79 of the Act of 1901. The requirement for ventilation should be replaced by a standard of purity; pure water should be used for steaming processes; the requirement that floors should be in a sound condition to prevent the retention and accumulation of water should be more strictly enforced; suitable and efficient respirators should be provided for persons working in roughing, sorting, hackling and carding processes, and an efficient system of ventilation introduced. Draft regulations are set out in detail.

Air Tests in Humid Cotton Weaving Sheds

Rep., app. pp. ix, 18. 1904

1904 *Cd.* 2135, *x*, 629 *sgd. May*, 1904

F. Scudder.

'To enquire into the ventilation of humid cotton weaving sheds.'

Section 94 (3) of the Factory and Workshop Act provides that 'the arrangements for ventilation shall be such that during working hours in no part of the cotton cloth factory shall the proportion of carbonic acid (carbon dioxide) in the air be greater than nine volumes of carbonic acid to every 10,000 volumes of air'. Manufacturers contended that while it was practicable to conform generally to the standard, it was not practicable to maintain it at all times in every part of the shed. They asked for a comprehensive enquiry and report by an independent chemist. The operatives declined to be associated with it, as no condition had been made that the standard would be made more stringent if the results showed that a higher standard of purity was practicable. The Report by Mr. Scudder on the air tests showed that installations planned and carried out by competent engineers to keep the air of a shed within the prescribed limit did in practice fully maintain the standard, notwithstanding inequalities due to local or accidental circumstances, provided that the appliances were kept in proper order and used to the full extent intended, and that their adequacy or efficiency was not impaired by subsequent alterations in structure or arrangement.

See *The Working of the Cotton Cloth Factories Act 1889;* 1897 C. 8348, xvii, 61.

Safe-Guards for the prevention of Accidents in the Manufacture of Cotton

Rep., apps. pp. 50. 1906

1906 *Cd.* 3168, *cx,* 7
sgd. June, 1906

H. S. Richmond

The reduction in the number of accidents between 1900 and 1904 inclusive occurred chiefly where the special guards advocated by a Report in 1899 (C. 9456, xii) had been used. The increase of accidents since that date was largely due to the increase of cotton spinning, sixty-five new mills with 5¾ million spindles being under erection in 1905. Since the new Factory Act of 1901 had come into operation several additional points of danger had been brought to light, and this report brought up to date in a more complete form the precautions which should be adopted.

See *Fencing Machinery at the Paris Exhibition.* Rep. Factories and Workshops. Ann. Rep.; 1902 Cd. 1112, xii, 45.

Factory and Workshop Act, 1901
Reps. of Enquiries

By Sections 79 and 80 of the Factory and Workshop Act, 1901, where the Secretary of State is satisfied that any manufacture, process or plant is dangerous or injurious to health, etc., he may make regulations. Before doing so he must publish them, receive any objection, and may appoint a competent person to hold an inquiry.

—— *Spinning and Weaving Flax and Tow and All Processes Incidental Thereto,* apps. pp. 22. 1906

1906 *Cd.* 2851, *xv,* 943

G. A. Bonner.

In roughing, hand hackling and sorting rooms, as well as in machine hackling, carding and preparing rooms, there is a considerable amount of dust which consists of decaying vegetable matter and silicious particles. Efficient exhaust ventilation is needed to protect the workers. The regulations provided also for artificial heat and for protection against moisture. Revised Regulations are given in the Appendices.

—— *The Process of Casting Brass,* apps. pp. 22. 1908

1908 *Cd.* 4154, *xii,* 743

W. Wills.

In 1896 it was reported 'that brass-workers as a class are extensively liable to diseases of the respiratory organs; and that the malady known as "brass-founders' ague" was due to the inhalation of the fumes given off by the molten brass at the time of pouring and in a less degree to the contamination of the workers' food with the fumes, and that the danger to health was proportionate to the amount of the zinc in the alloy'. Special Rules required 'means for facilitating the emission of the fumes by traps or louvre gratings or other like openings in the roof of the casting shop'. Experience has shown that when the atmosphere is foggy or humid, more adequate means of ventilation is required. More adequate washing accommodation should also be provided. See App. I for the Draft Regulations.

—— Generation, Transformation, Distribution and use of Electrical Energy in Premises under the Factory and Workshop Act, 1901, apps. pp. 36. 1908

1909 Cd. 4462, xxi, 641

J. Swinburne.

After the inquiry into objections to Draft Regulations had been in progress for some time, a Committee was set up of representatives of the Home Office and of the 200 objectors. They made draft regulations which were used by Mr. Swinburne in his amended draft for the Home Office. The three versions of the regulations are given in the Appendices.

—— Tinning of Metals, apps. pp. 22. 1909

1909 Cd. 4740, xxi, 729

E. T. H. Lawes.

The coating of metals with a mixture of tin and lead or lead alone was certified as dangerous in September 1908. Hitherto Rules covered cleanliness but not precautions for the removal of the sources of danger. The main controversy was over the use of lead in tinning hollow-ware, experiments having shown the presence of lead chloride in the fumes given off from tinning. The case for prohibition was supported by Dr. Legge and Miss Anderson. But since their report of 1907 manufacturers had introduced methods of ventilation which, if extended, would greatly reduce the dangers of lead poisoning. Mr. Lawes therefore rejected Clause I of the draft, which prohibited the use of lead in the

tinning of metal hollow-ware, and recommended instead that no tinning should be carried on except under an efficient draught.

—— Grinding of Metals and Racing of Grindstones, apps. pp. 22. 1909

1909 Cd. 4913, xxi, 685

A. H. Lush.

The Draft Regulations proposed were not objected to in principle by any party, the questions at issue being merely the exemption of particular trades and distributors or of meeting special difficulties. 'In a tenement factory properly so-called no workman is employed by the owner or any occupier of the factory, but all work for outside manufacturers. Each workman pays a fixed weekly sum to cover the rent value of his working space, and the cost of the power required to turn the grindstones or wheels and of artificial light. The power and light are sometimes supplied by a different person from the owner, and neither this person nor the owner is necessarily a manufacturer or in any way engaged in the trade of the factory. The workmen supply their own grindstones and wheels. There is no occupier of the factory as a whole, and it is often difficult to say who is the occupier of any particular part of it. In cases where a workman rents directly from the owner, he would appear to be in some sense the occupier of his own workplace; but he may in other cases be a sub-tenant of another workman, who rents a whole room or part of it, or an employee of a "little master". . . . The existence of the tenement factory has made the issue of regulations absolutely imperative for the Sheffield trades, because of the difficulty of enforcing the provisions of the Factory and Workshop Act in cases where no person can with certainty be made liable as occupier.' Wet and dry grinders were affected by diseases of the respiratory organs, and the dangers of the trade were not disputed. The regulations were redrafted so as to exclude those trades where there was occasional grinding of tools, etc., and the manufacture of needles, pins and fish hooks.

—— *Pottery Manufacture and Decoration of Pottery and any process incidental thereto.* pp. iv, 17. 1913

1912–13 *Cd.* 6568, *xxvi*, 59

A. H. Ruegg.

Draft Regulation 27 relating to the appointment of persons to see to the observance of regulations and to their records was re-worded by agreement between all parties, a proposal to reduce the temperature at which ovens might be drawn from 125° F. to 100° F. rejected, and employers recommended to provide ovens with cooling dampers, back clamping or other devices for hastening the operation of cooling.

Match Factory of Messrs. Moreland & Sons, Gloucester, with special reference to a recent fatal case of Phosphorus Necrosis

Rep. pp. 7. 1907

1907 *Cd.* 3373, *x*, 441
sgd. Feb., 1907

H. H. S. Cunynghame, B. A. Whitelegge.

In January 1907, Thomas Davis, employed in match factories for over 12 years, died from phosphorus necrosis. It was found that he had the habit of chewing tobacco whilst being exposed to phosphorus and that this was not prohibited by Special Rule. The Rule should be amended, but the abolition of the use of white phosphorus or making the machines completely automatic are the only alternatives which would eliminate the dangers to health.

See *Working of Special Rules for Lucifer Match Factories.* Mr. Goadby. Rep. *Phosphorus and Non-Phosphorus Matches.* Dr. Thorpe. Rep. Factory and Workshops. Ann. Rep.; 1908 Cd. 4166, xii, 367.

Tobacco, Cigar and Cigarette Industry

Rep. Factories and Workshops. Ann. Rep. 1906

1907 *Cd.* 3586, *x*, 1

L. A. E. Deane, E. J. Slocock.

The main object of the enquiry was the health of the workers and it was impossible to consider the industry an unhealthy one. The steaming processes were not considered healthy and it was felt advisable that girls and young women should as far as possible be kept out of the rooms in which they were carried on. In six of the largest factories there was a system of preliminary medical examination by the doctors specially appointed by the firms. The duties of doctors included daily attendance at the factory, where any of the workers could consult them as part of the Sick Club benefits. These doctors drew attention to the bearing of overtime on the normal health of workers. The conclusion was drawn that 8½ to 9 hours' work a day cannot be exceeded by women and girls without over-strain and fatigue.

Dangerous or Injurious Processes in the Coating of Metal with Lead or a Mixture of Lead and Tin

Special Rep., and a Rep. on *Experimental Investigation into the Conditions of Work in the Tinning Workshops*, apps. pp. 42. 1907

1908 *Cd.* 3793, *xii*, 765
sgd. June, 1907

Miss A. M. Anderson, T. M. Legge, G. E. Duckering.

'The risks in certain branches of the tinning industry had in no way diminished, and the actual effects of plumbism were more serious than had previously been imagined.' As it was not known how many processes in the tinning of metals were clearly injurious, or what Regulations were possible and necessary, a full investigation had to be made into a whole range of branches of the tinning trade, and a scheme of chemical experiments devised. The processes and the experiments are described and the first five of the twelve recommendations are as follows: '1. No lead shall be used in the tinning of metal hollow-ware. 2. No female person shall be employed in dipping or wiping. 3. No person under 16 years of age shall be employed in tinning processes. 4. No dipping shall be carried on unless the tinning bath is so enclosed and provided with exhaust draught as to prevent the fumes from entering the workroom. 5. No wiping, soldering, or polishing shall be done without the use of an exhaust draught, so arranged as to carry the fumes away from the worker as near as possible to the point of origin.' Other recommendations relate to medical examination, clothing, meal rooms, washing facilities, etc.

See *Dangerous or Injurious Processes in the Enamelling and Tinning of Metals.* Rep. Factory and Workshops. Ann. Rep.; 1903 Cd. 1610, xii, 1.

The Dangers Attendant on Building Operations

Dept. Cttee. Rep., mins. of ev., apps., index. pp. xxvi, 196. 1907

1908 *Cd.* 3848, *xi,* 469
apptd. July, 1906. *sgd. Oct.,* 1907

W. D. Cramp (*Ch.*), Batchelor, Haggerty, Jessup, Macfarlane, Shepherd, Stenning.

'*To inquire into the dangers attendant on Building Operations, and to prepare a draft for regulations embodying the precautions which may, in their opinion, be desirable for the safety of the workers.*'

Returns show that every year there were 2,000 accidents (mostly to labourers) on buildings in the course of construction, alteration and repair, of which more than 100 were fatal. That such a large incidence could be reduced was shown by the evidence given by a well-regulated firm (qq. 1–54) and by the number of accidents which were avoidable (qq. 263–343).

The serious dangers were due to insufficiency of plant, the use of defective material for scaffolding, coupled with unskilled and careless workmanship in the erection of scaffolds (qq. 1–54; qq. 263–343). Differences in kinds of equipment used, in the methods and traditions of working, as well as the number and size of firms, sub-contracting, etc., all add to the difficulties in making uniform regulations for all workmen in the industry. As the protection under the Factory Act is limited to certain cases, in spite of the difficulties the Committee felt that regulations should cover the whole industry. The question of enforcement of regulations did not come within the scope of the terms of reference, but it exercised the minds of most witnesses. Generally, the workmen objected to inspectors approved by local authorities, as they might not be independent and there would be a lack of uniformity, but most preferred inspectors appointed by the Government with the power of Factory Inspectors.

The recommendations took the form of draft regulations. Part I. Duties of Employers. Part II. Duties of Workmen, which specified that they should observe and co-operate with the details for safety laid down in Part I.

Humidity and Ventilation in Cotton Weaving Sheds

Dept. Cttee. Rep., pp. 22. 1909. Mins. of ev., apps., index. 1909

1909 Cd. 4484, *xv,* 635. *Mins. of ev., etc.*;
1909 Cd. 4485, *xv,* 657
apptd. Nov., 1907. *sgd. Jan.,* 1909

H. P. Freer-Smith (*Ch.*), Cross, Hartley, Roberts, Shackleton, Smith, Thomas.

'*To inquire and report*—(1) *What temperature and humidity are necessary in each case for the manufacture of different classes of cotton fabrics;* (2) *At what degrees of heat and humidity combined definite bodily discomfort arises, under the conditions of the work carried on by the operatives and what, if any, danger to health is involved by continuous work at those degrees; (3) What means of cooling humid sheds (where necessary) exist, whether combined with the means of humidifying or otherwise, which are both efficient and practicable, having regard to the conditions required for the manufacture of the several classes of goods; (4) What special arrangements, if any, are necessary in order to admit of the proper ventilation of dry weaving sheds without prejudice to the process of manufacture.'*

In the United Kingdom there are about 1,030 humid and 1,636 dry cotton weaving sheds. In the dry sheds particular classes of goods of better quality are made, in the humid sheds inferior yarns are used and the dampness is needed to prevent breakage and delays caused by the constant piecing together of the yarn. To prohibit humidity would interfere with the production of certain classes of goods and in many places would increase the labour required and reduce the wages of piece workers. Although the workers were well aware of this, they were prepared to face losses and they showed this opinion in a ballot organized by the operative leaders, in which 68,154 voted for the abolition of 'steaming', 3,094 against and 1,221 neutral. They contended, after seventy years' experience of regulations, 'that the introduction of humidity is the cause of great personal discomfort and detrimental to their health'.

The table of humidity in the Fourth Schedule of the Act of 1901 was very unrealistic. New maximum limits of wet bulb temperatures should be fixed by experiment, and to encourage the abolition of the use of artificial humidity, the standard of ventilation in humid sheds should be raised to 12 volumes of carbon dioxide in 10,000.

—— Second Report, mins. of ev., apps. pp. xxx, 70. 1911

1911 *Cd.* 5566, *xxiii*, 807

sgd. Jan., 1911

add Petavel.

This Report gives an account of the various ventilating and humidifying systems which had been inspected by the Committee. The Committee repeated its previous recommendations regarding temperatures and standard of ventilation. Cold draughts should be avoided, water for humidifying purposes purified, cloak rooms provided and temperature records kept. Details are given of the standard requirements needed for humidifying purposes.

In the three Memos. appended to the Report the employers' representatives, W. Hartley and T. Roberts, recommended the workers to accept a wet bulb temperature of 75° (see J. S. Haldane's evidence); the workers' representatives, J. Cross, D. J. Shackleton and F. Thomas, reiterated the workers' contentions as expressed in the ballot, but added that if abolition could not be secured, a wet bulb temperature should be fixed, and reconsidered again at the end of three years. The other members of the Committee, H. P. Freer-Smith, Professor Petavel and J. L. Smith, were mostly concerned with the application of an agreed standard and the time to be allowed before it became uniformally compulsory. The Appendices contain specialists' reports.

See *Regulations for Cotton Cloth Factories*. Factories and Workshops. Ann. Rep.; 1912–13 Cd. 6239, xxv, 565. Cotton Cloth Factories Act, 1911.

Florists' Workshops

Rep. pp. 8. 1909

1909 *Cd.* 4932, *xxi*, 677

A. H. Ruegg.

To inquire 'into the question of the application of the Factory and Workshop Act, 1901, to florists' workshops, and the necessity or advisability of granting certain special exceptions to this class of workshops.'

A decision of the Court of the King's Bench in Hoare *v.* Green indicated that florists' shops or workrooms had been 'workshops' within the meaning of the Act for a considerable time, though steps had been taken against them only recently. The application of the Factory Act to these workshops was beneficial, and only proved necessity would justify any exemptions from its complete operation. The recommendations concern the special requirements of the trade regarding meal times at different hours, permitted overtime, arrangements for the weekly half holiday, and the limits of employment inside and outside the workshop.

Dangerous or Injurious Processes in the Smelting of Materials containing Lead, and in the manufacture of Red and Orange Lead, and Flaked Litharge

Special Rep., apps. pp. 29. 1910

1910 Cd. 5152, xxix, 51

E. L. Collis.

'*An inquiry made into the various industries in which furnaces are used for the extraction of metals from materials containing lead, or in the preparation of oxides of lead.*'

'The industries concerned are (1) the smelting of ores containing lead, which includes the extraction of lead, silver or zinc in the form of spelter, from such ores; and (2) the production of red and orange lead, and of flaked litharge.' Lead smelting was made a dangerous trade in 1894, but the Special Rules applied only to cleaning flues. This had not been sufficient to affect the incidence of plumbism, which had increased in recent years. In other industries where exhaust ventilation for the removal of dust and periodical examination of the workers had been required there has been diminution of the disease. Regulations set out in the recommendations apply to 34 lead smelting factories, 8 spelter works, 17 red and orange lead factories and 8 flaked litharge factories.

Lead, etc., in Potteries

Dept. Cttee. Rep. Vol. I. Rep. pp. vii, 150. 1910. Vol. II. Apps. 1910. Vol. III. Mins of ev., index. 1910

1910 Cd. 5219, xxix, 85. Mins. of ev., etc.; 1910 Cd. 5278, Cd. 5385, xxix, 245 apptd. Sept., 1908. sgd. June, 1910

E. F. G. Hatch (*Ch.*), Burton, Buxton, Edwards, Moore, Parkes, Reid, Harcourt, Ward, Tuckwell (Miss G. M.).

'*To consider the dangers attendant on the use of lead in the various branches of the manufacture of china and earthenware, and in the processes incidental thereto, including the making of transfers, and to report how far these can be obviated or lessened.*'

Out of 63,000 workers in the pottery industry, 6,865 were on dangerous processes involving contact with lead, and 23,000 where there was danger from breathing clay dust and flint, etc. Contact with lead caused poisoning (plumbism), of which the principal forms were colic and gastric disturbance, anaemia, paralysis and infections of the brain. In addition, the breathing of dust, etc., gave rise to an excessive rate of lung diseases. Although the numbers of bad poisoning cases had declined between 1896 and 1900, improvement had not been maintained for the years 1902–8. Public attention to this had been widely aroused and there had been a definite agitation against the unrestricted use of lead compounds.

The conclusions drawn from evidence given by representatives of the manufacturers were that a great many articles of pottery could be manufactured in a high state of perfection with leadless glaze. In certain classes of common ware the costs were not appreciably increased, but in better classes of goods the excessive numbers of 'seconds' so increased costs that certain markets would be endangered. But where accuracy in reproduction was essential lead glaze could not be dispensed with. All agreed on the superiority of glaze made from raw lead, but there was divergence of opinion on the mechanical difficulties in producing low solubility glazes. If the pottery which could be made with leadless or low solubility glaze had lent itself to definition in its various branches, it might have been practicable to insist on the use of such glazes, but any attempt at classification would cause great disturbance in the trade. Prohibition of raw lead glazes was therefore not recommended 'at the present moment'. Encouragement should be given to those firms using leadless glaze by the relaxation of the health rules proposed. The public should be made aware of the desirability of insisting on leadless glaze pottery and Government Departments might well set the example. If the precautions in relation to lead processes which the Committee recommended were carried out, the risks should be reduced to the level in other industrial occupations.

Following an examination of the processes of manufacturers, the Committee propose a schedule of dangerous processes, a detailed code of recommendations applicable to them, and a similar code to be applied to employment in all departments of Potteries. These are set out in the form of draft regulations under Section 79 of the Factory and Workshops Act, 1901, on pp. 131–50 of the Report. A system of self-inspection through the appointment by the occupier of a person to enforce them is proposed.

In a dissenting Memo. Miss Tuckwell, whilst approving the proposals regarding safety, objected to any impression that a scheme of contributory insurance which imposed an additional tax on women workers was possible, and to the proposals for self-inspection. There should be more Factory Inspectors. Compensation equal to earnings should be a condition of permission to use glazes exceeding the 5 per cent standard. There should be a Schedule of articles to be made only with leadless glaze, and it should be gradually extended until within a given number of years the use of lead for china and earthenware was abandoned.

See *Employment of Lead Compounds in Pottery*, Dr. Oliver, T. E. Thorpe. Reps.; 1899 C. 9207, xii, 277. 1901 Cd. 527, Cd. 679, x, 683. *Methods of Determination of Dust and Lead in the air of workrooms*, G. E. Duckering. Rep. Factory and Workshops. Ann. Rep.; 1911 Cd. 5693, xxii, 407.

Bronzing. Conditions under which Bronzing is carried on in Factories and Workshops

Rep., apps. pp. 32. 1910

1910 *Cd. 5328, xxix*, 19

E. L. Collis, W. S. Smith, Rose E Squires.

'Bronzing' includes all processes in which metallic powders, either in the wet or dry state, are used to produce a metallic effect upon the surface of wood, paper, leather, etc. Bronze powders consist of copper and zinc with slight traces of lead, tin, arsenic and iron. Lithographic printers are probably the largest consumers of bronze powders used entirely in the dry state. Dust is an irritant injurious to health when inhaled over long periods. When exhaust ventilation is provided there is practically no escape of dust. Recommended that the voluntary regulations referring to the prevention and removal of dust and to personal cleanliness be made obligatory.

See also *Dangerous Trades*. Dept. Cttee. Interim Rep.; 1896 C. 8149, xxxiii, 1.

Accidents in Places under the Factory and Workshop Acts

Dept. Cttee. Rep. pp. v, 64. 1911. Mins. of ev., app., index. 1911

1911 *Cd. 5535, xxiii*, 1. *Mins. of ev., etc.*; 1911 *Cd. 5540, xxiii*, 71 *apptd. Nov.*, 1908. *sgd. Feb.*, 1911

F. D. Acland (*Ch.*), Carlisle, Cramp, Gill, Ramsay Macdonald, Tattersall, Taylor, Vivian, Wilson (Miss M.).

'To inquire into the causes and circumstances of the increase in the number of reported accidents in certain classes of factories and workshops, and other premises under the Factory Acts, and to report what additional precautionary measures are, in their opinion, necessary or desirable.'

While there had been some increases in reported accidents due to fuller reporting, and to an increase in the area over which the risk was spread owing to an expansion of industry, it was not possible to say whether there had been an actual increase of liability to accident. Amongst possible causes of increased risk put forward by witnesses were the increased speed and pressure of work through the speeding up of machinery at piece work; the use of unskilled labour on automatic machines; ambiguity in the regulations regarding the cleaning of machinery in motion, especially by children, and lack of co-ordination between the factory inspectorate. After examining the available statistics from various sources the Committee concluded that although the evidence consisted largely of inferences and probabilities, the accident risk for 1897–1907 probably remained constant, while the increase for 1907 was due to fuller reporting.

Telegraphists' Cramp

Rep.

1911 Cd. 5968. See p. 220.

'Shuttle-Kissing'

Rep., apps. pp. 24. 1912

1912–13 Cd. 6184, xxvi, 81
sgd. April, 1912

G. Bellhouse, W. W. E. Fletcher, D. J. Shackleton.

'To inquire into the alleged danger of the transmission of certain diseases from person to person in weaving sheds by means of the practice known as "shuttle-kissing".'

In order to thread a shuttle the mouth is placed over the eye of the shuttle, and a sudden and strong inhalation is made to bring the thread through it. This may happen as many as 450 to 500 times a day and the same shuttles may be 'kissed' by the weaver, the tenter, the tackler and the overlooker. The Home Office was already considering the practice when the Local Government Board received a copy of a 'Special Report on the Importance of Cleansing and Disinfecting the Shuttles' by Dr. J. Brown, M.O.H., Bacup, in which he stated that three persons who had used the same looms—not disinfected—had died from tuberculosis. Investigations of these and other cases did not bring to light evidence which was conclusive, although there was enough to show how unclean and objectionable the practice was. Alternative methods of threading the shuttle, such as the use of automatic suction, the use of a hook and a differently constructed shuttle were examined. It was agreed that the time was not ripe to prohibit the present shuttle, but the Committee hoped, with the aid of the inspectors, newer forms of shuttles would be gradually adopted.

Deep Excavations

Dept. Cttee. Rep., mins. of ev., app., index. pp. xi, 130. 1912

1912–13 Cd. 6261, xviii, 1
apptd. April, 1910. sgd. —

C. A. Harrison (Ch.), Squire, Wilson.

'To inquire into the dangers attending Deep Excavation in connection with the Construction of Docks and other similar works, and to consider and report what steps can be taken to minimize such dangers.'

Collapses of deep excavations involving serious loss of life were rare, but the existing law did not necessarily require all accidents occurring in the construction and repair of docks, ports, etc., to be reported. All deep excavations (those exceeding 10 feet in depth) should be supervised by an experienced person superior to the ganger, and should be suitably fenced, etc. Emergency ladders should be provided and life-saving and escape apparatus be at hand where the site was under water. Ambulance appliances should be provided at all works of deep excavation, and trenches inspected by a competent person, who should maintain a register of such inspections. This register should be available for H.M. Inspectors of Factories. There were specific recommendations concerning the storage, conveyance, charging and firing of nitro-glycerine explosives.

Metalliferous Mines and Quarries

R. Com.

apptd. May, 1910

H. Cunynghame (*Ch.*), Redmayne, Haldane, Ainsworth, Greaves, Thomas, Jones, Lewney, Lovett.

'*To inquire into and report upon the health and safety of persons employed in metalliferous mines and quarries.*'

The first Report is a formal presentation of the following volume of minutes of evidence, etc.; 1912–13 Cd. 6390, xli, 547.

—— Second Report, apps. pp. vi, 196. 1914. Mins. of ev., apps., index. Vols. II, III. 1914

1914 *Cd.* 7476, *xlii,* 27. *Mins. of ev., etc.*; 1914 *Cd.* 7477, *Cd.* 7478, *xlii,* 233 *sgd. June,* 1914

Metalliferous mining is an industry on a small scale. It lacks the homogeneity of coal mining, as it is subdivided into several distinct branches, each having methods of its own according to the 'natural' conditions and the size of the mine. Apart from the usual dangers attending mining operations the most serious one for the men was miners' phthisis, which arises from the inhalation of dust coming from the blasting of siliceous rock. Quarrying is a much more widely distributed industry and produces almost every variety of ore and stone. In general, the operations involved are much more simple than in mining and the methods do not vary a great deal from one quarry to another. On the whole, it is more healthy than mining, though there are the dangers from the inhalation of dust. The principal problems arise from the use of explosive and the danger to the eyes of flying particles of stone, and from the handling of sharp-edged stone, etc.

Since the passing of the Acts in 1872 and 1894 there had been no legislation of first importance affecting either industry. The Commission therefore made detailed recommendations for the simplification of the law, the strengthening of the inspectorate, provisions for supervision and management, safety and health regulations. There were memoranda by Jones, Lovett and Redmayne on inspection, non-fatal accidents in slate mines and the use of explosives in mines.

Conditions of Employment in the Manufacture of Tinplates with special reference to the process of Tinning

Rep., app. pp. 27. 1912

1912–13 *Cd.* 6394, *xxvi,* 105

sgd. ——

E. L. Collis, J. Hilditch.

'A tin plate is a thin sheet of iron or steel coated with tin, and possesses the strength of the iron or steel without liability to rust. The trade was established in Pontypool by Major John Hanbury in 1720.' The report gives a detailed description of the processes in the production of tin plate and the conditions to which the workers are exposed. For example, in the 'opening' process where women and girls are employed, weights of 60 to 70 lbs. are frequently handled by workers not more than 16 to 18 years of age, and a woman or a girl will open per day from 5,040 to 6,720 sheets, weighing from $2\frac{1}{4}$ to 3 tons. In the 'black-pickling' process, ten to twelve women handle about 80 tons of material per day. On the cold-rolling process, where night work is prohibited for women, it was common practice, in contravention of the Factory Act, to work male young persons on more than six nights in any two weeks, and they were 'often employed only on night work'. Tin-house workers run considerable risk of accident from splashing of molten metal, zinc chloride and grease; revolving shafting, pulleys and cog-wheels; chain gearing and belting; and rollers on dusting machines. While fumes, dust and temperatures add to the dangers of the trade, the precautions against excessive weight-carrying by young workers recommended for the Earthenware and China and Cotton Weaving industries should, with modifications, be adopted in the Tin Plate industry; draft new regulations for works in which tinning is carried on are set out in an appendix. Conferences and co-operation between worker and employer in every factory should be organized with a view to establishing and maintaining higher standards of safety.

Night Employment of Male Young Persons in Factories and Workshops

Dept. Cttee. Rep. pp. 18. 1912. Mins. of ev., apps., index. 1913

1912–13 *Cd.* 6503, *xxvi*, 41. *Mins. of ev.*, etc.; 1913 *Cd.* 6711, *xxiii*, 585. *apptd. July*, 1911. *sgd. Nov.*, 1912

Lord Ashton (*Ch.*), Murphy, Robinson, Astor, Henderson, Whitehouse.

'*To consider the question of the night employment of male young persons in factories and workshops; and to report whether any or all of the exemptions granted by or under sections 54, 55 and 56 of the Factory and Workshop Act, 1901, should be repealed.*'

In the course of a debate in the House of Commons in May, 1911, strong objection was raised to the grant by Order dated April, 1911, of permission to employ boys of 16 years and upwards at night in certain industries. The debate disclosed also the fact that there existed strong feelings against night employment of boys generally. Since 1802 Parliament had been averse to the employment of children and young persons on night work where it was not essential. Under Sections 54, 55, 56 of the Factory and Workshop Act, 1901, exemptions have been given at a minimum age of 14 to five trades and at a minimum age of 16 to eleven trades. No information was available as to the effect on health. Factory Inspectors had not noticed any ill-effects, though Dr. Acland of St. Thomas' Hospital stated that growing boys would suffer if they did not get the light and sunshine necessary for their health. Amongst masters and men night work was taken as a matter of course, not calling for special attention. The Board of Education was emphatic in stating that night work 'impaired seriously the energies of young men' and denied them educational activities.

In factories where work was carried on continuously 'shifts' were worked, and these differed according to the customs in different trades and localities, the work continuing sometimes 12 hours, sometimes 8 hours or less. The Committee favoured 3 shifts of 8 hours a shift. Though unnatural and undesirable in principle, night work was essential in industries where there were 'continuous processes', and it should be permitted for boys only in such cases. Separate recommendations are made for each industry affected. Boys on night work should undergo periodical medical examination, and employers should hold certificates showing that they complied with the conditions for such employment. In a Memo. W. Astor states that the recommendations in regard to iron mills and glass works ought not to be carried out until further enquiry shows what they would entail, in the face of foreign competition, in increased cost of production and the disturbance of trade conditions.

Hours of Employment of Winding Enginemen

Rep.

1913 *Cd.* 6710. See *Coal.* p. 135.

Celluloid

Dept. Cttee. Rep. pp. 29. 1913. Mins. of ev. 1913

1914 *Cd.* 7158, xv, 377. *Mins. of ev.*; 1914 *Cd.* 7159, xv, 407 *apptd. Oct.*, 1912. *sgd. Nov.*, 1913

Lord Plymouth (*Ch.*), Dobbie, Lloyd, Ollis, Robinson, Sachs.

'*To inquire and report as to the precautions necessary in the use of celluloid in manufacture and the handling and storage of celluloid and celluloid articles.*'

Celluloid is used increasingly as a 'most suitable' material, and as a 'substitute' material. It is highly inflammable, but the dangers have been somewhat exaggerated owing to attention having been concentrated on accidents occurring under exceptional circumstances. Shops and warehouses where there are 5 cwts. of celluloid articles or stores of raw celluloid, factories and workrooms with raw materials, and occupiers of premises where cinematograph films are handled, should register with the local authority, who should be responsible for enforcing specified regulations. Certain changes in the Factory Acts are also recommended.

Humidity and Ventilation in Flax Mills and Linen Factories

Dept. Cttee. Rep., apps. pp. 106. 1914. Mins. of ev., apps., index. 1914

1914 *Cd.* 7433, xxxvi, 1. *Mins. of ev.*, etc.; 1914 *Cd.* 7446, xxxvi, 107 *apptd. July*, 1912. *sgd. May*, 1914

H. P. Freer-Smith (*Ch.*), Cummins, Ewart, Petavel, Smith.

'*To inquire and report what amendment (if any) to the Regulations for the spinning and weaving of flax or tow and the processes incidental thereto is expedient in view of the Report of the Departmental Committee on Humidity and Ventilation in Cotton Weaving Sheds, or on other grounds.*'

Although operatives in both cotton and flax industries were exposed to moist atmospheres at high temperatures, which in flax spinning were generally in excess of those prevailing in the humid processes for cotton, while the Lancashire Operatives had agitated against artificial humidity and secured improvements in the Cotton Cloth Factories Act, 1911, Irish workers had petitioned that existing conditions should continue. As in the manufacture of fine linens a difference of two degrees between the wet and dry bulb temperatures had to be maintained, it was not possible to give linen weavers the full measure of relief recently granted to cotton weavers. It was recommended that the artificial humidity should cease when the wet bulb temperature reached 80° F. but it was hoped that methods would soon be found which would make 75 ° F. possible in all factories. In every wet spinning room where the wet bulb temperature was 75° F. and over, the ventilation should amount to the introduction of at least 1,000 cubic feet of fresh air per hour for every linear foot of trough serving one row of spindles, and the distribution of air should be made as uniform as possible. Other extended Regulations are given in detail.

Lead in Paint

Reps.

1915, 1920. See *Breviate 1917–39*, pp. 309–10.

Lighting in Factories and Workshops.

Reps.

1915–38. See *Breviate 1917–39*, pp. 312–13.

An Investigation of Industrial Fatigue by Physiological Methods

Interim Rep. pp. 34. 1915

1914–16 Cd. 8056, xxiv, 1
sgd. Aug., 1915

A. F. Stanley Kent.

The International Congress on Hygiene and Demography, held in Brussels in 1903, passed the following resolution: 'The various governments should facilitate as far as possible investigation into the subject of industrial fatigue'.

The term 'fatigue' includes 'the general lowering of the functions of the body as a result of extreme or prolonged activity. From the industrial point of view it is less important to understand the deep-lying causes than to be able to recognize and control the circumstances which have led up to them in the past and are likely to lead up to them in the future.' 'Any interference with the normal functions of the body brought about by an insufficient supply of fresh air (bad ventilation) or by an unduly humid state of the atmosphere, might lead to an increased production and lessened excretion of poisonous bodies, and thus to a more rapid development of the condition of fatigue.' 'Any failure to distribute the "rest intervals" properly throughout the working day so as to ensure the recovery of the tissues before exhaustion has become excessive will lead to a great increase in ultimate fatigue.' The report records the results of applying physiological experimental tests to laboratory and various classes of factory workers.

—— Second Interim Report. pp. 76. 1916

1916 Cd. 8335, xi, 9

The report deals with fatigue as the result of overtime, the influence of fatigue and overtime on output, and on food and feeding. Amongst the conclusions drawn from the experiments were the curious conditions of lowered efficiency exhibited by workers on Monday; inferior output of workers who go to work without breakfast and the high cost of the 'unsatisfactory' diet of the popular fish and chip food. During the middle periods of the day output is normally high, but is lowered by the working of overtime. This diminution is often so great that the total daily output is less when overtime is worked than when it is suspended. Thus overtime defeats its own object.

See Fatigue, Dr. Züntz and H. Joteyko. Reps. Factories and Workshops. Ann. Rep. Apps. II, III; 1904 Cd. 2139, x, 119.

Health of Munition Workers

Cttee. Interim Rep. Industrial Efficiency and Fatigue. pp. 121. 1917

1917–18 Cd. 8511, xvi, 1019
apptd. Sept., 1915. sgd. Feb., 1917

G. Newman (Ch.), Barlow, Bellhouse, Boycott, Clynes, Collis, Fletcher, Hill, Osborn, Squire (Miss R. E.), Tennant (Mrs. H. J.).

'To consider and advise on questions of industrial fatigue, hours of labour, and other matters affecting the personal health and physical efficiency of workers in munitions factories and workshops.'

In view of the immediate urgency of many of the problems which they were called upon to investigate, the Committee decided at an early stage of their inquiries to issue a series of Memoranda on various questions. (For a list of these Memos. see App., p. 450.) For the more directly industrial and statistical parts of these inquiries the Committee called in special investigators including B. Moore, P. Sargent Florence, H. M. Vernon, W. Neilson Jones, Professor Loveday, Captain M. Greenwood, S. H. Burchall, Captain T. H. Agnew, Miss J. Campbell and Miss L. Wilson. In the course of their inquiries the Committee found that there had been no systematic endeavour to discover by any method other than that of preconceived opinion (*a*) what is the best length for the working day; (*b*) what is the most economical arrangement for spells of work; (*c*) what are the real causes of lost time; and (*d*) what are the health requirements which are essential to a proper industrial organization. The firms who have made successful pioneer experiments have had few imitators, despite the success of some of the reforms which they have introduced.

Amongst the conclusions set out in the Memoranda were the following: if maximum output is to be secured and maintained, Sunday labour should be discontinued except for sudden emergencies, repairs, tending furnaces, etc. (Memo. 1); overtime should be restricted so that average weekly hours do not exceed 67 for adult males and 60 for women and boys under 16, and adequate breaks and ordinary factory holidays should be provided (Memo. 5); the experience of three years of war shows that hours should be reduced below this limit (Memo. 20); a system of welfare supervision, administered by an officer specially appointed, is essential in all munition works where women and girls are employed, and would be of advantage in munitions where 500 adult males or 100 boys are employed. The employment of women on night work, though at the moment inevitable, is undesirable and calls for particular care; the three shift system without overtime should be used, and all women and girls applying for work should be medically examined (Memo. 4).

Industrial Health and Efficiency. Final Rep.; 1918 Cd. 9065, xii, 195. See *Breviate 1917–39*, p. 314.

Factories and Workshops

Ann. Rep. pp. xiii, 83. 1919

1919 *Cmd.* 340, *xxii*, 31

H. M. Robinson.

An account of the work of the Department during the War 1914–18.

2. INDUSTRIAL RELATIONS, TRADE DISPUTES

Trade Disputes and Trade Combinations

R. Com. Rep., apps. pp. iv, 132. 1906. Mins. of ev., apps., index. 1906

1906 *Cd.* 2825, *lvi*, 1. *Mins. of ev., etc.*; 1906 *Cd.* 2826, *lvi*, 137
apptd. June, 1903. *sgd. Jan.*, 1906

Lord Dunedin (*Ch.*), Cohen, S. Webb, Lushington, Lewis.

'*To enquire into the subject of Trade Disputes and Trade Combinations and as to the law affecting them, and to report on the law applicable to the same and the effect of any modifications thereof.*'

The Commission was appointed following the judgment given in the Taff Vale case, as a result of which the trade union paid to the railway company damages amounting to £23,000. The Trade Union Congress passed a resolution that no member of a trade union should give evidence before the Commission. This did not involve the Commission in any difficulty, as the objections and proposals of the trade unions stood 'conspicuously before the world, not only in reported speeches but by the Bills introduced avowedly on their behalf in Parliament'. The main subjects of the enquiry were: (*a*) The liability of trade union funds to be taken in execution for the wrongful acts of agents of the union, (*b*) the statute law relating to picketing and other incidents of strikes, and (*c*) the law of conspiracy affecting trade unions.

(*a*) In 1900 the Amalgamated Society of Railway Servants and its officers were sued successfully in tort by the Taff Vale Railway Company, for having conspired to induce the workers of their Company to break contracts, and having conspired to interfere with the traffic of the Company by picketing and other unlawful means. The grounds for the judgment were that where a registered trade union has been invested with the statutory powers of the Act of 1871, it must be inferred that it was the intention of Parliament that such a trade union should be liable to be sued in its registered name. The Committee was satisfied that the law laid down involved no new principle and was not inconsistent with the Act of 1871. No statute had declared that trade unions should be liable to an action in tort and the liability had never been distinctly raised in Court, but theoretically the funds of the trade unions had always been subject to the general law of liability. 'The notion of a trade union having been intended to be especially exempted from action in tort is a misconception resting on no other foundation than long practical immunity.' A review in paras 15 to 31, of the law before 1871, of legal procedure, and of the report of the Erle Commission (1868–9 [4123] xxxi) leads to the conclusion that no Commission had recommended that unions should be exempt from actions for tort, nor had any Act or judge declared them to be so.

There was no ground for granting trade unions special exemption from liability for wrongs done to outsiders. But trade union branches were often in a semi-independent position and it would be a hardship if union funds were liable for unauthorized acts of branches. The benefit funds of a union were in law regarded as massed with other funds and liable in actions for tort; they should be legally separate, provided they were not available for militant purposes.

(b) Picketing is not defined by law, but is generally understood. Controversy turned on the methods of picketing, especially those made offences by law in order to protect persons from intimidation and molestation. The Act of 1875 had been interpreted to mean that it was a penal offence to 'watch and beset for the purpose of peacefully persuading'. In Mr. Whittaker's bill the trade union proposals were that 'it shall be lawful for any person or persons acting either on their own behalf or on behalf of a trade union . . . in contemplation of a trade dispute to attend for any of the following purposes at or near a house or place where a person resides or works, or carries on his business, or happens to be—(1) for the purpose of peacefully obtaining or communicating information; (2) for the purpose of peacefully persuading any person to work or abstain from working'. This would legalize the attendance of any number of persons, although attendance might constitute a nuisance or trespass. The real point brought out in evidence and not contradicted by the trade unions, was that 'watching' and 'besetting' for the purpose of peaceful persuasion was a contradiction in terms: picketing is always and of necessity in the nature of an annoyance to the picketed, especially as the Act placed no limit on the number of persons who might attend a house for this purpose or on the length of time they might stay.

(c) The law of conspiracy affecting trade unions was that 'no combination to commit any act, which, if done by one person, would not be an offence punishable by imprisonment, can be the foundation of criminal proceedings. The civil action of conspiracy . . . is that the conspiracy is not complete by mere agreement, but must result in something being done from which damage results in order that an action may lie.' It was obvious that during the discussion on the subject in 1875 no one was thinking of the civil action. The authoritative exposition of the law in the Taff Vale case makes the subject of civil action of supreme importance. It may be questioned whether an act done by a combination of persons can ever be the same as an act done by one. There was no doubt that it was a concession to trade unions, whose chief strength was in collective action. The Commission thought not only that it was reasonable to recognize this concession, but that the civil side should be equally dealt with.

The Majority, L. Dunedin, Cohen

and Webb, recommended that an Act should be passed declaring trade unions legal; that apart from breach of contract, strikes, including sympathetic strikes, and persuasion to strike should be legal, that an individual should not be liable for doing any act not in itself an actionable tort only on the ground that it is an interference with another person's trade, business or employment; that provision should be made for separating and making immune benefit funds; that protection should be provided for the central authorities of a union against unauthorized acts of branch agents, that trade unions should be able to become incorporated or to enter into enforceable agreements with other persons and their own members; that the 7th Section of the Conspiracy and Protection of Property Act, 1875, should be altered to 'Acting in such a manner as to cause a reasonable apprehension in the mind of any person that violence will be used to him or his family, or damage be done to his property'; and that an agreement or combination by two or more persons to do or to procure to be done any act in contemplation or furtherance of a trade dispute should not be the ground of a civil action, unless the agreement or combination is indictable as a conspiracy notwithstanding the terms of the Act of 1875.

There are a number of memoranda by various commissioners on legal cases and on civil action of conspiracy. Lushington and Lewis presented separate reports. Both dissent from the majority's proposals to legalize trade unions, to legalize the separation of funds, to give unions power to disavow the actions of branch agents and to become incorporated, and from the proposed re-wording of the picketing clause. The Commission called special attention to the evidence of Mr. G. R. Askwith on the case law involved.

See *Injunction granted by the Chancery Division of the Supreme Court of Judicature against Trade Unions, since the date of the House of Lords' Judgment in the case of Osborne* v. *The Amalgamated Society of Railway Servants.* Return; 1911 (247) lxxxix, 389. Trade Disputes Act, 6 Edward 7. c. 47.

Rules of Voluntary Conciliation and Arbitration Boards and Joint Committees

Bd. of Trade (Labour Department). Rep., apps. pp. xxv, 298. 1907

1908 *Cd.* 3788, *xcviii,* 1

A. Wilson Fox.

'Inquiries respecting existing Conciliation Boards have been addressed to the Department by persons interested in conciliation and arbitration, or by those contemplating the establishment of a Conciliation Board.' The Report deals with the rules and the nature of the work in the coal trade, other mining, iron and steel, engineering and shipbuilding, textiles, boots and shoes, building, co-operative societies, quarrying, pig iron, tailoring, transport and miscellaneous trades. Appendices classify the Boards according to the methods adopted for the settlement of disputes and show the number of cases settled by Boards and Committees for a period of 10 years. The number of Boards and Committees known to exist is 194, more than 1,250,000 workpeople being covered by the operations of conciliatory agencies. In addition, there are two Boards whose work is restricted to questions affecting employees of Co-operative Societies, and 15 District Boards not confined to any particular trade.

See *Proceedings under Conciliation Trades Dispute Act*, 1896. 14 Reps. 1897–1921.

Collective Agreements between Employers and Workpeople in the United Kingdom

Rep., apps., index. pp. xxxviii, 502. 1910

1910 *Cd.* 5366, *xx,* 1

sgd. Sept., 1910

D. F. Schloss and Labour Department.

The term 'collective agreement' is applied to those arrangements under which the conditions of employment are governed by the terms of a bargain made between employers or associations of employers and a group of workpeople employed by them, or an organization representing the interests of the work people. 'Collective bargains' include awards made by arbitrators or an umpire. Shop agreements may affect one firm and its employees, or one or more classes of employees. Collective bargaining prevails throughout the whole of our manufacturing industries, and to a very considerable extent in the docks and on the waterside, in transport and in sea fishing. Some 2,400,000 workpeople, or rather less than one-fourth of the total number employed are covered by Collective Agreements. The report discusses the chief subjects dealt with in agreements. The bulk of the volume is composed of detailed examples of agreements in force in the major industries.

Railway Strike (Employment of Military)

Correspondence between Home Office and Local Authorities. pp. 40. 1911

1911 (323) xlvii, 691

The correspondence and circulars which set out the circumstances leading up to the employment of the Military, in Liverpool, Manchester, Bristol, etc., during the Railway Strike, 1911.

Railway Conciliation and Arbitration Scheme of 1907

R. Com. Rep., apps., pp. 24. 1911. Mins. of ev., apps., index. 1911

1911 Cd. 5922, xxix, Pt. I, 663. Mins. of ev., etc.; 1912–13 Cd. 6014, xlv, 87 apptd. Aug., sgd. Oct., 1911

D. Harrel (Ch.), Ratcliffe-Ellis, Beale, Henderson, Burnett.

'To investigate the working of the Railway Conciliation and Arbitration Scheme, signed on behalf of the principal Railway Companies and of three Trade Unions of Railway employés at the Board of Trade on November 6th, 1907, and to report what changes (if any) are desirable with a view to the prompt and satisfactory settlement of differences.'

At a conference in November, 1906 the Amalgamated Society of Railway Servants drew up a 'National Programme' for England and Wales, which included a standard eight-hour day for all men concerned with the movement of vehicles in traffic and ten hours for the rest, except platemen, a minimum of nine hours rest between duties, overtime at time and a quarter, Sundays, etc., at time and a half, a guaranteed week's wages to full-time employees, and an advance of 2s. per week to all grades not receiving the eight-hour day. This 'Programme' was submitted to the Railway Companies in January 1907 by Mr. R. Bell, Secretary of the Amalgamated Society of Railway Servants, with a request that their directors should meet a deputation of the men accompanied by himself, but the Companies did not respond. Serious discontent showed itself in a ballot in which 76,925 votes were given in favour and 8,773 against a general railway strike to enforce the 'Programme', including the principle of 'recognition'. The Board of Trade intervened and although the two sides did not meet, secured their agreement to a scheme for conciliation and arbitration.

In evidence, J. H. Thomas said that the scheme was formulated by the Board of Trade and was submitted to the railway companies and to the men, 'all within a few hours', and pressure was brought to bear to avert a stoppage. The 'Scheme was set up practically two years after the men had originally formulated their programme'; and though signed in November, 1907, at the end of 12 months the machinery was not fully in operation (q. 1935). The Trade Unions complained that the scheme was inefficient through delays, the narrowing of the 'usual channels' of negotiation, the ineffectiveness of its Awards, which could be neutralized by 'changes in management', and because the men's secretary of the board must be an 'employee of the Company'. Their suggestions included direct recognition of the trade unions by the Companies, rights of appeal to the National Board and the removal of the restriction that their secretaries must be employees of the Company. Though the Companies did not agree that delays had been caused, they did agree that the Scheme might be simplified. They urged 'that the absence of discussion at the Conciliation Boards was due generally to the avowed inability of the men to depart from the terms of the National Programme'.

Proceedings by the usual channels and in the early stages had tended to become purely formal. 'The most important, if not the main evidence of the Companies and men concerned the "recognition" of the Unions', which the latter demanded and the former rejected. The Companies could not be expected to permit intervention between themselves and their men on questions of discipline and management. A more general adoption of negotiations by friendly collaboration between the Companies' officers and the trade union officials would be useful to both parties. Members of each Board should be at liberty to select a secretary from any source they might think proper. In Annex I the Commission gives its proposed new scheme in detail, and in Annex II the 1907 Agreements.

See *Railway Conciliation Boards*, Rep.; 1909 Cd. 4534, lxxvii, 73.

The Present Disputes Affecting Transport Workers in the Port of London and on the Medway

Rep., mins. of ev. pp. 50. 1912

1912–13 Cd. 6229, xlvii, 247
sgd. May, 1912

E. Clarke.

'*To inquire into and report upon the facts and circumstances of the present disputes affecting transport workers in the Port of London and on the Medway.*'

There were seven specific causes of dispute, all of which were dealt with in evidence by Mr. H. Gosling, of the National Transport Workers Federation. They related to the employment of non-union men, the refusal of employers to meet trade union representatives or to pay rates of wages which had been fixed by agreement. The facts and conclusions regarding each case are set out. Much of the trouble has been due to a breach in some cases and neglect in others of the provision in the Agreement for a decision by the Board of Trade in event of a difference between the Associations. The question of bringing within the operation of an Agreement between an employers' Association and a workmen's union an employer not a member of the Association could be dealt with only by legislation.

Transport Workers Strike. Certain disturbances at Rotherhithe on June 11th, 1912, and complaints against the conduct of the police in connection therewith

Rep.

1912–13 Cd. 6367. See *Police*. p. 367.

Profit-Sharing and Labour Co-Partnership in the United Kingdom

Rep., apps., index. pp. 160. 1912

1912–13 Cd. 6496, xliii, 853

D. F. Schloss, G. S. Barnes.

Profit-sharing is understood to involve an agreement between an employer and his workpeople under which the latter receive in addition to their wages a share, fixed beforehand, in the profits of the undertaking. A grant or bonus, therefore, made at the absolute discretion of an employer, and not upon any pre-arranged basis, is not a case of profit-sharing for the present purpose. It would be difficult, without a special enquiry, to determine in the less well-organized trades in which many of the profit-sharing schemes have been started, whether the wages paid are the full current district rates. Labour Co-partnership is an extension of Profit - sharing, enabling the worker to accumulate his share of profit in the capital of the business employing him, thus gaining the rights and responsibilities of a shareholder. A still further stage is found in some co-partnership schemes which provide for a direct share in the management as well as a share in the profits, one or more seats on the board of directors being expressly reserved for representatives of the workpeople. The results of annual inquiries made to keep up to date the detailed report of 1894 have been published in the *Board of Trade Labour Gazette* and the *Abstract of Labour Statistics*. The number of schemes now in operation is 133, and the number of workpeople employed in firms having such schemes being about 106,000. These 133 schemes are the survivors of nearly 300 profit-sharing arrangements of which 163 have been abandoned. The Report deals with profit-sharing and co-partnership in private firms, companies and co-operative societies, and the conversion of ordinary businesses into co-operative societies.

See *Profit Sharing and Labour Co-partnership Abroad*; 1914 Cd. 7283, xlvi, 1.

Industrial Disputes Investigation Act of Canada, 1907

Rep., apps. pp. 33. [1913]

1912–13 *Cd.* 6603, *xlvii*, 303
sgd. Dec., 1912

G. Askwith.

As a result of a dispute on the Canadian Pacific Railway in 1902, the *Railway Labour Disputes* Act, 1903, was

passed. This gave the Government power, when a strike was threatened, to refer the dispute to a Committee of Conciliation or, failing that, to a Board of Arbitration. The success of the Act was marked and following a prolonged strike of miners in Alberta, the Industrial Disputes Investigation Act, 1907 (The Lemieux Act), was passed. It requires any dispute arising in mining, transport and communication or public utility services to be submitted to a Board of Conciliation and Arbitration before a strike or lock-out could be declared. Thirty days' notice of any intended change in the wages or hours must be given; pending discussion by the Board, the relations between the parties must remain unchanged, and no strike or lock-out may be declared. The Act does not destroy the right of either side to terminate contracts or interfere with the organization of employers or workmen.

The virtue of the Act is not in its restrictions on the right to strike or to lock-out, nor has the imposition of penalties been satisfactory. Its essence is that by providing for impartial enquiry, it permits the public to obtain full knowledge of the causes of a dispute and gives time for an element of calm judgment to be introduced. Despite the differences between Canada and Great Britain, powers of investigation and recommendation would be an advantage in this country, at any rate in cases in which the public were likely to be seriously affected. A large number of trade unions might voluntarily afford time for investigation and recommendation; sympathetic strikes prior to an examination of the dispute would be unnecessary. The valuable portion of the Act is its promotion of the spirit of conciliation and even without the restrictive features aiming at delaying stoppages until after enquiry, it would be suitable and practicable in this country. An appendix gives the text of the Act.

See *Operation of certain laws in the British Dominions and Foreign Countries*

*affecting Strikes and Lock-outs with especial
reference to Public Utility Services;* 1912–13
Cd. 6081, lxxix, 1.

Industrial Agreements

Industrial Council. Rep. pp. 22. 1913.
  Mins. of ev., apps., index. 1913

1913 *Cd.* 6952, *xxviii*, 1. *Mins. of ev.,*
etc.; 1913 *Cd.* 6953, *xxviii*, 23
apptd. July, 1912. *sgd. July,* 1913

G. Askwith (*Ch.*) and 26 others.

'(1) *What is the best method of securing
the due fulfilment of Industrial Agreements;*
(2) *How far, and in what manner, Industrial
Agreements which are made between representative bodies of employers and of
workmen should be enforced throughout
a particular trade or district.*'

As there was no legal definition of
an 'industrial agreement' the Council
defined it as 'an arrangement arrived
at by employers and workpeople with
a view to formulating the general
conditions of employment in a particular trade or district'. Such agreements
could not be compared with commercial
contracts, because of the peculiar
conditions attached to them, some of
which are the numbers of persons
involved, the circumstances which surround trade movements, which make
it difficult to obtain a well-defined
authority to enter into a settlement, and
the difficulty of ascertaining beforehand
the exact wishes of those represented.
Their success had been mainly due to
the recognition on both sides of
the moral obligations involved. The
evidence given regarding the strikes
in the Northumberland Coal industry in
1916 in connection with the Eight
Hours Agreement, in the London
Taxicab trade, 1913, and of London
Carters (qq. 1–351) illustrate the difficulties which may surround agreements affecting large bodies of men.
In one case a large majority objected
to the agreement which had been
signed by their representatives, and
in another it was found that owing to
circumstances connected with the price

of petrol, the operation of one of the
clauses of the Award would probably
have made a considerable reduction
in the men's wages. 'The circumstances
leading up to the conclusion of an
agreement, and the circumstances subsequently existing will frequently be
found to indicate that some amount of
elasticity is inevitable.'

Many agreements contain no clause
for dealing with cases of disagreement
regarding interpretation, though most
industries provided for the consideration of disputes by voluntary Conciliation and Arbitration Boards and by
Joint Councils. These had worked
satisfactorily and in many cases where
they had failed recourse had been had
to the Board of Trade, or some neutral
authority to arbitrate in the matter.
The 'fulfilment of agreements' was
easiest and most successful in those
industries where there was the greatest
amount of organization both of employers and workers. But opinion was
divided as to the desirability of introducing any form of legislative compulsion to further trade organization
whether of workers or employers; or
to inflict monetary punishments or
prohibit the giving of assistance to
persons in breach. The majority were
in favour of the terms of the agreement
being enforceable at law, though many
disliked legislative interference with
their trade.

Collective bargaining based on consent met with the strongest approval.
Moral influences should in every way
be brought to bear in the strict carrying
out of agreements. But where a breach
is found to have been committed,
Associations should accept the findings
of a Tribunal. Parties to an agreement
should be able to apply to the Board of
Trade to cause an enquiry to be held,
to determine whether or not the agreement should be extended, and its terms
made obligatory upon persons not
members of the Associations represented by the signatories to the agreement.

Six members signed Memorandum
(1) disapproving of imposing agree-

ments on parties not signatories. In Memorandum (2) Mr. Ratcliffe-Ellis stated that it should be implied in every industrial agreement that enquiry by impartial tribunal should precede strikes and lock-outs, and that it should be made illegal to give assistance to any persons represented as signatories to agreements, who had contravened the terms of the agreement. In Memorandum (3) Mr. Siemens stressed the necessity for the ratification of an agreement by the parties concerned before its operation, and that ample provisions should be made for discussion on questions as they arise. Only in the ultimate stage should there be reference to an independent authority who should finally dispose of the matter. Witnesses include prominent representatives of employers and of trade unions.

Clyde Munition Workers

Ministry of Munitions. Rep. pp. 5. 1915

1914–16 Cd. 8136, *xxix*, 297

Lord Balfour of Burleigh, Macassey.

'*To enquire into the causes and circumstances of the apprehended differences affecting munition workers in the Clyde district.*'

Wherever friction between an employer and a workman arises in a particular munitions establishment, it seems to lead to a state of irritation amongst organized workers which becomes elevated into a question of principle affecting all employers and workers throughout the district. The Committee made a large number of recommendations on matters which had arisen in the Clyde district. Employers should not enter on a clearance certificate the reasons for a workman's dismissal, nor should a workman be entitled to leave for more highly paid work unless that work were more important in the country's interest; improvements to procedure should include the right of appeal from the decisions of Munitions Tribunals, and imprisonment for non-payment of fines

should be replaced by deductions from wages. There should be an official statement clarifying the position of workmen engaged on non-munition work in establishments making munitions in regard to clearance certificates, obeying domestic work rules and obeying foremen's orders.

3. TRUCK, PIECE WAGES, CHECKWEIGHING

Truck Acts

Dept. Cttee. Vol. I. Rep., apps. pp. iv, 142. 1908. Vols. II, III. Mins. of ev., index. 1908. Vol. IV. Précis of ev., apps. 1909

1908 *Cd.* 4442, *lix*, 1. *Mins. of ev., etc.*; 1908 *Cd.* 4443, *Cd.* 4444, *lix*, 147. 1909 *Cd.* 4568, *xlix*, 177

apptd. April, 1906. *sgd. Dec.*, 1908

T. Shaw (*Ch.*), Brotherton, Cawley, Delevingne, Maddison, Yarrow, Tennant (Mrs. M.), Walsh.

'*To inquire into the operation of the Truck Acts, and to consider and report what amendments, or extensions, of those Acts, or changes in their administration, are desirable; particularly whether fines and deductions from wages should be prohibited, and further to consider and report whether the practice of shop-assistants and certain classes of work-people being lodged and boarded by their employers gives rise to abuses needing remedy by an extension of the Truck Acts or by other action of the State.*'

The Act of 1725 required employers to pay the full wages or other prices agreed on in good and lawful money of the kingdom, and not to pay the said wages . . . or any part thereof in goods or *by way of truck*. The Act of 1831, which repealed a mass of legislation and became the leading statute, added that no condition was to be imposed in the contract of service, directly or indirectly, as to where, how, or with whom, wages or any part of wages were to be expended. The Act applied to a large number of trades specifically named, and so did not include masses of the population engaged in other trades not named, e.g. labourers engaged in the construction of railways. Truck continued to flourish until an inspectorate was set up by the Act of 1887, when more classes of workers were covered; but the question of deductions from wages was not dealt with. The Committee considered (1) workers outside the Acts; (2) deductions from wages; (3) miscellaneous, and (4) shop assistants and the living-in system.

Workers outside the Acts.—The Act of 1831 had been interpreted to cover contracts for 'work or labour' and not contracts for the 'results of labour'. In 1887 protection was given to persons not working under contract but selling articles made in the home with materials supplied by themselves, but it did not cover those to whom work was 'let out or given out to be done'. Where wages were paid in the 'current coin of the realm', there was often an obligation to spend it on goods at a shop owned by the persons providing the work and the raw materials. In the Midlands the lace clippers were outside the Act, as they were 'not bound to execute the work themselves'. In Donegal socks were knitted at 9d. and 10d. a dozen pairs and the truck master would give out the wool, take in the work, paying for it in tea (q. 1713). In Cornwall the truck master was the local draper, who supplied the wool for fishermen's guernseys and paid in drapery for work done. Similar instances were given of corset work near Bristol; glove work in Somerset, and the exquisite work from wool, often of the worker's own growing, in the Shetland Islands.

Deductions from wages covered fines, damage to goods, spoilt work, etc. The Act of 1896 attempted to protect the worker from harsh and unreasonable fines, and the factory inspectorate had been able to deal with most of the bad cases. But the phrase 'fair and reasonable' was open to many defini-

tions and the words 'due order and decorum' led to frivolous fines for having curlers in the hair, sneezing, etc. (qq. 1831–5). Workers maintained that fines were not a deterrent and that the moral effect was bad, as it often led to irritation and sense of injustice. Suspension or dismissal was put forward by some as the better alternative, though Mr. Bell preferred fines, as 'suspension is never less than one day, whereas a fine may be less than a day's wage' (q. 4834). Amongst employers there was more diversity of opinion, some regarded fining as an efficient deterrent, whereas suspension of a particular worker might disorganize the work of others, or dismissal of a man with special skill might create great hardship both to the employer and the employee. Officials in evidence agreed with some forms of penalties short of suspension or dismissal and pointed to difficulties which might occur if fines were abolished.

Deductions for damage were harshest in the unskilled and unorganized trades, or where bad work was the result of 'other causes'. In the toy balloon trade the number of finished balloons on which wages were assessed was influenced by weather conditions. In the pen trade women were paying up to half their wages for 'waste', and were so much in debt that regular weekly payments were being deducted from their wages. In the weaving trades workers complained of being penalized for damage outside their control; but employers stated that faults often occurred as a result of mutual emulation of workers trying to outvie one another in quantity of work done and amount of money earned. The majority of employers thought that workers should pay for damage caused by carelessness, incompetence and indifference. The 'official' view was that in assessing 'harshness and unreasonableness' regard should be had to wages earned and other circumstances of the case. Deductions for tools, machines, standing room, gas, etc., were made chiefly in the old established trades. Any proposed interference with existing customs would 'need tact and delicate handling on both sides' in order to sweep away a complicated and archaic system. Deductions in respect of benefits or other advantages included payments for housing, medicine, medical attendance, etc. The only serious complaint on housing came from the mining and Scottish bleaching trades, where it might be a condition of employment that the worker should live in the employer's house, rent being deducted from wages.

'*Living-in*' *by shop assistants* had ceased to exist to any appreciable extent, except in the drapery (Miss Bondfield, qq. 13093-243) and grocery trades. But over-crowding, unsuitable accommodation, bad food, dangers of lack of supervision for young girls and boys, etc., still existed and there was a request by the trade union representatives for its abolition, or for the application of the Truck Acts. A test advertisement for assistants had shown 23 in favour of living out, 8 against it and 14 indifferent. This, thought Mr. Edwin Jones (qq. 17990-3), represented the general feeling of male assistants.

The chief recommendations of the Committee were that the law should be consolidated; that the Truck Acts should cover outworkers; that fines should be abolished for young persons under sixteen, should not exceed 5 per cent of the week's wages and should be deducted only in the week in which they were imposed, that a list of those imposed should be sent to the Factory Inspector and posted in the works, and that workers should have a right of appeal. No deductions should be made in respect of materials which go into the substance of the fabric or product, nor in respect of tools, machinery, standing room, light, etc.; for the provision of mess rooms and similar facilities there should be separate charges; rent should be by free contract and separate from the contract of employment; the provision of house or lodging accommodation by the employer should be allowed; medical services should be by arrangement between worker and employer. The Central Authority should make regulations regarding the accommodation provided in living-in establishments, which should be inspected by the local authority.

In separate memos., Mr. Delevingne and Mr. Yarrow discussed equitable ways of dealing with fines, deductions and charges. In a Minority Report, Mrs. H. J. Tennant and Mr. Walsh made radical proposals: disciplinary fines, fines for bad work or injury to materials, and the living-in system should be abolished by law. They set out a much wider range of workers who should be covered by the Truck Acts and recommended that local authorities should be under a statutory obligation to appoint inspectors for the enforcement of the Truck Acts in shops.

See *The Truck System*. Com. Vol. I. Rep. App. XV; 1871 C. 326, xxxvi, 1. *Truck Acts and Checkweighing Clause in the Coal Mines Regulation Acts*. Memo. containing a collection of legal decisions; 1896 C. 8048, lxxvi, 1109. *Truck in the Shetlands*. Miss Meicklejohn. Rep. Factories and Workshops. Ann. Rep.; 1910 Cd. 5191, xxviii, 589.

Checkweighing in the Iron and Steel Trades

Dept. Cttee. Rep. pp. 15. 1907. Mins. of ev. 1907

1908 *Cd.* 3846, *xi*, 691. *Mins. of ev.*; 1908 *Cd.* 3847, *xi*, 707 *apptd. May, sgd. Nov.*, 1907

E. F. G. Hatch (*Ch.*), Ainsworth, Eccles, Hodge, Morgan, Walls, Wilson.

'*To consider and report what would be the best method of securing to workmen in the Iron and Steel Trades, who are paid by weight, the means of checking the correctness of the wages they receive.*'

Since 1894 there have been repeated requests for the weight of output to be checked by the workmen's independent representative, on similar lines to the system which was made compulsory in the mines by the Coal Mines Regulation Act of 1860. Opposition came from the employers in the steel smelting branch of the trade, where weighing every ingot would cause serious delays and a reduction in output. Sample checkweighing was, however, in operation and had been practised successfully since 1896 (qq. 3596–648).

The Committee recommended that where materials are normally weighed the men should have the right to appoint a checkweighman. In the case of ingots there should be test weighings at regular intervals of not less than 14 days under conditions agreed upon by the employers and men or in default of agreement determined by arbitration. Divulgence by a checkweighman of trade secrets should be made a criminal offence.

Checkweighing in Chalk Quarries and Cement and Limestone Quarries and Lime Works

Dept. Cttee. Rep., mins. of ev., app. pp. 37. 1908

1908 *Cd.* 4002, *xi*, 843
apptd. Aug., 1907. *sgd. Feb.,* 1908

E. F. G. Hatch (*Ch.*), Harston, Hartle, Morgan, Ryan.

'*To consider and report what would be the best means of securing to persons employed in lime and cement works and chalk quarries, who are paid by weight or measurement, the means of checking the correctness of the wages they receive.*'

The employers have no objection to the principle that workmen should have the right to check the measurements and weights on which their wages are computed, but the variety of materials, processes and practices makes it difficult to find methods of doing this. Workers paid by measure or weight should be allowed to appoint, at their own expense, a checkweighman to check tares and capacities of wagons. In cement works, where workmen are paid on the weight of the finished product, stock should be taken to allow an adjustment of wages at least once every six months.

The Checking of Piece-work Wages in Dock Labour

Dept. Cttee. Rep. pp. 10. 1908. Mins. of ev. 1908

1908 *Cd.* 4380, *xxxiv*, 467. *Mins. of ev.*; 1908 *Cd.* 4381, *xxxiv*, 479
apptd. Dec., 1907. *sgd. Oct.,* 1908

E. F. G. Hatch (*Ch.*), Anderson, Bellhouse, Harrington, Larkin, Morgan, Orbell, Sexton, Wignall, Gordon, Mead, Scrutton, Hardy.

'*To consider and report what would be the best means of securing to persons employed in dock labour who are paid by weight or measurement the means of checking the correctness of the wages they receive.*'

The workmen claimed that where materials were weighed, they should have the right to appoint a checkweighman and that in all other cases the employer should be required to show them or their representative a certificate to prove that they were being paid correctly. (J. Larkin said 'We do not want stevedores', q. 517.) In many cases the workmen had no means of checking the accuracy of their piece work wages or of compelling employers to prove it, and where they had doubted the figures had frequently to obtain evidence by indirect methods. In some instances adjustments had been made only after the employer had been threatened with legal action.

Workmen should have the right to appoint a checkweighman at their own expense; for goods not weighed the employer should be required to produce a certificate of quantities of goods handled by them; the stevedore should substantiate his certificate (if disputed) of the quantities on which he is paid. Workmen should be free to appoint as their representative either one of themselves, or someone not actually employed, such as a trade union official. The majority of the Committee regarded the shipowners' proposal, which involved the checking of merchants' weights and quantities, as an ideal solution, but outside their terms of reference. In a minority report Gordon, Mead and Scrutton said that without such a check it was impossible to deal with the problem satisfactorily. Hardy objected also to the examination of employers' accounts by someone not in their employ and possibly with less knowledge than the men on the work, and felt that it might lead to the abandonment of piece work, which some of the labour representatives on the Committee apparently desired.

Piecework Wages

Methods of applying the 'Particulars' Section of the Factory and Workshop
   Act, 1901. Rep. pp. 19.   1909

1909 Cd. 4842, xxi, 709

E. F. G. Hatch

'To inquire into and report on the question of the application of the "Particulars" Section of the Factory and Workshop Act to persons employed in Bleaching and Dyeing Works, Cartridge Works, and Chocolate Works, and to Platers in Shipbuilding Yards.'

A description is given of the five industries in question and recommendations were made for the workers to have access to the written particulars of their rates of pay, and where a gang system obtains or where an aggregate sum is divided amongst several workers in unequal shares, knowledge of the shares of each. There should also be some provision for enabling the worker to check the amount of completed work on which wages depend.

—— Foundries. Rep. pp. 7.   1913

1913 Cd. 6990, xxiii, 877

The request arose out of a deputation of Iron Moulders which had been received by the Home Secretary. The case was that whilst workmen generally knew the prices payable for piece work, cases did occur where a workman had

no means of knowing what the prices amounted to, as, for example where there was much changing about and a man was given patterns he had not previously handled, the rate of payment for which he might not know. Recommended that the 'Particulars Order' should be applied.

4. FAIR WAGES, HOME WORK, TRADES BOARDS

Fair Wages

Cttee. Rep. apps. pp. iv, 52.   1908.
   Mins. of ev., app., index. 1908

1908 Cd. 4422, xxxiv, 551. Mins. of ev., etc.; 1908 Cd. 4423, xxxiv, 607
apptd. Aug., 1907. sgd. Nov., 1908

G. H. Murray (Ch.), Bailey, Black, De La Bère, Fox, Hillier, King.

'To consider the working of the Fair Wages Resolution of the House of Commons of the 13th February, 1891, as embodied in Government Contracts, and to report whether any administrative changes, especially with a view to the prevention of evasion, the enforcement of the rate current in the district, and greater uniformity of interpretation and working, are desirable in order to enable the objects of the Resolution to be more effectually attained.'

The Fair Wages Resolution, passed by the House of Commons in 1891, was quoted by several Government Departments when placing contracts. Its object was to prevent sweating and to 'secure the payment of such wages as are generally accepted as current in each trade for competent workmen'. Trade union witnesses stated that in many industries working under Government contract this clause was ineffective because it did not cover many other conditions of employment. In unorganized and ill-organized trades there was no generally accepted rate; in isolated industries there was no district rate, and where the situation was changing owing to the introduction of women's work, women were often doing the same jobs as men at lower

rates of pay. It was difficult to find out
if the clause was being observed in those
cases where the contractor's name was
not published, and in sub-contract and
home work.

Suggestions that the words 'trade
union rate of wages' should be substituted for 'current wages' were
rejected on the ground that where the
trade union had established the rate,
that rate would be the current rate, and
that if it had not, the Government
could not enforce a rate which might
be above the market rate; in addition
the words would not provide for cases
where there was no trade union. The
fair wages clause should stay, but where
it did not or could not apply various
other methods, such as fixing wages
in the contract, wages boards, etc.,
should be used. Piece rates should be
fixed to yield more than time rates.
Co-operation and uniformity should
be established amongst the various
Government contracting departments
by the establishment of a committee
empowered to deal with problems
arising out of the placing of contracts.

Home Work
Sel. Cttee.

*'To consider and report upon the condi-
tions of labour in trades in which Home
Work is prevalent and the proposals,
including those for the establishment of
wages boards and the licensing of work
places, which have been made for the
remedying of existing abuses.'*

The Report for 1907 is a formal
presentation of the minutes of evidence;
1907 (290) vi, 55.

—— Report, proc., mins. of ev., apps.
pp. l, 216. Index. 1908

1908 (246) (246-*Ind.*) *viii*, 1.
re-apptd. Feb., o.p. July, 1908

T. Whittaker (*Ch.*), Arkwright, Bridge-
man, Bull, Boland, Brunner, Money,
Devlin, Dewar, Fell, Gooch, Hender-
son, Lamb, Law, Massie, Masterman,
Parkes, Richardson, Robinson, Samuel,
Trevelyan.

While it is not possible to say whether
sweating has decreased or not since the
Dunraven Committee reported in 1890,
it still exists in such a degree as to call
urgently for the interference of Parliament. Persons working for an employer in his home, whether members
of his family or not, are covered by
the Factory and Workshop Act, but
those who undertake work for others
and do it in their own homes are not,
being protected only by Section 108,
which gives the local authority power
to prohibit home work on 'premises
which are injurious or dangerous to the
health of the persons employed therein'.
This group of home workers consists
chiefly of single and married women
doing regular work as part or whole
time family breadwinners; women
working when the husband was unemployed — 'casual workers' — and
wives and daughters opting to increase
the family income. The circumstances
and earnings varied considerably, as
was shown by the evidence given by
separate groups of working women
(qq. 2782–3048, qq. 1788–2221). In
some cases it represented only such
time as could be spared from other
duties, but in others it represented
'almost ceaseless toil during all the
hours the workers are awake from
Monday morning until Saturday night'.
The earnings are low because much of
the work requires little training, can
be done at home, and as it is paid for
at piece rates, can be undertaken by old
and disabled persons. The supply of
labour for home work is thus large and
elastic. Sometimes the product faces
machine competition, or can be made
by the consumer himself if its price is
not low.

It is undesirable to prohibit home
work, but all home workers should be
registered, and provision of Section 9
of the Public Health Act, 1875, should
be extended to rooms in which home
work is done. No proposals which
fail to increase the incomes of home
workers can effect any appreciable
amelioration. It is as justifiable to fix
minimum wages as to fix minimum

standards of sanitation. An industry which cannot yield a minimum income to industrious workers is parasitic and should not continue, but the usual result is the reform of the industry. There should be experimental legislation covering home workers in the tailoring, shirtmaking, underclothing and baby linen trades and in the finishing processes of machine made lace. After enquiry Wages Boards, consisting of equal numbers of employers and employed, should be established in selected trades, and they should fix a general minimum time wage and such minimum piece rates as would enable an average worker to earn the minimum time rate. It should be an offence to pay or offer rates lower than those fixed.

The Sweated·Industries Bill, referred to the Committee, was not examined in detail, but was reported without amendment. Mary Macarthur representing the National Federation of Women Workers, Clementina Black, the Anti-Sweating League, Miss Squire, the Factory Inspectorate and Mr. Delevingne of the Home Office, gave evidence.

See *Outwork in 1907*. Chief Factory Inspector Rep.; 1909 Cd. 4633, xxi, 623.

Trade Boards Act Provisional Orders Bill

Sel. Cttee. Rep., proc., mins. of ev. pp. vi, 61. 1913

1913 (209) *xiv*, 765
apptd. June, o.p. July, 1913

J. Compton-Rickett (*Ch.*), Macdonald, Carlile, Wright, Nield, Pointer.

There were five Provisional Orders relating to sugar confectionery and food preserving, the shirt making, hollow-ware, linen and cotton embroidery and calendering and machine ironing laundries. There were no petitions against the first four Orders and these were confirmed. The Committee thought that the Order covering 'steam laundries' might induce such laundries to convert steam into some other form of power. The Order should cover all laundries, and petitions should be allowed from a wider group.

—— Report, Special Report, proc., mins. of ev., apps. pp. vi, 194. 1914
1914 (317) *x*, 609
apptd. June, o.p. July, 1914
del. Carlile.

The word 'steam' had been deleted, and the Order now covered all laundries. There was opposition from the trade on the grounds that there was no demand from the workers and that good as well as bad wages were paid. The Committee suggested that more information should be obtained about wages and conditions in the trade and recommended that any further Order should have a wider application.

5. CONDITIONS OF SEAMEN, POST OFFICE WORKERS, SHOP ASSISTANTS

Navy Rations

Cttee. Rep., apps. pp. 70. 1901

1901 *Cd.* 782, *xlii*, 551
apptd. May, 1900. *sgd.* ——

E. Rice (*Ch.*), Fellowes, Yorke, Bradford, Irvine, Smith.

'To investigate the general question of the victualling of the men of the Royal Navy.' The Letter of Appointment excludes from consideration the abolition of the system of savings or of canteens, or the Government management of canteens.

Rations in the Navy have been determined by the fact that ships have to stand victualled ready to put to sea under war conditions. This has meant the existence of reserve stocks of food in excess of peace requirements, that the rations lack variety because they must consist of food not subject to undue deterioration, and that when issued they may be older than is desirable. There can be no reduction in the size of reserves, but age limit beyond which they should not be issued should be fixed for the various articles. Two systems have arisen to offset these stern conditions. 'Savings' allows men to take cash in lieu of rations, and canteens cater for individual taste at times congenial to supplementary meals. That canteens are on the increase and Savings have doubled during the last 50 years shows that some adjustment should be made in the official rations and meal times, if there is not to be a further development outside official arrangements.

The framing of an ideal ration which the men will take and consume is very difficult in these conditions, but account has to be taken of the rising standards of life of the class of men on shore from whom the Navy is recruited.

The Committee recommended that milk and jam should be added and that there should be more tea, sugar, variety of meat, etc., and that the two unofficial meals should be added to the three official meals. If at any time revision of 'savings' price is considered, the Committee recommended three-quarters of the average cost price of each article. The responsibility of canteens should be with the Commanding Officers.

Continuous Discharge Certificates for Seamen

Cttee. Pt. I. Rep. pp. 8. 1900. Pt. II. Mins. of ev., app., index. 1900

1900 Cd. 133, *lxxvii*, 99. Mins. of ev., etc.; 1900 Cd. 136, *lxxvii*, 107
apptd. *April*, 1899. sgd. *March*, 1900

Lord Dudley (*Ch.*), Howell, Chalmers, Hall.

'To consider and report on the steps which should be taken with a view to the introduction of a system of continuous discharges for seamen.'

Certificates of discharge have been recognized by Statute since 1729, but in all the various experiments made in them since that time none have been general or compulsory. The Board of

Trade now issues a standard form which the captain is required to sign recording the discharge of a seaman for a single voyage. He is not required to give information regarding character, though in practice he does assess it in the discs at the bottom of the form by the letters 'V.G.', 'G.' or 'decline to report' (W. Murton, qq. 1–48). The disadvantage of this method is that it records one voyage only; gives no indication of a man's proficiency at sea, gives the master sole adjudication of a man's character; can be easily forged, and therefore gives no protection to the master when engaging a crew (J. Havelock Wilson, qq. 1419–544).

The employer's evidence was on the whole in favour of a continuous discharge certificate giving also a continuous record of character. Evidence by J. Havelock Wilson and other members of the seamen's trade union favoured legislation to make it compulsory for a seaman to have a continuous discharge book similar to that held by the Royal Naval·Reserve. They disagreed with character being recorded, as it gave too much power to the captain, and it singled seamen out for treatment which shoremen have sternly refused to accept. A continuous discharge book would protect the experienced men against those posing to be efficient after one voyage at sea. It should describe its owner and thus make forgery and false ownership of a book difficult. No man should be allowed to ship a sailor unless he could produce his book (J. Havelock Wilson, qq. 1419–544).

The Committee recommended: the form approved by the Board of Trade should be a continuous discharge certificate in book form, that it should be the only form prescribed, and that only upon the seaman's request should it be endorsed with a copy of the master's report on his character. Separate forms should also be provided for a report on character. The system should be introduced by stages.

Certain questions Affecting the Mercantile Marine

Cttee. Pt. I. Rep. pp. xiii. 1903.
Pt. II. Mins. of ev. 1903. Pt. III.
        Apps., index. 1903

1903 *Cd.* 1607, *lxii*, 1. *Mins. of ev., etc.*;
1903 *Cd.* 1608, *Cd.* 1609, *lxii*, 15
apptd. Jan., 1902. *sgd. May*, 1903

F. H. Jeune (*Ch.*), Anderson, Blake,
Burt, Chalmers, Denny, Howell,
Lloyd, Milburn, Wilson.

'*To enquire into and report upon the following matters:* (1) *The causes that have led to the employment of a large and increasing proportion of Lascars and Foreigners in the British Merchant Service, and the effect of such employment upon the reserve of seamen of British Nationality available for naval purposes in time of peace or war;* (2) *The sufficiency or otherwise of the existing law and practice for securing proper food, accommodation, medical attention, and reasonable conditions of comfort and well-being for seamen on British merchant ships;* (3) *The prevalence of desertion and other offences against discipline in the Mercantile Marine.*'

The decrease in the number of British seamen in merchant vessels between 1896 and 1901 was 4,597 and the increase in the number of foreign seamen in the same period was 5,168. In addition the increase in Lascars and other Asiatics amounted to 9,520. In evidence Havelock Wilson claimed that the numbers of foreign seamen were far larger owing to the fact that so many of them hid their identity under English names (q. 5230). The decrease in the numbers of British seamen was attributed to the superior attractions of shore employments. Speaking generally it was not thought that foreign seamen were employed because of their cheapness, although many British ships frequently recruited their crews from foreign ports, e.g. Antwerp and Hamburg. Lascars and other Asiatic seamen who are British subjects stand on a different footing. Lascars are in many cases hereditary sailors and have an additional claim

in view of the fact that British ships have displaced the native trading vessels.

As to whether the increase of foreign seamen gave any ground for apprehension in the event of war, because of the varieties of nationalities represented, it was doubted that there would be any shortage of men. Swedes, Norwegians and Danes represented one-third of the total of foreigners employed. It was probable that some merchant ships would be laid up, and their crews would be available for employment, and in any case, if freights and wages rose the effect would be to draw men from the shore to sea employment. At present the great mass of naval reserve men came from the fisherman and yachtsman class and from seamen of the coasting vessels. It is on these classes that reliance must be placed in times of war, rather than on the crews of the merchant marine, though there should be improved inducements and active recruiting in order to attract a greater number of seamen on foreign-going ships to join the Royal Naval Reserve. It was not thought that foreigners were driving out British subjects, thus compelling them to join the ranks of the unemployed, although the competition was regarded as most serious for those British seamen only imperfectly competent or whose best days had passed. To prevent any deterioration which such general tendencies might have on the British seagoing race, it was thought that steps should be made to ameliorate the lot of British seamen in order to induce the young to go and to remain at sea.

There should be a properly certified cook on every foreign-going vessel of 1,000 gross register and over; the scale of provisions recommended in the report should be universally adopted; the Board of Trade should have the power to inspect the provisions of any vessel whose probable voyage exceeds 21 days' duration; powers should be given to the Board of Trade to withhold the continuous discharge certificate of any seaman who wilfully fails to join his vessel after signing articles; a seaman should have the right of appeal against a master who 'declines to report' on character; efforts should be made to increase the numbers joining the Royal Naval Reserve, especially firemen; no foreigner should be engaged unless he could speak some English; he should be given facilities to become naturalized as a British subject after service of four years on British merchant ships. Comfortable quarters should be provided, though the evidence is conflicting and newer vessels have better accommodation; the provision of proper stoves and other special places for meals would be wise. The training ships and the training of boys on merchant ships should be encouraged. A system of voluntary examinations and certification of masters and officers in the elements of medical knowledge should be established.

Seamen's Wages

Cttee. Rep. pp. 8. 1905

1905 (334) *lxxi*, 179
apptd. Jan., sgd. July, 1905

A. Bonar Law (*Ch.*), Fergusson, Bloomfield, Heath, Milburn.

'*Copy of Report of the Committee appointed by the Board of Trade to consider the operation of the existing Provisions of the Law (Merchant Shipping Act, 1894, and the Merchant Shipping (Mercantile Marine Fund) Act, 1898) relating to the disposal of the wages of seamen who have deserted; the conveyance of distressed seamen and the recovery of expenses incurred in the relief and conveyance of such seamen; the collection of the wages and effects of deceased seamen; the collection of fines levied on seamen, due to His Majesty's Exchequer; and to report what, if any, Amendments to the Law are advisable.*'

It is the practice of the Master to retain the wages of seamen who have deserted, and as there is a serious number of desertions each year the sums retained are considerable. Owners should render an account of expenses caused by desertion and the balance should be paid to the Consul, Colonial Office or Superintendent as the case may be. Distressed seamen are usually wrecked seamen. Various cases in which the shipowners had contended that a seaman wrecked but in receipt of wages was not in distress had come before the Court, which had ruled that each case should be considered on its merits. The Merchant Shipping (Mercantile Marine Fund) Act, 1898, should be amended so as to make the liability of shipowners in such cases clear and to provide that the liability should extend to the cost of subsistence of seamen rescued at sea from wrecks until landed at a port either in the United Kingdom or abroad. The working of the Act with regard to the collection of the property of deceased seamen had been made difficult because of the changed conditions of trade since the Act was consolidated in 1894. In order to secure prompt settlement of the estates of deceased seamen, the Act should be amended so as to require property to be delivered from all British vessels registered in the United Kingdom. The simplification of the collection of fines should be made by an amendment to empower the Consul or Colonial Office before whom the seaman is discharged abroad, to receive the fines imposed and to credit the same in his account with the Board of Trade.

Supply and Training of Boy Seamen for the Mercantile Marine

Dept. Cttee. Vol. I. Rep. pp. iii, 8. 1907. Vol. II. Mins of ev., apps., index. 1908

1907 Cd. 3722, *lxxv*, 167. *Mins. of ev., etc.*; 1907 Cd. 3723, *lxxv*, 179
apptd. July, 1906. *sgd. Aug.*, 1907

H. E. Kearley (*Ch.*), Chalmers, Clarke, Devitt, Furness, Jones, Lewis, McLaren, Park, Runciman, Shankland, Watts, Wilson (J. H.), Wilson (C. H. W.).

'To consider and report upon the most practicable scheme for the supply and training of Boy Seamen of British Nationality for the Mercantile Marine.'

The steady decrease in the numbers of boys going to sea was shown by the fall in the number of indentures of apprenticeship from 18,303 in 1870 to 5,069 in 1905. In the days when sailing was predominant boys easily obtained employment at sea, but with the change to steam and the increasing severity of competition, shipowners declined to carry boys on the ground that it did not pay to do so, though there was an ample supply of boys wishing to go to sea. The prevailing view of the majority of witnesses was that any material increase, sufficient to replace in the near future any considerable proportion of the foreigners who serve in the Mercantile Marine, could be effected only by compelling shipowners to carry boys or by subsidizing the employment of boys. Compulsion, which would mean returning to the Navigation Laws, was not recommended. The amount of subsidy said to be adequate (£25) would be justified only if the numbers of foreign seamen became a serious objection on national grounds. In evidence Havelock Wilson said that foreign seamen were increasing and that they did constitute a threat (qq. 11046–57). Witnesses from the Admiralty stated that as a recruiting ground for the Navy, the Mercantile Marine would probably be more limited in the future because of the high degree of skill and training needed on battleships.

Improvements in food, cooking and accommodation and the bettering of the life at sea generally contained in the Merchant Shipping Act 'which became law last Session' may induce competent seamen to stay, and many who have left to return to sea employment. Shipowners should give a more extended trial to the indenture system. In view of the disinclination of shipowners to take untrained lads, considerable importance was attached to the work of the training ships and schools. During the year 1906 1,121 boys were sent into the Mercantile Marine and the Navy from 13 training ships, 397 of them from industrial and reformatory ships. But the efficiency of the ships was somewhat impaired by the prejudice some shipowners had against boys sent to them under magisterial warrants. The Committee concluded that any future increase in the supply of trained boys must be looked for from the ordinary training institutions, and that, subject to compliance with certain conditions, institutions engaged in training lads as sailors should be eligible for capitation grants. The average cost of a year's training was £30, and the grant should be £20 per annum, conditional upon two years' apprenticeship.

Desertion of Seamen from British Ships

Reports from Certain Foreign and Colonial Ports. pp. 26. 1909

1909 Cd. 4658, lxxviii, 23

In 1898, following a question asked in the House of Commons, reports on the numbers and causes of desertion of seamen from British ships were obtained from certain Colonial and Consular officers at certain ports (1899 C. 9265, lxxxvii). The statistics for 1908 showed that, notwithstanding the operation of the Merchant Shipping Act, 1906, the state of affairs had not materially altered. The chief factor determining the number of desertions was the attraction of higher wages, but the provisions of the Act, especially regarding the seamen's food, were not without influence. The Report gives figures for each port investigated.

Sight Tests

Dept. Cttee. Rep. pp. iv, 38. 1912. Mins. of ev., apps., index. 1912

1912–13 Cd. 6256, xlvi, 639. Mins. of ev., etc.; 1912–13 Cd. 6319, xlvi, 681 apptd. June, 1910. sgd. May, 1912

A. H. D. Acland (*Ch.*), Beck, Golding, Gotch, Hill, Nettleship, Parsons, Poynting, L. Rayleigh, Rücker, Sherrington.

'To inquire what degree of colour blindness or defective form vision in persons holding responsible positions at sea causes them to be incompetent to discharge their duties, and to advise whether any and, if so, what alterations are desirable in the Board of Trade Sight Tests at present in force for persons serving or intending to serve in the Merchant Service or in fishing vessels, or in the way in which these tests are applied.'

Colour vision tests had been introduced in 1877. Tests of form vision dated from 1894, and in 1909 the Board had decided that each eye should be examined separately, normal vision being required in one eye and at least half-normal in the other. This standard, which was enforceable from January 1914, should be retained by the Board, and any officer whose visual acuteness was below half-normal in his better eye should be considered incompetent. Various alterations in the colour tests were recommended. The approximate limits of colour defect compatible with safety could be tentatively placed at some luminosity ratio range such as that from ·87 to 1·15. Hill disagreed with these recommendations: there was no evidence that any casualties had been caused by defective form vision, and the need for higher standards had been exaggerated. With certain exceptions candidates should be examined with both eyes open.

Post Office Wages

Cttee. Pt. I. Rep., apps. pp. 43. 1904. Pt. II. Mins. of ev., apps., index. 1904

1904 Cd. 2170, *xxxiii*, 465. *Mins. of ev., etc.*; 1904 Cd. 2171, *xxxiii*, 511 *apptd. Aug.*, 1903. *sgd. May*, 1904

E. R. C. Bradford (*Ch.*), Booth, Brodrick, Burbidge, Fay.

'To enquire into the scales of pay received by the undermentioned classes of Established Post Office Servants, and to report whether, having regard to the conditions of their employment and to the rates current in other occupations, the remuneration of (a) Postmen, (b) Sorters (London), (c) Telegraphists (London), (d) Sorting Clerks and Telegraphists (Provincial) is adequate.'

After summarizing and commenting on the evidence the Committee set out what they considered to be General Principles. It was difficult to compare remuneration and conditions of work of the post office servants with workers in private industry, since payment by results and arbitrary promotion and dismissal were inapplicable, if not impossible, under the State. Postal workers were justified in resting their claims to remuneration on the responsible and exacting character of the duties performed and on the social position they filled as servants of the State. The State, for its part, did right in taking an independent course guided by principles of its own, irrespective of what others may do: 'neither following an example nor pretending to set one'. The public interest came first, but the terms offered should be such as to secure men and women of the requisite character and capacity, and ought to be such as to ensure the response of hearty service. The test of adequacy of the pay and conditions offered is in the numbers and character of those who apply to enter the service, their capacity and their contentment. On these tests, there is no lack of suitable candidates, nor complaints of their capacity, but there is widespread discontent. There is a just claim for the revision of the Tweedmouth settlement.

The Tweedmouth Commission (1897 (121) xliv), composed mainly of officials drawn from various departments, recommended the abolition of the existing system of classification, which carried with it allowances for special duties. This was accepted as the basis of the system of wage payment. The adjustments made in wages resulted in a higher average, but there was dissatisfaction because the remuneration of some duties which had received special remuneration were lowered under a uniform system. Moreover, uniformity of system as regards duties left untouched the differences of pay as regards place. Most of the complaints which the present Committee examined 'concerned the grievous inequalities felt under this system'. The dissatisfaction with the Tweedmouth Settlement has been aggravated by the general rise in wages and prices and in the standard of life, and by the great development of postal and telegraph business, which caused greater pressure of work.

The Committee agreed with much that had been said in support of a uniform rate throughout the country and that grading of the service as a whole would consolidate and simplify the organization, while removing much ground for discontent. The indoor staff should be welded into one service and allowances made for the cost of living, which should be contingent on the age of the officer and not on his length of service. The same arguments applied to postmen, although finer differences could be drawn. Sorters, telegraphists, counter clerks and counter clerks in London, and sorting clerks and telegraphists in the Provinces should be formed into one class of post office assistants, within which there should be grades of junior, senior and head assistants, with promotion based on length of service and competence. Women performing these duties should be similarly graded. The general scale of wages, for example, recommended for postmen in Central London was 22s. to 31s.; in the rest of London and for six great cities 21s. to 30s.; and in the rest of the country scales were based on population. For towns with a population over 25,000 there was a graded scale of extra allowances for those over 26 years of age. The scales are fully laid out in the Appendices.

Post Office Servants

Sel. Cttee. Rep., proc. pp. 194. 1907
    Mins. of ev. Vols. I, II. 1907

1907 (266) vii, 299. *Mins. of ev.*; 1906 (380) *xii*, Pt. I, 11, Pt. II
apptd. —, *o.p.* Dec., 1906. *re-apptd. Feb.*, *o.p. July*, 1907

Mr. Hobhouse (*Ch.*), Barker, Edwards, Hay, Hill, Meehan, Sutherland, Ward, Wardle.

'*To inquire into the wages and position of the principal classes of Post Office Servants and also of the Unestablished Sub-Postmasters; to examine, so far as may be necessary for the purpose of their Report, the conditions of employment of these classes; and to report whether, having regard to the conditions and prospects of their employment, and, so far as may be, to the standard rate of wages and the position of other classes of workers, the remuneration they receive is adequate or otherwise.*'

The Committee sat 68 times and of the 133 witnesses examined, 114 represented the principal classes of postal employees. The number and complexity of the points at issue were so great that some separate sixty-one subjects were dealt with, sixteen concerning the postal service as a whole and the rest the conditions and wages, etc., of forty-five different groups of employees.

The restrictions on civil rights, of which many witnesses complained, were a matter affecting the Civil Service as a whole and not just the post office workers. On the claim for early retirement and early pensions, the Committee stated that the work did not entail more than the normal strain and therefore retirement should not take place before the age of sixty-five. Other general questions considered were the hours of labour, including night duties, medical attendance, sanitation and inspection of buildings, special leave, confidential reporting, fines, stoppage of increment, promotion, substitution, age limit of clerkship, clerical duties and risk allowances. On the organization of the services as a whole the 'Committee would have desired to be free to suggest a complete and total revision of the compartments into which the postal service is divided. The complexity and number of the existing classes cannot be satisfactory either to the Department or to the staff and greater economy and efficiency would unquestionably result if a completely fresh start were possible. But with time the vested interests of existing classes have grown to such an extent that it would be unfair to large numbers of the staff to disturb them without grave reason. Your Committee have therefore contented themselves with making recommendations which will not only reduce the excessive number of classes and procure simplicity and regularity of grading, but will assign to each rank its proper description of work and pay.' The remainder of the report deals with the classification, conditions of work and pay of the various groups.

Post Office Servants (Wages and Conditions of Employment)

Sel. Cttee. Rep., apps. pp. iv, 290. 1913. Proc. 1913. Mins of ev., Vols. I–II. 1913. Apps. 1913. Index. 1914

1913 (268) x, 295. Mins. of ev., etc.; 1913 (268) x, xi, xii, xiii apptd. March, o.p. Aug., 1913

Mr. Holt (Ch.), Boyton, Brady, Dawes, France, Gilmour, M'Callum, Orde-Powlett, Wilson.

'To inquire into the Wages and other Conditions of Employment of the principal classes of Post Office Servants, of the unestablished sub-postmasters, and of such of the smaller classes as the Committee may think necessary; and, having regard to the conditions and prospects of their employment and, as far as may be, to the standard rate of Wages and the position of other classes of workers, to report what alterations, if any, are desirable.'

Questions affecting post office servants generally. (i) Vested interests.

An impression has grown up that the Post Office has allowed established officers to regard conditions of service, such as salary, hours of work, etc., as unalterable without the consent of the individual officers in each class concerned. This has hampered administration and the Committee in making recommendations for improving the service. Recognition of vested interests should be confined to ensuring to each officer the rate of pay held out to him when entering the grade in which he is serving. (ii) Wages Basis. No evidence was brought to show that wages were lower than in other similar occupations, and there was no difficulty in securing a sufficient number of competent recruits. (iii) Official recognition of Associations of Post Office Servants. The success or otherwise of previous Committees in settling the points at issue can be judged by the number of memorials presented to the Postmaster General; 45 in 1905, 533 in 1909, 825 in 1910 and 630 in 1911, and by the increasing number of Parliamentary Questions during this period. Underlying the great number of detailed problems dealt with by investigating committees was the problem of the 'special recognition' of the employees associations. In 1906, Sydney Buxton, the Postmaster General, had made considerable extensions of it, and although there were sometimes difficulties in deciding bona-fide representation, it was admitted that it had been an advantage to the Service as a whole; but its continued success would depend more on the spirit on both sides than on a recognition of, and adherence to, definite rules of procedure. To the employees' demand for representation on bodies affecting their interests, the Committee stated that it could not entertain the claim that the Postmaster General, who is responsible to Parliament for the proper conduct of his Department, should first consult the Associations concerning matters affecting the staff under review. (iv) Promotion. This should be given solely in the interests of the service and to the officer most capable of performing the superior duties: it should never be regarded merely as a reward for past services, for which the wages of the grade is the proper reward. There is no reason for relaxing the test imposed at the efficiency bar in any of the classes.

Recommendations deal with the pay and conditions of work of over forty classes of post office servants and on difficulties arising from the transfer of the staff of the National Telephone Company to the Post Office. They should come into force not more than six months after the presentation of the report; the recommendation for each class must be taken as a whole and no recommendation should be interpreted as involving a compulsory reduction of pay of any full time officer already in the service.

Post Office Servants

Cttee. 1st Rep. pp. 14. 1915

*1914–16 Cd. 7995, xxxii, 1009
apptd. July, 1914. sgd. June, 1915*

G. S. Gibb (*Ch.*), King, Stuart, Wilkins, Young.

'*To examine from the point of view of the Department and its employees the issue with regard to the wages and conditions of employment of Post Office servants raised by the Report of the recent Select Committee of the House of Commons presided over by Mr. Holt, and to advise what modifications, if any, are desirable in the decisions taken on its recommendations in these matters.*'

The Committee decided to deal only with the questions which depended exclusively on the interpretation of the Holt report and were not affected by war conditions, and therefore confined itself to recommending a large number of adjustments in the details of wages and conditions.

Telegraphists' Cramp

Dept. Cttee. Rep., apps. pp. 74. 1911

*1911 Cd. 5968, xli, 711
apptd. —, sgd. Oct., 1911*

J. N. Barran (*Ch.*), Davis, Leonard, Purves, Sinclair, Thompson.

'*To enquire into the prevalence and causes of the disease known as telegraphists' cramp, and to report what means may be adopted for its prevention.*'

'Telegraphists' cramp is a disease of the central nervous system, and is a result of the weakening or breakdown of the cerebral controlling mechanism in consequence of strain upon a given set of muscles. . . . The characteristic feature of the disease . . . is an involuntary violent and painful contraction of the muscles.' In this country it is associated mainly with the use of the morse instrument. In the early days this instrument was less generally used, but shortly after the transfer of telegraphs to the State in 1870, 30 per cent of the instruments in use were morse and by 1907 this had increased to 60 per cent. Telegraphists who had difficulty in manipulation were not unknown in the seventies and generally telegraphists who were unable to telegraph were transferred to other duties, but when after 1905 scales of pay were related to efficiency, cases of cramp attracted more attention. In 1908 the Industrial Disease Committee reported that it should 'be added to the Schedule as a subject for compensation'. A memorial from the Postal Telegraph Clerks' Association drew attention to the arrangements for instructing learners and the duties of junior telegraphists in the Central Telegraph Office.

The recommendations of the Committee take the form of a scheme for 'the admission into the service of fewer unsuitable learners; more uniform tuition, under close and careful watching, of those who are admitted; the more rigorous protection of young workers from conditions of undue stress; the steady substitution of mechanical forms of sending for the finer muscular movements demanded by the morse instruments; and the discovery and use of fresh forms of variation and relief for operators'.

Appendix No. I contains a Report of the Medical Sub-Committee.

Boy Labour in the Post Office

Standing Cttee. 1st Rep., app. pp. 18. 1911

1911 *Cd.* 5504, *xxxix*, 203
apptd. —, *sgd. Nov.*, 1910

M. Nathan (*Ch.*), Bruce, Chambers, Harvey, Hurcomb, Norway.

'*To consider measures for: 1. A reduction in the number of Boy Messengers by— (a) substituting other labour for that of boys; (b) greater use of electrical and mechanical appliances; (c) economy of numbers, by seeing that all are fully employed. 2. The absorption of a greater number into the Post Office or other Departments of State by—(a) lessening numbers taken into the Post Office by open competition; (b) arranging with War Office and Admiralty that special opportunities should be given to ex-Messengers to enter the more attractive branches of the military and naval services. 3. Increasing chances of outside employment by—(a) improving education; (b) utilizing labour bureaux, philanthropic societies and other institutions; (c) arranging for apprenticeship.*'

Before 1891, boy messengers had the first claim to vacancies for established postmen and porters and, in London, to sorterships also. It was then decided that they should no longer be appointed to sorterships; and as the number of vacancies for which they were eligible was reduced, it soon became necessary to introduce a system of weeding-out and only those boys whose conduct and health were thoroughly satisfactory were retained after the age of 16. The operation of the decision made in 1897 that half the vacancies for postmen and sorters should be reserved for ex-servicemen was practically suspended during the Boer War, but with the return of troops half the vacancies were again allotted to them. The age of entry for a boy is over 14, and of leaving 16, unless he is certain to obtain an established post. A large proportion must obviously leave each year, and many of them to find work for which they have no special training. In 1910 the number of boys employed was 15,790, the number ceasing to be employed during the year 6,782, while only 1,615 were absorbed into the Post Office at ages between 16 and 19. A review of the possibility of reducing the number of boys employed by the methods indicated in the terms of reference led to the conclusion that the numbers discarded were bound to be large as long as the reservation of posts for ex-servicemen continued. Various proposals for reducing the establishment and for absorption into the Post Office, the Services and the Post Office after Service would mean that 40 per cent would be left to find employment elsewhere. Mr. Norway dissented from the proposal that boys, for whom no permanent Post Office employment was likely to be found at the maximum age of 19, might be kept on after the age of 16 if their parents wished it.

See *Boy Labour. Poor Laws.* R. Com. Vol. XX; 1909 Cd. 4632, xliv, 921.

—— Second Report, apps. pp. 22. 1912

1911 *Cd.* 5755, *xxxix*, 221
sgd. Dec., 1911

add Mellersh.

A reduction of 1,284 boys had been accomplished in 18 months, bringing the total down to 14,506, and the number could be further reduced if there were more substitution by girls, army pensioners, postmen delivering telegrams, more telephone delivery, and by the use of bicycles. Further it was anticipated that, through a system of education and training, arrangements could be made for the absorption into the permanent service of the Post Office of a larger proportion of boys at the age of 16. Arrangements were being made to provide for some absorption into the wireless telegraphy branch of the Navy, and into the Army as line telegraphists, telephonists and electricians.

—— Third Report, apps. pp. 20. 1913
1913 Cd. 6959, xxxviii, 431.
sgd. July, 1913
add Francis, del Norway.

By December 1912 the numbers of boy messengers had been reduced to 13,680, and it was thought possible that the maximum number employed could be fixed at 13,000. The number of boys discharged at the age of 16 and without prospects of employment was 433 as compared with 4,322 in 1908–9. This reduction had been caused by (*a*) an increased absorption into the Post Office and branches of the Army and Navy; (*b*) by a more careful weeding out of the educationally and physically unsuitable, etc.; and (*c*) by an increased number of resignations, especially between 1911 and 1912, owing to better prospects in industry. As the Postmaster General pointed out, every improvement affecting morale, education or physique will improve the boys' chances of getting work outside the Department.

—— Fourth Report, apps. pp. 31. 1914
1914 Cd. 7556, xliv, 871
sgd. July, 1914

In 1913, except for 38 cases early in the year, no boy was discharged from the Post Office for lack of prospects.

—— Fifth Report, apps. pp. 22. 1915
1914–16 Cd. 8019, xxxii, 987
sgd. July, 1915

add Raven, del. Francis.

It was possible to absorb every boy messenger who was both willing and fit to enter the permanent service of the State; 52·6 per cent of boys ceasing to be messengers entered the public service.

Early Closing of Shops

Sel. Cttee. HL. Rep., proc., mins. of
    ev. pp. xvi, 213. 1901

1901 (369) vi, 1
apptd. Feb., o.p. Aug., 1901

Lord Avebury (*Ch.*), Duke of Marlborough, L. Salisbury, L. Stamford, L. Hardwicke, L. Romney, L. Verulam, Bishop of Winchester, L. Brassey.

'To inquire into the length of the hours of labour in shops; and whether any, and if so what, steps should be taken to diminish them.'

The Presidents of the College of Physicians and the College of Surgeons both gave evidence on the great and increasing evils of long hours. The only tradesmen's associations against the bill were the Off-Licence Holders and the London Pawnbrokers. The shopkeepers' witnesses were generally of opinion that little more could be expected of voluntary action and that only legislation would be effective, some shopkeepers anxious to close being unwilling to do so if their neighbours were open. Small shopkeepers were equally anxious to shorten hours and any legislation which merely regulated the hours of shop assistants would not satisfy them. The fact that Co-operative Stores invariably close early was some answer to the argument that the poorer purchasers would suffer from early closing. Earlier closing would be an immense boon to the shopkeeping community, and town councils should be authorized to pass Provisional Orders making regulations for closing, such orders to be submitted to Parliament before acquiring the force of law.

War Organization in the Distributing Trades in Scotland

Government Cttee. 1st Rep., app.
    pp. 11. 1915

1914–16 Cd. 7987, xxxvii, 475
apptd. June, sgd. July, 1915

J. D. White (*Ch.*), Arthur, Beaton, Brown, Clement, MacColl, MacKinder, Maule, Puckering, Sangster, Scruby, Stewart, Younger (Miss A.).

'*To consider how far, and by what means, it will be practicable so to readjust the conditions of employment in the Distributing Trades, both Wholesale and Retail, in Scotland, as to release a larger number of men for enlistment or other national services, with the minimum of interference with the necessary operations of those trades.*'

The number of males engaged in distribution was between 100,000 and 120,000, of whom one-half were males of military age. An appeal was made by the Committee to the public to shop as early as possible in the day, not to expect immediate service during busy hours, to carry home small purchases, to give the option of delivery of other goods on the following day, to send orders in writing where practicable and as long as possible in advance.

Reduction of staff by reorganization, economies in delivery, dinner hour closing, early closing, etc., and the substitution of men of military age by those above it or unfit, and by women and juveniles, should be accompanied by guarantee of re-instatement to those who join the services. The demand for school leavers was in excess of the supply. In many cases married women have been invited to return to work previously done by them. Shopkeepers were asked to adopt the statutory minimum of 74 hours per week for young persons in order to attract them to this occupation, to close during the lunch hour, and to obtain Closing Orders for early closing. In the wholesale trade much of the clerical work could be done by women.

—— Second Report. pp. 4. 1916

1916 *Cd.* 8222, *iv*, 299
sgd. March, 1916

The appeal to the public had been effective and the recommendation on closing should be made general through emergency legislation. A Question Paper was sent out to 11,000 employers and from the answers of the 4,306 who replied, it appeared that there were 2,000 men who could be recruited.

Shops

Cttee. Rep., apps. pp. 10. 1915

1914–16 *Cd.* 8113, *xxxv*, 733.
apptd. March, sgd. Oct., 1915

C. Harmsworth (*Ch.*), Bondfield (Miss M. G.), Squire (Miss R. E.), Bird, Burbidge, Giles, Hinds, May, Nicholson, Seddon, Wolff.

'*To consider the conditions of retail trade which can best secure that the further enlistment of men or their employment in other national services may not interfere with the necessary operations of that trade.*'

Where enlistment had already taken place the vacancies had been filled by men over military age or by women, though difficulties were experienced by women in those trades where physical strength was needed. Further reorganization was possible, including earlier closing hours and dinner hour closing. An appeal to the public to exercise consideration in their shopping had had considerable effects. The employment of women in the wholesale trade had released 'in London, at any rate' a remarkable number of men for enlistment in the forces.

Hours and Conditions of Work in Typewriting Offices

Rep. Factories and Workshops. Ann. Rep. 1910

1911 *Cd.* 5693, *xxii*, 407

H. M. Robinson, Miss A. M. Anderson.

The hours of work and conditions under which women were employed in typewriting offices were not such as to call for an extension of the Factory Act, the existing powers conferred by the Public Health Acts upon local authorities being sufficient to deal with sanitary matters. Duplicating work of a kind comparable with letterpress printing work was very little developed in these general typewriting offices and seemed likely to remain in letterpress printing works under the Act.

A considerable proportion of the work in public typewriting offices consisted of typing and copying of legal documents, evidence, etc., which occasionally came in late in the day at short notice and was required before the Courts sat on the following day; greater elasticity as to periods of employment was, therefore, required than would be possible under the Factory Act. All the representatives of the Clerks' Societies opposed an extension of it.

The number of women and girls employed in business houses is so far in excess of the number employed in typewriting offices that it would be unreasonable to place the latter under the Act without including the former and, owing to the nature of the work, it would be impossible to bring the typists in many business houses under the Act without also applying it to all female clerks.

6. COST OF LIVING, EARNINGS AND HOURS

Cost of Living of the Working Classes. Working Class Rents, Housing and Retail Prices together with the Standard Rates of Wages prevailing in Certain Occupations in the Principal Industrial Towns of the United Kingdom

Rep., apps. pp. 616. 1908

1908 Cd. 3864, cvii, 319

A. Wilson Fox.

The investigations were made to complete and supplement the memoranda on the cost of living of the working classes contained in *British and Foreign Trade and Industrial Conditions* (1903 Cd. 1761, lxvii and 1905 Cd. 2337, lxxxix). The object was to obtain a standard of comparison in regard to the cost of living which could be applied as between various districts of the United Kingdom and to foreign countries. The statistics given include index numbers showing for 75 towns the relative mean rent levels and relative retail price levels weighted in accordance with family budgets collected in 1904, as well as index numbers of prices and rents combined, of wages and of the approximate level of real wages. The tables do not show any close connection between the local variations of rent and price levels combined and the level of standard wages; and the relative levels of wages in the different trades show considerable differences.

Cost of Living. German Towns

Rep., apps., index. pp. lxi, 548. 1908

1908 Cd. 4032, cviii, 1

Precise comparison of the cost of living in Germany and in England is difficult, partly because of the difference in the habits and modes of living in the two countries. The cost of rent, fuel and food to an Englishman migrating to Germany and maintaining his own standard of living would be raised by one-fifth, while the expenditure of a German workman trying to maintain his standard in England would be reduced by less than one-half of that amount. In certain standard trades, German workers receive 17 per cent less in money wages in return for a week's work 10 per cent longer than the corresponding English workman's. The technical problems of making these comparisons and the results are set out in pp. xl–lii.

—— French Towns. Rep., apps., index. pp. liv, 430. 1909

1909 Cd. 4512, xci, 1

The same procedure is adopted for comparison with France. The national differences in housing and dietary are referred to on p. iv. If prices and rents had been charged at their respective levels in France, to enable him to maintain the same standard of life, the expenditure of the average British workman would have had to be increased by one-seventh and his hours of work would have been longer. The technical problems of making these comparisons and the results are set out in pp. xxxi–xlvii. The family budgets show the large contribution to family income made by wives and children, and the extent to which wives are engaged in occupation for gain.

—— *Belgian Towns.* Rep., apps., index.
     pp. xli, 218. 1910

1910 *Cd.* 5065, *xcv,* 43

Owing to the fact that the predominant types of housing in Belgium are more like those of England than those in France and Germany, and that the general level of prices is only slightly below that in English towns, the difficulties of comparison with Belgium are less than those with the other two countries. An Englishman trying to maintain his standard and mode of living unchanged in Belgium would find his expenditure on rent, food and fuel slightly diminished—by about 9 per cent—but his hours would be a fifth longer and weekly money wages a third lower.

—— *American Towns.* Rep., apps., index. pp. xcii, 533. 1911

1911 *Cd.* 5609, *lxxxviii,* 253

The special difficulties of comparison with the United States are due to its size and to its regional differences, and owing to the multiplicity of races amongst the immigrants, to differences in family budgets, which were presented on a nationality basis. An English workman's standard unchanged would cost about 2 per cent more in the United States, but his wages would be 130 per cent higher and his hours of work slightly less. Amongst the features of the family budgets are the large contributions

made by the children in the higher income classes, and the insignificant earnings of wives.

—— Report, apps. pp. 548. 1913

1913 *Cd.* 6955, *lxvi,* 393

F. H. McLeod.

This enquiry enabled comparison to be made between 1912 and the earlier results for 1905. Rents in the United Kingdom have changed only little since 1905, but retail prices have increased considerably. Probably the average increase in rent, fuel and food together may be about 10 per cent.

Wages and Hours of Labour. Part I. Changes in the Rates of Wages and Hours of Labour in the United Kingdom

     pp. lxxxviii, 222. 1894

1894 *C.* 7567, *lxxxi, Pt. II,* 1

The object of the report is to record the principal changes in market rates of wages and recognized hours of labour in the chief industries of the United Kingdom and to compute the actual effect of the changes reported on the weekly wages bill of the country. Followed by annual reports up to 1914–16.

—— *Part II. Standard Piece Rates of Wages.* pp. xvi, 232. 1894

1894 *C.* 7567–I, *lxxxi, Pt. II*

—— *Part III. Standard Time Rates of Wages.* pp. 278. 1894

1894 *C.* 7567–II, *lxxxi, Pt. II*

—— *Standard Piece Rates of Wages and Sliding Scales in the United Kingdom.* Rep. pp. xxv, 308. 1900

1900 *Cd.* 144, *lxxxii,* 1

In continuation of C. 7567–I. Information is given of the varied and complicated systems of calculating wages in many important British industries, and a key to the data given in the monthly and annual records of changes of wages published by the Department. The volume is of practical service in facilitating an understanding of the nature of the questions at issue between employers and employed in many trade disputes, which are often difficult to follow owing to the highly technical character of the points involved.

—— *Standard Time Rates of Wages in the United Kingdom.* pp. xii, 210. 1900

1900 *Cd.* 317, *lxxxii*, 335

In continuation of C. 7567–II. This and five succeeding reports between 1900 and 1914 deal with rates of time-wages and hours of labour in a large number of important industries; tables are given showing percentage variations in wages over lengthy periods.

Wages and Earnings of Agricultural Labourers in the United Kingdom

Rep., apps. pp. x, 296. 1900

1900 *Cd.* 346, *lxxxii*, 557

A. Wilson Fox.

The Report describes the various classes of agricultural labourers, their duties, and the terms of their engagements, hiring fairs, etc. An account is also given of the different ways in which the labourers' nominal wages are augmented, e.g. by piecework, extra earnings at harvest, etc., and by allowances in kind, such as free cottages, potatoes, fuel, etc., which are frequently an important factor of their total earnings. The rates of wages paid to the various classes of men in each county are given, and also their total earnings, including all cash payments and the value of allowances in kind. Charts show changes in the rate of wages over a period of 50 years. There is a section on migratory Irish labourers in England and Scotland.

—— Second Report, apps. pp. xii, 263.
[1905]

1905 *Cd.* 2376, *xcvii*, 335

In addition to information on rates of wages and yearly earnings, this report deals also with the cost of living of farm workers, the hours of work and general conditions of labour.

Earnings and Hours of Labour of Workpeople of the United Kingdom

Enquiry. I. *Textile Trades in 1906.* Rep., apps. pp. lxxiv, 250. 1909

1909 *Cd.* 4545, *lxxx*, 1

G. R. Askwith.

The continuous record of changes in the rates of wages requires to be supplemented at intervals by large scale investigation into weekly earnings. The statistical returns received cover 44 per cent of the 1,171,000 employed in the Textile Trades. The average wage for a full week in 1906 was 28s. 1d. for men and 15s. 5d. for women, an average increase since 1886 of 20 per cent for men and 22 per cent for women; but a comparison of 1884–8 and 1904–8 however shows increases of 16 per cent and 18 per cent respectively. Working time has fallen by 2 per cent.

—— II. *Clothing Trades in 1906.* Rep., apps. pp. lxvi, 237. 1909

1909 *Cd.* 4844, *lxxx*, 325

Of the total of 1,500,000 workers engaged in these trades in 1906, 789,000 (205,000 males and 584,000 females) were employed in factories and workshops, the rest working in their own homes for employers or on their own account. The statistics, which refer to those engaged in factories and workshops only, show average cash wages of 28s. 3d. for men, 13s. for women, 9s. 7d. for lads and 5s. 8d. for girls. The average yearly earnings would be approximately £37 per head.

—— III. *Building and Woodworking Trades in 1906.* Rep., apps. pp. xl, 188. 1910

1910 *Cd.* 5086, *lxxxiv*, 1

The return covered 14 per cent of the 1,250,000 workers employed, but in nearly every town of importance wage rates were fixed by agreement and were well recognized. The average earnings in the building trades were 31s. 6d. for men, 36s. 4d. for skilled men and 24s. 5d. for labourers. The earnings of men in works of construction (harbours, roads, etc.) were 27s., in sawmilling 27s. 1d., in cabinet making 32s. 1d.

—— IV. *Public Utility Services in 1906.* Rep., apps. pp. xxviii, 194. 1910
1910 Cd. 5196, *lxxxiv*, 229

The average annual earnings of all workers in these industries were £67 per head, varying from £78 in gas supply, £70 in water supply to £62 10s. in urban and £41 10s. in rural road and sanitary services.

—— V. *Agriculture in 1907.* Rep., apps. pp. xxvi, 58. 1910
1910 Cd. 5460, *lxxxiv*, 451

The average annual earnings of full-time adult male farm servants in 1907 were in England £47 15s., in Wales £46 16s., in Scotland £50 19s. and in Ireland £29 4s. The average weekly wage varied from 22s. in Durham to 16s. 4d. in Oxfordshire, 19s. 3d. in Glamorgan and 16s. 6d. in Cardiganshire. The average earnings of the predominant class of agricultural labourer in 1907 was greater than in 1898 by 5 per cent in England and 8 per cent in Scotland.

—— VI. *Metal, Engineering and Shipbuilding Trades in 1906.* Rep., apps. pp. lii, 200. 1911
1911 Cd. 5814, *lxxxviii*, 1

Returns were received covering one-half the 1,500,000 workers employed. The average weekly earnings of men varied from 42s. in tinplate manufacture to 31s. 4d. in the manufacture of light iron castings. In iron and steel manufacture the average was 39s. 1d., in shipbuilding 35s. 11d. There were wide differences of earnings within the occupations in iron and steel manufacture, 24 per cent of the men earning less than 25s. while 3 per cent earned £5 or more. The earnings in many important trades had risen in twenty years by 21 per cent; in pig iron manufacture the increase was 3 per cent, in shipbuilding 23 per cent. But 1886 was a depressed and 1906 a prosperous year.

—— VII. *Railway Service in 1907.* Rep., apps. pp. xxix, 258. 1912
1912–13 Cd. 6053, *cviii*, 1

The bulk of the employees in the industry were full-time male workers, nearly all of them being 'six-day' workers, except on electric railways, where one-half were 'six-day' workers. Average actual weekly earnings, excluding uniform and other allowances, varied from 45s. 11d. for engine drivers, 31s. 2d. for goods guards, 27s. 6d. for signalmen to 19s. 9d. for porters. Two-thirds had annual holidays of 3 to 6 days with pay.

—— VIII. *Paper, Printing, etc., Trades; Pottery, Brick, Glass and Chemical Trades; Food, Drink and Tobacco Trades; and miscellaneous Trades in 1906.* Rep., apps. pp. xxxv, 298. 1913
1912–13 Cd. 6556, *cviii*, 289

The average earnings of men working full-time varied from 23s. 4d. in the paper and printing trades, 29s. 2d. in the pottery, brick and chemical trades, to 26s. 4d. in food, drink and tobacco trades and 27s. 1d. in the miscellaneous trades. There were considerable variations round these averages—29.7 per cent in the paper and printing group earning from 20s. to 30s. as compared with 55.4 per cent in the food, drink and tobacco trades. The average weekly hours were under 50 for 17 per cent of the workpeople and between 54 and 60 for 43 per cent.

Miners' Eight Hour Day
Reps.

1907 Cd. 3505. See *Coal*. p. 131.

7. RESETTLEMENT OF EX-SERVICE MEN, LAND SETTLEMENT

Civil Employment of Ex-Soldiers and Sailors

Cttee. Rep., apps. pp. 73. 1906. Mins. of ev., index. 1906

1906 *Cd.* 2991, *xiv*, 143. *Mins. of ev., etc.*; 1906 *Cd.* 2992, *xiv*, 221

apptd. — 1905. *sgd. July*, 1906

E. W. D. Ward (*Ch.*), L. Cheylesmore, Elliot, Gifford, Harrison, Livesey, Miles, Walsh.

'(*a*) *To inquire into the position of the various organizations which at present assist pensioners and discharged soldiers and sailors to obtain civil employment.* (*b*) *To report whether by the co-ordination of existing agencies, or by other means, their work could not be extended.* (*c*) *To consider how the existing means of employing ex-sailors and soldiers may be improved and extended, and to report generally on the whole question of the civil employment of ex-sailors and ex-soldiers.*'

Previous Committees had reported that the Navy was well supplied from the training ships, but that the Army would get more recruitment if better prospects for civil employment were offered after a certain period of meritorious service. It was generally agreed that ex-service men were efficient workers, many employers stating that they were more satisfactory than civilian workmen. Recommendations had been made in favour of a greater employment of ex-service pensioners in the non-clerical branches of the Civil Service, and the appendices give an analysis of the kinds of work which have been given to ex-service men. The War Office keeps a register of candidates for employment, and the Navy enrols in the Royal Fleet Reserve men who have not earned long service pensions, and also makes a small grant to three employment agencies. But much of the work of finding employment for ex-service men is done by nine voluntary societies, such as the Army and Navy Pensioners and Time Expired Employment Society, the National Association for the Employment of Reserve and Discharged Soldiers, and the Incorporated Soldiers' and Sailors' Help Society. In addition, there are eight societies and agencies governed mainly by commercial as distinct from philanthropic principles. There is much overlapping and waste of resources and effort.

It was essential that there should be one association to take the place of the existing societies, with an advisory council consisting of members from the more important societies and departments. There should be a central office in London acting as an employment agency, with branches in counties and large towns. It should be assisted by, but not under the control of, the Admiralty or the War Office. The Government should direct the various Public Departments to fill vacancies in the appointments detailed in Appendices 2–5. Local Authorities should be urged to reserve a number of appointments for ex-service men. Every soldier should be required to learn some description of technical work during his military career and recommendations are made regarding their training and provision for welfare.

See *Steps taken to provide Technical Education to Soldiers to fit them for Civil Life.* Reps.; 1907 Cd. 3511, xlix, 415. 1908 Cd. 4059, xi, 135.

Provision of Employment for Sailors and Soldiers Disabled in the War

Cttee. Rep. pp. 8. 1915

1914–16 *Cd.* 7915, *xl*, 37

apptd. Feb., sgd. May, 1915

G. H. Murray (*Ch.*), Beveridge, Crutchley, Franklin, Henderson, Hodge, O'Brien, Price, Pullinger, L. Sandhurst, Scott (L.), Scott (R. R.), Symonds.

'*To consider and report upon the methods to be adopted for providing employment for soldiers and sailors disabled in the War.*'

As about 12,000 discharges were expected by December, 1915, the Committee considered the present position whereby the naval and military authorities assume responsibility for medical and surgical treatment of disabled men until they are discharged from the service. The decision to discharge is made as soon as it is clear that the man will not be able to return to active service and without much regard to the question whether his condition can be improved by further treatment. The State should assume responsibility for the free treatment of the discharged man and his restoration to health, where practicable. Arrangements for the supply of surgical appliances are sufficiently liberal, but a man requiring an artificial limb should be seen by an orthopaedic surgeon of repute. Where men are not able to follow their normal occupations they should receive training in polytechnics, technical institutes, trade schools, or by apprenticeship to employers who might be willing to train them. Local Education Authorities should help with the provision of training. There should be a 'central Committee responsible for the care of disabled soldiers and sailors, acting under the direction of some existing Government Department'. The proposed Central Committee should consider schemes for land settlement 'at the earliest date'.

Land Settlement for Soldiers and Sailors
Final Rep. Pts. I, II

1916 *Cd.* 8182, *Cd.* 8277. See *Agriculture.* p. 74.

Empire Settlement. Ex-Service Men
Rep.

1917–18 *Cd.* 8672. See *Migration.* p. 237.

8. EMPLOYMENT OF WOMEN

Accounts of Expenditure of Wage-Earning Women and Girls
pp. 96. 1911

1911 *Cd.* 5963, *lxxxix*, 531
G. R. Askwith.

'Since the summer of 1909, at the request of the Board of Trade, the executive officers of certain organizations, viz. the Women's Co-operative Guild, the Social Service Branch of the Young Women's Christian Association, the Women's Labour League, the National Organization of Girls' Clubs, and the Association of Teachers of Domestic Subjects, have made efforts to induce wage-earning women and girls to send in weekly detailed accounts of their expenditure to the Labour Department. One of the difficulties in their way has been the absence of any document showing how the results of their efforts may be tabulated and used to throw light on many important questions. It has, therefore, been thought advisable to publish in a convenient form the tabulated results of thirty complete accounts for one year which have been received by the Department. Twenty-three of the thirty correspondents who have kept these complete records lived at home with one or both parents, two were boarders, two lived with sisters also working, one shared rooms with a friend, two lived alone. Nearly all living at home with parents were quite self-supporting; some paid considerably more than their cost to their parents.' A detailed analysis of accounts of expenditure for one year of thirty women is given, but from so small a collection of samples no generalization or theories on expenditure were offered. A large collection of records would throw light on such questions as the value of unpaid services received by daughters at home, the increased cost of living of self-supporting women without family life or the relative importance to the woman worker of dress compared with food, present as compared with the future.

Women's Employment
Central Cttee. Interim Rep., apps.
pp. 42. 1915

1914–16 *Cd.* 7848, *xxxvii*, 669
apptd. Aug., 1914. *sgd. March*, 1915

Lady Crewe (*Ch.*), Mrs. M. Tennant, Lady Askwith, Miss M. G. Bondfield, Mrs. I. Chamberlain, Mrs. M. A. Gasson, Miss R. E. Lawrence, Miss A. S. Lawrence, Miss V. R. Markham, Lady Midleton, L. Montagu, Dr. M. Phillips, Mrs. E. Lyttelton, Miss M. R. Macarthur.

'*To consider, and from time to time report upon, schemes for the provision of work for women and girls unemployed on account of the war.*'

The Committee eased some early wartime unemployment problems by creating a Contract Department which advised on the placing of contracts so that unemployment was minimized, and undertook orders to be carried out by firms adversely affected by the war. Attempts were made to promote new openings for employment, e.g. the use of girls for work on the land. The provision of training and employment, i.e. relief work, for women unemployed because of the war, included local schemes for experimental workshops, Domestic Economy Training Centres in London; and a scheme for training Home Helps, based on the practice of Jewish Maternity and Sick Room Help, was adopted and extended to many London districts after an initially successful experiment at Plaistow. A central register for unemployed professional women had been opened.

Clerical and Commercial Employment

Cttee. Rep., apps. pp. 12. 1915

1914–16 Cd. 8110, *xiii*, 1
apptd. Oct., sgd. Nov., 1915

C. Harmsworth (*Ch.*), Delevingne, Fletcher, Goldstone, Henderson, Howard, Markham (Miss Violet R.), Paterson (Miss Mary M.), Phillips, Plender, Pryor, Sinclair, Whalley.

'*To consider the conditions of clerical and commercial employment with a view to advising what steps should be taken, by the employment of women or otherwise, to*
replace men withdrawn for service in the military forces.'

'A considerable proportion of the recruits still required for the prosecution of the war will be drawn from these occupations, and steps must be taken beforehand to organize the supply of substitutes systematically so that employers may not be left to make hasty arrangements when the emergency arises. The supply of substitutes will in the main have to be found among educated women.' Arrangements for organizing the supply and training of substitutes should be made in each commercial centre, and for this purpose local bodies should be formed representative of the local education authority and of the commerce of the district. Such a body might take the form either of a sub-committee of the education committee reinforced by representatives of business firms and other interests involved, or a special committee appointed *ad hoc* or any other form best adapted to local circumstances. In the present emergency the scale of wages payable to women should, as far as conditions permit and as the work deputed to them reasonably justifies, be based on the rate of wages paid to men who have been engaged in similar duties.

9. JUVENILES

Employment of School-Children

Inter-Dept. Cttee. Rep. pp. 25. 1901. Mins. of ev., apps., index. 1902

1902 Cd. 849, *xxv*, 261. *Mins. of ev., etc.*;
1902 Cd. 895, *xxv*, 287
apptd. Jan., sgd. Nov., 1901

H. H. S. Cunynghame (*Ch.*), Troup, Lindsell, Harrison, Smith.

'*To Inquire into the Question of the Employment of Children during School Age, and to Report what alterations are desirable in the laws relating to Child Labour and School Attendance and in the administration of those laws.*'

The Committee was set up as the result of serious facts disclosed by the Return on Wage Earning Children (1899 (23) (205) lxxv). Approximately 300,000 children combined paid work with school attendance, probably 50,000 worked 20 hours per week and a considerable proportion of this number worked 30, 40 and 50 hours per week. Many worked longer than the factory hours allowed for children of the same age. In evidence, Mr. Mundella argued that as the statutes regulating factories and mines could not apply to the thousands of little shops, etc., the Education Authority should be given powers, through bye-laws, to issue labour certificates to school children (q. 300). Though some witnesses argued for total prohibition, and others only for the prohibition of street trading for girls, the majority inclined to the view that light suitable work of approximately 20 hours per week was good for children. The Committee held that children's employment should be adjusted, not totally prohibited. Its recommendations were based on the assumption that training for manual work should begin before the age of 14, that education should continue after school leaving, that poverty ought not to be legally recognized as a test of the right to work, and that local authorities should be given powers to make bye-laws for employments not already covered by law, to license individual children for street trading and to prohibit night work. The public would support restrictions when conditions of play were more healthy and beneficial and were within the reach of the general mass of children.

See *Employment of Children Act, 1903*; 3 Edw. 7. c. 45.

Bye-laws made by the London County Council under the Employment of Children Act, 1903

Rep., apps. pp. 28. 1906

1906 Cd. 2809, xc, 1
sgd. Nov., 1905

C. Jones.

'*A local Inquiry with respect to the bye-laws made by the London County Council under the powers conferred on them by the Employment of Children Act, 1903, and with respect to the objections thereto.*'

On the recommendation of the 1902 Committee, the 1903 Act gave powers to Local Authorities to make bye-laws regarding the employment of children, and in pursuance of these powers the London County Council made a set of bye-laws (App. I). In spite of a large number of objections which were addressed to the Secretary of State, there was no effective opposition to them among the witnesses at the inquiry. Chester Jones confined himself to inquiring and reporting upon 'the amount of restriction on child labour that was permitted in the County of London and to discover where the line should be drawn'. Amongst the alterations he suggested were that the proposed limit of hours children should work when school is open to before 7 a.m. and after 7 p.m. throughout the year should be before 6 a.m. and after 6 p.m. and that the prohibition of street trading by girls under 16 should be replaced by licensing.

—— Report. Bye-laws made on the 29th January, 1910, apps. pp. 18. 1911

1911 Cd. 5497, lxiv, 219

S. O. Buckmaster.

After twelve months' experience new bye-laws had been proposed. The chief alterations were that the time before which a child should not be employed was fixed at 6.30 instead of 6 in the morning; that a boy should not be employed under the age of 13 (instead of 12) as a lather boy in a barber's shop, and that girls under the age of 16 should be entirely prohibited from street trading. The newsagents argued that if the papers were not delivered early trade would be diverted to the street or the stall, and milksellers that it would be so expensive to get the milk delivered. Boys' employment in barbers' shops should be restricted because the work was unhealthy, the proposals by the trade that the employment of boys should be licensed where the conditions were good being impracticable. S. O. Buckmaster confirmed the proposed changes.

Employment of Children Act, 1903

Dept. Cttee. Rep. pp. 23. [1910.] Mins. of ev., apps., index. 1910

1910 *Cd.* 5229, *xxviii*, 1. *Mins. of ev., etc.*; 1910 *Cd.* 5230, *xxviii*, 25 *apptd. July,* 1909. *sgd. April,* 1910

J. A. Simon (*Ch.*), Gladstone (Mrs.), Chambers, Gulland, Richards, Sherwell, Whitehouse, Bridgeman, Delevingne, Guinness, Law.

'*To inquire into the operation of the Employment of Children Act,* 1903, *and to consider whether any and what further legislative regulation or restriction is required in respect to street trading and other employments dealt with in that Act.*'

Section 2 of the Employment of Children Act, 1903, gives local authorities power to make bye-laws with respect to street trading by persons under 16, the expression 'street trading' including 'the hawking of newspapers, matches, flowers, and other articles, playing, singing, or performing for profit, shoeblacking, or any other like occupation carried on in streets or public places'. The most important is the hawking of newspapers, but although the sale of newspapers in the streets is undoubtedly street trading, the carrying of newspapers through the streets in order that they may be delivered at the doors of customers is not. In some cases boys ostensibly delivering may in fact be selling before 7 a.m., the time permitted (q. 1052). 'There is an absolute statutory prohibition against children engaging in street trading under the age of 11, but for children who have reached the age of 11, the statutory restrictions are prohibition of *night* work, and they are restrained from street trading only so far as bye-laws for this purpose have been made and put into force by the local authority, which is given power, with the approval of the Home Secretary, to make bye-laws for persons under the age of 16. Out of seventy-four county boroughs fifty had made bye-laws, but Leeds, Nottingham and Salford were amongst those who had not. In Scotland and Ireland no county borough had used the powers of the Act, which seemed to be a 'dead-letter'. But Manchester had been so successful that the Chief Constable said no legislation had done more good to the children than the supervision of street trading. More than 37,000 licences to engage in street trading are officially recorded, but there must be added those trading without a badge (qq. 7663–5) and those trading where the law is not observed. The effect of street trading upon the character of those who engage in it is only too frequently disastrous. The youthful street trader is exposed to many of the worst of moral risks. There was an almost equally strong body of testimony to the effect that, at any rate in crowded centres of population, street trading tends to produce a dislike or disability for more regular employment.

The majority of the Committee recommended there should be statutory prohibition of street trading by boys up to the age of 17 and by girls up to an age not less than 18. The definition of street trading should be revised to make it clear that the delivery of goods to regular customers is not covered by the term; the functions of local education authorities should be extended so as to include the administration of the law, either through school attendance officers or through specially appointed officers, as well as the giving of advice and assistance to children at or leaving school in the finding of suitable employment; street trading cases should be heard in the Children's Court, or, failing such a court, in a court of summary jurisdiction, and the penalties for illegal street trading revised.

In a Minority Report Bridgeman, Delevingne, Guinness and Law argued that a general prohibition might cause hardship in some cases and in others lead to other employment under conditions at least as undesirable and less subject to control. Powers should be given to local authorities to prohibit street trading by boys up to 18, e.g. newspaper selling, where there is alternative employment and in other cases to withhold licences where the trading has no beneficial purpose or to make them conditional on attendance at technical or continuation classes. Trading by girls should be prohibited up to 18, with a reservation for those of the coster-monger class. Local authorities should be required to appoint officers to enforce the act.

App. III is a Statement by the Committee on Wage-Earning Children, and includes a tabular statement of cases.

The Bye-law made by the Devon County Council under the Employment of Children Act, 1903, and on the objections thereto

Rep., apps. pp. 15. 1913

1913 Cd. 6988, xxiii, 885
sgd. June, 1913

S. Pope.

A bye-law which allowed parents to withdraw their children entirely from school during the time of religious instruction had been largely abused for the purposes of employment, but because of the desire to preserve liberty of conscience the Education Committee would not withdraw it. They were in favour of a bye-law which would prevent children from working on school days between the hours of 8.15 a.m. and 4.30 p.m. Opposition to this came chiefly from certain Boards of Guardians, Rural District Councils and farmers, but Mr. Pope thought that this could be met if the hours were altered to half an hour before school and half an hour after school; certain

light work, e.g. carrying small quantities of milk and farm produce for delivery on the way to school, should be excluded.

Hours and Conditions of Employment of Van Boys and Warehouse Boys

Dept. Cttee. Rep., apps. pp. 31. 1913. Mins. of ev., index. 1913

1913 Cd. 6886, xxxiii, 463. Mins. of ev., etc.; 1913 Cd. 6887, xxxiii, 495 apptd. April, 1912. sgd. May, 1913

G. Bellhouse (Ch.), Jackson, Walker.

'To inquire into the hours and conditions of employment of van boys and warehouse boys, and to report whether it is desirable that any, and if so what, means should be taken to regulate such employment.'

The term 'van boy' includes boys known as 'nippers' who accompany the driver on a van, cart, lorry or motor. His duty is to guard the van against theft, watch the horses and assist in the delivery of parcels. The returns of the Joint Advisory Committees of the Labour Exchanges to the Board of Trade showed that there were 1,155 van boys. There were 7 under the age of 13 and 25 over the age of 17; the general average hours worked was 70 per week, but specific cases showed excessive hours, for example, in the London area, where the figures ranged from under 60 to over 86. Starting wages were 7s. rising to 14s. a week. The problem was of limited application and arose chiefly in certain large towns and certain trades — railways, parcel delivery, delivery of aerated waters, biscuits, bread, laundry and milk, and in connection with shops. The work of warehouse boys was closely connected with that of van boys. W. H. Smith and Son seemed to be one of the biggest employers. In the London area alone they employed 100 boys. Their hours of work were 54, though in some cases they began at 2.30 a.m. Direct evidence from London, Manchester and Glasgow showed no cases where excessive hours had been worked.

Powers should be given to Local Authorities to make bye-laws to regulate the hours of employment for boys under 18 years; no boy under 16 should be employed before 6 a.m. or after 9.30 p.m., or for more than 70 hours inclusive of 1½ hours per day for meals, public holidays within the district to be allowed. Boys in warehouses where goods were collected, etc., should be subjected to the same regulations as van boys; in other warehouses, by Factory Acts, Shops Act, etc.

Boy Labour in the Post Office
Reps.

1911—1914–16. See *Labour*. p. 221.

Juvenile Employment
Memo. 13

1916 *Cd.* 8362. See *Labour*. p. 198.

Juvenile Eduction in relation to Employment after the War
Reps.

1916, 1917.   See *Breviate 1917–39*, pp. 338–9.

10. MIGRATION, EMPLOYMENT, WAR REFUGEES

Alien Immigration
R. Com.   Vol. I. Rep. pp. viii, 52. 1903. Vol. II. Mins. of ev. 1903.   Vol. III. Apps. 1903.   Vol. IV. Index, analysis of ev. 1904

1903 *Cd.* 1741, ix, 1. *Mins. of ev.*, etc.; 1903 *Cd.* 1742, *Cd.* 1741–1, *Cd.* 1743, ix, 61.
apptd. *March*, 1902. sgd. *Aug.*, 1903

Lord James (*Ch.*), L. Rothschild, Lyttelton, Digby, Gordon, Norman, Vallance.

'To inquire into—(1) *The character and extent of the evils which are attributed to the unrestricted immigration of Aliens,* especially in the Metropolis; (2) The measures which have been adopted for the restriction and control of Alien Immigration in Foreign Countries, and in British Colonies.'

Since 1880 there had been a marked increase of alien immigrants, mainly Jews from Eastern Europe escaping from the repressive enactments of the May Laws of Russia (1882). It was alleged that on arrival many of these immigrants were impoverished, dirty, and suffering from infectious diseases, and had amongst them criminals and prostitutes beyond the percentage of the native population. The regulations for controlling immigration were loosely applied and there was no means of checking the information supplied to the Board of Trade. No enquiry was made at the port of embarkation, concerning those coming to England, though most elaborate precautions were taken over those going to America, because shipping companies were responsible for the return of those defined in America as 'undesirables'.

Evidence showed that amongst the aliens in London, 2·7 were paupers, that crime had increased absolutely and relatively, and that they tended to overcrowd in the East End. Aliens went into the newer occupations of furniture making, tailoring and shoe-making, tended to do work which the native population found unsuitable or were unwilling to do, and overflowed into other trades, thus causing friction with Englishmen; and their industrial conditions were very poor. On the Continent aliens were on the whole subject to police regulations, but nothing in the nature of a right to enter was recognized. America had excluded certain defined classes, e.g. convicts, idiots, persons likely to become a public charge, persons whose ticket is paid for by the money of another, etc. Colonial regulations possessed characteristics similar to American ones, though much was based on the earliest Act in Natal,

1897, which adds an education test, mainly to restrict Asiatic immigration.

No case had been established for the total exclusion of aliens, but the right of residence should be placed under regulation which would prevent the immigration of undesirables, and allow for their repatriation, and prevent residence in districts already overcrowded. Immigrants should be subject to state regulation and control; a Department of Immigration established, with a staff of immigration officers. Alien immigrants found within two years to be undesirable, i.e. criminals, prostitutes, notorious bad characters, or chargeable on the public funds except through ill health, or without visible means of subsistence, should be ordered to leave. There should be medical examination at ports, with power to repatriate. If alien immigrants have contributed substantially to the overcrowding of an area, the area may be declared an area prohibited to newly-arrived aliens. In a memo. Digby deals with the difficulty of defining 'likely to become a public charge', and states that the special measures for prohibiting overcrowding would be unnecessary if the existing laws were properly enforced. Rothschild also thinks this power of prohibition unnecessary.

Alien Immigrants at the Port of London

Dept. Cttee. Vol. I. Rep., app. pp. 12. 1911. Vol. II. Mins of ev. 1911

1911 Cd. 5575, x, 87. Mins. of ev.; 1911 Cd. 5576, x, 99 apptd. —, sgd. March, 1911

R. C. Lehmann (Ch.), Alexander, Cawston, Cohen, Duncannon, Leach, Pedder, White.

'To enquire into the conditions under which alien immigrants are now inspected and held for the purpose of appeal in the Port of London, and to make proposals as to the best means of exercising the power possessed by the Secretary of State for the Home Department under section 29 of the Port of London Act, 1908, of requiring the Port Authority to provide accommodation for such immigrants, and to report generally upon the facilities provided for the reception of immigrants at other immigration ports.'

Under the Aliens Act only those alien steerage passengers are liable to inspection, detention and rejection who come to the United Kingdom on 'immigrant' ships carrying more than 20 such passengers. In 1906 these numbered 8,693 (chiefly Russian) but by 1909 they had fallen to 2,978 and in the first six months of 1910 to 1,385. Inspection takes place on the ship and is inconvenient to the immigration officers, to the shipping companies, whose boats may lose a tide and to the passengers, who may have to stay on deck in all weathers during the waits for inspection, etc. A receiving house should be provided at Tilbury, with accommodation in which up to 300 persons could rest and eat for a few hours, sleeping quarters for about 30 persons, and rooms for officials, etc. Transmigrants as well as immigrants should disembark there. The Port Authority had offered a shed which could provide these requirements and should be authorized to impose tolls.

See Expulsion of Aliens. Statement; 1911 Cd. 5789, x, 1.

Salvation Army Colonies in the United States and at Hadleigh, England, with Scheme of National Land Settlement

Rep. pp. 74. 1905

1905 Cd. 2562, liii, 359

H. Rider Haggard.

'To inspect and report upon the conditions and character of the agricultural and industrial settlements which have been established there by the Salvation Army, with a view to the transmigration of suitable persons from the great cities of the United States to the land and the formation of agricultural communities. . . . If these experiments are found to be successful, some analogous system might, with great advantage, be applied in transferring the urban populations of the United Kingdom to different parts of the British Empire. You should pay special attention to the class of persons taken by the Salvation Army, their training and success as agricultural settlers, and the general effect upon character and social happiness: you should also consider the financial aspect of the experiments. . . . You should proceed to Ottawa and discuss the subject with Lord Grey who has taken great interest in it, as well as with such local authorities as may be indicated to you by the Governor-General as likely to aid you with advice and assistance as to the application of the system in a British Colony.'

The report describes the experiments of the Salvation Army in founding settlements in the United States for persons without capital, and its colony at Hadleigh, Essex. The latter had a population of 500, with a further 200 persons in employment there. Some of the settlers came from the Army's 'surgical operations' who wanted to be trained on the land; some were respectable paupers who wanted to work, while a third group were weak and unsatisfactory persons whose labour was correspondingly expensive. Details of the work and earnings are given. The report also gives details of a scheme proposed by the Canadian government for a free grant of land sufficient for ten townships.

Agricultural Settlements in British Colonies

Dept. Cttee. Vol. I. Rep. pp. iii, 41. 1906. Vol. II. Mins. of ev., apps., index. 1906

1906 Cd. 2978, lxxvi, 533. Mins. of ev., etc.; 1906 Cd. 2979, lxxvi, 579 apptd. July, 1905. sgd. May, 1906

Lord Tennyson (Ch.), Davy, Fox, Holland, Lambert, Lawson, Llewellyn, Samuel, Webb (S.).

'To consider the suggestions made in Mr. Rider Haggard's Report on the Salvation Army Colonies in the United States and at Hadleigh; and to advise the Government whether any steps can usefully be taken for promoting agricultural settlements in the British Colonies of persons taken from the cities of this country.'

The report reviews the experience of and legislation on emigration and colonization, concluding with the test of successful colonization schemes proposed by Mr. Rathbone in evidence before a Committee of 1891 (1891 (152) xi): (1) that the colonists should be doing decidedly better than they were at home; (2) that after a few years they should still be living on and cultivating the land on which they were settled; and (3) the money advanced should have been repaid or at least that there should be no financial loss. General emigration schemes passed the test, but there was no instance of a colonization scheme strictly so named which had been successful. This was true even of the schemes of colonization by crofters and cottars from the Highlands, though they had received every help. For Englishmen going into an environment which they could easily assimilate the arguments were in favour of emigration. The colonies of the Salvation Army in the United States provided no guidance, and Mr. Haggard's proposals to settle families from English towns in a remote part of Canada should not be accepted.

The Committee recommended that no steps be taken by the Government at present to further any scheme of colonization; that a grant-in-aid should be given by the Imperial Government to the committees formed under the Unemployed Workmen Act for the purpose of emigration; that a special fund should be allotted for the purpose of assisting soldiers, after their terms of service, to emigrate to the British Colonies.

Herbert Samuel disagreed with the recommendation to give grants-in-aid. Emigration benefits individuals and it is an axiom of public finance that national funds ought to be spent only in order to secure a national advantage. But the proposal to encourage industrious men and women in the prime of life to leave the country because they were temporarily unemployed and therefore unproductive implied the theory that because there were persons unemployed, England must be over-populated, and that to remove some would solve unemployment. It took no account of the fact that the development of a country's natural resources and its foreign trade increases with the growth of its population and diminishes with its fall. H. Lambert's Reservation stressed the necessity of limiting aid to cases of real distress. Wilson Fox in a memo. repeats Samuel's warnings, and in a memo. on *Country-born Men in Large Towns* concludes that the submerged tenth of large towns are unsuitable for colonial life, while if rural depopulation is an evil, the existing rural population should be retained.

Empire Settlement. Ex-Service Men

Cttee. Rep., apps., index. pp. iii, 62.
1917

1917–18 *Cd*. 8672, *x*, 213
apptd. April, sgd. July, 1917

Lord Tennyson (*Ch.*) and 30 others.

'*To consider and report on the measures to be taken for settling within the Empire ex-soldiers who may desire to emigrate after the War. To collect and prepare for distribution to intending emigrants of this class information which shall show clearly the nature of any facilities afforded by the Governments of the Dominions and States. To advise as to the best methods of making this information accessible to the troops. To make recommendations as to the steps which should be taken by His Majesty's Government in concert with the Governments of the States and Dominions for the constitution of a Central Authority to supervise and assist such emigration.*'

Not long ago emigration 'was regarded as more or less a necessary evil which, during times of stress resulting from unemployment, was tolerated as a national convenience. Small account was taken of the fact that to it was largely due the rise of those Dominions and Colonies which to-day constitute the British Empire. If a subject of the Crown chose to leave these shores, it was a matter of comparative unconcern to the Home Government whether he settled elsewhere under the flag or in some foreign country. As a result, millions of men of British birth or parentage have become citizens of other lands. Only within the last few years have the problems of population begun to be studied in the light of Imperial necessities.' A new departure is needed, and emigration should be looked at from the point of view of the Empire as a whole; the interests of the individual countries must be subordinated and co-operative action taken.

The self-governing Dominions and States are interested in agricultural settlement at home because the type of emigrant they require comes from the agricultural districts of the United Kingdom. 'The plans for the employment and settlement of ex-service men on the land in England and Wales are as follows: So far as *employment* is concerned, the only proposals so far disclosed are: (*a*) the establishment of a minimum wage of 25*s*. per week for agricultural labourers; (*b*) the guarantee of a minimum price for wheat and oats from 1917 to 1922.' As regards *settlement*, legislation has been passed enabling the Board of Agriculture and Fisheries to acquire land for a small number of experimental smallholding colonies, intended primarily for ex-service men, in England and Wales up to a maximum of 6,000 acres in all. Land has already been obtained for two such colonies, 1,600 acres at Sunk Island, near Patrington, in Yorkshire, and 1,000 acres near Holbeach, in Lincolnshire. The Duke of Sutherland has presented the nation with the farm of Borgie, 12,200 acres; of which 200 acres are arable or can be reclaimed. It is proposed to form seventy holdings each with an arable area of six acres with an outrun of common pasture. 8,000 acres are reserved for afforestation.

Estimates are given of the probable numbers that the various Dominions could take: in the Prairie Provinces of Canada, in the first three years after the war, 90,000; in Queensland the preliminary scheme for soldier settlements provides for nearly 20,000 men; Western Australia 14,000 in agricultural pursuits; in New South Wales the Yanco scheme will provide for 1,000 farms, etc.

Preference in all the arrangements should be given to married men, and arrangements made for the widows and orphans of ex-service men. Suggestions are made for financial assistance to ex-service men; and for encouraging their settlement in those parts of the Empire where development depends on facilities for obtaining loan capital. A new Central Emigration Authority containing representation of Home and Overseas Governments and other bodies should be established without delay.

App. I contains a Memo. by P. L. Gell on *The Finance of Land Settlement*. See *Breviate 1917–39*, pp. 331–46.

Labour Bureaux

Rep., apps. pp. 32. 1906

1906 (86) *cii*, 363

A. Lowry.

In 1905 there were eleven Municipal Bureaux in London and ten in the Provinces; there were also two non-municipal ones in London and one in Ipswich. In many cases they had been connected with the machinery of some system of relief work for the unemployed, and there had been a tendency to regard them as a means of increasing employment, which they could not do, rather than as a means of finding it. The chief field of usefulness was in the unorganized trades. The Appendices contain a table of the kinds of workmen registered at the Bureaux. See *Agencies* and *Methods for Dealing with the Unemployed*. Rep.; 1893–4 C. 7182, lxxxii, 377. *Agencies and Methods for Dealing with Unemployed in certain Foreign Countries*. D. F. Schloss. Rep.; 1905 Cd. 2304, lxxiii, 471.

Distress Committees in Scotland

Reps.

1907 *Cd.* 3431, *lxxvi*, 1029. 1908 *Cd.* 3830, *lxxxviii*, 843. 1909 *Cd.* 4478, *Cd.* 4946, *lxxi*, 931

G. Falconar-Stewart.

Up to May 1909 sixteen Distress Committees had been established under the Unemployed Workmen Act, 1905, covering 42·59 per cent of the population of Scotland. The reports give details of the age, marital condition and occupation of the applicants, the duration of unemployment and the number provided with or assisted to find work.

State of Employment in the United Kingdom in October 1914

Rep., apps. pp. 41. 1914

1914–16 *Cd.* 7703, *xxi*, 25

H. Llewellyn Smith.

The Report is based on 43 per cent of the industrial population. The abrupt curtailment of production in August was met by the employers by putting their workpeople on half time rather than dismissing them. It soon became apparent that the continuance of our overseas commerce would make the restriction on production less serious, whilst those branches of industry supplying war materials were on full time. Taking July as a basis, there was no net increase of unemployment amongst males. Amongst women there was 6·2 per cent reduction of employment and a high percentage of women working short time, particularly in the cotton trade.

—— Report in December 1914. pp.10.
1915
1914–16 Cd. 7755, xxi, 67

There was a 10·7 per cent reduction in male employment since July and 10·6 per cent enlistment, therefore practically no net increase of unemployment. The improvement amongst women was marked by a 3·2 per cent reduction of numbers employed as against 6·2 per cent in October, 19·1 per cent working short time as against 26 per cent in October and 10·8 per cent working overtime as against 5·9 per cent in October.

—— Report in February 1915, apps.
pp. 19. 1915
1914–16 Cd. 7850, xxi, 77

The reduction in male employment was now 11·8 per cent and enlistment 15·4 per cent. The rate of absorption into industry of unemployed and unoccupied men was 3·6 per cent. Overtime had risen from 12·8 to 13·8 per cent. Amongst women the reduction in numbers employed since July was 1·5 per cent as compared with 3·2 per cent in December; short time had fallen to 12·6, overtime had increased to 10·9 per cent. There was now an actual shortage of women.

See Special Work of the Local Government Board Arising out of the War. p. 31.

Steps Taken for the Prevention and Relief of Distress Due to the War

Memo., apps. pp. 52. 1914

1914 Cd. 7603, lxxi, 877
apptd. Aug., 1914. sgd. ——

H. Samuel (Ch.), Birrell, Wood, Masterman, Pease, Burns, Long, Lewis, MacDonald, Benn, Murray, Tennant (Mrs.).

'To advise on the measures necessary to deal with any distress that may arise in consequence of the war.'

The Government Committee appointed by the Prime Minister was to be assisted by four sub-committees (on London, Agricultural Districts, Urban Housing and Women's Employment) appointed by the chairman, H. Samuel, President of the L.G.B., and by Local Representative Committees in counties and towns with a population of 20,000. The Intelligence Department of the L.G.B. was also to be assisted by two intelligence committees.

To prevent distress, Distress Committees had been urged to consider schemes of work in advance, local authorities informed that housing schemes could be undertaken to prevent unemployment in the building trades, and that works planned could be carried out and if necessary expedited; while the Road Board, Development Commission and Light Railways Commission were preparing schemes for possible use. Firms with Government contracts should expedite delivery by employing extra hands rather than by overtime. Employers should try to avert the sudden closing of works, and to replace men called up.

To relieve distress amongst the dependants of men on active service and amongst the civilian population, a National Relief Fund had been formed in a response to an appeal by H.R.H. the Prince of Wales. On the military side the fund would use as agents the Soldiers' and Sailors' Families Association and on the civil side the Local Representative Committees. To prevent overlapping, a common register of assisted cases should be kept. The guardians should continue to deal with all persons in the habit of receiving relief.

See National Relief Fund in Scotland; 1914–16 Cd. 8129, xxxi, 795. 1916 Cd. 8227, xiv, 445.

Belgian Refugees

Dept. Cttee. 1st Rep., apps. pp. iv, 62. 1914. Mins. of ev., index. 1915

1914–16 Cd. 7750, vii, 473. Mins. of ev., etc.; 1914–16 Cd. 7779, vii, 539
apptd. Oct., sgd. Dec., 1914

E. Hatch (*Ch.*), Bidwell, Bowerman, Cawley, Elliott, Gosling, Henderson, Lawrence, Lyttelton, Meiklejohn, Pease, L. Plymouth, Rey, Smillie, White, Williams.

'*To consider and report on questions arising from the reception of the Belgian Refugees in this country, particularly what action can properly be taken with a view to finding occupation for the Refugees which would not compete with the employment of available British labour.*'

In the flight from Belgium in 1914 caused by the German invasion, 110,000 persons arrived in this country. They consisted of three groups: those qualified to fill vacancies in industries in which there was a shortage of British labour, e.g. armaments, mining, agriculture, those qualified for and in need of employment where no opportunities existed in British industries, e.g. tailoring, printing, and members of the special professional and semi-professional classes for whom there is no chance of employment in their callings. Those of the first group should not be employed under conditions other than those prevailing for British workers, and those at work on Government contracts, on railways or in factories, etc., should be engaged through the Labour Exchanges. A Central Authority should be established to assist local refugees and employment committees to organize workshops, etc. The problem of the third group was referred to the Official Committee of Belgians.

App. I deals with the 'Conditions for finding employment for Belgian Refugees in the ordinary labour market.'

11. PROFESSIONS

Prohibition of Medical Practice by Companies Bill [H.L.]. Dental Companies (Restriction of Practice) Bill [H.L.]

Sel. Cttee. HL. Rep., proc., mins. of ev., app. pp. viii, 94. 1907

1907 (*HL*. 72) *vii*, 313
apptd. April, o.p. June, 1907

Lord Hylton (*Ch.*), L. Falkland, L. Knutsford, L. Ludlow, L. Colebrooke.

The short formal report states that the first Bill was reported without, and the second with, some amendments. According to the evidence, the two Bills dealt with the prohibition of unqualified persons from practising by means of companies formed under the Joint Stock Companies Act (qq. 10-27). An unqualified individual cannot assume a professional title gained by qualifications, cannot sign a death certificate, and has unlimited liability for damages for misconduct or malpractice. In all these cases the company has by law a privilege over the individual (q. 73). The Bill was designed to prevent this abuse, but in no way attempted to deal with the unqualified individual in medical practice.

In the case of the dental company there was no substance in the claim that the company could supply teeth cheaper than the qualified individual. These companies buy their materials from the same wholesale supplier at the same discount rates. Therefore no advantage can be gained except by making the sale of teeth the primary concern and it is 'to their interest to take out teeth regardless of a patient's real requirements, in order that dentures may be sold' (q. 182).

The Practice of Medicine and Surgery by Unqualified Persons

Rep. pp. 86. 1910

1910 *Cd.* 5422, *xliii*, 9

The General Medical Council had wanted a Royal Commission on this subject, but it had been thought advisable first to obtain information on the practices of bonesetters, herbalists, chemists, dentists, faithhealers, sellers of proprietary medicines, abortionists, and unqualified practitioners in venereal diseases and tuberculosis. It was difficult to say whether practice by unqualified persons was increasing. In 82 of the 217 towns considered it appeared that unqualified practice was either large or increasing; in 75 it existed to some extent; in 27 there was very little; while in only 30 was such practice stated to be non-existent. It was probable that a large number of ignorant people were deceived into believing that the persons they consulted were qualified.

Acceptance by the Board of Education of Dental Certificates from unregistered practitioners

Dept. Cttee. Rep. pp. 8. 1914

1914 *Cd. 7538, xxv,* 903
apptd. —, sgd. July, 1914

C. Trevelyan (*Ch.*), Newman, Phipps, Powell.

'*To consider what alterations, if any, are needed in the present practice of the Board with regard to the acceptance of certificates from unregistered practitioners in dentistry as to the condition of the teeth of candidates for recognition as teachers by the Board.*'

The Incorporated Dental Society complained that the Board's requirement that all candidates for recognition as teachers in public elementary schools whose teeth were defective must present a certificate of proper treatment from a registered dentist, and that only in exceptional circumstances did it accept one from an unregistered practitioner, deprived their members of patients and injured their reputation. The complaints had little foundation. Of the 12,000 persons recognized as teachers each year, about 320 annually are required to obtain dental treatment; and of these about one-third in the first instance submit the name of an unregistered practitioner. They are informed that the name of a registered dentist must be submitted. The Board should not agree to accept certificates from unregistered practitioners and in future where a candidate

satisfied the Board that he could not obtain one from a registered dentist, he should instead present one from a medical practitioner.

Public Veterinary Services

Dept. Cttee. Rep. pp. 15. 1913. Mins. of ev., apps., index. 1913

1912–13 Cd. 6575, xlviii, 251. *Mins. of ev., etc.;* 1912–13 *Cd. 6652, xlviii,* 267 *apptd. Aug.,* 1912. *sgd. Jan.,* 1913

A. Hopkinson (*Ch.*), Elliott, Read, MacMunn, Drake.

'*To inquire into the requirements of the public services with regard to the employment of officers possessing veterinary qualifications and to consider whether any further measures can with advantage be adopted for the selection and training of students with a view to such employment.*'

There was an inadequate supply of suitable candidates for civil veterinary appointments at home, in the Colonies and in India, the total number of students having dropped in 15 years by 40 per cent. A large number of them had the fixed objective of eventually engaging in private practice, but this had been reduced by the substitution of mechanical for animal transport. There was, however, an increasing demand for veterinary surgeons in the public services and, owing to the expansion of research into animal diseases, in research work. The problem was therefore one of attracting suitable students, and providing the training necessary for the public services without increasing the numbers of veterinary practitioners. Students possessing a suitable science degree should be granted exemption from one of the four years at present required for veterinary qualification; twelve scholarships should be offered each year, together with scholarships for advanced study, etc., and increased state aid given to veterinary educational institutions.

XI. SOCIAL SECURITY

1. Poor Law
2. Unemployment Insurance
3. Health Insurance

4. Workmen's Compensation
5. Old Age Pensions

1. POOR LAW

Industrial Training of Girls in the Separate and District Schools in the Metropolitan District

Rep. pp. 125. 1899

1900 *Cd. 237, lxxiii, 335*
sgd. Dec., 1898

Miss Ina Stansfeld.

'*To report upon the Industrial Training given to girls in the District and Separate Schools in the Metropolitan District, and, further, to submit my views on the working of the schools generally, the success or failure of existing arrangements, with such suggestions as I think desirable for future guidance.*'

There are four classes of girls in the poor law schools: infants, aged 3–7; full-timers, aged 7–11; half-timers, aged 11–14, and girls exempt from school. The most important training for the infants is conveyed through the kindergarten system and the child's ordinary play. The half-timers have household duties carefully graded to suit their age and strength, e.g. bedmaking, cleaning boots, acting as dormitory maids, washing up, etc. In some cases it is difficult to give them work distinctly different from that given to older girls, and to fit their domestic with their school work. Girls exempt from school were being trained for domestic work, but owing to differences in equipment and convenience of the buildings, the type and length of training varied from institution to institution. In West Ham and St. George's-in-the-East the buildings were so bad as to render the work of training ineffective. In many, girls bought materials and made their own outfits, were encouraged to shop, bank their savings and went to church unattended. But the most

efficient of matrons was hampered by the disturbing factors of 'Ins-and-Outs' and the sudden withdrawals by parents, etc.

The 1896–1897 Reports of the Metropolitan Association for Befriending Young Servants showed that 906 girls had been placed in service from 21 Poor Law Schools, and that their 'follow up' records showed good results. The fact that the demand for those trained in these schools far exceeded the supply was also an indication of the success of the training, even though allowance must be made for the general dearth of servants.

Miss Stansfeld made the following suggestions: cottage homes did not provide the same scope for training as did the associated and block system schools; the kindergarten should be universally adopted; 'half-timers' should be abolished; one year should be required for training and no girl should be sent out to service under 15 years of age. Matrons appointed to cottage homes should have received training in a hospital and a school or orphanage or training home.

Nursing of the Sick Poor in Workhouses

Dept. Cttee. Pt. I. Rep. pp. 41. 1902.
Pt. II. Mins. of ev., apps., index. 1902

1902 *Cd.* 1366, *xxxix,* 413. *Mins. of ev., etc.;* 1902 *Cd.* 1367, *xxxix,* 457
apptd. Jan., 1902. *sgd. Nov.,* 1902

J. G. Lawson (*Ch.*), Knollys, Downes, Fuller.

'*To inquire and report with regard to the Nursing of the Sick Poor in Workhouses:* (1) *As to any difficulties experienced in obtaining an adequate supply of properly qualified Nurses and Assistant Nurses, and how far these difficulties can be met;*

(2) *What regulations, if any, should be made as to the qualifications and training of Probationers; (3) What amendment, if any, is desirable in the Regulations as to the qualification of Superintendent Nurses; (4) Whether any, and if so, what provision should be made for defining more strictly the respective duties of the Master or Matron of the Workhouse and of the Superintendent Nurse.'*

The intake of probationers of 700 to 800 a year equalled the demand for nurses, but left no margin to make up for the 'wastage' or for the calls of special circumstances, such as the Boer War and the epidemic of small-pox and influenza, or for the increased opportunities in the District, Colonial and other nursing services. Recruits came, on the whole, from the same class as for non-Poor Law nursing ('daughters of private gentlemen, professional men, farmers and shopkeepers'). Although Poor Law nurses in training received a small remuneration whilst other trainees sometimes paid premiums, Poor Law training was less attractive because workhouse life was monotonous; there was only a small percentage of surgical cases.

To increase the supply of probationers and nurses there should be a Nursing Service of four grades, with opportunities of promotion. No more appointments of assistant nurses should be made. Probationers should be trained in either Minor or Major Training Schools, and should be enabled to qualify as Trained and as Superintendent Nurses. Qualified nurses should hold a Minor, Trained Nurses a Major, Training School Certificate. As counter-attractions to the non-Poor Law Nursing Services, paid servants- or pauper labour should do the house work in nurses' quarters, nurses should have separate bedrooms, leave of three weeks, etc., and in country workhouses, better pay. Superintendent Nurses should be trained nurses, with one year's service as such and a Midwifery Certificate. To avoid disputes of jurisdiction, the respective duties of Master, Matron and Superintendent Nurse are defined to give the latter control of the sick wards, nurses and non-nursing staff whilst in the wards. The Government grant should be increased, but be paid only for nurses whose qualifications are as laid down.

Method of Keeping Workhouse Accounts

Dept. Cttee. Rep., apps. pp. liii, 70. 1903

1903 Cd. 1440, *xxvi*, 567
apptd. May, 1901. *sgd. June,* 1902

J. S. Davy (*Ch.*), Downes, Lloyd-Roberts.

'To inquire and report with respect to (a) any difficulties in keeping the Workhouse Accounts prescribed by the Orders for Accounts and the Workhouse Regulation (Dietaries and Accounts) Order, 1900, and (b) any modifications in the Regulations as to the forms of account which appear desirable with a view to the necessary records being made as simple as practicable.'

The first Order prescribing a uniform system of books was made in 1835, no amendment being made till 1867. There has been no change of principle since its introduction, a fact which indicates its practical merits. It required no special knowledge of bookkeeping. The system was very complete, the forms being to a great extent dependent on one another, so that in order to simplify them, it was necessary to recast the whole system. The number of books has been reduced somewhat, but their form greatly simplified.

Outdoor Relief (Friendly Societies) (No. 2) Bill, 1900

Report to the Treasury. pp. 3. 1903

1903 (*HL.* 60) *xi*, 147

E. W. Brabrook.

It has been the practice of the Boards of Guardians to award outdoor relief without taking too strict account of any allowance received from Friendly Societies by applicants who had tried to help themselves by becoming members. To remove uncertainty as to the lawfulness of this practice, the Outdoor Relief Friendly Societies Act, 1894, changed the discretion into an obligation to disregard up to 5s. per week. Since Guardians have the duty of relieving every destitute person with an adequate sum, such a recipient who has made insufficient provision through his Friendly Society will be provided with a sum up to 5s. per week beyond what is adequate for his necessities.

Poor Law Medical Relief (Scotland)

Dept. Cttee. Vol. I. Rep. pp. vi, 129. 1904. Vol. II. Mins of ev., apps., index. 1904

1904 *Cd. 2008, xxxiii, 1. Mins. of ev., etc.*; 1904 *Cd. 2022, xxxiii, 137 apptd. July,* 1902. *sgd. March,* 1904

J. P. MacDougall (*Ch.*), Mackenzie, Barclay.

'*To inquire into and report on the methods and conditions under which Poor Law Medical Relief is at present administered in Scotland, and on what changes, if any, it is advisable to make in regard thereto, or in the regulations for distributing the sum contributed from the Local Taxation Account to the cost of Poor Law Medical Relief and Trained Sick Nursing, or in the Rules and Regulations for the Management of Poorhouses.*'

In 1902 a Bill had been introduced empowering the Local Government Board for Scotland to remove anomalies in the distribution of the grant-in-aid of poor law medical relief, and the Committee had been appointed to assist in framing a new scheme of distribution and more equitable rules. But the Bill had been withdrawn and the Committee had then been asked to suggest possible improvements of the Poor Law Medical Service.

There had been a gradual increase in total expenditure on medical relief from 3s. 4¼d. per pauper in 1851 to 11s. 3d. in 1902, but the grant had remained fixed at £20,000 since 1882, and was distributed on rules which could be altered only by legislation, proportionately amongst parishes which had a specified minimum of expenditure. The grant per £1 of expenditure had therefore fallen. Tested by modern standards, much in the administration needed reform, and over 100 recommendations are made. Indoor Relief.— The larger poorhouse hospitals have been coming into line with the most advanced general hospitals, but in many improvements were necessary, amongst which were separate and smaller wards for the sick, a minimum of 800 cubic feet per bed, sufficient beds for inmates requiring treatment, a maximum number of beds per ward, and segregation of phthisical cases. Untrained nursing by paupers, still existing in half the poorhouses, should be abolished, and replaced by nurses with a minimum of two years' training. The existing ratio of one nurse to sixty patients should be reduced to one to thirty at least. To increase the supply, probationers should be given a salary, three years' training followed by a uniform examination, and a grant should be made to enable selected poorhouses to become training centres. Outdoor medical relief.—All parishes should be required by statute to appoint a medical officer. The supply of medicines by medical officers in respect of salary or by druggists in return for a fixed annual payment should be discontinued. Grant-in-Aid.—The present 'minimum expenditure' as a condition of participation should be abolished, and vouched expenditure continue to be the basis of distribution until the recommendations of the Royal Commission on Local Taxation had been made law. No grant should be paid for indoor medical relief unless trained nursing is provided. The Board should be empowered to make orders for the administration of medical relief under the same safeguards as in England and Ireland. A draft of revised rules and regulations for the management of poorhouses is appended.

Methods of Administering Poor Relief in Certain Large Town Parishes of Scotland

Rep., apps. pp. xxxi, 43. 1905

1905 Cd. 2524, lxviii, 433
apptd. Dec., 1904. sgd. April, 1905

R. B. Barclay (*Ch.*), Penney, Stuart, Millar, Jeffrey.

'*To inquire into the administration of poor relief in the large centres of population in Scotland, and to consider and report whether the growth of pauperism might be retarded or checked by any change in the methods of administering relief. They also indicated that our investigations should, in the first instance at least, be confined to the parishes of Edinburgh, Leith, Glasgow, Govan, Greenock, Paisley, Dundee and Aberdeen, as these centres appeared to be mainly responsible for the large increase of pauperism.*'

Enquiries had been made into the administration of poor relief in the parishes of Edinburgh, Leith, Glasgow, Govan, Greenock, Paisley, Dundee and Aberdeen. In Scotland, excluding these parishes, there had been a decrease in ordinary (as opposed to lunatic) pauperism of 124 between 1894 and 1904; but an increase of over 9,000 had taken place in the parishes mentioned. If the pauperism in Greenock, Paisley and Dundee were regarded as normal, it appeared that that in Edinburgh, Glasgow and Govan was higher, and that in Leith and Aberdeen much higher, than their social conditions—age composition and housing—warranted. Relief, and especially indoor relief, was too easily obtainable.

Among the many changes in administration recommended were those in the constitution and procedure of Relief Committees. There should be more careful enquiry into the circumstances of applicants and into every re-application and more exhaustive medical examinations. A medical certificate should show whether the applicant was physically 'able to maintain' himself and those who were should not be offered indoor assistance. The workhouse test should be made more effective. Each parish council should draw up a scale of allowances and the Inspector of the Poor should make recommendations as to kind and amount of relief.

Vagrancy

Dept. Cttee. Vol. I. Rep. pp. vi, 123. 1906. Vol. II. Mins. of ev., index. 1906. Vol. III. Apps., etc. 1906

1906 Cd. 2852, ciii, 1. *Mins. of ev., etc.*;
1906 Cd. 2891, Cd. 2892, ciii, 131
apptd. July, 1904. sgd. Feb., 1906

J. L. Wharton (*Ch.*), Chance, Davy, Downes, Eardley-Wilmot, ˋShowers, Simpson.

'*To inquire and report with respect to England and Wales as to* (1) *the law applicable to persons of the vagrant class (i.e. the statutory provisions and the byelaws, rules, and regulations made thereunder);* (2) *the administration of the law applicable to these persons; and* (3) *any amendments which should be made in it or in its administration.*'

The complaint made thirty years ago that 'we are taxed to provide board and lodging' for vagrants 'who will not have households of their own, who have but one object in all their wicked and perverse lives—to exist without work at the expense of their industrious neighbours', and that in all the army of tramps 'there is no appreciable element of honest poverty or of penniless industry seeking work' might be repeated with considerable justice at the present day. The army of vagrants has increased in numbers and there is reason to fear that it will continue to increase if things are left as they are. The present system neither deters the vagrant nor affords any means of reclaiming him, and the Committee was 'unanimously of opinion that a thorough reform is necessary'.

Before the nineteenth century Parliament attempted to repress vagrancy by the enactment of a long series of measures of varying severity, but the result showed that isolated acts of punishment, however severe, did not prevent what was then, as now, a mode of life. In the last century milder counsels led to a twofold method of dealing with vagrancy. Certain acts were defined as offences, and cumulative punishments were prescribed; the status of the vagrant was definitely recognized, and food and shelter were provided at public expense to assist him on his wanderings, though to prevent a too free resort to this assistance the gift was surrounded with irksome conditions. A condition of success under this system was a consistent administration of the law throughout the country. But the Orders of the Central Authority issued to secure uniformity of treatment had failed to do so; and there has been a similar absence of consistency in the enforcement of the law by the police and the magistrates. Between the Poor Law and the police the vagrant has flourished. The police authorities treat the vagrant as a criminal, but do not punish him, while the Poor Law authorities treat him as a pauper but do not relieve him. The history of vagrancy in this and other countries indicates that the vagrant cannot be suppressed.

Casual wards could not be dispensed with at present, but should be placed under the control of the police authorities, who should take over all buildings, and close superfluous wards. To aid those *bona fide* in search of work, the police should issue tickets for a definite route, available for a month, entitling the holder to lodging, supper and breakfast in the casual ward. Short sentences should be discouraged. When the sentence is for less than 14 days, it should be limited to one day, and the conviction recorded. Lodging houses outside London, and shelters should be licensed and regulated. Sleeping out should be an offence whenever it takes place in buildings or enclosed premises, and is a danger or nuisance to the public; the methods of issue of pedlar's certificates should be made uniform, female vagrants received into the workhouses instead of the casual wards, and children of habitual vagrants sent to industrial schools and other places of safety. Habitual vagrants should be sent to labour colonies, which should be certified by the Home Secretary, councils of counties and county boroughs being given power to establish or contribute to them. They should be industrial and reformatory rather than penal, but the State should establish one colony of a penal type for those not amenable to the discipline of the industrial labour colonies. The real cause of vagrancy is beyond the power of the legislature or administrative action. If indiscriminate dole-giving ceased there would be no necessity for casual wards or labour colonies and vagrancy would come to an end.

In a memo. Eardley-Wilmot disputed the contention that the improvement in prisons had caused the increase of vagrancy (pp. 54-8). 'The causes were to be found in the social and economic conditions of the period under discussion.' Mr. Simpson suggested that in the Metropolitan area casual wards should be taken over by the Standing Joint Committee of the four surrounding counties, and not by the Metropolitan Police. The history of vagrancy is discussed in pp. 1-23 of the report and in the 1st-3rd days of evidence of Mr. Preston-Thomas. The Apps. give statistical material and reports on vagrancy in other continental countries.

See *Methods of Dealing with Vagrancy in Switzerland*. H. Preston-Thomas. Rep.; 1904 Cd. 2235, lxxxii, 593.

Poplar Union

Rep., app. pp. 75. 1906. Transcript shorthand notes. 1906

1906 Cd. 3240, Cd. 3274, *civ*, 1

J. S. Davy.

'A public Inquiry into the general conditions of the Poplar Union, its pauperism and the administration of the Guardians and their Officers.'

Although the population of Poplar had remained unchanged from 1894 to 1904, the number of indoor paupers rose from 2,623 to 3,465 and of outdoor paupers from 2,295 to 3,677. Expenditure on relief rose even faster, from £34,698 to £60,142 on indoor and from £12,395 to £24,399 on outdoor relief. In 1904 the indebtedness of the Guardians had reached almost the limit of their borrowing powers, which would require to be enlarged to meet the expenditure incurred in connection with the new schools they were erecting at Shenfield, Essex. Complaints were made by ratepayers as to the extravagance of the Guardians, and the great increase in their expenditure. Towards the end of 1904, the industrial depression became acute and 'on 19th November a resolution was passed by the Guardians to the effect that able-bodied men out of work applying for relief were to receive out-door relief in kind without being set to work'. An extraordinary increase in out-relief followed this decision.

In evidence, Mr. Crooks, chairman of the Guardians, was of the opinion that Poplar was getting poorer; Mr. Anderson, a Guardian and Secretary of the Stevedores Union, thought that although more permanent men were employed at the docks, the remaining casual labourers were an inferior class of men and really worse off than they used to be. Mr. Lansbury said that 'when people are casually employed they are naturally compelled to supplement their wages out of the rates'. Evidence seemed to show, as did Charles Booth's Survey in 1886, that Poplar was not quite the poorest part of London, that there were other unions with a higher proportion of casual labour, and therefore, that the disproportionate pauperism, and the exceptionally high rates of Poplar were due rather to the administration of the local authorities than to the exceptional poverty in the district. Serious mismanagement of the workhouse and serious abuses of contracts existed. The policy pursued by the Guardians has led to the pauperization of a great number of inhabitants and to subsidizing women's casual labour. While Mr. Crooks and Mr. Lansbury were directing their policy 'some of their colleagues had been guilty of misconduct in relation to the mismanagement of the workhouse, and that there has been a great want of business capacity in dealing with contracts'. The real question was how future Guardians were to be checked from carrying out a policy not in accordance with the intention of the Poor Law. Of their total expenditure, only a little over two-thirds was charged to Poplar rates, and the rateable value of that portion of the community which voted and paid rates was only one-fifth of the whole; and there is no representation on the Guardians of those who pay rates but cannot vote. Crooks and Lansbury advocated the transfer of all Poor Law work in the Metropolis to a central body, but on this the report of the Royal Commission on the Poor Laws must be awaited. Proposals which should be considered were that contracting should be taken out of the hands of the Guardians, that half-yearly returns of expenditure on consumable articles should be made, as recommended by the Committee on Workhouse Accounts.

See *Administration of the Guardians of the Hamlet of Mile End Old Town.* Rep.; 1908 Cd. 4011, xcii, 541.

Children under the Poor Law

Rep. pp. 25. 1908

1908 *Cd. 3899, xcii,* 455
sgd. Dec., 1907

T. J. Macnamara.

An investigation into the systems of maintaining and educating poor law children ten years after the Mundella Committee on *Metropolitan Poor Law Schools* (1896 C. 8032, xliii). The report explains and assesses the methods, including cottage homes, scattered homes and the district schools, by which the 69,000 poor law children are maintained and educated and gives information on after-careers, and the results of emigration.

Dock Labour in Relation to Poor Law Relief

Rep., apps. pp. 46. 1908

1908 *Cd.* 4391, *xcii*, 483
sgd. Sept., 1908

G. Walsh.

'*Enquiries as to the relation of casual labour at the docks in London and elsewhere to poor law relief.*'

The report describes the types of dock labour in London, Liverpool and Bristol, the proportion of skilled, permanent and casual labour, the methods of engagement, etc. Though there were great variations in conditions, even in the same port, dock labour was by no means completely casual and unorganized, a large proportion were skilled men in more or less regular employment. But a large number went to the docks because they preferred intermittent work which, together with the system of daily payments, did not conduce to thrift. Even the more highly skilled and regular worker often spent his wages recklessly. Dock labour was not subsidized by the poor rate, which was no more affected by it than by other types of manual labour. It was mainly the large number of casual workers, working an occasional day in the docks, who were a burden on the poor rates. They could not legitimately be called 'dock labourers', and the problem was rather that of casual labour as a whole. Various attempts had been made to regularize dock employment, but many, including the unions, who would otherwise welcome such a change, would

bitterly oppose it if it meant a reduction in the number employed. There was strong opposition to such schemes from skilled and unskilled workers, and from some employers, to whose advantage it was to have a large floating surplus of labour.

Poor Laws and Relief of Distress

R. Com. Rep. pp. xiii, 1238. 1909

1909 *Cd.* 4499, *xxxvii*, 1
apptd. Dec., 1905. *sgd. Feb.*, 1909

G. Hamilton (*Ch.*), Kelly, Robinson, Provis, Bentham, Downes, Gardiner, Loch, MacDougall, Nunn, Phelps, Smart, Bosanquet (Helen), Hill (Octavia), Wakefield, Chandler, Lansbury, Webb (Beatrice).

'*To inquire:* (1) *Into the working of the laws relating to the relief of poor persons in the United Kingdom;* (2) *Into the various means which have been adopted outside of the Poor Laws for meeting distress arising from want of employment, particularly during periods of severe industrial depression; and to consider and report whether any, and if so what, modification of the Poor Laws or changes in their administration or fresh legislation for dealing with distress are advisable.*'

The Royal Commission was finally appointed after questions had been asked in Parliament in August, 1905, criticizing the Unemployed Workmen's Bill as introducing methods of providing work outside the limits of the Poor Law. Though many investigations had been made into particular aspects of the Poor Law, this was the first comprehensive survey since 1834.

Majority Report. G. Hamilton, Kelly, Robinson, Provis, Bentham, Downes, Gardiner, Loch, MacDougall, Nunn, Phelps, Smart, Bosanquet (Helen), Hill (Octavia).

Pt. I. Procedure.—In view of the great scope of the investigation and the fact that there had been over 100 inquiries into Poor Law matters since 1834, the Commission decided to accept as far as possible the evidence and reports of recent and current enquiries.

Pt. II. Statistical Survey.—During the year ending 30th September, 1907, 526,449 men, 618,673 women and 564,314 children, a total of 1,709,436, received relief in some form. Just under one-third of these received outdoor and the remainder indoor relief. Rather under one-third were 'permanent' paupers, i.e. the aged, chronic sick, orphans and deserted children. A detailed review of changes in the numbers of the different classes of paupers, costs, changes in wages and the cost of living leads to the conclusion that despite moral and material progress, an expenditure on poor relief in 1905–6 of nearly £15 mn. or £15 16s. 6d. per pauper, and on poor relief, education and health together of £60 mn. had not decreased pauperism and that there still remained a large army of persons unable to support themselves. 'Something must be seriously wrong with our social organization.' The structure and voluminous character of the main body of the Report follows from the method the Majority elected to pursue. After a review of the development of the Poor Law from 1601 to 1834 (Pt. III) the discussion of each problem and branch of administration (Pt. IV) begins with a statement of the policy of 1834, then proceeds by way of a critical examination of the history and of the enquiries since that date to the evidence the Commission had itself taken and so to its conclusions and recommendations.

Pt. IV. Development and Present Condition of Various Branches.—The Royal Commission on the Poor Law of 1834 was faced with the increasing pauperism of the agricultural labourer, and guided by the experience of Friendly Societies, laid it down that the able-bodied should not be offered relief otherwise than in a well-regulated workhouse, and that the lot of the able-bodied should be less eligible than that of the independent workman. Their proposals for other classes were scantier, but they suggested proper classification and the impropriety of putting all classes of paupers under one roof (Pt. III, 143). It was the lifting of the burden of able-bodied pauperism through the work of the Poor Law Commissioners created by the Act of 1834 which made it possible for the administration to move in the direction of adapting treatment more closely to the needs of the different classes. The question is whether the demands for further specialization can be met without reverting to the evils which existed before 1834.

1. The Central Authority. A large responsibility for good administration rests upon the L.G.B., whose powers, though legally far-reaching, are limited by the control of the House of Commons and because the guardians are elected bodies. It should be placed in a more direct position of guidance and initiative by strengthening its powers, increasing the numbers and qualifications of inspectors, consolidating statutes and orders, and by giving it power to withhold central grants.

2. Local Authorities. The Act of 1894 swept away all ex-officio and nominated guardians provided for in 1834 and the alternative of co-option has failed. The central control envisaged in 1834 has not prevented great and unfair lack of uniformity in practice, the election of interested parties as members, or some over-large boards; there was a lack of popular interest in elections. The system of direct election has not given us local authorities with an adequate appreciation of their responsibilities and has led to evils which ought not to be perpetuated. The work of the guardians should be taken over by a new Public Assistance Authority, which should be a statutory committee of the county and county borough councils, one-half of whose members should be appointed from persons outside the council (Pt. IX, 20–23).

3. Officers. The Commission of 1834 stressed the importance of competent officers, and the Act of 1834 provided for the central approval of their

appointment, but little in the way of qualifications had been laid down. There should be examinations and qualifications for all higher officers, and a graded public assistance service should be set up.

4. Area of Administration. The combination of parishes into unions in 1834 was designed partly to make it possible to house the different classes of paupers in separate buildings, and it was assumed that the sick, the aged and children should be provided for in this way, but in the first year of their administration the Commissioners reported that it had 'been proved that the expense and loss of time in building new workhouses may . . . be saved . . . by assigning one or two classes to one separate workhouse within the district'. By 1839 they had concluded that few unions would 'find it desirable to maintain more than one establishment' and that there should be classification within institutions. Although the need for specialization was increasingly felt (e.g. by the Select Committee of 1861) the general mixed workhouse continued. The situation was complicated by the lack of competent nursing staff. Classification within the general workhouse, even where carried out, had not resulted in a proper treatment of the various classes. The area of administration should therefore be enlarged and this would also help to equalize burdens.

5. Indoor Relief. The Royal Commission of 1834 had intended that, as a deterrent measure, the able-bodied should be given relief in the workhouse, where they would be put to work. But they did not foresee that thousands of inmates of all types would be housed in urban workhouses where the absence of land, etc., made the provision of work difficult, that 'Ins-and-Outs' and other bad characters would use it as temporary lodgings, and that the workhouse might encourage the mental and moral deterioration of the inmates. In addition to the entire reorganization of the system of the general workhouse, there should be a periodic revision of

all indoor cases, powers of detention in certain cases, and a check on excessive expenditure on buildings, while the life of aged inmates should be 'made comfortable and as far as possible cheerful'.

6. Outdoor Relief. The intention in 1834 was that, with exceptions for emergencies, certain classes of widows, etc., outdoor relief to the able-bodied should generally cease, the restrictions being introduced gradually by the Outdoor Relief Prohibitory and Regulation Orders. But it had to be checked again by Goschen's Minute of 1869, and has once more developed. While some unions make sufficient enquiries and grant adequate relief, the majority do neither, with the gravest results (e.g. aged women being inadequately helped, much harm and little good being done to widows). The case paper system should be universally adopted, cases of widows should be considered individually, and the new Public Assistance Authority should have powers to remove neglected persons, to proscribe certain areas and to report unsanitary conditions.

7. Children. Since 1834 Poor Law policy had been one of education for independence, and though a few exceptional Poor Law schools were better than outside schools, some were criticized for being too isolated, others condemned as 'barracks'. Mrs. Nassau Senior's adverse report on them in 1873 and the recommendation of the Committee on the *Education and Maintenance of Pauper Children in the Metropolis* (1896 C. 8027, xliii) that the children should be removed from the care of the guardians gave a great impetus to boarding-out, cottage and scattered homes. There were still (1907) 62,426 indoor pauper children as compared with 16,221 sent out to public elementary schools. 'Effective steps should be taken to secure that the maintenance of children in the workhouse be no longer recognized as a legitimate way of dealing with them.' The extension of boarding-out, subject to fullest enquiry and supervision by competent

women officers, is strongly recommended, but children under the Poor Law should not be entirely transferred to the local education authority, since the training in the public elementary schools was unsuitable for their special needs. A large number of charitable agencies provided for the same class of children, but their work was not always safeguarded and there was no outside control. It should be considered whether all such agencies should not be supervised by and required to co-operate with the public authority.

8. The Able-bodied. The problem in 1834 was the reduction of able-bodied pauperism, to effect which the workhouse test was applied. In 1838 Chadwick stated that when an emergency in a manufacturing district made its use impracticable, labour by task was the next best test. But it proved as difficult to find work outside as inside the workhouse. All the experiments in test work, special schemes, work on farms and in colonies had succeeded or failed according to the amount of supervision they were given. But where, as in the labour yards, they were used as rough and ready means of dealing with able-bodied applicants the intermittent work attracted the loafer and they often became the centres of corruption. These difficulties led to the grant of 'sudden and urgent necessity' relief, and to its weekly renewal for prolonged periods until it sometimes became an allowance system. Attempts by charitable bodies, such as various distress funds started in the belief that poor law methods were inadequate or unsuitable, were harmful when not administered with proper safeguards. For many the workhouse had ceased to be a deterrent; the inmates lost the will to work and often stayed for many years, especially if the guardians did not 'call over' their inmates periodically or use their powers of discharge. A greater variety of occupation should be aimed at and methods of detention used for dealing with various classes of 'ins-and-outs'.

9. Causes of Pauperism. Many of the causes of pauperism are the same as in 1834—old age, drink, gambling, sickness, death of parents, etc. A review of the question of how far poverty and dependence are increased by the way the Poor Law is administered leads to the conclusion that the principle of making relief conditional on its recipients accepting a way of life likely to restore them to independence must be re-inforced in its application to the able-bodied and extended to the other classes.

Pt. V. Medical Relief.—No special system of medical relief was set up by the Act of 1834, reliance being placed on the general power to aid distress and on the voluntary activity of hospitals and dispensaries. There has been a great development since that date, though legislation has been limited chiefly to the Act of 1848, which enabled guardians to provide for accidents, sudden illness, etc., to the Metropolitan Poor Act, 1867, which, following a report by Mr. Farnall, established sick asylums and dispensaries, and to an Act of 1868, which enabled the central authority to order the provision of medical and surgical equipment without local consent. The system in existence in 1905 is almost entirely based on the orders of the central authority. 'Destitution' as a test of medical relief has come to mean 'inability to provide whatever medical treatment is necessary', and the progress of medical science and of public opinion has given the term 'necessary' a meaning unknown in 1834.

The Metropolitan Poor Act, 1867, was the real commencement of indoor medical relief, for it resulted in the establishment in London of separate Poor Law infirmaries with resident medical staffs and, under the pressure from the central authority, in large provincial unions also, as well as in the improvement of the sick wards in other unions. While in 1847 the qualification of a nurse was that she should be able to 'read written directions on medicine' and on the whole paupers were used, in 1865 the central authority recommended competent paid nurses, and by 1901 there were 183,000 trained nurses and 2,000 probationers in the workhouses and infirmaries. With these improvements, the separation from the workhouse and the pressure on the voluntary hospitals, some poor law infirmaries became well-equipped general hospitals supported by the State and by the rates, and they were used by a widening class of persons. Nevertheless, union sick wards often remained 'distinctly and strongly repellent'.

The present system of outdoor medical relief, based on the relief of destitution and aiming at encouraging independent provision through provident agencies, has on the whole remained unchanged since 1834: the unions contracted with doctors to provide attendance and medicines on an order from a Poor Law official. The situation has been complicated (1) by the existence in some large towns of free dispensaries; (2) by the existence of voluntary hospitals with out-patient departments; (3) by the development of the preventive work of the local sanitary authorities and, since 1866, of their powers of providing general hospitals, domiciliary service and medicines; and (4) since 1907, by the provision of medical inspection and medical treatment of school children by the education authority. Medical assistance, once almost entirely in the hands of one statutory authority, is now shared with the sanitary and education authorities.

As a result, there is a great deal of overlapping and inequality. A well-off sick person may get free or low cost treatment in a voluntary hospital while a poor labourer in an infirmary, or his relatives, may be charged. In some areas isolation and phthisis cases are dealt with by the health authority, in others by the Poor Law authority. The system is deficient in extent, deters some classes and does not reach numbers of persons by whom it ought to be used. There are defects of quality. The Public Assistance Authority

should appoint a Medical Assistance Committee, which should include representatives of the medical profession, the provident societies and other authorities.

One suggested remedy, a free medical service, is rejected on the grounds that it would be impossible to confine it to the poor, that ultimately the whole population would have to be provided for and that it would undermine the voluntary hospitals and provident societies. The proposal to transfer the Poor Law medical service to the sanitary authority in order to unify the two services is also rejected, because it would involve testing the means of patients, a task for which the sanitary authority has no staff, and because there are three times as many health authorities as Poor Law unions, so that the area of administration would become smaller. The Majority proposed instead that medical assistance should be re-organized on a provident basis, that the whole or part of the cost of treatment should be recovered if the patient could have afforded to become a member of a provident dispensary and had not done so. The great development of provident and benefit societies envisaged would require some concordat over the medical fees and the wage limit. Medical assistance could thus be available to all and the workmen would be encouraged to make independent provision for sickness, from which they would get substantial advantages.

Pt. VI. Distress through Unemployment. — Whilst the moral causes contributing to pauperism and unemployment have remained much the same as in 1834, the material influences have changed their scope and character. Trade cycles are now world-wide, invention is more rapid, trade unions have raised their standard of wages and employers the standard of efficiency required. There are a number of blind alley jobs for the young and a large proportion of the working class are in casual, seasonal and intermittent occupations, e.g. dock work. Chronic under-employment, as distinct from periodic unemployment, is the new problem. The Poor Law treatment of the able-bodied is defective, distress and other funds have done little good and much harm, and municipal relief works, which dealt with the same mixed class of applicants, also failed because of the difficulties of discrimination, supervision, etc. The Unemployed Workmen's Act should be discontinued for similar reasons.

The Majority's proposals consist of: (1) Permanent preventive measures. These include the establishment of a national system of labour exchanges; raising the boys' school leaving age to 15, together with more practical instruction and in conjunction with the labour exchanges, a special organization to give advice on employment. The Board of Trade should hold conferences to promote decasualization and public authorities should try to regularize their employment. Unemployment insurance should be promoted, with help from the public funds, but a general scheme is rejected in favour of one based on separate industries. It should not be compulsory or universal, as the State would have to administer it and voluntary bodies would oppose it. (2) A permanent system of assistance to the able-bodied. The responsibility for the public assistance of all necessitous persons should be in the hands of one authority only—a statutory Public Assistance Committee of each county and county borough council. Those requiring maintenance and work should be given Home Assistance, which should be conditional upon daily work and in some way less agreeable than the receipt of unemployment insurance benefit. There should be institutional and labour colony treatment and compulsory detention colonies managed by the Home Office for those requiring detention and discipline.

Pt. VII. Charities.—The aggregate income of charities is large and their practice, especially in the distribution of outdoor relief, varies greatly. There is much purposeless, indiscriminate giving and overlapping, and, except in a few towns, no common centre of enquiry and registration. They should be brought into the field of public work and co-ordinated. The principles of Goschen's Minute of 1869, which advised co-operation between the guardians and voluntary societies, should be generalized. Charities should be registered and Voluntary Aid Committees established in each area to relieve persons whose cases are not suitable for or are referred to them by the Public Assistance Committee.

Pt. IX. Invalidity Insurance. — Insurance against temporary unemployment does not meet the case of the person entirely incapacitated from wage earning, and some form of invalidity insurance is required. Such an insurance fund might be supported partly by contributions from employers and workpeople and partly by State subsidy. But more information is required before a definite scheme can be put forward.

On the proposals of 'certain of our colleagues who dissent from our report' and who had proposed the 'break up of the poor law', the Majority state that the question at issue was whether the work of maintaining those who have lost their independence could be safely entrusted to the authorities whose primary duty is something distinct, such as education or health. The subtle problems associated with assistance, especially when the family rather than the individual requires rehabilitation, could not be solved by sending off each unit to a separate authority for maintenance and treatment. What was needed was a disinterested authority, practised at looking at all sides of the question, and able to call in skilled assistance. Moreover, to thrust on to the educational and health authorities the difficult and delicate duties of dealing with broken down families was to court failure both in prevention and cure. Care must be taken not to multiply authorities giving relief, and not to abolish organizations specially qualified for certain classes of work.

Pt. IX of the report also reviews existing conditions and the changes proposed, and includes an indexed list of recommendations. There are memoranda of dissent by Downes, Loch, Helen Bosanquet, Octavia Hill and Nunn.

Minority Report. Wakefield, Chandler, Lansbury, Webb (Beatrice).

Part I. The Destitution of the Non-Able-bodied.

The General Mixed Workhouse.— The Poor Law Report of 1834 was concerned almost exclusively with the problem of able-bodied destitution. But the one positive recommendation which the Commissioners made with regard to children and the aged was that they should be provided for in entirely separate institutions, with separate rules, and independent management. Though the general mixed workhouse was condemned for the vicious conditions it created, it had grown to form the basis of the whole system of Poor Law relief, in spite of the L.G.B.'s constant efforts to supersede it with specialized institutions. This was because Parliament had placed the care of all classes of poor in each union under a single local authority, which was charged not with the treatment of any one of these classes, such as the education of children or the prevention and cure of sickness, but generally with the relief of the destitution of all of them. To the Boards of Guardians of 1835 and to their successors it seemed a waste of money to maintain a series of separate institutions, all having vacant places. Once the general mixed workhouse was established, the ease and apparent economy became in the hands of the destitution authority an obstacle to any alteration of policy by the Central Authority. For half a century guardians would not relinquish their care of the vagrant, and the Committee on *Vagrancy* (1906) had recommended

that they should be withdrawn from the Poor Law. The guardians were equally reluctant to join in schemes for building schools, and it also took persistent pressure on the part of the L.G.B. to get them to provide institutions for the sick poor. Even where guardians have been determined to break up the mass of pauperism, success has been imperfect because of the heterogeneous series of classes committed to their care. An equally disastrous incident of the mixed institution is the 'mixed official'—the Master— who can have no special training for all the various problems he has to deal with. To place under the management of one man and his wife an institution with so great a variety of functions is to abandon hope of obtaining expert training and specialized skill.

Outdoor Relief.—The common alternative to the general mixed workhouse, a small weekly allowance, is as old as the Elizabethan Poor Laws, and was scarcely criticized by the Report of 1834. The system has continued; 'no order has ever been issued regulating or controlling it' and the guardians 'have exercised unchecked their power of awarding doles'. Some guardians have framed bye-laws, which exhibit extraordinary diversity, others have scales of relief which are often disregarded. Most of them use the formula 'Each case on its merits', which conceals caprice, prejudice and favouritism, and instead of attempting a remedial policy have fallen into a slipshod habit of supplementing small and precarious incomes. With few exceptions, these doles are inadequate and unconditional. Outdoor relief has failed because there is no guidance or policy, because the relieving officer has a combination of heterogeneous functions without having proper qualifications for the job, because of the fall in status of membership of the guardians, and because of the overlapping with charitable organizations. There is nothing in the nature of providing for each case exactly the treatment appropriate to its needs.

Birth and Infancy.—Two authorities provide a service for birth and infancy, but there is no co-ordination between them and they operate on directly opposite principles. The Poor Law is restrictive in that by deterrent devices it confines help to relieving destitution. On the other hand the Health Authority tries to extend its services by offering medical and other services to every necessitous mother in the hope of diminishing infantile mortality. The public health service is growing in such a way that it will practically supersede the work of the Poor Law, but whilst the policies of the two authorities simultaneously receive the support of the L.G.B., the voluntary agencies continue to grow.

Children.—Three distinct authorities make provision for the children, the Guardians, the Home Office and the Education Authority. The 1834 Report recommended that separate residential institutions should be provided for the destitute children of school age, including orphans, deserted children, and children of able-bodied paupers, but this was ignored by the Poor Law Commissioners of 1835, who relegated to the workhouse all children on institutional relief and left in their homes, on small weekly allowances, all other children. From 1841 onwards the Central Authority have been persistently striving to get the policy reversed and to provide education and training by qualified teachers. Of the 186,000 Poor Law children of school age in England and Wales, 130,000 were on out-door relief, the majority suffering in health and character, and 3,000 were in the general mixed workhouse, as well as several thousands more in the sick wards of the workhouses. For the children of the vagrants, who do not get the benefit of the local health and education authorities, the Poor Law offers nothing but a bed with their parents in the casual ward.

The Home Office, acting through the magistrates and the police, were the first to rival the Poor Law. The industrial and reformatory schools, maintained mainly by a substantial government grant, were created as an alternative to sending children to prison, but they infringed on the sphere of the Poor Law when destitute children in danger of becoming criminals were sent to them. Of the 30,000 children provided for, the majority fall distinctly into the Poor Law group.

The general provision of education brought all children under the local education authorities, whose supervision revealed the incidence of sickness and tens of thousands of children destitute of medical attendance, and led to their inviting the health authorities to institute a medical examination of children in public elementary schools. While medical relief given by the Poor Law is almost always made dependent on the status of the parent, when given by the health authority it is based on the needs of the child. School feeding of 100,000 children was forced on the education authority because it soon became evident that a starving child could not be compelled to learn or to do physical exercise. The legislation of 1906–7 authorizing the local education authorities to give medical treatment and food to destitute children is a supersession of the 'destitution' authority by the education authority.

Curative Treatment of the Sick.—The 1834 Report contained no recommendations for the sick. The most that was done was to set aside a room in the workhouse or to contract with a local doctor to attend the patient in his home. From the one has grown the large infirmary of the urban union, from the other 3,713 district medical officers, an average of six for each union. These doctors are isolated in their work, often inadequately paid, and are at the beck and call of the relieving officer, who has the right to refuse a patient access to the doctor, or to refuse a fee to a doctor acting on his own initiative. In some unions there is a lavish and indiscriminate grant of medical orders by the relieving officer, while in others good administration has come to mean, not curing the sick, but restricting the number of such orders to a minimum. Such a policy leads to serious complication, particularly in relation to infectious diseases and the urgent service of providing treatment in the early stages of tuberculosis. Overlapping the medical work of the Poor Law are four classes of voluntary agencies for the domiciliary treatment of the sick— the free dispensary, the out-patient department of the voluntary hospital, the medical clubs and the provident dispensary. They differ widely in geographical distribution, in the service they render and the degree to which they infringe or overlap the Poor Law. But the greatest overlap comes from the local public health authorities operating under the various public health acts, and making provision for tuberculosis and isolation hospitals, the supply of medicines and anti-toxins, health visiting, municipal home nursing, diagnosis, and home aliment for persons prevented from working by reason of contact with an infectious disease. The Poor Law and Public Health medical services should be unified.

The Mentally Defective.—Mental defectives were scarcely mentioned in the 1834 Report, but separate statutory provision has since been made. County and county borough councils are the local lunacy authorities responsible for institutional provision. Where, as in most cases, a patient or his relatives do not pay direct to the council, the cost is claimed from the guardians, who endeavour to recover, so that he becomes a pauper even although part or whole of the cost is repaid to the Destitution Authority. The councils thus have no interest in economy, the guardians no connection with management and the three Government departments concerned no clearly defined responsibility for the service as a whole, with the result that the capital cost per patient in a lunatic asylum has risen as high as £500. As a result of this

lack of unified policy, in 1906 there were over 11,000 certified lunatics, idiots and imbeciles in the workhouses and 60,000 mental defectives in the ordinary wards, mixed in with other inmates and receiving no ameliorative treatment. The stigma of pauperism should be removed and, as recommended by the Royal Commission on the *Feebleminded* (1908), mental defectives completely withdrawn from the Poor Law and transferred to the local lunacy authority.

Charge and Recovery.—The public bodies making provision for the poor have definite legal powers for charging costs, but as these powers differ from service to service there is a 'chaotic agglomeration of powers' proceeding from no common principle. The guardians can charge against the person, or against other persons liable, while the public health charge is personal only, relations not being involved. Guardians often recover infirmary costs to a greater extent than the voluntary hospital. Elementary education is free except in the case of residential schools, where the charges are akin to Poor Law charges, while for reformatory and industrial schools the police make a weekly charge of 1s., 2s., 3s. according to means. The duty of making and enforcing assessments should be entirely separated from the work of assistance and should be in charge of a Registrar independent of the existing authorities.

Settlement and Removal.—The legal provision safeguarding the destitution authorities from having to maintain paupers from other areas has been modified by various statutes, but since it appears to give protection to a union it is difficult to see how it can be dispensed with as long as a destitution authority as such exists.

Grants - in - Aid. — Subventions are made for the Poor Law by the Central Authority to the county and borough councils who in turn pass them on to the guardians. There are two major fixed grants paid in lump sums under the Local Government Act, 1888, and the Agricultural Rates Act, 1896, and three separate smaller grants, one of 4s. per head per week for lunatics in asylums, etc., one in respect of teachers in Poor Law schools and one for the repayment of school fees for children sent from workhouses to public elementary schools. The amounts paid in the fixed grants bear no relation to the policy or to the relative efficiency and economy of the guardians, with the result that the poor rates vary in different unions from under 3d. to 2s. in the £. Subvention should take the form of grants and not of assigned revenues, should be conditional on efficiency, the total sum being distributed amongst the authorities according to their need and ability.

Scheme for Reform.—'The state of anarchy and confusion into which has fallen the whole realm of relief and assistance to the poor and to persons in distress' is generally recognized. On the other hand the newer specialized local authorities for education, health, lunacy, unemployment and pensions all attempt to provide for the needs of the poor, *according to the cause or character of their distress*, and every Royal Commission or Departmental Committee recommends some fresh development to their activities. The encouragement of such developments has the effect of denuding the Poor Law of groups for which they are responsible, e.g. the recommendation of the Committee on Vagrancy for penal colonies to be established under police administration. On the other hand to revert to a strictly deterrent, less eligibility principle, as so many witnesses had advocated, would mean that the newer developments would have to be abandoned. The condition of 'the lowest grade of independent labourer' is 'one of such inadequacy of food and clothing and other necessaries, that less eligible conditions would be demoralizing to children, physically injurious to the sick and brutalizing to the aged and infirm'.

The members of the Minority found 'difficulty in discovering or under-

standing' the purpose of the recommendations of the Majority in respect of functions and constitution of the bodies which they suggested, nor could they see how the area and functions of the Poor Law authority could be enlarged without enormously increasing the costly overlapping and rivalry of the local education and health authorities and thrusting back on to Poor Law those persons who had escaped through all the provisions of the newer services. The Majority's proposal that the feeble-minded should be removed from the Poor Law, but that the 'children found hungry at school' should be placed under it, was unfair, while the provision they recommended for the able-bodied was the widest departure from the principle of 'one and only one authority'. Past experience had shown that 'when a Destitution Authority departs from the simple function of providing bare maintenance under deterrent conditions, *it finds it quite impossible to mark off or delimit its services from those which are required by, and provided for, the population at large*'.

The chief recommendations were that the Poor Law Act of 1834 should be repealed; that the Boards of Guardians should be abolished; that their properties, liabilities, powers and duties should be transferred to the county and county borough councils; that the various classes of the non ablebodied should be separated from the able-bodied, and that the provision for (i) the children of school age; (ii) the sick and the permanently incapacitated, the infants under school age, and the aged needing institutional care; (iii) the mentally defective of all grades and ages; and (iv) the aged to whom pensions are awarded, should be assumed, under the direction of the county and county borough councils by education, health, asylums and pensions committees respectively. These committees should be authorized and required to provide institutional or domiciliary treatment conjoined with home aliment where this was indispensable. The law with regard to maintenance by relatives, the amounts to be charged, or exemptions made, should be considered by a Departmental Committee and be embodied in a consistent code. There should be a Registrar of Public Assistance, who should (i) keep a public register of all those in receipt of assistance, (ii) be responsible for assessing and recovering according to the law, (iii) sanction grants proposed by the committees concerned. Grants-in-aid should be made subject to the requirement of a 'National Minimum of Efficiency'.

To the existing Destitution Authority the governing consideration is not the actual mental or physical condition of the applicant, but his lack of material resources, i.e. his pecuniary destitution. For the local education, health or employment authority the test is personal or physiological destitution, the presence or absence of material resources being wholly irrelevant to the rendering of the appropriate treatment. After service has been rendered the question of charging and recovering arises.

The objections of the Majority to the proposals were (1) that the break-up of the Poor Law and transfer of its functions to specialized committees will tend to break up the family; (2) that they would involve a multiplicity of officers visiting homes; (3) that they would lead to a great extension of free treatment and in the numbers assisted, and (4) that the statutory rights of relief might be endangered. To this the Minority replied (1) that families are already disintegrating because they do not get preventive help soon enough, and that it will be to the interest of the specialized committees to maintain the family intact; (2) that the restriction of specialized officers to their own sphere will diminish their numbers and the questions they ask; (3) that the rise in expenditure will be temporary, but the savings permanent and that there will be economies through the Registrar's enforcement of charges, and (4) that the right to relief is accompanied

by the obligation to accept it in the most appropriate form, under penalty of removal in extreme cases.

Part II. The Able-bodied.

The 1834 Report not only practically left out of account all the various classes of non-able-bodied, but it did not concern itself with unemployment or under-employment. There were no statistics of unemployment, no statement as to the fluctuations of trade, no account of destitution caused by the new machines, and no estimate of the swarms of vagrants. The Poor Law Commissioners concentrated on the problem of the demoralized agricultural labourer by cutting off from the farmer all labour that he did not actually pay for, and depriving the labourer of all income that he did not actually earn. And for some 'undisclosed reason' they recommended that vagrants, who hitherto had been dealt with by the magistrates and the constables under the criminal law, should now be offered the discipline of the workhouse. There was to be one local authority, with one deterrent disciplinary method for all who applied for relief, irrespective of the causes of need.

In the towns the Outdoor Relief Prohibitory Order could not be applied uniformly to people suffering from fluctuating employment, and contrary to the principle of national uniformity stressed by the Royal Commission, during the century there came into being five different methods of treatment simultaneously applied. Two, maintenance in the workhouse and unconditional outdoor relief, still persist in spite of their condemnation in 1834; and three specialized methods, the outdoor relief test, the able-bodied workhouse test and the casual ward, failed to provide appropriate treatment. They were ineffective because no attempt had been made to define the various classes of the able-bodied or to deal with them according to the cause of their destitution. Professional vagrants were able to make use of the workhouse as a lodging house and the labour yard for occasional work, and so increased in numbers that casual wards were established throughout the country in an attempt to keep them out of the main workhouse. To the apathetic loafer the workhouse itself was more agreeable than work at the long hours and low wages of the unskilled labourer. The healthy able-bodied of all types receiving temporary outdoor relief without any task work in England and Wales numbered between 30,000 and 40,000, and the number in the general mixed workhouse (including Ireland) was probably more than 10,000. The Poor Law has not been able to deal effectively with the distress caused by a sudden contraction of employment. The extensive development of the various voluntary agencies has taken place because the public refuse to allow people to starve or the homeless to go without shelter. As a form of relief this work is without reproach, but it proved as useless as the Poor Law for permanently benefiting the persons relieved.

The provision of work by the municipalities started from Mr. Joseph Chamberlain's realization of the bankruptcy of the Poor Law and the utter inadequacy of the voluntary agencies to deal with the difficulties of hundreds of jewellers, silversmiths, electro-plate workers, etc., unemployed in Birmingham. In 1886 he stated that 'it was not desirable that the working class should be familiarized with the Poor Law'; in future unemployed persons normally in regular employment should be provided with work for wages by the town council. But this work was uncoordinated and unregulated and when Mr. Walter Long tackled the problem in 1904 there were no statistical or descriptive summaries of what had been done. In 1903 a group of experienced people administered the Mansion House fund by systematic investigation into the industrial status of each applicant. Distress Committees were set up all over London, and they were followed by similar ones throughout the country set up by the Unemployed Workmen's Act. These provincial committees, however, continued the policy of spasmodic municipal employment, which soon developed the same characteristics which had made other attempts at municipal relief ineffective. In London the Distress Committees distinguished themselves not so much for unemployment relief as for the establishment of rural colonies, the organization of labour exchanges and the removal of workmen to places where their labour was required. This was achieved through developing Mr. Chamberlain's policy of withdrawing the unemployed from the Poor Law.

At all times there is a considerable number of families in need of the necessities of life through the breadwinner being out of work. These persons approximate to one or other of the following types: 1. The permanent class—those who have been in situations of presumed permanency, e.g. cotton spinners; 2. those in discontinuous employment, who normally shift from job to job, e.g. bricklayers; 3. the under-employed—the casual hands, e.g. market porters; 4. the unemployables—those ousted or who wilfully withdraw themselves. In all these classes there are grades of skill and grades of conduct, but this does not affect trade. When there is work to be done even drunken, turbulent or negligent men are given employment if they have the requisite physical vigour. The task of dealing with such a problem is beyond the capacity of the local authority and should be undertaken by a national department.

The chief recommendations were that local authorities should be relieved of all responsibility for the able-bodied and the unemployed. There should be a Ministry of Labour with the duty of organizing the labour market so as to minimize unemployment. Steps to decasualize casual labour, to dovetail seasonal employment, or to suppress under-employment should be accompanied by full and honourable main-tenance, at the public expense, of any surplus labour thereby revealed. Work for some unemployed should be found by raising the school age to 15, by reducing the hours of work for railway, tramway and omnibus workers to not more than 60 a week, and by giving full maintenance to all mothers having the charge of children and in receipt of public assistance, on condition that they do not seek industrial employment. The Government should undertake a programme of capital expenditure for 10 years equal to £4 mn. a year, and it should be used exclusively in the lean years of the trade cycle for such undertakings as afforestation, coast protection and land reclamation. The Minority stated specifically that 'we do not recommend compulsory in-surance against unemployment', but as trade unions would benefit by more stable conditions of employment, the Government should offer a subvention not exceeding one-half of the sum actually paid as out-of-work benefit by the trade unions. For the residium of the unemployed, full maintenance should be given on the condition that physical and mental training was under-taken. The 'maintenance and training' division of the new Ministry should establish detention colonies, where men should be compulsorily detained after being convicted for vagrancy, mendicity, neglect to maintain the family, etc.

—— Report, *Ireland*. pp. v, 88. 1909
1909 *Cd.* 4630, *xxxviii*, 1
sgd. April, 1909

Majority Report. — An historical review of the establishment of the Poor Law system in 1838, despite Irish opposition, describes the distress caused by the Famine and the difficulties facing attempts in such circumstances to deal with the situation by indoor relief only. Though accommodation in workhouses was increased by tempor-ary additions, etc., to provide for 250,000 persons instead of 100,000,

they were full and overcrowded. The Poor Relief Extension Act, 1847, authorized the Guardians to grant either indoor or outdoor relief under special circumstances and for limited periods to such classes as the Central Authority might designate by Order, but the Central Authority might use these powers only in the event of the workhouse being full, etc. Outdoor relief to certain classes had to be sanc-tioned. The same reluctance to author-ize outdoor relief was shown in periods of distress, e.g. in 1879–80 and later, though sometimes it had to be sanc-tioned. The policy on government public works varied.

The Majority claimed that its general proposals were in accordance with the principles laid down by the Vice-Regal Commission, though there were differences of substance. The Vice-Regal Commission did not propose the amalgamation of unions or the abolition of the Boards of Guardians. The Majority proposed that the Public Assistance Authority should be a Statutory Committee of the county or county borough, half the members of which should be councillors and half other persons experienced in the work, and appointed by the council. The Public Assistance Authority should use local Public Assistance Committees as executive agencies. The Majority agreed with the Vice-Regal Commis-sion's recommendation that the general workhouse should be abolished, and the inmates classified, not *in* institu-tions, but *by* institutions. The required number of workhouses should be converted into specialized institutions and the rest closed. The Vice-Regal Commission had proposed a State Medical Service of full-time salaried doctors paid out of Parliamentary funds, and that the hospitals should be taken completely out of the Poor Law. The Majority rejected this proposal, and instead suggested the transfer of all infirmaries and hospitals to the County Public Assistance Authority, which would co-ordinate the medical institutions of their area, and organize an outdoor service, including the Medical Dispensary Service and the appointment of nurses for nursing in the homes of the necessitous. The Majority agreed with the proposals of the Vice-Regal Commission on the aged and infirm, and on the able-bodied inmates and vagrants, and the transfer of lunatics to the Asylums Authority. They agreed with the Vice-Regal Commission that the boarding-out of children should be extended, but stated that its efficiency depended on an adequate supply of suitable homes and foster parents and on adequate supervision, including medical supervision.

The position of England and Ireland in regard to unemployment was quite different. In England the mass of the population was occupied in industrial works, lived on daily wages, and unemployment was the main cause of distress. In Ireland the great majority of the population neither received a daily wage nor were wage earners, but were engaged on agricultural holdings and in service to cultivators. The Distress Committees under the Unemployed Workmen's Act, 1905, had not been successful in Ireland, and should be discontinued. Instead use should be made of Section 13 of the Local Government Act, 1898, which enabled local authorities to provide relief of exceptional distress, provided that they had an interest in economical administration by bearing a share of the cost. For similar general reasons, the proposals for Labour Exchanges and Unemployment Insurance made for England and Wales did not seem adapted to an exclusively agricultural country and any application to Ireland should be postponed until their results in Great Britain had been ascertained. It had not enquired into or had evidence on how the natural resources and industries of Ireland should be developed. Outdoor relief should be continued under proper safeguards. The Probate Duty and medical and educational grants should be re-apportioned on a more equitable basis. 'Four of our colleagues (the Minority) publish a separate report. They have already submitted proposals for Ireland in their dissent from our Report on England and Wales. The dissent attached to the Irish Report is therefore merely criticism of our recommendations, and all those who read and consider them will see that this criticism is neither fair nor accurate.'

Downes did not sign the Report on the ground that he was insufficiently acquainted with Irish affairs.

Minority Report.—Wakefield, Chandler, Lansbury, and Beatrice Webb argue that the Majority make recommendations different in character from those of the Vice-Regal Commission. These include the substitution of the Boards of Guardians by a new Public Assistance Authority which, though controlling the provision for and expenditure on the poor, would not contain a majority of elected representatives; the transfer to the Poor Law of the public health service, making the provision of school meals a Poor Law function, and the repeal of the Unemployed Workmen's Act without the establishment, until some indefinite future time, of any provision for unemployed workmen other than under the Poor Law. In the larger towns of Ireland the problem of unemployment presents much the same features as in Great Britain. The Minority support the proposals of the Vice-Regal Commission for a state medical service. They do not feel sufficiently conversant with Irish needs and Irish conditions to present any detailed criticism of the various reforms worked out by that Commission, but are convinced that Ireland is ready for the break-up of the Poor Law and that any attempt to set up a new authority would be a repetition of the mistake of 1838.

In a Memo. the Bishop of Ross and Sir H. Robinson say that they had life-long experience of Irish affairs and protest against the criticisms of the Minority, two of whom did not visit Ireland at all, the only member accompanying the Commission having stayed in Ireland for a shorter time than Sir G. Nicholls, whose haste they condemn.

—— Report, *Scotland.* pp. ix, 314. 1909

1909 Cd. 4922, *xxxviii,* 95
sgd. Oct., 1909

An appendix to the Report, by Prof. Smart, on the *History of the Scots Poor Laws prior to 1845* brings out the important differences in the historical background of the Scots and English Poor Laws. Amongst these were (1) the position of the church, which after the Reformation, had been given the care of the poor. Up to the beginning of the nineteenth century the main reliance was on church collections, compulsory assessments being regarded as auxiliary. (2) Relief to the able-bodied was prohibited, there were practically no poorhouses, and the system was essentially one of outdoor relief. The relief given was supplementary to relief from other sources. There was no central control, each parish being practically irresponsible in the reading of its duties. Whereas in England in 1834 the problem was one of profusion, and the reduction of able-bodied pauperism by the workhouse test, in Scotland the able-bodied were not relieved, and the problem was one of seeing that all persons legally entitled to relief should get it, and that it was adequate.

Majority Report.—Statistical Survey. —For the year ending 1907, 147,660 persons were relieved (34,829 men, 56,299 women and 56,532 children). The proportion of the population relieved, 20·0 per 1,000 was in 1906 3·3 per 1,000 below the English rate. A larger proportion of children was relieved in Scotland, since relief to widows with dependent children was more freely given, but partly for historical reasons and partly because of agricultural employment and the crofting system adult pauperism was relatively lower. Owing to the lower rate of pauperism, and the larger proportion of outdoor relief, expenditure per head

was lower than in England. The recent rise of expenditure had occurred for the same reason as in England—the development of indoor relief, of the more expensive forms of such relief, and an improvement in the standard of comfort in the institutions. It had increased more rapidly in large towns than elsewhere.

The Central and Local Authorities.— The powers of the L.G.B. for Scotland were unduly limited to supervision and restraint, and should be strengthened to enable it to exercise initiative and guidance in matters of principle. The status of the Board and its officers should be raised, it should be empowered to issue Orders and Regulations governing Public Assistance. In Scotland the parishes were still the units of Poor Law administration, though in burghs they were often combined to be co-terminous with the burghs. In burghs with a population of 7,000 and upwards, for purposes of Public Assistance, the area of the burgh should be the administrative area. In counties the parish should continue to be the area for outdoor relief, but for institutional relief, the administrative area should be the county, existing Poorhouse combinations being dissolved to facilitate this. The Local Government (Scotland) Act, 1894, transferred Poor Law duties from parochial boards to the parish councils. In the larger burghs the system of direct election had failed to attract capable social workers and leading citizens. The Public Assistance Authority should be a statutory committee of the county council or of the town council in the case of burghs with a population of 7,000 and upwards, composed one-half of councillors and one-half of persons of experience in Public Assistance; in counties Parish Councils should be retained for administering outdoor relief.

Qualifications for Relief.—The inability to relieve the able-bodied was productive of great anomalies and hardship, and the law had worked only because common sense had led to its not being stretched to breaking point; it was often openly disregarded. In law an able-bodied man could not have his sick wife or children treated under the Poor Law, unless they were lunatic or imbecile. A woman living with her husband could not obtain midwifery relief, but if living in adultery could.

Poorhouses and Indoor Relief.—The Royal Commission on the Poor Laws (Scotland), 1844 [557] was strongly opposed to the compulsory creation of 'workhouses' in the English sense, the poorhouses they thought desirable being of an entirely different character. The Poor Law Act of 1845 made this provision permissive, but partly under the pressure of the Central Authority, especially after 1870, the poorhouse was used as a test of physical disability and a means of checking improper applications for relief, so that by 1906 the workhouse population was similar to that in England. There was no proper classification of inmates, and the workhouse had most signally failed with the 'test' class. The general poorhouses should be abolished, and institutional assistance given in separate appropriate institutions. Treatment should be curative and reformative and powers taken to detain 'Ins-and-Outs'.

Outdoor and other forms of relief.— The recommendations are in general on similar lines to those for England. Home Assistance should be given after thorough inquiry, and should, with other sources of income, be adequate and conditional. The case paper system should be universally adopted, and the L.G.B. for Scotland should be empowered to prescribe the conditions of Home Assistance. The system of boarding-out children had long been in operation, and should be extended as far as possible, but it should be carefully regulated. Children should be boarded with strangers rather than relatives, should not be boarded with paupers, the suitability of the foster-parents should be carefully investigated, and the homes should be in the country rather than the town. In the relief of unmarried mothers a distinction should be made between a woman of good character with her first child, weak minded women and women of loose character. The first should have institutional treatment away from the poorhouse, the second should be dealt with in accordance with the recommendations of the Commission on the Feebleminded, and the third be liable to compulsory detention.

Medical Relief. — Comprehensive recommendations were made for a block grant, accommodating the sick poor in detached buildings properly equipped and staffed, for the extension of nursing in the Highland and Islands, the better supply of hospital accommodation based on the needs of each area, co-operation between statutory and voluntary bodies for framing schemes and delimiting functions, and the promotion of medical aid based on insurance.

The Able-bodied Unemployed. — The preventive measures prescribed for England applied also to Scotland— viz. decasualization of labour, Labour Exchanges, and a system of insurance against unemployment. For relief of distress, there should be one authority in each area—in large burghs the Public Assistance Authority, elsewhere the parish councils. First applications for assistance for temporary causes should be made to the Voluntary Aid Committee, chronic distress being dealt with by the statutory bodies. The necessitous unemployed should be classified according to their need for temporary assistance with work, for long period maintenance and training, and for detention and discipline.

Recommendations are also made for giving the Public Assistance Authorities and parish councils powers to secure the continuous treatment of aged and bedridden persons and the feeble-minded, and powers of detention for vagrants, 'Ins-and-Outs', and of persons persistently refusing to maintain themselves and their families, etc.

Minority Report. — The Minority 'agree with the Majority in holding that the whole system of dealing with the unemployed and the necessitous calls for reform in Scotland at least as urgently as in England', but state that the measures the Majority propose would leave the evils unremedied. The Minority disagree with the Majority's proposal to set up a new Destitution Authority, which should administer relief only at the period of destitution, and have under its charge all classes of paupers from the sick and the aged to the unemployed workman and the vagrant. This would lead to the perpetuation of the general mixed workhouse, of outdoor relief doles, and an abandonment of any hope of preventing unemployment or destitution (p. 281). The Minority's proposals therefore follow the lines of those they made for England. The Scottish Poor Law should be abolished. The legal prohibition on relief to the able-bodied did not prevent that relief, but led to its being given in a demoralizing way, accounted for the absence of any public organization dealing with them, and caused a 'plague of vagrancy'. Labour Exchanges had not been set up, and the Distress Committees, with limited funds and jurisdiction, had not been really successful. As in England, unemployment should be dealt with by a national authority, on the lines proposed in that Report and here repeated. In some respects Scotland was in advance of England in its provision for necessitous children, especially in boarding-out arrangements. But one-third of the boarded-out children in towns were underfed and not properly clothed. The whole of the public provision for children should be handed to the local Education Authority. The medical service in many parishes was deplorably insufficient and could not be remedied by transferring the Poor Law Medical Service to the new authority. They agreed with Dr. McVail that it should be merged with the Public Health Service to form a united Medical Service and taken out of the Poor Law altogether. All grades of mentally

defective persons should be taken out of the Poor Law and dealt with in separate institutions by the Lunacy Authority. In place of the Poor Law, which should be abolished, there should be an adequate enlargement of the existing specialized bodies who were in fact dealing with the causes of destitution.

In a special Chairman's Memo., the Chairman (G. Hamilton) commented on the procedure of Royal Commissions which gave a dissenting minority 'the last word'. As the Commission has made three separate reports, on England, Ireland and Scotland, the Minority have had 'three last words'. 'The latter part of what purports to be their report on Scotland is not a report upon that country or dealing with the peculiarities of the system in force in that country, but is an enlarged and varied edition of the original proposals intermingled with a new set of comments and criticisms upon the proposals of the Majority.' He did not as Chairman feel justified in refusing to accept the document, in spite of protests from his colleagues against it, but the use made of the customary procedure by the Minority was manifestly unfair. He was unwilling to reassemble the Commission in order to give the Majority an opportunity to reply to a series of statements they had not seen or considered when they dispersed. He therefore gave a brief account of the points at issue by stating the matters on which the Majority and Minority were agreed, those on which they differed, and the causes of the difference. Amongst the differences stressed were the objection of the Majority to the Registrar proposed by the Minority, on the ground that he would be in a position to override the elected body, and that the division of responsibility between him and his authority would be an impossible one. Another comment was that under the scheme of the Minority, the family would in a large number of cases be disintegrated as each item of it is sent off to a separate Committee, and that a large part of the 'population will be under official surveillance from the cradle to the grave'.

The reports, memoranda and evidence, reports of special inquiries and appendices, etc., of the Commission comprise 53 separately numbered papers, covering a wide variety of subjects. Amongst this mass of documents there are both papers and evidence of historical importance. Examples are: evidence by Beveridge and Bowley on unemployment, labour exchanges, and public works; by Sexton and Eleanor Rathbone on casual dock labour (Cd. 5066); by Tawney and Urwick on Boy Labour (Cd. 5068); a report by McVail on Poor Law Medical Relief (Cd. 4573); and evidence by Newsholme on Medical Services (Cd. 5068); reports by Thomas Jones and Miss Williams on Outdoor Relief and Wages (Cd. 4960) and by Steel-Maitland and Miss Squire on the relation of Industrial and Sanitary Conditions and Pauperism (Cd. 4563); evidence by Miss Mason and Miss Stansfeld on Boarded-out Children and Maternity Wards (Cd. 4625); by Chance on the Elberfeld system (Cd. 4755); and by H. V. Toynbee on Case Work (Cd. 4593). Three important papers by Loch, Mrs. Webb and Prof. Smart on the History of the Poor Law are to be found in Cd. 4983, which is entitled *Memoranda by Individual Commissioners*. The search for the material is made unnecessarily difficult because the Majority and Minority Reports used 20 different types of footnote reference to the evidence and other papers, some of them being inadequate and uncertain guides. Use should be made not only of the *General Consolidated Index* (Cd. 5443), but also of the *Alphabetical Lists of Oral and Non-Oral Witnesses* (Cd. 5442). In App. I, p. 448, is given a full list of the papers and their reference numbers, the question numbers included in volumes of evidence, etc., arranged as far as possible to show the structure of the inquiry.

The Administration of Outdoor Relief

Dept. Cttee. Rep., apps. pp. 62. 1911

1911 *Cd. 5525, xxxix, 1*
apptd. March, sgd. Dec., 1910

S. B. Provis (*Ch.*), Davy, Jerred, Smith.

'*To enquire and report whether any, and if so what, amendments should be made in the Orders issued by the Poor Law Commissioners, the Poor Law Board, and the Local Government Board, relating to the Administration of Out-door Relief in England and Wales.*'

The Royal Commission on the Poor Laws had recommended that there should be one consolidated Outdoor Relief Order. Three differing sets of Regulations were in operation in 1910. (1) Relief under a Prohibitory Order, that is, an Order contemplating the normal application, in the case of an able-bodied person, of the 'workhouse test'. (2) Relief under a Regulation Order, that is, an Order not excluding the use of the 'workhouse test' for able-bodied men. In some cases the operation of this Order has been temporarily affected in periods of stress by the issue of a 'Modified Workhouse Test Order'; and (3) Relief under combined Prohibitory and Labour Test Orders, allowing the use of a 'labour test' in the case of able-bodied male applicants for relief, but preserving the requirement of a 'workhouse test' in the case of able-bodied women, other than widows with children or widows in the first six months of widowhood. Of 644 Unions, 274 are under the Prohibitory Order alone, 254 under the Prohibitory and Labour Test Orders combined, 116 under the Regulation Order.

The Draft Order proposed took the form of a Prohibition Order, but defined the persons to whom outdoor relief might be given without test; these included widows with families and the aged and infirm. An important innovation was the introduction of the case paper system. There is an appendix giving the text of Outdoor Relief Orders issued from 1841.

Poor Law Orders

Dept. Cttee. 1st Rep., apps. pp. 89. 1913

1913 Cd. 6968, xxxviii, 241
apptd. Jan., 1911. sgd. July, 1913

S. B. Provis (Ch.), Davy, Jerred, Smith.

'To examine the Orders issued by the Poor Law Commissioners, the Poor Law Board, and the Local Government Board under the Acts relating to the Relief of the Poor and for the time being in force, with a view to their consolidation with amendments into one or more new Orders, and from time to time to report the result of such examination, together with recommendations as to the provisions to be included in the new Orders.'

The General Consolidated Order, 1847, covered a large part of the Guardians' administration, but contained a large number of regulations, to which numerous amending orders had been added. In view of the magnitude of the task it seemed better to deal with the articles in groups and to issue separate orders for the groups in a form in which they could ultimately be combined into a general consolidated order. The report presents two such draft orders, one governing the administration of workhouses and the other a Nursing Order.

Machinery and Engineering Staffs at Poor Law Institutions

Dept. Cttee. Rep., apps. pp. iv, 38. Mins. of ev., apps., index. pp. 139. 1909

1909 Cd. 4502, xxxvi, 607. Mins. of ev., etc.; 1909 Cd. 4503, xxxvi, 649
apptd. Oct., 1907. sgd. Jan., 1909

A. Lowry (Ch.), Kitchin, Hooper.

'To inquire and report—(1) As to the machinery for lighting, heating, laundry, and other purposes, installed at some representative Poor Law Institutions in London and elsewhere, as to any matters incidental to the running of the machinery, including the classes, numbers, and remuneration of the officers employed, and as to the way in which Poor Law Institutions compare in these respects with other places where such machinery is in use; (2) As to the most economical kinds of machinery which may be installed for these purposes at Poor Law Institutions, regard being had to cost of running and efficiency of service as well as to cost of purchase, and to any special considerations attaching to particular classes of institutions; and (3) As to the classes, numbers and remuneration of the officers required, and as to any other matters incidental to efficient and economical administration where such machinery is in use.'

Poor Law institutions differ considerably in date and type, ranging in size from those for 20 to those for 2,000 inmates. They had installed a great variety of equipment for heating, cooking, laundering, lighting, etc., which could have been simplified had there been more systematic central supervision and control. Coal was the largest single item of consumption, costing in the case of the Bethnal Green institution more than a rate of $1\frac{1}{2}d.$ in the £. The daily consumption of water per head at infirmaries varied from under 20 to over 80 gallons. There were similar differences in the consumption of gas and electricity. There were large differences in the pay, hours, size and organization of the engineering staffs, which were sometimes excessive in number and cost.

There should be more systematic central supervision of engineering work in all Poor Law institutions, based on adequate records and returns and the appointment of an engineering inspector. More systematic check should be exercised over the quality and quantity of coal consumed. The engineer in charge of a large institution should be given more control over his department, appointments to his own staff, etc. Suggestions are made as to the number of staff and their wages.

2. UNEMPLOYMENT INSURANCE

Unemployment Insurance. Proceedings of the Board of Trade under Part II of the National Insurance Act, 1911
1st Rep., apps. pp. viii, 82. 1913

1913 *Cd. 6965, xxxvi, 677 apptd. —, sgd. July, 1913*

W. H. Beveridge.

'*The proceedings under Part II of the National Insurance Act, 1911, covering a period of about nineteen months, from the passage of the Act, on December 16th, 1911, to the end of the first "insurance year" on July 12th, 1913.*'

The Report by W. H. Beveridge sets out in detail the creation of the administrative machinery, the issue of regulations and insurance cards and the experience of claims. Provision was made for compulsory insurance against unemployment in the 'insured trades', building, construction of works, shipbuilding, construction of vehicles, ironfounding and certain branches of saw-milling. Employers and workmen each paid 2½d. per week or part of a week, and the State contributed one-third of the total receipts from employers and workmen. The benefit was 7s. per week after the first week of unemployment, for a maximum of 15 weeks in any 12 months. There were various conditions governing the receipt of benefit, and grounds for disqualification. For the encouragement of voluntary insurance through associations, a Parliamentary grant, under certain conditions, of not more than one-sixth of the associations' expenditure on unemployment benefit up to 12s. per week, was to be made. The amount of voluntary insurance had increased since the Act.

From the administrative point of view, the prosperity of 1913 had probably been the most important factor enabling the scheme to be launched at all. The number of employment insurance books issued corresponds to about 2¼ million workpeople holding books at any given time, of which less than one-fifth were previously insured against unemployment. About 400,000 individuals made 560,000 claims, one-quarter being made through associations of workmen. The total expenditure on benefit claims between 8th January and 11th July, 1913, was £235,458. This represented 774,494 payments, which was surprisingly large at a time of high employment, and was due to the extent of transitional unemployment. Much could be done by the Labour Exchanges towards reducing unemployment by shortening the intervals between jobs. Further, there was an uneven distribution of unemployment, which was greater in the south of England than in the rest of Great Britain, where there was an unsatisfied demand for labour. The year's experience had shown that compulsory insurance in scheduled trades was practicable, and that it could be introduced without destroying voluntary insurance. The invested balance was £1,610,000 and the insured trades could look forward to entering the next period of depression with a reserve fund of some millions (p. 46).

3. HEALTH INSURANCE

Application of the National Insurance Act to Outworkers

Cttee. Vol. I. Rep. pp. 21. 1912.
Vol. II. Mins of ev., apps., index. 1912

1912–13 *Cd. 6178, xlii, 369. Mins. of ev., etc.; 1912–13 Cd. 6179, xlii, 391 apptd. Jan., sgd. May, 1912*

E. F. G. Hatch (*Ch.*), Barnes, Bentinck, Paterson (Miss), Toulmin.

'*To consider and advise what special orders, if any, should be made by the Insurance Commissioners under the powers and provisions of the First Schedule, Part I (c), of the National Insurance Act with regard to its application to outworkers, and what regulations, if any, should be made under Schedule III (10) in connection with the contributions of such outworkers as are insured under the Act.'*

The Insurance Act defined an outworker as a person to whom articles or materials are given out to be made up, cleaned, washed, altered, ornamented, finished, or repaired, or adapted for sale in his own home or on other premises not under the control or management of the person who gave out the articles or materials. But there is a large number of persons spoken of colloquially as outworkers who do not come under this definition. The total number known to be employed in the scheduled industries in Great Britain in 1910 was 92,000, the largest numbers employed being 72,000 in the wearing-apparel and 4,000 in the lace and lace curtain trades.

Only three of the thirty - three employers' representatives who gave evidence were definitely opposed to the inclusion of any outworkers, and their opposition would be modified if contributions were proportionate to work done. Twelve were against the inclusion of married women who were the wives of insured persons: some trades employed a large number of them. If employers did not have to pay contributions for married women, such women would be given unfair advantage over others dependent on earnings. Married women should be included. To avoid the consequent danger of a concentration of work in fewer hands, the contributions of outworkers who were only partially employed should be in proportion to work done. If an outworker were fully employed by one person, the contributions should be the same as those for an inworker. Contributions should be at full rate for all outworkers whose average earnings for a full week exceeded 30s. for men and 17s. 6d. for women, and at a lower rate for lower earnings.

Married Women Outworkers

Rep., apps. pp. 24. 1913

1912–13 *Cd.* 6600, *lxxviii*, 655
apptd. — 1912. *sgd. Jan.*, 1913

S. Pope.

'The Objections raised against the Draft Special Order including Married Women Outworkers within the Provision of Part I of the National Insurance Act.'

The Hatch Committee had recommended that an Order should be made. The Order to include married women outworkers had come into force in July, 1912. The main cause of the opposition to it was the belief of the employers in certain trades that they had to pay disproportionate contributions on the small earnings of married women, who formed a large proportion of female outworkers. They maintained that they could not afford these contributions and would have to concentrate work in fewer hands, although their knowledge of the working of Scheme B, under which contributions varied with work, was small. There was a tendency to make the Act an excuse for concentrating the outwork.

The outworkers, as a class, would desire insurance if they could feel sure of their employment and of qualifying for benefit. The arguments in favour of the Special Order were conclusive, and it would be undesirable to exempt any trades. The solution was a relaxation of Scheme B, the proposed amendments to which would both keep the low wage-earners in work, and also bring them within reach of the benefits of the Act. The employer would pay exactly the same contribution on an amount of work, whether it were done by one or by several workers.

Outdoor Staff

Inter-Dept. Cttee. Rep. pp. 9. 1912

1912–13 *Cd.* 6231, *xlii*, 359
apptd. April, 1911. *sgd. May*, 1912

F. Mowatt (*Ch.*), Haldane (Miss), Morant, Tedder, Bradbury, Leathes, Glynn, Hughes, Leishman.

'To consider and report upon the Outdoor Staff (other than Auditors) which it will shortly become necessary to appoint

for the purposes of Part I of the National Insurance Act, 1911, with reference more particularly: (1) to the character and scope of the duties to be performed (due regard being had to the arrangements already under consideration for making use of the services of Pension officers); the qualifications to be required in candidates for appointments, and the classification, grading and rates of remuneration of the officers required. (2) To the methods by which such Staff should be recruited; to what extent officers possessing the necessary qualifications can be obtained by transfer from the existing public service or by open competitive examination; and to what extent it may be necessary to have recourse to selection from outside the public service (or to limited competition between selected candidates); and the principles upon which such selection should be exercised.'

As the Act was to become operative from July 15th, the outdoor staff should be appointed immediately. There should be four Chief Inspectors, one for each part of the United Kingdom, drawn from public departments with experience of controlling outdoor staff. The numbers and salaries of the various grades are recommended. Inspectors and insurance officers, where not obtained by transfer from other departments, should be interviewed, and those suitable tested by examination. Women should be eligible, and their salaries fixed in the light of the Report of the Royal Commission on the Civil Service.

Appointment of Audit Staff

Inter-Dept. Cttee. 1st Rep., app. pp. 7. 1912

1912–13 Cd. 6232, xlii, 321
apptd. —, sgd. May, 1912

H. J. Gibson (*Ch.*), Bunbury, Mair, Malcolm.

'*To consider and report upon the method of recruitment to be adopted and the terms of service laid down for the audit staff under section 35 of the National Insurance Act, 1911. Whether it is desirable that such*

staff should consist wholly of salaried officers giving their whole time to the public service or partly of such officers and partly of part-time officers remunerated by fees and in the latter alternative to what extent, if at all, it may be desirable to employ persons already holding appointments as Public Auditors under the Friendly Societies Acts, and to make recommendations as to organization and remuneration of the audit staff and as to the character and scope of the audit generally.'

In view of the impossibility of close control of the administration of benefits by approved societies, audit of their accounts should be quarterly. As the work will be uniform, specialized and large in volume, the auditors should not be drawn from a panel of public auditors, but should be full time established civil servants. Grades and salaries are proposed.

—— Second Report. pp. 3. 1912

1912–13 Cd. 6243, xlii, 329
sgd. May, 1912 .

A whole time staff is recommended also for Scotland, Ireland and Wales.

Employment under the Crown

Inter-Dept. Cttee. 1st Rep., apps. pp. 20. 1912

1912–13 Cd. 6234, xlii, 333
apptd. March, sgd. May, 1912

M. Nathan (*Ch.*), Wilson (Miss M.), Bradbury, Baddeley, Dannreuther, Raven.

'*To report, with reference to the various classes of employment in the public service —(1) To what extent the conditions of employment as regards sick pay and pensions in the event of permanent disablement are such as to enable advantage to be taken of the provisions of paragraph (b) of Part II of the First Schedule and of section 47, as applied by subsection (2) of section 53 of the National Insurance Act, 1911; and (2) What modifications (if any) it may be desirable to introduce by legislation or otherwise into such conditions of employment, with a view to enabling more extended advantage to be taken of such provisions as regards—(a) members of the permanent Civil Service, (b) other employees of public departments; and (3) How far the Exchequer can be recouped the cost of any additional advantages to be given for such purpose—in so far as such cost may exceed in value the consequent saving in respect of the employer's contribution—by adjustments of salaries or wages or otherwise.'*

With the exception of certain classes, the terms of employment of male established officers were such as to secure them benefits not less favourable than those conferred by the Act. Those terms which did not do this should be altered so as to bring sickness benefits into line with those of the majority of established servants. Individual cases of hardship should be rectified by amending the Superannuation Acts. The extent to which sick leave privileges for unestablished servants were more or less valuable than the insurance benefits depended upon the rates of pay. But in no case was disablement pension given and it was therefore necessary to insure all unestablished persons earning under £160 per annum and all unestablished manual workers.

—— Second Report. pp. 4. 1912

1912–13 Cd. 6315, xlii, 353
sgd. June, 1912

A difficulty arose from the compulsory retirement of women on marriage and the consequent liability to have no pension granted, but the majority served under conditions which excepted them from the Act. Some established women, however, did not receive the full benefits available, and their sick-leave privileges should be increased in order that they too might be excepted. These, and the other recommendations, would result in the exception of all established Civil Servants, other than established Admiralty workmen.

—— Third Report. apps. pp. 11, 1913

1914 Cd. 7176, lxxii, 609
re-apptd. June, 1913. *sgd. Oct.,* 1913

Although it would be to the advantage of the unestablished employees to bring them under the provisions, the cost to the Exchequer would be considerable. Only those persons employed mainly on professional, clerical or supervisory duties, or receiving board and lodging in part remuneration, should come under section 47, all other classes compulsorily insurable being left to the ordinary operation of the Act.

The officers of the Public Trustees Department are in the unique position of being in the personal employment of the Head of the Department and paid out of a lump sum allowance he receives from the Treasury. Pending the establishment of a contributory scheme for the Department, classes other than messengers should be given extra sick leave advantages.

Existing Conditions in Respect of Medical Attendance and Remuneration in Certain Towns

Rep. pp. 6. 1912

1912–13 Cd. 6305, lxxviii, 679
sgd. July, 1912

W. Plender.

The number of medical practitioners in the six selected areas was 265. Of this number 51, of whom 40 reside in Cardiff, refused access to their records. The large proportion of refusals in Cardiff out of a total of 96 practitioners in that City made it impossible to regard information obtained as in any way indicative of the medical experience in that City. The results shown were therefore confined to Darlington, Darwen, Dundee, Norwich and St. Albans. The tables show gross remuneration from residents inside and outside the towns, and the deduction made to arrive at net income.

Supply of Medicines to Insured Persons

Dept. Cttee. Vol. I. Rep. pp. 18. 1913.
Vol. II. Mins of ev., apps. index. 1913

1913 *Cd.* 6853, *xxxvi*, 777. *Mins. of ev., etc.*; 1913 *Cd.* 6854, *xxxvi*, 795 *apptd. Feb., sgd. June,* 1913

J. S. Whitaker (*Ch.*), Davies, Ledlie, Schuster, Shaw.

'*To enquire and report whether, having regard to the interests of insured persons in obtaining an efficient and rapid supply of drugs, medicines, and appliances, and to the conditions under which those articles were supplied before the passing of the National Insurance Act,* 1911, *any alteration is necessary in the conditions laid down by Section* 15 (5) (iii) *of the National Insurance Act, in respect of the matter.*'

The National Insurance Act, 1911, prohibited medical practitioners from supplying drugs and medicines to insured persons, except in special cases; and in the dispensing of medicines, it laid down two conditions, (1) that dispensing should be done only by persons or firms legally entitled to carry on the business of chemist or druggist; and (2) that medicines should be dispensed either by or under the direct supervision of a registered pharmacist or by a person who, for three years immediately prior to the passage of the Act had acted as a dispenser to a duly qualified medical practitioner or a public institution.

Four groups of persons adversely affected by the Act, drug store proprietors, doctors' dispensers, apothecary's assistants, and army dispensers, represented that they had been discriminated against unreasonably and that without their service insured persons were inadequately served; that in certain areas (e.g. Bradford, Leeds, Manchester and Nottingham) insured persons had experienced serious inconvenience because the firms permitted to contract for the dispensing of medicines were unable to cope with the demand. Persons who could not be registered under the Pharmacy Acts had hitherto dispensed medicines not containing scheduled poisons to the satisfaction of their customers and without detriment to the public, and persons of this class were more familiar with the requirements of the insured population than were the registered chemists.

No change should be made in the provisions of the Act which required that the dispensing of medicine should be done only by persons or firms entitled under the Acts of 1868 and 1908 to carry on the business of chemist or druggist. If the Act is amended to allow drug store proprietors to dispense for insured persons medicines not containing poisons, the legislation should not confer a statutory right upon persons not at present possessing that right, but should only authorize an Insurance Committee to make arrangements, if it sees fit, with persons who have been, *bona fide*, engaged in business as drug store proprietors. The Insurance Act should be amended to permit persons to dispense medicines for insured persons, without the necessity of being supervised by a registered pharmacist, if they have (*a*) a thorough practical knowledge of dispensing, (*b*) a sufficient degree of general intelligence and education, and (*c*) some knowledge of chemistry, and of the nature and physical properties of drugs. The dispensing of drugs by persons not specifically qualified should in practice be under the direct supervision of a registered pharmacist. Definite proposals should be submitted to the Pharmaceutical Society by the War Office and the Society of Apothecaries to carry into effect, as regards qualified military dispensers and certified assistants to apothecaries, the powers conferred by the Poisons and Pharmacy Act of 1908.

Reasons why certain Insured Persons become Deposit Contributors

Rep. pp. 9. 1913

1913 *Cd.* 7034, *xxxvi*, 767 *sgd. June,* 1913

E. A. Gowers.

The chief reasons were ignorance or indifference as to the relative advantages of the alternatives and a belief that an Approved Society required subscriptions for benefits outside the Act. There was a group who felt it beneath their dignity to join a society.

Proposals for Facilitating the Payment through the Post of Benefits under the National Insurance Act

Inter-Dept. Cttee. Rep., app. pp. 11. 1914

1914 *Cd. 7245, lxxii, 627 apptd. June, sgd. Dec., 1913*

T. H. Elliott (*Ch.*), Harris, Harvey, King, Bunbury, Gates.

'*To consider proposals for providing a special form of Postal Order or Draft for the use of Approved Societies under the National Insurance Act for the payment of benefits.*'

The approved societies suggested to the Postmaster General the issue of special postal orders having attached to them a receipt form, which, after signature by the payee, could be returned to the approved society. Recommended that a special order form should be introduced and that the societies should contribute towards the expense involved.

Sickness Benefit Claims under the National Insurance Act

Dept. Cttee. Rep. pp. vii, 87. 1914. Mins. of ev., apps. Vols. I–IV. 1914. Index. 1914

1914–16 *Cd. 7687, xxx, 1. Mins. of ev., etc.;* 1914–16 *Cd. 7688, Cd. 7689, xxx, 97.* 1914–16 *Cd. 7690, Cd. 7691, xxxi, 1 apptd. Aug., 1913. sgd. July, 1914*

C. Schuster (*Ch.*), Carter, Davies, Fulton, Ivens (Miss M. H. F.), Macarthur (Miss M. R.), Mosses, Shaw, Thompson, Warren, Watson, Whitaker, Wilson (Miss M.), Wright.

'*To enquire into and report upon the alleged excessive claims upon and allowances by approved societies in England in respect of sickness benefit, and any special circumstances which may cause any such claims or allowances.*'

The machinery is working as smoothly as could have been expected, and there was little evidence of fraud or malingering. The 2,608 societies approved varied from great centralized societies and affiliated orders with hundreds of thousands of members to small local clubs. Some were highly centralized, in others the efficiency depended on local administration. The membership of some was a representative sample of the insured population, of others a selected group which might have specially bad health risks. Many of the old societies' members had been carefully selected by medical examination, and were familiar with the principles of insurance: but the societies had admitted many new members neither familiar with them, nor with any great interest in friendly society administration. While on the whole the experience of men's societies had justified the actuaries' estimates, there were excessive claims due to mismanagement of various kinds.

Many medical practitioners had worked for the old friendly societies, their relationship with them was close, and their certificates were often accepted by the societies without question. This contract practice was now replaced by a new relationship, and there were many doctors on the panel who had had no previous experience of the work, and some were hostile and lax. Many of them had given medical certicates not justified by the circumstances. This had been due partly to uncertainty as to whether 'incapacity to work' meant inability to follow the usual occupation, included convalescence, etc., and partly to a desire to do the best for the patient irrespective of incapacity, as well as to a desire to win the good will of patients, etc.

Some millions of the insured persons had already been insured through the friendly societies, and despite the provisions of Section 72 of the Act, large numbers had continued to contribute to the private friendly society side as well as the 'approved' side, and for many the combined private and state benefit was near or at full wages. Societies should make arrangements to ensure uniformity of administration and strict supervision from the centre. The results of the segregation of persons with special health risks into particular societies and branches should be redressed by creating a Special Risks Fund, aided by a State grant, out of which payments could be made to societies with a deficiency from this cause. The uncertainty of the meaning of incapacity for work had led both to the admission of improper and refusal of proper claims, and should be removed by a statutory definition to mean incapacity by disease or bodily or mental disablement from following the usual employment.

The scale of benefits often made it an advantage to badly paid women to declare on the funds, a situation which could be remedied only by improvement in their economic conditions. Uniform rules should be made to determine the nature of the household work permissible during the receipt of benefit. There were doubts, which led to great variety of practice, as to whether both women incapacitated by pregnancy and those by pregnancy with other sickness were entitled to benefit. Some societies excluded both, and some women exposed themselves to risk by continuing to work when they should not do so. There should be a new benefit for pregnant women in respect of the last four weeks of pregnancy, financed by a Treasury grant. Inexperience in conducting women's insurance and an under-estimate of the incidence of illness had led to a general excess of claims, which could not be met either by raising contributions or by reducing benefit. A portion of the sums now going to the redemption of reserve values should be diverted to the societies for this purpose.

The defects in medical certification should be remedied by greater precision, rigid dating, a clearer understanding by doctors and societies of their respective duties, and by insured persons of their obligation to furnish all necessary information. A special inquiry should be made in the near future into the limitations in scope of medical benefit, with particular regard to the provision of hospital facilities, for second opinions, for major surgical operations, and to care of the eyes and teeth. As soon as possible whole-time medical referees should be appointed to advise in cases of doubt and to review periodically the certificates granted.

In a memo. Mary Macarthur states that the reforms proposed were inadequate to meet the needs of an effective National Health Service. Administration should be removed from the friendly societies and trade unions and transferred to a national society. Special provision should be made for the needs of women. A Royal Commission should be appointed to investigate the case of pregnant women and a Medical Committee to consider the reform and extension of medical treatment. Mosses recommended a whole-time state medical service to secure the independence of doctors in the administration of sickness benefit. Wright thought that women's benefits should be administered solely by women officials.

Drug Tariff under the National Insurance Acts

Dept. Cttee. Vol. I. Rep., apps. pp. 31. 1915. Vol. II. Mins. of ev., index. 1915

1914–16 Cd. 8062, *xxix*, 657. *Mins. of ev.*, etc.; 1914–16 Cd. 8063, *xxix*, 689 *apptd. Feb., sgd. Sept.*, 1915

R. Bailey (*Ch.*), Adams, Cox, Gilmour, Tocher, Vernon, Vivian, Woolcock.

'To consider and report what margin of profit (apart from discounting) is yielded by the present Drug Tariff, what revision, if any, of prices is required to place that tariff on a commercial basis, and whether any extension or re-arrangement of the list of priced drugs and mixtures is desirable; to make such investigations as they may think necessary for this purpose either generally or in particular areas, and to submit a tariff in accordance with their recommendations.'

Each Insurance Committee sets aside for medicines 2s. per head of the insured population per annum, but no economy on its part can effect any saving, nor is it concerned with any rise of prices, since a maximum is set to its payments. The medical profession did not co-operate in discussions on the drug tariff, which was fixed by pharmacists without real scrutiny. The tariff provides a price for every ingredient in a prescription and for a dispensing fee for the prescription as a whole; but this structure resulted in serious inequalities and injustice to individual chemists. Owing to the method of allowing for establishment charges, there was a variation of yield between chemists which depended on the conduct of practitioners in prescribing; and the dispensing fee was not scientifically graded solely by the degree of professional skill required in dispensing the several classes of medicaments. The tariff proposed was arrived at after considering the results of an investigation of prescriptions dispensed in 1913–14, of chemists' businesses to arrive at profits earned, and a dispensing test. It should be annually revised. There are three dissents on various points.

Approved Society Finance and Administration

Dept. Cttee. Interim Rep., apps. pp. 39. 1916

1916 Cd. 8251, xiv, 25
apptd. Jan., 1916. sgd. May, 1916

G. H. Ryan (Ch.), Anderson, Appleton, Bunbury, Davies (F. C.), Davies (I.), Kinnear, Macarthur (Miss M. R.), McNicol, Mann, Neill, Nugent, Douglas-Pennant, Platt, Ritson (Miss M.), Thompson, Watson, Williams, Woods, Rockliff.

'To consider and report upon any amendments in the financial scheme of the National Insurance Acts which experience of the administration of Sickness, Disablement, and Maternity Benefits may suggest as desirable, within the existing limits of contributions and benefits, and apart from further Exchequer Grants, before the completion of any valuations of Approved Societies; and, further, to consider how far the work of Approved Societies could be simplified and its cost reduced, without detriment to the interests of insured persons, by amendment of the Acts and Regulations; and to make recommendations thereon.'

The National Health Insurance Scheme contemplated one fundamental departure from a flat rate insurance system in that insured persons were encouraged to segregate themselves into societies which might have high or low proportions of members below average health, or engaged in unhealthy or exacting occupations, or affected by local conditions. The prosperous societies were to enjoy the greater part of their surpluses, while less fortunate ones with a membership engaged in hazardous occupations were in an unsatisfactory position. The claims of women, especially married women, were permanently in excess of contributions. A number of societies would be seriously in deficiency. Since the terms of reference excluded changes in benefits, contributions or increased Exchequer grants, £1,800,000 of the income of the Sinking Fund should be diverted to increasing the net contribution income of societies for the payment of benefits to women, married women, men affected by war service, societies with special occupational risks, etc. Small societies with less than 1,000 members should be liable to pool up to

50 per cent of contingency funds into a national pool. Valuations should be triennial.

—— Further Report, apps. pp. ix, 88. 1916

1916 *Cd.* 8396, *xiv*, 65 *sgd. Oct.*, 1916

add Tuckfield.

Voluntary societies were selective, those who joined them choosing the scale of benefits, contributions, etc., which suited them. National insurance was compulsory, included all classes of the industrial community, and had fixed contributions and benefits. The Act aimed at a standard of uniformity and precision probably inconsistent with the administration of benefits through varied approved societies. Exceptional treatment had been provided for a number of classes, but the demand for some of these arrangements was small and they should be withdrawn. There were only 28,000 voluntary contributors; no new entrants should be accepted. Large classes of employers who paid wages during sickness made no use of the arrangements of section 47, which should be repealed, as should section 53 covering persons in the employment of the Crown. Women on marriage had not used the options provided and should be offered new ones, e.g. a marriage benefit of £2, with free medical benefit for one year. The arrangements for foreign going seamen, who received medical attention without deduction from wages and who were subject to different insurance conditions when doing shore jobs, should be simplified. The right of transfer should not be taken away, but a fee should be charged.

—— Final Report, apps. pp. 17. 1917

1917–18 *Cd.* 8451, *xvii*, 395 *sgd. Dec.*, 1916

Section 63 of the Act provided that where the normal sickness rate exceeded the 'standard rate' by more than 10 per cent, an inquiry could be demanded to determine whether this was due to specified preventible causes, with a view to reimbursing societies. Some societies showed an habitual excess, since conditions encouraged the segregation of insured persons into societies with distinctive occupational hazards. This test should be abandoned and the Insurance Commissioners given power to hold such an inquiry where a prima facie case had been made.

The plea for sickness benefits for sufferers from venereal diseases was justified from the points of view of the community, the societies, and the individuals concerned. But the contention that the societies should give benefits to tuberculous people after they had resumed work was rejected. The title to sickness benefit as a statutory right depended upon the criterion of incapacity to work. The campaign against tuberculosis should be national, and while the societies could assist, they should not take on any substantial new burden.

4. WORKMEN'S COMPENSATION

Compensation for Injuries to Workmen

Dept. Cttee. Vol. I. Rep., apps. pp. 236. 1904. Vol. II. Mins. of ev., index. 1904. Vol. III. Memo., apps. 1905

1904 *Cd.* 2208, *lxxxviii*, 743. *Mins. of ev., etc.*; 1905 *Cd.* 2334 *Cd.* 2458, *lxxv*, 487

apptd. Nov., 1903. *sgd. Aug.*, 1904

K. E. Digby (*Ch.*), Browne, Smith, Chalmers, Barnes.

'To enquire and report—(a) What amendments in the law relating to compensation for injuries to workmen are necessary or desirable, and (b) To what classes of employments, not now included in the Workmen's Compensation Acts, those Acts can properly be extended, with or without modification.'

The Workmen's Compensation Act, 1897, introduced a great change into the contractual relations of employers and employed by giving the workmen a legal right to be relieved of some part of the loss due to industrial accidents.

(a) Although the Act has a bad name for litigation, the amount is small compared with the number of cases settled out of court. It has had no appreciable effect either in improving or diminishing safety. A number of mutual accident benefit societies have ended through the withdrawal of employer's contributions. Many small employers were now involved, and because insurance was not compulsory, the workman might lose his security through their insolvency. Some difficulties had arisen regarding the employment of aged and maimed persons. The Committee make detailed recommendations to deal with difficulties which had arisen from the definitions of accident, place of work, building, of the liability of sub-contractors, misconduct, and of earning capacity, etc. The medical referee should not be a practitioner in private practice paid by fee, but a salaried officer. The County Court should be given powers to protect widows and dependents from improvident or oppressive settlements for lump sums.

(b) A great part of the most dangerous trades, covering 7¼ mn. workpeople, were already covered. The Act should be extended, after considering the circumstances of each class, to include those where the dangers and numbers of accidents were greatest. The principle should be applied to seamen by amendment of the Merchant Shipping Act, and a special inquiry should be made into the fishing industry. Carriers and persons employed in workshops with five or more workpeople should be included. The extension of the Act, especially to small employers, would increase the risks due to the insolvency of employers, which could not be met except by substituting the security of a solvent insurance fund for the personal liability of individual employers. Some witnesses proposed a system of national insurance, and if insurance were compulsory an increase of benefit might be obtained if workmen also contributed. The Act could not be regarded as otherwise than a step in the direction of a more comprehensive scheme.

Compensation for Industrial Diseases

Dept. Cttee. Rep. pp. 24. 1907. Mins. of ev., apps., index. 1907

1907 Cd. 3495, xxxiv, 1045. Mins. of ev., etc.; 1907 Cd. 3496, xxxiv, 1075 apptd. Aug., 1906. sgd. May, 1907

H. Samuel (Ch.), Cunynghame, Allbutt, Legge.

'To inquire and report what diseases and injuries, other than injuries by accident, are due to industrial occupations, are distinguishable as such, and can properly be added to the diseases enumerated in the Third Schedule of the Workmen's Compensation Bill, 1906.'

Those symptoms which were due to a cause which operated at a definite moment of time were regarded as the result of 'accidents'; others were the result of 'diseases' or injuries not being injuries caused by 'accident'. Two other tests applied to any disease or injury considered were (i) did it incapacitate for more than one week? and (ii) was it so specific to an employment that the cause could be established in individual instances? Under the Workmen's Compensation Act of 1906 the burden of proving whether a disease was occupational could be laid upon either the workman or the employer, according to the nature of the disease. The committee reviewed a large number of diseases, some of which were and others of which were not recommended for inclusion in the Schedule.

—— Second Report. pp. 4. 1908.
Mins. of ev., apps. 1908

1908 *Cd.* 4386, *xxxv*, 1. *Mins. of ev., etc.*; 1908 *Cd.* 4387, *xxxv*, 7
sgd. Oct., 1908

Glassworkers' cataract, and tele-graphists' cramp should be added. The definition of eczema given in the first report was modified.

Post Office. Facilities for Insurance under the Workmen's Compensation Acts

Dept. Cttee. Rep. pp. 11 [1907]. Mins. of ev., apps., index. 1907

1907 *Cd.* 3568, *lxviii*, 163. *Mins. of ev., etc.*; 1907 *Cd.* 3569, *lxviii*, 175
apptd. March, sgd. June, 1907

Lord Farrer (*Ch.*), Cochrane, Davies, Denman, Hewby, Kirkwood, Turpin.

'*To consider whether it is practicable, and, if practicable, whether it is desirable, for the Post Office to provide facilities for the insurance of employers in respect of their liabilities under the Workmen's Compensation Acts, either generally or subject to limitations. And further, to consider whether it is desirable that steps should be taken to encourage the use of the present life insurance system of the Post Office; and, if so, what steps.*'

By the Act of 1906 about six million more workmen will come under the Workmen's Compensation Acts. The necessity of Post Office intervention must lie amongst those small employers, other than a residuum unwilling to insure at all, who are anxious to insure but have difficulty in doing so. Extensive facilities are provided by competitive companies who gave a pledge to undertake insurance for all classes. Apart from the impossibility of establishing any scheme before the Act came into force, it was undesirable for the Post Office to undertake such insurance as principal, either generally or for limited classes, or as agent. Sub-postmasters working on commission are free and should be encouraged to become agents for companies. The Post Office could offer to distribute an alphabetical list of such accident insurance companies as complied with the conditions laid down in the Employers' Liability Insurance Companies Bill now before Parliament. Denman dissents on the ground that the list would inevitably be taken as guaranteeing the respectability of the companies.

Compensation for Industrial Diseases

Dept. Cttee. Rep. pp. 10. 1913. Mins. of ev., apps., index. 1913

1913 *Cd.* 6956, *xviii*, 649. *Mins. of ev., etc.*; 1913 *Cd.* 6957, *xviii*, 659
apptd. April, 1912. *sgd. July,* 1913

E. J. Griffith (*Ch.*), Allbutt, Ruegg, Legge.

'*To inquire and report whether the following diseases can properly be added to those enumerated in the Third Schedule of the Workmen's Compensation Act, 1906, viz.: (1) Cowpox; (2) Dupuytren's Contraction; (3) Clonic Spasm of the Eyelids, apart from Nystagmus.*'

It was suggested that miners suffering from clonic spasm of the eyelids had been refused certificates because they did not exhibit nystagmus, i.e. oscillation of the eyeballs. There was a considerable divergence of opinion and experience. The term 'nystagmus' should be replaced by 'miner's nystagmus in miners and other'. Cowpox, of which the incidence is not great and recovery from which takes only ten days, and Dupuytren's Contraction, which is found in all sections of the community and not dominantly amongst lace twist-hands, should not be scheduled. Writer's Cramp does not disable sufferers from following other occupations; compensation should be payable for not more than 12 months.

5. OLD AGE PENSIONS

Aged Deserving Poor

Dept. Cttee. Rep., apps. pp. 1, 93. 1900

1900 *Cd.* 67, *x*, 1.
apptd. Aug., 1899. *sgd. Jan.,* 1900

E. W. Hamilton (*Ch.*), Brabrook, Provis, Humphreys.

'To *obtain information bearing upon certain questions raised in connexion with the Report, dated 26th July, 1899, of the Select Committee of the House of Commons on the Aged Deserving Poor.*'

The object of the inquiry was to arrive at an estimate of the cost of the Old Age Pensions scheme prepared by the Select Committee on the *Aged Deserving Poor* (1899 (296) viii). By an examination of the available statistics and the aid of a house-to-house sample in 28 representative poor law unions, an estimate is made of the numbers of persons aged 65, and deductions are made for probable failure to satisfy the qualifying conditions. For England and Wales these deductions are: conviction for serious offences in the previous 20 years, 2 per cent; receipt of poor law relief other than medical, 27 per cent; incomes above 10*s.*, 37 per cent; inability to prove thrift, etc., 10 per cent of the remainder. Similar calculations are made for Scotland and Ireland. Taking into account the probable increase in number of the aged, a pension of 5*s.* to 7*s.* would cost the United Kingdom £10,300,000 in 1901, £12,650,000 in 1911 and £15,650,000 in 1921. If the pensionable age were 70, the cost would be reduced to £5,950,000, £7,450,000 and £9,550,000. The estimates of ultimate costs might be affected by increased length of life.

See *Old Age Pensions*. Table and Preliminary Memo.; 1907 Cd. 3618, lxviii, 385. This revises the estimates made by the Departmental Committee, in the light of subsequent changes in the numbers of pensionable age, etc.

Aged Pensioners Bill

Sel. Cttee. Reps., proc., mins. of ev., apps., index. pp. xvi, 571. 1904

1903 (276) *v*, 393
apptd. May, *o.p.* July, 1903

G. Lawson (*Ch.*), Brown, Channing, Crean, Flower, Goulding, Hutton, Lloyd-George, Lawson, O'Shee, Pemberton, Pilkington, Reid, Remnant, Shackleton, Skews-Cox.

The Bill, which proposed to give persons over the age of 65 a pension of five shillings a week, was reported without amendment. The Committee limited the evidence it took to matters which had arisen since Mr. Chaplin's Report (1899 (296) viii): (1) further experience gained by the continued operation of Old Age Pension Laws in Denmark, New Zealand and Victoria; (2) the views expressed at conferences of trade unions, friendly and co-operative societies; (3) recent investigations made in certain workhouses as to the number of aged inmates who could leave such workhouses if provided with pensions; (4) the accuracy of the estimate made by Sir E. Hamilton's Committee in 1900, as tested by the Census of 1901 and the extent to which such estimate could be affected by certain variations from the scheme upon which these estimates were based.

It would not be reasonable to leave to an elected body the task of deciding on the merits of its constituents, and the decision on the qualification of any person for a pension should be in the hands of special commissioners for suitable areas. The 'receipt of poor relief' disqualification should be so amended as not to exclude aged persons in receipt of relief at the date of the Act, if they had not received it for 20 years before they reached the qualifying age. In order not to discourage thrift, it might be advisable to give distributing officers discretion as to amount, so that applicants might not be deprived of the fruits of thrift. All the materials available had been exhausted to enable Parliament to arrive at a decision; points on which there was still uncertainty could be settled only by the actual experiment.

See *Old Age Pensions, Australia.* R. Com. Rep.; 1907 Cd. 3341, lvi, 863.

Workmen's Insurance (Germany); 1908 (102) xcvi, 1189. *Old Age Pensions, New Zealand and Germany*; 1908 (159) lxxxviii, 391.

Old Age Pensioners and Aged Pauperism

Memo. pp. 41. 1913

1913 *Cd.* 7015, lv, 683

The paper gives statistics bearing on the decline of aged pauperism and its relationship to the operation of the Old Age Pensions Act. In England and Wales in 1911, 29·7 per 1,000 of the population were over 70, while in 1912 three-fifths of them, or 17·8 per 1,000, were old age pensioners. Between 1906 and 1913 the numbers of paupers over 70 declined by 74·8 per cent (indoor by 19·8 per cent, outdoor by 94·9 per cent). The total sum paid in pensions was the equivalent of a rate of 9*d.* in the £1. There were considerable variations between different areas. The proportion of the population who were pensioners varied from 9·4 per 1,000 in Hampstead to 40·8 per 1,000 in Cardiganshire, the proportion of those over 70 who were pensioners ranged from one-quarter in Bournemouth to four-fifths in Northamptonshire.

XII. HEALTH

1. General, Nursing and Medical Services
2. Sewage Disposal
3. Particular Problems and Diseases
4. Food Purity, Drugs, Patent Medicines

1. GENERAL, NURSING AND MEDICAL SERVICES

Public Health and Social Conditions

Memos., etc. pp. iv, 109. 1909

1909 *Cd.* 4671, *ciii*, 669

J. S. Davy, A. Newsholme, C. F. Adair Hore.

sgd. May, 1909

A statistical analysis, with tables and 59 charts, many of the statistical series extending from 1850–1908. The statistics included deal with natural increase, marriage and fertility rates; mortality rates at various ages and urban and rural; infant and child death rates; deaths from 'killing' diseases and in different occupations; the period of the working life; wages and prices, decline of agricultural labour; trade union unemployment, 1860–1908; occupations of distress committee applicants. The information on pauperism deals with the relation of pauperism to population, unemployment, and rateable value, and its geographical distribution. The causes of the rise of cost of relief 1857–1907 (76 per cent for indoor, 52 per cent for outdoor) include specialization of treatment, staffing improvements, advance of science, specialization of institutions, etc.

Nursing of the Sick Poor in Workhouses

Rep.

1902 *Cd.* 1366. See *Poor Law*. p. 242.

Registration of Nurses

Sel. Cttee. Rep., proc., mins. of ev., apps. pp. viii, 107. Index. 1904. Rep., proc., mins. of ev., apps., index. pp. xiv, 234. 1905

1904 (281) (281-*Ind.*) *vi*, 701. 1905 (263) *vii*, 733

apptd. June, o.p. July, 1904. *re-apptd. March, o.p. July*, 1905

Mr. Tennant (*Ch.*), Ambrose, Balfour, Douglas, Hobhouse, Hutchinson, Mount, L. Morpeth, Pierpoint, Stirling-Maxwell, Tuke.

'To consider the expediency of providing for the Registration of Nurses.'

The 1904 report is a formal presentation of the minutes of evidence. The appendices include a paper handed by Dr. Fenwick on behalf of the British Nursing Association supporting, and one handed in by C. Burt on behalf of the Central Hospital Council for London, opposing registration. The former argues that since Dr. Acland's proposal of registration fifteen years earlier, nursing had become a skilled calling, but that it was still possible for an untrained person to call herself trained; registration would furnish a guarantee of the technical efficiency of every trained nurse and midwife. Mr. Burt's paper argues that registration would have to be based on examinations and would leave out of account the personal qualities which cannot be so tested.

The Report of 1905 states that 'amidst many divergent views met with in this evidence, there is a general opinion in favour of some change in the conditions under which nursing is carried on'. But upon the question of what changes in the conditions of nursing are desirable, unanimity could not be found. 'The principal suggestions laid before the Committee are: (a) Registration of individual nurses. (b) Registration of training schools for nurses. (c) Licensing of nursing homes, institutions and societies which supply or employ nurses. Your Committee are agreed that it is desirable that a Register of Nurses should be kept by a Central Body appointed by the State, and that, while it is not desirable to prohibit unregistered persons from nursing for gain, no person should be entitled to assume the designation of "Registered Nurse" whose name is not upon the Register.'

The Working of the Midwives Act, 1902

Dept. Cttee. Vol. I. Rep., apps. pp. iv, 51 [1909]. Vol. II. Mins. of ev., index [1909]

1909 Cd. 4822, xxxiii, 19. Mins. of ev., etc.; 1909 Cd. 4823, xxxiii, 77 apptd. Dec., 1908. sgd. Aug., 1909

A. W. FitzRoy (Ch.), Hobhouse (Mrs.), Champneys, Davy, Downes, Fremantle, Pedder.

'To consider the working of the Midwives Act, 1902, and in particular with reference to the supply of midwives and the cost of training, the remuneration of medical men summoned on the advice of midwives under the rules in pursuance of the Act, and the delegation of their powers by county councils under the Act.'

It was estimated that there were about 15,000 practising midwives, that they attended about 50 per cent of births, the proportion varying from 11 per cent in Newcastle, and 25 per cent in London to 93 per cent in St. Helens. No general shortage of midwives was likely, though in 15 out of 50 counties and 17 county boroughs out of 71 a deficiency was anticipated. The question was one of distribution.

The date of prohibition of practice by uncertified women should not be postponed. As the maintenance of an adequate supply was mainly a problem of distribution, no state subvention was needed. There should be co-ordinated action by local authorities and voluntary agencies in the establishment of county nursing associations. The combination of midwifery with district or school nursing might be an advantage in rural districts, and where other arrangements could not be made, guardians should appoint district midwives. In some institutions the cost of training was too high; local authorities should be authorized to contribute to the cost of training of midwives for work in their areas.

Medical practitioners summoned on the advice of a midwife should be given a secure expectation of payment, the scale of fees being laid down by the L.G.B., the poor law authority being responsible for payment, with powers to recover. County councils' powers of delegation to district councils have been detrimental and should be withdrawn; where delegation is still exercised, it should be revoked.

App. III is a memo. by A. Newsholme.

Asylum Officers' Superannuation Bill

Sel. Cttee. Reps., proc., mins. of ev., apps. pp. xvi, 98. 1909

1909 (257) *vi*, 587.
apptd. April, o.p. Aug., 1909

J. Henderson (*Ch.*), Collins, Hazleton, Horniman, Priestley, Richards, Roch, Stanier, Tuke.

The 'instability of asylum service', the unrest occasioned by constant change of attendants, and the consequent difficulty of maintaining and retaining staff has arisen chiefly because of the lack of assured pension on a recognized basis in the service. Commissions in 1891 and 1900 had called attention to the importance of these matters for attracting and keeping suitable persons in the service. The principle of assured pensions had already been recognized in the case of the civil service, poor law officers, the police and prison officers. But although 'optional powers' had been used by a large number of local authorities, there was no uniform scale of pensions operating throughout the public asylums of the United Kingdom. The Committee were strongly and unanimously of the opinion that such contributory pensions should be compulsory, and that aggregation of pensions for officers moving from one asylum to another should be arranged. It accepted the principles and amended the Bill 'in such a way as to apply to the special exigencies and requirements of the asylum service'.

See 1909 9 Edw. 7. c. 48.

Asylum Officers (Employment, Pensions and Superannuation) Bill

Sel. Cttee. Rep., proc., mins. of ev., apps. pp. xxii, 167. Index. 1911

1911 (239, 242) (239, 242-*Ind.*) *vi*, 307
apptd. May, o.p. July, Aug., 1911

C. Roberts (*Ch.*), Bathurst, Black, Brocklehurst, Cotton, Craig, Craik, Dickinson, Hayden, Higham, Jones, M'-Callum, Redmond, Remnant, Rutherford, Stanier, Wardle, L. Wolmer.

'The Bill restricts the hours of duty of nurses and attendants in asylums to 60 hours per week, and amends the provisions of the Asylum Officers Superannuation Act, 1909, with a view to securing better terms of pension for the staff in asylums.' Dr. Cook, of the Lunacy Commission, thought that the average number of hours for the asylums was 84 per week. In view of the special stress and strain of the work this number of hours was excessive and ought to be diminished, but there was no unanimity for the 60 hours even amongst the Unions, who seemed to be divided between 60 and 70 hours per week (Shuttleworth, q. 441. Bankart, q. 587). It was generally argued that if a 60 hour week were made compulsory, a three shift system would have to be introduced. The existing hours of work could not be defended and ought to be diminished. There was no objection to the principle of the statutory limitation of hours and the ordinary case against Parliamentary interference with the hours of adult labour did not apply. There should be a maximum of 70 hours a week for the day staff and 60 for the night staff, calculated over a period of a fortnight, and an appeal should be made to Visiting Committees to use individual discretion when fixing hours under local conditions.

The Act of 1909 conferred the right of pension at the age of 55 when 20 years' service had been completed. The present Bill proposed to confer the pension after 25 years' service irrespective of age. In view of the fact that 'women may enter asylum service at the age of 21 or 22, but at 46 or 47 a woman is less fit for asylum service than a man of equal age' and that, to quote Dr. Cook, 'hardly any women can stand being in an asylum from the age of 18 to 55', the Committee recommended that the change proposed in the Bill should be for women only.

Highlands and Islands Medical Service

Cttee. Vol. I. Rep., apps. pp. 55. 1912. Vol. II. Mins. of ev., index. 1913

1912–13 Cd. 6559, *xlii*, 581. *Mins. of ev., etc.*; 1913 Cd. 6920, *xxxvii*, 213 *apptd. July, sgd. Dec.*, 1912

J. A. Dewar (*Ch.*), Tullibardine (Lady), Grierson, Lindsay, Mackenzie, McVail, Miller, Orrock, Robertson.

'*To consider at an early date how far the provision of medical attendance in districts situated in the Highlands and Islands of Scotland is inadequate, and to advise as to the best method of securing a satisfactory medical service therein, regard being had to the duties and responsibilities of the several public authorities operating in such districts.*'

In many parts the medical attention received by the majority of the people was insufficient, even when measured by the wholly inadequate standard accepted by an impoverished population. The people were unable to pay fees or maintain voluntary insurance, and could not take advantage of the Insurance Act; their dwellings were grossly insanitary, their food inferior, and many had a primitive belief in traditional 'cures'. The exodus of the healthy and enterprising had inevitably meant that the unfit formed a larger proportion of the population.

Although there were too few doctors in some districts, the obstacles to an adequate medical service lay rather in defective transport facilities and the very bad conditions of medical service. But the nursing and hospital services were quite inadequate: the number of nurses should be increased and their organization improved, while cottage hospitals should be established at convenient centres. The medical facilities provided through the parish council were necessarily inadequate, since the proportion of the grant-in-aid received by the parishes had been decreasing in spite of their rising expenditure. With a properly administered additional Imperial grant, the necessary public medical services could be correlated so as to provide a more satisfactory financial basis for general medical practice. A central authority representative of the various central departments concerned with the medical services, and the subordinate District Committees should administer the grant. Each centrally recognized practitioner should be assured of a minimum income of £300 per annum, with travelling allowance.

Prohibition of Medical Practice by Companies Bill. [H.L.] Dental Companies (Restriction of Practice Bill) [H.L.]

Rep.

1907 (HL. 72). See *Professions*. p. 240.

The Practice of Medicine and Surgery by Unqualified Persons

Rep.

1910 Cd. 5422. See *Professions*. p. 240.

Acceptance by the Board of Education of Dental Certificates from unregistered practitioners

Rep.

1914 Cd. 7538. See *Professions*. p. 241.

2. SEWAGE DISPOSAL

Sewage Disposal

R. Com. Interim Rep., *Treating and Disposing of Sewage*. pp. xiii. 1901. Mins. of ev., index. 1901. Apps. 1901

1901 Cd. 685, *xxxiv*, Pt. I. *Mins. of ev., etc.*; 1901 Cd. 686, *xxxiv*, Pt. I, 15. *Apps.*; 1901 Cd. 686-I, *xxxiv*, Pt. II, 1 *apptd. May*, 1898. *sgd. July*, 1901

Lord Iddesleigh (*Ch.*), Carey, Cotton, Foster, Harding, Killick, Ramsay, Russell, Power.

'To inquire and report: I. (1) *What method or methods of treating and disposing of sewage (including any liquid from any factory or manufacturing process) may properly be adopted, consistently with due regard for the requirements of the existing law, for the protection of public health, and for the economical and efficient discharge of the duties of Local Authorities; and (2) If more than one method may be so adopted, by what rules, in relation to the nature or volume of sewage, or the population to be served, or other varying circumstances or requirements, should the particular method of treatment and disposal to be adopted be determined; and II. To make any recommendations which may be deemed desirable with reference to the treatment and disposal of sewage.*'

The problem before the Commission was that land available, especially in the industrial centres, is either of unsuitable quality, inadequate in area or obtainable only at prohibitive costs, and that present knowledge regarding purification by artificial processes opened out possibilities not hitherto thought practicable.

Mr. A. D. Adrian, Assistant Secretary to the L.G.B., gave valuable evidence on the history and the law relating to the problem, and on the practices of the L.G.B. There were three historical periods. (1) The period from 1842-57, when the prompt removal of sewage from the neighbourhood of dwellings was regarded as of first importance, the use of a river outfall being preferable to its retention near houses. In consequence of doubts as to the effect on public health of the irrigation of large surfaces with liquid manure, the best system of disposal was by underground pipes for subsequent distribution by hose or jets. (2) The period 1858-70 marks the abandonment of the notion of possible injury to health as a consequence of the irrigation of land by sewage, and the growth of the belief that ideal systems of sewage disposal should aim at a profitable utilization by direct application to the land, thus facilitating the protection of rivers from contamination. (3) From 1870 the dominant idea was that the prevention of the pollution of streams was an indispensable requisite of every system of sewage disposal which laid claim to efficiency.

The Royal Commission on *Discharge of Sewage of the Metropolis into the River Thames*, 1884, warned that 'certain parts of organic matter of the sewage were removed by chemical precipitation' and that 'liquid so separated required futher purification... by its application to land'. The L.G.B., guided by this recommendation when giving its sanction for money borrowed, required that schemes should 'provide for the application of the sewage or effluent to an adequate area of suitable land before its discharge into a stream'. This gave rise to the problem of finding suitable land at reasonable cost, together with the demand for further knowledge on the use of chemical purification.

This preliminary Report reached conclusions concerning the efficiency of different soils and artificial processes for purifying sewage, and the problem of protecting rivers from pollution. No land was entirely useless for the effective filtration of sewage, but peat and stiff claylands were generally unsuitable. It seemed possible to produce, by artificial processes, effluents which could be safely discharged into streams, and the L.G.B. would be justified in modifying the law regarding the application of sewage to land. The Rivers Pollution Prevention Act of 1876 had not been effectively executed and a new department should be established having powers to take action where local authorities had failed to do so.

—— Second Report. pp. 153. 1902
1902 *Cd.* 1178, *xlix*, 1

Consists of ten technical and scientific reports.

—— Third Report. 1. *Trade Effluents*. 2. *A New Central Authority*. Apps. pp. xxix, 12. 1903. Mins. of ev., index. pp. 321. 1903

1903 *Cd*. 1486, *xxxi*, 1. *Mins. of ev., etc.*; 1903 *Cd*. 1487, *xxxi*, 43

Discusses the relations between local authorities and manufacturers in regard to the disposal of manufacturing effluents. The state of the law was unsatisfactory; in the majority of cases purification by the local authority was practicable, while it was often difficult for manufacturers. It should be the duty of the local authority to provide sewers for trade effluents as well as domestic sewage, subject to safeguards. Cases may arise in which the local authority should be relieved of the duty wholly or partly, and be empowered to make a special charge. Disputes should be referred to the Central Board proposed in the First Report. River Boards should have the duty of inspecting water supplies for pollution and reporting to the Central Board, which should be empowered to make orders for the removal or diminution of the danger.

—— Fourth Report. Vol. I. Report on *Pollution of Tidal Waters with special reference to Contamination of Shell-Fish*. pp. xliv. 1904. Vol. II. Mins. of ev., index. 1904

1904 *Cd*. 1883, *xxxvii*, 1. *Mins. of ev., etc.*; 1904 *Cd*. 1884, *xxxvii*, 45

The discharge of sewage into tidal waters was brought specially to the notice of the Commission by the L.G.B. because of the serious outbreaks of enteric fever which were attributed to the contamination of shell-fish. Sewage and trade effluents were usually discharged in an unpurified condition into tidal waters and shell-fish, which had become contaminated by sewage, could convey enteric fever, etc., to human beings. Further, the discharge of unpurified sewage, besides creating offensive putrification and deposits, could poison fish and render water incapable of supporting life. Legislation was required to protect the rivers and the shell-fish trade. There should be a competent authority with power to prevent the taking of shell-fish from polluted areas for consumption and to enforce restrictions concerning pollution. The authority should be vested in the River Boards, subject to appeal to a central authority. Further bacteriological researches were essential. No shell-fish should be imported if procured from polluted localities.

—— ——. Vols. III, IV. Parts I-V

1904 *Cd*. 1885, *xxxvii*. 1904 *Cd*. 1886, *xxxviii*. 1904 *Cd*. 1886-I *to Cd*. 1886-IV, *xxxviii*.

These are technical reports on the chemical, bacteriological, engineering and other aspects of land sewage.

—— Fifth Report, index. pp. 238. 1908. App. I, mins. of ev., index. pp. 803. 1908. App. II, Summary of ev. pp. 227. 1908

1908 *Cd*. 4278, *liii*, 749. *Mins. of ev., etc.*; 1908 *Cd*. 4279, *Cd*. 4280, *liv*, 1

The report deals chiefly with the relative merits of the various methods of purification of sewage of towns. Up to the date of the Commission the experiments in purification by chemical methods were on too limited a scale for conclusions to be drawn. The Commission therefore initiated systematic and detailed investigations, bacteriological and chemical, of the treatment of sewage on land of various kinds. The results of these investigations are given in five appendices to this report. These experiments proved that it was practicable to purify sewage of towns to any degree required either by land treatment or by artificial filters and that there was no essential difference between the two processes. The main questions for a town proposing to adopt a system were, first, what degree of purification was required in the circumstances of the town, and the character of the river or stream into which its refuse is to be discharged. The conditions of each case vary to such an extent that the necessary control could not be exercised by any direct enactment enforced by the ordinary Courts. Ultimate control should be vested in an adequately equipped Central Administrative Authority, and that as far as practicable the local River Boards should, in accordance with regulations framed by the Central Department, act as the first tribunal.

—— ——. Apps. III–VIII.

1908 *Cd. 4281, Cd. 4282, lv.* 1908 *Cd. 4283 to Cd. 4286, lvi*

These consist of technical reports and reports on special investigations and experiments.

—— Sixth Report, apps. *Disposal of liquid refuse from distilleries.* pp. 86. 1909

1909 *Cd. 4511, xlvi, 793*

Although treatment of distillery refuse was a particularly difficult problem, manufacturers stated that they were willing to spend money on purification. They asked the Commission to consider the question of some standards of purity up to which it would be safe for the riparian proprietors to receive effluents into their streams. Hitherto it had been impossible to comply with the standards 'which seemed to demand that refuse should be converted into pure water or a liquid identical with that of the river'.

Recommendations again stressed the need for a central authority responsible for the standards, with powers elastic enough to adapt them to particular local conditions. It was found that the treatment of distillery waste could produce a satisfactory effluent and that pot ale could be evaporated and sold as manure at about £5 per ton. Where distilleries were situated in sewered towns, the sewers should be utilized for waste disposal.

—— Seventh Report. Vol. I. Report. *Nuisances due to excessive growths of green sea-weeds in sewage polluted estuaries, with special reference to Belfast Lough.* pp. 13. 1911. Vols. II, III. Mins. of ev., apps. 1911

1911 *Cd. 5542, xli, 1. Apps.;* 1911 *Cd. 5543, Cd. 5543–1, xli, 25*

Pollution of Belfast Lough by sewage was said to have caused the excessive growth of *Ulva lattissima* (sea lettuce), which when decaying on the shore give off large quantities of sulphuretted hydrogen and so caused nuisance. Belfast Corporation had submitted a costly scheme of purification to the L.G.B., which asked the Commission for information on the problem. Other places, including Poole and Southampton, were examined.

It was not established that the removal of the effluent would stop the nuisance, as other conditions favourable to the growth of the *Ulva* were present. Various remedies were proposed, but the removal of sewage pollution could not be a complete and certain remedy.

—— Eighth Report. Vol. I. Report. *Standards and tests for sewage and sewage effluents discharging into rivers and streams.* pp. 17. 1912. Vol. II. App. 1913

1912–13 *Cd. 6464, xlvi, 613. App.;* 1913 *Cd. 6943, xxxix, 807*

Statute law recognized no graduated standards of purity for sewage effluents. 'Under the Rivers Prevention Pollution Act, 1876, in the case of sewage entering non-tidal waters, the duty is imposed on the local authority of adapting the best practicable means to render the sewage harmless before it enters the river, and no local circumstances may be taken into account.' The object of the Commission was to devise a system whereby the local authority should not be required to incur any greater expenditure on sewage disposal than would be necessary to prevent nuisance. Investigation showed that the volume and other conditions of a stream go far to determine the standard of purification necessary in individual cases. The standards arrived at are set out. The law should be altered so that a person shall be allowed to discharge sewage matter into a stream provided it satisfies the requirements of the prescribed standard laid down by a Central Authority.

—— Ninth Report. Vol. I. Report. *I. Disposal of liquid wastes from manufacturing processes. II. Disposal of liquid and solid domestic refuse in rural areas.* pp. 190. 1915. Vol. II. Mins. of ev., apps. pp. 160. 1915

1914–16 *Cd.* 7819, xxxv, 333. *Mins. of ev., etc.*; 1914–16 *Cd.* 7820, xxxv, 539

I. *Disposal of liquid wastes from manufacturing processes.*

The character of liquid trade waste varies with each trade, but speaking generally it is of a highly polluting nature, especially as in the woollen trade where water acts as a solvent and carries away the impurities from the wool; it is more foul and polluting than strong domestic sewage. Liquid wastes can be highly objectionable when they contain chemicals of a corroding and poisonous nature. The volume also presents a special problem, as is shown by a single factory, where during a working day of ten to fourteen hours the 500,000 gallons discharged are equivalent to the daily volume of domestic sewage of a town with a population of about 17,000 persons.

Most of the larger authorities do receive into their sewers a large number of trade effluents of small volume, without conditions, and in some cases with special conditions; but smaller authorities show considerable reluctance because of the danger that the costs for treating trade waste may exceed the rateable value of the trades for all purposes.

Under the Rivers Pollution Prevention Act, 1876, the L.G.B. cannot proceed against a manufacturer unless there are known means of purification which 'are reasonably practical and available under all circumstances of the case'. This provides no encouragement for a manufacturer to discover methods of dealing with waste, if by so doing he is saddled with the burden of providing them at his own expense, although there are many cases where it would benefit a manufacturer if he could contribute the money spent on pure water to some larger scheme, as it would enable him either to re-use the purified water or abstract profitable waste products, as for example, grease from wool. Efficient means of purification were available for some, but not all trade wastes; in the present state of knowledge some could not be thoroughly purified. The requirement of the existing law that trade wastes should be rendered harmless was therefore impracticable and local authorities have had to exercise their discretion. There were wide differences in trade wastes, and separate standards should be prescribed for different trades. The report suggests the standards suitable for a large number of trades.

In order to give a greater measure of security to the manufacturer and a greater measure of uniformity in administration, the law should be altered so that, before proceedings are taken against a manufacturer the River Board or Sanitary Authority should specify the degree of purification which they propose to demand; the manufacturer should have the right to appeal, when settled the requirements should remain in force for ten years, and any infringement should be referred by the Court to the Central Authority. Further guidance should be given to the Central Authority and to manufacturers by the publication of general rules in regard to the degree of purification to be demanded for various trade wastes. There should be provisions for the regulation of new sources of pollution.

II. *Disposal of liquid and solid refuse in rural areas.*

In rural areas the main fact is the abundance or scarcity of water. Where it is abundant, water carriage is the most satisfactory. The most appropriate methods where a water carriage system is impossible are discussed.

In a Memo. Sir William Ramsay expounded. the methods for disposal of sewage in gardens.

—— Final Report. *General Summary of conclusions and recommendations.* pp. 19.
1915
1914–16 *Cd.* 7821, *xxxv*, 705

Gives full summaries of conclusions of the separate reports.

In a Memo. Sir William Power urged that Watershed Authorities should definitely be charged with control of volume as well as of quality of water in their rivers and that details should have been given of the procedures they would adopt.

3. PARTICULAR PROBLEMS AND DISEASES

Physical Deterioration

Inter-Dept. Cttee. Vol. I. Rep., apps. pp. v, 137. 1904. Vol. II. Mins of ev. 1904. Vol. III. Apps., index. 1904

1904 *Cd.* 2175, *xxxii*, 1. *Mins. of ev.*, etc.; 1904 *Cd.* 2210, *Cd.* 2186, *xxxii*, 145 *apptd.* Sept., 1903. *sgd, July,* 1904

A. W. Fitz Roy (*Ch.*), Fox, Legge, Lindsell, Onslow, Struthers, Tatham.

'*To make a preliminary enquiry into the allegations concerning the deterioration of certain classes of the population as shown by the large percentage of rejections for physical causes of recruits for the Army and by other evidence, especially the Report of the Royal Commission on Physical Training (Scotland), and to consider in what manner the medical profession can best be consulted on the subject with a view to the appointment of a Royal Commission, and the terms of reference to such a Commission, if appointed.*'

Extended terms. '(1) *To determine, with the aid of such counsel as the medical profession are able to give, the steps that should be taken to furnish the Government and the Nation at large with periodical data for an accurate comparative estimate of the health and physique of the people; (2) to indicate generally the causes of such physical deterioration as does exist in certain classes; and (3) to point out the means by which it can be most effectually diminished.*'

A controversy arose in the press out of statements made by Sir F. Maurice that only two out of every five men who wished to be soldiers were in the ranks at the end of two years. It was not possible to draw any conclusion about the mass of the population from statistics relating to Army recruits, since the class from which they were drawn varied with the state of trade, the Army was not attracting so good a class of recruit, and the statistics were defective in other ways. The grave state of things disclosed made it important to have complete and accurate comparative data on the health and physique of the population. This work was unsuitable for a Royal Commission. A permanent anthropometric survey organization should be established on the lines suggested by Prof. Cunningham, but in addition to its long-period work on the population at large, every elementary school child should be examined at two selected ages, on tests to be approved and standardized by a consultative committee. A Register of Sickness based on revised Poor Law Medical Returns and other sources should be compiled and maintained.

Part II

Following Dr. Eichholz (q. 435) a distinction is drawn between physical defect, which was established, and progressive physical deterioration, which was not. There had been a great improvement in social conditions and standards of life, but there remained a considerable class of persons who were physically degenerate. The Committee examined a wide range of causes and symptoms, making a large number of recommendations (which foreshadowed

later developments in the social services).
These included: local authorities should
notify a date after which overcrowding
in excess of a fixed standard of persons
per room could not be allowed, should
preserve open spaces in areas contiguous with other towns and in
process of urbanization, and provide
open spaces in some proportion to the
density of population; the ordinary
householder should be made aware of
his responsibilities in regard to domestic
smoke pollution; counties and all towns
above a certain population should have
full time medical officers. Enquiry
should be made into the sterilization of
milk, which should go direct from
farms to milk depots for distribution;
to eliminate the loss of infant life
through improper feeding, girls and
mothers should be given systematic
instruction; the L.G.B. should be
empowered to fix purity standards for
all food and drinks. By a combination
of municipal and voluntary effort,
arrangements should be made to feed
habitually underfed school children.
A systematized medical inspection of
school children should be the duty of
every school authority. There should
be organized games for school children,
together with methodical physical exercise in the open air or in a special
shed; an organized medical service in
factories, with power to re-examine
after 16 and to deal with insanitary
conditions, and medical examination
of young persons entering mines.
The sale of cigarettes, etc., to children
below a certain age should be prohibited. A scientific enquiry should
be made into the physiological aspects
of fatigue, the extent and effects of
syphilis, and into the increase of lunacy
in Ireland.

The members of the Committee all
held official positions, and most of
the witnesses were official or scientific
experts. Important evidence by Cunningham, Eichholz, Kerr, Booth and
Rowntree. In a memo. Loch criticized
the poverty measurements of the last
two.

Vaccination Expenses

Dept. Cttee. Pt. I. Rep. pp. 27. 1905.
Pt. II. Mins. of ev., apps., index. 1905

1905 Cd. 2420, xl, 385. Mins. of ev., etc.;
1905 Cd. 2421, xl, 413
apptd. Sept., 1903. sgd. April, 1904

E. H. Llewellyn (Ch.), Lithiby, Low,
Vallance.

'To inquire and report with regard to
(1) The payments at present made under
the Vaccination Order, 1898, in respect
of the remuneration, costs, and expenses
of Public Vaccinators and Vaccination
Officers; and (2) Whether any, and if so
what, alterations should be made in relation
to the remuneration, costs, and expenses of
these officers.'

After 1872 the annual poor rate
expenditure on public vaccination in
England and Wales had declined to
£72,655 in 1899, but had risen to
£237,500 in 1900, the first complete
year under the Vaccination Act, 1898.
Nearly half the Boards of Guardians
had asked that steps should be taken
to reduce the cost. The main causes of
the rise of cost were the increased
fees paid to public vaccinators, an
increased amount of vaccination due
to a revival of confidence in it after the
report of the Royal Commission (1889–
1896), and the substitution of domiciliary for stational vaccination. A re-
arrangement of duties and a scale of
fees are proposed (para. 91). Public
vaccinators should be given fixity of
tenure. In some districts a whole-
time salaried officer could be appointed,
in others the duties amalgamated
with those of District Medical Officer
or Medical Officer.

Medical Inspection and Feeding of Children attending Public Elementary Schools

Rep.

1906 Cd. 2779. See Education. p. 318.

The Relations of Human and Animal Tuberculosis. (Bovine Tuberculosis)

R. Com. Interim Rep. pp. 7. 1904

1904 Cd. 2092, xxxix, 129
apptd. Aug., 1901. sgd. May, 1904

M. Foster (Ch.), Woodhead, Martin, McFadyean, Boyce.

'To inquire and report with respect to Tuberculosis: 1. Whether the disease in animals and man is one and the same; 2. Whether animals and man can be reciprocally infected with it; 3. Under what conditions, if at all, the transmission of the disease from animals to man takes place, and what are the circumstances favourable or unfavourable to such transmission.'

At the Congress on Tuberculosis held in London in July, 1901, 'Professor Koch called in question the correctness of the belief which was widely held that tuberculosis can be transmitted from animals to man. The views expressed by Professor Koch on this subject had numerous opponents among scientific men; but, having regard to the great importance of the matter, it was decided to acceded to a request made by the Congress that there should be an inquiry with respect to it. A Royal Commission was accordingly appointed.' (L.G.B. Ann. Rep. 1901–2; 1902 Cd. 1231, xxxv.) The Commission decided to begin by conducting their own experimental investigations. Bovine animals had been either injected or fed with strains of tuberculosis material of both human and bovine origin. The diseases caused by both strains were identical and no means of distinguishing between the two had so far been discovered. It would therefore be unwise to take any legislative action on the assumption that human and bovine bacilli, and the diseases caused by each, were different.

—— Second Interim Report. Pt. I. Rep. pp. 98. 1907. Pt. II. Apps. Vols. I–IV. 1907

1907 Cd. 3322, xxxviii, 1. Apps.; 1907 Cd. 3584, xxxviii, 99. 1907 Cd. 3660, xxxix, 1. 1907 Cd. 3661, Cd. 3378, xl, 1. 1908 Cd. 3758, lvii, 1 sgd. Jan., 1907

Parallel investigations were carried on at Walpole and Blythwood Farms, Essex. Sir James Blythwood lent the farm and house indefinitely 'without any payment of rent whatever'. The report contains a detailed account of experimental results. A positive answer could be given to the second term of reference: the human body could be infected by bovine tuberculosis. Bovine animals and man could be reciprocally infected. A very considerable amount of disease and death, especially among the young, was due to the consumption of cow's milk containing tubercle bacilli, the presence of which could be detected. More stringent measures to prevent the sale and consumption of such milk were necessary. Apps. consist of scientific memos.

—— Third Interim Report, app. pp. 38. 1909

1909 Cd. 4483, xlix, 365
sgd. Jan., 1909

add W. H. Power (Ch.), del. Foster (Ch.).

Tuberculosis involving the udder was comparatively common; in such cases the milk always contained tubercle bacilli. But investigations had been made into six naturally infected cows which showed no sign of disease of the udder during life. After slaughtering the udders were examined, and in only one case was slight evidence of tuberculosis of the udder discovered. Three of the cows obviously suffered from the disease and their milk contained tubercle bacilli. Since it was also found that the faeces contained tubercle bacilli, the presence of infected cows with healthy cows in the cow-shed was dangerous. Apps. consist of technical memos.

—— Final Report. Pt. I. Rep., memo. pp. iv, 54. 1911. Pt. II. Apps. Vols. I–VII. 1911–15. Supplemental Vol. Rep. 1913

1911 *Cd.* 5761, *xlii*, 173. *Apps.*, etc.; 1911 *Cd.* 5790, *xlii*, 231. 1911 *Cd.* 5791, *Cd.* 5893, *xliii*, 1. 1911 *Cd.* 5894, *Cd.* 5975, *xliv*, 1. 1913 *Cd.* 6904, *xl*, 71. 1914–16 *Cd.* 7941, *xxxvii*, 255. 1913 *Cd.* 6796, *xl*, 105

sgd. June, 1911

All the conclusions were based on the Commission's own researches. There were only slight cultural differences between human and bovine bacilli with which to justify the conclusion that they were distinct organisms. The Commission preferred to regard the two types as varieties of the same bacillus, and the lesions they produced as manifestations of the same disease. There was no doubt that human tuberculosis was in part identical with bovine tuberculosis. In many cases of the former the lesions contained, and were caused by bacilli indistinguishable from the bacilli causing bovine tuberculosis. A considerable proportion of the tuberculosis affecting children was of bovine origin, especially that which affected the abdominal organs and the cervical glands. The results of the investigations into tuberculosis in adolescents and adults were, however, very different: bovine bacilli were very rarely found in the lesions. Even so two adult fatalities due solely to the bovine bacillus had been found.

The need for stricter Government regulations to guard against the sale of food from tuberculous animals was again emphasized. Apps. consist of technical memos.

Treatment of Soldiers Invalided for Tuberculosis

Cttee. Preliminary Rep. pp. 5. 1908

1908 *Cd.* 3930, *xi*, 165 *apptd.* —, *sgd. Nov.,* 1907

E. W. D. Ward (*Ch.*), Keogh, L. Lucas, Seely, Summerbell, Tuke.

'*To consider the care and treatment after discharge from the Army of soldiers invalided for tuberculous disease.*'

The Committee reject both the existing method of discharging from the Army any man suffering from tubercle of the lung and thereafter disowning all responsibility for him and a proposal for a central military sanatorium, but recommend that the Army should obtain the use of 200 beds in civil sanatoria at an annual cost of about £20,000.

Tuberculosis

Dept. Cttee. Interim Rep. pp. 28. 1912

1912–13 *Cd.* 6164, *xlviii*, 1 *apptd. Feb.,* 1912. *sgd.* ——

W. Astor (*Ch.*), Addison, Bardswell, Davies, Fraser, Latham, Mackenzie, McVail, Maguire, Newman, Newsholme, Niven, Paterson, Philip, Richards, Stafford, Walker (Miss J.), Whitaker, Willis, Henderson.

'*To report at an early date upon the consideration of general policy in respect of the problem of tuberculosis in the United Kingdom, in its preventive, curative, and other aspects, which should guide the Government and local bodies in making or aiding provision for the treatment of tuberculosis in sanatoria or other institutions or otherwise.*'

The National Insurance Act, 1911, to come into force 15th July, 1912, requires the County and County Borough Insurance Committees set up by the Act to provide for insured persons tuberculosis treatment in sanatoria or otherwise, and provides for the purpose 1*s.* 3*d.* per person, plus 1*d.* per person from the Exchequer, a total of £880,000. £1,500,000 is made available for sanatoria, etc. Any organized scheme must be available for the whole community, and must provide for preventive diagnosis, treatment and research. Cases of pulmonary tuberculosis are divided into six classes according to the degree of impairment of working capacity and sanatoria should be used where there is prospect of restoration or of arrest of the disease.

The first unit of the scheme is the Tuberculosis Dispensary, designed to act as a common centre for diagnosis and treatment and in the charge of a full-time Tuberculosis Officer. There should be one dispensary for every 150,000 to 200,000 population in urban and for smaller populations in rural areas. The second unit consists of sanatoria, etc., for institutional treatment. There should be one sanatorium bed for every 5,000 persons, a total of 9,000. Sanatoria should contain not less than 100 beds, at a cost of £150 per bed. Provision should be made for 200 beds for pulmonary and 2,000 beds for osseous tuberculosis in children.

Capital grants for dispensaries should be up to 80 per cent of the amount required, with a maximum of £1 per 750 population, or an average of £240 per dispensary, and of 60 per cent of the cost of sanatorium beds, with a maximum of £90 per bed. Insurance Committees should make arrangements with authorities for the maintenance of a fixed number of beds, and with dispensaries for an annual lump sum payment, in both cases for a term of years. The co-operation of medical practitioners in the working of the scheme should be secured. County and County Borough Councils should have primary administrative responsibility. In view of the heavy incidence of pulmonary tuberculosis in Ireland, the disease should be compulsorily notifiable there.

—— Final Report. Vol. I. pp. 17. 1913. Vol. II. Apps., index. 1913. 1912–13 Cd. 6641, xlviii, 29. Apps., etc.; 1912–13 Cd. 6654, xlviii, 47 sgd. March, 1913
add Stockman, Smith. del, Henderson.

The Local Government Boards and Insurance Commissioners for the various parts of the United Kingdom had approved the recommendations of the Interim Report. Since it was issued, a central grant had been made of half the estimated cost of treating non-insured persons and the dependents of insured persons, and 6d. per insured person of the 1s. 3d. provided by the Act had been allocated to the remuneration of medical practitioners concerned with domiciliary treatment.

Amongst the preventive measures recommended are the compulsory isolation of persons in a high state of infective activity, the disinfection of premises likely to harbour tubercle bacilli; the improvement of housing; town planning and garden cities, and inquiry into the occupational incidence of the disease. The findings of the Royal Commission on bovine tuberculosis show that it can cause tuberculosis in man and especially in children. Steps should be taken to eradicate tuberculosis from herds, cows with diseased udders or in the advanced stages being slaughtered, and in the meantime steps taken to protect milk during distribution. Sterilization and pasteurization can render infected milk harmless, but opinion is divided on whether milk so treated is otherwise satisfactory. Tuberculosis — pulmonary, osseous, glandular, etc.—is widespread amongst children; more institutions are needed, and there should be a widespread application of open air treatment in institutions, schools, classes, etc. £200,000 should be provided for such institutions. A central advisory council with an executive committee should advise on the use of the research funds, employ competent investigators, etc.

The Appendix volume consists of memoranda, many by experts.

Care and Control of the Feeble Minded

R. Com. Vol. VIII. Rep. pp. xxiii, 512. 1908. Vols. I–IV. Mins. of ev., 1908. Vol. V. Apps. 1908

1908 *Cd.* 4202, *xxxix*, 159. *Mins. of ev., etc.*; 1908 *Cd.* 4215, *xxxv*, 83. 1908 *Cd.* 4216, *xxxvi*, 1. 1908 *Cd.* 4217, *Cd.* 4218, *xxxvii*, 1. 1908 *Cd.* 4219, *xxxviii*, 1
apptd. Sept., 1904. *sgd. July*, 1908

Lord Radnor (*Ch.*), Byrne, Chadwyck-Healey, Hobhouse, Needham, Donkin, Dunlop, Greene, Burden, Dickinson, Loch, Pinsent (Ellen F.).

'*To consider the existing methods of dealing with idiots and epileptics and with imbecile, feeble-minded or defective persons not certified under the Lunacy laws, and . . . to enquire into the expediency of amending the constitution, jurisdiction and working of the Commission in Lunacy and of other Lunacy authorities in England and Wales, or adopting some other system of supervising the care of lunatics and mental defectives.*'

For circumstances of appointment, see 131 H.C. Deb. 4 s. col. 966, 967. The 513 pages of the report contain a searching analysis of every aspect of the problem, leading to a complete scheme embodied in 213 recommendations, some of far-reaching character and involving important legal changes.

There were large numbers of mentally defective persons whose training was neglected, over whom no sufficient control was exercised, and whose irresponsible lives were productive of crime and misery, of much injury and mischief to themselves and to others, and of much continuous expenditure wasteful to the community and to individual families. The local 'permissive' system of public education for a limited section of mentally defective children was not supplemented by subsequent supervision and control, and was, in consequence, misdirected and unserviceable. Large numbers of people were committed to prisons for repeated offences; lunatic asylums were crowded with patients who might be treated in other ways more economically and efficiently, and there were at large numbers of uncontrolled mental defec-

tives of all ages, exposed to constant moral danger to themselves, who become a lasting source of injury to the community.

The Commission used the term mentally defective to cover two classes: lunatics, i.e. those who from disorder of the mind or decay of faculties have lost the power of managing their affairs, and idiots, imbeciles, feebleminded and moral imbeciles, i.e. those in whom the brain is undeveloped and will remain undeveloped throughout life. A detailed study is made of the definition of these types. As there were no statistics on which trustworthy estimates of the numbers involved could be made, medical investigators were appointed to inquire into 16 typical districts (11 in England, 4 in Ireland, 1 in Scotland). On the basis of their results it was estimated that apart from certified lunatics, in England and Wales ·46 per cent or 149,628 persons were mentally defective, 44·45 per cent of whom urgently needed provision in their own interest or for the public safety. The proportions for Scotland and Ireland were ·26 per cent and ·57 per cent respectively.

The principles the Commission adopted as the basis of its solution of the problem were as follows: (1) The powers of protection and supervision relating to lunatics should be extended to the mentally infirm and all other classes of mental defectives. This principle was new to English law. (2) Steps should be taken by the local authority to ascertain the number of defectives, 'who they are and where they are', and to bring them into relation with the local authority. This principle also was new. (3) The real claim of these persons to aid was their mental condition, and they should be treated primarily on the grounds of their defect, and not as paupers or criminals. The three methods of oversight, certification and detention should be used, according to the needs of the particular person. (4) Protection of the defective person should be continued as long as was necessary for his good. If necessary, protection should take the form of segregation and detention. (5) One central authority should be created to be the general guardian of all mentally defective persons. (6) The privileges enjoyed by lunatics, etc., regarding the protection of property should be extended to all mentally defective persons. (7) There should be the closest co-operation between the new central authority and the Chancery Division of the High Court.

In applying these principles to England and Wales, the following recommendations were made. A Board of Control, which should include medical and legal commissioners, should supervise all mentally defective persons, regulate their accommodation, maintenance, education and control, register, inspect and visit all hospitals and houses where they are maintained. The country should be divided into eight districts and assistant commissioners appointed to each. The local authorities should be the councils of counties and county boroughs, who should ascertain the numbers of mental defectives in their area and make provision for them. They should exercise their powers through a statutory committee called the Committee for the Care of the Mentally Defective, which should take over the duties of the Asylums Visiting Committee and some of those of the Education Committee. In London the authority should be a statutory committee of the L.C.C., and should take over the relevant duties of the Metropolitan Asylums Board. As the childhood and schooling of mental defectives could not be separated from their later life and no age could be given for its termination, the education of such children should be the responsibility of the new committee and not of the education committee. Besides providing special classes, homes, colonies, etc., the committee should have power, in certain circumstances, to take mentally defective persons into wardship up to the age of 21. There should

be powers to separate and detain weak-minded persons guilty of offences and on whom repeated punishment has had no effect; their treatment and discharge should be re-organized. Questions of the offence should be kept separate from questions of defect and treatment. Recommendations are made on the legal procedure in such cases, on securing medical certificates, on transfer after conviction to the care of the committee, instead of to prison. Arrangements should be made for the voluntary care of mental defectives at the request of parents or guardians; for the erection of intermediate hospitals, colonies, reception wards and for boarding out.

The annual cost of providing for mental defectives in the scheme proposed was estimated at £1,173,000 as compared with £541,000. The 4s. grant should be discontinued, and a block grant paid on the principles suggested by Balfour of Burleigh, or alternatively, as half the cost of maintenance and management.

The general principles should be adhered to in Scotland and Ireland, allowance being made for differences in the immediate problems. In Scotland the General Board of Lunacy should become the Board of Control, and the local authority, the District Board of Lunacy, should become the District Board for the Care of Mentally Defective Persons. The duties of the Inspectors of the Poor with regard to Lunacy should be extended to all cases of mental defect and their services placed at the disposal of the new District Board. In Ireland the central authority should be the Commission for the Care of the Mentally Defective, and the local authorities the councils of county and county boroughs acting through statutory committees. The general financial arrangements proposed for England and Wales should be applied to Scotland and Ireland, except that Ireland should be given a grant-in-aid for ten years towards the cost of the necessary accommodation.

In dissents, Dunlop objects to the

proposals for Scotland as being much more extreme than is called for, and Greene thought that the Commission should have made a clear pronouncement on the insufficiency of the law to protect defectives from sexual allurements and attacks and that positive and unqualified prohibition with punitive sanction was necessary. Vol. VI contains the reports of the enquiry, the first of its kind, designed to ascertain the number of defectives and epileptic persons in 16 selected areas.

Vols. I–IV. Mins. of ev., etc.; 1908 Cd. 4215, xxxv, 83.   1908 Cd. 4216, xxxvi, 1.   1908 Cd. 4217, Cd. 4218, xxxvii, 1.   Vol. V. Apps.; 1908 Cd. 4219, xxxviii, 1.   Vol. VI. Reps., etc.; 1908 Cd. 4220, xxxviii, 351.   Vol. VII. Rep., etc.; 1908 Cd. 4221, xxxix, 1. Vol. VIII. Rep.; 1908 Cd. 4202, xxxix, 159.

See *Mental Deficiency Act, 1913.* 3 & 4 Geo. 5. c. 28. *Lunacy Act (Scotland), 1913.* 3 & 4 Geo. 5. c. 38.

Infant and Child Mortality

L.G.B. 39th Ann. Rep. Supplement. Rep., apps. pp. 142. 1910

1910 *Cd. 5263, xxxix,* 973

A. Newsholme.

The object of the Report was to determine whether the reduction of infant mortality implies any untoward influence on the health of survivors to later years; to indicate the communities which are characterized by a continuing high rate of infant mortality; and to assess the relative value of the different factors of excessive infant mortality. A heavy infant death rate implies a heavier death rate up to the age of five, and it is doubtful whether any greater 'weeding out' is exercised by a larger than by a lighter infant death rate.   App. I gives the statistical evidence for this conclusion. The continuance of a high mortality rate in certain districts, e.g. Northumberland, Durham, Glamorgan, Lancashire, implies the prevalence of adverse

conditions which are a source of national weakness. While infant mortality is always higher in crowded centres of industry, a study of the causes of death and the fact that some urban areas have low rates show that much of it is preventible. Part III sets out the mutual responsibility of local authorities and parents. The chief reasons for a low infant mortality rate are efficient domestic and municipal sanitation, good housing and intelligent mothering. The recommendations include: the general adoption of the Notification of Births Act, better training and help for midwives, more health visitors. The authorities which should urgently improve their sanitary administration are named. App. II gives statistics for the separate counties.

See other supplements. *Infant and Child Mortality,* 2nd Rep.; 1913 Cd. 6909, xxxii, 1. *Maternal Mortality in Connection with Child Bearing;* 1914–16 Cd. 8085, xxv, 157. *Child Mortality at ages 0–5;* 1917–18 Cd. 8496, xvi, 1. This is based on statistics of 245 provincial towns and 29 metropolitan boroughs. Diagrams show the geographical distribution of infant deaths within particular areas. Specific improvements of the Maternity and Child Welfare Services are recommended. *Infant Mortality in Lancashire;* 1914 Cd. 7511, xxxix, 371.

Venereal Diseases

R. Com.

apptd. Nov., 1913

Lord Sydenham (*Ch.*), Jones, Digby, Fitzroy, Morris, Collie, Newsholme, Horsley, Lidgett, Mott, Scharlieb (Mary), Lane, Snowden, Creighton (Mrs. L.), Burgwin (Elizabeth M.).

'*To inquire into the prevalence of Venereal Diseases in the United Kingdom, their effects upon the health of the community, and the means by which those effects can be alleviated or prevented, it being understood that no return to the policy or provisions of the Contagious Diseases Acts of 1864, 1866, or 1869 is to be regarded as falling within the scope of the inquiry.*'

The First Report is a formal presentation of the following volume of minutes of evidence, etc.; 1914 Cd. 7475, xlix, 113.

—— Final Report, apps. pp. vi, 191. 1916. Mins. of ev., index. 1916
1916 *Cd.* 8189, *xvi*, 1. *Mins. of ev., etc.*; 1916 *Cd.* 8190, *xvi*, 215
sgd. Feb., 1916

The incidence rate of venereal diseases in the Forces is not greater than in normal times, but after a war an excessive incidence is bound to occur, and it is imperative that action should be taken without delay. The statistical information available is not adequate, but the numbers who had been infected with syphilis are not below 10 per cent of the population in large cities, while for gonorrhea the proportion is much larger. The report gives a detailed medical account of the diseases, the means by which they are transmitted and their effects. These include an enormous annual loss of child life, ophthalmia neonatorum, sterility in women, etc. The medical evidence establishes that by early and efficient treatment the diseases could be brought under control and reduced within narrow limits.

Except in the case of the Army and Navy, provision for the treatment of the diseases is extremely deficient. Extended facilities for diagnosis by laboratory methods should be organized and made available by county and county borough councils. The best modern treatment, both institutional and out-patient, should be made available to the whole community under conditions such that those affected will not hesitate to take advantage of it. It should be free, central grants of 75 per cent of local expenditure being provided. Compulsory notification should not be put into force at present, but should be reconsidered after experience of the operation of the scheme. Infected men in the Services whose time has not expired should be detained until they are pronounced free of infec-

tion. Advertisements of remedies for venereal diseases should be prohibited; venereal disease should constitute a ground for nullity, with safeguards for the legitimacy of children. A communication by a medical practitioner made bona fide to an interested person with a view to preventing or delaying marriage with an infected person should be a privileged communication.

There are numerous recommendations concerning better statistical information, the training of medical students, more careful instruction in all grades of education on moral conduct in sexual relations, and the preparation of teachers in training colleges to give such instruction though there should be no detailed sex instruction in elementary schools. The National Council for the Prevention of Venereal Disease should be recognized by the Government as an authoritative body for spreading knowledge. 'We are deeply sensible of the need and importance of appeals to conscience and honour.' Continuous efforts must be made to keep the question before the public mind.

Prevention and Treatment of Venereal Diseases

Memo. pp. 4. 1917

1917–18 *Cd.* 8509, *xxxviii*, 363

A memorandum by the L.G.B. summarizing the recommendations of the Commission, the action taken by the L.G.B. and the progress made with schemes of treatment.

Vivisection

R. Com.

apptd. Sept., 1906

Lord Selby (*Ch.*), Lockwood, Church, Collins, McFadyean, Chalmers, Ram, Gaskell, Tomkinson, Wilson.

'To enquire into and report upon the practice of subjecting live animals to experiments, whether by vivisection or otherwise, and also to enquire into the law

relating to that practice, and its administration: and to report whether any, and if so what, changes are desirable.'

Six Reports were formal presentation of the following volumes of minutes of evidence, etc.; 1907 Cd. 3326, Cd. 3462, xli, 649.   1908 Cd. 3757, Cd. 3955, Cd. 4147, lvii, 283.   1912–13 Cd. 6113, xlviii, 373.

—— Final Report. pp. v, 139. 1912
1912–13 *Cd.* 6114, *xlviii*, 401
sgd. March, 1912

add A. J. Ram (*Ch.*), del. Lord Selby (*Ch.*), Tomkinson.

Under the Act of 1876 no experiment calculated to give pain to an animal was to be performed except under licence by the Secretary of State, or in certain circumstances, by a High Court Judge. All such experiments were to be directed towards the advancement or testing of knowledge, and were subject to the restrictions that the animal must be under an anaesthetic, that if serious injury were inflicted or if pain were likely to continue afterwards, the animal must be killed before recovery from the anaesthetic, that such experiments were not to be made for the purpose of illustrating lectures, or made without anaesthetics on dogs, cats, horses, mules, asses. These restrictions could be dispensed with by means of statutory certificates of various types for different purposes, which could be granted only to licensed persons. The Home Secretary could appoint inspectors, and require the registration of any places where experiments were performed. There were three inspectors for Great Britain and for Ireland.

(*a*) Administration. Many complaints have been made against the administration of the Act. It was said that there had been disregard of pain by licensed experimenters, that some unlicensed experiments were made (qq. 8790, 10262). There had been a considerable body of criticism through anti-vivisectionist societies. Mrs. Lind-af-Hageby's book *The Shambles of Science*, withdrawn from circulation after a libel action, had been reprinted with the libellous sections omitted (q. 9105). Serious misgivings in the public mind had arisen from the grant of licences to two doctors holding extreme or untenable views. Though open to some criticism, the Act had been administered so as to afford a large protection to animals, without impeding research. With rare exceptions licensed experimenters had complied with the law loyally and in good faith. (*b*) The scientific results of experiments. After a review of the contributions to knowledge and technique both generally and in relation to particular diseases, the Commission concluded that the great preponderance of medical and scientific opinion was against the opponents of vivisection. Valuable knowledge had been added which could not have been obtained without the experiments and which had helped to reduce disease and mortality in man and animals. The value of the experimental method was demonstrated by new institutions such as the School of Tropical Medicine, the Research Fund for the Investigation of Cancer, research into tuberculosis, etc. (*c*) Immunity from pain. In the majority of Certificate A experiments the animals did not suffer pain, but subsequent results might produce suffering. (*d*) The morality of experiments. Experiments on animals, adequately safeguarded by law, faithfully administered, were morally justified and should not be prohibited. Inoculation might be painless primarily, but lead to suffering later. Limits should be placed on such suffering.

The chief recommendations were: the Home Office inspectorate should be increased; the Home Office consultations with the Association for the Advancement of Medical Research regarding the grant of certificates should cease; instead, there should be an advisory body appointed by the Home Secretary from persons suggested by the Royal Society and the Colleges of

Surgeons and Physicians. The persons selected should not themselves hold licences and their names should be published. Experimenters should be asked for special records in certain cases. There should be additional restrictions regulating the painless destruction of animals which show signs of suffering after an experiment, further limitations in the use of curare, and a stricter provision on the definition and practice of pithing.

In a memo. Lockwood, Collins and Wilson argued that the law should be amended to provide (1) for the undivided responsibility of the Home Secretary, and (2) for the killing of any animal on the advent of real or obvious suffering. In a separate reservation Wilson said that while in the main the accusations of infringement of the Act had not been proved, the useful results claimed had been greatly over-estimated, and the relief of human suffering small compared with the pain inflicted on animals to secure it.

Work in Connection with the War at present undertaken by the Medical Research Committee

Interim Rep. pp. 6. 1915

1914–16 Cd. 7922, xxxi, 533
sgd. May, 1915

The Report gives an account of the way in which the resources of the Council were used during the war. See 1st Ann. Rep.; 1914–16 Cd. 8101, xxxi, 539 and succeeding Ann. Reps.

Artificial Limbs

Dept. Cttee. Rep. pp. 12. 1919

1919 Non-Parl. Min. of Pensions
apptd. Feb., sgd. May, 1919

H. Guedalla (Ch.), Cockerill, Smith, Kenderine, Johnson, Cohen.

'To consider and advise whether, and if so in what respects, the existing arrangement for supply, fitting, repair, and refitting of artificial limbs should be modified particularly with a view to minimizing the delay experienced by limbless men in getting their requirements attended to. Whether it would be advantageous to the Ministry to provide and maintain one or more institutions for the supply and repair of artificial limbs and to employ partially disabled and limbless men on their work; whether the supplies of surgical instruments are satisfactory, or in what way could they be improved.'

The outbreak of war found British limb makers unable to cope with the demand, and the types supplied were not always suitable. Types should be standardized and supplied at prices laid down by the Ministry. Fitting centres should be under State control, and medical men should have opportunity to study at them. Repairs should be done at the centres, the State paying the costs. A government factory was not recommended.

Artificial Limbs

Committee. Report. pp. 10. 1921

1921 Non-Parl. Min. of Pensions
apptd. July, sgd. July, 1921

A. Williamson (Ch.), Pollard, Sinclair, Leahy, Atkinson, Meech, Webb.

'To enquire into the arrangements for the supply and repair of the various types of artificial limbs which are provided under the Royal Warrants and Orders in Council; and into the comparative advantages of the metal limbs.'

The Ministry's new standard pattern of wooden limb would prove satisfactory in most cases, but special cases, e.g. where very heavy legs were required, would have to be considered. The very light Desoutter limb should be supplied on the advice of the surgeon. The amount of refund to persons obtaining limbs for themselves should be the cost of what the surgeon certifies as suitable. The Ministry should be responsible for repairs and travelling expenses. There should be additional limb fitting centres at orthopaedic clinics.

Reports on Public Health and Medical Subjects (New Series)

Between 1909 and 1919 inclusive the Local Government Board issued 124 reports on Public Health and Medical subjects. Of these 18 concerned food, e.g. *Facing and other Methods of Preparing Rice for Sale*, the *Presence of Calcium Sulphate in Baking Powder and Self-Raising Flour*, *Bacterial Food Poisoning and Food Infections*. Over 30 reports dealt with the *Sanitary Circumstances* of a particular district; others with particular infections and diseases. There were a number on flies as carriers of infections. All except three are Non-Parliamentary Publications, and are listed in the *Catalogue* of Non-Parliamentary Publications, revised to 31st Dec., 1920, issued by H.M.S.O. in 1921, pp. 108–13. This series followed a long series of Medical Inspectors' Reports, listed on pages 120–5.

4. FOOD PURITY, DRUGS, PATENT MEDICINES

Epidemic Arsenical Poisoning Attributed to Beer

Rep., apps. pp. 25. 1901

1901 *Cd.* 459, *ix*, 255
sgd. Jan., 1901

G. S. Buchanan.

Gives a detailed account of the epidemic of 1900 and of cases where symptoms of poisoning were present in the deaths from other diseases to which beer drinkers are subject. It also describes the steps taken by the authorities to arrest the epidemic.

Arsenical Poisoning from the Consumption of Beer and other articles of Food and Drink

R. Com. 1st Rep. Pt. I. Rep. pp. vi, 10. 1901. Pt. II. Mins. of ev., apps., index. Vol. I. 1903

1901 *Cd.* 692, *ix*, 283. *Mins. of ev., etc.*;
1904 *Cd.* 1845, *ix*, 1
apptd. Feb., sgd. July, 1901

Lord Kelvin (*Ch.*), Dyke, Church, Thorpe, Bonsor, Whitelegge.

'To ascertain with respect to England and Wales; (1) The amount of recent exceptional sickness and death attributable to poisoning by arsenic; (2) Whether such exceptional sickness and death have been due to arsenic in beer or in other articles of food or drink, and, if so, (a) to what extent; (b) by what ingredients or in what manner the arsenic was conveyed; and (c) in what way such ingredients became arsenicated; and (3) If it be found that exceptional sickness and death have been due to arsenic in beer or in other articles of food or drink, by what safeguards the introduction of arsenic therein can be prevented.'

In 1900 3,000 persons died in Lancashire as a result of poisoning traced to beer contaminated with arsenic derived from sulphuric acid used in the manufacture of brewing sugar. Certain illnesses sometimes regarded as arising from heavy drinking may also be attributed to the presence of small quantities of arsenic in beer.

The introduction of arsenic can be avoided by the use of stringent tests. The statutory powers of the Medical Officer of Health under the Sale of Food and Drugs Act are limited to goods on sale and do not extend to the stage of manufacture, while the Customs Officers' powers are for preventing fraud on the revenue and not for testing for purity. Pending further consideration, the Board of Inland Revenue should specially detail the ingredients liable to become contaminated and prescribe tests for them.

—— Final Report. Pt. I. Rep. pp. iv, 52. 1903. Pt. II. Mins of ev., apps., index. Vol. II. 1903

1904 *Cd.* 1848, *ix*, 399. *Mins. of ev., etc.*;
1904 *Cd.* 1869, *ix*, 455
sgd. Nov., 1903

The Report discusses the 1900 outbreak of arsenical poisoning, the relation of beri-beri to arsenic, tests for arsenic in food and substances used in its manufacture, the ways in which food may be contaminated and the precautions which should be taken. There is little control over the manufacture of food. Control over sale is concerned with fraudulent adulteration rather than contamination, there are no official standards of impurity, and prosecutions are not against the manufacturer, importer or intermediate vendor, but against the retailer, who in the majority of cases had nothing to do with the contamination.

There should be more extended administration by the Local Government Board, which should have a scientific officer with access to laboratories. With the assistance of a Board of Reference of scientific men, official standards should be prescribed for foods, ingredients and substances used in their manufacture. The Sale of Food and Drugs Acts should be amended so that a defendant retailer could attach a manufacturer or intermediate vendor to the prosecution if he alleged that the article was sold in the condition in which it was received, or that the contamination was due to an ingredient. Medical Officers should have power to suspend the sale of suspected foods or ingredients.

Milk and Cream Regulations

Dept. Cttee. Rep. pp. iii, 72. 1901.
    Mins. of ev., app., index. 1901

1901 *Cd.* 491, *xxx*, 371. *Mins. of ev., etc.*; 1901 *Cd.* 484, *xxx*, 447 *apptd. Jan., sgd. Jan.,* 1901

Lord Wenlock (*Ch.*), Cowan, Craigie, Farmer, Murphy, Thorpe, Voelcker, Barham.

'*To enquire and report as to what regulations, if any, may with advantage be made by the Board of Agriculture under section 4 of the Sale of Food and Drugs Act,* 1899, *for determining what deficiency in any of the normal constituents of genuine milk or cream, or what addition of extraneous matter or proportion of water, in any sample of milk (including condensed milk) or cream, shall for the purposes of the Sale of Food and Drugs Acts,* 1875 *to* 1899,

raise a presumption, until the contrary is proved, that the milk or cream is not genuine.'

The prevalence of the adulteration of milk and the ease and readiness with which 'separated milk' obtained by methods of comparatively recent invention, could be added to 'tone down' the milk supply, suggested the need for more stringent regulations and the fixing of legal minimal limits. Of the three main classes of witnesses, the traders generally favoured laissez faire or a low statutory limit, while the producers were mostly concerned with a specified fat content. The third class, the public analysts, in practice were free and did work to divergent standards, but generally desired a uniform legal standard.

The Committee rejected limits varying between different districts, limits varying with the season, and different limits for different grades of milk. Regulations should be made under Section 4 of the Act, that the solids in milk should amount to 12 per cent, and that 3·25 per cent should be milk fat; adulteration should be presumed if the total milk solids were less than 12 per cent and non-fatty milk solids less than 8·5 per cent. The addition of artificial thickening should raise a presumption that the cream was not genuine. Limits were fixed for condensed milk. Steps should be taken to identify and ear-mark skimmed milk.

In a reservation Farmer suggested that owing to seasonal and daily variations of yield, and to the fact that this was more in evidence on the small farm, seasonal limits should be fixed for the two six month periods. In a Minority Report Barham stated that the Committee had been more concerned with defining the quality of 'average' than that of 'genuine' milk, that the majority of witnesses were in favour of a 3 per cent fat content. A low standard well worked was better than a high standard administered with laxity. He therefore recommended a seasonal standard of 3 per cent fat content for July-February and 2·75 for March-June.

The Use of Preservatives and Colouring Matters in the Preservation and Colouring of Food

Dept. Cttee. Rep., mins. of ev., apps., index. pp. xxxvi, 497. 1901

1902 *Cd. 833, xxxiv, 579*
apptd. July, 1899, sgd. —

H. Maxwell (*Ch.*), Thorpe, Bulstrode, Tunnicliffe.

'*To inquire into the use of preservatives and colouring matters in the preservation and colouring of food and to report* (1) *Whether the use of such materials or any of them, for the preservation and colouring of food, in certain quantities, is injurious to health, and if so, in what proportions does their use become injurious.* (2) *To what extent, and in what amounts, are they so used at the present time.*'

With the progress of chemistry, natural oils, sugar, salt, vinegar, etc., used to prevent or retard food decomposition were being replaced by chemicals known as 'anti-septics'. A test of 4,251 samples showed 39 per cent containing chemical preservatives, 71 samples containing more than one preservative. Whilst there was an extensive colouring of food the use of lead chromate, vermilion and Scheele's Green, all more or less poisonous, had disappeared, though sulphate of copper was used extensively with peas.

In urban conditions, the use in perishable goods of some preservatives, not necessarily chemical, might be necessary, and total prohibition might lead to food being withheld or consumed in a state of incipient putrifaction. The extent of the harm done depended on the agent used, the chief danger being the cumulative effect of small doses in many different goods. The use of any preservatives in milk or in dietetic preparations for infants or invalids, or in cream and butter of any preservatives other than boric acid,

etc., in proportions exceeding 0·25 per cent and 0·5 per cent respectively, or of formalin or formaldehyde, or copper salts for greening should be prohibited. As suggested in 1896, a scientific court of reference, or alternatively the L.G.B. should be empowered to schedule preservatives, etc., inimical to health.

See L.G.B. Ann. Rep. Supplement. W. G. Savage. Reps.; 1910 Cd. 5312, xxxix, 1.

Butter Regulations

Dept. Cttee. Interim Rep. pp. 7. 1902. Mins. of ev., apps. 1902

1902 *Cd. 944, xx, 123. Mins. of ev., etc.;*
1902 *Cd 1039, xx, 131*
apptd. July, 1901. sgd. Jan., 1902

H. Plunkett (*Ch.*), Anderson, Cameron, Craigie, Dunn, Gibbons, Gilchrist, Hickey, Kearley, Thomson, Thorpe.

'*To enquire and report as to what regulations, if any, may with advantage be made under Section 4 of the Sale of Food and Drugs Act, 1899, for determining what deficiency in any of the normal constituents of butter, or what addition of extraneous matter, or proportion of water in any sample of butter shall, for the purpose of the Sale of Food and Drugs Acts, raise a presumption, until the contrary is proved, that the butter is not genuine.*'

The large number of prosecutions in respect of an alleged excess of water in butter was attributed to the absence of Regulations. The weight of evidence was against leaving the question to public taste through the operation of supply and demand. The difficulty appeared to be that Irish salt firkin butter frequently contains up to 20 per cent water, which is a higher percentage than in any other butter coming on the market. This is due to the traditional method of making butter with brine. It is sold in Lancashire, Yorkshire and South Wales and is liked for its low price, distinctive flavour and long-keeping qualities. In carefully made butter the proportion of water is found to range from 10 per cent to 15 per cent. The Committee recommended the adoption of a limit of 16 per cent, on the assumption that butter containing a larger percentage of water than 16 per cent, will escape the operation of this limit provided that a sufficient disclosure is made to the purchaser.

See *Prevention of Butter Adulteration.* 2nd International Dairy Congress, Paris, 1905. Rep.; 1907 Cd. 3689, xvii, 149.

—— Final Report. pp. 28. 1903. Mins. of ev., apps., index. 1904

1903 Cd. 1749, *xvii*, 349. *Mins. of ev., etc.*; 1903 Cd. 1750, *xvii*, 379 *sgd. Dec.*, 1903

The second part of the enquiry resolved itself into what regulations should be framed for the purpose of directing an analyst when to raise the presumption that a sample of butter had been mixed with foreign fat. This led to an inquiry into the chemical nature of butter.

Butter fat is sharply distinguished from the vast majority of the natural fats, and in particular from those substances which are or may be used to mix with butter, by the circumstance that a considerable proportion of its acids, when separated by chemical means from the glycerin, are readily soluble in water. Other methods of discriminating between butter and margarine, or detecting a mixture of the two, are also used by the analysts. But the difficulty is that butter does not have a constant composition, which sometimes makes it difficult to establish the presumption, on the basis of a deficiency in the normal proportion of some one or other of its constituents, that the butter has been mixed with foreign fat. After having before them the tabulated results (see Apps.) of some thousands of determinations, more particularly of the volatile acids contained in butters of very variable origin, the Committee recommended that the figure 24 arrived at by the Reichert-Wollny method should be

the limit below which a presumption should be raised that butter is not genuine; that the use of 10 per cent of sesamé oil in the manufacture of margarine be made compulsory and that steps should be taken to obtain international co-operation. Craigie and Gilchrist did not agree with the limit of 24 being fixed without further enquiry, Dunn preferred the limit of 23, Hickey, in a separate report, stated that a majority of witnesses were against a fixed limit and rejected it accordingly. The Apps. contain Reports on *The Composition of British Butter*, T. E. Thorpe, and on *Water in Butter*, Committee of the Governors of the Munster Dairy School.

Butter Trade

Sel. Cttee. Rep., proc., mins. of ev., apps. pp. xl, 459. Index. 1906

1906 (245) (245-*Ind.*) *vii*, 1 *apptd. March, o.p. July*, 1906

E. Strachey (*Ch.*), Dalziel, Cornwall, Courthope, Lonsdale, Steadman, McMicking, Scott, Stuart, Williams, Warner, L. Morpeth, Beach, Flynn, Lundon.

'*To consider whether any, and if so what, further Legislation is required in order to secure the better conduct and control of the Trade in Butter and Butter Substitutes.*'

The legislature has always recognized that butter is an article of food by itself and has made special provisions for the regulation of trade. No mixture of margarine and butter which contains more than 10 per cent of butter fat may be made; imported margarine and adulterated butter must be labelled accordingly, and butter with 16 per cent of water is presumed not genuine. The evidence on adulterated butter and the irregularities connected with the sale of margarine showed some need for amendment in the law. In natural butter, curd is a normal constituent, but curd extracted from margarine is used as an adulterant and there is no statutory power under which a presumptive limit could be fixed. Blended or factory butter (butter mixed with butter) should not be prohibited, but should not contain more than 16 per cent moisture. Milk-blended butter should not be prohibited, but it is not butter and should be sold under a special name, the factories and wholesale premises dealing with it being registered and open to inspection. The addition of any fat not derived from milk should be prohibited. Margarine, whether from home sources or imported, should not contain more than 16 per cent moisture and when sold retail should be labelled margarine.

See *Irish Butter Industry*. 1910. p. 394.

Shellfish other than Oysters in Relation to Disease

L.G.B. 39th Ann. Rep. Supplement. Rep., apps. pp. viii, 243. 1911

1910 *Cd.* 5313, *xxxix*, 651

H. T. Bulstrode.

The supplement is a continuation of the Report on '*Oyster Culture in Relation to Disease*' submitted to the Board in 1894. The frequent outbreaks of enteric fever and gastro-enteritis are attributed to the sewage-contaminated laying beds, which have received little attention since it was pointed out in 1896 that there was urgent need for reform. The Report is based on a comprehensive study of the shellfish beds around the coast of England.

Short Weight

Rep.

1914 (359). See *Trade*. p. 127.

Schedule A to the Pharmacy Act, 1868. (Poisons)

Dept. Cttee. Pt. I. Rep. pp. xv. 1903. Pt. II. Mins. of ev., apps. index. 1903

1903 *Cd.* 1442, *xxxiii*, 1. *Mins. of ev., etc.*; 1903 *Cd.* 1443, *xxxiii*, 17
apptd. June, 1901. *sgd. Nov.*, 1902

H. Maxwell (*Ch.*), Cross, Thorpe, Tilden, Stevenson, Harrison, Hills.

'*To consider the First Schedule annexed to the Pharmacy Act, 1868, and to report the alterations therein which they deem expedient; and also to consider whether a third sub-division might not properly be added to the Schedule, containing substances which, whether sold by pharmaceutical chemists or not, should be labelled or otherwise distinguished, and, if so, to enumerate the substances which, in their opinion, should be so treated.*'

Since the passage of the Act, there had been a greatly increased use in agriculture and horticulture of poisons which could legally be sold only by a registered chemist or druggist. Prosecution of unregistered sellers by the Pharmaceutical Society had been effective in some areas but not in others, and where successful, e.g. against seedsmen, had caused farmers loss and inconvenience. Arsenic was transported in large quantities under conditions of laxity. Preparations for use in agriculture and sanitation should be placed in a third part of the schedule, the traffic in arsenic regulated, and changes made in Part I of Schedule A.

Cross thought there should be greater latitude in the sales of these substances for agricultural purposes. Hills, in a Minority Report argued that the demand for relaxation did not come from users but from unregistered persons who desired to sell the poisons. There was no ground for relaxation of restrictions, the Pharmaceutical Society's administration did not interfere with their use in agriculture. There should be efficient supervision of every shop selling poison by retail.

Poisons and Pharmacy Bill [H.L.]

Jt. Sel. Cttee. Proc., mins. of ev., apps., index. pp. xiii, 82. 1908

1908 (150) *ix*, 521
apptd. —, *o.p. May*, 1908

Lord Haversham, L. Saltoun, L. Stanley, L. Lawrence, L. Monk-Bretton, Atherley-Jones, Baring, Idris, Kennedy, Tuke.

The restriction of the sale of poisonous material to registered chemists had caused much inconvenience to farmers and gardeners in districts where there was no such qualified tradesmen. The Bill proposed a relaxation of this restriction to allow for the sale of poisons needed in agriculture, by a person holding a licence from a local authority. The Bill was reported with amendments.

Use of Cocaine in Dentistry

Cttee. Rep. pp. 7. 1917

1917–18 Cd. 8489, viii, 151
apptd. Nov., 1916. sgd. Feb., 1917

C. Hobhouse (Ch.), Baldwin, O'Grady, Ruegg, Bayliss.

'To consider the authorizations granted for the use of cocaine in dentistry, and to advise whether or not they should be continued or modified, and if continued in what cases and with what conditions.'

In the Autumn of 1915 the attention of the Home Office was drawn to the prevalence of the use of cocaine amongst soldiers in the London area, whereupon the importation of cocaine was prohibited, except under licence. This cut off supplies from 6,500 unregistered dentists—one-half the whole number of practising dentists—who have to use some other anaesthetic. No evidence was found of a cocaine habit amongst the people, but the drug was so potentially dangerous that restrictions should be put upon its sale. Preparations containing more than 1 per cent of cocaine required for dental work should be procurable only by registered dentists and members of an approved Dental Association, and only from registered chemists and other licensed persons, on condition that they were used for dental purposes only. Unregistered dentists practising bona-fide and satisfying their local authority should be entitled to be registered for the right to purchase preparations containing not more than 1 per cent of cocaine.

Patent Medicines

Sel. Cttee. Rep., proc., mins. of ev., apps. pp. lviii, 782. Index. 1914

1914 (414) (414-Ind.) ix, 1
re-apptd. June, o.p. Aug., 1914

H. Norman (Ch.), Bathurst, Cawley, Chapple, Dalziel, Hayden, Ingleby, Glyn-Jones, Jones, Lawson, Lynch, Magnus, Newton, O'Grady, Hill-Wood.

'To consider and inquire into the question of the sale of Patent and Proprietary Medicines and medical preparations and appliances, and advertisements relating thereto, and to report what amendments, if any, in the Law are necessary or desirable.'

The law regarding patent medicines was chaotic, being contained in fragmentary form in parts of overlapping statutes, no government department was officially concerned with the sale or advertisement of these articles, nor was any person charged with the duty of seeing that the law was carried out. The difficulties in the way of successful prosecutions were almost insuperable.

The 'remedies' on sale varied from genuine scientific preparations and unobjectionable remedies for simple ailments to secret remedies making fraudulent claims, causing injury by leading sick persons to delay proper treatment, containing disguised large proportions of alcohol, professing to cure diseases, e.g. cancer and consumption, incurable by medicaments, or being sold for improper purposes, e.g. abortifacients (the latter sometimes resulting in blackmail). Names were invented, composition changed and persons of social position and even medical practitioners induced to give unfounded testimonials. At least £2 mn. was spent on advertising, and although some of the better press exercised some censorship, many papers and journals did not; and successful prosecutions were sometimes not reported. It was a grave and growing evil, practically uncontrolled by law, except as regards scheduled poisons and gross impropriety.

Amongst the Committee's proposals

were: the administration of the law should be co-ordinated under one department, the L.G.B. or a Ministry of Health, if created, and a competent officer, aided by inspectors, appointed to deal with enforcement. All manufacturers, proprietors and importers of patent medicines and medicated wines should be registered, and a full statement of ingredients and therapeutic claims sent to the department, the Government Chemist checking their accuracy by confidential analysis. A

Commission should be appointed to permit or prohibit in the public interest or for non-compliance, any such secret remedy, any aggrieved person having a right of appeal to the High Court.

The distinction made under the Stamp Acts between the name of an ailment and of an organ should be removed; false descriptions, advertisements of abortifacients inviting correspondence with vendors, and claims to cure certain diseases, should be prohibited.

XIII. HOUSING

Housing of the Working Classes

Jt. Sel. Cttee. Rep., proc., mins. of ev., apps., index. pp. xviii, 173. 1902

1902 (325) v, 801
apptd. Feb., o.p. Aug., 1902

Lord Camperdown (Ch.), L. Carrington, L. Hampden, L. Hatherton, L. Wenlock, L. Sandhurst, L. Lamington, Bond, Collings, Crean, Hay, Kearley, Macnamara, Tuke.

'To consider the Standing Orders relating to houses occupied by persons of the labouring class and the Clauses usually inserted in Private and Local Bills and Provisional Order Confirmation Bills in pursuance thereof; and to report whether any amendments should be made in such Standing Orders and Clauses, and especially whether any and what provision should be made for better securing the re-housing of all persons of the labouring class who may be displaced in connection with the undertakings to which the Bills relate, whether displaced under the powers given by the Bills, or otherwise.'

As evasions of the Standing Orders had taken place, the Home Office had asked that they should be re-worded. The Committee recommended that where houses of the working classes were proposed to be taken, the Central Authority should be notified of every case in London, and outside London of cases in which thirty persons were displaced in any one borough, urban

or rural district. The Central Authority should have full discretion in settling schemes and power to fix the rents of the new houses, which should be suitable for the working classes and not too ambitious in character. The Committee submitted two new model clauses, and three Standing Orders (pp. ix, xiii, xv).

Housing of the Working Classes Acts Amendment Bill

Sel. Cttee. Reps., proc., mins. of ev., apps. pp. cxxiv, 467. 1906. Index. 1907

1906 (376) (376-Ind.) ix, 1
apptd. April, o.p. Dec., 1906

J. Dickson-Poynder (Ch.), Dunne, Mackarness, Morrell, Rowlands, Vivian, Bethell, Lane-Fox, Lockwood, Smith, Ginnell.

A Rural District could not adopt Part III of the Housing of the Working Classes Act, 1890, without the consent of the county council, which had to take into account the probability of the houses being provided without the use of the Act, the rate liability, etc. In only nine cases had the Act been adopted. The Bill, which aimed at promoting the building of houses by removing the restriction, was reported without amendment.

Special Report.—The Act of 1890

was intended primarily for towns and only incidentally for rural districts, in which it was a dead letter. The diminution of population in some and stagnation in other country districts were due to many causes not dealt with by the Bill, including the lack of supervision of existing houses. The insanitary condition of much cottage property was due to the perfunctory administration of the ample powers rural districts possessed. There was little or no inspection in many rural districts, which refrained from claiming the grant of one-half the salary of the medical officer in order to retain the full right of appointment and dismissal; in 337 cases appointments were annual. The office of inspector of nuisances was subject to similar conditions and often combined with and subordinate to that of the surveyor of highways. Such officers were reluctant to cause friction with the appointing authority or to propose plans which might increase the rates.

The shortage of cottages was due to the fact that the cost of building, exclusive of land and water supply, was £150-£170, which necessitated a rent of 3s. 7d., as compared with the prevailing agricultural rents of 1s. to 2s. 6d. While richer farmers and landowners could afford to provide cottages as a means of securing agricultural labour, the poorer farmer was reluctant to mortgage his farm to subsidize rents.

The administration of public health and housing legislation should be transferred from rural districts to county councils, which should be required to appoint a statutory public health and housing committee to which its powers should be delegated. They should also be required to appoint a full-time medical officer and inspectors; to prepare and maintain by house-to-house survey a register of all houses and tenements, their age, sanitary condition, state of repair, number of rooms and occupants, etc., and to make bye-laws for every district. Rural district councils should have concurrent powers with county councils under

Part III of the Act. The L.G.B. should have a special housing and public health Department, with a staff of inspectors; and should be empowered, on complaint by rural local authorities or by householders of default by a county council, after enquiry to make an order enforceable by *mandamus* and to appoint persons to execute such order at the county council's expense. The acquisition of land compulsorily on the basis of rateable value should be made easier, the rate of interest on loans for housing, etc., reduced to the lowest rate at which the Treasury could borrow and the period of redemption lengthened. Exchequer grants should be made to necessitous areas and allocated at the discretion of the L.G.B.

House-Letting, Scotland

Dept. Cttee. Rep. Vol. I. Rep. pp. 26. 1907. Vol. II. Mins. of ev., apps., index. 1907

1907 *Cd. 3715, xxxvii, 1. Mins. of ev., etc.;* 1908 *Cd. 3792, xlvii, 1 apptd. Nov., 1906. sgd. Aug., 1907*

Lord Guthrie (*Ch.*), Binnie, Cox, Dobbie, Esslemont, Howden, Stirling-Maxwell.

'*To inquire into and report upon alleged grievances connected with the letting of working men's dwellings in Scotland.*'

Since 1890 there had been nine Bills dealing with the grievances. For the purpose of the inquiry the Committee regarded as workmen's dwellings those let at not more than £20; four-fifths of the houses occupied by workmen in Glasgow were rented at not more than £16.

'The grievances complained of by the tenants of workmen's dwellings are mainly, *first*, the Scotch system of letting by missives for yearly tacks— that is, the practice of letting all but the poorest class of working men's houses for a whole year, to tenants whose occupation requires them to shift their residences frequently throughout the year, as compared with the weekly or monthly lets of similar houses to similar tenants in England; *second*, the practice of calling upon the occupants of working men's dwellings to contract for such yearly houses four months before the term of entry; and *third*, the demand made on working men to pay their rates, both municipal and parish council, in one sum, in winter, when work is scarcest and when household expenses are highest.' Landlords complained of the cost and slowness of the procedure for evicting undesirable or non-paying tenants; the local authorities of the loss of rates, under direct collection, through failure to pay, and of excessive allowances to ratepayers pleading poverty.

The recommendations included: 'that no agreements for tenancy of such houses, verbal or written, made more than two months prior to the date of entry, shall be binding; that it shall be sufficient, in weekly lets of such houses, to give three days' notice; in monthly lets, one week's notice; and, in all other lets, one month's notice of termination of tenancy'. Owners liable for rates should be entitled to an allowance for cost of collection and loss, and for periods of non-occupation. Rating authorities should be empowered to collect rates from owners of houses under £10, and to collect tenant's rates by instalments. Furniture, etc., of tenants should be exempt from diligence of creditors for rent, rates, etc., up to £10. In a memo. Binnie recommended that the owners' allowance for collection should be 15 per cent and that since in 1904 20,887 Glasgow ejectment orders had cost landlords 570 years' rent, plus arrears, the procedure should be simplified, as in London.

App. I. *Practice of Compounding for Rates in the Administrative County of London*. E. Harper.

Moveable Dwellings Bill [H.L.]

Sel. Cttee. HL. Rep., proc., mins. of ev., apps. pp. viii, 88. 1909. Rep., proc. pp. xv. 1910

1909 (*HL*. 199) *x*, 195. 1910 (*HL*. 146) *ix*, 141
apptd. May, 1909, *re-apptd.* March, *o.p.* July, 1910

Lord Salisbury (*Ch.*), L. Northumberland, L. Russell, L. Liverpool, L. Zouche, L. Clifford, L. Farrer.

Apart from a small number of persons who use moveable dwellings as a pastime, van-dwellers are of two classes, showmen and the gipsy class. For showmen no legislation was required. Mr. Horne, the chaplain of their Guild, stated that there were 4,000 vans and 12,000 souls. The trade was perfectly honest and respectable and its members were well-to-do and in some cases even thriving. There was no complaint against them, but the showmen sometimes complained that localities used existing restrictions to prevent shows.
The gipsy class should be distinguished from tramps—the large nomad population coming from the cities to do hop-picking, pea-picking, etc., who sleep under hedges, in barns and casual wards, and not in vans, and who are a 'terror to the neighbourhood'. Gipsies were cleaner than the East End hop-pickers, but had primitive views as to the rights of property, especially in respect of what grows and moves on the earth in a more or less wild state, and were given to petty pilfering. Where they congregated in numbers, e.g. the commons in Surrey, problems of sanitation might arise. The case for further legislation had been made out.
The Bill proposed that moveable dwellings should be registered, that sanitary regulations should be prescribed by the L.G.B., and that the local authorities should have powers to prohibit the encampment of moveable dwellings if they were considered dangerous or a nuisance to public health.
The Committee rejected the registration of moveable dwellings as impracticable and a policy of hunting them from place to place as inequitable. County councils should have power,

where van dwellers were of such numbers as to involve the evils described, to provide camping grounds, on which regulations could be enforced, the users being charged a small fee; and where such grounds were provided, to prohibit the use of commons, open spaces, roadside wastes, etc. Powers of compulsory purchase of land were not recommended.

Back - to - Back Houses. Relative Mortality in Through and Back to Back Houses in certain Towns in the West Riding of Yorkshire

Rep., app. pp. 48. 1910

1910 *Cd. 5314, xxxviii*, 893

L. W. Darra Mair.

In 1906 Dewsbury Town Council asked the L.G.B. to approve bye-laws containing a provision permitting, under certain restrictions, the erection of back-to-back houses. The L.G.B.'s conditions for sanction that the amount of air space provided should equal the minimum required by its model bye-laws for 'through' houses was objected to because this would have meant 20 ft. instead of 10 ft. between the blocks of four. The L.G.B. therefore decided upon the inquiry.

The basis was a comparison of death rates in structurally sound back-to-back and through houses of a similar class, situated in healthy areas in thirteen towns in the West Riding. The statistics were taken over ten years, and corrected for variations in age and sex composition. There was a 15 per cent to 20 per cent excess in death rate, even in good back-to-back houses over that in through houses, though this was not evident where the former had cross ventilation through being built in blocks of four; but for all types of back-to-back houses there was excessive mortality from diseases of the chest and those associated with the growth of young children. Though back-to-back houses had lower rents than through houses, the difference is recouped in better health.

Intercepting Traps in House Drains

Dept. Cttee. Rep., apps. pp. 77. 1912.
Mins. of ev. 1912

1912–13 *Cd. 6359, xxix*, 723. *Mins. of ev.;* 1912 *Non-Parl. Min. of Health apptd. Oct.*, 1908. *sgd. Dec.*, 1911

L. W. Darra Mair (*Ch.*), Malet, Pearson.

'*To inquire and report with regard to the use of intercepting traps in house drains.*'

'The investigation nominally originated with a proposal of the Willesden Urban District Council to adopt a series of building bye-laws, in which the requirement as to the provision of the intercepting trap was to be omitted. The L.G.B. refused their assent to this proposal, but promised an enquiry.'

The report consists of a detailed technical investigation, which concluded that the intercepting trap had serious disadvantages and that its necessity on bacteriological or epidemological grounds had not been established. The characteristic of sewer air of practical importance is its smell, and as offensive odours affect the comfort and probably the health of individuals, public health authorities should reduce the possibility of its penetrating to the atmosphere. The question whether in order to prevent such a nuisance in exceptional cases the intercepting trap is or is not required in any locality must be considered by the local authority in the light of local conditions.

Rent Increases in Scotland

Rep.

1914–16 *Cd.* 8111. See *Breviate 1917–39*, p. 449.

XIV. EDUCATION

1. **General: Schools, Scholarships**
2. **Health of School Children, Curriculum**
3. **Teachers' Salaries and Training**
4. **Universities, Scientific Institutions**
5. **Galleries, Museums, Public Records**

1. GENERAL: SCHOOLS, SCHOLARSHIPS

Special Reports on Educational Subjects

A Series of reports edited by M. E. Sadler. For a full list see App. II, p. 451.

Education Board Provisional Order Confirmation (London) Bill. [H.L.]

Sel. Cttee. Reps., proc. pp. v. 1901

1901 (322) *vi*, 279
apptd. Aug., o.p. Aug., 1901

J. Gorst (*Ch.*), Boland, Griffith-Boscawen, Emmott, Jones, Morton, Platt-Higgins, Powell.

In the acquisition of sites in populous districts by the London School Board, the greatest care should be taken to provide for the re-housing of the people displaced and that each re-housing should take place, wherever possible, before the houses to be acquired are demolished.

Children under Five Years of Age in Public Elementary Schools

Reps. pp. iii, 155. 1905

1906 *Cd.* 2726, *xc*, 29
apptd. April, 1904

'*An inquiry relative to the age of admission of infants to Public Elementary Schools and the curriculum suitable for very young children.*'

Five women inspectors—Miss Munday, Miss Bathurst, Miss Callis, Miss Heale, Miss Harrington—made visits of inspection and submitted separate reports. These are summarized in an Introductory Memo. by Cyril Jackson.

There had been a careful examination of some thousands of children and opinion was unanimous that those between the ages of three and five received practically no intellectual advantage from school instruction, the mechanical teaching seeming to dull their powers of imagination. The children admitted later could soon attain the same standard as those who had been educated for two years. Children under five should be given not formal education, but opportunities for free expression. If they had good homes it would be better to keep them there, but those of poorer parents are improved in physique by the regularity of school life, and should go to nursery schools rather than ordinary schools. The best informed teacher is not necessarily the best for babies. There should be special training for infant teachers.

Education Rates

Rep.

1907 *Cd.* 3313. See *Local Government.* p. 48.

School Attendance of Children below the Age of Five

Consultative Cttee. Rep., ev., apps. pp. 350. 1908

1908 *Cd.* 4259, *lxxxii*, 527
apptd. — sgd. —

A. H. D. Acland (*Ch.*), Benson, Bryant (Mrs. S.), Cleghorn (Miss I.), Glazebrook, Gray, Hibbert, Hobhouse, Jackman, Manley (Miss L.), Mansbridge, Moore, Paton, Reichel, Sadler, Sandford, Shackleton, Sidgwick, Sidgwick (Mrs. E. M.), Waller, Went.

'To consider and advise the Board of Education in regard to the desirability, or otherwise, both on educational and other grounds, of discouraging the attendance at school of children under the age of (say) five years, on the assumption that, in the event of the change being found generally desirable, the moneys now payable by the Board of Education in the shape of grants in respect of the attendance of such children, should still be payable to Local Education Authorities, in greater relief of their expenditure in educating the children over five years of age.'

The practical results of the inquiry by the women inspectors were embodied in Article 53 of the 1905 Code, which stated that 'where the local authority had so determined in the case of any school maintained by them, children under five years of age may be refused admission to that school'.

Although it had been the practice for children between the ages of 3 and 5 to attend school if their parents wished, and about one-third of them did so, there was diversity of opinion as to what age was most desirable in the interests of the child and the community. Many medical authorities held that the public elementary school was not the proper place for young children, some maintaining that a poor home was preferable to the atmosphere of existing classrooms (pp. 27-32). Most other witnesses, e.g. teachers, agreed that the ideal home was preferable to school, but that the school was better than poor homes, the dangers of the street or the undesirable 'minder', etc. The decision to admit or to exclude children had to a large extent been influenced by local conditions, some authorities just accepting the tradition, some, where accommodation was adequate, being influenced by grant payments, while others, faced with a growing population and pressure on space, had excluded the under fives, and used the space for the older children in the hope of avoiding capital expenditure on new buildings.

The conditions of home life in many large towns made it necessary to provide opportunities for the training and education of great numbers of little children, whose parents should be encouraged to make use of them. To turn children out of school was to abandon them to poor homes, the street, etc., whilst, given the conditions of the nursery school, the modern crèche and kindergarten, children could be brought under trained staffs into a free, healthy environment which would be so beneficial to their health, morals and educational chances. The Committee recommended nursery schools attached to public elementary schools, in which there should be no mental pressure, no formal lessons and no undue physical discipline. No teacher of infants should have more than 30 children, unless assisted by nurse attendants or school helps. There should be a great improvement in the building of nursery schools, and present accommodation should be improved by removing galleries and heavy furniture. Grants should be made equal to those for older children, in order to allow purely educational motives to influence local authorities. In order to stop any mental over-pressure of the children, higher grants should be based on age and not on attainment.

Devolution by County Education Authorities

Consultative Cttee. Rep., apps. pp. vi, 81. 1908

1908 *Cd. 3952, lxxxii, 439 apptd. —, sgd. Feb., 1908*

A. H. D. Acland (*Ch.*), Benson, Bryant (Mrs. S.), Cleghorn (Miss I.), Gray, Hibbert, Hobhouse, Jackman, Manley (Miss L.), Mansbridge, Moore, Paton, Reichel, Sadler, Sandford, Shackleton, Sidgwick, Sidgwick (Mrs. E. M.), Waller, Went.

'To consider and advise the Board of Education what methods are desirable and possible, under existing legislation, for securing greater local interest in the *administration of elementary education in administrative counties by some form of devolution or delegation of certain powers and duties of the Local Authority to district or other strictly local committees.'*

Under existing legislation it is not possible to frame schemes of devolution of great variety and extent. (i) Under Schedule I A (6) of the Education Act, 1902, an education committee may appoint local sub-committees with all the powers entrusted to the Education Committee itself, save the power of raising rates or borrowing. Of 61 counties concerned, 32 have appointed such committees. (ii) Under Section 7 (1)(a) or Schedule I B (4) of the Act, the authority may issue to the managers of its schools directions which may either leave them with little or no discretion or may devolve wide powers upon them. In 22 counties the only devolution is to individual bodies of managers. (iii) Counties unwilling to grant more than a limited discretion to managers of single schools may give more freedom to managers of schools grouped under Section 12 of the Act: 7 authorities have grouped schools in that way. Bodies of managers of grouped schools may be formally constituted sub-committees of the Education Committee.

The arguments in favour of devolution were based on the need to enlist local interest, those against it on economy and educational and administrative efficiency. There are a certain number of counties where local sub-committees might be an advantage. Systems of devolution which have been adopted have no apparent connection with the geographical or social conditions of the counties, personal and educational traditions having nearly as close a bearing upon it. An advanced system of devolution which postulated the existence of a considerable number of efficient and interested educationalists would not be successful where these are not forthcoming. Those counties which retained a centralized form of administration should study the details in the report.

Partial Exemption from School Attendance

Inter-Dept. Cttee. Vol. I. Rep. pp. iv, 18. 1909. Vol. II. Mins. of ev., apps., index. 1909

1909 Cd. 4791, xvii, 731. *Mins. of ev., etc.;* 1909 Cd. 4887, xvii, 753 *apptd. July,* 1908. *sgd. July,* 1909

C. Trevelyan (*Ch.*), L. Clifford, L. Sheffield, Rea, Lindsell, Bellhouse, Cross, Garnett, Gee, Oldroyd.

'(1) To inquire into and report upon the extent to which existing enactments relating to partial exemption from compulsory school attendance are taken advantage of in urban and rural areas in England and Wales; the occupations in which children so exempted are employed; and the effect of such occupations upon the general education and industrial training of the children. (2) To consider the practical effects of legislation providing for the abolition or restriction of half-time employment upon industries and wage-earning, and upon education organization and expenditure. (3) To report whether and to what extent, in view of these considerations, it is desirable to amend the law by raising the age at which partial exemption from attendance at Public Elementary Schools is to be permitted, or by raising the minimum age for total exemption concurrently with affording facilities for partial exemption.'

The law governing partial and total exemption from attendance at school was rather complicated and uncertain. Subject to certain exceptions, the ordinary obligation on the parent under the Education Acts is to send his child to school between 5 and 14 years of age, but all Education Authorities are required to make bye-laws and some half-dozen of them fixed 13 as the school leaving age. No child between the ages of 5 and 11 can obtain exemption, except for a reasonable excuse, such as that it is under efficient instruction in some other manner, is ill, or resides, e.g., more than two miles from the nearest school. Under certain conditions, partial exemption could be claimed at 12 for employment under the Factory Acts, and total exemption if a prescribed standard of efficiency had been reached, but the majority obtain partial exemption by satisfying the alternative of a given number of attendances. There was a material difference between the nature of partial exemption in the textile districts, where a child worked half of the week in the mill and the other half in school, and the agricultural districts, where a child was allowed entire exemption from school during the summer and part of the autumn.

In 1906–7 the average numbers of partial exemption scholars were 34,306 employed in factories, 3,800 in agriculture and 9,254 in other employments, e.g. as domestic helps (principally at home), errand boys, carters and milk boys, golf caddies, hawkers, or in dairy work, dressmaking, tailoring, rag sorting, hurdle making, sea-fishing. Although there had been a rise in the numbers of half-timers, they were used very little for subordinate industries where the half-time system was not already the custom in the staple industry of a district. The problem was really confined to certain parts of the textile industries in Yorkshire, Lancashire and Cheshire, and to certain agricultural districts.

The half-time system which began with the Education Clauses of the Factory Acts 1833 and 1844, was the only effective system of compulsory education before 1870. The situation was now reversed; the half-time system deprived children of educational opportunities, and was now condemned by all those considering it from the educational point of view. Half-time depends more on custom than on provable necessity. All partial exemption (from January, 1911), total exemption under the age of 13 and the Attendance Certificate for total exemption should be abolished. Total exemption at the age of 13 should be granted only for the purposes of beneficial or necessary employment, the ordinary condition being attendance at a continuation class, or as an alter-native, the passing of Standard VI. While no reliable estimate could be made of additional total costs due to the changes, it is not likely to be serious.

Attendance, Compulsory or Otherwise at Continuation Schools

Consultative Cttee. Vol. I. Rep., apps., index. pp. 324, xxvii. 1909. Vol. II. Summaries of ev., index. 1909

1909 Cd. 4757, xvii, 1. Summaries of ev., etc.; 1909 Cd. 4758, xvii, 353 apptd. — sgd. —

A. H. D. Acland (Ch.), Bryant (Mrs. S.), Chapman, Clay, Cleghorn (Miss I.), Durham (Miss F. H.), Glazebrook, Hibbert, Hobhouse, Jackman, Manley (Miss L.), Mansbridge, Moore, Paton, Reichel, Sadler, Shackleton, Sharples, Smith, Tuke (Miss M. J.), Went.

'To consider Clause 8 of the Education Bill for Scotland recently introduced, and to advise as to its applicability to England and Wales; and, whether apart from or in addition to such legislative change, to consider and advise the Board of Education as to whether any means, and if so what, can be devised, in respect of rural areas and of urban areas respectively, for securing (i) that a much larger proportion of boys and girls should on leaving the Public Elementary School commence and continue attendance at Evening Schools than at present do so; and (ii) that employers and other persons or bodies in a position to give effective help shall co-operate in arranging facilities for such attendance on the part of their employés, and in planning suitable courses and subjects for the schools and classes.'

The Parliamentary discussions on Clause 8 of the Education Bill coincided in point of time with the Inquiry, and the Education (Scotland) Act, 1908 was passed before the report was printed. As finally passed, it made it the duty of the school board to provide continuation classes for children above 14, and they were empowered to require attendance up to 17. At the most critical period of their lives a majority of boys and girls are left without guidance and care. There are 170,000 between 12 and 14 who have left school and attend no day classes, others still at school but engaged part-time in wage earning occupations, while 74 per cent of 2,000,000 between 14 and 17 receive no continued education. They lack technical, physical and mental training. An enquiry by Mr. R. H. Tawney, confirmed by other evidence, shows that new developments in industry are multiplying non-educative, blind alley employments for boys and girls. Apprenticeship is declining and there is a large class of boys and girls who are neither apprentices nor learners, which constitutes the chief argument for continuation schools.

The work of the continuation schools must be based on that of the day schools, where smaller classes, better provision of playing fields and organized games, and more fully trained teachers are required. Except in the case of boys in agriculture and girls in rural districts, exemption from school below 14 should be abolished. Juvenile Employment Registries should be established to advise children up to 17 on the choice of employment. Compulsory continuation schools will be ultimately advantageous, but it is best to proceed by local option. The local authority should be required to provide continuation classes, and empowered to make bye-laws requiring attendance, limiting the hours of work and education combined, and forbidding street trading under 17. Separate bye-laws might be made for boys and girls, and for those in special occupations. It should be the statutory duty of employers to enable their employees up to 17 to attend. The cost of raising the school age to 13 would be £53,000, of raising it to 14 £489,000, exclusive of loan charges, and of universal compulsory continuation classes up to 17 £2,625,000.

Cost of School Buildings

Dept. Cttee. Rep., abstracts of ev., apps., index. pp. iii, 114.   1911

1911 *Cd. 5534, xvii,* 9
apptd. Feb., sgd. Dec., 1910

L. A. Selby-Bigge (*Ch.*), Kershaw, Clay.

'*To inquire and report*—(*a*) *Whether the cost of buildings for Public Elementary Schools can properly, and with due regard to their suitability and durability, be reduced by the use of materials or methods of construction different from those ordinarily employed at present; and, if so,* (*b*) *What steps should be taken to facilitate the adoption of such materials or methods, and whether any alteration in the law is required for the purpose.*'

Standards of ventilation, lighting, heating, sanitation and general comfort, as well as methods of instruction, classification and staffing had undergone such a rapid change that it had amounted to little less than a revolution since 1870. Buildings soon became outmoded and good structures had to be extensively remodelled to meet the changed requirements. In addition, movements of population have made 15-20 years a consideration in the life of a school building. In 1870, 8 sq. ft. at a cost of £5-£6 a place was considered sufficient, while in 1911 the minimum for children over 8 was 10 sq. ft. at a cost of £10 per place. Much saving can be effected by good designing, attention to details and to the 'useful life' of school buildings. Hardly any other materials than bricks and stones had been used, and the committee was much embarrassed in their enquiry by the small number of buildings erected on novel lines which were comparable with school buildings. Local Authorities should be encouraged to submit specific proposals for the use of novel materials or methods, a condition of approval being the periodical inspection of the structure. To facilitate experiments, such buildings should be exempt from bye-laws, and the buildings regulations of the Board of Education should be revised. Loans should be granted for 30 years until further experience is available as to the durability of such structures.

Building Regulations for Public Elementary Schools being Principles to be Observed in Planning and Fitting up New Buildings in England; 1914 Cd. 7516, lxiv, 53.

Educational Endowments

Dept. Cttee. Vol. I. Rep. pp. 43. 1911. Vol. II. Mins. of ev., apps., index. 1911

1911 *Cd.* 5662, *xvii*, 125. *Mins. of ev., etc.;* 1911 *Cd.* 5747, *xvii*, 171 *apptd.* —, *sgd. March,* 1911

C. Trevelyan (*Ch.*), Bickersteth, Bowyear, Harris, Henderson, Hughes (Miss), Jones (F. A.), Jones (W.), Lindsell, Parker, Pember, Pitts, Rogers, Bridgeman.

'*To inquire into the administration of (a) Endowments the income of which is applicable, or is applied to or in connection with, Elementary Education, and (b) small Education Endowments other than the above, in rural areas, the application of which to their proper purposes presents special difficulties; and to consider how far under the existing law it is possible to utilize them to the best advantage; and whether any and, if so, what changes in the law are desirable in the direction of conferring upon County and other Local Authorities some powers in respect of such Educational Endowments or otherwise.*'

Endowments up to the end of the seventeenth century were generally established in places which then possessed a considerable population and contemplated subjects not now regarded as elementary. Where the endowment was sufficient and where the place was suitable secondary education developed, but where these conditions did not exist, by the beginning of the nineteenth century the education given had become indistinguishable from the elementary education. Throughout the nineteenth century the financial requirements of elementary education were increasing, and endowments for purely elementary education were absorbed in the developing system, but were outmoded

as the costs were taken over by the State, e.g. trusts for the payment of poor children's school fees when all school fees were abolished. The Education Act, 1902, cast on the Board of Education an enormous amount of detailed work in connection with the endowments which a central department could not perform efficiently.

The powers of the Board of Education regarding endowments should be transferred by order to county councils, including the L.C.C., except that it should retain control of those solely for religious education, the sites and buildings of non-provided schools, etc., and should determine appeals. The range of objects to which trust funds could be applied should be widened. There are reservations by various members.

Examinations in Secondary Schools

Consultative Cttee. Rep., summaries of ev., apps., index. pp. xviii, 596, xi. 1911

1911 *Cd.* 6004, *xvi*, 159 *sgd.* —

A. H. D. Acland (*Ch.*), Bowerman, Bryant (Mrs. S.), Chapman, Clay, Cleghorn (Miss I.), Cookson, Durham (Miss F. H.), Easterbrook, Fitzpatrick, Hibbert, Mansbridge, Moore, Paton, Reichel, Sadler, Tuke (Miss M. J.), Turnor, Jackman, Sharples.

'*To consider when and in what circumstances examinations are desirable in Secondary Schools (a) for boys and (b) for girls.*'

Examination at entrance and during school life are of minor urgency and are dealt with in notes A and B after the main report. They were approved of as being well-recognized machinery which was adapted to the particular schools and particular districts in which the schools were situated. But a warning was given that no internal examination should be held merely to obtain results, either for the award of prizes, or for any other purpose than to help forward the general course of instruction and to be of real educational value.

External examinations were the 'crux of the whole problem' and the report is mainly confined to them. The problem was complicated by its history, by the delay which occurred before the organization of secondary education was undertaken by the State, and by the number and variety of bodies, educational and professional, which had in the meantime become actively concerned with the matter.

After the middle of the nineteenth century external examinations developed in three ways: (1) the introduction of open competition by examination in the Indian and Home Civil Service as a means of preventing patronage; (2) the reform of the Universities of Oxford and Cambridge after 1854 and 1856, when the removal of restrictions in the election of scholars stimulated the better boys in schools; and (3) the establishment of external examining bodies such as the College of Preceptors (1853), the Oxford Delegacy and Cambridge Syndicate for Local Examinations (1858), followed by other university boards and specialized bodies. While the objects are the same, there is much overlapping. For example, in 20 towns the 4 main examining boards hold independent local examinations, in 26 towns, 3 bodies hold examinations; in 84 towns, 2 of these bodies hold examinations. Professional, commercial and other similar bodies are naturally concerned with distinct purposes, but there is no consultation between them on the common ground of early and preliminary education. One result of this multiplicity of examinations with no adequate system of equivalents is that children try to safeguard themselves by taking several of them. In 2 training colleges in 1910, 124 entrants had taken 2, 9 had taken 3 and 1 had taken 4 examinations. Undue emphasis was placed on them and an undesirable competitive spirit created between schools and schoolmasters. Any development of a wide and modern curriculum can be seriously endangered if a school as a whole or its pupils individually are under pressure to work for individual examinations. Moreover, the isolation of the examining bodies from the schools and from the system of inspection conducted by the Board of Education had in many cases the undesirable effect of fragmenting the higher classes and retarding the work of the schools.

The Committee recommended the establishment of a widely representative Examinations Council which would supervise all external examinations in recognized secondary schools throughout the country. The fundamental principles underlying an improved system were: intimate connection between examinations and inspection, the reduction in their number and examinations of a type which would emphasize and assist the principle that secondary schools should provide a liberal education. Only two external examinations should be taken by ordinary pupils; one at about 16 years— the Secondary School Certificate—to replace the existing variety, the other— the Secondary School Higher Certificate—to be a less uniform test of more specialized education. Specialization should not be carried too far. Concentration on science should not mean the exclusion of all literary subjects.

Jackman, who did not sign the report, objected that establishment of a Secondary School Certificate exclusive to those who had attended for three years would be detrimental to those children who had no opportunity of obtaining one. It was tantamount to telling the public that any continuation of education in other than approved secondary schools would not help the advancement of their children. The Board could diminish the evils by making grants depend on the limitation of the number of examinations.

Playgrounds of Public Elementary Schools

Dept. Cttee. Rep., abstracts of ev., apps., index. pp. 171. 1912

1912–13 *Cd.* 6463, *xxi*, 779
apptd. —, *sgd. Oct.*, 1912

J. C. Iles (*Ch.*), Dale, Maclachlan, Newman, Phipps.

'(*a*) *Whether it would be consistent with due regard to educational and hygienic considerations that the minimum standard of playground accommodation for new Public Elementary Schools prescribed in the Building Regulations of the Board of Education—viz. 30 feet per head of accommodation—should be modified or adjusted according to the size, design, or situation of schools, the proximity of recreation grounds or open spaces, the density of population, the cost of land, or otherwise: (b) How far it is possible or desirable to define more precisely the standard of playground accommodation which the Board of Education will require under the Code of Regulations for Public Elementary Schools in the case of existing schools, or to regulate the practice of the Board of Education in dealing with cases in which the playground accommodation is considered to be insufficient.'*

For new schools the Committee recommended that the shape of playgrounds should be more carefully scrutinized; that except in very small schools, playgrounds should be separate for boys and girls; that girls and infants need not be separate; for older children, where no other provision for games is made, 30 sq. ft. should be provided, where there is other provision, 20 sq. ft. For existing schools 10 sq. ft. should be classed as insufficient after 1920, and 15 sq. ft. after 1925. Enlargement of buildings, except in unusual circumstances, should not be allowed if it would result in a reduction of playgrounds below the limits set for new schools.

Scholarships for Higher Education
Consultative Cttee. Interim Rep. pp. x, 74. 1916

1916 *Cd.* 8291, *viii*, 327
sgd. Jan., 1916

A. H. D. Acland (*Ch.*), Bowerman, Cleghorn (Miss I.), Cookson, Douglas (Miss M. A.), Easterbrook, Fitzpatrick, Goldstone, Hadow, Leathes, Paton, Powell, Robertson (Miss H.), Tawney, Turnor, Urquhart.

'*To consider the existing provision of awards — whether by Local Education Authorities, by the Governing Bodies of Secondary Schools, Universities and Colleges, by the Trustees of Endowments, or otherwise—for assisting pupils (other than those who have declared their intention to become teachers in State-aided Schools) to proceed from Secondary Schools to Universities or other places for Higher Education; and to report how far such provision is adequate in character, extent and distribution, and effective in meeting educational needs, and what measures are necessary and practicable for developing a system of such Scholarships and Exhibitions in organic relation to a system of National Education.*'

The Committee had just begun its enquiry when war broke out in 1914 and the sittings were suspended: war, however, underlined the importance of scientific and technical instruction, and in 1916 a Committee of the Privy Council on 'Scientific and Industrial Research' was set up and at the same time the enquiry was resumed, its field being now narrowed to 'scholarships in reference to industrial, commercial and agricultural needs'.

The proper aims of the scholarship system were primarily to train persons to serve the national needs in the best possible way, and to secure educational equality of opportunity; and subsidiary to these aims were the encouragement of learning and the reward of merit. Stressing the importance of secondary education at the 16–19 stage as the best training for university studies, the Committee regarded this as a weak spot in our national system of education. The secondary school system was very unequally developed in different parts of the country—of the 5,000 needed to maintain the undergraduate population, only 3,148 came from grant-aided secondary schools. Public schools should devote more energy to scientific training. The scholarship system should be supported from Government funds (tentative figures being suggested) and should be re-planned. The methods of award should be improved, a competitive examination being retained but not mechanically assessed, and the results checked by other means. The number and variety of awards should be increased (especially for women) with maintenance grants where necessary; they should be tenable not only at universities but also at various types of technical colleges, and open to pupils not only from secondary schools but also from works-schools, evening classes, etc. The scholarship syllabus should in some cases be restricted to mathematics and science papers (except for one on general English); the universities' requirements should be similarly modified. Tenure of scholarships should be prolonged in suitable cases, e.g. where the scholar could benefit from training in scientific research; and an effort should be made to bring home to a wider public the value of advanced training and research in scientific and technological fields.

2. HEALTH OF SCHOOL CHILDREN, CURRICULUM

Physical Training (Scotland)

R. Com. Vol. I. Rep., apps. pp. 119. 1903. Vol. II. Mins. of ev., index. 1903

1903 *Cd.* 1507, *xxx*, 1. *Mins. of ev., etc.*; 1903 *Cd.* 1508, *xxx*, 123
apptd. March, 1902. *sgd. March*, 1903

Lord Mansfield (*Ch.*), Cochrane, Glen-Coats, Craik, Stewart, Alston, Fergusson, McCrae, Ogston.

'*To enquire into the opportunities for physical training now available in the State-aided schools and other educational institutions of Scotland; and to suggest means by which such training may be made to conduce to the welfare of the pupils; and, further, how such opportunities may be increased by Continuation Classes and otherwise, so as to develop, in their practical application, to the requirements of life, the faculties of those who have left the day schools, and thus to contribute towards the sources of national strength.*'

Physical training throughout elementary schools was inadequate in quantity and quality. As a rule only one half-hour a week was allotted to it, although there were one or two very exceptional cases where three hours were given to it without detriment to the ordinary work. In the industrial schools and reformatories for boys eighteen out of twenty-three provided some form of physical training and the disciplinary results were highly commended. At twelve of these schools for girls there was instruction in physical drill, swimming, dancing and free gymnastics. In the training colleges physical exercises and drill were made a necessary part of the curriculum in 1901, but it was not a sufficiently prominent feature and not enough time was given to it. In the higher class day schools it was found that as the pupil advanced he received less physical training, except where there was a cadet corps and there was military drill. In these schools generally the provisions were as unsatisfactory as in the elementary schools. With respect to the universities, the lack of physical training 'gives rise to serious regret'. More attention had been given to the feeble-minded and crippled who, after medical examination, were put into special classes where there was a course of training of physical exercises and manual occupations.

One of the chief hindrances to the general development of physical training in elementary schools was the 'utter lack of system and want of qualified teachers'. The habit of mind produced by former Codes, which regulated payments by the number of subjects taken up, had not disappeared; teachers were accustomed to measure their success by the number of subjects taken. Parents had a mistaken idea arising from the system existing before the Education Act of 1901, when exemption from school attendance could be gained at ten years of age, provided that the fifth standard was then passed. It became the object to attain this exemption, often with the very worst results on the pupil.

Many children 'are too long confined to the atmosphere and surroundings of the school-room . . . would be benefited by being occupied for four or five mornings or afternoons in the week in physical exercises, games, or such light instruction as might be given in conversational form to large numbers at a time, . . . this might be effected without any increase of home lessons'. 'There might be less book work done from day to day, . . . but it would give better intellectual results.' If the wider aims of the Code and of education were recognized, there would be ample time for physical exercise. There is a marked contrast between elementary schools and industrial schools, whose children in this respect have advantages not enjoyed by elementary school children. A large amount of new school accommodation should take the form of playgrounds, gymnasia or recreation halls. Voluntary assistance should be enlisted in the organization of games, and School Boards should set up voluntary games committees. No scheme is more likely to revive that voluntary assistance than the institution of places of recreation, which would be the common meeting-ground of a group of schools.

More time and more facilities for physical exercises should be given in all educational institutions, including continuation classes. A minimum of two hours per week up to one out of every two school openings should be given to physical exercises, games, etc., but local authorities should have power to assign any proportion of time up to one out of every two school openings. There should be medical inspection, systematic records of physical and health statistics should be kept, and a small number of medical and sanitary

experts added to the inspecting staff. Where there were cases of insufficient feeding, there should be co-operation with the voluntary agency to provide suitable food, without cost to public funds. Should this prove inadequate, powers should be given to provide a meal and to demand payment from the parents to meet the cost price. A skilled Committee should be appointed to prepare a model course for a National System of Physical Training for Scotland. Training College grants should be conditional upon their providing systematic training in giving physical instruction, and the possession of a certificate in physical instruction should in due course be a condition of recognition as a teacher in any state-aided school. Auxiliary agencies such as the Cadet Corps and the Boys' Brigades should be encouraged. The Appendices contain reports on the physical examination of school children.

Model Course of Physical Exercises

Inter-Dept. Cttee. Rep., apps. pp. 51. 1904

1904 Cd. 2032, xix, 411
apptd. —, sgd. March, 1904

J. Struthers (Ch.), Blacker, Deverell (Miss E. M.), Fox, Jackman, Kerr, Stewart, Tuke, Whitton.

'To examine the Model Course now in use, to judge how far it should be modified or supplemented, and to consider what principles should be followed, in order to render a Model Course, or Courses, adaptable for the different ages and sexes of the children in public elementary schools.'

The Model Course was not suitable chiefly because it 'did not appear to follow any well-defined general principles governing the integration of physical exercise with general education. The syllabus proposed should be the basis of physical exercise for children of all ages, but teachers should be free to propose amendments and enlargements. All teachers should receive more training in health and hygiene, but formal lessons should be given by specially qualified instructors, of whom there was an increasing supply. The syllabus required no special apparatus, but playground space and halls were indispensable. The almost complete lack of facilities for physical training in many schools should be remedied by the local authorities as soon as possible.

Medical Inspection and Feeding of Children attending Public Elementary Schools

Inter-Dept. Cttee. Vol. I. Rep., apps. pp. vii, 147. 1905. Vol. II. Mins. of ev., apps., index. 1905

1906 *Cd.* 2779, *xlvii*, 1. *Mins. of ev., etc.*; 1906 *Cd.* 2784, *xlvii*, 157 *apptd. March, sgd. Nov.*, 1905

H. W. Simpkinson (*Ch.*), Parsons, Jackson, Lawrence (Maude), Walrond.

'(1) *To ascertain and report on what is now being done and with what result in respect of Medical Inspection of Children in Public Elementary Schools.* (2) *And further, to inquire into the methods employed, the sums expended, and the relief given by various voluntary agencies for the provision of meals for children at Public Elementary Schools, and to report whether relief of this character could be better organized, without any charge upon public funds, both generally and with special regard to children who, though not defective, are from malnutrition below the normal standard.*'

1. In addition to London, 48 areas had a definite system of medical inspection and in 18 others there was work organized by teachers and sanitary inspectors. School medical officers had been appointed in 85 areas, but were frequently also in private practice. In some areas nurses were provided by the authority or by voluntary associations. The school medical officer did not inspect each child, but those referred to him by teachers as suffering from defects likely to affect their education, e.g. defects of sight, uncleanliness, infectious disease, physical

unfitness to attend, etc. The cost varied from $\frac{1}{20}d.$ to $\frac{1}{10}d.$ rate. There have been specially beneficial results regarding eyesight and infectious disease. There was room for improvement. The local authority inspected and called defects to the notice of parents, but did not provide treatment; it had no power to force them to take remedial steps. Owing to poverty, and more often apathy and indifference, a large percentage of cases went untreated; this would improve as parents became more conscious of the value of immediate attention to the results of inspection.

2. The Committee took account of the work of the Physical Deterioration Committee, though that committee was not restricted by the condition that no charge was to be laid on public funds. Local authorities had no power to spend money on feeding school children, which was in the hands of voluntary agencies. These existed in 55 out of 71 county boroughs and in 38 boroughs and 22 urban districts. The problem in country districts was different, being that of ensuring adequate midday meals for children from a distance. Examples are given of the methods used in different areas, and of the part played by the authorities, teachers and the voluntary agencies.

The local authority should be informed of all feeding of its school children and of all funds received. Any organization for the purpose should be permanent, even if its operations were intermittent. Provision should be made for meals throughout the year on every school day, the more destitute being fed regularly rather than large numbers irregularly. The advice of the school medical officer should be sought on the selection of children. The meals should be orderly and given an educative effect. Teachers should not be required to serve or supervise meals. Most meals were provided free, but when some children paid and some did not, they all tended to become free. Efforts should be made to secure contributions from parents, who should be reminded of the actual cost. In view of the conflict of evidence, the Committee was unable to decide how successful school restaurants would be, but wished experiments to be made.

See *Cases of Children attending Public Elementary Schools who are without adequate nourishment.* Circulars; 1905 Cd. 2505, lx, 307. *Methods in great Continental and American cities for dealing with underfed children.* Statement; 1906 Cd. 2926, xc, 531. *History of Medical Inspection.* Chief Medical Officer. Ann. Rep.; 1910 Cd. 4986, xxiii, 1.

Education (Provision of Meals) Bill, 1906; and the Education (Provision of Meals) (Scotland) Bill, 1906

Sel. Cttee. Reps., proc., mins. of ev., apps., index. pp. xliv, 288. 1906

1906 (288) *viii,* 71
apptd. March, o.p. July, 1906

Mr. Lough (*Ch.*), Bridgeman, Collins, Craig, Craik, Dickson-Poynder, Henderson, Macnamara, McKean, Priestley, Powell, Roberts, Trevelyan, Whitbread, Dolan.

'The inadequate feeding of the children attending Public Elementary Schools has forced itself into recognition as a real evil in some large towns, although the evidence submitted tends to show that such evil is limited in extent and more or less spasmodic in regard to period of occurrence.'

The main causes are social conditions in which many of the poorer people in large towns live, or lack of employment. Other causes are: work which prevents anyone from being at home to prepare the midday meal; intemperance, thriftlessness and ignorance regarding the preparation of suitable food.

Hitherto the voluntary agencies have been almost exclusively responsible for feeding the children in need, but they have laboured under the difficulties of precarious financial support, inadequate facilities for the preparation of and the giving of meals, and have no statutory power of recovery from parents, or means of punishing neglectful parents except through the agency of the Society for the Prevention of Cruelty to Children. The proposal, which has not been seriously suggested, of providing meals out of rates or Exchequer grants as part of a statutory duty would obviously result in the extinction of all voluntary agencies, which would be deplorable from every point of view, as well as involving a large addition to the already burdened rates.

The local Education Authority should be empowered to organize and direct the provision of a midday meal, to establish Committees composed of representatives of the authority and of voluntary subscribers, to deal with canteens, to raise loans and spend money on the provision of accommodation and officials and for the preparation, etc., of meals. Recourse to rates, which should not exceed $\frac{1}{2}d.$ in the £, should be allowed only where the resources of the local voluntary funds and of the parents are insufficient to cover the costs. Where possible, payment for meals should be insisted upon. Where costs have to be recovered from parents the Guardians or the Society for the Prevention of Cruelty to Children should be empowered to prosecute. Teachers should not be required to take part in the dispensing of meals. The Proceedings give the three draft reports considered by the Committee.

See *Working of the Education (Provision of Meals) Act.* Rep.; 1910 Cd. 5131, xxiii, 393. 1911 Cd. 5724, xviii, 269. *Grant Regulations;* 1914 Cd. 7461, lxiv, 143.

Employment of School Children
Rep.

1902 *Cd.* 849. See *Labour.* p. 230.

Juvenile Education in relation to Employment after the War
Reps.

See *Breviate 1917–39,* pp. 459–60.

Co-ordination of the Technological Work of the Board of Education

Dept. Cttee. Rep.

unpublished
apptd. Nov., 1900

'To consider the best means of co-ordinating the technological work of the Board of Education with that at present carried on by other educational organizations.'

'Much valuable evidence was elicited from public bodies interested in this subject, and we obtained the most cordial assistance from the officers of the City and Guilds of London Technical Institute, who are engaged in the promotion of this teaching by a very extensive series of examinations conducted throughout the country. In consequence of the work of the Committee the following resolution has been passed by the Council of the Institute: "That provided an arrangement be made for co-operation between the Board of Education and the Examination Department of the City and Guilds of London Institute, by which the examination of the Institute receives the recognition of the Board, the Board of Education be requested to nominate four representatives to act on the Institute's Examinations Board".'

See Bd. of Education. Ann. Rep. p. 67; 1901 Cd. 756, xix, 1.

Industrial Training of Girls in the Separate and District Schools in the Metropolitan District

Rep.

1900 *Cd.* 237. See *Poor Law.* p. 242.

Agricultural Education in England and Wales

Dept. Cttee. Rep., apps. pp. iv, 48. 1908. Mins. of ev., index. 1908

1908 *Cd.* 4206, *xxi,* 363. *Mins. of ev.,* etc.; 1908 *Cd.* 4207, *xxi,* 417
apptd. March, 1907. *sgd. July,* 1908

Lord Reay (*Ch.*), L. Barnard, L. Belper, L. Moreton, Acland, Davies, Lamont, Latham, Medd, Middleton, Somerville, Staveley-Hill.

'To inquire as to the provision which has now been made for affording scientific and technical instruction in agriculture in England and Wales, and to report whether, in view of the practical results which have already been obtained, the existing facilities for the purpose are satisfactory and sufficient, and, if not, in what manner they may with advantage be modified or extended.'

While at the time of the last direct enquiry into agricultural education in 1887–8 there were only four or five institutions providing courses in agriculture, there were now at least 24. Improvements in management of grass land, in use of fertilizers, and in other activities, could be traced to their work, but the great majority of farmers had still not been reached. The higher institutions were limited by lack of funds, which were inadequate for agricultural education generally.

A grant should be made to Oxford University for its work in agriculture; the number of higher institutions was sufficient, but they should be better equipped. The facilities for agricultural instruction of a lower grade were unorganized, unsystematic and inadequate. Winter agricultural schools, courses, lectures, etc., and the use of itinerant instructors based on farm institutes were recommended. Fifty or sixty winter agricultural schools were needed to provide courses for lads of 17–20. The central authority for higher, etc., agricultural instruction should be the Board of Agriculture, not the Board of Education, which should control agricultural teaching in primary, secondary and evening schools where it was in continuation of that given in primary schools. The Board of Agriculture should be aided by a consultative committee and the local authority should set up an agricultural education committee or sub-committee consisting chiefly of representatives of agriculture and agricultural colleges, etc. There are many recommendations on research courses at higher institutions, scholarships, etc. Increased State funds were needed.

In a supplementary report Medd said that the system would not be complete till it provided for the continuous education of lads up to 17 or 18, and that local authorities should establish intermediate schools of agriculture.

See *Distribution of Grants for Agricultural Education and Research*. Rep.; 1910 Cd. 5388, vii, 561, and succeeding Ann. Reps.

Agricultural Education in England and Wales

Memo. pp. 5. 1909

1909 *Cd. 4886, xlvii,* 15
sgd. Sept., 1909

Lord Carrington, W. Runciman.

The aim was to improve and to extend specialized agricultural education, and to ensure a close relationship between such instruction and the practice and progress of the industry. A Rural Education Conference would be established to discuss agricultural education and to exchange views. The educational work would be divided between the Board of Agriculture and Fisheries, which would deal with and distribute the Parliamentary grants to the Agricultural Colleges and other independent institutions, while the Board of Education would be concerned with instruction by the county and other local authorities. An Inter-Departmental Committee consisting of responsible officers of the two Boards would be set up to correlate their duties.

—— *Revised Arrangements*. Memo. pp. 2. 1912

1912–13 *Cd.* 6039, *lxv,* 335

W. Runciman, J. A. Pease.

In view of the large additional sums available for agricultural education and research, Farm Institutes will be transferred from the Board of Education to the Board of Agriculture and the Board will be the Government Department concerned with advances from the Development Fund in aid of Farm Institutes.

Rural Education

Conference. 1st Rep., *County Staffs of Instructors in Agricultural Subjects*, app. pp. 9. 1910

1910 *Non-Parl. Bd. of Agric. and Fish., Bd. of Education*
apptd. June, sgd. Nov., 1910

H. Hobhouse (*Ch.*).

'*As to whether it is desirable that each county should have its own staff of instructors in Agriculture, Horticulture and other allied subjects, or whether it is possible that the services of a single staff should be made available for groups of contiguous counties; as to the training and qualifications which such instructors should possess in order to enable them to secure the confidence of agriculturists; and as to the manner in which the staff should be composed for each county or group of counties in England and Wales in view of the different branches of rural industry followed in each locality.*'

The great majority of counties have some separate staff of their own. Where there is a grouping of counties it is for the purpose of establishing or assisting to maintain a joint college or institute and arises out of association with a centre for agricultural education and research. The independent staff of the county is often supplemented, and their work often supervised, by the staff of the centre with which the county is in association.

It should be a general principle that every county should either be associated, in combination with other counties, with an efficient centre, or if not in combination, should have a minimum efficient staff of its own. Details are given of the various classes and qualifications of officers which should be included in this minimum. Higher agricultural education should be concentrated in a few official centres.

—— Second Report, *The Qualification of Teachers of Rural Subjects*, apps. pp. 23. 1911

1911 *Cd.* 5773, *viii*, 553
sgd. *May*, 1911

H. Hobhouse (*Ch.*).

'*To call attention to the lack of teachers properly qualified for giving instruction in rural subjects in the Elementary Schools, and the means which should be taken to raise the standard of efficiency in these subjects.*'

The curriculum in rural schools should be less purely literary. As the children in country schools are rarely more than 13 years old, observation, nature study and manual work are important. Their teachers should have a broad general education, together with a familiarity with country life and rural science. The instruction should be part of ordinary teaching done by regular members of the staff, and not specialized instruction by peripatetic teachers. The recommendations of the Hobhouse Departmental Committee on *Training College Courses of Instruction* (not published) for an optional course in rural science and an opportunity for picked teachers to take a third year at an Agricultural College, though adopted, proved ineffective.

To enable teachers to specialize, training college courses should be extended to three years, one of which might be in an institution giving instruction in agricultural subjects; local education authorities should be required to provide classes and vacation courses in rural subjects, free of charge and with ordinary pay; the pay of county teachers should be nearer that obtaining in towns; the curriculum of rural secondary schools should include rural subjects for bursars and intending teachers. Increased Treasury grants should be given for these purposes.

—— Third Report, *A Suggested Type of Agricultural School*, apps. pp. 27. 1911

1911 *Cd.* 5774, *viii*, 577
sgd. *May*, 1911

H. Hobhouse (*Ch.*).

'*As to whether there is any place in the system of Rural Education either generally or in particular counties in view of special local conditions, for schools giving to boys leaving Elementary Schools a three-years' Course from the age of 12 or 13 in the Theory and Practice of Agriculture, together with continued general education.*'

So far as the boys intending to become farm labourers were concerned, there was no demand for schools intended to make them more efficient labourers; they should go on to the land as soon as possible after leaving elementary school. But it was essential that manual instruction and nature study should be extended in the upper classes of the elementary schools. In addition, as an experiment, rural continuation day schools should be set up to which boys working on the land could go for a period every week to receive not only general education but instruction in elementary science and rural economy.

The class of boys who intended to become farmers or small occupiers required something more than elementary education. There was a small number of secondary schools giving specialized instruction, but even if these were encouraged the experimental establishment of a new type of school which would specialize in agricultural education—'Higher Grade Rural Schools', akin to existing 'Higher Elementary Schools'—should be tried. Liberal grants from the central authority would be necessary if these recommendations were to be adopted at all extensively.

—— Fourth Report, *The Consolidation of Rural Elementary Schools*, apps. pp. 13. 1912

1912–13 *Cd.* 6055, *xi*, 129
A. W. Chapman (*Ch.*).

'With a view to improving the education given in Elementary Schools in Rural Districts, to suggest that the "tops" or parts of the "tops" of such Schools should in selected areas and as an experiment be consolidated.'

There were a few instances in this country, but no definite conclusions could be drawn from them. Consolidation could be effected either by drawing all or some of the children from several elementary schools into a central school, and giving them the ordinary elementary education, or by selecting older children only and giving them special training connected with rural life. Great educational advantages might be derived from either type, but nothing more than experimental application of the principle should be tried at first. Any extra cost incurred by local education authorities should be met by the central government.

—— Fifth Report, Courses in Agricultural Colleges, apps. pp. 31. 1912

1912–13 Cd. 6151, xi, 143
sgd. Feb., 1912

H. Hobhouse (Ch.).

'To consider and advise as to the considerations which should be borne in mind in the framing of courses occupying not less than two sessions at institutions devoted to the higher study of agriculture, and to report on the main characteristics which such courses should possess in order to render them suitable to those students who intend to take up practical farming or the management of landed estates.'

For intending farmers, the minimum length of a course should be five, the normal six terms. Instruction should be provided in chemistry, elementary physics, mechanics, botany, animal physiology, keeping in mind that the knowledge given should be of value to the student as a farmer, and is not intended to train him as an agricultural chemist or botanist. There should also be contact with the practical processes of farm work. Geology,

entomology and mechanical engineering, which have been taught, should be left for those who will qualify as experts. For students intending to manage estates there should in addition be forestry, agricultural valuations, rating, taxation, law, estate bookkeeping, building construction and in some cases advanced surveying and levelling. All counties should award senior agricultural scholarships.

—— Sixth Report, Co-ordination of Agricultural Education, apps. pp. 17. 1912

1912–13 Cd. 6273, xi, 175
sgd. June, 1912

H. Hobhouse (Ch.).

'To consider and advise as to the co-ordination of the work of the Agricultural Staffs employed by counties and by collegiate centres serving the area in which the County is situated having regard to: (1) The necessity for linking up local work with that of institutions responsible for higher education and technical advice; (2) The advantages of co-operation between counties in making provision for certain branches of agricultural instruction and in establishing farm institutes and schools; (3) The need for maintaining the supervision of Local Education Authorities over the Agricultural Staffs employed within their administrative areas.'

The Board had announced its intention of making a special grant to 12 institutions which would act, for as many areas, as centres of agricultural research and technical advice to farmers. In these 12 divisions local lectures and classes outside the institution should be co-ordinated by a joint council consisting of representatives of county councils, institutions engaged in agricultural education, agricultural societies, etc.

See Constitution of the Advisory Councils for Agricultural Education in England and of the Agricultural Council for Wales. Memo.; 1914 Cd. 7118, lxxi, 15. Agricultural Education and the improvement of Live Stock in Wales. C. B. Jones. Rep.; 1916 Cd. 8222, iv, 299.

—— Seventh Report, *Manual Instruction in Rural Elementary Schools and the Individual Examination of Children in Rural Elementary Schools*, apps. pp. 23. 1913

1912–13 Cd. 6571, xi, 193
sgd. Dec., 1912

H. Hobhouse (*Ch.*).

'*That this Conference should consider— (a) the possibility and advisability of introducing Manual Instruction throughout the whole of a child's School Life into the Rural Elementary Schools as a new method of teaching rather than as a new subject; (b) whether a system of periodic, independent, individual Examination of children in Rural Elementary Schools should be initiated.*'

By manual instruction was meant cookery, laundry work, housewifery, dairy work and gardening for girls, and gardening, handicrafts and light woodwork for boys. Much had been done in introducing these subjects and much success had been achieved by capable teachers, but it would be impossible to introduce it on a large scale until there were suitably trained teachers. The county education authorities should do all they can to introduce the manual method of teaching and the Board should give increased grants for the purpose. Examinations should not be re-introduced, but there should be more informal inspection.

—— Eighth Report, *Manual Processes of Agriculture*, apps. pp. 27. 1913

1913 Cd. 6871, xv, 757
sgd. May, 1913

H. Hobhouse (*Ch.*).

'*To enquire into the methods which Local Education Authorities adopt with the object of promoting efficiency in the performance of Manual Processes, e.g. Ploughing, Hedging, Ditching, Sheep shearing, Milking and Basket-making, and to advise as to any further action that may appear to be desirable for the purpose of developing skill in workmen employed in agriculture.*'

There were no complete data on which to base any calculation as to the number of counties providing instruction in the manual processes of agriculture. Monmouthshire had a system whereby children were instructed at different centres during school hours and in Wiltshire children were taught milking and thatching. Other counties should consider similar schemes; farmers should combine instruction with paid work during holidays; holidays should be arranged during the period when most work is required of the boys.

Provision for instruction for boys over school age and for men varies considerably. In the 30 counties where some form of instruction is given the methods used are (a) Farm schools or agricultural colleges; (b) employment of itinerant inspectors, and (c) work through a local agricultural society. Instruction should be more generally provided and more thorough; for men employed on the land, classes should be more in the nature of assistance rather than formal instruction; there should be competitions in the local societies and the expenditure of local education authorities on money prizes should be regulated.

See *Principles and Methods of Rural Education*. Memo.; 1911 Non-Parl. Bd. of Education.

Practical Work in Secondary Schools

Consultative Cttee. Rep., apps., ev., index. pp. xvi, 411. 1913

1913 Cd. 6849, xx, 291
apptd. —— sgd. ——

A. H. D. Acland (*Ch.*), Bowerman, Chapman, Clay, Cleghorn (Miss I.), Cookson, Douglas (Miss M. A.), Durham (Miss F. H.), Easterbrook, Fitzpatrick, Goldstone, Paton, Powell, Reichel, Robertson (Miss H.), Sadler, Sharples, Tawney, Tuke (Miss M. J.), Turnor, Urquhart.

'*To consider to what degree education by means of practical work (or things) should be encouraged and developed in Secondary Schools and in particular to consider the following questions:—(a) To what extent is it desirable that the education of boys in Secondary Schools should include instruction in hand-craft, either in the ordinary school course, or in certain classes, as local circumstances and requirements may indicate, and what lines should such instruction follow? (b)—(i) Is it desirable that Courses of Domestic Economy or Housecraft should form part of the education of girls in Secondary Schools during the whole or the main part of school life? or (ii) Could this form of education be more usefully concentrated upon the year or two years immediately before leaving school? or (iii) Should it be deferred till after the close of the Secondary School Course, at any rate where the leaving age is under 17?'*

Education by means of practical work was taken to mean 'education by means of subjects in which bodily activity is, to a greater or less extent, involved and in which the pupil learns by doing'. There is no long experience in educational handwork except in kindergarten work, though there are an increasing number of well-equipped and well-staffed elementary schools in urban districts where the methods have a stimulating effect on the school work of the ordinary pupil which more than makes up for the time taken for them. Handwork, as a constituent of a liberal education, should form part of the education of the normal child and should be given a definite place in secondary schools and associated with the rest of school work. It should be taken up to the age of 16.

In order to foster independence and initiative the taste of each pupil and the pace at which he naturally works should be taken into account. The plan of keeping a class together at the same stage, and even at the same piece of work, is educationally unsound. Classes should, therefore, be sufficiently small to admit of individual instruction, and the range of work should be fairly wide. Constructive practice and instruction in theory should go hand in hand; as the pupil's age increases, more importance will naturally attach to the latter. The teaching of principles should be based as far as possible on practical operations, the pupil being encouraged to deduce his own conclusions and to test them practically. A number of suggestions are given of the value of paper, cardboard and plastic modelling, woodwork, metal work, cookery, etc., and the correlation of handwork with other school subjects as, e.g., geography, arithmetic, physics, etc. All the suggestions presume that the fullest freedom to experiment is allowed to the teacher.

The country environment of rural secondary schools should be fully utilized and a rural basis given to their work. Natural science should be made more practical in character, but the dangers of over-emphasis of practical work pointed out by Mr. E. H. Smith (Sexey's School, Blackford) should be avoided. But the introduction of manual work and the teaching of science from a practical point of view required suitably qualified teachers, and the Board of Education should call a conference of head teachers of rural secondary schools with this in mind. The work of these secondary schools should be freed from the rigid control of external examinations. The controversy as to the proper relationship between the teaching of science and domestic subjects was not closed, and after reviewing the evidence, e.g. of Mrs. Stephen Priestman (Leeds High School) and Miss McCroben (Girls' High School, Wakefield), the Committee concluded that the teaching of domestic subjects should be preceded by two years of science.

The Universities have done little to train teachers in handwork. There is no university or college diploma for school handicrafts. Such teachers must be given an efficient training, should be specialists of good general education, be regular members of staff and of equal status. The work should not be relegated to artisan teachers. No regular means exists for training men students in these subjects. The ideal would be a diploma course following a degree course and universities should give increased facilities for this work. The time has now come when every secondary school should provide for the teaching of some branches of educational handwork, should make them an integral part of its curriculum, and give them a position on the same level with other subjects studied.

In a Prefatory Note, L. A. Selby-Bigge commends the Report as a valuable aid to school authorities and those authorities who work under the Board's Regulations may count upon a sympathetic consideration of any experimental courses which they may submit for approval. The Appendices contain *Syllabuses of Work in Various Handwork Subjects* and an *Historical Sketch of the Development of Constructional Handwork as an Educational Subject.*

Provision of Funds for Reformatory and Industrial Schools

Rep.

1906 *Cd.* 3143. See *Prisons, etc.* p. 370.

Reformatory and Industrial Schools

Rep.

1913 *Cd.* 6838. See *Prisons, etc.* p. 370.

Reformatory and Industrial Schools in Scotland

Rep.

1914–16 *Cd.* 7886. See *Prisons, etc.* p. 372.

3. TEACHERS' SALARIES AND TRAINING

Training College Courses of Instruction

Dept. Cttee. Memo.

unpublished
apptd. 1901
H. Hobhouse (*Ch.*).

'*To draw up specimen Two Year Courses of Instruction for Students in Training Colleges, with a view to ensuring that every student who leaves College shall have been through some Course which shall prepare him in the best manner for some one or other of the various types of Elementary Schools.*'

See *Qualification of Teachers of Rural Subjects*, p. 322. *Circular to Training Colleges providing for a Two-Years' Continuous Course of Study.* Bd. of Education. Ann. Rep. Vol. III; 1901 Cd. 758, xx, 1.

The Teaching of School and Personal Hygiene to Students in Training as Teachers in Scotland

Rep., apps. pp. 16. 1907

1907 *Cd.* 3443, lxv, 55
sgd. March, 1907
W. L. Mackenzie.

'The object of the course is to assist the teacher in discovering such gross mental or physical defects as may unfit, or tend to unfit, the child for school work. The teacher is not expected to become a doctor, or to assume the functions of a doctor. It is intended only that he should be put in the attitude to observe, that he should know enough of the common school diseases and defects to prevent him from pressing incapable children or retaining sick children at school, and that he should be trained to appreciate the limits of mental work, the limits of physical exercise and, generally, the conditions that unfit the child for the one or the other.' The report describes the methods of instruction used. They should tend towards the observation of the actual child and away from generalized physiology and anatomy.

Superannuation of Teachers

Dept. Cttee. Rep. on the First Reference, app. pp. iii, 16. 1914

1914 *Cd.* 7364, xxv, 837
apptd. July, 1912. *sgd. April*, 1914

J. W. Wilson (*Ch.*), Wright, Heath, Orange.

'1. *To consider and report whether, and by what amount, the total cost of the proposed amendments of the Elementary School Teachers (Superannuation) Act, 1898, will fall short of the equivalent of a perpetual annuity of £200,000 accruing from 1st April, 1912. 2. To consider and report upon the methods by which the system of superannuation of Elementary School Teachers might be further improved without incurring an expenditure from public funds in excess of the surplus (if any) remaining from such annuity of £200,000.*'

Since the total cost of the amendments was equivalent to an annual charge of £279,237, it was decided to discontinue the enquiry.

—— Report on the Second Reference.
pp. iv, 42. 1914

1914 *Cd.* 7365, *xxv*, 857
sgd. March, 1914

add L. Farrer.

'*To consider and report upon the best system by which provision can be made for the superannuation of teachers in secondary and technical schools and institutions, schools of art, colleges and schools for the training of teachers, pupil-teacher centres and other schools and institutions (not being Universities or University colleges) which are aided by grants from the Board of Education, and upon its cost both immediate and ultimate.*'

Unless there were funds in addition to those indicated in the terms of reference, no satisfactory scheme of pensions for secondary school teachers, etc., was possible, and the only course would be to include them in the elementary teachers' scheme. The Government had indicated its intention of providing additional funds for secondary education, and the existing schemes should be brought within a common framework before a chaos of local variations was produced. Any scheme should provide an adequate

minimum, should not impede the free circulation of teachers, the benefits intended for old age should be reserved for old age, and there should be some choice of benefits. The scheme proposed followed the lines of the Federated Universities Superannuation Scheme, and was based on contributions by teachers and the authorities, with some state subvention. The scheme should be compulsory and the whole teaching staff should be included. A central committee should determine the main conditions of the insurance policies which might be taken out. About 15,000 teachers would be affected, while the annual premiums, half of which would be borne by the employers and half by the teachers, would amount to £250,000.

Farrer disagreed because the scheme would impose on local authorities without their consent an annual expenditure of £170,000, because it divided teachers into two classes, and because the taxpayer's money would be paid to insurance companies. A simple alternative would be for the State to provide teachers with a minimum subsistence maintenance for old age and disablement.

4. UNIVERSITIES, SCIENTIFIC INSTITUTIONS

Report to Accompany Statutes and Regulations made by the Commissioners appointed under the University of London Act 1898,

apps. pp. 9. 1900

1900 *Cd.* 83, *lxvi*, 57
sgd. Feb., 1900

Davey, London, Roberts, Jebb, Foster, Busk, Barlow.

Neither the Royal College of Music nor the Royal Academy of Music were willing to become a School of the University except upon conditions not in the power of the Commission to accept. In these circumstances Trinity College and the Guildhall School of

Music were not made Schools of the University, but a certain number of teachers were 'recognized' as teachers of the University. A 'Faculty of Law' was not created because the four Inns declined to take part in the University. The Incorporated Law Society of the United Kingdom decided to appoint two representatives upon the Senate in accordance with the Act. Under Section 80 of the Statutes the Commissioners introduced words to provide for 'common courses of instruction for internal medical students in the preliminary and intermediate portion of their studies under Appointed or Recognized teachers at one or more centres'. Two new Faculties in Engineering and in Economics and Political Science (including Commerce and Industry) were recommended. The Training Colleges were not included.

The Organization of Oriental Studies in London

Treasury Cttee. Rep., apps. pp. v, 156. 1909. Mins. of ev., index. 1909

1909 *Cd. 4560, xxxv, 235. Mins. of ev., etc.;* 1909 *Cd.* 4561, *xxxv, 397 apptd. April,* 1907. *sgd. Dec.,* 1908

Lord Reay (*Ch.*), L. Redesdale, Lyall, Guest, Raleigh, Turner.

'*To consider generally and in detail*—(1) *The present allocation of grants by the several Government Departments for the purposes of instruction in Oriental languages.* (2) *Having regard to present facilities for Oriental studies, and the importance of the interests involved in the formation of a thoroughly adequate scheme for the teaching of Oriental languages in London, in what way the general organization of a School for this purpose would most advantageously proceed.* (3) *What funds and resources at present applied in London to the teaching of Oriental languages would be rendered immediately available for the establishment of such a School by the co-operation of existing agencies.* (4) *What additional funds from Government or other sources would be required for its establishment and maintenance, provision being made*

in the first instance for the adequate remuneration of its teachers. (5) *What recognition should be given by the various Government Departments to the knowledge of selected Oriental languages, as attested by approved certificates, diplomas, or degrees.'*

There were Government-supported Schools of living Oriental languages in most of the important Continental countries, but in England there were only the facilities provided by a few colleges and societies. To meet the urgent need for suitable teaching in London for those about to take up employment in the East and in Africa, a School of Oriental Studies, with a name and a home of its own, should be built up from the nucleus of oriental teaching already existing at University and King's Colleges. This School, which should be incorporated into the University of London, should ultimately be greater than that of any other country. On the foundation of the School the Government should make a grant for living Oriental languages only.

Proposed School of Oriental Languages in London

Dept. Cttee. Interim Rep., apps. pp. iii, 33. 1911

1911 *Cd.* 5967, *xviii,* 707 *apptd. March,* 1910. *sgd. June,* 1911

Lord Cromer (*Ch.*), L. Curzon, Strong, Nicolson, Lyall, Heath.

'*To formulate in detail an organized Scheme for the institution in London of a School of Oriental Languages upon the lines recommended in the Report of Lord Reay's Committee of* 1909.'

The report was almost wholly confined to a consideration of the site and buildings required for the School. It was agreed that it would be difficult to find a site with greater advantages than that of the London Institution, and that the buildings could be suitably adapted at a cost of about £20,000 or £25,000. Pending further report on the constitution of the School, the only recommendation was that it should be established under a Royal Charter.

See *London Institution Transfer Bill.* Sel. Cttee. Rep.; 1912–13 (306) vii, 577.

University Education in London
R. Com.

apptd. Feb., 1909

Lord Haldane (*Ch.*), L. Milner, Romer, Morant, Currie, M'Cormick, Sargant, Creighton (Mrs. L.).

'*To inquire into the working of the present organization of the University of London, and into other facilities for advanced education (general, professional, and technical) existing in London for persons of either sex above secondary school age; to consider what provision should exist in the Metropolis for University teaching and research; to make recommendations as to the relations which should in consequence subsist between the University of London, its incorporated Colleges, the Imperial College of Science and Technology, the other Schools of the University, and the various public institutions and bodies concerned; and further to recommend as to any changes of constitution and organization which appear desirable; regard being had to the facilities for education and research which the Metropolis should afford for specialist and advanced students in connection with the provision existing in other parts of the United Kingdom and of Our Dominions beyond the Seas.*'

The first three Reports and the Fifth Report are formal presentations of the following volumes of minutes of evidence, etc.; 1910 Cd. 5166, xxiii, 643. 1911 Cd. 5528, Cd. 5911, xx, 5. 1912–1913 Cd. 6312, xxii, 591.

—— Fourth Report. pp. 6. 1911

1912–13 *Cd.* 6015, *xxii*, 581
sgd. Dec., 1911

The housing of the University of London was the sole subject of the Fourth Report. The accommodation provided at the Imperial Institute Buildings at South Kensington was inadequate and unsuitable for many of the purposes for which it was used. The adoption of any scheme for the reorganization of the University which might be recommended would be seriously delayed if steps had not previously been taken to provide a site and buildings more adequate and more central to the University institutions. Among other things, a great hall for university functions, proper accommodation for the Senate, Committees, the Principal, for the social and corporate life and for libraries, should be provided. In view of the scarcity of available land in central London the early acquisition of a site was particularly urgent; if any opportunity should be missed, many years might elapse before another arose.

—— Final Report, app., index. pp. xxviii, 218. 1913

1913 *Cd.* 6717, *xl*, 297. *Mins. of ev., etc.*;
1913 *Cd.* 6718, *xl*, 543
sgd. March, 1913

The organization of the University was very defective and not calculated to promote the highest interests of university education. The defects arose from two sources. (1) The relation between the internal and external sides of the University. This was largely due to departures from the recommendations of the Gresham Commission made in the Schedule of the University of London Act, 1898, which reduced the Senate in size and gave it all the executive powers of the University; reduced the Academic Council to a Standing Advisory Committee for Internal Students and placed the External Council in an equal position. Neither Council was able to get anything done without the consent of the other and questions on which they were most divided were decided by the votes of Senate members least able to consider the needs of the case. The root cause of the trouble was the incompatible ideals of the Academic and External Councils (representing internal and external sides). The former believed that training in a university under university teachers was the most important; the latter considered that examinations were adequate tests of education. This difference caused dissension in the Senate in which the representatives of Convocation claimed control of external examinations. The Commissioners rejected this claim. The external degrees should eventually be abolished and replaced by full university education open to poor but capable students.

(2) The variety and complete financial independence of the teaching institutions led to duplication of departments, work and institutions, while the Senate's power to prescribe curricula limited the best teaching of the stronger schools. The University has no control over the teachers in its schools, its power of visitation is rarely exercised, and the greater teaching institutions cannot be brought into proper academic relations with the University. University College and King's College are incorporated in the University, and are the only institutions represented in Senate; unincorporated schools are jealous of the incorporated Colleges. The Faculties have limited powers and its members are of very unequal academic standing. Owing to the necessity of providing for institutions of different aims and standards, the internal examinations are rapidly becoming external in character, and are progressively out of touch with the work of the best teachers.

The necessary conditions of reform were that students should enter with a sound general education, that there should be homogeneity of university classes, a university quarter, a Professociate appointed and paid by the University, professorial control of teaching and examinations, and complete financial control by the University of all the institutions within it. The supreme power of the University should be vested in a widely representative Court; Senate should be a small body of 15, a large proportion being nominated by the Crown, to work out university policy; the Academic Council, consisting of Deans of Faculties and university teachers, whose advice should be taken by Senate on any educational matter affecting the University as a whole. No reorganization less radical than this will suffice. The Constituent Colleges of the University should, following the precedent of the University and King's Colleges, be incorporated in the University, and financial and educational control of the work should be with the University. Each of them will be managed by a Delegacy. The first constituent Colleges are named. The basis of the teaching organization should be the Faculties (consisting of professors and other teachers), which should determine the courses of study and control the examinations, the award of degrees and formulate the needs of the Faculty. The University quarters should be at Bloomsbury, central buildings be erected there and certain Colleges should move to it. Many of the difficulties of the University would not have arisen if it had had sufficient income. Estimates are given of the sums needed to carry out the reform. Institutions not Constituent Colleges might qualify as Schools of the University if the University were represented on the governing body, its principal teachers formed an Academic Board, and in the case of teachers not appointed by the University, if the University were represented on the appointing committee. No such schools may confer the title of Professor or Reader. The practice of recognizing teachers in such schools not appointed by the University would cease. The general supervision of curricula for students in Schools of the University and other students, not being students in Constituent Colleges, should be undertaken by a Committee appointed by Senate. The area within which institutions could be recognized as Schools of the University should, with certain exclusions, be extended beyond the existing 30-mile radius to include Middlesex, Surrey, Kent, Sussex, Essex and Hertfordshire.

A large number of detailed recommendations are made on the work and organization of the Faculties, including the Medical Faculty, the termination of colonial examinations, students' hostels, students' Representative Council, etc.

Mins. of ev., etc.; 1910 Cd. 5166, xxiii, 643. 1911 Cd. 5528, Cd. 5911, xx, 5. 1912–13 Cd. 6312, xxii, 591. 4th Rep.; 1912–13 Cd. 6015, xxii, 581. Final Rep., Mins. of ev., etc.; 1913 Cd. 6717, Cd. 6718, xl, 297.

The University of Wales and the Welsh University Colleges

Dept. Cttee. Rep. pp. xxxvi. 1909. Mins. of ev., apps. 1909

1909 *Cd.* 4571, *xix*, 663. *Mins. of ev., etc.;* 1909 *Cd.* 4572, *xix*, 699 *apptd. July,* 1907. *sgd. June,* 1908

T. Raleigh (*Ch.*), Rhys, MacAlister, Ogilvie, McCormick, Hill.

'*To enquire and report as to*—(1) *The quality, character and results of the educational work accomplished by the University of Wales and its constituent Colleges, so far as it is work which can properly be described as of a University standard:* (2) *The financial position of the University and the Colleges and the manner in which their resources are utilized:* (3) *The lines on which any development of the work of the Colleges should proceed:* (4) *The probable requirements of the Colleges for staff or otherwise in order to enable the work to be carried out effectually in the future.*'

The history of university education in Wales was reviewed, and the courses of study, degrees, accommodation and financial position of the constituent colleges—Aberystwyth, Bangor, Cardiff and St. David's—were considered in detail. The University of Wales (Charter 1893) had aimed at promoting co-operation between the Colleges, and had wisely refrained from attempting to impose central control upon them. It should continue to be a co-ordinating body and leave the teaching to the Colleges. Further enquiry by the University into the question of specialization was necessary. The population of Wales was not sufficient to maintain more than one university.

There was a very creditable record of work in all the branches of university education. Few students left the Colleges without a fair mastery of their subjects and the statistics of graduation were good. But the salaries of the teaching staff were inadequate and, at least in the case of Professors and Heads of Departments, should be raised. The Colleges would benefit immensely if they were enabled to devote more funds to libraries and equipment, and there should be more financial provision for postgraduate study. Private donations were increasing and grants from local authorities to students had done much to extend university education. Suggestions are made for the further development of this work. It was for the Treasury to decide how far the needs of the Colleges could and ought to be provided for by increased grants.

See *Grants in Aid.* Advisory Cttee. Rep.; 1916 (62) viii, 433. University Education in Wales. *Breviate 1917–39,* p. 490.

National Medical School for Wales at Cardiff

Dept. Cttee. Interim, Final Reps., apps. pp. 36. 1916

1916 (62), *viii,* 433 *sgd. Aug., Dec.,* 1914

H. F. Heath (*Ch.*), Addison, Davies, Newman, Stocks.

'*To consider any application for a Special Grant in aid of the Medical School at Cardiff and to advise the Treasury as to the appropriate amount and conditions of such Grant; and to consider and report upon the plans for the erection of new buildings for the purpose of the Medical School.*'

The University of Wales had been offered up to £90,000 towards buildings for a Medical School at Cardiff, subject to conditions which included an adequate grant for a first-rate up-to-date medical school. The Committee recommended that any consideration of a grant should be conditional upon the authorities complying with points regarding the plans raised by Dr. Addison and Sir George Newman (App. I) and to the Committee's approval of further plans. The constitution of a Medical Board was recommended. This Board should be required to submit a curriculum to the Council of the University College of South Wales and Monmouthshire and the Medical Board should have financial control of funds available from whatever source. Appointments of professional lecturers should be made on recommendation by the Medical Board or, where a hospital appointment is also concerned, by a Joint Committee of the Medical Board and the hospital.

In the Final Report estimates are given for grants for ten years, beginning with £4,565 for the first year and increasing to £8,115 by the tenth year.

Scottish Universities

Dept. Cttee. Rep., apps. pp. 44. 1910. Mins. of ev., index. 1910

1910 Cd. 5257, xxvi, 159. Mins. of ev., etc.; 1910 Cd. 5258, xxvi, 203 apptd. —, sgd. Aug., 1909

Lord Elgin (Ch.), Haldane (Elizabeth), Digby, Reichel, Forsyth, Woodhead, Douglas.

'To consider the statement of claims to additional State assistance and estimates of the amounts needed for the respective services, which have been supplied by the Scottish Universities at the request of His Majesty's Government, and to report for what objects and to what extent assistance, if any, should be granted from public funds in the interests of the proper development of the work of the Universities.'

The grants to Scottish Universities under the Acts of 1889 and 1892 were

insufficient. In the last thirty years £1 mn. raised from private sources had been spent on buildings, etc., but since no provision had been made for upkeep, the charge on the Universities' funds was serious. Further provision was needed for equipment, etc., for higher work, and for improved methods of teaching. The claims were for £55,000, but capital expenditure should be met, as need arose, outside any annual grants. The additional annual grant should be £40,000, divided between the Universities of Edinburgh and Glasgow (£12,500 each), Aberdeen (£9,000) and St. Andrews (£6,000). The University Courts should administer the grants and submit reports and accounts to the Treasury.

Amongst the suggestions made were that a definite proportion of the additional annual grant (e.g. one-fourth) should be spent on provision for higher work, and that women medical students should be admitted to university medical classes and degrees. On the difficulties of the relationship between the Court of St. Andrews and the Council of the University College of Dundee, the Committee recommended that the proper place for the Medical School was at Dundee, which should receive £1,500 of the grant of £6,000 to St. Andrews, and £3,000 in lieu of a grant from the University Colleges (Britain) Grant.

Royal College of Science (Including the Royal School of Mines)

Dept. Cttee. Preliminary Rep. pp. 10. 1905

1905 Cd. 2610, lxi, 423 apptd. April, 1904. sgd. Feb., 1905

R. B. Haldane (Ch.), Abney, Carbutt, Church, Leech, Magnus, McDermott, Mowatt, Ogilvie, L. Reay, Rücker, Webb, Wernher, White.

'To inquire into the present and future working of the Royal College of Science including the School of Mines: to consider in what manner the Staff, together with the buildings and appliances now in occupa-

tion or in course of construction, may be utilized to the fullest extent for the promotion of higher scientific studies in connection with the work of existing or projected Institutions for instruction of the same character in the Metropolis or elsewhere: and to report on any changes which may be desirable in order to carry out such recommendations as they may make.'

While admirable work in training teachers in the methods of teaching science and in research has been done at the Royal College of Science, increased facilities for advanced instruction and research, particularly in application to industry, were an urgent national necessity. The accommodation and equipment in the School of Mines and the City and Guilds Technical College were inadequate for the purpose in view. The conditions of success for a new College of Applied Science equipped for the most advanced training and research were gifts of a capital sum and a site at South Kensington, the amalgamation of The Royal College of Science (including the School of Mines) and the City and Guilds Technical College under a common government and administration, and the creation of new departments of engineering by new foundation or transfer from other colleges. The moment was opportune for such a scheme, and the Committee had approached persons and bodies who had made munificent offers.

—— Final Report. Vol. I. Rep., app. pp. v, 33. 1906. Vol. II. Mins. of ev., apps., index. 1906
1906 Cd. 2872, xxxi, 391. Mins. of ev., etc.; 1906 Cd. 2956, xxxi, 431
sgd. Jan., 1906
del. Carbutt.

The circumstances which had led to the enquiry were the approaching completion of the new buildings of the Royal College of Science and the consequent discussion of its functions and scope, and the offer through Lord Rosebery of a school of advanced instruction in Applied Science on the South Kensington site. The principal sphere in which Britain lagged behind other countries was that of the highest technological education, the main obstacles to which were the indifferent attitude of employers, and the lack of facilities and of co-ordination of existing technological institutions. The conditions necessary for the provision of a new school, which was urgently needed, had been guaranteed. The scheme proposed to include the work of the Royal College of Science, the Royal School of Mines, the Central Technical College, and departments to be established on the additional site at South Kensington.

The composition and functions of the governing body of the new institution, which should be established initially as a School of the University of London, were given. The relations of the School and of the University were the subject of considerable disagreement, and while this should not delay the establishment of the new School, a Royal Commission should be appointed to enquire into the question. The new College should enter into negotiations with King's College and University College for the co-ordination and where necessary transfer of engineering and technological work.

McDermott, White, Abney and Leech thought that the suggestion of further enquiry into the changes in the University organization which might be necessitated by the advent of the School, would prejudice the work of the new governing body. The latter should be entrusted with the organization of the School for at least five years. Lord Reay and Mr. Rücker wanted incorporation of the School into the University as soon as possible.

Royal College of Art
Dept. Cttee. Rep., apps. pp. 61. 1912
1911 Cd. 5810, xviii, 549
apptd. April, 1910. sgd. July, 1911
E. K. Chambers (Ch.), Anderson, Brown, Cockerell, Frampton, Holroyd, Ricardo, Warner.

'*To consider and report upon the functions and constitution of the Royal College of Art and its relations to the Schools of Art in London and throughout the country.*'

The purpose for which the College was founded in 1837—the encouragement of the study of art in relation to industry—still held good, though the development of local schools of art led to its reconstruction in 1852 rather for the purpose of training teachers of art than for training designers. In 1901 it was reorganized on two main principles: division into the four schools of architecture, ornament and design, decorative painting, and sculpture and modelling, each under a Professor, and the encouragement of technical work in craft classes. Designers for the 'handicraft' industries such as glass-painting, jewellery, pottery and engraving, making costly productions for a limited public gained the greatest benefit from the College courses, but on the industrial design for the factory industries it had had little influence.

The training of industrial designers should be undertaken by the provincial schools of art in direct relation to the industries of their areas, and there should be a liberal provision of scholarships to enable students to attend them. They should also undertake the training of teachers of art. When a system of provincial colleges had been established, the Royal College should become an institution of advanced study, offering a one or two years' course. Immediate improvements were necessary, but when the reorganization had been carried out, new buildings should be provided to replace the existing ones, which lack the dignity and convenience worthy of a national institution.

Administration by the Meteorological Council of the Existing Parliamentary Grant

Cttee. Rep.

1940 *Cd.* 2123. See *Government*. p. 26.

National Physical Laboratory

Cttee. Rep. pp. 12. 1908. Mins. of ev., apps., index. 1908

1908 *Cd.* 3926, *xxix*, 959. *Mins. of ev.,* etc.; 1908 *Cd.* 3927, *xxix*, 971 apptd. Dec., 1906. sgd. Dec., 1907

G. W. Balfour (*Ch.*), Noble, Barry, Crossley, Chalmers.

'*To inquire generally into the work now performed at the National Physical Laboratory, with special reference to: (i) The character of the mechanical, physical and chemical tests undertaken there; (ii) The possibility of their interfering unduly with the business of other agencies; (iii) The desirability of publishing the results of all such testing work; and to report: (1) Whether having regard to the industrial interests of the country generally, and to those of private agencies, any change is desirable in the scope of the work of the Laboratory, and (2) On what lines any further development of its business should proceed.*'

The previous Committee (1898 C. 8976, xlv) had laid down correctly the scope of the Laboratory as including not only physical research bearing directly or indirectly on industrial problems and the standardization and verification of instruments but, under proper restrictions, the testing of materials. Complaints had been made that some of the testing work carried out by the Laboratory was inconsistent with the recommendations of that Committee and was an encroachment on the sphere of private enterprise. The fears of the private testing establishments were exaggerated, but a more precise formulation of the testing work to be undertaken by the Laboratory was desirable. There should be no restriction on its 'investigatory testing', but it should not undertake 'contractual testing', i.e. testing whether materials were in accordance with contracts, except for Government Departments, in arbitration cases, and in special tests which could not be adequately carried out in private establishments.

The rule, based on the recommendation of the Committee of 1898, that all results should be published immediately, even where it was paid for by private individuals—this being regarded as the mark of work which the Laboratory should undertake—deterred manufacturers from submitting investigations of great importance: it was too rigid, and should be relaxed. The Laboratory should have discretion in withholding the publication of results for a limited period of years, charging a higher fee to the individuals concerned. Noble and Barry recommended that the restriction on contractual testing should end after ten years.

Solar Physics Observatory

Dept. Cttee. Rep., mins. of ev., apps.
1911

1911 *Cd. 5924, xviii,* 611
apptd. April, sgd. June, 1911

T. L. Heath (*Ch.*), Dyson, Schuster, Glazebrook.

'*To consider the alternative schemes for locating the Solar Physics Observatory at Fosterdown and at Cambridge respectively, and to report which of the two schemes is likely to secure the best results for an annual expenditure of approximately the same amount as is now incurred for the work done under the direction of the Solar Physics Committee.*'

The site occupied by the Solar Physics Observatory at South Kensington was required for permanent buildings and sufficient ground could not be reserved for it. The conditions necessary in a new site were that the Observatory should be at an elevation of not less than 250 feet; it should not be in a smoke area; it should be away from river valley mists, and not upon clay (chalk or gravel would be satisfactory); it should not be exposed to violent winds, and should have as clear a horizon as possible, especially east, south and west; there should be a water supply for photographic purposes. Fosterdown comprised 12 acres

on the crest of the North Downs, a mile and a quarter from Caterham railway station. The main part of its elevation was from 750 to 795 feet. The site belonged to the Government, and there were many military works and buildings which might be utilized. The site in Cambridge is south of ground occupied by the University Observatory, it is a field of four acres at an elevation of 70 to 75 feet.

The Cambridge site was recommended because of the prospect of the establishment of a real school combining the study of solar physics and astrophysics. There should be a grant for buildings and a fixed annual inclusive grant-in-aid, provided that the University agree to the Professor of Astrophysics being the Director of the Solar Observatory, that the Astronomer Royal and the Director of the Meteorological Office were *ex officio* members of the Committee; that the University undertook the necessary routine work laid down in the report, and that an annual report on the work and expenditure were presented to the Treasury. Glazebrook dissented, and recommended the Fosterdown site.

5. GALLERIES, MUSEUMS, PUBLIC RECORDS

National Gallery (Purchase of Adjacent Land) Bill

Sel. Cttee. Reps., proc., mins. of ev.
pp. vi, 11. 1901

1901 (260) *vii,* 1
apptd. June, o.p. July, 1901

A. Akers-Douglas (*Ch.*), L. Balcarres, Paulton, Whitmore, Burns.

The Bill dealt with the acquisition of a small piece of land on the west side of the National Gallery. The Committee was strongly impressed with the need for acquisition by the Government as soon as possible of other lands adjoining those acquired under the Bill in order that the National Gallery should be more effectively protected.

Chantrey Trust

Sel. Cttee. HL. Rep., proc., mins. of
ev. app., index. pp. xvi, 219. 1904

1904 (357) v, 493
apptd. June, o.p. Aug., 1904.

Lord Crewe (Ch.), L. Carlisle, L.
Lytton, L. Windsor, L. Ribblesdale,
L. Newton, L. Killanin.

'To inquire into the administration of
the Chantrey Trust; and, if necessary, to
make recommendations.'

By his will, dated 31st Dec., 1840, Sir
Francis Chantrey left £105,000 to be
'devoted to the encouragement of
British fine art in painting and sculpture
only', and the President and Council
of the Royal Academy were nominated
as the purchasing body. As a national
collection of modern British art it is
incomplete and largely unrepresentative, especially of many brilliant and
capable artists of the last quarter of
the 19th century. It contains too many
pictures of minor importance and
purely popular character, and too few
which reach the degree of artistic
distinction aimed at by Sir Francis.
In evidence, Professor Brown stated
that 'there is little work in that collection which I should send a student to
study' (q. 1974). The Council held
that the injunction in the will to encourage British artists and pay liberal
prices debarred them from making any
purchases except from the artists or
their families. No work had ever been
bought at an auction or from a dealer,
and with five exceptions, all of them
had come from some exhibition of the
Royal Academy.

An unduly narrow construction had
been put upon the will and too exclusive
a preference shown to Academy exhibitions to the neglect of other
exhibitions. There should be greater
flexibility in method, by selection
from studios, by purchase from private
owners, auctions and dealers, and
there should be powers to purchase
works executed abroad by British
artists living in Great Britain. A

Committee of three composed of the
President, ex officio, of a Royal Academi-
cian, and an Associate of the Royal
Academy should be appointed to
replace the Council as the purchasing
body.

National Gallery

Cttee. of Trustees. Rep., apps. pp. 78.
1915. Mins. of ev., index. 1915

1914–16 Cd. 7878, xxix, 317. Mins. of
ev., etc.; 1914–16 Cd. 7879, xxix, 395
apptd. Nov., 1911. sgd. Dec., 1913

Lord Curzon (Ch.), Vincent, Benson,
Holroyd.

'To enquire into the Retention of Important Pictures in this Country, and other
matters connected with the National Art
Collections.'

The export or exodus of pictures
from private collections—facilitated in
the case of pictures settled as heirlooms,
by the provisions of the Settled Land
Act, 1872, and accelerated by death
duties and other forms of taxation—was
causing serious apprehension. Appendix V gives a list of over 500 old
masters which have left this country
quite recently. Appendix VII gives
a list of painters wholly or imperfectly
represented in the National Gallery.

The present annual provision of
£5,000 for the National and Tate
Galleries combined, supplemented in
some cases by extraordinary grants, was
totally inadequate for building up the
national collection. The Committee
investigated the position of the various
galleries and decided that to avoid
duplication and to build up a representative collection the four collections
in the metropolis, the National and
Tate Galleries, the National Portrait
Gallery and the Victoria and Albert
Museum Collection should be treated as
one organic whole. Some transfer and
rearrangement would be necessary.
The problem of the Chantrey Bequest
should be solved. There are in the
Tate 150 British works of art hung
there simply because they have been

purchased by the President and Council of the Royal Academy. The administration of the Trust and the choice of works of art have been the subject of much criticism. Although the President of the Royal Academy was satisfied with the selection, which he did not think would be improved, other witnesses said that many of the Chantrey pictures were of inferior merit and were a discredit to the walls of the gallery.

The Parliamentary Grant should be increased to £25,000; the Trustees should not be required to return any unspent balance, and should be able to apply for extraordinary aid for a limited number of masterpieces. The Trustees and Director of the National Gallery should approach confidentially owners of collections containing pictures desirable for the nation, and in event of their sale to the nation, the proceeds should be exempt from aggregation for the purpose of estate duty. If the increased annual grants were not made, the alternatives of a tax on the gross proceeds of sales of works of art at auctions or the allocation to the galleries of the proceeds of death duties upon them should be considered. It would be inadvisable to place any restriction or duty on the export of works of art. The Trustees of the National Gallery should notify the Treasury and the Chantrey Trustees that they were no longer willing to accept pictures in the selection of which they had no-choice, and failing legislation, they should exercise more efficaciously their rights of storage. The administration of the Chantrey Bequest should be transferred to the Trustees of the Tate Gallery. The powers and system of loans should be greatly extended. There were a number of recommendations on the administration of the Galleries. Appendices I–III are by Lord Curzon on *The Chantrey Purchases*, the *Friends of Art* and *Oil Paintings in the Victoria and Albert Museum*. Appendix IV contains a note on *Frames* by R. H. Benson.

The Board of Manufactures

Dept. Cttee. Vol. I. Rep. pp. 23. 1903. Vol. II. Mins. of ev., apps., index. 1903

1904 *Cd.* 1812, *xxx*, 1. *Mins. of ev., etc.*; 1904 *Cd.* 1813, *xxx*, 25 *apptd. Sept.*, 1902. *sgd. Aug.*, 1903

A. A. Douglas (*Ch.*), Maxwell, Armstrong, Mackenzie, Buchanan.

'*To enquire into the constitution, powers and duties of the Board of Manufactures, with special reference to the administration of the grants made by Parliament for purposes of Art in Edinburgh, and to report whether, and in what way, such administration may be improved.*'

The Board had its origin in the 15th article of the Treaty of Union, 1707, and at first its purpose was to encourage and aid improvements in the woollen, linen, flax and fishing industries. Its duties at the date of the Committee's enquiries were confined to the encouragement of art and the management of the National Gallery and National Portrait Gallery (of Scotland) and other institutions. It should be reduced in size and reconstituted as a Board of Trustees. Funds should be provided for the purchase of pictures, the building of a new National Gallery and related purposes.

Rearrangement of the Victoria and Albert Museum (Art Division)

Cttee. Rep., app. pp. 36. 1908

1908 *Cd.* 4389, *xxix*, 809 *apptd. Feb.*, *sgd. July*, 1908

C. H. Smith (*Ch.*), Benson, Day, Powell, Wedgwood.

To prepare a scheme of arrangement 'for the whole of the Art Museum which will provide the greatest facilities for study, primarily to those interested in the commercial manufacture of objects of a kind represented in the collection—craftsman, manufacturers, designers and students, and secondarily to those interested in Art without regard to its relation to industrial production—artists, students of art, of history of manners and customs.'

'The Museum was originally founded as an instrument for stimulating the improvement in this country of such manufactures and crafts as require and admit of decorative design.' As the collections grew the original purpose became obscured. The Board of Education was now anxious that the precise purpose intended to be fulfilled by the Museum should be clearly realized and co-ordinated. The Committee prepared a scheme for this based on the instructions they had received from the Board. Consideration should be given to the transfer of oil paintings and water colours having no real connection with applied art to the National and Tate Galleries.

Geological Survey and Museum of Practical Geology

Dept. Cttee. Rep.

unpublished

To inquire into the organization of the Geological Survey and Museum of Practical Geology. 'The Board are carrying out the suggestions and recommendations which have been made.'

See Bd. of Education. Ann. Rep.; 1901 Cd. 756, xix, 1.

The Science Museum and the Geological Museum

Dept. Cttee. Rep., apps. pp. 32. 1911

1911 *Cd. 5625, xviii,* 517
apptd. March, 1910. *sgd. March,* 1911

H. Bell (*Ch.*), Dobbie, Geikie, Glazebrook, Laing, Mcdonnell, Ramsay, Ripper, White.

'*To consider and report upon various questions in regard to the present condition and the future development of the valuable Collections comprised in the Board's Science Museum at South Kensington and Geological Museum in Jermyn Street. In particular the Committee are asked to advise (a) as to the precise educational and other purposes which the Collections can best serve in the* National interests; (*b*) *as to the lines on which the Collections should be arranged and developed, and possibly modified, so as more effectively to fulfil these purposes; and* (*c*) *as to the special characteristics which should be possessed by the new buildings which it is hoped will shortly be erected on the South Kensington site to house these collections, so as to enable the latter to be classified and exhibited in the manner most fitted to accomplish the purposes they are intended to fulfil.*'

The collections in the Science Museum ought to give illustration and exposition of the various branches of science and of their applications in the arts and industries, and to benefit students and others to whom the subjects are of professional importance or general interest. Detailed examination of the collections led to the suggestion that some objects should be removed and that all of them should be brought up to date. Proper organization was impossible in the existing buildings. An advisory committee of experts should be established. The Geological Survey Office and Museum of Practical Geology were cramped in their existing buildings; they should be removed to South Kensington and housed with the Science Museum as part of a single scheme.

—— Report, apps. Part II. pp. 17. 1912

1912–13 *Cd. 6221, xxii,* 375
sgd. April, 1912

This report deals with the buildings required to house the collections. The co-operation of the Trustees of the British Museum, who had agreed to the establishment of the building for the Museum of Practical Geology and the offices and library of the Geological Survey, on part of the site allotted to the National History Museum, had made possible the concentration of national collections representing geological science in London. Details are given of the proposed new Science Museum building, which was to be connected with the new Geological Museum.

Local Records

Cttee. Rep. pp. iv, 51. 1902. Apps., index. 1902

1902 *Cd. 1335, xlix,* 413. *Apps., etc.;*
1902 *Cd. 1333, xlix,* 469
apptd. Aug., 1899. *sgd. Oct.,* 1902

J. Bryce *(Ch.)*, Bishop of Winchester, Mowatt, Lyte, Ilbert.

'To enquire and report as to any arrangements now in operation for the collection, custody, indexing and calendaring of local records, and as to any further measures which it may be advisable to take for this purpose.'

Local records are documents of historical importance and interest which belong to a particular place and have not been collected in a central depository. Although the legislature often determined who the legal custodians were to be, few directions were given as to the manner in which they were to be preserved. There was no system or uniformity either for security or accessibility. Some were intelligently looked after, others neglected or badly housed or where well-housed, often unlisted. Most interested bodies were in favour of local centralization. The boroughs and counties should be the record authorities, but it would be preferable if boroughs and ecclesiastical authorities would arrange to deposit their records in the county depository, retaining the right of ownership. Each record office should be in charge of a custodian trained in paleography, there should be a uniform system of classifying and indexing, and institutions, etc., should be encouraged to deposit their records in the county depository. Any legislation required to give effect to the proposals should in the first instance be permissive.

Public Records

R. Com. Vol. I. 1st Rep. Pt. I. Rep. pp. vi, 53. 1912. Pt. II. Apps. 1912. Pt. III. Mins. of ev., apps., index. 1912

1912–13 *Cd. 6361, xliv,* 13. *Mins. of ev., etc.;* 1912–13 *Cd. 6395, Cd. 6396, xliv,* 73 *apptd. Oct.,* 1910. *sgd.* —

F. Pollock *(Ch.)*, Evans, Firth, James, Kenyon, Lee, Owen, Tedder, Williams.

'To inquire and report—(1) as to the working of the Public Records Act, 1 & 2 Vict. c. 94, the Public Records Act, 40 & 41 Vict. c. 55, the Public Records Act, 61 & 62 Vict. c. 12, the Order in Council of March 5, 1852, and any other Acts of Parliament and Orders in Council and Treasury Minutes concerning the custody and control of the Public Records of England and Wales, as well as all rules and regulations now in force at the Public Record Office; (2) as to all arrangements now in operation for the collection, control, custody, preservation from decay or injury, classification, description, cataloguing, indexing, calendaring, publishing, making accessible and disposing of the Public Records of England and Wales; (3) as to the Record Publications (texts, calendars, reports and lists) since the year 1838, illustrating the national history of England, Scotland, Ireland and Wales; (4) as to the custody of local records of a public nature; (5) as to the Record Office establishment and the training of archivists; and (6) as to any further measures which it may be advisable to take for these purposes.'

During the last 20 years much useful work has been accomplished in the arrangement of the records and the issue of calendars or other official publications by the present Deputy Keeper and his staff. At the same time, there are defects in the custody, arrangement and description of the records; in the facilities provided for students in the search rooms; in the methods adopted for producing the records and for their supervision, preservation, cleansing and repair. Large masses of records known as Chancery Masters' Documents, Exchequer Port Books and Coast Bonds and Judicial Writs are stored in bulk under very unsatisfactory conditions, and these, together with other classes, such as the State Papers 'Supplementary' and 'Miscellaneous' and the records of the High Court of Admiralty, require immediate attention. Owing to inadequate organization, the statutory provisions regarding the disposal of valueless records have not been carried out, and many public records have been destroyed which might have been useful to historical scholars. Only Record Officers with special knowledge of historical literature and research should be on the Committee of Investigating Officers.

Seals attached to documents should be preserved, there should be more catalogues, more printed lists and temporary manuscript lists. There should be more accommodation in the Search Rooms, which should be open weekdays including Saturday, until 5 p.m. There should be more reference books. With marked exceptions, the staff do not hold that position as historical students of proved competence which might be expected of men constantly engaged in handling interesting historical material. Candidates for appointments should have a good general education, but should not be regarded as eligible unless they have fair proficiency in Latin, French and History and thereafter have a year's special training in a university or similar place of study and passed a relevant qualifying examination. The opportunities and methods of promotion lack elasticity and stimulus. More funds are needed to carry out these and the preceding proposals.

The unarranged, undescribed and inaccessible state of many public records and delays in publication are due to the absence of control by a body of expert advisers. The Master of the Rolls has become only the titular head, and should be replaced by a commission of nine, three representing the judiciary, three the public offices, and three historical interests. A permanent Board of Historical Scholars should direct the publication of calendars and other historical materials.

The public records relating to Wales are badly arranged, no separate series of publications has been devoted to them. If transferred to a Record Office for Wales, they should be in an accessible place near to one of the University Colleges.

—— Vol. II. Second Report. Pt. I. Rep. pp. viii, 96. 1914. Pt. II. Apps. 1914. Pt. III. Mins. of ev., index. 1914 1914 Cd. 7544, xlvi, 189. Mins. of ev., etc.; 1914 Cd. 7545, Cd. 7546, xlvi, 293 sgd. June, 1914

The Commission lists (pp. 2–4) those recommendations in its First Report which had and those which had not been carried out. This Report concerns records in departmental archives or elsewhere outside the Public Record Office. The records of many courts and departments are unarranged or badly arranged, are in a decayed condition, insecure, in attics or corridors and injured by damp, etc., or are not properly listed. The public departments are imperfectly acquainted with the statutory definition of a public record and they lack definite organization. The cost of the unsatisfactory and unscientific custody of the outlying public records is greater than that of the Public Record Office itself.

The Commission lists those records for which better custody is required, those which should be transferred to the Public Record Office, and the courts and departments where improvements in organization or structural changes are required. Departmental records not in the Public Record Office should be entrusted only to trained record keepers. The national archives should be reorganized by establishing departmental and district record offices as branch repositories supervised by the Commission of Government recommended for the Public Record Office itself.

—— Vol. III. Third Report. Pt. I. (Local Records.) Rep. pp. v, 46. 1919. Pt. II. Apps. 1919. Pt. III. Mins. of ev., app., index. 1919

1919 *Cmd. 367, xxviii, 1. Mins. of ev., etc.;* 1919 *Cmd.* 368, *Cmd.* 369, *xxviii,* 53 *sgd. April,* 1918

The Commissioners begin by listing the recommendations made in their First and Second Reports which have not yet been carried out and repeat their recommendations for a permanent Commission of Government for the Public Record Office. This report is concerned with local records of a public nature. The objects to be attained are that they should be safely kept in convenient places under adequate supervision, and that they should be properly arranged and accessible to the public on reasonable terms. None of these conditions is generally satisfied. A large mass of judicial records of various courts and district registries is or ought to be preserved in numerous repositories. Those which are extant are often in want of adequate accommodation, proper arrangement and expert description, but as a class they have been practically lost sight of for a long time, and having often been allowed to remain in the custody of some practising solicitor, a large part of them cannot now be accounted for. The irresponsible and unskilful custody which has directly contributed to a loss of a large part of the whole series should no longer be tolerated. Large classes of records of non-corporate and disfranchised towns have disappeared. The condition of non-judicial local records is more satisfactory, but leaves much to be desired.

Recent experience does not give much hope that merely permissive legislation will be sufficient, and the scheme presented requires general legislation. A moderate degree of sufficiency and security uniformly required and enforced, is preferable to a more ambitious plan resting on the discretion of local authorities. No remedy short of a central controlling power will suffice. All local records of a public nature should be brought under the control and superintendence of the Master of the Rolls. The duty of keeping and maintaining them in proper condition should be enforced by legislation, and a special section of the Public Record Office established to inspect and supervise local records.

Amongst the very numerous recommendations are better provision for custody and care of specified records; preparation of a catalogue on a systematic plan by county authorities; proper repositories under a skilled archivist for the older county and borough records; proper custody of the records of expired commissions and statutory trusts; recovery by county councils of public records in private hands; and a new repository near the Imperial War Museum for departmental records relating to the war.

1st Rep., Mins. of ev., etc.; 1912–13 Cd. 6361, Cd. 6395, Cd. 6396, xliv, 13. 2nd Rep., Mins. of ev., etc.; 1914 Cd. 7544, Cd. 7545, Cd. 7546, xlvi, 189. 3rd Rep., Mins. of ev., etc.; 1919 Cmd. 367, Cmd. 368, Cmd. 369, xxviii, 1.

XV. SOCIAL PROBLEMS

1. Children
2. Charities
3. Betting

4. Intemperance, Licensed Trade
5. Sunday Closing, Sunday Trading

1. CHILDREN

Prevention of Cruelty to Children (Amendment) Bill [H.L.]
Sel. Cttee. HL. Rep., proc. pp. vii. 1903

1903 (*HL.* 57) *viii,* 5
apptd. March, o.p. May, 1903

Lord Alverstone (*Ch.*), L. Ancaster, L. Belper, L. Lamington, L. Monkswell.

The Bill sought to remedy defects in the Prevention of Cruelty to Children Act, 1894, and to render incest, which was punishable in Ecclesiastical Courts only (although a crime in Scotland and most civilized countries) punishable in certain cases by criminal proceedings.

See 1904 4 Edw. 7. c. 15.

Juvenile Smoking Bill [H.L.]

Sel. Cttee. HL. Rep., proc. pp. x. 1906

1906 (HL. 155) ix, 145
apptd. May, o.p. July, 1906

Lord Beauchamp (Ch.), L. Bishop of Ripon, L. Aberdare, L. Heneage, L. Biddulph.

'To consider the Juvenile Smoking Bill [H.L.], and to consider the question of juvenile smoking generally, and its effect on the physical condition of children; and to report whether any, and if so, what alterations in the law are desirable or practicable with a view to stopping the sale of tobacco and cigarettes to children below a certain age, and to report to the House.'

It was the unanimous opinion of the witnesses, including representatives of the tobacco trade, that juvenile smoking, which was increasing rapidly, indirectly produced a number of ills, including habits of drink. There were no signs of physical deterioration in girls, because they were entirely free from the habit. The Committee were unable to recommend the Bill referred to them, but recommended with certain additions, a Bill as drafted by Sir Ralph Littler. This included prohibition of the sale of any description of cigarettes to a child under the age of sixteen years; children found in possession of cigarettes should be liable to conviction; police should be empowered to stop youths smoking in any public place, and should confiscate any tobacco found on them, and local authorities should be allowed to extend this power to park-keepers and school-masters.

Infant Life Protection

Sel. Cttee. Rep., proc., mins. of ev., apps. pp. viii, 103. 1908. Index. 1908

1908 (99) (99-Ind.) ix, 147
apptd. Feb., o.p. March, 1908

J. E. Ellis (Ch.), Allen, Bright, L. Cecil, Gulland, Taylor, Power.

'To inquire and report as to the desirability of extending the provisions of the Infant Life Protection Act, 1897, to homes in which not more than one infant is kept in consideration of periodical payment, and of altering the limit of age prescribed by Section 2 of the Act.'

The provision of the Act allows for supervision 'where a child under two years of age has been received for a lump sum', but there is no provision for a child under five years of age received for a periodical payment. This distinction confuses the public mind and should be abolished in order to make the administration of the Act simpler. The lack of inspection where there was only one child has led to a large trade being carried on for adoption. For example, out of 386 advertisements in one month, 375 related to one child (qq. 197–206). More supervision is needed, as cruelty and neglect can be more easily concealed from neighbours than where there are two or more children in a 'baby farm'. The age limit should be raised because for health and other reasons many children do not start school at the age of five; they would then remain with one supervisory authority until they were more definitely connected with the education authorities.

The provisions of the Act should be extended to homes where one child is kept and there should be supervision until the child is seven years old.

Bastardy Orders

Sel. Cttee. Rep., proc., mins. of ev., apps. pp. xii, 69. 1909

1909 (236) vi, 717
apptd. May, o.p. July, 1909.

H. Whitbread (*Ch.*), Corbett, Herbert, King, Kennedy.

'*To inquire and report as to the Law relating to the making and enforcement of Orders under the Acts relating to Bastardy, and to report whether any and, if so, what amendments are required in the same.*'

The evidence given shows that there was a general and well-founded consensus of opinion that the objects to be aimed at were (1) to secure adequate care and maintenance of the child until it could be expected to earn something for itself, and (2) to facilitate the process by which mothers, guardians and others might recover from the male parent expenses incurred in connection with the birth and maintenance of the child. Procedure under the Bastardy Laws was uncertain and difficult, and the powers of the guardians should be enlarged. Guardians could claim maintenance for a woman only after the birth of her child; pre-natal expenses had to be borne by the ratepayers. Application for maintenance after the birth often resulted in no payment, as for example, in 1907, in the Dewsbury Union, where out of fifteen illegitimate children born, only three orders were obtained, eleven of the children having died or having been removed (q. 34). Difficulties were experienced where a mother on leaving the workhouse had to go through the procedure of getting an affiliation order made to her, after it had been taken out by the guardians in the first place.

The recommendations followed those of the Royal Commission on the Poor Laws. The Justices should have power (*a*) to make a Bastardy Order, which may be enforced by the mother or by the guardians or by the person maintaining the child or by the person appointed by the Court to receive payment from the father; (*b*) on application by the mother or guardians after the birth of the child, to order reimbursement of expenses incidental to birth, including expenses due to illness or loss of work, within a period not

exceeding one month previous to confinement; and to order such payments to be made by instalments; (*c*) to dispense with the mother's evidence in cases of the mother's death or insanity when the paternity is admitted by the father; (*d*) to vary the weekly sum mentioned in the order within a limit of 10*s.*, and to order that payments made under any Bastardy Order be made to a third person appointed by the Court; (*e*) to assign the custody of the child to a person other than the mother; (*f*) to order payment of a lump sum, to be invested upon trust for the benefit of the child, in place of a weekly payment; (*g*) in special cases to order the father to contribute for the whole lifetime of a cripple or mentally defective child.

After considering the objections to a Bill introduced by Mr. H. Herbert, designed to make a deceased man's estate liable for future maintenance, the Committee confined itself to the above recommendations and reported the Bill without amendment.

2. CHARITIES

War Charities

Rep.

1916 *Cd.* 8287. See *Breviate 1917–39*, p. 502.

3. BETTING

Betting

Sel. Cttee. HL. Rep., proc., mins. of ev. pp. vi, 38. 1901

1901 (370) *v*, 347
apptd. May, o.p. Aug., 1901

Lord Durham (*Ch.*), L. Derby, L. Harewood, L. Cobham, L. Gordon, L. Aberdeen, L. Peel, L. Bishop of Hereford, L. Newton, L. Davey.

'*To inquire into the increase of Public Betting amongst all classes, and whether any Legislative measures are possible and expedient for checking the abuses occasioned thereby.*'

The Report was a formal presentation of minutes of evidence with the recommendation for re-appointment next Session. Two witnesses had been called. J. Hawke, of the National Anti-Gambling League, gave evidence on his own investigations of street betting, especially amongst boys, the methods of the bookmakers, the organized scouting done to protect them from the police and from people suspected of being 'splits' (q. 6) and on coupon betting, etc. G. H. Studfield, the representative for the Jockey Club, discussed the various forms of betting—e.g. post and ante-post betting and the part played by the newspapers. He was of opinion that the present statutory powers, if properly enforced, 'would absolutely suppress all street betting whatsoever'.

—— Report, proc., mins. of ev. pp. xviii, 188. 1902. Index. 1903

1902 (389) (389-*Ind.*) *v*, 445
re-apptd. Jan., o.p. June, 1902

Greater prosperity amongst the working classes and the facilities provided by the press, bookmakers and tipsters had resulted in an increase of betting, though the Betting Houses Act had driven betting on to the street, and it was therefore more in evidence before the magistrates. There was a decrease of the habit of large-scale betting amongst owners and breeders of horses. It had spread to athletic and football meetings, and was contrary to the true interests of amateur sport. The Committee did not regard betting as a crime, but deplored its increase. It rejected suggestions that bookmakers should be licensed and that totalisators should be established, but recommended that advertisements of racing tipsters and circulars be made illegal, that betting should be localized on the course and higher penalties imposed for street betting offences.

Lotteries and Indecent Advertisements

Jt. Sel. Cttee. Rep., proc., mins. of ev., apps. pp. xviii, 106. 1908

1908 (275) *ix*, 375
apptd. March, o.p. July, 1908

Lord Beauchamp (*Ch.*), L. Hutchinson, L. Llandaff, L. Ramsay, L. Herschell, Beckett, Craig, Duncan, O'Malley, Wilson.

'To consider and inquire into the law (1) as to lotteries, including the sale of lottery bonds, competitions for prizes which involve an element of chance, and advertisements relating thereto; (2) as to indecent literature and pictures, and advertisements relating to things indecent and immoral; and to report what amendments, if any, in the law are necessary or desirable.'

The Gaming Act of 1802 and the Lotteries Act of 1823 have been effective in preventing the holding of lotteries in Great Britain. Most of the prosecutions in recent years appear to have been instituted under Section 41 of the Act of 1823, which makes it an offence to sell any ticket or chances, or shares of tickets or chances, in any lottery, foreign or otherwise, or to publish proposals or schemes for the sale of tickets or chances in a lottery. Further legislation is now required in view of the development of prize competitions introduced to the public mainly by proprietors and editors of newspapers and periodicals, in which the element of chance largely predominates, and for which entrance fees are charged or coupons required. It was stated by witnesses that the scale of the limerick competitions—in one case there had been 200,000 entries at 6*d.* each—were so great that, even with a large staff, the judges could not make any assessment based on the skill of the competitor.

The Committee was urged to widen the definition of a lottery to include even those competitions in which an element of skill was required. But rather than alter the well-tried definition 'a distribution of prizes by lot or chance', they recommended 'that it should be made illegal for any proprietor, publisher or editor of any newspaper or periodical to charge any form of entrance fee, including the purchase and return of coupons for prize competitions'.

As it was doubtful whether the word 'publish' included the word 'print', it had been difficult to obtain a process against persons in this country who printed circulars relating to foreign lotteries. The majority of such circulars are printed abroad, and then sent over in bulk to be addressed and posted in England. Section 41 of the Act of 1823 should be made to apply to 'publishing and printing in the country, and also to sending through the post or any other means of distributing, any circular or advertisement relating to a lottery in this or any foreign country'.

The Vagrancy Acts of 1824 and 1838, which deal with the offence of wilfully exposing to view in any street, road or highway or any public place or window or any other part of the shop any obscene print, picture or indecent exhibition, had been effective, though the police asked for powers to search at night as well as in the day-time. Traffic in indecent and obscene postcards had been considerably checked under these Acts, but the police experienced difficulties with establishments open to the public without entrance fees, in which stereoscopic machines containing photographs may be seen for 1d. and $\frac{1}{2}d$., many of them being of an objectionable character and calculated to demoralize the crowds of children and young people who frequent them. If the main recommendation of the Committee were adopted, the Magistrates would have no difficulty in deciding, when the case warranted, on the suppression of such exhibitions.

The Law of Libel Amendment Act, 1888, makes it unnecessary, in the indictment of the publisher of an obscene book, to set out in full the passages to which objection is taken, but it is still necessary in the prosecution of a person for obtaining and procuring such a book for the purposes of sale. The provision in question should be made to apply also to such cases.

The Post Office (Protection) Act of 1884 makes it illegal to send indecent or obscene literature, etc., through the post, but as the Postmaster-General has no power to open letters or packages unless he obtains the warrant of the Home Secretary, the post office can deal only with postcards and open letters. The Committee were unable to recommend any wide powers to the Postmaster-General. It was thought that the trade in such goods from abroad could be checked only by international agreement.

The Indecent Advertisements Act, 1889, does not make it an offence to place any picture or printed matter of an obscene or indecent nature in the letter box of any house or shop, nor state that advertisements of medicines, or appliances for procuring abortion, promoting miscarriage or preventing conception are to be deemed indecent, nor does it refer to advertisements printed in newspapers or periodicals. These omissions should be repaired in a new Bill. Existing legislation, so far as it relates to the publication and sale and advertisement of obscene and indecent literature, pictures and other matters of the same nature, should be repealed, and a new Bill should be introduced to provide a uniform method of procedure in the prosecution of all such offences. Provisions should be made to protect medical men and registered chemists acting *bona fide* in the ordinary course of their profession or business. Exemption from the operation of the Act should be given to any books of literary merit or reputation or any genuine work of Art, and since no definition of these can be devised, the decision should be left to the discretion of the magistrates.

4. INTEMPERANCE, LICENSED TRADE

Inebriates Detention in Reformatories and Retreats

Dept. Cttee. Rep. pp. iii, 39. 1908.
Mins. of ev., apps., index. 1908

1908 *Cd.* 4438, *xii*, 817. *Mins. of ev.,*
etc.; 1908 *Cd.* 4439, *xii*, 861
apptd. April, sgd. Dec., 1908

J. Dickson-Poynder (*Ch.*), Adkins, Bramsdon, Branthwaite, Bridgeman, Bruce-Porter, Donkin, Mercier, Rose.

'To inquire into the operation of the Law relating to Inebriates and to their detention in Reformatories and Retreats, and to report what amendments in the law and its administration are desirable.'

As any recommendation for increased powers of detention might involve expenditure of public money, it was necessary to investigate the possibility that treatment by drugs was a practicable alternative. No mode of treatment by drugs could be enforced by Act; it would be impossible to lay down by statute the various modifications required for individual cases or to force on a voluntary inmate a mode of treatment to which he objected. And the medical officer of an institution was free to adopt any mode of treatment he thought desirable.

The Habitual Drunkards Act, 1879, legalized the establishment of Retreats, licensed by the local authorities, for the reception of voluntary inmates. No retreats had been established out of public funds. The two defects of the Act were that there was little or no accommodation for poor inebriates and that many persons became inmates only at a late stage when they were irreformable and when ruin or ill health led to pressure by relatives. The power of licensing retreats should be transferred to the Secretary of State. The State and local authorities should provide retreats for poorer persons and have powers to enforce contributions. The severity of the legal conditions deterred many inebriates from becoming voluntary inmates: provision should be made to enable them to apply to a Justice of the Peace to be placed under voluntary guardianship. The Act of 1879 had been shorn of all compulsory features, and in 1898 public opinion was still unwilling to face compulsory detention of non-criminal inebriates. There was, however, a large class of inebriates who committed no public offences, but brought poverty and degradation on themselves and on relatives. A Judicial Authority should be empowered, upon petition by relatives, voluntary guardians, etc., to make an order for compulsory guardianship and, if necessary, compulsory detention.

The Inebriates Act, 1898, aimed at replacing by prolonged detention the useless, repeated short terms of imprisonment given to inebriate offenders. Less than 1.5 per 1,000 persons convicted of drunkenness had been detained under its provisions. The success of the Act had been limited: some magistrates had been ignorant of or unwilling to enforce it, there were difficulties in defining an 'habitual drunkard', the requirement of three previous convictions in 12 months was inappropriate, and the maximum sentence of three years, which had become the normal, was too long for reformable cases. There should be a change in definition and procedure and the requirement of three previous convictions should be abolished. Fixed maximum sentences should be discontinued and replaced by graduated measures, varying from discharge on probation to committal to a reformatory for periods not exceeding six months followed by a probation period, and to committal for longer periods up to three years. The Act envisaged that criminal inebriates would be sent to State reformatories and 'police court recidivists' to certified reformatories. Contrary to expectations, the former class had proved more amenable to discipline, while a proportion of the latter had to be sent to State reformatories, which had come to control refractory inmates only. The State should purchase all existing reformatories at a cost not exceeding £150 per bed; and provide for the accommodation and maintenance of all inebriates committed by the Courts. A Treasury grant should be given to help After-Care Associations to assist released inebriates.

—— *Scotland.* Dept. Cttee. Rep. pp. 55. 1909. Mins. of ev., apps., index.
1909
1909 *Cd.* 4766, *xxvi*, 573. *Mins. of ev., etc.*; 1909 *Cd.* 4767, *xxvi*, 601 *apptd. Nov.*, 1908. *sgd. June*, 1909
W. Bilsland (*Ch.*), Carswell, Clouston, Dewar, Falconer (Mrs. A.), Grant (Miss E.), M'Hardy, Macpherson, Scott-Moncrieff.

Terms of Reference, see Cd. 4438.

This Report follows closely that on England and Wales, many of its recommendations being in identical or in closely similar terms.

Inebriates fall into four distinct groups: those known to the police, and for whose treatment the State should be responsible; those known to the parochial authorities, who should deal with them; poor persons of otherwise respectable character, who cannot pay the cost of treatment in a retreat, for whom town and county councils should be responsible; and well-to-do persons who could be provided for out of their own resources. Early and minor deterioration of the brain due to alcoholic excess could be recovered from, but from later and more organic changes complete recovery was not possible. Measures should therefore be taken to arrest the evil in its early stages.

As in England and Wales, the failure of the Habitual Drunkards Act, 1879, was due to its being entirely permissive and to the insufficiency of retreats for poor persons. Public opinion had been adverse to interference with the liberty of the subject, but the witnesses were agreed on the necessity of some measure of compulsion. The Sheriff should be empowered, on the petition of relatives, friends or guardians, to make an order for compulsory guardianship or committal to a retreat for six months, with power to increase the period up to three years. The conditions of guardianship should be laid down by the Secretary of State, to whom the licensing of retreats should be transferred. There were only two licensed retreats in Scotland; the increased number required should be provided by local authorities acting singly or jointly.

The number of offenders committed to reformatories was insufficient and the results were disappointing because offenders were sent too late for reform to be possible. As in England, this was due to the difficulty of proving a man to be an habitual drunkard, to inconvenient procedure, to the failure to bring habitual drunkenness to the notice of the Court and to the small number of reformatories. Where an inebriate has been convicted of specified offences three times within the preceding twelve months, the Court should be empowered to order compulsory guardianship, imprisonment or detention in a reformatory. The State should provide accommodation for and maintain inebriates committed by the Courts, and should make grants to After-Care Associations. Some recommendations are additional to those made for England and Wales. In order to enable parish councils to deal with certain 'ins-and-outs' the Sheriff should have power, on the application of a parish council, to order the detention of pauper inebriates in a poorhouse for a term not exceeding three years. Steps should be taken to protect the property of an inebriate from his own dissipation of it by powers of appointment of a *curator bonis* to look after his estate, as in the case of an insane person.

The Duties of the Metropolitan Police

Rep.

1908 *Cd.* 4156. See *Police.* p. 365.

Licensing (Consolidation) Bill [H.L.]

Jt. Sel. Cttee. 1st Rep., proc., mins. of ev., apps. pp. xxx, 89. 1910. Index. 1913. (2nd Rep. on Consolidation Bills, see *Perjury*, p. 376)

1910 (321) (321-*Ind.*) *vi*, 389
apptd. March, o.p. Nov., 1910

The Lord Chancellor (*Ch.*), L. Ridley, L. Stanley, L. Kinnaird, L. Mersey, Cave, Hindle, Roberts, Simon, Younger.

The Licensing (Consolidation) Bill should be allowed to proceed, as it now represents simply the present law. The Appendix outlines the amendments for improving or making clear the language of existing Acts and for remedying an anomaly under the existing law with respect to licensing jurisdiction in county boroughs, and gives the definition of a new licence.

Proposals for the State Purchase of the Licensed Liquor Trade (England and Wales)

Advisory Cttee. Rep. pp. 6. 1916
1916 *Cd.* 8283, *xii*, 529
sgd. April, 1915

H. Samuel (*Ch.*), L. Cunliffe, Simon, Bradbury, Coates, Harmood-Banner, Plender, Snowden, Whittaker.

'The Committee were appointed to advise the Government on the financial arrangements that would have to be made if it should be decided by the State to purchase the properties of the Breweries in England and Wales, to control the branches of the retail liquor trade not so purchased, and to prohibit temporarily the retail trade in spirits, while permitting the continuance of the sale of beer below a certain alcoholic strength. They understand that the purchase would be effected by the issue of Government stock in exchange for the securities or properties to be bought. The Committee understand also that they are

not asked to enter into the broad questions of policy, either general or financial, involved by these proposals, and that they are to view the purchase as a purely commercial transaction, and without prejudice to the issue how far a licence to sell exciseable liquor can or cannot rightly be regarded as property.'

'Taking into account the present position and future prospects of the trade, together with the compulsory character of the proposed purchase, the Committee are of opinion that the property which is to be acquired should be bought by the exchange of £100 of Government 4 per cent stock for every ascertained £100 worth of liquor-trade securities or properties.'

Commissioners would have to be appointed to determine values, and an authority set up to conduct the trade on behalf of the State. The undertakings should not be purchased as a whole, but securities of each class purchased from their holders at the average of the middle prices quoted during the three years ending 30th June, 1914. The proposals provide for concerns whose shares are not dealt in, the purchase of public houses, etc., on the basis of the actual profits of each house, temporary compensation arrangements during the war, etc. The approximate total cost would be £250 mn. for England and Wales.

Proposals for the State Purchase of the Licensed Liquor Trade. Scotland

Advisory Cttee. Rep. pp. [4]. 1916

1916 *Cd.* 8319, *xii*, 535
apptd. —, sgd. April, 1915

T. M. Wood, Munro, Dickson, Adamson, Maclay, Mann, Andrews.

'*To consider and advise the Government as to the methods and principles upon which compensation should be awarded on the following suppositions: (a) That the Government should decide to obtain control of the liquor trade by purchase. (b) That the Government should decide to prohibit the retail sale of spirits with or without wines, but permit the retail sale of beer not exceeding a certain alcoholic strength.'*

The Scottish problem was quite distinct from that of England and Wales, where possession of public houses would be given by the purchase of breweries which owned them. In Scotland, breweries were merely creditors of the public house licensees, which numbered 6,700, with 3,400 licensed grocers in addition. In Scotland, the principles of compensation of the Licensing Act, 1904, did not apply, the licence being merely an annual grant. Further, by 1920 the principle of local option would be in force, and might result in the extinction or reduction of licences. The annual profits of the trade as a whole should be fixed, the division of the sum being left to the trade, but without more information no suggestion could be made of the fair number of years purchase to be used as a multiple. The capital value had been assessed, before the 1913 Act, at £8,788,000 and of grocers' licences at £1,470,000. Distilleries should not be purchased. If the sale of spirits were prohibited, compensation should be on the basis of an allowance per gallon on the probable loss of sales, with a set-off in the case of publicans for consequential increases in the sales of beer.

State Purchase and Control of the Liquor Trade

Rep.

1918 *Cd.* 9042. See *Breviate 1917–39,* pp. 506–7.

5. SUNDAY CLOSING, SUNDAY TRADING

Sunday Closing (Shops) Bill. [H.L.]

Sel. Cttee. HL. Rep., proc.; mins. of ev., apps., index. pp. xiii, 175, 28. 1905

1905 (344) *viii,* 9
apptd. March, o.p. Aug., 1905

Lord Avebury (*Ch.*), Duke of Northumberland, L. Derby, L. Stanhope, L. Gordon, L. Bishop of Rochester, L. Belper, L. Sandhurst.

The majority of the witnesses expressed a strong opinion that the public would suffer no inconvenience if the Bill became law. The Committee concurred in this opinion and stated that it would be of great benefit to the country generally and that it commended itself both to the reason and the conscience of the community. A clause allowed for the exemption of an area, in special circumstances. Reported to the House with amendments.

Sunday Trading

Jt. Sel. Cttee. Rep., proc., mins. of ev., apps. pp. xxvi, 282. Index. 1906

1906 (275) (275-*Ind.*) *xiii,* 29
apptd. March, o.p. July, 1906

Lord Avebury (*Ch.*), Duke of Northumberland, L. Beauchamp, L. Bishop of Wakefield, L. Weardale, Burke, Edwards, Gulland, Samuel, Doughty.

'To inquire into the subject of Sunday trading.'

Maintaining Sunday as a day of rest is of great importance not only on religious and moral grounds, but because one clear day's rest in seven is necessary to the preservation of the health and strength of the community. But any new legislation passed to prevent the increase in Sunday shopping will have to provide some exemptions, if hardship is to be prevented amongst costermongers, street hawkers and small shopkeepers not employing an assistant.

The law is said to be unworkable in Scotland, and in England ignored by most local authorities on the grounds that it was invidious to act on certain provisions of the Act of Charles II while ignoring others, and that the fine of 5s. was too small to be effective. Of the total prosecutions in England, 78 per cent were in Hull, 10 per cent in Swansea and 12 per cent for the rest of the country. The Chief Constable of Swansea said 'they bring their money into Court, hand it in and walk out again'. But he was joined by the Chief Constable of Hull in saying that the local authorities were supported by public opinion in their attempts to enforce the law, and that little if any inconvenience had been experienced.

Complaints were made by those who observe the law against those who set the law at defiance. To meet the problem of certain Jewish traders, areas might be scheduled in any Act permitting a Jew who closed his shop on Saturday to trade until midday on Sunday. In Scotland the public houses have been closed on Sunday for over 50 years with complete success. Public opinion is in favour of a more thorough Sunday closing than in England.

If the law were effectually enforced it would constitute a protection to many who were virtually compelled to work on Sunday, and under slightly increased pressure the habits of the people would adjust themselves to a more considerate attitude towards the trading community. The general principle of the Act of 1677 should be maintained; penalties imposed are inadequate; regulations permitting exemptions from the Act, e.g. the sale of milk and cream, newspapers, refreshments, should be drawn up by the local authorities, and confirmed by the central authority; one day's rest in seven for shop assistants should be secured by law.

Police Forces (Weekly Rest Day) Rep.

1908 (353). See *Police*. p. 367.

XVI. LEGAL ADMINISTRATION, POLICE, LAW

1. Legal Administration, Procedure, Legal Aid to the Poor
2. Police
3. Prisons, Prisoners, Reformatory and Industrial Schools, Probation
4. Civil and Criminal Law
5. Law of Property
6. Divorce
7. Civil Order, Censorship, Miscellaneous Regulatory Powers
8. War Losses.

1. LEGAL ADMINISTRATION, PROCEDURE, LEGAL AID TO THE POOR

Jurisdiction of the Metropolitan Police Magistrates and County Justices in the Metropolitan Police Court District

Dept. Cttee. Rep., mins. of ev., apps., index. pp. xiv, 111. 1900

1900 Cd. 374, *xl*, 659
apptd. Dec., 1898. *sgd. Aug.*, 1899

Lord Belper (*Ch.*), Poland, Dugdale, Whitmore, Lushington.

'*To enquire into the jurisdiction of the Metropolitan Police Magistrates and County Justices respectively in the Metropolitan Police Court District; and to report whether any and what limitations in lieu of or in addition to those contained in* Section 42 *of the Metropolitan Police Courts Act*, 1839 (2 & 3 *Vict. cap.* 71) *should be made by legislation or otherwise in regard to their respective jurisdictions, and generally whether any and what measures are required in order to meet the needs of the Metropolitan Police Court District as regards the exercise of magisterial jurisdiction.*'

The Act of 1839, which established the Metropolitan Police Courts, prohibited the County Justices in the area, other than the Police Court Magistrates, from taking fees for exercising jurisdiction, except in such matters as were specified. Some County Justices had begun to exercise jurisdiction over other classes of cases, in which claimants and informants saved fees which would otherwise have been payable in the Police Courts; and this power was confirmed by the High Court. The anomaly of two distinct sets of Courts sitting in the same district with concurrent jurisdiction, levying different fees and imposing different penalties could not be defended. The growth of London and of the volume of legislation affecting its citizens had led to a great pressure of business in the Police Courts, causing serious delays and additional expense (qq. 941–944). The London Standing Joint Committee had issued a statement suggesting changes in the law to make clear the powers of the Justices and there was a desire to relieve the congestion of work (qq. 746–779).

The number of Police Magistrates should be raised to the permitted maximum and the areas of the police districts re-arranged to equalize the work and relieve the busiest courts. There should be no interference with their powers of administering criminal justice. The jurisdiction of the County Justices should continue to be exercised within distinct limits, be clearly defined to prevent any clashing of authority, and recommendations are made to this end (Lushington dissenting from the proposal that they should deal with School Board summonses). They should be able to apply to the Secretary of State for power to sit as a Petty Sessional Court and the Police Magistrates should cease to adjudicate on matters allotted to it. (Whitemore considered that the Secretary of State should first satisfy himself as to the competence of the County Justices and that the powers granted should be revocable.) The fees payable should be on the Police Court scale and paid into the Police Fund, from which provision should be made for the remuneration of the Clerks of the Petty Sessional Courts.

Metropolitan Police Court Jurisdiction in Middlesex

Dept. Cttee. Vol. I. Rep. pp. 8. 1904.
Vol. II. Mins. of ev. 1904

1904 *Cd.* 2215, *xxxiv*, 343. *Mins. of ev.*;
1904 *Cd.* 2216, *xxxiv*, 351
apptd. March, sgd. July, 1904

Lord Belper (*Ch.*), Bosanquet, Simpson, Arkwright.

'To consider and report whether any alteration of the boundaries of the Metropolitan Police Court Districts where they extend into the County of Middlesex is desirable; and, if so, whether any re-arrangement of the Police Court Districts is, in consequence, required.'

Since 1840–1 parts of the County of Middlesex have been included in the Metropolitan Police Court Districts, which overlap the boundaries of the Administrative County of London, established in 1888. Officials attending court on behalf of the local Education Authority have to attend courts in two different counties. In prosecutions under bye-laws a Metropolitan Police Court magistrate may have to administer two different sets of laws, one for Middlesex, the other for London. Appeals from his court go to Middlesex Quarter Sessions if arising in Middlesex, to London Quarter Sessions if arising in London. Arguments in favour of continuing Police Court jurisdiction over these areas would apply in principle equally to even more extended adjacent areas similar in population. Any increase of work entailed by taking the cases now sent to the Metropolitan Police Courts could be undertaken without difficulty by the County Petty Sessional Courts. Police Court Districts should be restricted to the area within the County of London boundary. In the case of Acton and Chiswick, the transfer of jurisdiction should be deferred until some Court or Courts had been provided in those districts.

County of Suffolk Bill

Sel. Cttee. Rep., proc., mins. of ev. pp. vi, 6. 1904

1904 (273) *vi*, 25
apptd. July, o.p. July, 1904.

Mr. Stuart-Wortley (*Ch.*), Quilter, Round, Hobhouse, Price, Tomkinson, Soames.

The Bill 'to make better provision for the administration of Justice at Sessions of the Peace and for the transactions of County Business', was reported without amendment.

See 1904 4 Edw. 7. c. clvii.

Poor Prisoners' Defence Bill

Sel. Cttee. Reps., proc., mins of ev., apps. pp. xii, 64. 1903. (Also Reps. printed separately. 1903 (254).)

1903 (264) *vii*, 595
apptd. March, o.p. July, 1903

Mr. Bousfield (*Ch.*), Atherley-Jones, Black, Bowles, Duke, Griffith, Kimber, Leese, Redmond, Solicitor-General for Scotland, Arkwright, Nussey.

In criminal matters, where the prosecution is conducted by experienced solicitors and counsel, it is contrary to the ordinary requirements of justice that no legal advice should be given to the prisoner. A prisoner without means ought to be in no worse position to establish his innocence than one with means. In Scotland these principles have been widely applied with success for many years. But 40 per cent of prisoners tried plead guilty, and it would not be worth while to tempt them with an offer of solicitor and counsel to try for an acquittal. The operation of the Bill should be limited to cases in which, having regard to the nature of the defence raised, it appears desirable in the interests of justice that the prisoner should have legal aid. Solicitor and counsel should be assigned to the prisoner and as it seemed unlikely that sufficient voluntary help from solicitors would be forthcoming, both should be paid out of public funds.

As arrangements of the kind already exist in Ireland, the Bill should not apply to Ireland.

Allowances to Prosecutors and Witnesses in Criminal Prosecutions

Dept. Cttee. Rep. pp. xx. 1903. Mins. of ev., apps. 1903

1903 *Cd.* 1650, *lvi*, 357. *Mins of ev., etc.*; 1903 *Cd.* 1651, *lvi*, 377
apptd. May, 1902. *sgd. April,* 1903

J. E. Dorington (*Ch.*), Lawrence, Merrifield, Simpson.

'*To inquire and report what changes are desirable in the regulations made under the Act* 14 & 15 *Vict. c.* 55, *s.* 5, *respecting Allowances to Prosecutors and Witnesses in Criminal Cases, and what Amendments, if any, are desirable in the law as to the circumstances in which such allowances can be made.*'

It is generally agreed that the present allowances to ordinary prosecutors and witnesses are inadequate and involve a considerable number of witnesses of the poorer classes in serious loss, but there is divergence of opinion as to whether they should be based on the principle of equality of payment to all witnesses or should indemnify them for trouble and loss of time. The Committee rejects both the principle of compensation for loss and proposals to divide witnesses into classes, with graduated payments, as in Scotland and Ireland. Its proposals aim at making such payments as will secure the efficient administration of justice while preserving from loss the witness of the poorer class who earns a daily wage.

For an ordinary witness the allowances should not exceed 7s. per day and 5s. per night, provided that he should not generally be paid more than the amount of wages lost, and that the minimum should be 1s., this to be the general allowance for unemployed persons. Travelling expenses should be the fare actually paid and should be third class. Seamen detained on shore should receive the amount actually and reasonably paid for maintenance. Allowances paid to interpreters and to expert witnesses, i.e. those previously unacquainted with the case, but giving evidence because of special knowledge of the subject, should be at the discretion of the Court. The allowances to professional witnesses (mainly doctors, accountants and lawyers), i.e. those giving evidence as to facts which have come to their notice in their ordinary practice and not in the first instance with a view to prosecution, have been inadequate, and should be based on one guinea per day in the place of residence and two guineas a day for evidence given in some other place. Allowances are also set out for police witnesses and warders.

In a memo. Humphrey-Owen and Roberts state that the maximum allowances for ordinary witnesses, especially the reduced rate for less than four hours' attendance, would not meet the case of miners, artisans, mechanics and small shopkeepers, and recommend a graduated scale like those in force in Scotland and Ireland, English County Courts and the Old Northern Circuit.

Sheriff Court Procedure

Dept. Cttee. Rep., mins. of ev., apps., index. pp. 74. 1904

1905 *Cd.* 2287, *lxiv*, 451
apptd. —, *sgd.* —

C. S. Dickson (*Ch.*), L. Darling, Rutherfurd, Ure, Fraser, Ritchie, Spens.

'*To inquire and report as to the following matters*: 1. *The forms of writs and pleadings and the rules of procedure in the civil courts of the Sheriff.* 2. *The forms of writs and the rules of procedure in the criminal courts of the Sheriff.* 3. *The procedure for review of and appeal from decrees, interlocutors and orders in the civil courts of the Sheriff; and sentences in the criminal courts of the Sheriff.* 4. *The constitution of and rules of procedure in arbitration either at common law or under the Land Clauses Acts, and other statutes.*'

The procedure of the Court was examined with a view to simplifying it in the light of the altered circumstances of the times. Of the Statutes, Sheriff Mackay said that 'the present procedure is a good working system, but experience had pointed out some defects, and the consolidation of the Procedure Statutes is required' (q. 117). The thirteen recommendations included the following: the extension of jurisdiction of the Small Debts Courts to actions for sums up to £20 instead of up to £12; the Debts Recovery Court should not be kept as a separate court, but all cases over £20 and under £50 should be dealt with by the Ordinary Court; the jurisdiction of the Sheriff Court should be extended to cover actions for separation and aliment, to regulate the custody of children, etc.; and the Statutes dealing with Sheriff Court procedure should be consolidated and codified. In Common Law arbitrations the provision of the English law that where no particular mode of arbitration is specified, a single arbitrator should be used, should be extended to Scotland.

See Acts; 1907 7 Edw. 7. c. 51. 1908 8 Edw. 7. c. 65.

County Court Procedure

Cttee. Rep. pp. 37. [1909]

1909 (71) *lxxii*, 311
apptd. July, 1908. *sgd. Feb.*, 1909

Lord Gorell, Channell, Atkinson, MacDonell, Chalmers, Bridgeman, Cleaver, Ellett, Bonsey.

'*To consider the relations now subsisting between the High Court of Justice and the County Courts, and to report whether any and what alteration or modification should be made in those relations and consequently in the jurisdiction and practice of the County Courts.*'

Although originally founded as small case courts, County Courts have been given a large number of extra duties, e.g. in Equity and Admiralty cases, Workmen's Compensation, Bankruptcy, etc. These, with an increase of ordinary work, have heavily taxed their strength to carry out their primary duty of enforcing small debts and claims by simple, inexpensive machinery. At the same time there has been dissatisfaction with the system under which the civil work of the High Court outside London has been dealt with and a great diminution of business on Circuit.

The problem to be determined was the best way of dealing with that work which was, or ought to be, disposed of in the provinces and was beyond the present jurisdiction of the County Courts. The suggestions the Committee rejected were (1) that the County Courts should become part of the High Court, with unlimited jurisdiction in actions, subject to the rights of transfer to a superior branch of the High Court; (2) that the County Courts should retain their present constitution, but should have unlimited, or much enlarged jurisdiction in actions, subject to the right of transfer; and (3) that provincial courts should be established for cases not left to the County Courts. It adopted instead the principles that the Circuit system should be remodelled so as to concentrate the civil work in centres, and that more time should be allowed, and more convenient arrangements made for the disposal of business. The High Court judges should be in sufficient strength to deal adequately with all the work which ought to be done by them; the number of King's Bench Judges was insufficient. Any scheme for the improvement of civil business throughout the country would be more easy of adoption if the principle of the separation between the civil and criminal business were adopted and the County Courts other than those of easy access to London were given limited jurisdiction in matrimonial cases. Detailed recommendations were made for the alteration of County Court practice, for producing better administration and the saving of time. Three notes added by members of the Committee showed concurrence with the main recommendations but disagree-

ment on details; Bonsey did not sign the report for reasons stated in a note.

High Court of Justice (King's Bench Division)

Jt. Sel. Cttee. Rep., proc., mins. of ev., apps. pp. x, 156. 1909. Index. 1910

1909 (333) (333-Ind.) viii, 1.
apptd. July, o.p. Dec., 1909

Lord Cawdor (*Ch.*), Akers-Douglas, Ellis, Kennaway, Haldane, Whittaker, Duke of Devonshire, L. Belper, L. Welby, L. Courtney.

'To consider the state of business in the King's Bench Division of the High Court and report thereon, and whether any increase is desirable in the number of Judges of that Division, and to make such recommendations as they see fit.'

Owing to the serious arrears in the King's Bench Division the King's Bench judges, in a communication to the Lord Chancellor, asked that two new judges should be appointed (q. 1). The situation could not be dealt with by the appointment of Commissioners. Two additional judges should be added, in the first instance on the footing that vacancies subsequently occurring should remain unfilled unless sanctioned by Parliament, until the present establishment is reached, and that the reforms for better organization of the business in London and on circuit should be carried into effect.

Coroners

Dept. Cttee.

apptd. Dec., 1908

M. D. Chalmers (*Ch.*), Morris, Shephard, Bramsdon, Willcox.

'To inquire into the law relating to coroners and coroners' inquests, and into the practice in coroners' courts.'

The First Report is a formal presentation of the following volume of minutes of evidence, etc.; 1909 Cd. 4782, xv, 389.

—— Second Report. Part I. Rep. pp.
22. [1910.] Part II. Mins. of ev. 1910.
Part III. Mins. of ev., apps. 1911.

1910 *Cd.* 5004, *xxi*, 561. *Mins. of ev.,*
etc.; 1910 *Cd.* 5139, *xxi*, 583; 1911 *Cd.*
5492, *xiii*, 649
sgd. Dec., 1909

'The Law relating to Coroners is
antiquated,' and 'is not very well
suited to the changed conditions of
modern life.' The duties are discharged
by three classes of coroners, the county,
borough, and franchise coroners. Franchise coronerships are inconvenient
and anomalous. They were created
by Charter from the Crown granted
to individuals or to a corporation.
They now constitute islands in the
jurisdiction of the county coroner as,
for example, in Norfolk, where one
franchise coroner's district is scattered
over the county and consists of twenty-
three patches of exclusive jurisdiction.
The total number of coroners' jurisdictions is 360.

The qualifications of a coroner are
(1) in a county, that he should be
required to have 'land in fee sufficient
in the same county whereof he may
answer to all manner of people',
which could mean that the freehold
ownership of a grave was sufficient;
(2) that he should be a 'fit person,
and not an alderman or councillor of
the county or county borough'. Fit
person is not defined, though the
majority of coroners have legal or
medical training. It was recommended
that the franchise coronerships should
be abolished as they fall vacant;
that the holding of land as a qualification should be abolished and a professional training prescribed.

The field of jurisdiction and the
procedure and practice of the coroner's
court were reviewed in great detail
and many recommendations were made
to define the powers and to facilitate the
efficient working of the courts. For
example: *Jurisdiction.* Fire Inquests: in
the City of London these have worked
well, and they should be extended to
the whole country. Treasure Trove:

no inquest should be held except on
the order of the Treasury. Post-
mortem examination without inquest:
for example, sudden death from heart
disease by person not under medical
treatment; the coroner should have
power to order and pay for a post-
mortem, which might remove the need
for public inquiry. Second Inquest:
a coroner should himself have powers
to apply for one. Coroners as substitute for Sheriff: where the coroner is
not a lawyer, it would be a better plan
to call in the nearest adjacent sheriff
when a substitute was needed. *Procedure*
and Practice. There is no authority
with powers to make rules of procedure; wide and flexible powers to
make such rules should be given to
the Lord Chancellor and the Home
Secretary, assisted by a small committee
of coroners. The coroner should have
more direct powers over exhumation,
removal of the body, backing warrants
and the production of exhibits. Jurors'
List: there is no legally prescribed
list, and in an emergency passers-by
may be called in. The Parliamentary
Voters List or the Burgess Roll is
usually the index to persons liable to
be called to serve. Rules should be
made, and there should be some time
exemption before one person can be
called to serve again. Failure to agree:
if twelve cannot agree on a verdict 'the
coroner may order them to be kept
without meat, drink or fire until they
do agree'. He should be empowered
to accept a three-fourths majority, or
to discharge the jury and appoint a
fresh one. Perverse Verdicts: the
coroners should not be compelled to
accept a perverse verdict. Two actual
examples are: 'The man died from stone
in the kidney which stone he swallowed
while lying on a gravel path in a state
of drunkenness', or 'A child three
months old found dead, but no evidence
to show whether born alive'. He
should have the power to apply to a
judge in chambers to set aside the
verdict and authorize a new jury to be
summoned. Riders to verdicts are
very often sensible, but are sometimes

unreasonable and mischievous. They should be separated from the verdict, and the coroner should be free to record his dissent from it. Certification of death: certificates should not be accepted from the medical practitioner unless he has inspected the body. It should be a statutory duty to report all uncertified deaths to the coroner. The verdict of felo-de-se, the only effect of which is to induce juries to find a verdict of temporary insanity without any evidence to justify it, should be abolished. In cases of suicide the verdict should be that 'the deceased died by his own hand' (stating how). The jury should be at liberty to add to their verdict that there is no evidence to show the state of his mind, or that at the time of taking his life he was 'of unsound mind'. The coroner's power to exclude the public from an inquest should be retained. A fresh Consolidation Act was recommended.

—— Deaths Resulting from the Administration of Anaesthetics. Rep. pp. 8. 1910

1910 Cd. 5111, xxi, 785
sgd. March, 1910

There had been an increasing number of deaths under (not necessarily from) anaesthetics, some of which were preventable. Every death under an anaesthetic should be reported to the Coroner, who should have discretion whether or not to hold an inquest. The absence of any regulation for the administration of anaesthetics was a serious menace; it should be a criminal offence for an unqualified or unsupervised person to administer a general respirable anaesthetic. One person should never attempt both to operate and administer gas. The administration of anaesthetics which had a prolonged effect should be confined to qualified medical men, but the restrictions on the use of drugs like cocaine depended upon the various uses to which they were put. Registered dentists should be confined to the use of nitrous oxide gas for dental operations. Adequate training in anaesthetics should be obligatory for all medical students. Knowledge of anaesthetics was still inadequate, and a small standing committee should be set up under the authority of the Home Office.

—— Danger Arising from the Use of Flannelette for Articles of Clothing. Rep. pp. 6. 1910

1910 Cd. 5376, xxi, 793
sgd. Aug., 1910

In 1907 the Registrar General showed separately the deaths attributable to flannelette and in the three months ending January 1910, 176 deaths were recorded. Whilst flannelette was an important contributing cause to deaths by burning, carelessness with matches, candles, open fires and the absence of fire-guards were the real causes. Prohibition of an article of clothing in such common use was thought to be undesirable, and no recommendations were made beyond making it a penal offence to describe material as non-inflammable which did not stand up to tests. What was required was a cheap process for diminishing inflammability. In view of the tests which were being made, the Committee anticipated improvements in the manufacture of flannelette in the near future.

County of London Quarter Sessions

Dept. Cttee. Vol. I. Rep., apps. pp. 41. 1909. Vol. II. Mins. of ev. 1909

1909 Cd. 4828, xxxi, 329. Mins. of ev.; 1909 Cd. 4829, xxxi, 371
apptd. March, sgd. July, 1909

Lord Alverstone (Ch.), Troup, Cave, Hanson, Harris, Smith.

'To consider and report what place would be the most suitable, having regard to convenience and economy, for transacting the Quarter Sessions business of the County of London and what, if any, improvements could be made in the arrangements for the *trial of criminal cases and the hearing of appeals.'*

Before 1888, Quarter Sessions for Middlesex were held at Clerkenwell, appeals being heard in the Guildhall, Westminster, and for Surrey at Newington; after the creation of the County of London, this separation of courts survived, though in a somewhat altered form. (See Mr. Gomme's statement on the History of the County of London Quarter Sessions in App. VIII.) The principle that all the Sessions' business of the County of London should be transacted in one place had been, in practice, accepted and the Committee confined themselves to considering a single place. It was recommended that 'it is not possible to use the buildings of the Central Criminal Court, whether by amalgamating the criminal business of the Sessions with that of the Central Criminal Court, or by interposing the sittings of the Quarter Sessions between those of the Central Criminal Court. If regard is had to economy only, it is desirable that a new Sessions House should be built on the site at Newington. If regard is had chiefly to convenience, a site in the central district above described would be most suitable for all classes of persons connected with the Sessions.

The trial of criminal cases and the hearing of appeals cannot be expeditiously and satisfactorily carried on if a large number of justices—the average attendance on the first day of a session is between 25 and 30—take part in the proceedings. There should be a rota consisting of a limited number of magistrates selected from the Petty Sessional Divisions of the County. It would be of advantage to form a third court for the hearing of appeals in civil matters.

Selection of Justices of the Peace

R. Com. Rep. pp. iv, 16. 1911. Mins. of ev., apps., index. 1910

1910 Cd. 5250, *xxxvii*, 647. Mins. of ev., etc.; 1910 Cd. 5358, *xxxvii*, 669 apptd. Nov., 1909. sgd. July, 1910

Lord James (*Ch.*), L. Chichester, L. Robert Cecil, L. Hamilton, Dyke, Hobhouse, Mowatt, Williams, Troup, Verney, Simon, Adkins, Ashton, Bridgeman, Henderson, L. Jersey.

'To consider and report whether any and what steps should be taken to facilitate the selection of the most suitable persons to be Justices of the Peace, irrespective of creed and political opinion.'

As the Lord Lieutenant is virtually the head of the magistracy in his county it is natural that the Lord Chancellor should seek his assistance when appointing Justices of the Peace; it is in this way that the 'custom' and not the 'right' had become established. Attempts to claim on behalf of the Lords Lieutenants any absolute rights have usually evoked vigorous protest from the Lord Chancellors and others. For example, the present Lord Chancellor stated that 'it would be intolerable if he were required to bear the whole responsibility for appointments which the law entrusts solely to him, but were constrained to act upon the opinion of someone else'. But, he said, there were only a few cases where appointments had been made without the concurrence of the Lord Lieutenant (pp. 5, 6).

The methods pursued by the different Lords Lieutenants in obtaining the necessary information about those whom they recommend as suitable to fill the office of Justice of the Peace varies widely, but the persons most usually consulted are the Chairmen of Quarter and Petty Sessions, the Clerk of the Peace and the Clerks to the Justices. Some Lords Lieutenants would also rely upon the advice which they would get from a large circle of personal friends. Some Lords Lieutenants seem to work systematically, others to be guided by one or two personal friends whose political predilections might influence his choice. Such influence was to be regretted. There was ground for the suggestion that the methods used were insufficient and the results unsatisfactory. As the result of this system and of the property qualification not abolished till 1906, there was a preponderance on the County Benches of Justices of one political complexion. In addition, the office was desired because of the social distinction it was thought to confer. In some cases lists of persons were drawn up by political agents with the object of encouraging party support, and sent to the Lord Lieutenant. The evils of this system of selection of judicial officers were apparent; the attributes of ability, impartiality and high character were frequently absent or deficient.

The appointment of Justices of the Peace should continue to be with the Crown. The Lords Lieutenants of Counties should retain the practice of recommending to the Lord Chancellor, for his approval, persons to be appointed Justices of the Peace, subject to the following conditions: (i) That the Lord Chancellor should nominate within each county one or more small representative Committees, to inform and advise the Lord Chancellor and the Lord Lieutenant. (ii) That the persons to be selected as members of the Committees, and the practice and procedure of the Committees, should be left to the discretion of the Lord Chancellor. The Lord Chancellor should have power to appoint similar Committees in boroughs. It is not in the public interest that there should be an undue preponderance of Justices drawn from one political party. The Lords Lieutenants and the Lord Chancellor should refuse to receive any unasked-for recommendations from members of Parliament, candidates, political agents or associations. Working men with a knowledge of conditions of life in their own class should be appointed to the County as well as to the Borough Benches. There are memoranda by Adkins and Ashton, and by Verney.

The Trial of Stinie Morrison
Rep., app. pp. 15. 1911

1911 *Cd.* 5627, *xxxviii*, 823
sgd. April, 1911

G. Cave.

'*To hold an inquiry into the incidents attending the arrest of Stinie Morrison and his detention at Leman Street Police Station on the 8th January last, and into the statements with regard thereto made by the police officers who were witnesses at the trial, and to report whether, in my opinion, any of the statements made by them were false.*'

In the trial for the murder of Leon Beron on Clapham Common in Jan., 1911, the evidence of five police officers conflicted with that of one police officer, on the words used to Morrison at the time of his arrest. This enquiry into the details of the circumstances and statements of the officers in the police station on the day of the arrest, and the individual characters of the two officers chiefly concerned led to the conclusion that the five officers made true statements and the one officer Greaves an untrue one: although, it was added, he did not deliberately swear to what he knew to be false.

Salford Hundred Court of Record
Dept. Cttee. Rep., mins. of ev., apps., index. pp. vi, 49. 1911

1911 *Cd.* 5530, *xl*, 783
apptd. Oct., sgd. Dec., 1910

Lord Mersey (*Ch.*), McCall, Maddison.

'*To enquire into the practice, procedure and area of jurisdiction of the Court of Record of the Hundred of Salford, and to report how far the Court is now of benefit to the parties for whose use it is intended, whether any changes in its practice or procedure are desirable, and whether any parts of the Hundred of Salford, now within its district, should be wholly or partially exempt from its jurisdiction.*'

In 1868 the two Courts of Record, the Hundred of Salford and the

Borough of Manchester, were amalgamated, with extended jurisdiction, into one Court, 'The Court for the Hundred of Salford'. In the years following several Orders were made by her late Majesty in Council, excluding wholly or partially from the jurisdiction of the Court various boroughs included by the Act of 1868. Applications from the Councils of Stockport and Todmorden for exclusion were before the Council, and a clause for exclusion was in the Heywood Corporation Bill. The statistics and evidence, and the repeated applications for exclusion made it quite clear that inconvenience and hardships have arisen in the practice of the Court, but it performed a large amount of useful work. To abolish it would mean the appointment of an additional County Court Judge, and an additional burden on the Exchequer. As inconvenience and loss have been caused to many defendants residing at a distance from the Court, its territorial jurisdiction should be limited to the areas of the County Courts of Manchester and Salford, and leave for service out of the area should be granted only if the Registrar were satisfied that a material part of the cause of the action arose within the jurisdiction and that its trial in the Salford Hundred was most convenient for both parties.

Salford Hundred Court of Record Bill

Sel. Cttee. Rep., proc., mins. of ev. pp. iv, 6. 1911

1911 (257) *vii*, 779
apptd. July, o.p. Aug., 1911

J. A. Pease (*Ch.*), Gordon, Low, Gill Tyron.

The Committee found that the preamble of the Bill, which was based on the recommendations of the Mersey Committee, was proved and reported the Bill with amendments. There was a statement in evidence regarding the constitutional maxim that the Crown

could not by prerogative, create or limit the power of existing Courts created by statute.

See 1911 1 & 2 Geo. 5. c. clxxii.

Minor Legal Appointments in Scotland

Dept. Cttee. Vol. I. Rep., app. pp. 27. 1911. Mins. of ev., index. 1911

1911 *Cd. 5602, xxxv,* 665. *Mins. of ev., etc.;* 1911 *Cd. 5603, xxxv,* 693 *apptd. Feb.,* 1910. *sgd. March,* 1911

Lord Salvesen (*Ch.*), Mackenzie, Maconochie, Mackay, Haldane, Mitchell, Watt.

'To inquire into the conditions of tenure of office, remuneration, duties, and hours of work in Session and Vacation of the following officials, namely: (1) The Principal, Depute, Assistant and Ordinary Clerks of Session, (2) The Clerks of the Bill Chamber of the Court of Session, (3) The Assistant and Depute Clerks of Justiciary, (4) The clerical staff of the Crown Office, (5) The Depute-Keeper of the Minute Book and of the Register of Edictal Citations of the Court of Session, (6) Extractor of the Court of Session and staff of his Office, (7) Clerk of Teinds and staff of his Office, and (8) Sheriff Clerks Depute; and to consider and report whether any alterations in the present arrangements are advisable; and also to inquire into the organization and control of the various offices concerned, and to report as to the best methods of organizing these offices so as to promote efficiency.'

The Committee discussed each office separately and made separate recommendations for general easement either by extra appointments, by transference of work, and by some increase of salary and by rights to pensions. To minimize political appointments of minor officials, and to provide for promotion from the bottom upwards, all future entrants should pass one of the examinations specified, and the whole staff not holding Crown appointments should be given the status of a Civil Servant.

In a memo., in which Mitchell

concurred, Haldane said that the recommendations were not strong enough to break down the present system of separate and independent offices so as to produce in its place one with a regular and progressive scheme of promotion based not on seniority, but on efficiency. Watt thought that the proposals were inadequate. To continue the system of watertight compartments with a constant importation of outsiders to nearly all the important posts was to perpetuate the evil. The offices should be formed into a consolidated service, with the status, etc., of civil servants, no outsiders being appointed to any posts except as in other Government Departments, and these should be approved by the Civil Service Commissioners. Entrance should be by open competitive examination.

Conditions of Employment of the Present Members of the Engrossing Staff in the General Register of Sasines, Edinburgh

Dept. Cttee. Rep. Vol. I. Rep. pp. 19. 1913. Vol. II. Mins. of ev., apps. 1913

1913 *Cd. 6789, xxxix, 743. Mins. of ev., etc.*; 1913 *Cd. 6790, xxxix, 763 apptd. —, sgd. Dec., 1912*

G. M. Paul (*Ch.*), Lamb, Mackenzie.

'*To inquire into and report upon the conditions of employment of the present members of the Engrossing Staff in the General Register of Sasines, Edinburgh.*'

The Engrossing Clerks in the Sasines Office had for many years protested against the principle of piecework. In order to earn their incomes they had to work unduly hard a few months of each year, whilst at other times they were idle; they had no sick pay, no regular holidays or pensions, no promotion and no recognition for long service. They asked for admission to the Civil Service, with the benefits resulting by amalgamation with the Commissioned Staff.

The Committee agreed with the conclusions of previous Committees that because of the rules of the Civil Service there could be no amalgamation with it. Writing was a manual occupation, requiring no training and a young man could earn twice as much as an older man, whose speed slowed down with age. The piecework system of payment should be continued, but recommendations were made to measure payments by, or alternatively to make a retiring allowance proportional to length of service. The Committee suggested a reduction of staff in order to give more regular employment, and the use of temporary staff in busy times.

See *Minute Regulating terms of Employment*; 1913 Cd. 6813, lii, 525.

Delay in the King's Bench Division

R. Com. 1st Rep. pp. 5. 1913. Mins. of ev. 1913

1913 *Cd. 6761, xxx, 683. Mins. of ev., etc.*; 1913 *Cd. 6762, xxx, 689*

apptd. Dec., 1912. sgd. —

Lord St. Aldwyn (*Ch.*), Goschen, Darling, Henry, Cornwall, Acland, Coward, Craig, Morton, Roberts (G. H.), Roberts (S.).

'*To inquire into the complaints of delay in the hearing of actions and appeals and Crown Cases in the King's Bench Division of the High Court of Justice and whether any reforms should be adopted.*'

Very little evidence was found of delay in particular cases, but so far as the work of the King's Bench Division in London was concerned the complaints of general delay were fully justified. The Report gives a brief explanation of the changes in the number and duties of the Judges of the King's Bench since 1830, and in the number of cases standing for hearing at the commencement of the Michaelmas sittings in each year from 1908 to 1911 inclusive. At the commencement of Hilary sittings, 1913, when there were 17 Judges, there were 918 cases to be disposed of, viz. 647 actions for trial, 263 cases for hearing in the Divisional Court and 8 Bankruptcy Appeals, an increase of no less than 317 cases since the commencement of Hilary sittings, 1912. This increase was undoubtedly partly due to a quite exceptional loss of judicial power in 1912 from the illness of some of the Judges. In these circumstances 17 Judges were not sufficient to overtake arrears. The number of Judges should be maintained at 18 until cases standing for hearing could be heard within a reasonable time from the date of their entry, and adequate measures could be adopted for preventing the recurrence of arrears.

—— Second and Final Report. pp. 48. 1913. Vol. II. Mins. of ev., apps., index. 1913

1914 Cd. 7177, xxxvii, 1. Mins. of ev., etc.; 1914 Cd. 7178, xxxvii, 49 sgd. Nov., 1913

The attention of the Commission was called to proposals for changes of a sweeping character, including the substitution of provincial or district Judges of different grades for Judges holding Circuits, Chairmen of Quarter Sessions, and Recorders, and involving a complete re-organization of the tribunals of the country. But an investigation into the whole judicial system, and of the present distribution of population and its needs in the administration of Criminal and Civil Justice, was outside the scope of the Commission, and 'neither Parliament nor public opinion would sanction such a revolution in order to remedy the complaints' the Commission was appointed to consider.

The primary cause of delay arose from the long continued struggle between London and the provinces for the time of the Judges. Owing to the centralizing tendency in legal as well as in other business, this had become keener in recent years, and had resulted in an increase in the number of causes to be tried in London, and a decrease of those to be tried in the smaller Assize towns. The Circuit system was devised when travelling was slow and country folk rarely moved far from their homes, and it was of importance to have at 56 selected places, at regular times, Judges and a Bar available for the trial of prisoners and civil cases. But the development of the means of locomotion and communication during the last 30 years had led to an immense change in the habits of the population and to a tendency to concentrate business in a few centres. Except in such centres as Liverpool, Manchester, Leeds, Birmingham and Cardiff, there was no local Bar; few barristers who had a leading position in the London Courts go on Circuit regularly. The centre of the Bar was therefore London; and except for the causes tried in the cities named, all London and most important non-jury causes were tried in London.

The recommendations were directed to that kind of easement which would prevent delays. For example, the Circuits and London work should be allotted through a rota fixed by the Judges, allowing for at least 10 Judges in London during the sittings. In case of illness, etc., there should be relief by a Supernumerary Judge or Commissioner and no Judge should be diverted from his regular work; the long vacation should be reduced to two months. Circuit: (a) Criminal Work. Grand Juries should be abolished both at Assizes and Quarter Sessions. Quarter Sessions should be empowered to hold Sessions more frequently. Judges should direct prisoners wrongly committed to Assizes to be tried at Sessions preceding his Assizes. It should be made unnecessary to hold an Assize where there were not more than three prisoners committed to trial, unless the Judge were satisfied that it ought to be held. He should then be empowered to direct that any prisoner committed for trial should be tried in a county other than that in which the offence had been committed. The Monmouth Assize should be transferred to Newport. (*b*) *Civil Work*. Causes should be entered not later than three weeks before the date mentioned in the Order in Council for the Assize at all places except the last town on each Circuit and Manchester, Liverpool and Newcastle, at which places they might be up to the day preceding the commencement of work. The Judge should be empowered to alter the venue of any cause entered for trial to the last place on Circuit, unless at least four causes have been entered at the place originally fixed for the trial. *London:* Definite lists of each class of work should be issued, with the names of the Judges allotted, at the commencement of each sitting. One Judge should be in charge of each class of the Special, Common and Non-Jury Lists and should not leave London. Two other Judges should be assigned to each List and should not be diverted to other work, except at such times as they go on Circuit. Hours should be more strictly adhered to, and with certain exceptions, sufficient business should be placed in the List for Saturdays to occupy all the Judges in London. There should be 18 Judges for two years to test the effect on the transaction of business. They should retire at 72 and they should receive pensions after 5 years' service. Recommendations on practice and procedure were made to speed up the work.

In a note Mr. Morton objected to the suggestion that prisoners could be transferred for trial from one Assize to another, and he suggested that there should be 19 Judges.

Jury Law and Practice

Dept. Cttee. Vol. I. Rep. pp. iv, 56. 1913. Vol. II. Mins. of ev., apps., index. 1913

1913 Cd. 6817, xxx, 403. *Mins. of ev.,* etc.; 1913 Cd. 6818, xxx, 463 apptd. Dec., 1911. sgd. —

Lord Mersey (*Ch.*), Blackwell, Burchell, Gwynne, Hobhouse, Davies, Parry, Snowden.

'*To inquire into the law and practice with regard to (a) the constitution of juries and the conditions on which in civil cases a special jury is allowed; (b) the qualifications and mode of selection of jurors; (c) the preparation of the jury lists and the summoning of jurors; (d) the conditions of jury service; and to report what amendments are necessary or desirable.*

The present state of the jury law is not satisfactory, 'much of it is little more than custom, and the rest, contained in a series of over 30 statutes, is in many respects confused and obscure'. The purposes for which a jury can be called are so numerous, that many of them can be known only to lawyers. Broadly, there are two kinds of juries: (1) juries of presentment or inquiry, e.g., grand juries presenting accusations to judges, magistrates and recorders at assizes, including the Central Criminal Court, and Quarter Sessions, and coroners' juries giving verdicts after inquisitions; and (ii) juries of issue or assessment giving verdicts in the ordinary civil and criminal courts. The 'grand' jury hears the evidence for the prosecution and makes 'presentments of accusations' against persons committed by the magistrates for trial at the assizes or quarter sessions. If a presentment is duly made, a 'petty' jury hears evidence for the prosecution and the defence, and decides by its verdict whether the person charged is guilty or not guilty. Petty juries are either 'special' or 'common'. Qualifications for the common jury are those set out in the Juries Act, 1825, but a special juror must be entitled to be called esquire, merchant or banker (though there is no meaning attached to these terms), and must have a higher rateable value qualification. Jury Lists are in law made by the overseers of the poor or churchwardens of every parish or township, but in practice by a salaried official. In London the selection of the panel is made by the under-sheriff on a grouping system. Outside London there is no uniformity in the practice followed. In some places there is a regular method of selection, in others it is conducted entirely at the discretion of the summoning officer. The extent of the claims of common jury service or those liable is indicated by the fact that if it were possible to go through the jury book by rotation, turns of service would come in London every 12 years, in Caernarvon every 7 years, in Sussex every 20 years.

The chief complaints against the jury system from the administrative point of view were (i) the responsibility placed on those who make the lists, (ii) the time and form of publicity given to them; posting them on the church door for the first three Sundays in September was not considered adequate, especially for those persons wishing to claim exemption; and (iii) the absence of any provision for the interchange of information between the various summoning authorities, so as to ensure that no person is compelled to serve too soon on another jury, etc. As means of justice, juries have been criticized on grounds of their quality, competence, impartiality and value. As a result of modern education, quality was thought to be better; their competence was questioned in 'commercial cases and cases of the very complicated nature that arise out of modern business, which it is perfectly impossible to try with a jury' (Channell, q. 1595). The committee regarded it as serious that, despite the views of those competent to speak, their impartiality was questioned, e.g. as against labour organizations and persons holding different political opinions from the jurors. The value of trial by jury was unquestioned in criminal cases, but in civil cases it was thought it could be far less absolute.

Amongst the forty-five recommendations were: that the division of juries into special and common should be maintained, that trial by jury should remain as of right in all criminal cases,

but in common law civil cases only where the parties to an action agree to such mode of trial; that in cases affecting personal character, it should remain as of right to either party to an action; that in all other common law actions it be left for the Master or Judge to determine. The preparation of the Jury List should continue as at present; notice should be sent to persons whose name appears for the first time. For common jurors the leasehold and freehold qualifications should be abolished, and except in the City of London the rating qualification should be reduced; for special jurors the qualification of 'banker', 'merchant', 'esquire' should be abolished, but the rating qualification raised. The panel of jurors should be chosen by some uniform and mechanized system. The age of liability to service should be raised. Out-of-pocket expenses should be paid by the State.

R. S. Gwynne, M.P., and E. Harrison, K.C., signed a memo. stating that the terms of reference did not include whether the jury system should be abolished and therefore disagreed with curtailments of the rights. In a Minority Report, E. W. Davis, E. A. Parry and P. Snowden argued that four reforms were urgently needed. (1) The abolition of the Special Jury, as this distinction did not exist on the criminal side; (2) the present Jury List, whose preparation is intricate and operation unsatisfactory, should be replaced by one based on the parliamentary register; (3) the officer summoning all juries should be a permanent official and not a solicitor in private practice; (4) the selection of jurors from the Jury List should be by some automatic system.

Justices' Clerks' Fees and Salaries

Conference. Rep. pp. 26. 1914

1914 Cd. 7495, xxxvi, 897
apptd. Nov., 1907. sgd. Dec., 1908

Cunynghame, Simpson, Pedder, Hobhouse, De Rutzen, Willis - Bund, Brevitt, Roberts, Whiteley, Ellett.

'*To form a Conference on the subject of the salaries and fees of Justices' Clerks.*'

The Conference decided that it would be possible to establish a uniform scale of charges for all Courts of Summary Jurisdiction apart from the Metropolitan Police Courts, and recommended the table of fees given on p. 6. It was also recommended that the Secretary of State should remain the ultimate authority for fixing fees and salaries. In Boroughs the Justices should appoint the Clerk and fix or vary his salary; in Counties the Justices of each Petty Sessional Division should appoint the Clerk, and the Standing Joint Committee fix and vary the salary. Clerks should be remunerated by salary. It was undesirable that Justices should appoint one Clerk for ordinary work and another for all work connected with licensing.

Indictments Bill [H.L.]

Jt. Sel. Cttee. 2nd Rep. on Consolidation Bills, proc., mins. of ev. pp. viii, 28. 1915

1914–16 (291, 292) *iv*, 121
apptd. June, o.p. July, 1915

Lord Loreburn (*Ch.*), L. Sanderson, L. Parmoor, L. Wrenbury, L. Muir-Mackenzie, Cave, Jardine, O'Connor, Roberts, Yate.

The Bill ensured that in every indictment the alleged offence should be charged in the simplest possible language, avoiding technical language, unnecessary repetition and undue length. For example, an ignorant prisoner should be told 'You are indicted for having stolen a duck' (qq. 7, 8) instead of hearing a lengthy document read. The Bill did not alter the substantive law.

Rules and Forms Under the Criminal Justice Administration Acts, 1914

Dept. Cttee. Reps., app. pp. 10. 1915

1914–16 Cd. 7853, *xiii*, 151
apptd. Sept., 1914. *sgd. Jan., March,* 1915

J. Dickinson (*Ch.*), Graham-Campbell, Blackwell, Simpson, Douglas, Sanders.

'*To prepare a draft of rules and forms to be made under the statutory powers given by the Criminal Justice Administration Act,* 1914, *and also, if any such rules appear to them to be required, a draft of rules under the Affiliation Orders Act,* 1914.'

In view of the extensive alterations made by the Criminal Justice Administration Act, the necessary arrangements could not be made by the date of its commencement. The Committee recommended its postponement, and the replacement of the Summary Jurisdiction rules and forms by a new single set.

The provision for the collection and payment of money under the Affiliation Orders Act, 1914, which required the appointment of a Collecting Officer, was not as workable as the provisions under Section 30 of the Criminal Justice Administration Act which empowers the Court to direct payment through the court officials or any other person or officer 'if it thinks fit', and does not necessarily require the intervention of the third person. Section I of the Affiliation Orders Act, 1914, should be repealed. Section 30 of the Criminal Justice Administration Act should take its place.

2. POLICE

Police Superannuation (Scotland) Bill

Sel. Cttee. Reps., proc., mins. of ev., apps., index. pp. xiv, 180. 1901

1901 (356) *vii*, 19
apptd. March, o.p. August, 1901

The Lord Advocate (*Ch.*), Brown, Caldwell, Colville, L. Dalkeith, Dewar, Farquharson, Maxwell, McIver, Nicol, Smith, Stirling - Maxwell, Stopford - Sackville, Tennant, Wilson.

The Bill proposed to assimilate the law relating to police pensions and allowances in Scotland to that in England. The difference between the scales was considerable. The Scottish Act had been based on the assumptions that the numbers of the force would remain stationary, that the average age at retirement would be 55, and the pension £46, whereas the force increased by 1 per cent per annum, average age of retirement was 45, and average pension £60. The chief constables giving evidence on behalf of the police thought that there should be no great difference in the attractiveness of the two services, but there seemed to be no considerable drain from the Scottish services. Some local authorities opposed the Bill. The Committee did not recommend it, because of the burden thrown on the rates, but did not offer any other Bill, and were against optional scales as opening local authorities to harassing pressure.

The Duties of the Metropolitan Police

R. Com. Vol. I. Rep., apps. pp. viii, 460, xxx. 1908. Vol. II. Mins. of ev. 1908. Vol. III. Mins. of ev., apps., index. 1908

1908 *Cd.* 4156, *l*, 1. *Mins. of ev., etc.*; 1908 *Cd.* 4260, *l*, 501. 1908 *Cd.* 4261, *li*, 1.

apptd. May, 1906. sgd. June, 1908

D. B. Jones (*Ch.*), Isaacs, Whitmore, Dickinson.

'*To inquire into and report upon the duties of the Metropolitan Police in dealing with cases of drunkenness, disorder and solicitation in the streets, and the manner in which those duties are discharged, with power to make recommendations thereon.*'

The primary object of the police force in the capital of a modern state is the prevention of crime and the detection and punishment of offenders if crime be committed. The duties of each member of the Metropolitan Police Force derive from duties imposed upon them as constables at

Common Law, by statute and by the Regulations of the Commissioner.

At Common Law neither drunkenness nor solicitation in the streets appears by itself to be an offence. Under statute they can be determined only by the provisions of the Acts. The wording of the Metropolitan Police Act, 1839, is 'while drunk shall be guilty of riotous or indecent behaviour'; the Licensing Act, 1872, refers to 'every person found drunk in any highway or public place', though giving no power of arrest without warrant, and to persons 'drunk while in charge of any carriage, horse, cattle or steam engine . . .' when powers of arrest are given. The Licensing Act, 1902, refers to people drunk and incapable of taking care of themselves or 'while having charge of a child apparently under the age of seven years'. Some of the difficulties for the police are due to the want of precision in the meaning of the word drunk, which is obviously a matter of degree. In the Metropolitan Police Act, 1829, disorder is referred to thus: 'all loose, idle and disorderly persons whom he (police officer) finds disturbing the public peace or whom he (police officer) shall have just cause to suspect of evil designs'; while the Metropolitan Police Act, 1839, adds 'just cause to suspect of having committed or being about to commit any felony, misdemeanour or breach of the peace, and all persons whom he shall find between sunset and the hour of eight in the morning lying or loitering in any highway, yard or other place, and not giving a satisfactory account of themselves'. Under these Acts the power of arrest is wider than the jurisdiction of the magistrate, as being 'loose, idle and disorderly' is not a punishable crime unless there is some specific act constituting an offence, so that if the magistrate dismisses a case it does not necessarily mean that the policeman was wrong in bringing it to court: the magistrate can bind the person over to keep the peace. Other offences are set out in the

Act of 1839, and there are also various offences which have been defined in the bye-laws of local authorities.

Solicitation can be dealt with under the Vagrancy Act, 1824: 'every common prostitute wandering in public streets . . . and behaving in a riotous and indecent manner . . . shall be deemed an idle and disorderly person . . . and shall be deemed a rogue and a vagabond'. The Metropolitan Police Act, 1839, refers to 'Every common prostitute or night walker, loitering or being in any thoroughfare or public place for the purpose of prostitution or solicitation, to the annoyance of the inhabitants or passengers'; and the Vagrancy Act, 1898, to 'Every male person who knowingly lives . . . on the earnings of prostitution, or in any public place persistently solicits or importunes for immoral purposes . . .'.

The Commissioner of Police frames Orders and Regulations. These are modified from time to time in the light of experience gained, and they form a code of rules binding on all members of the Force. The Police are therefore invested with rights and are subject to duties by virtue of their office. They are protected by statute from persons who assault or resist them in the execution of their duties, but they are not themselves immune from the jurisdiction of the Courts of Justice, for any breach of the law committed by them in the discharge or intended discharge of their duties. The Report sets out in detail the duties of the police and the procedure they should follow in regard to street offences, arrests, taking statements, searching prisoners, charges, bail, etc., pointing out the amount of discretion he must exercise.

The Commission gave every person of the Metropolis who conceived that he had substantial grounds for complaining of the action of individual officers or constables, an opportunity of stating their case. Analysis of the complaints showed that they related to five stages in the regular process of the exercise by the Police of their powers. 1. Unjustified arrests; 2. the manner in which the prisoner is apprehended and his treatment on the way to the station; 3. the proceedings in the charge room; 4. the prisoner's treatment at the station, and 5. the conduct by the Police of the case at the Police Court. No evidence was offered by the L.C.C. or by any Metropolitan Borough. The evidence of the Police Court Magistrates was to the effect that as a rule the police dealt with street offences honestly, efficiently and with discretion, although there were individual cases of police misconduct. They did not believe there was any systematic or widespread bribery by prostitutes or bookmakers. Five hundred complaints from individuals were received and each one was examined; many were irrelevant, but of the nineteen special complaints selected for inquiry, the conduct of the police was correct in eleven cases, and in eight cases there was misconduct more or less serious, or errors of judgment on the part of the constables and officers concerned.

Having regard to the number of men in the police force (17,000) and the number of arrests (119,000 during any one of the last four years) the Commission had no hestitation in coming to the conclusion that the Metropolitan Police Force discharge their duties with honesty, discretion and efficiency, and carry out the arrangements for dealing with street offences in a thoroughly satisfactory manner. The instances of individual misconduct afforded no reasonable ground for lessening the general confidence of the community in the integrity and efficiency of the police force as a whole. A qualified officer acting under the direct superintendence of the Chief Commissioner should be appointed for the purpose of dealing with complaints against the police by private persons. The inquiries should be conducted at New Scotland Yard or a convenient Police Station.

Police Forces (Weekly Rest Day)
Sel. Cttee.

'To inquire and report whether, having regard to the conditions of service in Police Forces in the United Kingdom, it is desirable that provision should be made, by legislation or otherwise, for granting to every constable one full day off duty in seven; what, if any, alterations in the conditions of service and police administration should accompany this change; what would be the cost, and how it should be borne so as not to increase the charge on imperial funds— and to whom the Police (Weekly Holiday) Bill was committed.'

The Report for 1908 is a formal presentation of the minutes of evidence; 1908 (353) (353-Ind.) ix, 679.

—— Report, proc. pp. ix. 1909

1909 (132) *viii*, 339
re-apptd. Feb., o.p. May, 1909

J. E. Ellis (*Ch.*), Armitage, Harvey, Hedges, Lockwood, Nannetti, Priestly, Remnant, Wiles, Wilson.

The Police (Weekly Holiday) Bill proposed to enact that 'save on occasions of public emergency, no constable or other peace officer shall be called upon to perform duty on more than six days in any week'. Mr. Kempster, proprietor and controlling editor of the Police Review, which had a circulation of 18,000 copies, gave evidence in support of the Bill, on the basis of nearly 2,600 replies to questions inserted in the paper. As Reading had adopted the provisions of the Bill and had found them to be highly successful, it was thought that other local authorities could do the same without legislation. An Act requiring a universal one day rest in seven would add to the rates, and as the matter had not been generally demanded by local authorities, the Committee did not recommend the Bill, since it applied to the whole of England and Wales. The need was not so pressing in the country as a whole as it was in London, where the Committee decided it was absolutely essential without delay, in spite of the fact that it would entail a considerable addition to the numbers of the Metropolitan Police, and a corresponding increase in its cost to the ratepayer.

Transport Workers Strike. Certain disturbances at Rotherhithe on June 11th, 1912, and complaints against the conduct of the police in connection therewith
Rep. pp. 6. 1912

1912–13 Cd. 6367, *xlvii*, 297
apptd. June, sgd. July, 1912

C. Jones.

The disturbance along the route where the police usually accompanied meat from the docks, was caused by 'lodging house boys' and not by workmen on strike. Stones, broken glass and other missiles were thrown at the drivers and at the police (100 glasses were missed from the public houses in the vicinity). In order to get through the night without riot or probable loss of life, the Superintendent found it necessary for the police to clear the crowd away. They did so, and in the process some persons were necessarily roughly handled, and no blame is attached to the police for what happened at Mill Pond Bridge. In the subsequent pursuit some members of the Police Force employed were guilty of excesses, and though there were no serious injuries, some persons 'have undoubtedly a right to complain of the treatment they received'.

3. PRISONS, PRISONERS, REFORMATORY AND INDUSTRIAL SCHOOLS, PROBATION
Scottish Prisons

Dept. Cttee. Rep. pp. iv, 26. 1900. Mins. of ev., apps., index. 1900

1900 Cd. 218, *xlii*, 89. *Mins. of ev., etc.*; 1900 Cd. 219, *xlii*, 119
apptd. Aug., 1899. sgd. May, 1900

Lord Elgin (*Ch.*), Carmichael, Scott-Moncrieff, Tuke, Smith.

'To enquire concerning—(*a*) the provision made in Scottish prisons for the nursing and accommodation of sick prisoners; (*b*) the sufficiency of the accommodation provided in the prisons of Scotland for ordinary prisoners; (*c*) juveniles and first offenders, and to what extent they should be treated as classes apart; (*d*) the sufficiency of prison dietary; (*e*) prison labour and occupation, with special reference to the physical condition and the moral improvement and training of the prisoners.'

In an unsigned Memorial, presented to the Secretary of State for Scotland, asking for an inquiry into Scottish Prisons similar to the Gladstone Enquiry on Prisons 1895-8, certain charges were made regarding the paucity of the prison staffs, nursing arrangements, inferiority of salaries, etc. The Committee dismissed as untenable most of the charges made, and found no fault with the general treatment of prisoners, but criticism was offered on points of detail. The treatment of sick prisoners was generally successful and humane, and there had been no wilful neglect. To guarantee to the public that deaths in prison were in no way the fault of prison officials, there should be post-mortems in every case of sudden death or death from unascertained cause. It was essential that the power of removal of sick prisoners to public hospitals should be preserved, as the alternative of maintaining staffs and equipment in prison hospitals would be too expensive. Warder staffs should be trained to deal with minor complaints, and there should be a Medical Commissioner on the Prison Board. The Committee rejects gross charges that corruption results from permitting the association of prisoners for medical reasons. Association should not be absolutely forbidden, provided there were proper election and adequate supervision. Its should not be permitted in sleeping cells except on the express recommendation of the Medical Officer.

Punishments were not too many nor excessive, but the use of the figure of eight handcuff ought to be restricted as much as possible.

There was no permanent deficiency of accommodation for the normal prison population, but the increase in drunkenness had caused some overcrowding amongst those serving short sentences. Police cells were not suitable for the housing of juvenile offenders and the Youthful Offenders Bill, which makes provision for places of confinement separate from prisons and police cells, was approved. Dr. Dunlop's proposals concerning diet should be adopted and this should ensure that all prisoners would be adequately fed. It was unlikely that prison labour had much educative or reformative influence, though stone-breaking, physical drill and garden work were good for the prisoners. It was more possible to help to prepare young women for honest work.

Prison Libraries

Dept. Cttee. Rep., apps. pp. 33. 1911

1911 *Cd.* 5589, *xxxix*, 745
apptd. April, sgd. Oct., 1910

M. L. Waller (*Ch.*), Birrell (Miss O.), Raleigh, Simpson, Stanley, Thomson.

'To consider what are the principles which should govern the supply of books to the prisoners in H.M. Prisons and to the inmates of H.M. Borstal Institutions, regard being had to the reformative purposes of prison treatment and to the maintenance of the progressive stage system. And to report what, if any, amendment of the existing rules and practice on the subject is desirable.'

The library of every prison is placed in the charge of the Chaplain who once a year makes out a list of books he wants to put in it; prison libraries in general are under the supervision of the Chaplain Inspector of Prisons. In convict prisons the same numbers and kinds of books are allowed to a prisoner during the whole of his stay, but in local prisons there is a 'progressive stage system' by which books are allowed on a graduated scale based on 'industry and good conduct'. For administrative purposes the books are in five classes: (1) Devotional, e.g. Bible, prayer book; (2) School, e.g. history, language lessons, arithmetic; (3) Moral Instruction, e.g. the *Narrow Way*, the *Roman Catholic Penny Catechism*, *Pilgrim's Progress*; (4) Secular, which has come to mean educational or technical in the narrow sense, and (5) Library Books, i.e. all books other than those above.

In the majority of prisons, including all the small ones, the appearance of a prisoner of any substantial degree of education is a rare event. The table in App. III shows the favourite authors amongst the six favourites in each prison. Mrs. Henry Wood tops the list with 58, Charles Dickens 46, G. H. Henty 20, Rider Haggard 20, Sir W. Scott 19. There is a great demand for magazines with pictures, especially amongst the illiterate. Amongst the 'professional' men in prisons there is a demand for such books as Mill, Macaulay, Gibbon, etc.

Whilst it is true that in making the selection of books the 'reformative object' must be kept in mind, it would be a mistake to try to do this 'by the clumsy expedient of books which point an obvious moral'. Good description by good novelists of 'the incidents of a society in which certain standards of manners and conduct are habitually observed' and stories of a healthy bracing outdoor nature by such authors as Marryat, Fennimore Cooper are to be desired. The term 'books of secular instruction' should be replaced by the term 'books of education', and Chaplains should use a wide discretion in supplying them. In every prison there should be a series of small 'trade manuals', a few technical treatises and some technical magazines. For moral instruction *The Narrow Way* should not be regarded as indispensable for Anglicans, and besides books whose basis is religious, there should

be works of an ethical or philosophical character. For the six convict prisons and three borstal institutions the capitation grant should be raised from 1*s*. 3*d*. to a maximum of 1*s*. 6*d*. The reason for this in the case of the convict prisons is not shortage of books, but the fact that they contain prisoners who have already served long sentences of penal servitude, have read an enormous number of books and are acquainted with the contents of the bulk of the library. Selecting books is too big a task for one man. There should be, for the use of the Chaplains, an official catalogue, similar to that in a large free library in London. There are other recommendations on the details of administration, distribution and the care of books.

The Treatment of William Ball in H.M. Prison, Pentonville, and the Circumstances connected with his Removal to Colney Hatch Asylum

Rep., app. pp. 7. 1912

1912–13 *Cd.* 6175, *lxix*, 1
sgd. April, 1912

G. Savage.

William Ball was sentenced at Bow Street on the 22nd Dec., 1911, to two months' imprisonment for wilful damage. At the date when the sentence had expired he was certified insane and was removed to Colney Hatch Asylum. It was suggested that his insanity was due to the treatment he had received in prison, and in particular to forcible feeding. Sir G. Savage, who was asked by the Home Secretary for an entirely independent medical opinion, stated that his opinion was that 'both in the prison and in the asylum Ball was kindly and properly treated, and his insanity could not be attributed to any treatment to which he was subjected'. The only mistake that had been made was that his wife was not informed of the earliest symptoms of his mental disorder.

Lilian Lenton's Case

Correspondence of the Home Office with the Royal College of Surgeons and Sir Victor Horsley with regard to the case of Lilian Lenton. pp. 17. 1913

1913 (190) *lii*, 435
o.p. July, 1913

Miss Lenton, a suffragette, was charged before the Justices sitting at Richmond with setting fire to a building in Kew Gardens, and was committed to Holloway Prison on remand for one week. She went on hunger strike for three days, was forcibly fed and then discharged because of her collapsed physical condition. On 18th March a letter appeared in *The Times* stating that Miss Lenton's condition was due to the fact that whilst being forcibly fed food had been poured into the lungs. The correspondence was concerned with a denial, by the authorities concerned, of the truth of the allegation.

The English Convict. Charles Goring

Statistical Study. pp. 440. 1913. Abridged edition. pp. 275. 1915

1913 *Non-Parl. Home Office*

The Report is mainly concerned with the relative parts played in the production of the criminal by constitutional qualities and environmental conditions. The influence of the latter is significant; conviction of crime is associated with a constitutional rather than circumstantial condition. This tendency to crime is affected by heredity to the same extent as other physical and mental conditions in man. The study points to the fact that crime can be combated most effectively by the segregation and supervision of the obviously unfit where the conditions of modern existence are less severe. Left to themselves, such people drift to the criminal population and fill the prisons, but in most cases they can be made strong enough to resist the hopeless drift which leads to penal servitude.

Provision of Funds for Reformatory and Industrial Schools

Inter-Dept. Cttee. Vol. I. Rep., apps. pp. vi, 47. 1906. Vol. II. Mins. of ev. 1906

1906 *Cd.* 3143, *liv*, 1. *Mins. of ev.*; 1906 *Cd.* 3144, *liv*, 55
apptd. May, 1905. *sgd. Aug.*, 1906

T. Cochrane (*Ch.*), Aitken, Davies, Milne.

'To inquire into the system by which funds are at present provided for Reformatory and Industrial Schools; and to report what, if any, changes in that system appear to be required; due regard being had to efficiency, economy, and proper adjustment as between Imperial and other funds respectively.'

While the costs of these institutions had steadily increased, the Treasury grant had remained unaltered since 1862, but liberal subscriptions and legacies such as were received in the early years of the movement had declined as the responsibility of the State for the schools was increasingly recognized. Profits from the work of the inmates had fallen off owing to the general raising of the standard of education, physical training and industrial training given to them. In former days many boys were employed in wood chopping, paper bag making, etc., which brought considerable revenue but were of no permanent benefit to them. There was increased difficulty in obtaining help from local authorities, owing to the new burdens imposed on them by the Education Act of 1902. The recommendations give the details of a revised scale of grants estimated at an additional cost of £41,060.

Reformatory and Industrial Schools

Dept. Cttee. Rep., app. pp. 114. 1913. Mins. of ev., index. pp. v, 542. 1913

1913 *Cd.* 6838, *xxxix*, 1. *Mins. of ev., etc.*; 1913 *Cd.* 6839, *xxxix*, 117.
apptd. March, 1911. *sgd. May*, 1913.

E. J. Griffith (*Ch.*), Allen, Blackwell, Churchill (Mrs. Winston), Crooks, Lyttelton, Newman, Player (Mrs. H. D.), Russell, Talbot (Lady M.), Waller, Whitehouse.

'To inquire in general into the constitution, management, discipline and education of Reformatory and Industrial Schools in England and Wales, and to include in their inquiry: the adequacy of the Inspectorate; the relation of the Schools to the Education Committees and other local authorities; the qualifications of Superintendents and other officers, their remuneration and the practicability of any scheme of superannuation; variation in the types of Schools, and whether further provision is necessary for the proper grading of boys and girls; the suitability of ships for use as Schools; the preparation given boys for entry into industrial or other careers, and the training and disposal of girls; the care of boys and girls after leaving the Schools, and the relation of the Schools in this connection to existing institutions for the welfare of young persons; the provision for physical training, recreation and play-time in the Schools; the opportunities for conference and co-operation between managers and officials of the Schools; the medical care of the Schools; the methods of maintaining discipline and encouraging good conduct, and the extent to which further regulations with regard to punishments are desirable; the relations with parents and the methods of obtaining payment from them.'

The broad distinction between the two types of school is that young offenders sent to reformatory schools must have been convicted of offences punishable in the case of adults with imprisonment or penal servitude, while children sent to industrial schools have not, but have been found begging, or with bad parents, with no home, residing in a disorderly house, etc. Those sent to reformatories must be over 12 and under 16 years old, and sentence must terminate at 19; while those sent to industrial schools must be under 14, but may be detained up to 16.

In 1911 the main provision for the 30,000 children in the schools or under supervision was by voluntary bodies— all the 37 reformatories and 90 of the 112 industrial schools being voluntary institutions. The Home Office had powers of inspection and certification of schools and the main proportion of the income came from the Treasury. Schools were ceasing to be built by voluntary effort, and the local authorities had not made extensive use of the powers granted to them in 1870 and 1908. The schools varied greatly in efficiency and the shortage of accommodation made the Central Authority hesitant in closing the more inefficient of them. Lack of progress was due to the shortage of funds, and the small amount of power that the Central Authority had in enforcing changes of which the managers failed to see the value and urgency. Further, the magnitude and importance of the work amongst this number of children, equal at any one time to the whole prison population, had not been sufficiently recognized.

The schools needed the continual guidance and stimulus of a strong and active united authority. No member of the Home Office devoted his exclusive attention to the schools and the care of children. Local authorities should be encouraged, with Treasury help, to provide new schools or to acquire existing ones, but any drastic modification of management would involve special difficulties where they were denominational. And the schools owned by local authorities showed the same variations of efficiency as voluntary ones.

The recommendations included the creation of a special branch of the Home Office for Reformatory and Industrial Schools, and for the administration of the Probation Act as it affected children; additional grants at the discretion of the Central Authority; certification based on the observance of a detailed schedule of conditions outlined in the recommendations (e.g. higher professional status of. staffs, with superintendents approved by the Home Office, more time in the school room, systematic medical care, freer discipline, prohibition of non-educational employment, P.T., games and holidays). Inspection was to be divided between the Home Office and the Board of Education, and the Home Office was to appoint two Medical Officers. More attention was to be given to the classification of the children and to after-care supervision, etc. Magistrates should be allowed to commit young offenders to reformatories without convicting. A sum of £10,000 should be provided to assist the children to find employment, to supervise them whilst in it and to help them when their wages are insufficient for self support. The cost to the Treasury of the proposed increased maintenance grants per child, plus a variable grant distributed at the discretion of the Central Authority, and certain other grants would be £73,000. There should be an Advisory Committee to assist the Central Authority.

All signed the Report. Five separate Memos. emphasized particular aspects of the problem, e.g. complete control by the Home Office, complete control by the Board of Education, extension of the age to 21. A Memo. by J. H. Whitehouse stated that two vital weaknesses of the system were that the majority of the schools were under private management with insufficient funds and resources generally, and that they were divorced from the general educational life of the nation. They had outgrown their original intention as places of detention and punishment, their function now being recognized as mainly educational. They should be regulated and supervised by the Board of Education in the same way as elementary and other schools maintained by the local authority.

Reformatory and Industrial Schools in Scotland

Dept. Cttee. Rep. pp. v, 111. 1915. Mins. of ev., apps., index. 1915

1914-16 Cd. 7886, xxxiv, 491. *Mins. of ev., etc.*; 1914-16 Cd. 7887, xxxiv, 609 *apptd. May, 1914. sgd. March, 1915*

A. A. Allen (*Ch.*), Alexander, Husband (Miss A.), Mackenzie (Mrs. H. L.), Maclay, Maxwell, Stuart, Mackenzie (K. J.), Neilson, Rose.

'*To inquire into the constitution, control and inspection, management, discipline, education, staffing, and remuneration of the staffs of Reformatory and Industrial Schools in Scotland; into the provision made for different types of children; into the number and character of committals; into the care of boys and girls after leaving the Schools; into the financial position of the Schools, including the cost of maintenance; into the proportion borne by the Exchequer and local authorities respectively of the expenditure on assistance from public funds; and into the extent to which a proper contribution is obtained from parents.*'

The Scottish inquiry covered much the same ground as did the English one, as in most respects the problem was the same in both countries and much of the evidence applied to both. The differences concerned chiefly special features of the administration of the law and the financial condition of the schools. The recommendations followed the same principles of upgrading the general conditions of living, staffing and education, with a prohibition of remunerative work and abolition of conviction as a preliminary to committal. The main recommendation, however, was the reverse of the English one. It was considered that as the main function of the institutions was an educational one, the powers and duties (including inspection) of the Secretary for Scotland, except those relating to committals and discharges, should be transferred to the Scottish Education Department. As in England, the costs of running the schools had increased and they had been equally hampered by lack of funds. The lower contributions of Scottish local authorities was due not to parsimony, but to the fact that the Scottish schools were conducted at lower cost. The annual grants by the State should be increased by £13,500 (of which £8,230 should be a variable grant) and the minimum contributions of local authorities raised by £8,500.

The Minority Report signed by Mackenzie, Neilson and Rose wished the schools to remain under the Scottish Office, as child delinquency was part of the problem of delinquency of all kinds. If responsibility were handed to the education authority, there might be a tendency towards assimilating arrangements to those of day schools. While work performed for remuneration should be regulated, work technically not educative, e.g. potato lifting, was not always harmful, and as this was regularly done by boys in country districts, there would seem to be no reason why those maintained at public expense should not earn something towards their keep. The chief points in separate Memos. were, that there should be more elasticity in management and financial responsibility by the local authority, according to local circumstance; corporal punishment should be abolished; the age of entry to ships' schools should be eleven years; the training of elementary school teachers was not sufficient for industrial residential schools; emigration should not be encouraged as a means of disposal.

Probation of Offenders Act, 1907

Dept. Cttee. Rep. pp. iv, 15. [1910]
    Mins. of ev., apps., index. 1910

1910 Cd. 5001, xlv, 819. Mins. of ev., etc.;
1910 Cd. 5002, xlv, 839
apptd. March, sgd. Dec., 1909

H. Samuel (Ch.), L. Lytton, Acland, Troup, Dickinson.

'To enquire whether full advantage has been taken during the past year of the powers conferred by the Probation of Offenders Act, 1907, and, if not, what are the difficulties which have stood in the way of their more general use. And, in the case of those Courts where the Probation Officers are appointed by the Secretary of State, to advise me whether the existing arrangements for their appointment and remuneration are satisfactory, and whether any steps should be taken to secure the better organization of their work, and their more frequent employment in suitable cases.'

The Act placed at the disposal of the criminal courts of the United Kingdom new official machinery for dealing with persons who have offended against the law, by a method of personal supervision by specially chosen men and women of strong character who could exercise good influence. In 1908, nearly one in nine of all offenders charged before courts of summary jurisdiction with indictable offences were placed on probation. The Act had not been in operation long enough to allow an opinion to be formed of its results, but it was shown by the evidence given by those working the provisions that the Act could be most effective. Courts had made unequal use of it, owing to the diversity of opinion amongst magistrates on its advantages over previous procedure: most of the objections were ill-founded.

The work should be extended, and Courts should appoint full-time officers to be assisted by part-time paid or honorary workers, a directory of probation officers should be prepared and revised annually by the Home Office; the Home Office should keep in touch with the work through an officer specially charged with the duty. Salaries rather than fees should be paid to probation officers. A probation period of less than six months is in most cases of little use, and in a large number of cases twelve months is desirable. The help of local social agencies should be enlisted.

See Probation of Offenders Act, 1907. Memo.; 1908 Cd. 3981, lxxxix, 477.

4. CIVIL AND CRIMINAL LAW
Naturalization Laws

Inter-Dept. Cttee. Rep., app. pp. 148.
[1901]

1901 *Cd. 723, lix, 351*
apptd. Feb., 1899. sgd. July, 1901

K. E. Digby (*Ch.*), Villiers, Fitzpatrick, Davidson, Cox.

'To report upon the doubts and difficulties which have arisen in connection with the interpretation and administration of the Acts relating to Naturalization, and to advise whether legislation for the amending of those Acts is desirable, and, if so, what scope and direction such legislation should take.'

The law relating to naturalization is concerned mainly with conditions under which rights, privileges and duties constituting the status of a British subject are acquired and lost. Persons are invested with that status at birth, or subsequently acquire it by the operation of Statute Law. The main conditions required by the Naturalization Act, 1870, are a certain period of residence, or service with the Crown for five years, and intention to reside in the United Kingdom. The rights and duties which constitute the status of a British subject are mainly the political rights and the capacities for the acquisition and holding of property, and those personal rights and privileges which he carries with him into foreign countries. The principal of these are (1) the privilege of protection, subject to any paramount obligation which he may be under to any state of which he is also a subject or citizen; (2) the right and liability to become a party to proceedings in the British Consular Courts established under the Foreign Jurisdiction Act, 1890.

The fundamental principle is that any person born in His Majesty's Dominions is from the moment of birth a British subject, whatever the nationality of his parents or the circumstances determining the locality of his birth. Cases of double nationality acquired at birth are due mainly to the differences between those countries whose law is derived mainly from feudal principles, and those countries whose law comes more directly from Roman sources, the former regarding the place of birth as the determining factor in constituting the relation of sovereign and subject, while the latter took the nationality of the parent. The Statute Law of most countries has introduced modifications, but only some assimilation of all the various systems would guard against cases of double nationality. It is expedient to ensure as far as possible that a person who acquires British nationality shall thereupon cease to be a subject of the country to which he previously belonged. It makes provision for the case of a British subject becoming a subject of a foreign country by his own act, but it cannot provide that a person, on becoming a British subject, shall cease to be a subject of a foreign state. A natural-born British subject, such as a person who is born in a foreign country but whose father was born in His Majesty's Dominions, or a naturalized British subject if also subject to a foreign country, could not be protected against military service while actually in the state which claimed his allegiance. Similar complications arising over the status of children born on ships, wives, widows, etc., are set out in the Report.

The existing Statute Law relating to the acquisition and loss of British nationality should be consolidated; the existing law as to the acquisition of British nationality by parentage should be re-enacted in simpler form, with the exception that, where the father was born out of His Majesty's Dominions, a child also born out of such Dominions should not be a British subject; that a person born on a British ship in foreign waters should be a British subject, but a person born on a foreign ship in British waters should not be a British subject; provision should be made by legislation enabling the Secretary of State, or Governor of a British possession, to confer the status of a British subject upon persons who fulfil the requisite conditions in any part of the British Dominions; the conditions necessary for acquisition and loss of status of a British subject, or for persons under disability should remain as at present, with certain modifications. In a Note D. Fitzpatrick points out the necessity of making provision for the complications which arise under voluntary naturalization, e.g. where a person accepts service under a foreign state, or has nationality conferred on him by a foreign state as an honour. The Appendix contains the laws of some British colonies and possessions.

Debtors (Imprisonment)

Sel. Cttee. Rep., proc., mins. of ev., index. pp. xxx, 418. 1909. Index. 1909

1909 (239) (239-Ind.) vii, 281
apptd. March, 1908. *o.p. July*, 1909

Mr. Pickersgill (*Ch.*), Brooke, Byles, Collins, Delany, Duncan, Ferens, Gibbs, Hodge, Keswick, Phillips, Rendall, Wadsworth, L. Willoughby de Eresby, Wills.

'*To inquire into the existing Law relating to the Imprisonment of Debtors, and to Report whether any Amendments are desirable.*'

Under Section 5 of the Debtors Act, 1869, any County Court may commit to prison for a term not exceeding six weeks or until payment of the sum due, any person who has, or has had, since the date of an order, the means to make payment. A majority of County Court judges think that power to give judgment for the recovery of a debt should be accompanied by powers to enforce it. The alternative of execution against goods was useless and would injure the credit now given to the working classes, who needed credit from landlords and others as much as merchants required it for business. A short period of imprisonment caused far less suffering than the breaking up of a home due to selling goods under an execution warrant. The alternatives of bankruptcy, appointment of receivers and attachment of wages were rejected. The effectiveness of the committal

procedure was shown by the steady decrease in the numbers going to prison as compared with the number of warrants of committal issued.

Section 5 was criticized because it allowed such wide powers of discretion to the judges that different practices had grown up in different parts of the country. The draft report in the Proceedings (p. xiii) gives the discussion on the burdens to the community caused by imprisonment and quotes Judge Parry, 'Imprisonment for debt is really made the means of *blackmailing* relatives and friends of the debtor'. The Debtors Act was being abused. Temptations held out by moneylenders and their touts had grown enormously and there had been a great increase in the numbers of vendors of jewellery, expensive watches, etc., on the instalment system at prices often much above their market value, forms of trading which rested mainly on the power of committal. In spite of the Gaming Acts, judgments had been obtained for sums due in respect of gaming or betting transactions.

Recommendations were made for uniformity of administration. These included a reduction of the power to imprison from 42 to 21 days; that except in the case of debtors who are not artisans, power to commit should rest on the debtor having at the time of hearing, means in hand or falling due; that judges should be instructed, having regard to wages, house rent and other conditions of their district, to treat a minimum income as needed for necessaries, and should not commit unless they have evidence that a debtor has means over and above such income. The Committee agreed with the memorandum to the County Courts and Debtors Acts Amendments Bill, which set forth that no committal should be made for money lent or for goods sold or lent on hire, unless lent or sold for trade purposes or unless the goods were necessaries for the support or maintenance of the debtor or his family.

Perjury Bill [H.L.]

Jt. Sel. Cttee. 2nd Rep., proc., mins. of ev., apps., index. pp. xxx, 89. 1910. Index. 1913. (1st Rep. on Consolidation Bills, see *Licensing*, p. 348)

1910 (321) (321-*Ind.*) *vi*, 389
apptd. March, o.p. Nov., 1910

The Lord Chancellor (*Ch.*), L. Ridley, L. Stanley, L. Kinnaird, L. Mersey, Cave, Hindle, Roberts, Simon, Younger.

The Bill not only consolidates the Statute Law, but also codifies the Common Law relating to perjury. The amendments are for the most part designed to simplify the law in the direction of making punishments uniform. There are a number of enactments scattered through the Statute Book making false declarations punishable, the offences are not in their nature substantially different, but the punishments affixed appear in each case to have been chosen haphazardly. For example, false declarations under the Government Annuities Act, 1882, renders the offender liable to twelve months imprisonment and under the Merchandise Marks Act, 1887, to seven years penal servitude. The amendments for securing uniformity and generalizing the law so as to make it applicable to false statements under future as well as past Acts, go beyond codification and consolidation in the strictest sense, but codification would hardly be worth while without such changes.

Forgery Bill [H.L.]

Jt. Sel. Cttee. Rep., proc., mins. of ev., apps. pp. xlix, 199. 1914. Index. 1916

1913 (180) (180-*Ind.*) *vi*, 695
apptd. April, o.p. June, 1913

Lord Loreburn (*Ch.*), L. Zouche, L. Stanley, L. Ashby, L. Ashton, Cave, Nield, O'Connor, Radford, Roberts.

Amendments are set out in the Appendix. They aimed at improving the form of the Bill or bringing it into closer conformity with the existing law, and simplifying the law in the direction of making procedure uniform. Whilst the Bill was satisfactory as a measure of pure consolidation, it brought into prominence the many anomalies and inequalities in the existing law of forgery. The Bill should not be allowed to proceed.

The Committee accepted the Draft Bill (No. 2) prepared by the Advisory Committee (set up by the Lord Chancellor in 1909 to advise on Criminal Law Consolidation). The Advisory Committee's memo. is in App. III, p. ix. This Bill does not make punishable any act or create any offence which is not punishable already. The chief alterations are to standardize punishments—mostly in the direction of reducing them—and to group under a general description, such as 'valuable security' and 'document of title', a large number of documents now specially dealt with in various statutes. The inevitable effect of adopting general terms is that the punishments applicable to the documents specially dealt with are extended to a few others of a similar character.

Larceny Bill [H.L.]

Jt. Sel. Cttee. on Consolidation Bills. Rep., proc., mins. of ev. pp. x, 63. 1916

1916 (99) *iii*, 507
apptd. April, o.p. July, 1916

Lord Loreburn (*Ch.*), L. Sanderson, L. Parmoor, L. Wrenbury, L. Muir-Mackenzie, Solicitor-General, Nield, Roberts, O'Connor, Radford.

The Bill consolidates the statute law so far as it relates to larceny triable by indictment and codifies the common law relating to larceny. It brings into prominence certain anomalies and inequalities which are undesirable and illogical, e.g. a lark is, but a canary is not, capable of being stolen at common law, and it reproduces substantially the common law definition of larceny taken from numerous judgments. Hitherto there has been no statutory definition of larceny (q. 34). See mins. of ev. for a discussion of the definition.

5. LAW OF PROPERTY

Land Registry (New Buildings) Bill

Sel. Cttee. Rep., proc., mins of ev. pp. iv, 2. 1900

1900 (253) *vii*, 141
apptd. April, o.p. July, 1900

Mr. Akers-Douglas (*Ch.*), Lockwood, Ure, Trevelyan, Faber.

Compulsory first registration, under the Land Transfer Acts, in the London district will increase the work. This, together with other growth in work, makes more accommodation necessary. Bill reported without amendment.

Conveyancing Bill [H.L.], Married Women's Property Bill [H.L.], Settled Land Bill [H.L.]

Sel. Cttee. HL. Rep., proc., mins. of ev. pp. x, 58. 1906

1906 (*HL.* 136) *ix*, 53
apptd. April, o.p. June, 1906

Lord Davey (*Ch.*), L. Halsbury, L. Knutsford, L. Selby, L. Stanley, L. Macnaghten.

The Bills were reported with amendments. The evidence relates to the Bills clause by clause.

Land Transfer Acts

R. Com.

apptd. July, 1908

Lord St. Aldwyn (*Ch.*), L. Beauchamp, L. Faber, Evans, Buckmaster, Stewart-Smith, Cave, Gregory, Pennington, Shackleton, Wood.

'*To consider and report upon the working of the Land Transfer Acts, and whether amendments are desirable.*'

The First Report is a formal presentation of the following volume of minutes of evidence, etc.; 1909 Cd. 4510, xxvii, 733.

—— Second and Final Report. pp. vii, 56. 1911. Mins of ev., apps., index.

1911

1911 *Cd.* 5483, *xxx*, 1. *Mins. of ev., etc.*;
1911 *Cd.* 5494, *xxx*, 65
sgd. Jan., 1911

del. Pennington.

The object of the Land Transfer Acts is to simplify, expedite and cheapen the transfer of land, not merely for the advantage of the present owners, but in order to facilitate the increased ownership of land and houses by the poorer classes. The main evils the Acts were designed to remedy are the risk of loss of deeds, fraud by duplication or concealment of deeds, the complexity and cost of deeds and abstracts of title, and the fresh re-investigation of title on every fresh dealing with the land, entailing unnecessary trouble, delay and expense. The Registrar claims that the advantages obtained by Registration with Absolute Title simplifies procedure and therefore quickens the business connected with the sale, reduces the costs, simplifies the deeds and guarantees security. Yet the system is not widely used. In the administrative County of London, where registration was gradually made compulsory between 1899 and 1902, there were 132,028 Registrations, but in the rest of England and Wales where it is voluntary there were only 8,592 Registrations. The Registrar explained that this reluctance was due to the unfortunately hostile attitude of the legal profession, which was unaccustomed to the new procedure and disinclined to assist it, or recommend it to their clients. The complaints handed in against the working of Registration were examined by the Registrar. He declared two-thirds of them practically negligible and of the rest, the complaints arose out of doubtful or debateable points or unavoidable anomalies, or cases relating to faults of administration. Out of the vast amount of cases of all kinds dealt with by the Registrar it could not be assumed that there would be no cases of complaint. The 33 recommendations for amendments to the Acts included the following: That the length of title now required to be shown for Registration with Absolute Title, to be reduced from 40 to 20 years. After not less than 12, or more than 20 years' probation, a Possessory Title in a compulsory area, if undisputed, to ripen into an Absolute Title to the first transferee for value in cases not exceeding £10,000 in value. If undisputed after 10 years, a leasehold Possessory Title should confer a 'Good Leasehold' Title. Compulsory enfranchisement of copyholds and the abolition of the need for technical words of limitation on the words 'in fee simple' in conveyances of land in fee simple, are also recommended.

Registration of Title in Scotland

R. Com. Reps. pp. 46. 1910. Mins. of ev., apps., index. 1910

1910 *Cd.* 5316, *lviii*, 67. *Mins. of ev., etc.*; 1910 *Cd.* 5357, *lviii*, 113 *apptd. May*, 1906. *sgd. July*, 1910

Lord Dunedin (*Ch.*), Dundas, Prosser, Clark, Chisholm, Fortescue-Brickdale, Ferguson, Kennedy.

'*To inquire into the expediency of instituting in Scotland a system of registration of title.*'

Chairman's Report.—Dunedin, W. J. Dundas, J. Prosser. The only system which is to any practical extent in operation in Scotland is one of registration not of absolute but of possessory or provisional title. This leaves unregistered conveyancing to live alongside of it in respect of the same subjects, and so deprives registration of title of one of its chief advantages. Only a system of registration of absolute title would have any attraction in

Scotland, but it would be impracticable to introduce it for the whole of Scotland instead of the existing arrangements, which should be amended so as to facilitate the ultimate adoption of a true system of title. Registration should be introduced tentatively in a limited area.

Report.—J. S. Clark, S. Chisholm. From time immemorial the deeds relating to practically every unit of feudal property in Scotland have been carefully and exhaustively examined by the Keeper of the Sasine Office and his assistants. Accordingly, the only deed the Keeper would require would be the deed granted in any future transmission by death or sale. If registration of title is adopted, the immediate effect would be to abolish in almost every case in the future (*a*) the examination of the progress of titles, (*b*) the preparation of the inventory of titles, (*c*) searches and (*d*) notorial documents. A system of registration of titles must be of immediate absolute title or its equivalent with very rare exceptions, and must take into account the incidents of the ownership of land, and the essence of it is the examination of the progress of titles at the Sasine Office once for all. The system should be tried out in a limited area selected by the Secretary for Scotland.

Report. — C. Fortescue - Brickdale, R. M. Ferguson. The main idea of the registration of title is 'that the Government shall keep a register or list constantly corrected up to date, of owners of land and real rights, showing the lands they hold, the nature of their rights, and also of the burdens and obligations for the time being affecting them: that this list or register shall have absolute validity and shall be on all occasions and for all purposes complete legal proof of the rights and liabilities recorded in it'. The establishment of registration of title would go a long way towards removing not only the present drawbacks 'on all dealings with real estate and heritable security, as compared with dealings with other kinds of property, but one of the most formidable obstacles in the way of that most desirable of social reforms— increased ownership of land and houses among the poorer classes'. The system of registration of title should be introduced without delay, but it should not be compulsory immediately over the whole country.

Report.—Sheriff Kennedy. A system of registration should, as soon as practicable, be introduced into a limited area, (*a*) largely urban, (*b*) sufficient in extent to secure economy and efficiency and (*c*) containing such variety of properties as fairly to test the system.

Compulsory Taking of Land (Insanitary Property)

Sel. Cttee. HL. Rep., proc., mins of ev., apps. pp. iv, 32. 1913

1913 (*HL.* 66) *viii*, 9
apptd. Jan., o.p. June, 1913

Lord Donoughmore (*Ch.*), L. Bath, L. Stanhope, L. Craven, L. Camperdown.

The London County Council had bought land for schools on the terms of the Land Clauses Act. They wanted, where there was slum property, to buy on the terms of Section 21 of the Housing Act, 1890. The committee did not approve of the Housing Act being used for this purpose, but thought if it is required to cheapen the process of the acquisition of sites for educational and kindred purposes, there should be simplified procedure under the Land Clauses Act.

Trusts Bill

Sel. Cttee. Reps., proc., apps. pp. xciv, 14. 1908

1908 (355) *x*, 1155

Mr. Beale (*Ch.*), Cave, Clancy, Hazel, Hills, Micklem, O'Connor, Radford, Rendall, Stewart-Smith.

The Committee submitted the Bill to the criticism of His Majesty's Judges and other legal authorities (First Special Report) and in view of the criticisms made concluded that it was practically impossible to report it without some modification of the principle on which it was framed (Second Special Report). With the aid of these criticisms it was thought possible by the majority so to recast it that 'qualified or partial codification might be a great convenience to the legal profession while preserving in the fullest manner the equitable jurisdiction of the courts in regard to trusts'. The criticisms referred to are set out in the Appendices to the Second Special Report. In App. 8 A. Underhill, Conveyancer to the Court, stated that 'This Bill is entirely misconceived in principle. Private trusts are the invention and the principal subject of judicial equity. To crystallize equity (the very nature of which is to modify legal rights in particular cases where they would cause injustice, and necessarily implies large judicial discretion) seems to me a negation of its first principles.'

6. DIVORCE

Divorce and Matrimonial Causes

R. Com. Rep., index. pp. viii, 207. 1912. Vols. I–III. Mins. of ev., index. 1912. Apps., index. 1912

1912–13 *Cd.* 6478, *xviii*, 143. *Mins. of ev., etc.*; 1912–13 *Cd.* 6479, *xviii*, 359. 1912–13 *Cd.* 6480, *xix*, 1. 1912–13 *Cd.* 6481, *Cd.* 6482, *xx*, 1
apptd. Nov., 1909. *sgd. Nov.,* 1912

Lord Gorell (*Ch.*), Balfour (Lady), Burt, Guthrie, Treves, Tindal-Atkinson, Tennant (Mrs. M.), Brierley, Spender, Archbishop of York, Anson, Dibdin.

'*To inquire into the present state of the law and the administration thereof in divorce and matrimonial causes and applications for separation orders, especially with regard to the position of the poorer classes in relation thereto, and the subject of the publication of reports of such causes and applications; and to report whether any and what amendments should be made in such law, or the administration thereof or with regard to the publication of such reports.'*

In the House of Lords on the 14th July, 1909, Lord Gorell pointed out that separations were being obtained instead of divorces and that this was having a bad effect on the moral standards of the working classes, who were inclined to commit bigamy or live in sin because they were not able to obtain a decree enabling them to remarry. There had been no previous full-scale investigation and the present position was exactly the same as it was after the Act of 1857. The Royal Commission on the Law of Divorce (1852–3 [1604] xl) had examined only two witnesses and the 1857 Act which followed had transferred the Canon Law of the Ecclesiastical Courts to the civil system then set up. The position was as follows: A husband could obtain a divorce for adultery by his wife. The wife could obtain a divorce if her husband committed incestuous adultery, adultery plus bigamy, rape, sodomy, bestiality or adultery coupled with such cruelty as would have given judicial separation in the Ecclesiastical Courts, also adultery plus desertion for two or more years (or its equivalent of failure to comply with a decree for restitution of conjugal rights plus adultery).

A review of the evidence from representatives of religious bodies and of theological witnesses showed that there was no general consensus of Christian opinion on the subject and that lay witnesses based their views not on ecclesiastical opinions but on general Christian principles coupled with common sense and experience of life. The suggestion of some witnesses that the Act of 1857 should be repealed on religious grounds, and marriage made absolutely indissoluble was therefore rejected, especially as the State must deal with all its citizens whatever their religious views. The legislature must act on unfettered consideration of what was best for the interests of

society, morality and of the parties and their families. The present procedure was beyond the reach of the poorer classes, with lamentable results; there was a need and a substantial demand for reform.

The chief recommendations include the following: (1) The decentralization of sittings for the hearings of divorce and matrimonial cases to an extent sufficient to enable persons of limited means to have their cases heard by the High Court locally. The country should be divided into districts corresponding to the circuits, with a Court presided over by a commissioner with all the powers of a judge. This procedure should be limited to cases where the joint income of petitioner and respondent did not exceed £300 and assets £250. (2) The powers of the Courts of Summary Jurisdiction to make orders for permanent separation should be abolished; if permanent separation is necessary, there should be a right of application to the High Court by simple processes. Courts of Summary Jurisdiction should grant separation orders only when they are necessary for the immediate protection of wife or husband or the support of the wife and children with her. The grounds for orders should include cruelty (defined so as to include infecting the applicant with venereal disease, compelling a wife to submit to prostitution), habitual drunkenness, desertion and refusal or neglect to maintain. (3) Men and women should be placed on an equal footing with regard to grounds for divorce. There can be no adequate reason why two persons who enter into matrimonial relationships should have a different standard of morality applied to them; and where two standards exist, there is a tendency to accept the lower for both parties. (4) The law should be amended to add, in addition to adultery, five other grounds for divorce which are generally recognized as in fact putting an end to married life: desertion for three years and upwards, cruelty, incurable insanity after five years' confinement, habitual drunkenness found incurable after three years from the first separation order, imprisonment under commuted death sentence. (5) The addition of grounds for decrees of nullity in certain cases of unfitness for marriage: undisclosed state of venereal disease in communicable form, undisclosed pregnancy by some other man at time of marriage, and under certain conditions, unsoundness of mind or incipient unsoundness which becomes definite six months after marriage, epilepsy or recurrent insanity, of which the other party was ignorant at the time of marriage. (6) Limits should be placed on the publication of reports of divorce and other matrimonial causes by empowering the judge to close the Court if the interests of decency, morality, humanity and justice required it; to order that certain portions of evidence, etc., should not be reported. There should be no publication of a report of a case until after it had finished, no publication of pictorial representations of witnesses, parties, etc. (7) The extension of the protecting clauses of the Act of 1857 with regard to the position of clergy of the Church of England on re-marrying divorced persons.

In a note Mrs. Tennant disagrees with the addition of the grounds of habitual drunkenness (as it was provided for under cruelty) and of a commuted death sentence, and with the proposal that the Court should have power to grant a decree of divorce where only a decree of separation is desired. Mr. Spender's qualifying note included suggestions for reducing the period of desertion from three to two years; making all sentences of five years and upwards grounds for divorce; converting a decree of separation into a decree of divorce after a lapse of two years; the restrictions on publicity should not be interpreted as a rule of secrecy which prevents access to the Court records by the parties involved.

The Minority Report, signed by the Archbishop of York, Sir William Anson and Sir Lewis Dibdin, stated 'that it cannot be questioned that in a democratic country like ours public opinion must prevail; but they did not consider that the demand was as widespread as the recommendations of the majority report suggested. The points of agreement, however, were on costs and court procedure; on nullity of marriage in the cases of unsound mind, epilepsy, recurrent insanity, venereal disease, pregnancy of a woman at the time of her marriage by a man other than her husband, who is ignorant of the fact, and of wilful refusal to consummate the marriage; presumption of death; and equality as between men and women in obtaining a divorce.

7. CIVIL ORDER, CENSORSHIP, MISCELLANEOUS REGULATORY POWERS

Preservation of Order at Public Meetings

Dept. Cttee. Vol. I. Rep., apps. pp. 23, 1909. Vol. II. Mins. of ev. 1909

1909 Cd. 4673, xxxvi, 83. Mins. of ev.; 1909 Cd. 4674, xxxvi, 107
apptd. Feb., sgd. April, 1909

H. Hobhouse (Ch.), Compton-Rickett, Simpson, Astbury, Butcher, Barnes, Fox.

'To consider the duties of the Police with respect to the preservation of order at public meetings, and to report whether any, and if so what, alteration in practice is desirable, regard being had especially to the importance of securing uniformity throughout the country.'

In November 1908 a disturbance occurred at a Liberal political meeting at Ingatestone, Essex. The Chief Constable had been warned that this might occur and had been asked to send police to the meeting. He had replied 'I am not allowed to take any part in a political meeting, so cannot come inside the hall' (App iv). This led to a series of questions in the House of Commons (Austen Chamberlain, q. 2) and to the inquiry.

For the purposes of the inquiry a public meeting was defined as 'any lawful meeting called for the further-ance of discussion of a matter of public concern, to which the public or any particular section of the public is invited or admitted, whether the admis-sion is general or restricted'. This would not include a shareholders' or a committee meeting. Where a private meeting is held in a public building, the building for the time being becomes non-public, but where a public meeting is held on private premises the persons present have no more right to remain, when requested to leave by the pro-moters of the meeting, than if they had been invited to enter a private house by the occupier of the house. The duties of the police at public meetings are not defined by any public statute, but are generally speaking 'to keep the King's peace'. They have no power to enter except by leave of the occupier of the premises, or the promoters of the meeting, or when they have good reason to believe that a breach of the peace is being committed. There was however great diversity of prac-tice throughout the country, though roughly classified there emerged the following distinct principles—(1) That it is unwise for the police to interfere inside political meetings any further than they are bound to do in order to prevent actual breaches of the peace (the Liverpool system); (2) that it is expedient to assist the promoters of public meetings to keep order inside, but that this is a special duty of the police which must be paid for by the persons desiring their assistance (the Manchester system); (3) that keeping order inside public meetings is part of the ordinary duties of the police, for which no payment ought to be asked (the Birmingham system).

The Committee preferred the non-interference principle, but felt that the police should be allowed discretion to adopt the methods most suitable to their districts. The Committee also agreed that under the Public Meeting Act, 1908, which states that 'any person who at a lawful public meeting acts in a disorderly manner for the purpose of preventing the transaction of the business for which the meeting was called together, shall be guilty of an offence punishable on summary con-viction', the promoter or steward of the meeting should prosecute and not the police.

Employment of Military in Cases of Disturbances

Sel. Cttee. Rep., proc. pp. iv.   1914

1914 (454) *vii*, 173
apptd. July, *sgd.* Aug., 1914

E. Griffith (*Ch.*), Butcher, Cave, L. Hugh Cecil, Greenwood, Herbert, Beach, McGhee, Pollock, Pringle, Red-mond, Richardson, Roberts, Stanley, Ward.

'*To report in what circumstances and on what conditions His Majesty's Military Forces should be employed to deal with Disturbances or Threatened Disturbances of the Peace among the Civil Population.*'

'Your Committee have considered the matters referred to them, but as it will not be in their power to make a full Report in the present Session, they have agreed to recommend that a Committee on the same subject be appointed in the next session of Parlia-ment.'

For circumstances of appointment see 61 H.C. Deb. 5s. cols. 994–1023. 1114.

Stage Plays (Censorship)

Jt. Sel. Ctee. Rep., proc., mins. of ev., apps. pp. xl, 375. 1909. Index. 1910

1909 (303) (303–*Ind.*) *viii*, 451
apptd. July, *o.p.* Nov., 1909

H. Samuel (*Ch.*), Harcourt, Law, Lockwood, Mason, L. Plymouth, L. Willoughby L. Newton, L. Redesdale, L. Gorell.

'To inquire into the Censorship of Stage Plays as constituted by the Theatres Act, 1843, and into the operations of the Acts of Parliament relating to the licensing and regulation of theatres and places of public entertainment, and to report any alterations of the law or practice which may appear desirable.'

Feeling in literary and dramatic circles against the censorship of stage plays was expressed in a letter to The Times in October 1907, and signed by seventy-one persons of literary repute. They protested against the office of censorship 'which was instituted for political, and not for so-called moral ends to which it is perverted, against power lodged in the hands of a single official—who judges without a public hearing, and against whose dictum there is no appeal—to cast a slur on the good name and destroy the means of livelihood of any member of an honourable calling'. They asked that licensing of plays should be abolished (App. A).

Before 1737 powers of censorship sprang from the Royal Prerogative; in that year the Act 10 George II, c. 28, was carried through Parliament by Sir Robert Walpole in order to restrain the political and personal satire which was then prevalent on the stage. The Act conferred upon the Lord Chamberlain an unfettered power of veto on the performance of any plays with no indication of the grounds upon which he was to act. The Theatre Act, 1843, gave additional powers to local authorities to license theatres. When the Bill was passing through the House of Lords words were inserted restricting, though vaguely, the Lord Chamberlain's powers of prohibition to cases in which 'he shall be of opinion that it is fitting for the preservation of good manners, decorum or of the public peace so to do'. These words form the only provision which now gives statutory direction to the operation of the censorship.

With rare exceptions, all dramatists of the day ask for the abolition of the censorship and they are supported by many men of letters. On the other hand managers of theatres ask for the control over plays prior to their production. They feared, and so did the actors' organizations, that control by local licensing authorities, or control through prosecutions, would render their position intolerably uncertain. Mr. C. Frohman, in App. C, p. 375, wrote: 'In America we have no censor, and I do not see that the absence of one causes any inconvenience to managers'. A large body of public opinion, of which the Speaker of the House of Commons may be regarded as representative, expressed the view that its abolition would involve serious risk of a gradual demoralization of the stage.

The Committee considered that where ideas or situations are represented through the personality of actors they may have a more powerful and deleterious effect than a printed book and therefore public interests require that theatrical performances should be regulated by special laws. Because of the risks involved, producers should have access, prior to a play's production, to a public authority empowered to license plays. But censorship with powers to veto before production is open to grave objection. Coercion into conformity with conventional standards is contrary to the 'axiom underlying all our legislation that only through the toleration of that which one age thinks to be error can the next age progress further in the pursuit of truth'. Many hold the view that the theatre is for recreation, others that it is a vehicle by which great ideas of profound importance may be communicated by the thinkers to the citizens. It is clearly not the duty of the State to enforce by law the opinions of those who hold the former view upon those who hold the latter. Conferring the right of reference to arbitration on an aggrieved author is not the way out. Where the question is, 'By what means the State on behalf of the community is to prevent the performance of improper plays?' to refer the decision of a

Minister of State on such an issue to an outside arbitrator for approval or reversal 'is contrary to the sound principles of government'. In view of the danger that official control over plays before their production may hinder growth of a great and serious national drama, the Committee concluded that the licensing authority should not have the power to impose a veto on the production of plays. But if the law is to allow the production of unlicensed plays, it must take steps to safeguard the community against the evils that might ensue. Experience has shown that the danger of the drama of ideas becoming a drama of indecencies is not unreal.

The public authority should have power by summary process to suspend the performance of unlicensed plays of improper character and where they are of such a character, the producers should be liable to heavy penalties. This power of *ex post facto* control should not be entrusted to local authorities, or to the licenser of plays, or to another branch of the Executive Government. The authority should be, in cases of indecency, the Courts of Law; but in other cases, a mixed committee of legal and lay members of the Privy Council. Detailed recommendations are made for implementing these conclusions. The duty of licensing plays should not be transferred to the Home Secretary as a Minister accountable to Parliament, and the office of Examiner of Plays should continue. It should be the Lord Chamberlain's duty to license plays, unless he considered that it could reasonably be held that they were indecent, did violence to religious sentiment, represented in an invidious manner a living person, etc. A stricter guard than hitherto might be exercised against indecency in plays of a frivolous type; the ban on characters from the Scriptures should not be maintained. The Lord Chamberlain would be well advised to set up a Consultative Committee.

Licensing of Music Halls for music and dancing dates from the passing of the Disorderly Houses Act, 1751, and is still based upon the Act. The Statute applied to London and Westminster and to the districts within 20 miles of those cities. The Local Government Act, 1890, and the Public Health Acts Amendment Act dealt comprehensively with licensing powers of local authorities. Since the Lord Chamberlain's censorship extends only to stage plays, he has no control over the nature of the performance in music halls. In some parts of the country a music hall has been granted a stage play licence as well as a music and dancing licence, but in London and many places elsewhere, music halls have a music and dancing licence only. This has led to a controversy between managers of theatres and managers of music halls as to the right of the latter to produce 'sketches', which the Committee proposed to resolve by a single Dramatic and Music licence for both classes of houses, giving them freedom to produce whatever entertainment they thought best. There was no reason of policy for the State maintaining a statutory differentiation which had become unreal. The licensing of theatres should be transferred to the L.C.C. These proposals are equally applicable to Scotland.

Amongst those giving evidence were G. Bernard Shaw, Granville Barker, J. M. Barrie, J. Galsworthy, Sir William S. Gilbert, Gilbert Murray, G. K. Chesterton, O. Stoll, Beerbohm Tree, F. Whelen.

Cremation

Dept. Cttee. Rep., mins. of ev., apps. pp. 67. 1903

1903 Cd. 1452, xxiii, 577
apptd. Oct., 1902. sgd. Jan., 1903

C. E. Troup (*Ch.*), Byrne, Parsons.

'To be a Committee to prepare a draft of the Regulations to be made by the Secretary of State in pursuance of the powers given him by Section 7 of the Cremation Act, 1902.'

As the Report was a preface to the Draft Regulations and Forms, which were the Committee's substantive proposals, it was limited to a discussion of the conditions under which cremation took place, and the regulations required to reduce to a minimum the risk of cremation being used to destroy evidence of murder by violence or poison. After considering the practice of the Cremation Society, the Committee recommended that before cremation took place two medical certificates should be required, or a certificate given after a post mortem by a pathologist, or by a coroner after an inquest.

Daylight Saving Bill

Sel. Cttee. Reps., proc., mins. of ev., apps., index. pp. xvi, 188. 1908

1908 (204) (204-*Ind.*) *vii*, 73
apptd. March, o.p. June, 1908

E. Sassoon (*Ch.*), Harrison-Broadly, Hutton, Holt, Nugent, Pearce, Pirie, Philipps, Richards.

The effect of the proposals in the Bill would be to move the usual hours of work and leisure nearer sunrise; to promote the greater use of daylight for recreative purposes of all kinds; to lessen the use of licensed houses; to facilitate the training of territorial forces; to benefit the physique, general health and welfare of all classes of the community; to reduce the industrial, commercial and domestic expenditures on artificial light. The Committee recommended an alteration of one hour in April and September, Greenwich mean time to remain the same.

Mr. William Willett, F.R.A.S., builder in London and Brighton, etc., was the sole promoter of the scheme (qq. 1–204).

Daylight Saving Bill

Sel. Cttee. Reps., proc., mins. of ev., apps. pp. xviii, 239. Index. 1909

1909 (265) *vii*, 1
apptd. March, o.p. Aug., 1909

Mr. Tomkinson (*Ch.*), Bennett, Haworth, Hayden, Herbert, Kavanagh, Macpherson, Magnus, Morrison-Bell, Nicholls, Norman, Pearce, Renton, Stone, White.

There were grave doubts as to whether the objects of the measure could be realized by legislation, without causing serious inconvenience. The Bill should not be proceeded with. It was noted that the efforts made by those in favour of daylight saving had already, in many cases, caused a shortening of the hours of work.

Summer Time

Cttee. Rep. pp. 23. 1917

1917–18 *Cd.* 8487, *xviii*, 641
apptd. Sept., 1916. *sgd. Feb.*, 1917

J. W. Wilson (*Ch.*), Davies, Delevingne, Duncan, Lonsdale, Morton, Nugent, Pettigrew, Samuel, Stanier.

'*To inquire into the social and economic results of the Summer Time Act, 1916, and to consider (1) whether it is advisable that Summer Time should be reintroduced in 1917 and in subsequent years, and, if so, (2) whether any modifications in the arrangements are required, and (3) between what dates Summer Time should be operative.*'

The first Summer Time Bill came before Parliament in 1908, but no Act was passed until 1916, two years after the First World War had started. Information was collected by questionnaires, and the replies received were over 76 per cent of the number of letters sent out. It was almost universally stated that the extra hour had been used for the purpose of outdoor recreation and pursuits, and in particular for the cultivation of allotments and gardens. The police authorities reported that there had been a definite improvement in public morals and order and there was also a slight decrease in road accidents. The Trade Unions were favourable. The women's organizations, though they complained of the children going to bed late, thought that this was out-weighed by the advantages of the extra hour and there was no evidence to show any bad effects on the children through loss of sleep caused by the extra hour. There was a marked decrease in the consumption of gas and electricity. More difficulty was ex-perienced in the agricultural districts and the Act was ignored on many farms, but in spite of this the majority of farmers were in favour of the renewal of the Act. In Ireland the town was for and the country against the Act. Summer Time should be re-introduced in 1917 and in subsequent years.

8. WAR LOSSES

Insurance of British Shipping in Time of War

Rep.

1914 *Cd.* 7560. See *Sea Transport*, p. 159

Government War Risks Insurance Scheme

Aircraft Insurance Cttee. Rep. pp. 12. 1915

1914–16 *Cd.* 7997, *xxxvii,* 487 *apptd. June, sgd. July,* 1915

F. H. Jackson (*Ch.*), Beck, Heath, Owen, Ryan.

'To consider, without prejudice to the question of Policy, whether a scheme can be devised to cover loss and damage by bombardment and aircraft in so far as such loss and damage are not covered by the terms of the ordinary fire insurance policy. Any scheme prepared must be on the basis of reasonable contribution being paid by the owners of property insured towards the cost of insurance.'

The recommendations are based on the assumption that it is possible to suggest rates of premium to cover loss arising from raids or air bombardment in the light of recent experience. It is not possible to fix rates against loss due to general conflagrations in congested districts. The rates should be the same for all districts. An agreement in the form of Schedule III should be made with Fire Insurance Companies, whereby they will issue, on behalf of the Government, policies against air-craft risks or aircraft risks and bom-bardment. They will also undertake initial proceedings in connection with the adjustment of claims. A State Insurance Office should be established to issue policies, to settle finally, and pay all claims arising out of policies. This Office should be administered by experts, including representatives from Lloyds, the Fire Insurance Offices and the Government. The Companies should receive 10 per cent of the gross premiums, and brokerage of 5 per cent should be paid to the agent or broker.

Defence of the Realm Losses

Reps.

1916–20. See *Breviate 1917–39,* pp. 545–546.

XVII. IRISH PAPERS

This section includes, with certain exceptions, those papers which deal exclusively with Irish matters, whether the investigating body were appointed from Westminster or Dublin Castle. A commission or committee may, however, investigate a problem general to the United Kingdom, e.g. Local Taxation or Canals and Inland Waterways. In such cases, in order to give a complete account of the investigation as a whole, that report is dealt with along with the main inquiry, but a cross-reference is given in this section to show its place in the stream of inquiries on Irish problems. Thus, an account of the Vice-Regal Commission on *Poor Law Reform in Ireland,* 1906, is followed by a cross-reference to the report on Ireland made by the Royal Commission on *Poor Laws,* 1909, since the two documents must clearly be read together. This arrangement greatly simplifies the search of a reader particularly interested in Irish papers.

1. (a) MACHINERY OF GOVERNMENT

Circumstances of the Loss of the Regalia of the Order of Saint Patrick

Vice-Regal Com. Rep., apps. pp. xi, 9. 1908. Mins. of ev. 1908

1908 *Cd.* 3906, *xi*, 881. *Mins. of ev.*; 1908 *Cd.* 3936, *xi*, 905
apptd. Jan., sgd. Jan., 1908

J. J. Shaw (*Ch.*), Starkie, Jones.

'*To investigate the circumstances of the loss of the Regalia of the Order of Saint Patrick and to inquire whether Sir Arthur Vicars exercised due vigilance and proper care as the custodian thereof.*'

The Crown Jewels were in the safe on June 11th, 1907, when Sir Arthur Vicars showed them to the librarian of the Duke of Northumberland. There is no evidence from that date until the 6th July, when their loss was discovered, that they were seen by anybody. On the 3rd July, the office cleaner reported that the office door was open on her arrival, and on 6th July she reported that the door of the strong room was open on her arrival. No action was taken until 2.15 p.m. of the 6th when Sir Arthur had occasion to send the messenger to the safe in the strong room. Having considered the provisions for the safe keeping of the jewels, and the inactivity of Sir Arthur on the occasions immediately preceding the disappearance of the jewels, when he knew that the office and strong room had been opened at night by unauthorized persons, the Committee were of the opinion that Sir Arthur Vicars had not exercised due vigilance or proper care as the custodian of the Regalia.

Boundary Commission (Ireland). Representation of the People Bill 1917. Redistribution of Seats

Rep., apps. pp. 11. 1917

1917–18 *Cd.* 8830, *xiv*, 1
apptd. Oct., sgd. Nov., 1917

J. W. Lowther (*Ch.*), Robinson, Jerred.

'*To determine, for the purposes of the Representation of the People Bill now before Parliament, the distribution of members as between counties and boroughs in Ireland, and the boundaries of such counties and boroughs and of the divisions thereof.*'

The Commissioners were instructed to proceed on the basis that the number of members, apart from University representation, should remain at 101, and that the existing constituencies should not be altered except when necessary for this purpose. In order to give effect to the principle of 'one vote, one value' it was necessary to advise a standard unit of population, which was 43,000. To prevent the hardship and disturbance which would follow if this were rigidly applied, 30,000 should entitle a borough or county to separate representation, 73,000 to two members, etc., and certain other adjustments should be made.

Department of Agriculture and Technical Instruction (Ireland)

Dept. Cttee. Rep. pp. viii, 155. 1907. Apps. 1907. Mins. of ev., index. 1907

1907 *Cd.* 3572, *xvii*, 799. *Mins. of ev.*, etc.; 1907 *Cd.* 3573, *Cd.* 3574, *xviii*, 1.
apptd. March, 1906. *sgd. May*, 1907

K. E. Digby (*Ch.*), Dryden, Ogilvie, Brown.

'To inquire and report whether the provisions of the Agriculture and Technical Instruction (Ireland) Act, 1899, constituting the Department, and the methods which the Department has followed in carrying out those provisions, have been shown by experience to be well suited to the conditions of Ireland; whether any, and, if so, what changes are desirable in those provisions and methods; and to report also upon the relations of the Department to the Council of Agriculture, to the Agricultural Board, and to the Board of Technical Instruction; upon its relations to local statutory bodies; upon the funds at its disposal, and the modes of employing them; and upon its position in regard to other Departments, especially those charged with educational functions.'

The Agricultural and Technical Instruction (Ireland) Act, 1899, established a Department of Agriculture and Other Industries and Technical Instruction for Ireland, with the Chief Secretary as President and a Vice-President whose position in practice has come to resemble that of permanent head of a Department. Existing powers under many statutes were transferred to it and further powers were given the Lord Lieutenant to transfer from other Departments administrative powers which appeared to him analogous. Provision was made for the constitution of a Council of Agriculture, an Agricultural Board and a Board of Technical Instruction comprising members nominated by the Department and county councils. This was done to give an independent character to the new Department and to dispel the suspicion that it was a 'Castle Board'. Powers were given to the Department 'to make or cause to be made, or aid in making, such enquiries, experiments and research and collect or aid in collecting, such information as they may think important for the purpose of agriculture and other rural industries'. Provisions were made for laying the foundations of the relations between the Department and the newly created local authorities. Besides the three

new bodies there was also constituted a Consultative Committee for the purpose of co-ordinating educational administration. The income from the Endowment Fund was £166,000 but with other sums it amounted to £180,000.

The Act of 1899 aimed at new machinery for creating the same conditions as had effected a beneficial revolution in the conditions of agriculture and industry in other parts of Europe. In Ireland this depended on the introduction of a better system of agricultural and technical education, and bringing home to small cultivators the benefits to be derived from improved methods of farming and distribution. The central object was to spread instruction by co-operating with local committees in the appointment of itinerant instructors. Since there were few persons so qualified, steps had to be taken to train them. The Report gives a detailed account of the training of instructors, and of their work. County Advisory Committees had initiated schemes for the improvement of livestock, bulls, store and milking cattle, swine, poultry and horse breeding, and had encouraged agricultural and industrial shows. Encouraging seed testing, creameries, winter-dairying, cheesemaking, forestry, fishing, etc., were amongst the Department's activities. The steps taken to improve technical education are also detailed.

On the constitution of the Department the Committee rejected the suggestion, made by some concerned with what they considered the ideal machinery for the government of Ireland, that it should be controlled by an elective Board. Continuity is best secured by responsibility being vested solely in the head of the Department, with the subordinate officials responsible to him. The President (the Chief Secretary), as the Minister responsible to Parliament, is properly at Westminster, but takes little part in the actual administration. The Vice-President who directs the policy of the

Department should be in Ireland. He should not be capable of sitting in Parliament, should not be a permanent, pensionable civil servant, but should be appointed for five years, with powers of reappointment. He should be independent of party politics. In the actual work of the localities persons of different political and religious views had worked together without friction. The Committee also rejects proposals for removing the nominated element in the Council and Board of Agriculture. The prohibition on 'teaching the practice of trade' is unduly restrictive and should be removed. Sea fisheries should be placed in the same position as inland fisheries regarding financial aid, and the power to obtain agricultural and trade statistics given. The system of training Irish itinerant instructors has been attended with marked success, and was well suited to the conditions of Ireland.

—— Minority Report, apps. pp. xii, 165. 1907

1907 Cd. 3575, xvii, 963
sgd. June, 1907

W. L. Micks.

It was not possible to assess whether the Department and its methods suited the conditions of Ireland without understanding the causes which had brought about the conditions. An historical account of English administration in Ireland from the time of Henry VIII precedes the detailed examination of the work of the Department, in the course of which the use of itinerant instructors is criticized on the ground that their districts were too large, and that a system of supervision of smaller areas by intelligent local farmers would be more effective. The suppression of industries in Ireland had thrown the population into agriculture, particularly cattle raising, where the openings for employment were restricted. It was necessary to start industries in Ireland. The Act of 1899 was too narrowly conceived. The powers of the Con-

gested Districts Board, conferred on them because they had to deal with destitution and poverty, covered both industry and agriculture, should be extended to the whole of Ireland and its Agricultural Council should be elective. The Department was not suited to the conditions of Ireland, and should be confined to educational functions. A new Development Board should be established, with the same powers for all Ireland as are possessed by the Congested Districts Board. It should be provided with £1 mn. annually, for development purposes. It should be a purely Irish Department, separate from the Imperial Government and Parliament, made responsive to Irish opinion by being in the charge of five Commissioners, one chosen by the parliamentary representatives of each Province and one nominated by the Irish Government.

Dublin Corporation Bill and the Clontarf Urban District Council Bill

Jt. Sel. Cttee. Rep., proc. pp. 17. 1900

1900 (301) vi, 895
apptd. March, o.p. July, 1900

V. Kay-Shuttleworth (Ch.), L. Pirbright, L. Llandaff, L. Welby, L. Wenlock, Mowbray, Whitmore, Harwood.

There should be one administration to control the drainage and sewers and sewerage of Dublin, Rathmines and Rathgar and Pembroke, and there should be a joint drainage board which would distribute the burdens of the system of drainage.

Irish Valuation Acts

Sel. Cttee.

'To enquire and report what changes in the Irish Valuation Acts are desirable in order to enable a Re-valuation of Rateable Property in any District to be made on a basis equitable to all Classes of Ratepayers and to be brought into force in an effective manner.'

Two Reports are formal presentations of the minutes of evidence, etc.; 1902 (370) vi, 57. 1903 (33) vi, 19.

—— Report, proc., app. pp. 28. 1904

1904 (130) vi, 271
re-apptd. March, o.p. April, 1904

G. Murray (Ch.), Clancy, Colomb, Craig, Devlin, Douglas, Duke, Goulding, Haslett, Hemphill, Lee, Lough, M'Killop, Maxwell, Randles.

The principle of the net annual value applies in towns in Ireland as in England and in Scotland, but in the case of agricultural land the test of the rent obtained from tenants in the open market fails because of the peculiarities of the Irish land system. The Committee did not consider the problem, because the Irish Land Bill had introduced a system of land purchase under which a large proportion of holdings would 'change hands during the next twenty years'. It would be inexpedient to attempt any alteration in the value of agricultural land while this was going on. The Committee agreed that the value of a licence should be included in valuation; that in Ireland there were special difficulties in removing the exemptions of religious institutions, but if the exemptions were abolished, it should be done concurrently in all three Kingdoms; that the centralized machinery for valuation should be maintained in Ireland, and that a general revaluation should be made to clear away accumulations of anomalies.

Remission of Surcharges (Dublin) Bill

Sel. Cttee. Rep., proc. pp. iv. 1909

1909 (197) viii, 411
apptd. Feb., o.p. June, 1909

Mr. Menzies (Ch.), Barrie, Glendinning.

The purpose of the Bill was to discharge certain surcharges made upon the accounts of the Municipal Corporation of Dublin in respect of payments made for the purposes of the public libraries of the City of Dublin. The Committee went through the Bill and made amendments.

Local Taxation

R. Com. Reps. Ireland. 1902

See Local Government, p. 46, for account of reports, and App. I, p. 447, for list of reports and volumes of minutes of evidence relating to Ireland.

1. (b) HOME RULE: CONSTITUTION AND FINANCE

Irish Finance

Cttee. Rep., app. pp. 34. 1912. Mins. of ev., apps. 1913

1912–13 Cd. 6153, xxxiv, 5. Mins. of ev., etc.; 1913 Cd. 6799, xxx, 1
apptd. —, sgd. Oct., 1911

H. W. Primrose (Ch.), Bishop of Ross, L. Pirrie, Adams, Gladstone, Jackson, Plender.

'(1) To ascertain and consider the financial relations between Ireland and the other component parts of the United Kingdom as they exist to-day, paying especial regard to the changes that have taken place both in Revenue and Expenditure since 1896, the date of the Report of the Royal Commission. (2) To distinguish as far as possible between Irish Local Expenditure and Imperial Expenditure in Ireland. (3) To consider, in the event of Irish local affairs being entrusted to an Irish Assembly with a responsible Executive, how the revenue required to meet the necessary expenditure should be provided.'

The Annual return of Revenue and Expenditure (England, Scotland and Ireland) dissects the Exchequer accounts in order to show as far as possible the true revenue and true expenditure of each part of the United Kingdom, but the statistical difficulties are such that it can give only an approximate idea and could not serve as a firm basis for the permanent financial relations between Great Britain and Ireland, if true revenue were taken as the determining factor. The 'true' revenue of Ireland in 1910–11 was about £10,300,000 and expenditure on Irish services £11,300,000, an excess of £1,000,000. Since 1895–6 the true revenue had grown by 28 per cent and Irish expenditure by 91 per cent. The Royal Commission of 1895–6 on the *Financial Relations between Great Britain and Ireland* (1896 C. 8262, xxxiii) had emphasized that Ireland suffered in her financial partnership through being compelled to keep pace in expenditure with a country many times richer. The cost of the postal services had risen by 74 per cent because unified postal administration had led to the provision in Ireland of enlarged postal facilities required by Great Britain. The charge for Old Age Pensions equalled a third of the true revenue, because the population of 4,000,000 contained the survivors of a population which 70 years earlier was 8,000,000 and because 70 per cent of the Irish population lived in rural conditions as compared with 20 per cent in Great Britain.

A review of earlier schemes led to the conclusion that 'collected' revenue was not suitable as a standard of the funds to be placed at the disposal of an Irish Government, and that since Irish expenditure exceeded Irish revenue, the difficulties of fixing what should eventually be the contribution of Ireland to Imperial expenditure were such that the question should be deferred. The 'original' scheme of 1893 was superior to others, which involved an apportionment of all revenues, since it proposed that the Imperial Government should retain the revenues from and control of Customs, out of which it should defray the Irish share of Imperial services, and that the Irish Government should retain all true Irish revenue and control all other taxes.

The Committee rejected the principles of earlier schemes in favour of giving the Irish Government full power of imposing and levying all taxation in Ireland, subject to such reservations as might be necessary to guard against tariff changes that might prejudice the relations with foreign powers or trade between Great Britain and Ireland. Any disadvantages which might arise from a weakening of the customs unity of the United Kingdom were outweighed by the advantage of making the Irish Government completely responsible for the administration of Ireland and of ending the extravagance due to the assimilation of the scale of Irish with that of British expenditure. It would avoid the necessity of apportioning liability for local expenditure, and remove every point of financial contact which might give rise to friction. Irish expenditure would be £12,400,000 and revenue £10,350,000. To meet the deficit, all Old Age Pensions already granted should be taken over by the Imperial Exchequer. Recommendations were also made for avoiding double death duties and double income tax.

Government of Ireland Bill

Outline of Financial Provisions. pp. 8. 1912. Memo. pp. 6. 1912. Memo. pp. 6. 1913

1912–13 *Cd.* 6154, *Cd.* 6486, *lxix*, 679. 1913 *Cd.* 6844, *lii*, 921

The Irish Exchequer will defray the whole cost of the present and future Irish services, with the exception of the Reserved Services (Old Age Pensions, National Insurance, Labour Exchanges, Land Purchase, Collection of Taxes and Royal Irish Constabulary for six years). During the period in which the yield of Irish taxes is less than the cost of Irish services, the Imperial Exchequer will collect all Irish taxes and transfer to the Irish Exchequer the transferred sum, i.e. the amount needed, with Post Office revenue, to cover the cost of the Irish services, plus a surplus for a period of years.

The Irish Parliament will be given the following powers of varying taxation: it may add to the rates of excise duties, customs duties on wines and spirits, etc., levied by the Imperial Parliament, add not more than 10 per cent to Income Tax, Death Duties and Customs Duties other than on wines and spirits, and levy any new taxes other than Customs Duties. It may reduce taxes. Any additional revenue from these taxes will be added to and any loss of revenue through reduction of taxes will be deducted from the transferred sum. When Irish revenue has equalled Irish expenditure for three years, Parliament will consider fixing the Irish contribution to common Imperial expenses, and the transfer to Ireland of the control and collection of such taxes as seem desirable.

The memo. sets out the financial estimates on the basis of these proposals. Memos. Cd. 6486 and Cd. 6844 give estimates on the basis of later information.

Disturbances, The Rising. See pp. 442–6

Government of Ireland

Headings of a Settlement. pp. 1. 1916

1916 Cd. 8310, xxii, 415

The Government of Ireland Act, 1914, was to be brought into operation as soon as possible after the Bill had been passed. The Act would not apply to the excluded 'six counties', in which the executive power of His Majesty was to be administered by a Secretary of State, with officers and departments not in any way responsible to the new Irish Government. The number of Irish members in the United Kingdom House of Commons would remain unaltered at 103, and the Irish House of Commons would consist of the members of the United Kingdom House of Commons for constituencies other than the excluded areas. The number of Irish Senators would be reduced proportionately to the population of the excluded area;

they would be nominated by the Lord Lieutenant. A High Court Judge would be appointed by the Imperial Government to sit in Belfast and all appeals, whether from Dublin or Belfast, would go to an Appeal Court in Dublin consisting of judges appointed by the Imperial Government.

The Act should remain in force for the period of the war and twelve months thereafter, or be extended by Order in Council if Parliament had not meanwhile made permanent provision for the government of Ireland. At the close of the war there should be an Imperial Conference, at which the permanent settlement of Ireland should be considered.

Irish Convention

Report of the Proceedings, apps. pp. 176. 1918

1918 Cd. 9019, x, 697
apptd. May, 1917. sgd. April, 1918

H. Plunkett (Ch.).

'The terms of reference to the Convention are set forth in the following passage from a letter on the subject which was lately addressed to the leaders of the principal Irish parties in the House of Commons:
' "Would it be too much to hope that Irishmen of all creeds and parties might meet together in a Convention for the purpose of drafting a constitution for their country which should secure a just balance of all the opposing interests, and finally compose the unhappy discords which have so long distracted Ireland and impeded its harmonious development?" ... "The Government therefore propose to summon immediately on behalf of the Crown a Convention of representative Irishmen in Ireland, to submit to the British Government a constitution for the future government of Ireland within the Empire." '

The Convention was called as a result of a letter of 16th May, 1917, from Mr. Lloyd George, Prime Minister, to Mr. W. Redmond, M.P., leader of the Irish Nationalists, in which he outlined a scheme for Home Rule for Ireland excluding the six counties of Northern Ulster, the exclusion to be subject to reconsideration after five years. If the scheme were not acceptable, he suggested as an alternative, a Convention of Irishmen of all parties (similar to the Convention which preceded the Union of South Africa) for the purpose of producing a scheme of Irish self-government.

Letter of transmission from Chairman.—Sir Horace Plunkett, in a letter transmitting the Report of Proceedings to the Prime Minister, explained that the Convention had worked for eight months, and in view of the difficulties caused to the war and peace efforts by the unsettled Irish question, it was decided not to waste time by protracted debate on majority and minority reports, but to issue a full account of the Convention's proceedings and its conclusions, whether unanimous or otherwise. Contrary to hopes, though its accuracy was not challenged, it was not unanimously adopted. There was thus no reasoned majority report, but two minorities, the Ulster Unionists and a minority of the Nationalists presented detailed reports covering the whole field. The effect of this procedure was to minimize the agreement reached and to maximize the disagreement.

If the adherence of the Ulster representatives could have been secured, there was hope of a unanimous report. Those from a portion of Ulster claimed that if Ireland had the right to separate itself from the rest of the United Kingdom, Ulster had the right to separate itself from the rest of Ireland. But since no section of the rest of Ireland would accept partition even as a temporary expedient, the Ulster representatives remained in the Convention only in the hope that some scheme of Home Rule might be found to modify the determination of those they represented to have no part in an Irish Parliament. No agreement was found, and they presented a scheme based on the complete exclusion of Ulster (App. XIV). The alternative to an unanimous report was agreement between a majority of Nationalists, the Southern Unionists and the Labour representatives. This was secured, save for two representatives of Labour and a minority of Nationalists who, however, differed only in one important particular from the majority. The Southern Unionists, led by Lord Middleton, accepted self-government for Ireland with full powers over all internal legislation and direct taxation, subject to (1) special representation of the Minority in the Irish Parliament; (2) representation in the Imperial Parliament and (3) the control of Customs remaining with the Imperial Parliament as vital to its control over external trade policy. They would accept no scheme which was incompatible with Ireland's full participation in any future scheme of United Kingdom federation. (1) was accepted by the Nationalists; (2) was also accepted by the Nationalists, provided the representatives were elected by the Irish Parliament and not direct by the constituencies, and this was agreed. (3) was the most difficult, since the Southern Unionists agreed on this point with the Ulster representatives, but the Nationalists felt that the equivalent of Dominion status required full control of Customs and Excise, though they agreed to a free trade arrangement between the two countries. Pending a decision of the whole question, it was agreed that the imposition of these duties should remain with the Imperial Parliament, but that the proceeds should be paid in full to the Irish Exchequer. The majority of the Labour representatives, while supporting this agreement, objected to the principle of nomination and to the inadequate representation of Labour in the Upper House.

Reports of Proceedings and of various groups of representatives.—The Report of the Proceedings gives a draft scheme presented by the Bishop of Raphoe and the conclusions arrived at on each point by a sub-committee of nine, together with the final scheme as accepted by 44 votes to 29. The Report of the Irish Unionist delegates states that they had assumed that to meet their views, any proposals would provide for the supremacy of the Imperial Parliament, the maintenance of fiscal unity, the protection of the rights of the Unionist minority, and the safety of the industrial enterprises of Ulster. The scheme proposed did not provide for these and in addition denied the right of the Imperial Parliament to impose conscription in Ireland without the consent of the Irish Parliament, and gave Ireland the right to raise and maintain a military force. The Provost of Trinity College and the Bishop of Armagh did not vote for the majority scheme because it involved either the coercion of Ulster, which was unthinkable, or the partition of Ireland, which would be disastrous. They had put forward a federal scheme based on Swiss or Canadian precedents, which might ensure a united Ireland with provincial autonomy for Ulster or any other Province that desired it. The minority of the Nationalists proposed a scheme for an Irish Parliament with full powers in all Irish matters, including taxation, but with religious safeguards, and with no powers in foreign affairs, the Army and Navy, etc. They conceded additional representation of the minority, representation at Westminster, free trade between the two countries, and the suspension for a term of years of the right to raise a local defence force and of the transfer of control over Customs. The majority of the Nationalists while they did not press their objection at the moment, reaffirmed the claim to full fiscal autonomy. The majority of the Labour representatives accepted the scheme, but objected to the nominated element in the Senate. The Earl of Dunraven regretted that no provision was made for a Grand Committee of the Irish Parliament to supervise matters affecting Ulster, but otherwise accepted the scheme as leading towards Federation, which was the best principle. The Southern Unionists stated that it was their unaltered conviction that Legislative Union was the best system for Ireland, but that they accepted the scheme as a result of the appeal of H.M. Government. An Irish Parliament could be established with safety only by the participation of Irishmen of all classes and creeds and with the safeguards agreed by the Convention but not provided in the Act of 1914. They further stated that Ireland must occupy the same position in any United Kingdom federation as any other part of it, that Customs should remain with the Imperial Parliament, and representatives be sent to Westminster.

2. (a) AGRICULTURE, DRAINAGE, FISHING

Irish Butter Industry

Dept. Cttee. Rep. pp. 35. 1910. Mins. of ev., apps., index. 1910

1910 Cd. 5092, vii, 835. Mins. of ev., etc.; 1910 Cd. 5093, viii, 1
apptd. April, 1909. sgd. March, 1910

J. R. Campbell (Ch.), Carroll, Brown, L. Carrick, Wilson.

'To inquire into and interpret the principal forms of trade description (as defined by Section 3 of the Merchandise Marks Act, 1887) at present applied, in the United Kingdom, to different grades of butter; and to suggest what additional measures, if any, it is desirable for the Department to take in the interests of the Irish butter industry, with special reference to the prevention of loss or injury to the industry from the use of false trade descriptions.'

Irish butter was originally known by names derived from localities or packages, as for example, 'Cork Firsts', 'firkins', 'kitts', 'butts', 'cloth lumps', etc., but the principal descriptions now are 'creamery', 'dairy' and 'factory' butter. Each name indicates a mode of manufacture. Creamery means unblended butter made from cream separated by centrifugal force from commingled milk supplies. Dairy butter means butter made at the farmer's homestead, and factory butter is blended, reworked or subject to any other treatment, but not so as to cease to be butter. Irish creamery butter is regarded by the trade as the best Irish butter, and harm is caused by the attempts which are made to sell blended butters under names which suggest they may be creamery butters, as when butter is sold as 'Irish Creamery'. The recommendations were designed to protect creamery butter as traditionally defined, by suggesting a set of regulations to be drawn up by the Department of Agriculture, to which the manufacturers of creamery butter should be legally obliged to conform. No premises should be used for making creamery butter unless registered and inspected, the description 'creamery' should not be applied to butter not produced on registered premises, and all such butter should be marked 'Irish Creamery Butter' and given a creamery number. The Department should also seek powers to regulate the general conditions under which butter is produced in order to protect the interests of the industry.

Butter Regulations. Butter Trade. Reps. See *Food Purity*, p. 300.

Irish Flax-growing Industry

Dept. Cttee. Rep. pp. 23. 1911.
    Mins of ev., apps., index. 1911

1911 *Cd.* 5502, *xxvi*, 1. *Mins. of ev., etc.*;
1911 *Cd.* 5503, *xxvi*, 31
apptd. Dec., 1909. *sgd. Jan.,* 1911

J. R. Campbell (*Ch.*), Barbour, Crawford, Stewart (J. W.), Stewart (J.), Lane, Gordon, Hinchcliff.

'*To inquire into the present state of the flax-growing industry in Ireland and the causes which are contributing to the decline of that industry, and to submit recommendations.*'

In 1847, the date of the earliest official record, the acreage under flax was 58,312; in 1910 it was 45,974. In the intervening years there had been great fluctuations — during the American wars when cotton was scarce

the area reached 301,693 acres—but there is no indication that the decline indicated by the 1910 figure has been arrested. The reasons for these fluctuations were that flax is not an essential part of a farmer's usual rotation of the temporary grass, grain and green crops, but is grown only when the prices appear attractive. If the price is good he grows more, if bad he grows less, and it is the opinion of farmers in general that flax-growing is a 'gamble'. A run of bad seasons has a detrimental effect because the scutch mills may become dismantled; and the art of growing and handling flax can be so lost as to make it exceedingly difficult to revive the industry. Some of the reasons given for the decline of flax-growing were: flax-sick land, defective cultivation, inferior seed, careless handling and the inefficiency and increased cost of labour.

At present only one-fifth to one-fourth of the fibre used in Irish mills is home-grown. Irish flax possesses a special degree of strength and spinning qualities so well adapted for thread and other yarns that they are almost a necessity in certain branches of the Irish linen industry. It is most important that the art of growing and handling it should be kept alive. For continuous success the grower must produce high-class fibre, and should not attempt to compete with the inferior Russian article, which can be produced in large quantities at low cost.

Recommendations are made that the Department of Agriculture should investigate the production of better seeds from Irish crops, the problems of retting, the provision of technical advice to any syndicate which would buy and ret flax on the courtrai system and to owners of scutch mills. The selling of flax at scutch mills is unsatisfactory, and should be discontinued. Where it would not interfere with private enterprise, the Department should consider direct aid for the erection of new or renovation of old scutch mills.

Irish Milk Supply
Vice-Regal Com.

apptd. Nov., 1911

P. J. O'Neill (*Ch.*), Woodhouse, Moorhead, Wilson, O'Brien, Campbell, Mettam, Everard (Lady), McNeill (Miss M.).

'*To inquire into the alleged scarcity in the supply of Milk in some parts of Ireland, and to report upon the causes of the deficiency where it exists, its effects upon the public health, and the means whereby the deficiency can be remedied; and also to inquire into and report upon the dangers of contamination and infection in the present Milk supply, and the methods best adapted to guard against these dangers.*'

The First and Second Reports are formal presentations of the following volumes of minutes of evidence, etc.; 1913 Cd. 6684, Cd. 6937, xxix, 5.

—— Final Report. pp. vi, 61. 1913. Mins. of ev., apps., index. 1913

1914 *Cd.* 7129, *xxxvi*, 601. *Mins. of ev., etc.*; 1914 *Cd.* 7134, *xxxvi*, 669 *sgd. Oct.*, 1913

In large towns the problem is not the scarcity of milk, but the unwillingness or inability to pay the price demanded for it. In a poor man's budget, money spent on milk is grudged and instead is often spent on foods inferior as a means of sustenance, but frequently this is due to ignorance or to the conviction that milk sold in the poorer districts is inferior in quality and not worth the money. Evidence did go to show that there had been laxity on the part of the authorities concerning adulteration. In the small towns and the rural areas the change in habits of feeding were due to the scarcity of milk. Where experiments had been made to supply it, either by voluntary effort or through the initiative of an individual, the consumption had increased. But where no milk is available people come to rely on other things, they cease to appreciate its value, and the ensuing fitful demand for it in turn affects the supply.

The longevity as well as the poverty of the Irish peasant class is well known, and it follows that good health must have been the result of nourishing and inexpensive food. Thirty years ago the diet of a labouring man was—breakfast: stirabout made with oatmeal (more solid than porridge), milk, buttermilk, wholemeal bread made with buttermilk; dinner: potatoes, butter, buttermilk, bread, milk; supper: potatoes and buttermilk. In 1908, in County Mayo, it was as follows—breakfast: tea, one pint (and in a majority of cases without milk for several months in the year) and sodden bread baked with water; sometimes buttermilk mixed with water; dinner: from August to March, potatoes, salt fish or milk if they have it; when there is no milk, which is usual till the middle of May or June, shell-fish soup or sugar on porridge or coffee; tea: same as breakfast; supper: same as dinner, in smaller quantities. For men working away from home, for breakfast and dinner, cold tea with or without milk, and bread.

The scarcity of milk which exists in the rural districts in the greater part of Ireland is due to many causes. (1) The loudest and bitterest complaints arise in the districts with the most milk and the most creameries—farmers will not break bulk, but send all the milk to the creamery. When in the past they set their milk at home, there was not only a local supply of milk but plenty of sweet skimmed milk with 1 per cent cream, as well as the buttermilk. The effects of the change in butter making have been as fundamental as the passing of hand-weaving in the linen and woollen industries. (2) On much of the rich pasture land fat cattle are considered more profitable than milch cows. The complaint in Counties Antrim and Armagh and parts of County Down is that there would be large quantities if a proper system of selection in breeding milch cows were encouraged by the Department of

Agriculture. In Cork and Limerick it is alleged that the tendency of the Department is to encourage the breeding of store cattle at the expense of the milch cow. In Connemara and Donegal the land is said to be too poor to support milch cows. The Galloway cow, a notoriously poor milker, was introduced because it could subsist on poor pasture. (3) Scarcity is almost universal in the winter because the farmer says that winter dairying does not pay, the chief difficulties being those of getting suitable labour and the cost of feeding stuffs. (4) Scarcity of milk in the fertile County of Meath is attributed to the fact that labourers find difficulty in getting cow-plots. The cost of keeping a cow, £10 a year, is practically prohibitive.

Local authorities should contribute towards the cost of infant milk depots; milk clubs should be formed in rural districts to organize a regular demand for milk; winter dairying should be encouraged by cow-testing and record-keeping associations; cow-plots should be provided; standards of cleanliness and purity, etc., should be encouraged through inspection and enforcement of the Dairies Order and loans should be granted for the improvement of cattle byres.

Foot-and-Mouth Disease in Ireland in the year 1912

Rep., apps. pp. 74. 1913

1914 Cd. 7103, xii, 793

The last appearance of foot-and-mouth in Ireland was in 1883 and 1884 when the number of animals affected was 115,641. As during the 28 years of immunity precautionary measures were always taken when there were any outbreaks in England, the tracing of diseased animals at Liverpool to Swords, County Dublin, in June, 1912 caused consternation and surprise. The Report gives an account of the outbreaks at 68 places between June and November, and the steps taken to isolate and prevent the spread of the disease.

Irish Pig-breeding Industry

Dept. Cttee. Rep. pp. 18. 1915.
Mins. of ev., apps., index. 1915

1914–16 Cd. 7890, vi, 855. Mins. of ev., etc.; 1914–16 Cd. 8004, vi, 879 apptd. Oct., 1914. sgd. April, 1915

J. S. Gordon (Ch.), Boyd, O'Mara, Clune, Willington, Roulston.

'To inquire into the present state of the pig-breeding industry in Ireland, with special reference to the causes which contributed to the recent decrease in the number of pigs in Ireland; and to submit recommendations.'

During the period 1851–1910 the average number of pigs in Ireland was about 1,250,000, the variation from year to year being slight. The pigs produced are disposed of at home either through Irish bacon curers or by killing for home consumption (1,458,000 in 1910), or are exported alive (324,000). The quantity of bacon and hams exported annually is approximately one-fifth of the total imported to Great Britain. The highest figure reached was 1,450,128 in 1882; the lowest was in 1913, when the figures fell to 1,060,360. The cause of this shrinkage was the concurrently low prices of pork and the high prices of feeding stuffs, accentuated by a poor yield of potatoes in 1912. The adverse effect of shortage of potatoes was emphasized in that it was 'the current price for potatoes, and the price of "bonhams" during the autumn and winter months, that determines whether a grower will sell his potatoes or keep them for feeding to pigs'.

The more general factors militating against the stability of the industry are (1) the difficulties experienced by large farmers in getting farm servants who are willing to undertake the care and feeding of pigs—though this does not hamper small holders; (2) the conditions of marketing live pigs in the South, and dead pigs in the North; (3) fluctuations in prices, which were open to daily manipulation in the small markets; (4) combinations amongst the buyers, e.g. curers; (5) the increase of store cattle raising and poultry keeping—small holders' wives preferred poultry to pigs; (6) want of proper pig styes in connection with rural district council cottages and (7) the effect of sanitary restrictions in the towns.

The farmers who breed regularly a certain number of pigs obtain the best results. Pig keepers should discontinue the practice of giving up pig breeding and feeding when pork prices are low and commencing again when pork prices are high. To improve pig breeding, the price paid by the Department for suitable boars should be increased. The maximum value of the premium should be raised to enable county committees to increase premiums to suitable applicants; and the committees should be empowered to sanction an increase of service fees. Other recommendations are made to pig breeders on breeding, rearing, feeding and marketing, the improvement of pig styes on small holdings; householders in urban districts should be allowed to keep pigs where they would be no danger to public health.

Conditions on which a Grant will be made to the Irish Agricultural Organization Society, from the Development Fund

Treasury Letter. pp. 1. 1913

1913 Cd. 6735, liii, 3

The Treasury recommended an advance of £2,000 by way of grant for the period up to 1st July, 1912, in aid of current work, and further assistance in future years on condition that the Society added to its governing body eleven persons nominated by the Development Commissioners, and that no co-operative society engaging in co-operation other than that of a purely agricultural nature should be affiliated to the Society.

Agricultural Credit in Ireland

Dept. Cttee. Rep. pp. xvi, 407. 1914.
Mins. of ev., apps., index. 1914

*1914 Cd. 7375, xiii, 1. Mins. of ev., etc.;
1914 Cd. 7376, xiii, 431
apptd. Jan., 1912. sgd. April, 1914*

G. Murnaghan (*Ch.*), Anderson, Bailey, Bastable, Finlay, Gill, Kavanagh, Knox.

'To inquire into the existing system of credit available for the rural classes in Ireland; to suggest what, if any, improvements not involving financial assistance from the Exchequer, should be made in the system; and to consider especially the form of agricultural credit most suitable to the requirements of the occupiers of land affected by the Land Acts in the western districts, and throughout the country generally.'

The Joint Stock Banks, though willing, are unable from the nature of their business to deal with the special requirements of small farmers and of the agricultural industry generally. The large deposits in Post Office Savings Banks prove that there are ample funds in rural districts for agricultural credit, but an economic injury is done to Ireland by the transfer of £13 mn. of Irish savings to London for investment in Government securities. The best method of using the funds for reproductive purposes would be to organize co-operative credit societies to which they could be gradually transferred. As the majority of depositors in Trustee Savings Banks belong to the urban rather than the rural population, the possibility of using any of the funds for rural credit purposes is small.

The number of moneylenders has greatly increased, and legislation has effected little diminution in the evils connected with the system. The greatest economic and social injury is caused not in cases of reckless small borrowers or of persons of high social position, but of the small and medium farmers and traders who, finding themselves in temporary financial difficulties and wishing to conceal their position, borrow from moneylending firms whose circulars through the post and advertisements in the press are so widespread. More drastic legislation and stricter enforcement of present legislation would accomplish much, but the establishment of a sound system of co-operative credit attracting the confidence of the industrious farmer would be more effective. Trust and credit auctions are one of the worst methods resorted to by Irish farmers who need ready cash. A farmer will take a cow to auction, where it may be bid for by a son or relative, who gives the auctioneer a bill for three to six months, the nominal purchaser often driving back the cow to the field from which it came. When the bill falls due the process is repeated. No legislation would prevent evasion by collusion; the evil should be counteracted by co-operative credit. The gombeen man, the local moneylending shopkeeper, who lends at high rates of interest, has almost disappeared. Shop indebtedness arising from the demand for a higher standard of comfort is not harmful if the amount is moderate. Although shopkeepers have often saved farmers from bankruptcy, long credit can lead to serious abuse, especially when it is for feeding stuffs which could be grown by the farmer himself.

The Loan Fund Board system was originally intended for industrial workers, but 70 per cent of the borrowers are now farmers and agricultural labourers. The maximum length of loans, repayment by instalments, limitation of amount to £10, and comparatively high rates of interest are unsuitable for agriculture. Their history is one of central and local mismanagement, defective legislation and in some districts heavy losses. The functions of the Board should be transferred to the Department of Agriculture and the local societies transformed into co-operative credit societies.

The Credit Societies organized by the Irish Agricultural Organization Society have done much good, £550,000 having been lent in nineteen years. Some of the stronger ones furnish admirable examples of what can be accomplished under good local management, but there have been faults due to the carelessness of local committees, lack of efficient secretaries, inadequate inspection and over-reliance on State loans. Of the 76 societies which have survived, 45 per cent are unsatisfactory. In view of the difficulty of inducing medium and large farmers to undertake unlimited liability, Credit Societies based on shares and limited liability should also be established. Deposits and loans should approximately balance. Trading operations and banking operations should not be combined in a single society. The failure to attract deposits is due to competition of the Post Office Savings Banks, which offer security and secrecy, the distrust of local committees, the widespread reluctance of persons with savings to allow the fact to become known to their neighbours. The total of £30,000 deposits in all Ireland after nineteen years is disappointing. The confidence of depositors would be increased by the establishment of a system of Credit Societies under an Agricultural Credit Section of the Department of Agriculture, with reorganized methods of audit, inspection and supervision, combined with full local responsibility for management. The rate of interest in deposits is not so influential a factor in attracting savings as security: it should not exceed 3½ per cent.

The Land Loans are the only systems of long-term loans for land improvement available to all farmers and landowners fulfilling the prescribed conditions, but many small farmers (those with a Poor Law valuation of under £7) are ineligible. The outstanding loans, amounting to £11,500, advanced to credit societies by the Department of Agriculture and the Congested Districts Board, should be withdrawn gradually. Rural industries are handicapped by lack of facilities for obtaining capital at a reasonable rate; the Department of Agriculture should assist the banks with full information on these matters.

The tendency of a peasantry to incur over-indebtedness is a danger from which the new tenant-purchasers should be protected, consistently with their need, in suitable cases, to obtain long-term loans upon the only security they have, their land. The net mortgage indebtedness of Irish land is increasing by £1 mn. per annum. A complete system of registry of title is essential. The limitations on mortgaging imposed by the Land Act, 1903, are desirable. New holders should make the most of their land by work rather than by pledging it. The development of the agricultural loan schemes of the Board of Works, Department of Agriculture and Congested Districts Board should prove sufficient in the majority of cases not met by the Banks, and these should be thoroughly tested before any attempts based on Continental systems are made.

Note by the Chairman and Prof. Bastable; by Finlay objecting that the proposals for the organization and inspection of credit societies by the Department of Agriculture will fail to attract the deposits or to stimulate self help, and will compete with the Irish Agricultural Organization Society. Both Knox and Anderson support Finlay. Kavanagh signed the report in deference to the knowledge of his colleagues but feels that the existing facilities for agricultural credit are sufficient, and that it would be harmful to increase them.

Food Production in Ireland

Dept. Cttee. Rep. pp. v, 21. 1915.
   Mins. of ev., apps., index. 1916

1914–16 Cd. 8046, v, 799. *Mins. of ev.,*
etc.; 1914–16 Cd. 8158, v, 827
apptd. June, sgd. Aug., 1915

T. W. Russell (*Ch.*), Bagwell, Barrie, Bastable, Boland, Boyd, Campbell, Downes, Field, Gill, Gordon, L. Bishop of Ross, McDonald, Murnaghan, O'Connor, O'Neill, Montgomery, Plunkett.

'*To consider and report what steps should be taken by legislation or otherwise for the sole purpose of maintaining and, if possible, increasing the present production of food in Ireland, on the assumption that the war may be prolonged beyond the harvest of* 1916.'

The main objects to be aimed at in effecting an increased supply of food in Ireland were as follows: (*a*) a material increase in the area under tillage, not only with a view to the direct production of more human food, but also to its indirect production by increasing the amount of fodder available for cattle. (*b*) The maintenance, increase and improvement of breeding stock of all kinds. (*c*) The improvement of the farmers' position in regard to the means of obtaining the use of machinery and implements. (*d*) The conservation of the artificial manure supply of the country. (*e*) The maintenance of the Irish fishing industry. Higher prices had already favourably affected acreage, as shown by the figures for the crop return of 1915 as compared with 1914. A further increase could be expected by the Government guaranteeing for one year a minimum price for wheat and oats. The livestock had been adversely affected by foot-and-mouth disease, but it was thought that the Live Stock Act, 1915, which gave the Department of Agriculture powers to stop the slaughter and export of breeding stock, would safeguard the stock and the cattle trade. The County Committees should promote and take charge of the schemes to enable small holders to get loans for machinery and implements. The system of loans for the provision of fishing boats and gear should be extended.

Seven separate notes deal with such points as the length of the period for the minimum price, the encouragement of sugar beet, improved equipment and facilities, and reduced rates for the transport of livestock. The Minority Report of Sir Horace Plunkett was written after eleven members of the committee had voted against—four voted for—a clause embodying what he maintained to be 'the principle at issue'. This was a claim on behalf of the Agricultural Organization Society, that 'any hopeful scheme for increasing the production of food in a country where eighty-five per cent of the farms are small holdings, must depend at least as much upon voluntary effort as upon governmental action; that the Society has proved its ability to organize the voluntary effort of the agricultural classes upon the co-operative system, which is the only plan suitable for combination among farmers; that, before the creation of the Department, it had effected a more radical reform in the methods of Irish dairying than is now required in the methods of tillage; and that, where farmers have used their co-operative organization for the purpose of enabling them to adopt a more intensive cultivation, a remarkable increase in food production has actually taken place. It is maintained that not only a permanent improvement in Irish agriculture, but also an immediate increase in the production of food can be brought about by the Department and the Society helping each other while each does its own work independently.'

In this Minority Report Plunkett argues that food production could be increased by compulsion, inducement or persuasion. Compulsion is rejected. The Majority's proposals for a guarantee against loss if farmers are called upon to grow emergency crops and for the maintenance of livestock are endorsed. A more productive farming demands a reorganization on the basis of continuous cropping. For this more labour will be needed, but the supply had decreased and was unevenly distributed. It should be mobilized by Labour Exchanges, but a minimum wage at the moment would make the farmers unwilling to develop the industry. The modern implements and machinery required should be acquired by small holders through co-operative organizations. A Joint Committee of the Department and the Irish Agricultural Organization Society should be set up to plan and carry out a joint campaign.

Irish Forestry

Dept. Cttee. Rep. pp. v, 60. 1908. Mins. of ev., apps., index. 1908

1908 *Cd.* 4027, *xxiii*, 601. *Mins. of ev., etc.*; 1908 *Cd.* 4028, *xxiii*, 669 *apptd. Aug.*, 1907. *sgd. April*, 1908

T. P. Gill (*Ch.*), L. Castletown, Redmond, Bishop of Ross, Montgomery, Bailey, Fisher, Campbell.

'To inquire into and report upon the following matters relating to the improvement of forestry in Ireland, viz.—(1) The present provision for State aid to forestry in Ireland; (2) The means whereby, in connection with the operation of the Land Purchase Acts, existing woods may be preserved, and land suitable for forestry acquired for public purposes; and (3) The financial and other provisions necessary for a comprehensive scheme of afforestation in Ireland.'

While Ireland is particularly suitable for tree growing, forestry has been so neglected by the Government that the percentage under woodlands (1.5 per cent, or 300,000 acres) is the lowest of any country in Europe save one, and is being wastefully diminished under the indirect influence of the Land Purchase Acts. At least one million acres of woodland is essential, and 700,000 acres suitable for plantation and unsuited to other uses are available, 200,000 being plantable in large blocks. The Land Purchase Acts made no effective provision for dealing with woodlands on estates being sold to tenants, or with general questions of drainage, roads, access involved in handling woods, or for the acquisition of waste land, not part of tenants' holdings, suitable for forestry.

There should be a national scheme of afforestation. The State should acquire, plant and manage as a State Forest 200,000 acres of land plantable in large blocks, and should **acquire and** manage the larger woods passing from their present owners under the Land Purchase Acts. Smaller woods should be purchased and managed by county councils. Private owners should be encouraged to plant portions of their holdings. The Department of Agriculture should assist in the organization of the timber trade and forest industries by expert assistance and instruction. The net expenses of the scheme, including land purchase, would rise from £45,000 per annum in the first decade to £74,600 in the third decade, and would thereafter decline, till a surplus appeared in the sixth, the return becoming 4½ per cent on the sum invested. The Irish Quit and Crown Rents might be used for the scheme, together with an annual grant of £13,600 for fifty years and £8,600 for ten years.

Bann and Lough Neagh Drainage

Rep. pp. 30. 1906

1906 Cd. 2855, xcvi, 901

A. R. Binnie.

The problem of the Bann and Lough Neagh Drainage arises not so much from engineering difficulties as from the conflicting • interests involved. Whilst there was consensus of opinion that the large winter floods, which submerged the land for some months, were the principal cause of complaint, some wanted all floods prevented, others said partial flooding was beneficial, but because of the considerable traffic on it, no one wanted any reduction in the summer level of Lough Neagh. One fact is indisputable, that the summer floods of a temporary nature will occur on the Blackwater and Upper Bann when the lake is at its summer level.

The drainage of the Lower Bann had previously been considered in the light of the maintenance of the Lower Bann Navigation, but its trade was insignificant, it violated the first principles of canal engineering, the amount of water passing down the canalized river in the winter months against upward traffic militated against any commercial success for the navigation. The Lower Bann Navigation should be abandoned. A scheme is proposed for the construction and reconstruction of weirs and sluices and for excavations which would maintain the summer level of Lough Neagh at 46 feet above datum and cope with the flow of flood water and preserve the salmon and eel fisheries. Estimates for the work are given on page 17.

See *Drainage of Lough Neagh and the Lower Bann*. F. J. Dick. Rep. pp. 7. 1904; 1904 Cd. 2205, lxxix, 21. *Bann and Lough Neagh Drainage*. J. D. Bell. Land Valuer. Rep. pp. 17. 1907; 1907 Cd. 3534, lxvii, 61.

Arterial Drainage (Ireland)

Vice-Regal Com. Rep. pp. 26. 1907. Mins. of ev., apps., index. 1907

1907 Cd. 3374, xxxii, 1. *Mins. of ev., etc.*; 1907 Cd. 3467, xxxii, 27

apptd. Sept., 1905. sgd. Feb., 1907

A. R. Binnie (*Ch.*), Andrews, Brown, Dillon, Ryan.

'*To inquire into and report upon the methods of initiating, executing and maintaining schemes of Arterial Drainage in Ireland under the Statutes now in force, and their practical working; whether any reforms or alterations of the existing methods, or consolidation of existing Statutes, are desirable, and, if so, what legislation is necessary for carrying them into effect.*' Extended terms—to inquire '*into the Drainage Areas of the River Barrow; the Lough and River Erne; and the Lough and River Corrib.*'

The Allport Commission on Arterial Drainage (1887 C. 5038, xxv) recognized the general necessity for arterial drainage. They went into the matter so thoroughly that there is nothing fresh which could be added (q. 4). The problem in 1907 was that drainage schemes were coming to a standstill because present legislation was becoming obsolete.

Under the Drainage Code of 1842

proprietors of lands could present a memorial to the Board of Works, and after the assent of one-half of the owners the Board could proceed with a scheme. On completion the cost was divisible amongst the proprietors in proportion to benefit received. Considerable schemes were undertaken and 120 districts were formed. But the Act did not get a fair trial because of the famine relief work. The ultimate financial result of the drainage scheme was £1,041,938 charged to proprietors and £1,348,678 being either a free grant or remitted by the State. The Code of 1863 reversed the policy regarding the promotion of schemes. Their initiation and execution, instead of being undertaken by the Board, were now left to the proprietors. The Board's obligation was to approve them, to prepare the Provisional Order constituting the district, advance the money, and to make the Final Award charging on the lands improved the expenditure incurred. Sixty-three drainage districts had been formed, but the figures show that whereas excess of actual over-estimated expenditure was borne by the State under the 1842 code, under the 1863 code it was borne by the proprietors. The Act of 1863 contemplated the existence of a few large landowners who would agree amongst themselves whether a Drainage District should be formed, but with the recent legislation the land is passing to a large number of tenant occupiers, and this makes it impossible to raise the preliminary expenses of a scheme, or to get the necessary assents for the initiation of one.

Arterial drainage is of special importance in Ireland. The mountains usually rise in the maritime counties, great portions of the Midlands being flat and of low elevation, so that a small obstacle will cause flooding out of all proportion to the impediment. Drainage is therefore of vital importance to protect the farmer. Yet for the reasons given, the initiation of new drainage schemes is at a standstill.

Recommended: '(i) the formation of a Government Drainage Department, whose functions should be to define the boundaries of the several catchment basins in Ireland, to ascertain the nature, extent and cost of the drainage works required therein, to determine the constitution of the body which shall be responsible for the maintenance of works when executed, and be the guardian for the expenditure of public money; (ii) the creation of Conservancy Boards for the large or "major" catchment areas, which should have charge of the main outfall works, and exercise control over the subordinate Drainage Committees in their area with a view to securing harmony of action and unity of purpose; and (iii) Drainage Committees for small or "minor" catchment basins, and for Drainage Districts in the large watersheds. These latter would be largely under the control of the County Councils.'

Irish Inland Fisheries

Vice-Regal Com. Rep. pp. 17. 1901. Pt. I. Mins. of ev., index. 1901. Pts. II., III. Apps. 1901

1901 Cd. 448, xii, 1. Mins. of ev., etc.; 1901 Cd. 450, Cd. 451, Cd. 452, xii, 19 apptd. Aug., 1899. sgd. Jan., 1901

S. Walker (Ch.), Don, Cunningham, Esmonde, Fitzgerald, M'Intosh, Green.

'To inquire into the present condition of Inland Fisheries, that is to say Fisheries in Lakes, Rivers and Estuaries in Ireland, and the Laws relating thereto.'

The object of the enquiry was to consider the principle of preserving the supply of salmon and trout for the use of the public and maintaining the benefits accruing therefrom. Although the estimated yield of the salmon fisheries was £300,000, of which £200,000 could be taken as earnings of fishermen, it was felt that the supplies were declining, possibly owing to the capture of the fish by engines and nets in estuaries and tidal waters, by nets in fresh water portions of the rivers, through killing by dynamite and by various forms of river pollution, and the capture of immature fish. The recommendations included the establishment and maintenance in each province of Ireland, by the Fishery Authority, of a central hatchery; for more accurate statistics, more scientific investigation, more protection of the spawning grounds, more efficient fish-passes in mill-dams, etc.; an efficient working of the closed season and a better and more independent bailiff system, etc. Cormorants and mergansers should be excluded from the operation of the Wild Birds' Protection Act.

Irish Inland Fisheries

Dept. Cttee. Rep. pp. v, 24. 1912.
 Mins. of ev., apps., index. 1913

1912–13 Cd. 6433, xxvii, 161. Mins. of ev., etc.; 1912–13 Cd. 6545, xxvii, 191 apptd. Jan., 1911. sgd. Sept., 1912

D. Harrel (Ch.), Ross, Wrench, Mahaffy, Gwynn, Calderwood, Green.

'To enquire into the effect which changes in the ownership of land in Ireland under the Land Acts have had or may be expected to have on the Fisheries of the country, and in particular on the Salmon Fishing Industry, and to make recommendations as to what steps, if any, it may be desirable in the circumstances for the State to adopt in the interests of Irish Fisheries.'

The Irish Land Purchase Acts, which were passed to enable tenants to purchase the fee simple of their holdings, have not affected the fishing rights in tidal waters—which are usually Crown rights subject to the recognized public right of fishing—but have brought about a considerable change in the ownership of fisheries in non-tidal waters. With very few exceptions tenant purchasers have not made profitable use of their fishing rights, and do not appear to have grasped the importance of fishery preservation. Netting is carried on to an excessive degree and poaching is widely prevalent, with most disastrous effects. The reduction of stocks threatens grievous injury to the industry.

The recommendations set out the details of reconstructed Boards of Conservators and proposals for increasing their revenues. Other recommendations concern the powers of Boards to take over and administer unused or misused fisheries, combination amongst tenant purchasers for the protection and letting of their fisheries, the abolition of netting in fresh waters, limitation of drift netting at sea, protection of fisheries, etc.

The Rev. Dr. Mahaffy submitted a memo. on Trout Fishing, and a note by J. Gwynn stated that netting fish in estuaries was a livelihood to many men. The Conservators should have power to limit the number of nets and to vary the licences.

Shell-fish Layings on the Irish Coast, as respects their Liability to Sewage Contamination

Rep., app. pp. x, 148. 1904

1904 Cd. 1900, xxvii, 481

T. J. Browne, E. J. McWeeney.

This scientific investigation was made as a result of outbreaks of enteric fever in England and Ireland thought to be caused by the consumption of oysters from fisheries polluted by sewage. Some areas in which shell-fish are laid are grossly polluted, for example, the estuaries of the Liffy, the Lagan and the Newry rivers, and there are also large numbers of layings whose purity is open to doubt. On the other hand there is a great stretch of coast line in the South and the West where there is almost illimitable scope for the extension of the industry under suitable hygienic conditions.

2. (b) LAND AND LAND LAW, CONGESTED DISTRICTS

The Present Condition of Tenant Purchasers under the Land Purchase Acts

Rep. pp. 30. 1903

1903 (92) lvii, 333

W. F. Bailey

'An Inquiry into the condition of tenant purchasers who have acquired their holdings under the various Land Purchase Acts, and into the condition of their farms.'

That the holdings of tenant purchasers, including their houses and buildings, have largely improved in all parts of Ireland as regards cultivation, treatment and general condition is unquestionable. On one estate in Mayo by reclamation the occupiers had added from 50 to 100 per cent to the cropping capacity of their little holdings. Where improvement has not taken place and conditions are stationary, it is commonly due to some unavoidable misfortune, such as the dying of cattle, or sickness or death in the family, etc. This first shows itself in the general neglect of the houses, caused by the 'pinch of poverty' and 'want of hope'. The great differences in the size of holdings are mainly due to the prevailing local practices. For example, what is considered ample in one district may be quite insufficient in another. Holdings should in general conform to the character of the district. The tendency to sell, sub-let or sub-divide has decreased. Where occupiers' interests in holdings are sold, purchase price is very much influenced by the practices of the district. Tenant purchasers in a progressive district get a larger price than the vendors of non-purchased holdings. On an estate in Antrim the feeling was that holdings have declined in value, but generally there has been no undue rise in the prices paid for interests sold by tenant purchasers. General solvency and credit have also improved, and this is most marked in the localities where people were worse off in former times. They have paid off their debts to the shopkeepers and bankers, stocks have increased, and loans are more easy to get. Improved financial circumstances are indicated by the hesitation and great care taken in accepting a loan. An agent for artificial manures in Mayo said 'it was not like old times. They do not want . . . credit now—they

pay in cash.' The moneylender—the 'gombeen man'—has disappeared. There are, however, some estates, e.g. in Londonderry, Leitrim, Kerry and Donegal, where people are not better off and where solvency and credit has not improved.

State-aided land purchase does not mean that the State can divest itself of all responsibility. Widely scattered over the country are groups of purchasers who have made little improvement in their material condition by becoming owners, and who live in poverty without hope and without incentive. The explanation probably lies in their sunken circumstances before and at purchase. There is a need for a specially organized State Department responsible for giving advice to tenants, especially those where no progress has been made, for the periodic inspections of holdings in general and for the protection of communal interests, as, for example, the cutting of turf, the use of spent bogs, forestry, etc. Arrangements should be made, e.g. through rural banks, for supplying the small purchaser with capital on easy terms.

See *Investment of Funds under the Control of the Supreme Court.* Special Committee of the Dublin Stock Exchange. Statement; 1906 (171) c, 605.

Irish Land Purchase Finance

Dept. Cttee. Rep. pp. 19. 1908

1908 *Cd.* 4005, *xxiii*, 267
apptd. Nov., 1907. sgd. Feb., 1908

W. Runciman (*Ch.*), Schuster, Heath, Blain, Duncan, Davies.

'To enquire into the difficulties which have arisen in connection with the provision of the funds required for the purposes of the Irish Land Act, 1903; and to report how far these difficulties can be diminished or removed without imposing any additional charge on the Exchequer.'

Previous Acts had failed because of the difficulty of devising a scheme for voluntary land purchase which should provide that the landlord would obtain a price for his land at which he would be ready to sell, while allowing the tenant a sufficient reduction in his rent in the shape of an annuity, to induce him to buy. The Act of 1903 provided for a bonus to the landlord over and above the purchase money paid by the tenant up to a limit of a total of £12 mn. and for a reduction below the level of previous enactments of the annuity which the tenant purchaser paid for his advance. The money was advanced at 2¾ per cent over a lengthened period for repayment with ½ per cent sinking fund.

The main difficulty is the charge for Excess Stock, i.e. the difference between the face value of the stock and the sum realized on issue. The amount of stock so far issued is £23,750,000, and the sum realized £20,911,000. If the probable amount required to complete land purchase, £160 mn. (instead of the £100 mn. originally estimated), is raised on the same terms, the annual charges for excess stock would be £705,000. As the cash proceeds of issue so far amount to £20 mn., the issue of a further £140 mn., even if spread over a period of years, must have a depressing effect on the price. The terms of reference do not permit the suggestion that the extra charge should be borne by the Exchequer, and in any case the taxpayer's contribution is sufficient and could not be equitably increased to relieve the Irish ratepayers of a charge on them imposed by the Act. On the other hand, Land Purchase must continue. The landlords say they would not be willing to sell at lower terms than they now receive, and the tenant will not buy unless his annuity payments are below the rents he is paying (20-25 per cent in the case of second-term rents). In addition, agreements between landlords and the tenants on which advances have not yet been made, involving £40 mn., have already been arrived at, and the bonus of £12 mn. will be insufficient.

An announcement should be made that no fresh agreements should be made under the Act. No alteration could properly be made in the terms on which the pending agreements were concluded, but no stock should be issued so long as money market conditions are unfavourable, cash advances being limited to the amount the National Debt Commissioners may be able to provide in exchange for stock. As regards future agreements, no scheme of land purchase will be sound unless the finance is self-supporting. The tenant's annuity, which should be sufficient to cover interest charges and sinking fund, should be raised to 3⅝ per cent. The bonus was under-estimated, and the limit of £12 mn. should be extended. Power should be taken to issue a 3 per cent Guaranteed Stock, which seems slightly more attractive, but it should not be issued below par. In order not to halt land purchase altogether, if it could not be issued at par or above, the landlord should be given the option, should he elect to take it, of accepting his purchase money in 3 per cent stock at the face value.

See *Irish Land Act 1903.* Statement; 1906 (171) c, 605. Estates Commissioners. 1903-5. Rep.; 1906 Cd. 2742, xxv, 183. See succeeding Ann. Reps.

Congestion in Ireland

R. Com. Final Rep., apps. pp. xii, 222. 1908

1908 *Cd.* 4097, *xlii*, 729
apptd. July, 1906. *sgd. May,* 1908

Lord Dudley (*Ch.*), MacDonnell, Colomb, Mowatt, O'Donnell, Bryce, Kavanagh, O'Kelly, Sutherland.

'*To inquire into and report upon the operations of the Acts dealing with congestion in Ireland; the working of the Congested Districts Board, and the Land Commission under these Acts, and the relations of the Board with the Land Commission and the Department of Agriculture and Technical Instruction; what areas (if any) outside the districts now scheduled as congested require to be dealt with as congested; what lands are most conveniently situated for the relief of congestion; what changes in law or administration are needed for dealing with the problem of congestion as a whole, for facilitating the migration of the surplus population from congested areas to other lands, and generally for bettering the condition of the people inhabiting congested areas.'*

Reports one to eleven are formal presentations of the minutes of evidence. See App., p. 450.

The term 'congested' as applied to the very poor districts of the West of Ireland appears to have been first used in 1882 (q. 5). In order to allow the Congested Districts Board set up by the Act of 1891 to concentrate its energies upon counties where there was a large amount of exceptional poverty, no electoral division was scheduled unless its average rateable value did not exceed 30s. per head, and a fifth of the population of the county lived in such divisions. In addition, a small number of the divisions where the rateable value exceeded the figures were scheduled by the Lord Lieutenant. The districts scheduled consisted of one-sixth of the total area (3,626,381 acres) with one-ninth of the population (506,000) and one twenty-seventh of the total valuation of Ireland. As a whole the population is not dense, and the areas are not congested in the ordinary sense of the word. The term means little more than 'exceptionally poor'. The average value of agricultural holdings is 3s. 6d. per acre as compared with 12s. 1d. for the rest of Ireland. The trouble is not the scarcity of land, but the scarcity of any but the poorest land.

Nine-tenths of the population in the congested districts are dependent on the land for a living, but over three-quarters are living on holdings too small (i.e. below £10 valuation) to support them in a proper standard of living. They have consequently to supplement the produce of their hold-ings from other sources, such as seasonal migratory labour in England, fishing on the seaboard, and some home industries, or to live below a proper standard; and the majority do both. No redistribution of population within the scheduled areas would relieve congestion to any considerable extent. And many of the holdings are not only too small, but owing to historical circumstances, are also greatly sub-divided and intermingled.

The Board was empowered to aid migration from the congested districts and the settlement of the migrant in his new home, and to aid agriculture, forestry, fishing, weaving, etc. The Report reviews the work of the Board in these fields. The first thing to do was to enlarge the size of as many holdings as possible. As it proved impossible properly to amalgamate and enlarge holdings still in the hands of a landlord, the Board passed to its most important function, that of the purchase and resettlement of estates. It made many purchases. Amongst its difficulties were that tenants did not want to give up their holdings in exchange for new ones on untenanted land several miles away; that those living near untenanted grazing lands disapproved of using them for relieving the congestion in other parts of the country; and it was often essential for it to hold estates for a considerable time before re-sale, in order to make improvements which would permit the re-arrangement and enlargement of holdings. Progress was slow after 1905 because it could not purchase the amount of land it desired without more funds, and had to hold estates it was improving for longer than would otherwise have been necessary. Suggestions for increased funds were not met.

The policy of the Board has been on sound lines, and the best hope for the congested districts lies in the development of its work, especially in land settlement. The Board should be continued. There are areas outside those scheduled which are in as much need. The present test for scheduling should be abolished, and the scheduled area extended to include all Connaught, the counties of Donegal, Kerry and Clare, and the Rural District of Bantry, Castletown, Schull and Skibbereen. The population of the new area was 1,159,000. Outside the area the relief of congestion should be entrusted to the Estates Commission and the Department of Agriculture. The Board should have complete control of land purchase in their area, no estate passing by direct purchase from landlord to tenant without its consent.

While the minimum size of an economic holding must vary with the quality of land, the skill of the occupier and other factors, £10 was a fair average minimum valuation of an economic holding. Two-thirds of the 130,000 holdings in the proposed new area fell into this category, but after deducting small holdings which were in fact economic, those not really agricultural (e.g. fishermen's and labourers' allotments), those bought by tenants under the Land Purchase Acts, and those in areas of land so poor that no resettlement could make them economic, the maximum size of the problem of enlarging holdings involved dealing with 80,000 holdings and would require additional land with an annual valuation of £450,000. The amount of land available within the area was not sufficient and the Board should have powers of compulsory purchase.

Various categories of the 'Grasslands', i.e. large tracts of grassland, whether held by landlord, tenant or tenant purchaser and used mainly for grazing by the permanent or temporary occupier, are the chief source of fresh land, but the total amount is barely sufficient. Unless there were a radical change in public opinion, congested areas could not be relieved by migration east of the Shannon, and the Board would be forced to rely upon the land available in its own area. Every holding given to the son of a tenant or to any other person not already a land owner would therefore help to perpetuate the congestion. There has been vigorous opposition from the sons of tenants and from landless men living in the neighbourhood of the grasslands to the introduction of migrants from a distance. The claims of farmers with totally inadequate holdings and those of landless men are in conflict and the Committee 'have no hesitation in deciding that the former should prevail'. If the claims of landless men are persisted in, the problem of congestion as a whole cannot be solved, no matter what powers and what funds are given to the Board.

The breaking up of the grasslands used for grazing and their redistribution amongst the small occupiers will require the substitution of mixed farming, and this offers the best prospect of improvement in the position of small farmers. The price paid for land taken compulsorily should be such a sum as, after paying off all charges suitable for redemption by the State, will yield the landlord his average net profit, including where appropriate compensation for sporting rights, allowance being made for the effect of existing economic and natural causes on probable receipts for five years. The average net income should be capitalized at the rate of interest obtained by the National Debt Commissioners for investment in authorized securities of as much money as is required for the purpose. As the Board will be dealing with 80,000 holdings with an annual value of £350,000 and will need new land valued at £450,000, a total of £800,000, and will have to deal with other holdings requiring resettlement, the annual value of the land to be dealt with will be about £1 mn.

Other recommendations include: restriction on the power of small holders to mortgage their holdings; the encouragement of co-operative agricultural marketing and credit; the encouragement of fishing, including continuous fishing, and deep-sea fishing on some parts of the coast; the establishment of fishing villages; the encouragement of industries connected with fishing or with local raw materials, e.g. barrel making, net making, kelp making.

The Board should consist of 20 members, and should be made a corporation. It should be equipped for buying and re-selling land to the value of £1 mn. each year. It will be necessary for it to hold an average estate for two years. Its annual income, to cover loss on estates, work on fisheries, industries, roads, etc., should be £300,000.

Memo. by MacDonnell. — The Board's operations will be on a large scale and involve substantial losses, and it will have to proceed in the face of opposition from landless men. The work could best be done by the Estates Commission, which is already experienced, but if this proposal is not acceptable, the Board should be non-elective and free from local pressure. The Board's area should not be extended. Half the additional areas proposed are not congested. In the existing area there are 50,000 congested holdings and as at three times the existing rate of progress it will take 23 years to remove congestion, the extra burden of dealing with another 30,000 should not be added. Financial proposals are made and it is claimed that the arrangements would make it possible to complete the work on the existing area in 25 years at a cost of £4 mn.

Memo. by Colomb.—Disagrees with the Report on (1) the effects of breaking up the great grasslands, which would be adverse; improved agricultural knowledge of the small farmer was essential; (2) the constitution of the Court for dealing with questions arising out of the price paid for the land. He also stresses the importance of educating children in preparation for agricultural and industrial pursuits. O'Donnell and Kavanagh favour giving the Estates Commission compulsory powers for dealing with congestion outside the new area.

3. TRANSPORT

Canals and Waterways

R. Com. Rep., *Ireland*

1911 *Cd.* 5626. See *Transport*, p. 147.

Railways (Ireland) Amalgamation Bills

Jt. Sel. Cttee. Rep., proc. pp. 23. 1900

1900 (293) *viii*, 255
apptd. March, o.p. July, 1900

Lord Spencer (*Ch.*), L. Chelmsford, L. Glanusk, L. Hawkesbury, Pierpoint, Osborne, Montagu, Buchanan.

A large number of petitions were received in connection with the Great Southern and Western, and Waterford, Limerick and Western Railway Companies Amalgamation Bill, the Midland Great Western Railway of Ireland Bill, and the Great Southern and Western and Waterford and Central Ireland Railway Companies Amalgamation Bill. The Bills were considered and amendments made.

Irish Railways, Including Light Railways

Vice-Regal Com.

apptd. July, 1906

C. Scotter (*Ch.*), L. Pirrie, Poë, Sexton, Jekyll, Acworth, Aspinall.

'*To inquire into the present working of Railways in Ireland, including Light Railways, and to report how far they afford, separately or in conjunction with other means of transit, adequate facilities for the cheap and rapid transport of goods and passengers within the Island and to Great Britain; what causes have retarded the expansion of traffic upon the Irish lines and their full utilization for the development of the agricultural and industrial resources of the country; and, generally, by what means the economical, efficient, and harmonious working of the Irish Railways can be best secured.*'

The First, Second, Third and Fourth Reports are formal presentations of the following volumes of minutes of evidence, etc.; 1907 Cd. 3633, xxxvii, 49. 1908 Cd. 3896, xlvii, 331.   1908 Cd. 4054, Cd. 4205, xlviii, 5.   1909 Cd. 4481, xxvii, 199.

—— Fifth and Final Report, apps. pp. vi, 127. 1910

1910 Cd. 5247, xxxvii, 1
sgd. July, 1910

Majority Report: Scotter, L. Pirrie, Poë, Sexton. The Irish railway system, exclusive of Light Railways and Tramways, is worked by sixteen companies. The seven principal companies comprise sixty railways which were formerly separate undertakings.

Part I. Trunk Railways.—This part of the Report consists of a review of complaints made by various bodies and persons against the companies. Since Irish local rates are non-competitive and cross-channel through rates competitive, the Irish share of through-rates was lower than the sum of Irish local rates, especially as the cross-channel through-rates were based on the shortest distance between any two points. All railways having termini in Dublin charged station to station rates, instead of including collection and delivery, though the companies said that at many stations the traffic was too small to justify the maintenance of cartage staff and plant. The rates for transport of cattle were said to be too high, especially the extra charge of 33 per cent if cattle were sent by passenger train. The complaints of the existence of secret rebates showed much misunderstanding, but on two lines there had existed for two or three years a system of rebates which were not recorded as required by statute. Temporary low rates had been used to eliminate competition by coastal steamers, and had afterwards been withdrawn. The Great Southern and Western Amalgamation Act had been advantageous, but had led to anomalies. Proposals for subsidies to particular rates were rejected by the Committee on the ground that it would be difficult

to select between the competing claims of different industries, and would lessen the companies' incentives to efficiency. As receipts for the carriage of livestock amount to 7·6 per cent of total traffic receipts, the companies would be well advised to enter into arrangements with the cattle trade for insurance against loss or damage. The internal rates of Continental countries and their export rates to the English market were relatively lower than the Irish rates, but the companies argued that the export rates on agricultural produce could be lower if Irish farmers took up winter dairying. Although there had been a great increase of British imports of foreign agricultural produce, those from Ireland had grown much more slowly. Other factors, e.g. regularity of supply, volume of consignments, packing, co-operation, etc., largely accounted for this, but a reduction of railway rates would stimulate such exports.

The complaints that internal rates are too high, and in particular that local rates are higher than the Irish proportion of through rates cannot be dealt with by reducing the non-competitive rates to the competitive level, nor by raising the competitive rates to the level of the non-competitive, since either course would mean loss of revenue. Though trade and industry could benefit by reduction of rates, railways are commercial undertakings, and the net profits of the companies would not permit substantial reductions, nor would the increased volume of traffic be sufficient to compensate. Under existing conditions no substantial reductions in rates and fares can be looked for, though they might be made if railways were unified, and if the resources of the country developed so as to offer produce in greater volume and with greater regularity.

The introduction of English capital and the ownership of certain railways by English railway companies had been an advantage to the poorer country and had in many cases been supported by Irish local opinion. But opinion outside Belfast was hostile to it, and was in favour of complete separation. Proposals were received for 83 new railways or extensions, but in few cases were the immediate prospects of traffic such as to justify them. Four proposals for linkage between main lines could be made with small outlay.

As regards internal traffic Irish railways are essentially non-competitive, since the traffic resources of the country are limited and Irish railways have been planned to give each line a non-competitive district of its own. Unification of the Irish lines would not affect the competitive character of through traffic between Ireland and Great Britain, but it would by the lowering of cost of conveyance, increase the competitive pressure on other forms of transport. Commercial companies, when they extinguish competition, are likely also to extinguish the public benefit which competition gives. A single public administration would be able to negotiate better with British companies about through rates and the extension of the facilities required to develop the resources of Ireland. Railway experts have agreed that amalgamation, partial or complete, is desirable; and economies in working, administration and finance would result from it. Public opinion is in favour of unification under some form of public control.

Part II. Light Railways.—The Light Railways have no working capital, nor any means of raising any, and cannot provide for exceptional outlay on permanent way or rolling stock without depleting revenues or burdening the public rates. They need unification even more than the ordinary lines, and should be absorbed in a general scheme of unification.

Part III. Conclusions and Recommendations.—The necessity of reform is not dependent on proof of the complaints made against the companies, for although there have been defects in administration, the results are what might be expected from commercial undertakings pressed on the one hand by heavy capital obligations and on the other by narrow resources of traffic. While they exist as commercial concerns they cannot make the reductions of rates which the economic conditions of the country require. Mere amalgamation would be inadequate, since the benefits would go to the increase of dividends instead of to reductions of rates. It must be accompanied by public ownership. The Commission rejected both public ownership with administration by a Government Department and compulsory amalgamation with a controlling Government interest, in favour of acquisition and administration by an Irish elected authority, the interest on capital being guaranteed by the State and charged on the net revenues. Any deficit should be charged against an annual grant from the Exchequer, and if this were insufficient in any year, from the proceeds of a general rate struck by the Irish Authority. The Irish Authority was to consist of a Board of 20 directors, 12 being elected by the ratepayers by a system of indirect election, two each nominated by the Treasury and Lord Lieutenant, the remainder being chosen by various commercial and trading associations. The general terms of purchase should be those prescribed by the Railways Act, 1844, with supplementary provision for the purchase of non-profit earning lines.

Minority Report: Jekyll, Acworth, Aspinall. On the evidence as a whole, the railways are entitled to an acquittal, though advantages would follow from a change of system. Substantial reductions of rates, especially through rates, would naturally stimulate exports, but those enjoyed by countries competing with Ireland are the result of a large volume of traffic, regularly sent in a form convenient to handle. Countries far less well circumstanced in climate, fertility and situation than Ireland have secured the advantages in this way, and Ireland could obtain similar results, e.g. by winter dairying. There is little evidence of retardation in the expansion of traffic traceable to general defects of management, but development would be assisted by improved organization and methods in agriculture and industry. The main defect in the railway system lies in its subdivision among a number of independent companies; the number should be reduced with a view to concentration into a single company in not more than four years. The amalgamation should be voluntary in the first instance, and should be assisted by legislation enabling railways to combine under the authority of an Order in Council, instead of by a separate Act of Parliament in each individual case. If necessary, limited financial aid should be given. The railways should continue to be privately owned. Failing voluntary agreement within three years, they might be compelled to amalgamate in not more than four years, on terms fixed by arbitration. To deal with the possibilities of monopoly, the supervision of such a unified system should be exercised by a Government Department capable of bringing pressure on the company. The powers now exercised by the Board of Trade under the Railway and Land Traffic Act, 1888, Section 31, should be transferred to the Department of Agriculture to enable them to deal with complaints, to make representations to the company and to assist traders in dealing with it.

Formal Reps. not cited. Mins. of ev., etc.; 1907 Cd. 3633, xxxvii, 49.   1908 Cd. 3896, xlvii, 331.   1908 Cd. 4054, Cd. 4205, xlviii, 5.   1909 Cd. 4481, xxvii, 199.   5th and Final Rep. Mins. of ev., etc.; 1910 Cd. 5247, Cd. 5248, xxxvii, 1.

4. LABOUR

Street Trading by Children (Ireland)

Inter-Dept. Cttee. Rep., mins. of ev., apps., index. pp. xv, 187.   1902

1902 *Cd. 1144, xlix,* 209
apptd. March —, sgd. June, 1902

F. F. J. Cullinan (*Ch.*), Bagwell, Fagan, Mulhall.

'*To enquire into the Question of the Employment of Children during School Age, especially in Street Trading in the large centres of population in Ireland, and to Report upon the alterations in the Law and other steps that may be desirable.*'

In Dublin there were 433 boys under 16 selling chiefly newspapers, and 144 girls selling newspapers, fruit or fish. In Belfast there were 1,240 boys and 45 girls, in Cork, boys only, 114. Police returns showed that as a rule these children were well disposed, but their lot was a wretched one. The principal dangers were late hours in the streets, truancy, insufficient clothing, entering licensed premises to find sale for their goods, obstructing, annoying, importuning passengers, begging, fighting with other children, playing football or games in the streets, using bad language, playing pitch and toss and smoking. Councils of counties and county boroughs should be empowered to prohibit street trading by persons under 16 or to permit it subject to the holding of a licence. No licences should be granted to children under 11, street trading by girls should be discouraged, and street trading on Sunday should be prohibited by Act for both boys and girls. Councils should be empowered to provide clothes, homes or lodgings where necessary. To deal with non-attendance at school, the retention of a licence should be dependent on the production of a certificate of fair average attendance. Day Industrial Schools should be established.

Conditions of Employment in the Linen and other making-up trades of the North of Ireland

Cttee. Rep., app., mins. of ev., index. pp. xxviii, 191.   1912

1912-13 *Cd. 6509, xxxiv,* 365
apptd. July, 1911. *sgd. Nov.,* 1912

E. F. G. Hatch (*Ch.*), Cohen, Streatfeild (Mrs. L. A. E. D.)

'*To inquire into the conditions of employment in the making-up of articles of linen, cotton and similar fabrics, including the processes of embroidering and thread-drawing and other incidental processes, in Belfast, Londonderry and other places in the North of Ireland, with special reference to hygienic conditions of working, rates and methods of payment, and earnings, and to report thereon.*'

The investigation took place as a result of the annual report for 1909 by the Belfast Medical Officer of Health, who stressed the fact that out-workers in the linen and cotton trades had to work unduly long hours, to the detriment of their health, for small rates of pay. There are some 22,000 women workers employed in the factories, and it was thought that the number of out-workers far exceeded this. In Belfast there were 3,400, in Lurgan, 1,400, and besides considerable numbers in the neighbourhood of Belfast, there were large numbers scattered through the urban and rural districts of Northern Ireland. Out-workers consisted mainly of widows and spinsters, and married women; in country districts they were the wives and daughters of farm labourers and small farmers. To such women the work was indispensable; for the most part they were people supplementing small pay. The principal processes were broad and narrow hemming, thread-drawing, vice-folding, hemstitching, top - sewing, thread - clipping, lace - undercutting, scalloping, button-holing, etc. There were no standard rates for piece workers, and many processes were in direct competition with machine work. Some employers tried to show that the competition of employers was sufficient to ensure the out-worker good pay, but the Committee did not find this proved. The supply of out-workers was ample, while the employers' demand varied. Sample investigations, and factory investigation by the Committee were made before it was decided that the majority of the out-workers earned from $\frac{1}{2}d$. to 2d. an hour, although there were some relatively good rates varying from 3d. to 4d. an hour. In evidence a number of employers admitted that a rate under 2d. an hour was 'sweating'. A meeting of the principal employers in Belfast, which was informed that the Committee had sufficient evidence to lead it to recommend the establishment of a Trades Board, passed a resolution saying that they would raise no objection to it, provided the system applied to all other places in the United Kingdom in competition with Belfast.

The Trades Boards Acts should be applied to the processes specified; rates of pay should be clearly marked on work distributed to out-workers through agents; shop-keepers used as agents should be replaced by salaried employees directly responsible to the firms; the protection of the Truck Acts should be given; the local authorities should be given prescribed lists of out-workers; workers should not take work from factories for evening work, beyond their legal period of employment; the provisions of the Employment of Children Act (that no child should work for gain between 9 p.m. and 6 a.m.) should be strictly enforced by the urban authorities.

5. POOR LAW, SOCIAL INSURANCE

Financial Provisions of the Poor Law Superannuation (Ireland) Bill, 1901

Rep. pp. 8. 1902

1902 Cd. 925, *xxxvii*, 757
sgd. Nov., 1901

C. E. Howell.

The report sets out actuarial estimates of the cost of the scheme and the assumptions on which they were made. The percentage deductions from salaries would provide £49,800 for persons at 65, while the pensions on the conditions proposed by the Bill would cost £189,100, leaving £139,300 to be provided for by the rates. To make the fund solvent would require a present payment of £443,700 to the body administering the scheme, or alternatively, a loan for 40 years, involving a half yearly rate charge of £9,345.

Poor Law Reform in Ireland

Vice-Regal Com. Vol. I. Rep. pp. ix, 82. 1906. Vol. II. Apps. 1906. Vol. III. Mins. of ev., index.   1906

1906 Cd. 3202, li, 349. Mins. of ev., etc.; 1906 Cd. 3203, li, 441. 1906 Cd. 3204, lii, 1.

apptd. May, 1903. sgd. Oct., 1906.

W. L. Micks (Ch.), Murnaghan, Bigger.

'To inquire into, and investigate and report on the following subjects:—I. Whether any Poor Law Unions could be dissolved with advantage to the ratepayers, and without hardship to the sick and destitute poor; and if any such dissolution be deemed desirable, what arrangements by amalgamation of Unions or otherwise should be substituted therefor. II. Whether, in the event of any Unions being amalgamated and the Workhouses thereof being no longer required for Poor Law purposes, such Workhouses could with advantage be taken over by County Councils for auxiliary lunatic asylums under Section 76 of the Local Government (Ireland) Act, 1898, or could be otherwise utilized for any public purpose. III. Whether it would be possible, either by an arrangement for the maintenance of paupers in adjoining workhouses, or by combining a number of Unions for the purposes of indoor relief, to make better provision for the classification and treatment of the inmates, specially the aged and infirm, sick, lunatics and children chargeable to the said Unions, and whether any changes in the law and procedure as to the administration and chargeability of relief would be desirable in the event of such combination of Unions being carried out. IV. Whether having regard to the number and capacity of Workhouses, Hospitals and Infirmaries existing in any County, Union, District or locality, and to the other provisions for the relief of the sick poor, any additional accommodation is now required for the proper treatment of the sick poor, and if additional accommodation is necessary, how it might be best provided. V. Generally to inquire and report whether any, and what administrative and financial changes are desirable in order to secure a more economical system for the relief of the sick, the insane and all classes of destitute poor in Ireland, without impairing efficiency of administration.'

The Royal Commission of 1833–6 on the Condition of the Poorer Classes in Ireland came to the conclusion that the English workhouse system, designed to make the idle seek employment which could be obtained, would be unsuitable for Ireland, where there was widespread destitution and there were able-bodied and healthy men willing and anxious to work even for two pence a day but unable to find it. Their recommendations were twofold. First, employment was to be provided by developing the resources of the country, by reclaiming waste land, drainage, improvement of labourers' cottages and allotments, bringing agricultural instruction to the doors of the peasantry, enlargement of landlords' leasing and charging powers to encourage land improvement, giving powers to the Board of Works to undertake public works, etc. The emigration of those for whom no work could be obtained was to be assisted by the State, by landlords who had evicted tenants and by a national rate. Secondly, the sick, infirm and lunatic were to be supported in institutions, and relief districts, with Boards of Guardians, established. The Government of the day did not accept the recommendations for promoting employment by developing the country's resources, though in the seventy years which followed most of them have been unconsciously adopted. Instead, George Nicholls was sent to Ireland to enquire whether the English workhouse system could be applied to Ireland, and although he had never been in the country before, he recommended the establishment of the Poor Law and the workhouse system. Despite the fact that much of the population was little above the low water mark of utter destitution, he said that destitution should be proved before assistance was given and that to any Irishman confinement of any kind would be more irksome than to an Englishman. He expected a painful transition period during which the tenancy of small holdings and allotments would be replaced by employment by day-labour for wages. The Act of 1838, which followed his recommendations, provided for relief only in the workhouse, but the sufferings of the expected transition continued, the small tenants did not turn themselves into day labourers, and want of employment continued. The standard of life of a large proportion of the population was still very low. That it was not so low as before the Famine was due to the reduction of the population from 8,175,000 in 1841 to 4,450,000 in 1901. The Vice-Regal Commission agreed with the conclusion of the Commission of 1833–6 that the low level of subsistence throughout Ireland could not be relieved by any Poor Relief Law, but only by the development of the country's resources.

The existing system of keeping many different classes in the same workhouse should be abolished, the 159 workhouses closed as such and the various classes of inmates, except children, segregated into separate institutions. The existing hospitals of workhouses should be continued and cottage hospitals provided in remote districts. All such hospitals should be cut off completely from the Poor Law. In view of the incidence of tuberculosis, disused workhouses might be adapted and used as supplementary sanatoria. Qualified medical officers would be needed for the hospitals and these should be obtained by the establishment of a State Medical Service of full-time salaried doctors paid by the State, selected by competitive examination and for the present limited to Irishmen. A Dispensary Medical

Service would facilitate the hospital scheme, and there should be an extension of District Nursing. The aged and infirm should be placed in disused workhouses converted into almshouses, the insane removed to asylums under the control of the Asylum Authority, unmarried mothers sent to institutions under religious or philanthropic management and kept apart from the other classes. All infants should be placed in nurseries under religious or philanthropic management, or where disused workhouses are used, under Poor Law control. All children between infancy and a maximum limit of age (fifteen) should be boarded out. Guardians should be empowered to levy a rate for outdoor relief. The cost of boarded-out children should be a union charge, of the aged, sick, infants, unmarried mothers and lunatics a county-at-large charge. The Irish Grants-in-Aid should be increased as recommended by the Royal Commission on Local Taxation, and be apportioned on the basis recommended by the Minority members. Temporary Commissions should be appointed to reconstitute the Poor Law Official Service and to prepare schemes for carrying out the recommendations.

Murnaghan dissents from the proposal to make the County the area of rating for Poor Law purposes.

Poor Laws and Relief of Distress
Rep. *Ireland*

1909 *Cd.* 4630. See pp. 260, 449.

Extension of Medical Benefit under the National Insurance Act to Ireland

Cttee. Rep. pp. 15. 1913. Mins. of ev., apps., index. 1913

1913 *Cd.* 6963, *xxxvii*, 1. *Mins. of ev., etc.*; 1913 *Cd.* 7039, *xxxvii*, 17 *apptd. Feb., sgd. July*, 1913

A. St. Ledgers (*Ch.*), Bradbury, Devlin, Glynn, Lardner, Maguire, Micks, Stafford, Barrie.

'*To consider and report as to the advisability of applying to Ireland the provisions of the National Insurance Act, 1911, with respect to Medical Benefit, and as to the alterations, legislative or otherwise, which in the event of such provisions being applied would be desirable in the systems for affording medical relief at the present existing.*'

In Ireland the system of poor law dispensaries developed under the Medical Charities Act. All poor persons are entitled to the services of the dispensary doctor, and a very large proportion of the working classes has, in practice, been held to come within that description. In rural districts there are large areas where the dispensary doctor is the only doctor, so that there could be no effective choice of doctor, and the labourer would not be willing to pay 1½d. more per week to get substantially what he now gets for nothing. In towns the same conditions apply to the very poor and there is insufficient evidence to determine the extent to which private medical practice exists amongst the working class population in towns. Only in Belfast could it be ascertained that the fee charged for a private patient was 2s. 6d. Resistance to the 'pauper taint' was indicated in the use by the trade unions and friendly societies of the contract system for securing medical attendance for members and their families. Only in the big towns and amongst the better paid workers was there a demand for an insurance scheme.

Before the Act, there had been controversy between the societies and the doctors about the inadequacy of the medical remuneration. When it was introduced, Irish doctors, stimulated by the vigorous controversy in England, terminated their contracts with the societies, and continued their work under provisional arrangements at higher rates. Societies were faced with paying the medical bills of their members or leaving them to resort to dispensary treatment. The doctors'

position is difficult, since payment on the English scale would be beyond the resources of the societies. Unless, therefore, the medical benefit is extended to the large urban districts, the working class will be forced back on the dispensaries. The doctors are willing to accept a scheme on the British system, and to include, on terms, dependants. The societies were unwilling to accept, except in the case of Belfast, any scheme which excluded them. A private conference, called by the Committee, between the medical profession and the societies was abortive, as the doctors' minimum terms were far in excess of what the societies could pay.

The Committee recommended the provisional and interim arrangement, for raising the contributions in six county boroughs to the English rate, and that the Exchequer grant of 2s. 6d. per insured person should be paid to societies to enable them to enter into arrangements for providing medical benefit to members and dependants or to members only. The societies should give alternative benefits for the additional contributions, for if they were obliged by statute to provide medical benefits, they would be handicapped in negotiating with a body which had a monopoly of the service. The scheme proposed would meet the demand for medical benefits in places where it is most persistent, but is not suitable for rural districts and smaller towns, nor as a permanent arrangement in the six county boroughs.

A general scheme would involve the creation of a state medical service, which is necessarily bound up with the reform of the poor law and its dispensary service. The funds of the Medical Charities, with National Insurance contributions and grants raised to the English level, would be adequate for this purpose, and this is the real solution of the problem.

In Notes, Bradbury, Micks and Stafford say they would have preferred a national medical service. In view of the failure to get doctors and societies to agree on terms, Barrie thought the matter should be deferred.

Application of the National Insurance Act to Outworkers in Ireland

Cttee. Vol. I. Rep. pp. 23. 1914. Vol. II. Mins. of ev., apps., index. 1914

1914–16 *Cd.* 7685, *xxxi*, 637. *Mins. of ev., etc.*; 1914–16 *Cd.* 7686, *xxxi*, 661 *apptd. June*, 1912. *sgd. July*, 1914

E. F. G. Hatch (*Ch.*), Barrie, Dickie (Mrs. M. L.), Paterson (Miss M. M.).

'*To consider and advise, having regard to the special provisions as to outworkers in Ireland in section* 81 (4), *what special orders applicable to Ireland, if any, should be made by the Irish Insurance Commissioners jointly with the Joint Committee under the powers and provisions of the First Schedule, Part I (c), of the National Insurance Act with regard to its application to outworkers; and what regulations applicable to Ireland, if any, should be made under Schedule III (10) in connection with the contributions of such outworkers as are insured under the Act.*'

Outworkers in the underclothing and shirtmaking industries are chiefly the daughters of farmers and carters, and do the work as a subsidiary occupation for six months in the year. Their maximum earning capacity in an 8–9 hour day varies from 5*s.* to 9*s.* a week, the price for making two dozen shirts ranging from 2*s.* 6*d.* to 4*s.* 6*d.* a dozen, according to the class of shirt. Often the work is done by the combined efforts of members of the family. Two-thirds of the shirtmaking is done by outworkers and one-third in the factories, but factory work is on the increase. The proportion of home to factory work in underclothing is six to one. Mr. Macartney-Filgate, the Inspector for Industries, thought that attempts to impose the insurance scheme where the work was so spread out, and the output per worker so small, would destroy an industry which **brought a subsidiary** income to the family. Hosiery and hand-knitting, home-spuns, crochet, sewing machine embroidery, handloom and silk weaving, handloom tapestry, carpet-making, embroidery were all occupations carried on in much the same way as shirtmaking, except that in some, such as home-spuns, the workers made their own raw materials. Some witnesses argued that the exclusion of partially employed outworkers would constitute a threat to the employment of full-time outworkers who were insured, while others contended that the extra cost to the employer if they were included would lead to a diminution of valuable part-time work.

As no practicable scheme which would enable the peasant outworkers to benefit from inclusion under the Act could be suggested, no change was recommended for those not mainly dependent on their outwork. Unless medical benefit is extended so as to include these partially employed outworkers, they will obtain very little benefit in return for small contributions. If it is so extended, then all outworkers in the districts to which the extension is made should be made eligible for benefit.

Application of the Government of Ireland Act, 1920, to National Health Insurance

Dept. Cttee. Rep. pp. 27. 1922

1922 *Cmd.* 1575, *ix*, 457 *apptd. Oct., sgd. Dec.*, 1921

A. W. Watson (*Ch.*), Dale, Gwyer, Glynn, Kinnear, Strohmenger.

'*To consider and report upon the steps necessary to carry out the provisions of the Government of Ireland Act, 1920, in respect of National Health Insurance.*'

In view of the agreement of 6th December, the Committee decided to restrict its report as far as possible to the transfer of National Health Insurance to Northern Ireland, and to assume that the Health Insurance scheme would remain in operation until the

Governments of Northern and of Southern Ireland respectively decided otherwise. A great number of persons resident in either Northern Ireland or Southern Ireland were members of societies whose head offices were situated in a part of Ireland other than that in which they reside, or were members of societies with head offices in Great Britain. Members of Irish societies had gone to reside in Great Britain. Of the 750,000 insured persons in Ireland, 201,000 were members of societies with headquarters in Great Britain, while of the 276,000 insured persons in Northern Ireland, 107,000 were members of societies with headquarters in Southern Ireland, 119,000 of societies with headquarters in Northern Ireland and the remainder in societies with headquarters in Great Britain. Amongst the recommendations made to deal with the situation were the following. Two-ninths of the cost of benefits in either area of Ireland will be charged to the relevant Exchequer, the State charged being the country of actual residence. Payments made to residents in each part of Ireland will be drawn from the separate Insurance Fund for that part. Approved societies must keep separate benefit registers, and separate membership registers so that the State contribution to administration costs can be properly assigned. Any approved society which has members in both parts of Ireland, e.g. one near the border between the two parts of Ireland, should be allowed to relinquish the approval for the other part, with provision for existing members. The apportionment of the Irish National Health Insurance Fund will depend on the apportionment of the approved societies' assets, which has to be made on the basis of an actuarial valuation and will take some time. In the meantime new Funds will have to be opened for Northern and Southern Ireland, and a provisional apportionment of 80 per cent of the assets should be made on the basis of relative numbers of insured persons resident in each part.

6. HEALTH

Public Health of the City of Dublin

Cttee. Rep. pp. 17. 1900. Mins. of ev., apps. 1900

1900 Cd. 243, *xxxix*, 681. *Mins. of ev., etc.*; 1900 Cd. 244, *xxxix*, 707 *apptd. Feb., sgd. May*, 1900

C. P. Cotton (*Ch.*), Meade, Moore, Swan, Thomson, Dowd.

'To make inquiry under the provisions of Section 209 of the Public Health (Ireland) Act, 1878, as to the cause of the high death rate in Dublin, and to recommend measures for adoption with the view of improving the health of the city.'

In 1891 the average density of population was 65·6 per acre, 37 per cent of the population occupying accommodation of the fourth or poorest class, and 28 per cent third class accommodation. In 1869–78 the mean death rate in Dublin was lower than that of Liverpool and Manchester, though higher than that of London, but since then there had been a material reduction in England and Wales, while that of Dublin had not decreased, its rate of 29·5 per 1,000 being considerably higher than that of London and any of the thirty-three large towns in England and Wales. Dublin contains a larger proportion of the poorer classes than London. There is an excess of mortality between the ages of five and thirty-five, and in deaths due to phthisis and other constitutional diseases, diseases of the respiratory system and of the brain and nervous system. In Dublin there exists in exceptional degree several of the conditions associated with high mortality. A considerable portion of the population lives in large dilapidated tenement houses, each room being occupied by a separate family, with water inconvenient of access, inadequate water closet accommodation, foul back yards, etc. 'Conditions favourable to strict cleanliness find no place in most of the houses occupied by the Dublin poor.' Poverty, with its concomitants of insufficient and unsuitable food and scanty clothing, lowers vitality and has a marked influence on the death rate. The conditions of many cowsheds, dairy yards and ill-kept private slaughter houses give rise to serious risk.

The recommendations include: water should be laid on to each floor of tenement houses and separate sanitary accommodation provided for at least every two familes; no stables should be let as dwellings without a licence; schemes of housing for the poorer classes undertaken, if necessary outside the city; all streets and lanes should be scavenged, all dust bins covered and emptied into covered carts, and an additional destructor provided. The regulations as to dairies and cowsheds should be vigorously enforced, an abattoir provided and private slaughter houses reduced in numbers, and the sanitary condition of public elementary day schools improved. The notification of infectious disease should be made compulsory in districts round Dublin, and there should be voluntary notification of pulmonary consumption. The duties of medical officer of health discharged by the sixteen dispensary doctors should be transferred to a full time assistant medical officer. Changes in legislation proposed include the grant of powers to limit the number of inhabitants of a house, and to prevent houses being turned into tenement houses unless they are structurally fit.

The Report is reprinted in the Supplement to the Ann. Rep. L.G.B. Ireland, 1900–1; 1902 Cd. 1260, xxxvii, 429.

Sanitary Circumstances and Administration of Cities and Towns in Ireland, and Precautionary Measures respecting Plague taken by Local Authorities at Various Ports

Reps. Supplement to the 29th Ann. Rep. of the L.G.B. pp. 324. 1902

1902 Cd. 1260, xxxvii, 429

Contains fifty-five reports on cities and towns in Ireland.

Typhoid Fever in Limerick City and Prison

Reps. pp. 8. 1902

1902 Cd. 1331, xlvii, 137

S. Woodhouse, J. A. MacCullagh.

Woodhouse.—Two prisoners in Limerick male prison developed typhoid fever, and owing to the length of time they had been in prison, could not have contracted it outside. There had been an epidemic of 48 cases in the city, not following any particular line of drainage or milk supply. The prison drainage system had been remodelled 9 years ago; the dairy from which milk was obtained was in a healthy condition. The public water supply had long been suspected as at least liable to pollution; —that used in the prison had been passed through a filter and of late boiled if used for drinking.

MacCullagh.—The outbreak in the city could not be traced directly to milk, as the milk drunk by the victims came from 23 different sources. In July the water supply in the Newcastle reservoir was low, and supplemented by water from Rebogue, which is not filtered. There is little doubt that the contagion was conveyed by water. The intake of water at Clareville pumping station should be improved. The dairies and cowsheds in the Park district were dirty and insanitary, with heaps of manure everywhere, cesspools in front of every house, etc. In the lanes and smaller streets of Limerick most houses have no sanitary arrangements of any kind. Many tenement houses have no sanitary arrangements. The Council undertook to deal with the manure heaps at Park and to inspect the lanes and streets referred to. Although the Infectious Diseases (Notification) Act, 1889, had been adopted as from 1899, only 7 cases had been notified.

Cancer in Ireland

Special Rep., etc. Supplement to the Thirty-eighth Detailed Ann. Rep. of the Registrar-General. Ireland. pp. 45.
1903

1903 *Cd.* 1450, *xvi*, 709

The death rate in Ireland from cancer, though lower than in England and Wales and in seven other European states, had increased, as it had done in the other countries. In 1864 it was 2.7, in 1897 5·8 and 1901 6·5 per 10,000 living. The statistical investigation and notes on the details of over 200 cases show that in many instances cancer recurs in the same family, that other members of the family suffer from tuberculosis, that cancer has supervened where there has been irritation of the lip consequent on smoking clay pipes, that in some instances it has shown itself amongst different families living in the same house, or amongst successive occupants of the same house, etc.

Outbreak of Enteric Fever at Brentry Certified Inebriate Reformatory

Rep. pp. 8. 1908

1908 *Cd.* 3938, *xii*, 1141

R. W. Branthwaite.

Brentry, an inebriates reformatory with 235 inmates and 30 officers, in 1906–7 had 28 cases of enteric fever, which occurred in irregular batches. The water was pure, the cows kept on the estate were free from disease, and though the drainage system had some defects, which were remedied, no pollution of water or food arose from that source. Recently admitted inmates were examined and found to be in good health. The source was traced to the contamination of milk after sterilization. The chances of contamination were by rats or the dairy officer; both were eliminated, leaving Mrs. X, an inmate who had become a dairy-maid. She had had an attack six years earlier, and proved to be a 'carrier'.

Since her removal from dairy work, there had been no more cases.

Belfast Health

Com. Rep., apps. pp. viii, 141, 11. 1908

1908 *Cd.* 4128, *xxxi*, 699
apptd. Feb., 1907. sgd. April, 1908

T. W. Harding (*Ch.*), Chalmers, Mair, Cowan, Flinn.

'To make inquiry and report to Us as to the following matters and things in so far as regards the city of Belfast, that is to say: 1. The cause or causes of the high death-rate. 2. The administration by the several authorities charged therewith of all general Acts and Orders relating to the Public Health and the prevention of disease and of all provisions of local Acts conversant with the same or similar matters, and of all other Acts and Orders, whether general or local, which directly or indirectly affect the public health of the city. 3. The measures they recommend for adoption with a view to the improvement of the health of the city.'

The death rate from all causes in Belfast is about the same as that of Manchester, is lower than that of Dublin and Liverpool, but not so low as that of other large cities of the United Kingdom. The mortality from enteric fever and phthisis and to a less extent from nervous diseases is, however, excessive. The mortality from enteric fever has no parallel in the United Kingdom. It is distributed over the city irrespective of water supply or sanitary conditions, and is due to the consumption of shell fish from the grossly contaminated shores of Belfast Lough. The treatment of sewage, within the practicable limits of cost, will fully safeguard the shell fish; powers should be obtained to prohibit the gathering of them for human consumption. Phthisis is excessive as compared with English and Scottish cities, but is not exceptional for an Irish one, but whereas the death rate in Manchester was low at ages under 35 and high at ages over 55, in Belfast it was the reverse; and in Belfast mortality was greater amongst females than males at ages between 5 and 35, in Manchester it was greater amongst males at all ages over 20. This needs thorough investigation. Belfast, like other local authorities in Ireland, is without adequate information regarding the details of deaths, and cannot cope with its sanitary problems without it. The precedent of the English and Scottish Registrations Acts should be followed.

Although great improvements have been made in the catchment areas, the water supplies from Woodford and Stoneyford need careful treatment, including modern methods of filtration. The early development of the Mourne supply, the catchment area of which is uncultivated and free from human habitation, should be the main feature of future policy. Although the Water Commissioners have done excellent work, the water supply should be in the hands of Belfast Corporation, which is the authority responsible for public health, and has wider financial resources. This repeats the recommendation of a Royal Commission on the *State of the Municipal Affairs of the Borough of Belfast* (1859 Sess. 1 [2470] xii). The relief of the main intercepting sewers in time of heavy rainfall and the prevention of flooding, cutting off the discharge of sewers to the foreshores and concentration of sewage to two other main outfalls, and the removal of suspended matter before discharge should be completed. In the meantime the removal of the accumulation of *Ulva* should be efficiently organized.

The existing organization of a Medical Superintendent Officer of Health, with fourteen District Medical Officers whose first duty is to attend the sick is unworkable, and should be replaced by the appointment of a special medical staff for public health work, as in England and Scotland. The whole responsibility should be placed on the Medical Officer, a bacteriologist and veterinary surgeon being placed under

his direction. The number of Sanitary Sub-officers should be increased.

Other recommendations include the prohibition of double tenancy of houses unless there is separate sanitary accommodation for each part let independently, and improvements in the removal of refuse and in street cleansing. The Dairies, Cowsheds and Milkshops Order should be more stringently enforced, and the inspecting staff augmented. Fresh legislation is needed to prevent the distribution of contaminated milk.

Many of the schools of Belfast are in an extremely unsatisfactory condition. Thirty per cent are without playgrounds, many are overcrowded, the average floor space per child is lower than in Dublin, Cork, Limerick, Waterford and Ireland as a whole. Some are filthy, the lavatory accommodation is inadequate generally and often wholly absent. Many of the schools are under the management of religious bodies, which use the buildings for their denominational purposes at other than school times. No effective progress will be made until the ratepayers take their share of the burden of education. In the meantime, the corporation should rigorously enforce its powers, and require its regulations to be observed in all new schools.

The special incidence of phthisis mortality in women aged 25–45 suggests an occupational influence. While there has been an improvement in some processes as to temperature and humidity (in weaving sheds and wet spinning rooms) little progress has been made in preventing excessive dust in carding tow. Many mills are still far behind the standard of the best in ventilation.

Public Health and Medical Services in Ireland

Irish Public Health Council. Rep. pp. 24. 1920

1920 *Cmd.* 761, *xvii*, 1075
sgd. —

C. Bigger (*Ch.*), and the sixteen members.

'*To formulate proposals, with a view to the submission to Parliament of an Irish Public Health Bill, which would*, inter alia, *place the public health services in Ireland on a wider and more comprehensive basis, and, where necessary, make mandatory on the local health authorities the various adoptive and permissive health enactments.*'

There is a considerable lack of co-ordination and a certain amount of overlapping in the administration of the public health and medical services. Several central authorities in Ireland deal more or less independently with health matters. For example, the L.G.B. for Ireland controls the Board of Guardians in relation to the administration of its dispensaries, infirmaries and fever hospitals, the rural and urban sanitary authorities in the administration of the Public Health Acts and the county councils in relation to county infirmaries, sanatoria, medical treatment of school children, etc.; the Irish Insurance Commission is important in the administration of sickness, disablement, maternity benefits, etc. In local matters there is even greater lack of co-ordination between the Boards of Guardians, the sanitary authorities and the county councils, with the result that few persons, apart from the officials directly concerned, understand the various sources from which advice or assistance can be obtained. Government grants to local authorities for various services are not uniform and are administered by authorities with varying degrees of powers; all these grants should be in the hands of one body. The system of keeping records and the services of medical practitioners and nurses, etc., engaged upon the schemes, would be more economic and efficient if organized on a county basis under one local authority. The present hospital system is disjointed and unsatisfactory, the various classes of institutions in each county being controlled by different authorities, and the formalities to be observed in obtaining admission varying according to the type of institution. All rate-aided hospitals should be co-ordinated under one county health authority and voluntary hospitals should be given financial assistance. The Adoptive Acts relating to the notification of infectious diseases should be made mandatory.

The recommendations are framed to effect a co-ordination of the central control of all the health services, the re-organization of the local administration to place it on a county basis, and the reform and extension of the medical services. There should be a Ministry of Health or Central Health Authority for Ireland, to which should be transferred the powers and duties of the L.G.B. for Ireland, of the Irish Insurance Commission, of the Irish Registrar General, of the Inspector of Lunatics and certain health powers of the Chief Secretary. Power should be taken to transfer to it by Order the medical duties in connection with the Ministry of Pensions, of the Home Office under the Factory Acts, etc., and also Veterinary Medical Services. The Council was divided on the form in which the Ministry should be organized, one group recommending a Ministry on the English model, in which case the Chief Secretary would be Minister, as required constitutionally, with a permanent Vice-President in charge, the other a Board, with the Chief Secretary as President, and a Chairman and permanent members, which they thought most suited to the Irish constitutional situation. Within the Ministry there should be a Health Council to control and direct the general policy and principles of administration, and it should consist of representatives of local Boards of Health, the medical, dental and veterinary and nursing professions, and of approved societies.

The local unit of administration should be a Board of Health in each county and county borough and to it should be transferred all health matters including the medical treatment of insured and poor persons, maternity, child welfare and school medical services, and hospitals and institutions. The general sanitary powers in the rural districts and urban districts with a population of less than 5,000 should also be transferred. The Health Boards should be comprised of one-half members of the county and county borough councils, the rest being composed of representatives from insured persons, medical practitioners, nursing and other voluntary organizations. There should be a Medical Officer of Health to each local Board.

The Dispensary Medical System established under the Medical Charities Act nearly 70 years ago should be divorced from Poor Law administration and linked with a county medical hospital system under the control of the Board of Health. Treatment should be provided for (a) insured persons on a contributory basis; (b) those unable to contribute to the cost of treatment; (c) those not compulsorily insured, on a contributory basis. There should be an Irish Medical Service to include both the medical and surgical staffs of county institutions, Medical Officers and medical practitioners responsible for treating the classes named, paid by the State, and appointed as a result of competitive examinations arranged by the Central Authority. The establishment of this service was advocated by the Vice-Regal Commission on Poor Law Reform, 1906, and by the Committee to consider the extension of medical benefits to Ireland, 1913. The principle has been approved by the medical profession. Provision should be made for the transference, as far as possible, of medical practitioners now connected with the health services. The question of the inclusion of the dependants of insured persons and of voluntary contributors should be considered at an early date.

The scheme should be financed by a contribution of 2d. per week from insured persons, including voluntarily insured persons, and after deducting this and the receipts from paying

patients and from other public sources, the rest should come on the 'Hobhouse Principle', one half from the rates and one half from the State. The present cost, excluding Insurance charges, to the rates of £654,000 and to the State of £396,000 would be increased by £100,000 and £358,000 respectively.

7. HOUSING

Housing Conditions of the Working Classes in the City of Dublin

Dept. Cttee. Rep. pp. iv, 30. 1914. Mins. of ev., apps. 1914

1914 Cd. 7273, xix, 61. Mins. of ev., etc.; 1914 Cd. 7317, xix, 107
apptd. Nov., 1913. sgd. Feb., 1914

C. H. O'Conor (Ch.), Watt, MacCabe, Delany.

'To enquire:—I. How far the existing accommodation for the housing of the working classes is inadequate in view of the ordinary requirements of the working classes in the city; II. The general circumstances of the working classes in Dublin with special reference to the amount of rent they can reasonably be expected to pay for suitable accommodation; III. To what extent it is possible by the exercise of the powers granted by the existing law to remedy the housing conditions of the working classes in the City; IV. The finance of housing schemes which have been carried out by the Municipal authorities or other agencies for the city workers, and the class of accommodation provided by such schemes; V. What measures (including any legislative amendments) you would suggest for dealing with the housing problem in the City, and the probable cost of any of the schemes so suggested.'

I and II. In 1891 the population of Dublin was 240,000, by 1911 it had risen to 304,802. Excluding domestic servants, it was estimated that the working classes comprised 194,250, or 63 per cent of the population. The figure approximated closely to the 194,870 of the population occupying accommodation at not more than four persons per room in Dublin.

Of this working population 118,000 live in tenement houses and 10,000 in second and third class small houses. Most tenements were built to accommodate one family, are exceedingly old structures, and have not been converted to give facilities to their present occupants. Seventy-eight per cent of the lettings are for one room, i.e. 20,108 families. The highest number of persons occupying one tenement was ninety-eight. Entrance is by a common door, water supply is generally from a single tap in the yard, which also contains the common closet. Some of the structures of the second and third class houses are so bad as not to deserve the name of house. They usually consist of one room and a kitchen, with a common tap and lavatory for many houses. They are even worse than the tenements, as they are usually in dark alleys between high buildings. On being questioned as to why they lived in such houses the women said that landlords did not like children.

The wages of the heads of families living in these premises ranged from fifteen shillings to thirty shillings and the rents from one shilling to six shillings, with a few at ten shillings. Taking all groups of houses together, 5,600 heads of families earn not more than 15s. per week, and 9,000 15s. to 20s., whilst 13,200 heads of families paid less than 3s. per week rent. From the figures it would appear that there was no relation between rent and wages, as people had to take what they could get. These conditions cannot be compared with those of other industrial cities, as Dublin had no predominating industry apart from brewing, distilling, soda water and biscuit manufacture, and transport connected with the port; the number of factory workers is very small, unskilled labourers predominating.

III. The Report reviews the powers possessed by the Corporation and the bye-laws made under various Acts. The plea of the Corporation that their powers were insufficient would have had more force if they had administered rigidly their existing powers. Sir Charles Cameron (Medical Superintendent Officer of Health) had taken on himself dispensing power regarding the closet accommodation required in bye-laws relating to tenement houses. There were over 5,000 tenements with only one closet each for from twenty to forty persons. Generally, tenement property is owned by a large number of small owners. Fourteen members of the Corporation owned or were interested in tenement houses and some in small houses as well, and though some of the property owned by three members was unfit for human habitation, yet they nevertheless received a 25 per cent rebate, one of the conditions of which was that it should be fit. Other dwellings receiving rebates were also unfit. Sir Charles Cameron had on his own authority dispensed with conditions of the bye-laws, on the ground that strict enforcement would inflict hardship and lead to evictions. Had judicious but firm administration been exercised during the past 35 years, a better state of affairs could have been produced without inflicting undue hardship. Want of firm administration has permitted the occupation of unfit houses at rents altogether excessive for the accommodation provided, has hindered the erection of sanitary dwellings by private enterprise by permitting the competition of insanitary ones, and has contributed to the low social conditions of the poorer classes.

The Corporation has from the beginning taken advantage of its powers to provide houses. It had provided dwellings and lodging houses for 7,600 people, i.e. 2·5 per cent of the population, and has further schemes to house 6,480 persons; this compared favourably with other towns. But the schemes were incomplete and scattered. And it had had to pay a high price in compensation—£10,000 per acre in one case and an average of £4,070. The price was fixed by arbitration.

IV. The Corporation schemes involve an annual expenditure of £20,000–£21,000, while rents yield £10,000–£12,000, leaving a net deficit of £10,000, representing a rate of over 2½d. in the £. Details are also given of the experience of social agencies and companies providing houses.

V. Any scheme for reform must contemplate the complete break-up of the tenement system. Every working class family should have a self-contained dwelling of sufficient size to prevent overcrowding, which permits separation of the sexes, and water closet accommodation for the sole use of each family. To replace the third class tenement and small houses and to relieve the overcrowding in the first and second class tenement houses would require 14,000 houses. At £250 per cottage to cover all expenses, this would cost £3,500,000. Though present rents are about 3s., the working classes could probably pay 3s. 7d., but the cost would be 5s. 5½d., a loss to be borne by the rates of 1s. 5½d. in the £1, which would be too great a burden, as the rates are now 10s. 5d.

The State should give a grant to assist the urban workers similar to the one given to assist rural workers under the Labourers Acts, namely 16 per cent of the total amount required for annual repayment of principal and interest, with a right to revise every ten years. This would cover the difference between the economic rent of 5s. 5½d. and the 3s. 7d. the people could pay. Further suggestions were made regarding the provision of sanitation, the licensing of tenement houses, re-housing in the city, and re-housing outside the city.

In a Memorandum MacCabe protested against any criticism of the sanitary administration of the Corporation, stating that no regulation could do more than prevent the evil becoming absolutely intolerable. He advocated a Civic Survey on the grounds that a Town Plan was essential to any extensive building scheme.

8. EDUCATION

Irregularities in the Office of the Commissioners

Copy of 'Extracts from Minutes of the Proceedings of the Commissioners of National Education (Ireland), and other Documents, in relation to recent action taken by the Most Reverend W. J. Walsh, D.D., Archbishop of Dublin, respecting alleged irregularities in the transaction of business in the Office of the Commissioners, and to the withdrawal or amendment of Letters alleged to have been incorrect'. Return to an Order. pp. 34. 1901

1901 (261) lvii, 103

Documents arising from complaints in the Press by the Archbishop of Dublin of the way in which the transition in the payment of teachers' salaries on bases which included payments by results to one of consolidated salaries was handled.

Primary Education in Ireland

Rep., apps. pp. 103. 1904

1904 Cd. 1981, xx, 947
sgd. Sept., 1903

F. H. Dale.

'To inquire and report how typical Irish Elementary Day Schools compare with similarly circumstanced Public Elementary Schools in England as regards Premises, Equipment, Staffing and Instruction; and to what causes differences in economy and efficiency appear to be chiefly due.'

The majority of Irish schools are rural and the children are from poor families. There is no supervision by the local authority, little voluntary effort and 5,000 of the schools are 'non-vested'. There is an insufficiency of classrooms, while the state of repair, toilet accommodation and standard of cleanliness were below English standards. Under the Irish Rules desks need be provided only for a proportion of the children, so that in most schools visited only about one-half of the children could be seated. The majority of country schools compared favourably with accommodation in English country schools, because they had been built for a greater number of children than there were in attendance. In the country attendance was bad during bad weather and because of seasonal work. In Mayo and the West of Ireland children take care of the holding whilst the parents migrate to England as labourers in the summer months. There is a larger proportion of trained teachers in Ireland, but the general average of salaries is lower, not only because there are so few urban schools in Ireland, but because rate-aided schools do not exist.

The more important conclusions and recommendations include the following. Premises and Equipment.— The premises of the Irish town schools are markedly inferior to those of the English both in the requirements essential for proper sanitation and in their convenience for purposes of effective teaching. This inferiority has been chiefly caused (i) by excessive economy in building, (ii) by the absence of a local authority, such as exists in England, responsible for the supply of schools, and competent to raise rates for the purpose. The absence of such an authority has also led both to (a) inordinate delay in the provision of suitable school buildings, and (b) serious waste of money owing to injudicious methods of expenditure. In order to bring the premises of these town schools up to the English level it would be necessary (i) to adopt better building plans for all new schools; (ii) to make considerable structural improvements in many existing schools; (iii) to establish local bodies with the power of rating and the responsibility for school supply. The majority of country schools compare not unfavourably in essentials with English country schools, but a few are below the standard of the worst English ones, and in the majority there are defects in repair, cleanliness and heating. These are due to Irish rural poverty and want of organization in the distribution of state and local aid. The former should be allotted to districts on the basis of need, while for the latter Associations of Managers drawing local aid for a large district and distributing it on the basis of need should be formed.

Staffing.—The Irish Monitors, unlike the English Pupil Teachers, do not form part of the recognized staff of a school, so that only such numbers are required as would fill vacancies amongst the adult staff. The actual number is much in excess of this. Their education is defective and much of the expenditure on training colleges is rendered unprofitable. The formation of classes for their instruction by well qualified teachers is an urgent need. It is undesirable that the selection of teachers for promotion should rest with the Government Inspectors. Weighting should be given to the size of schools in determining teachers' salaries, but the control of the Central Office over appointments should be greater than in England, as no financial penalties fall on Irish managers in consequence of an unsuitable appointment.

Instruction. — The instruction in Irish schools is adversely affected by certain fundamental defects. (i) The multiplication of small schools, often unsuitably staffed and organized. The number of elementary schools has increased, although the population has diminished, the increase taking the form of separate schools for Roman Catholics and ˙Protestants, different sects of Protestants, and children of different age and sex. This has led to a high rate of expenditure without a corresponding measure of efficiency. The primary cause is the strong preference for a denominational system of education, so that the aim of the National School system of providing schools for children of all persuasions has not been achieved. In addition, the Central Office in Ireland has not exercised the same control over the supply of schools as has been the case in England, while the system of grants of the full salaries of individual teachers instead of capitation grants based on attendance has relieved local managers of financial responsibility. Pending the devolution of greater financial responsibility on to the local managers, the Central Office must exercise more control than is necessary in England. (ii) Except amongst the clergy, there is little interest in Primary Schools. (iii) The staffing is inadequate and badly distributed. (iv) Attendance is more irregular than in England. In towns compulsory attendance has been beneficial, though it has not been rigorously enforced. In rural districts it could not be applied, but attendance could be improved if children were taken to school in covered carts.

Intermediate Education (Ireland)
Rep., apps. pp. iv, 98. 1905

1905 Cd. 2546, xxviii, 709
apptd. May, 1904. sgd. Feb., 1905

F. H. Dale, T. A. Stephens.

'To enquire into and report upon the system of Intermediate and Technical Education in Ireland—the latter so far as it is connected with the former—with a view to ascertaining whether any organic or other changes in that system are desirable.'

Intermediate education is defined as the education of scholars between the ages of 13 and 19, and most of it is provided by schools in connection with the Board of Intermediate Education. Although many children pass from the primary to the intermediate schools, no provision is made for suitable transference, so that there is practically universal overlapping in the form of undue retention of scholars in the primary schools beyond the age at which they should commence their intermediate education. There is a great deficiency of scholarships and bursaries to enable poor children of ability to transfer from the National to the Intermediate schools, and a con-

siderable local deficiency of schools for supplying a systematic course of intermediate instruction in its lower grades. This want of co-ordination is due to the fact that there is no one authority with powers to survey the system of education as a whole. The Board of National Education has neither the power nor the knowledge to deal with the children in its schools whose primary education has been completed and are able to profit by further study elsewhere. The Board of Intermediate Education is precluded from any investigation of the previous training and needs of National School pupils which form one of its main sources of supply. The necessary co-ordination can be secured only by legislation, but it is essential to any successful attempt to remedy the defects. Further, the Department of Agriculture and Technical Instruction has assisted in the erection and equipment of laboratories in intermediate schools, but this has meant that such schools have had to deal with two authorities which make grants on principles inconsistent with one another, while a school recognized by the one may be refused recognition by the other. The administration of funds for Science and Art should be transferred to the new Central Authority. The Central Authority should take measures to remedy the deficiency of local schools for children up to 16, and to arrange for the instruction of monitors in lower grade intermediate schools; and the system of scholarships should be reconstructed. The defects in the connection of the universities with intermediate education should be remedied by the equalization of the final school examinations held by the State and the entrance examinations to the universities. For this purpose the Central Authority should form a small Consultative Committee which includes representatives of the universities.

The premises and equipment of the larger boarding and day schools are on the whole satisfactory, but 40 of the 110 schools with fewer than 50 pupils fall below, often well below, a proper standard as regards rooms, playgrounds, sanitation, etc. This is partly the result of the over-multiplication of small schools, generally Protestant and often privately-owned, and conducted in unsuitable private houses. The number of teachers employed is in general adequate. But especially in small Protestant schools, there is a large number of ill-paid, inexperienced assistants who do not intend to remain in the profession.

The amount paid in grant in 1903 was £57,000, allocated on the results of individual examinations (the Results Fees system). Not only do the grants bear no relation to the cost of educating the pupils, but the work of the school as a whole is not tested nor is efficiency secured; and the grants are unduly variable. There is no differentiation between the curricula of schools, a continuous course of study is provided for only a small number of pupils, and the organization of the school and the education of the child are subordinated to an external examination and to monetary rewards. The Intermediate Board's proposal to remedy this by a permanent inspectorate would not achieve this object so long as the grant system remains unchanged. The Act should be amended to remove the compulsion on the Central Authority to make its grants largely on the individual results basis. Grants should be paid only to recognized schools, and recognition should depend on satisfying the requirements of the Central Authority regarding premises, staffing, inspection and examinations. The grants should take the form of a block capitation grant. The total, £70,000, would mean a payment of not less than £6 per child. The schools should be inspected, the examination system should include both an internal examination and the external School Certificate examination of two grades, Lower and Higher, determined by the ages at which the children leave.

The conditions for establishing a profession for intermediate teachers similar to that of elementary teachers do not exist, since there are no analogous conditions regarding standard of qualification, provision for training, registration and recognition of training, whilst the remuneration is lamentably low. For the registration of Intermediate schools and teachers the Common Register established for the United Kingdom should be used. The steps taken to provide training should be generously conceived and should in the present state of knowledge comply with the agreed desiderata—training should be subsequent to graduation, should include instruction in the mental and moral sciences bearing on education, and include practical training, practical and written examination, and a probationary period in a recognized school. Regard should be paid to the special conditions in many Irish schools, e.g. Convent schools. Any scheme for raising suddenly the salaries of assistant teachers is impracticable, but much might be done by gradually eliminating unqualified persons, and the establishment of a pensions fund. To encourage the employment of registered teachers, a bonus of £5 per year for ten years should be paid to schools for each such teacher employed.

See *Proposed Grant of £40,000 per annum*. Correspondence between the Chief Sec. of State for Ireland and the Catholic Headmasters' Association; 1913 Cd. 6924, l, 771.

Primary Education (Ireland). System of Inspection

Vice-Regal Cttee. (Com.)

apptd. Jan., 1913

S. Dill (*Ch.*), Kelly, Wilkinson, Coffey, Harrison, Henly, Kavanagh, Kettle.

'*To inquire into the system of inspection and other matters connected with the Board of National Education in Ireland.*'

The First, Second and Third Reports are formal presentations of the following volumes of minutes of evidence, etc.; 1913 Cd. 6829, xxii, 235. 1914 Cd. 7229, Cd. 7480, xxxviii, 5.

—— Final Report. pp. 52. 1914

1914 Cd. 7235, xxviii, 1081
sgd. Jan., 1914

There was widespread discontent amongst the teachers against the lack of uniformity in inspection and the Merit Mark System, which was determined by inspection, to which salaries and promotion were tied. Some of the reasons for lack of uniformity were: too much responsibility left to individual inspectors' appraisal of a school when on short visits, without an examination of the children; the impressionist style of inspection depending on the inspectors' tastes; tests made when the children were new to their work; adverse criticism on attendance when the weather had been bad, and fault finding instead of friendly criticism. An unfavourable report by an inspector, especially if based on physical conditions, etc., outside the control of the teaching staff, had the effect of jeopardizing their future prospects, without their having any means of appeal.

There were grave defects in uniformity in inspection and the following are some of the recommendations made: that the present system of grading and promoting teachers be modified, so as to provide for more rapid promotion of able and promising teachers; that the present system of assigning Merit Marks to schools and teachers be abolished; that increments within the grade be automatic in the absence of an adverse report; that promotion of teachers should be in the hands of the Chief Inspectors, who should have regard to seniority, professional merit, general attainments and the circumstances in which the teacher works. Machinery was suggested for the reorganization of the inspectorate, including a redistribution of districts giving sole responsibility for a district to one inspector, for a thorough examination of schools from 'time to time' and for the consideration of un-favourable reports against schools and teachers.

Primary Education (Ireland) 1918

Vice-Regal Cttee. Vol. I. Rep. pp. 44. 1919. Vol. II. Summaries of ev. 1919

1919 Cmd. 60, xxi, 741. Summaries of ev., etc.; 1919 Cmd. 178, xxi, 789 apptd. Aug., 1918. sgd. Feb., 1919

Lord Killanin (*Ch.*), O'Donnell, Tuam, Goligher, Martin, Doyle (Miss M.), Haslett, Joyce, Judge, Nunan, O'Neill, Ramsay, Headlam, Wyse, Kennedy, Macken, Strahan.

'*To inquire and report as to possible improvements in the position, conditions of service, promotion and remuneration of the teachers in Irish National Schools, and in the distribution of grants from public funds for Primary Education in Ireland with a view to recommending suitable scales of salaries and pensions for different classes of teachers, having regard to the character and length of training necessary, the special qualifications obtained, the nature of the duties which have to be performed, and other relevant considerations.*'

The Committee interpreted its terms of reference as directing them to concern themselves only with making proposals for suitable scales of salaries and pensions for the different classes of teachers in Irish National Schools, and they regarded an enquiry into the managerial system, so fundamental a part of the scheme of primary education in Ireland, as excluded.

In Ireland three-fourths of the schools are rural ones, and most of them are small—only one-twelfth contain over 100 pupils — and their efficiency and the quality of the teachers are of highest importance. There is regrettable public indifference to the work of the National Schools, which shows itself in bad or irregular attendance. In many cases average attendance is not more than 60 per cent of those on the rolls, some leave school at the age of 10, and many never go. The School Attendance Act, 1902, which local councils may or may not put into operation, is either not used or is ineffective. Bad attendance interferes with the work of the school, retards the classes and is unfair to the teacher. But if more children are to attend school, the schools must be ready to receive them and the defects of heating, equipment, sanitation, etc., remedied.

The normal scale proposed is a commencing salary of £100 for men and £90 for women, rising by annual increments to £200 and £170 respectively, with special increments not less than every three years, after the receipt of three very favourable annual reports, and higher increments for very satisfactory service for teachers at the maximum. There are further increment for principals according to the size of the school. The staffing of large schools should be improved. All trained teachers should be eligible for appointment as principals of schools of less than 50 where no trained assistant is employed; appointment as principal of other schools should require five, seven and ten years' experience, according to size. A non-contributory scheme of pensions is proposed. These improvements are no more than are necessary for placing the profession on a sound basis, and substantial State aid will be necessary. The defects of the scheme of 1900 arose from the need not to increase expenditure and subsequent improvements have been delayed by the theory that grants should be 'equivalent to' those in England, rather than based on needs.

No untrained man teacher should in future be appointed nor, without the sanction of the Board, any untrained woman, unless otherwise qualified and unless no trained woman is available. Teachers of small schools under 20 should always be women, no new small school under 10 should be recognized, small schools should be amalgamated where they exist within one or two miles of each other and where

amalgamation would not entail any religious inequality or disadvantage to any religious denomination.

The general rate of remuneration of teachers is altogether insufficient and a number of barriers can vexatiously hinder their advancement. The replacement of the payment by results system by a system of grades, in which the possibilities of promotion were affected by the average attendance of the school was beneficial in many ways, but was defective because it confined the greater number of teachers—i.e. all assistants and principals of schools with under 70 average attendance — to the lower grades. Out of 7,782 principal teachers, 6,372 are unable, however efficient, to rise to the highest grade. For these reasons the number of men candidates for entry to training colleges is small and so few are capable of passing a good entrance examination that inferior candidates have to be admitted. There is a large number of women applicants, but many are not up to a desirable standard. Increased State grants are needed to make the improvements necessary, and under the scheme proposed any efficient teacher (in schools over 20) will be able to reach early in life a suitable salary which will not depend on averages; and he will be able to rise to the top of his profession, though his financial reward will vary with the size of his school.

Although primary education is a national service and State grants for capital expenditure should be continued, localities should show their interest by contributing a local rate. All county and county borough councils should be obliged to appoint a Schools Committee, with duties and powers of enforcing the School Attendance Acts throughout Ireland, and of maintaining, repairing, heating, etc., schools unless provision is otherwise made. They should have power to aid medical and dental treatment of school children, to provide meals for necessitous children, and to provide school books, garden plots, etc. National schools should require attendance from children between the ages of 6 and 14, and no school should be regarded as efficient if not open 180 days in the year. School vans should be provided by the State, where necessary, to bring children to the nearest National school.

There are four reservations. Martin, Goligher, Haslett and Headlam regretted that the Managerial System had not been dealt with. Headlam and Gordon Strahan felt that the recommendation of higher salaries for teachers was not sufficient and that educational reconstruction involving the co-ordination of educational authorities under a Minister responsible to Parliament was desirable. Martin, citing the serious deficiencies in Belfast, urged that as the voluntary system was ineffective, there should be a new partnership between the State and the local authority. Four members concurred with this. Headlam argued that 'In the case of Ireland we cannot proceed on the lines of purely educational needs, for all religious needs have to be conciliated, as well as purely educational needs provided for', and that in the circumstances the principle of equivalent grants, illogical though they appear, seemed the only possible system.

Intermediate Education (Ireland)

Vice-Regal Cttee. Rep., apps. pp. 60.
1919

1919 *Cmd. 66, xxi,* 654
apptd. Aug., 1918. *sgd. March,* 1919

T. F. Molony (*Ch.*), Starkie, Marshall, Corcoran, Hennessy, Henry, Thompson, White (Miss H. M.), Ryan (Miss M.), Beaven, Steele (Miss B.), Headlam, Fletcher, Ensor.

'*To inquire and report as to any improvements which may appear desirable to be made in the conditions of service and in the methods of remuneration of teachers in Intermediate Schools in Ireland, and in the distribution of the grants made from public funds for Intermediate Education, and as to the best means in the public interest of effecting such improvements.*'

Although the report by Messrs. Dale and Stephens drew attention to the unsatisfactory position of Irish Intermediate teachers, it was not until 1914 that a Treasury grant of £40,000 was authorized. The participating schools were divided into two groups, those under Roman Catholic management and those not under Roman Catholic management, and the grants made separately to the schools of each group, on the conditions that the total number of qualified lay teachers was not less than one-fortieth of the number of pupils, that the salaries were not less than the prescribed minimum, and that certain other conditions as to hours of work, security of tenure, etc., were complied with. The grant could be withheld for non-compliance, but although it was reported that those under Roman Catholic management had not complied with conditions, the grant was not disturbed. In practice, schools which did not employ any qualified lay teachers, and some that employed no lay teachers had shared in the grant, while in other schools the whole grant was passed to lay assistant teachers. And some school managers, who were given discretion in the disposal of the grant received provided they paid minimum salaries to any qualified teachers employed, used only a portion of it on salaries. Although there had been some further improvements, these were far from adequate to induce young men and women to undergo the course of training of about seven years needed to enable them to qualify for registration. The disabilities of the new profession created by the establishment of the register concern security of tenure, hours of work, remuneration and pensions. Amongst the recommendations were: that as a rule there should be no dismissal during efficiency and good conduct, and that there should be a right of appeal in event of dismissal; that the Central Authority should not approve timetables making excessive demands, that no school should receive a grant unless it paid the minimum salary to all full time teachers up to the number required by the Central Authority, and that unless for reasons the Authority deemed sufficient, there should be at least one fully registered teacher for each 40 pupils. Pension rights should be confined to registered teachers. There should be no difference between the salaries of men and of women.

In Ireland there are separate departments for primary, intermediate and technical education: intermediate education cannot be properly organized unless these are co-ordinated, and that is impossible until there is a single Central Authority. There should be an Advisory Committee for intermediate education. All existing grants for intermediate education should be amalgamated; payment by results should be abolished and in substitution for it a capitation grant at a flat rate for all pupils between prescribed ages who have attended regularly, should be paid to all schools recognized by the Central Authority and maintaining a reasonable standard of efficiency. Efficiency should be tested mainly by inspection of the school as a whole, account being taken of examinations. The present system of three examinations should be replaced by two examinations, the Intermediate Certicate and the Leaving Certificate. No public funds are provided to enable children to pass from the primary to the intermediate school. Bursaries should be offered to remedy this. The grants are inadequate; nothing effectual can be done for teachers' salaries without more money, and Ireland is not receiving aid proportionate to that received by England and Scotland. Rate aid for intermediate education is essential, but as some areas are very poor, it should take the form not of a local rate, but a flat rate levied over the whole country. Cost of administration should be borne by the Treasury.

There were six reservations dealing with security of tenure, equal pay for women teachers, the proportion of lay teachers, etc.

In a Minority Report, Henry, Williams and McHugh, while agreeing with most of the main Report, state that the arrangements proposed for security of tenure are inadequate, and that they do not believe that a Catholic's right of appeal to a publicly constituted tribunal would affect the efficiency, dignity or freedom of Catholic schools. The Majority Report does not insist on the proportion of lay teachers to be employed, and this will go far to undo the improvements made in the position of Catholic lay teachers. The various branches of education should be co-ordinated, not under a Minister on the English plan, but under the present Board of Commissioners enlarged to be more representative of Irish educational bodies and institutions.

University Education in Ireland
R. Com.

apptd. July, 1901

Lord Robertson (Ch.), L. Ridley, Healy, Madden, Jebb, Butcher, Ewing, Rhys, Smith, Starkie, Ward.

'To inquire into the present condition of the higher, general and technical education available in Ireland outside Trinity College, Dublin, and to report as to what reforms, if any, are desirable in order to render that education adequate to the needs of the Irish people.'

The First, Second and Third Reports are formal presentations of the following volumes of minutes of evidence, etc.; 1902 Cd. 826, Cd. 900, xxxi, 29. 1902 Cd. 1229, xxxii, 5.

—— Final Report. pp. v, 74. 1903. Mins. of ev. 1903

1903 Cd. 1483, xxxii, 1. Mins. of ev., etc.; 1903 Cd. 1484, xxxii, 81 sgd. Feb., 1903

No university in Ireland admitted Roman Catholics to degrees before

1793, when the degrees of the University of Dublin were thrown open to all, and for fifty years many Irish laymen were educated at Trinity College. In 1845, the three State endowed Queen's Colleges of Belfast, Cork and Galway were established; these were undenominational, all Professors being forbidden to teach any doctrines or to make any statement derogatory to the truths of revealed religion and injurious or disrespectful to the religious convictions of any portion of their class, etc. Although the authors of the scheme contemplated that the colleges at Cork and Galway would necessarily be mainly Roman Catholic, the Roman Catholic hierarchy became hostile to them, as well as to Trinity College, as involving danger to faith and morals. As the Queen's Colleges were not accomplishing their object, the Royal University was founded in 1879 to give Roman Catholics access to examinations and degrees. It is an examining university, with no power to require attendance at any college or other institution, and by convention all appointments in the university, from Senate to Hall Porter were made in such a way as to keep an even balance between Protestants and Roman Catholics. The three Queen's Colleges, the Roman Catholic University College, Dublin, and Magee College, Londonderry, were 'approved' institutions. Fellowships with emoluments attached were assigned, and really constituted an indirect endowment; University College, Dublin, which had no State endowment, receiving 15 and Magee College 1. Only a minority of candidates passing the examinations have been taught in the five Colleges, the rest preparing themselves by private study, cramming institutions, etc.

While the Royal University has stimulated learning, particularly amongst women, who were admitted to all degrees equally with men, it has not achieved its object. It was created to meet the religious difficulties but has neither solved them nor met educational needs. The divorce of examination for degrees from teaching violates an essential academic principle and should be ended. The selection of Senators, Fellows and Examiners with a view to maintaining even religious balance, instead of on the basis of academic qualifications in indefensible. Neither the Queen's Colleges nor University College, Dublin, have any direct representation on Senate, nor have their Professors any clear function in arranging the programme of degree subjects. The creation of a purely examining university has destroyed much of the good work being done by the Queen's University, the number in attendance at all three Queen's Colleges having declined. Nor is it supported by the Roman Catholic hierarchy or population.

The consideration of a Roman Catholic College within the University of Dublin was excluded by the terms of reference; the proposal to establish a Roman Catholic University was rejected. The Royal University should be reconstructed as a Federal teaching university, with constituent colleges, each with a large measure of autonomy, so that they could develop on their own lines while conforming to the common standard of culture prescribed by the University. The constituent colleges should be the three Queen's Colleges, together with a new University College of first rank, for Roman Catholics at Dublin, which should include the Catholic University School of Medicine. Attendance at classes at one of the four colleges should be required from all candidates. Courses at the Royal College of Science at Dublin should be recognized as qualifying, in whole or part, for certain degrees. Degrees should be open to women on the same terms as men. Recommendations are made for the government of the University and for the protection of the Roman Catholic religion in the new University College.

Eight Notes are appended. Two regret that Trinity College and the University of Dublin were excluded from the terms of reference, as this closed the door to a permanent solution. Others, though thinking the proposals the best practicable, doubted if they would be accepted by Roman Catholics. Two saw difficulties in the introduction of a denominational College into what had hitherto been an undenominational University.

Trinity College, Dublin, Estates Commission

Vice-Regal Com. Rep. pp. 69. 1905. Mins. of ev., apps. 1905

1905 *Cd. 2526, xxvii, 81. Mins. of ev., etc.;* 1905 *Cd. 2527, xxvii, 157 apptd. June,* 1904. *sgd. April,* 1905

G. Fitzgibbon (*Ch.*), Healy, Trench.

'(1) *To inquire into and report upon the relations subsisting between the Grantees and Lessees and the Occupying Tenants, since the date of the passing of the Trinity College, Dublin, Leasing and Perpetuity Act,* 1851; *and* (2) *To inquire into and report upon the means by which the Purchase by the Occupying Tenants of their Holdings pursuant to the provisions of the Land Purchase Acts may be facilitated without diminishing the Average Net Rental derived by Trinity College as Head Landlord.'*

The Report first sets out in detail particulars of the College estates, the several interests therein, and the conditions under which tenants held land from the College. 'We cannot suggest any means by which sales can be facilitated if the income to be derived from the investment of the redemption money is to be equal to the full amount of the rents redeemed, since this could be attained only by sales at impossible prices or by investment of redemption money at impossible rates.' The Commission therefore interpreted the 'average net rental' which was not to be reduced as meaning the annual income from the investment of redemption prices, together with the income from the annual indemnity grant of £5,000. The indemnity grant was available only to make good loss of income which had actually resulted from sales to tenants. On the basis of estimates of the rates of purchase, the total amounts likely to be received as purchase and redemption money, and the rate of interest likely to be received from the investment of redemption money, the Commission concluded that the whole indemnity grant would be sufficient to make good the loss on the redemption of £30,000 a year if the money could be invested at 3½ per cent, but not sufficient to cover the actual annual rental of £32,500 at 24 years' purchase.

Recommendations are made respecting the position of grantees, subgrantees, lessees and occupying tenants. If grantees were given advances sufficient to enable them to sell to occupying tenants at rates specified, the Purchase Acts could be brought into operation, without diminishing the College income, on all lands other than those subgranted. To enable sub-granted lands to be purchased by occupiers, there must be provided from the Land Purchase Aid Fund a capital sum of £150,000, sufficient to give sub-grantees the fair value of their interest. All mesne owners on each sub-granted estate should be obliged to sell their interests at the same time. The amount of money available from the Land Purchase Fund is insufficient to complete the sales for which advances on agreements have been sanctioned. The completion of sales is delayed, and until they are complete further sales cannot be effected. Where, as in the case of the College estates, large superior interests must be redeemed and large rents continue to be paid until the redemption prices have been paid, the immediate landlords cannot sell without losing income during the period of delay. Under pressure of this difficulty, selling landlords had declined to sell unless the purchasing tenants agreed, pending the completion of sales, to pay a rate of interest which equalled, or in some cases exceeded, the existing rents. It is therefore recommended that provision should be made for the prompt payment of advances upon or immediately after the order sanctioning the advance, or failing this, that the Land Commission should be empowered to pay in Guaranteed Two and Three-Quarter Per Cent Stock a sum equal in value *at the price of the day* to the amount to which the recipient was entitled. As the indemnity fund, in so far as not required to make good loss actually incurred, is an accumulating fund, to avoid any loss of interest, punctual payment of it should be unconditionally secured.

Trinity College, Dublin, and the University of Dublin

R. Com.

apptd. June, 1906

E. Fry (*Ch.*), Palles, Raleigh, Rücker, Jackson, Butcher, Hyde, Coffey, Kelleher.

'To *inquire into and report upon the present state of Trinity College, Dublin, and of the University of Dublin, including the revenues of the College and of any of its officers and their application; the method of government of the University and of the College; the system of instruction in the College and the teachers by whom it is conducted; the system of University examinations, and the provision made for post-graduate study and the encouragement of research; and also to inquire and report upon the place which Trinity College, Dublin, and the University of Dublin now hold as organs of the higher education in Ireland, and the steps proper to be taken to increase their usefulness to the country.'*

The First Report is a formal presentation of the following volume of statements and returns; 1906 Cd. 3176, lvi, 607.

—— Final Report. pp. vi, 90. 1907. Mins. of ev. 1907

1907 *Cd.* 3311, *xli*, 1. *Mins. of ev., etc.*; 1907 *Cd.* 3312, *xli*, 87 *sgd. Jan.*, 1907

The relation of Trinity College and the University of Dublin is a matter of some difficulty. Whether the College and University be two bodies, or one body under two aspects, their government has been conducted as that of one institution. It has been and still is a satisfactory organ for the university education of the Episcopalian Protestants of Ireland. But it has not been satisfactory to the Roman Catholic population, nor to Presbyterians partly for historical reasons and partly because they are resident mainly in Ulster, where they have their own institutions and Queen's College, Belfast. In 1903 the College offered to both Roman Catholic and Presbyterian communions the right to have their own Divinity School, with professional privileges similar to those enjoyed by the Church of Ireland, and their own chapel. Neither accepted the offer. Out of 266 students who entered the college in 1905–6, only 35 were Roman Catholic and 18 were Presbyterians. In 1906 the Standing Committee of Roman Catholic Archbishops and Bishops stated that they would accept either a university for Catholics, a new Catholic College in the University of Dublin, or a new Catholic College in the Royal University, but that on no account would they accept mixed education at Trinity. In view of this, no solution by alteration in the constitution of the College to make it more acceptable to Roman Catholics is practicable, nor is the creation of a new University in Dublin. On the creation of a new College the Commission was divided. Five Commissioners thought that the University of Dublin should be remodelled to include Trinity, the three Queen's Colleges and a new Roman Catholic College in Dublin, while a fifth agreed that this was the best solution, but did not recommend it because the Colleges were hostile. Three rejected this in favour of a reconstruction of the Royal University as a teaching institution consisting of the three Queen's Colleges and a new Roman Catholic College in Dublin. One opposed the creation of any new College. If a new College is created,

Trinity College should be empowered to co-operate with it by recognizing the teachers and the courses it provided.

A number of changes in the internal organization and work of Trinity College are recommended to increase its usefulness, for reasons not connected with the religious question. The College Board, consisting of the Provost and the seven Senior Fellows, has the sole management of the estates and revenues; but it has become a body of elderly men, their average age being over seventy and the average time which has elapsed since their graduation between fifty and fifty-one years. The twenty-four Junior Fellows have no part in it, whilst there are Professors of great eminence who are neither Fellows nor members of Senate. The Board should be reconstituted to consist of not more than 15 nor less than 9 members, the Provost and *ex officio* members being reduced to one-fourth of the total; one-half should be elected from Fellows by Fellows and Professors voting together, and one-fourth by Professors not Fellows. The College Council should be replaced by an Academic Council and by Boards of Studies. The disparity in office and remuneration between Senior and Junior Fellows should be removed. The former fill the senior administrative offices, but this distinction will disappear with the change of government proposed. The present system of election to Fellowships based on competitive examination causes a waste of intellectual power: candidates should be able to present any published or unpublished work. A fixed number of Fellowships should be assigned to Professors. The main Professorships should be elected by an Electoral Board selected from outside as well as inside the College.

Other recommendations are: as too much of the time of scholars is taken up with routine work, the accounts should be simplified and a Chartered Accountant employed; the scope of studies should be widened, no candidate should be admitted to graduation except after a period of study within the College or attendance at lectures by teachers recognized by the University. The office of Lady Registrar of Women Students should be made permanent, and to provide for those whose parents did not wish them to be educated in a mixed College, the University should be empowered to recognize teachers in Women's Colleges within thirty miles of Dublin. Recommendations are also made regarding the Medical and Divinity schools, the teaching of law, and the establishment of a whole-time Professor and a lecturer in Irish language and literature who should be expected to devote all their time not occupied in teaching to the study and editing of the Irish MSS. of the College. The number of public examinations should be reduced, research encouraged and special courses for degrees for research established. The recommendations should be put into effect by an Executive Commission with power to make statutes and orders, which should be laid before both Houses and require the approval of the Sovereign in Council.

In separate Notes (I) Fry, Rücker and Butcher support the creation of a Roman Catholic University College in Dublin as part of a reconstructed Royal University; (II) The Lord Chief Baron, Raleigh, Jackson, Hyde and Coffey propose a widened University of Dublin to include Trinity, the Queen's Colleges and a new Roman Catholic University in Dublin, though failing this, Hyde and Coffey would accept two teaching Universities in Dublin.

See University Education Ireland Act, 1908; 8 Edw. 7. c. 38 for the establishment of the National University, Dublin and Queen's University, Belfast.

Irish Universities Act, 1908

Dublin Commissioners. Final Rep. pp. 14. 1911. Belfast Commissioners. Rep. pp. 4. 1911

1911 *Cd. 5877, Cd. 5929, xxi, 485*
sgd. July, 1911

Dublin:—C. Pallas (*Ch.*), Walsh (Archbishop), Rhys, Jackson, Windle, Anderson, Coffey, Boland, Gwynn. Belfast:—D. MacAlister (*Ch.*), Dill, Hamilton, Martin, Rücker, Symington.

The Irish Universities Act, 1908, provided for the foundation of two universities having their seats at Dublin and Belfast, for the dissolution of the Royal University and of Queen's College, Belfast. The National University of Ireland was to include as constituent colleges the University College of Dublin, and the Queen's Colleges of Cork and Galway, to be renamed respectively University College, Cork, and University College, Galway. Queen's College, Belfast, was reconstituted the Queen's University of Belfast. The task of the two bodies of Commissioners was to draft statutes of government of the new universities, to arrange for the transfers of property, first appointments, etc. The Dublin Commissioners decided that the buildings of the Royal University should be allocated to the University College, Dublin, that £40,000 of the £150,000 provided by Parliament should be used for new buildings for the University, and the remainder for buildings and equipment for the Colleges.

University of Dublin (Trinity College)

R. Com. Rep. pp. 31. 1920. Extracts from ev., etc. 1921

1920 *Cmd. 1078, xiii, 1189. Extracts from ev., etc.;* 1921 *Cmd. 1167, xi, 487 apptd. March, sgd. Nov.,* 1920

A. Geikie (*Ch.*), Ross, Shipley, Townsend, Joly.

'*To consider the application made by the University of Dublin for financial assistance from the State, and for this purpose to enquire into the financial resources of the University and of Trinity College, Dublin, into the administration and application of* those resources, into the constitution of the University and the College, and to make Recommendations.*'

While many of the recommendations of the Royal Commission of 1907 had been carried out, full effect has not been given to the proposals to abolish the distinction in duties and remuneration between Senior and Junior Fellows, or to end the exclusion of Professors and Junior Fellows from the Governing Board, on which the Provost and Senior Fellows still retain a majority. A number of distinguished scholars are still employed on routine accountancy work and no chartered accountant has been appointed. No pensions scheme has been adopted. Nevertheless, the range of studies has been widened, especially in pure and applied science, a number of lectureships created, and by the exercise of powers conferred by Letters Patent, 1911, and Ordinances of 1916 and 1920, some revisions made in the constitution, and the gap between Senior and Junior Fellows narrowed. But the war reduced the number of men students by one-half, and so diminished the fee incomes of members of staff that Tutor Fellows had to borrow £10,000 from the College, though a Treasury grant made up some of the losses.

Especially with the development of Science, the continued dominance of the Provost and Senior Fellows on the Governing Body is unreasonable: there should be a much larger representation of Science. Scholars should be relieved of clerical work and finance, and greater use made of professional assistants. Incomes of Fellows and Professors are drawn from numerous sources, some of them subject to unpredictable variation. All fees should be paid into a Common Chest, and all Professors, Lecturers and other members of the teaching staff paid fixed salaries. Vacant Professorships should be widely advertised and the appointment should be permanent. The salaries of whole-time Professorships should be £1,000, and those of

Lecturers and others as specified in Part VI of the Report. The proposals of the Commission would involve an additional annual expenditure of £49,000, and capital charges of £113,000, and it unanimously recommended the grant of these sums from public funds.

Royal Hibernian Academy and the Metropolitan School of Art, Dublin

Cttee. Rep., mins. of ev., apps., index. pp. xxiv, 98. 1906

1906 Cd. 3256, xxxi, 799
apptd. July, 1905. sgd. Nov., 1906

Lord Plymouth (Ch.), L. Westmeath, Holmes, Madden, Boland.

'To enquire into the work carried on by the Royal Hibernian Academy and the Metropolitan School of Art in Dublin, and to report whether any, and, if so, what measures should be taken in order to enable these Institutions to serve more effectually the purposes for which they are maintained.'

The Royal Hibernian Academy was founded under a Royal Charter in 1823 for 'the better cultivation and advancement of Fine Arts in Ireland'. It acquired buildings by private donations and from 1832 it has received a Government grant of £300. But the Academy is poor, its income other than the Government grant of £300 per annum being derived from exhibition entrance fees and commission on sales of pictures. The receipts from admission fees fell from £522 in 1884 to an average of £269 in the ten years preceding the enquiry. With decreasing attendances, the commission on sales fell in the same period from £125 to £39, with the result that fewer pictures are sent and of recent years two-fifths of the pictures have had to be invited from England, the Academy paying the cost of transport and insurance. The Life class is attended by only 17 students, 16 of whom are women, and nearly all of them are drawn from the Metropolitan School of Art; and

the teaching given was severely criticized. Many witnesses considered the site unsatisfactory, the buildings unattractive, and for Life classes, inadequate. The buildings in Lower Abbey Street, held on perpetual lease at 10s. per annum, although most conveniently situated for the transport of the city, are located in a once fashionable area now occupied by hotels and commercial establishments. It would be more favourably situated if it were transferred to the area around Leinster House, where similar institutions are closely grouped. There is not sufficient justification for rebuilding it near Merrion Square. The Dublin Metropolitan School of Art was established in 1760 by the Dublin Royal Society, which at that time received grants from the Irish Parliament. In 1853–4 it was amalgamated with the School of Design, previously conducted by the Board of Trade, in 1900 was transferred to the Department of Agriculture and Technical Instruction and now received a grant of £4,300 and is directly controlled by the Central Authority. It provides training for art as applied to industry, for school teachers and for all branches of the Arts to students coming from any part of Ireland.

The Committee recommended that a grant should be made to the Academy to make the third gallery suitable for exhibition purposes, and for other necessary repairs; that the title of the Metropolitan School of Art should be changed to the Royal College of Art for Ireland, that the Life School of the Academy should be transferred to the Metropolitan School to form one school, that a Professorship of Painting should be established in connection with it, and that an outside Committee should be appointed to direct the work of the Life Schools of Painting and Sculpture.

—— Minority Report. Mr. Justice Madden and Mr. Boland protested against the idea, supported solely by official witnesses, of superseding in Ireland a Royal Academy of Art as a teaching body by a school taught by paid masters in connection with a Government department. The building in Abbey Street could be sold at a profit to assist the Academy to be rehoused nearer the other institutions 'where you have the infection which comes from the best students, and the influence of one creative faculty on the others'. It is the duty of the State to provide a building suitable for the purpose for which the Academy obtained its Charter.

9. LAW, POLICE, PRISONS, PUBLIC ORDER, THE RISING

Under Sheriffs and Bailiffs (Ireland)

Vice-Regal Cttee. Rep. pp. 10. 1919

1919 *Cmd.* 190, *xxx*, 185
apptd. Oct., 1918. *sgd. May*, 1919

T. L. O'Shaughnessy (*Ch.*), Fottrell, Headlam, Seddall, Gamble.

'(*a*) *To enquire into and report upon the duties discharged by Under Sheriffs in Ireland, and to report whether any, and if so what, changes are recommended in the present remuneration of Under Sheriffs, and the fees at present received by them in respect of the duties of their office, and the arrangements made for the discharge of such duties; (b) to enquire into and report upon the present system of the appointment of Under Sheriffs, and to report if any, and if so what, change is recommended in reference to such appointments; and (c) to enquire into and report upon the present system of appointment of Bailiffs by Sheriffs, and to report if any, and if so what, change is recommended.*'

The Under Sheriff is appointed by and is entirely dependent upon the High Sheriff, who is appointed every year. The Under Sheriffs, the Incorporated Law Society and other bodies criticize this anomalous tenure of office. This official, who performs the duties historically associated with the post of High Sheriff, should be appointed by the Lord Lieutenant, should be a barrister or solicitor of five years'

standing or have five years of specified legal experience. He should be granted fixity of tenure, and the responsibility for the duties he performs should be legally transferred to him. These duties are outlined. Permanent status and an increased fixed salary are recommended.

The Bailiff is not a full-time officer, has no regular salary, but receives certain statutory fees. His position is similar to the Civil Bill Officer's. The two posts are sometimes combined in the same person. These two offices should be combined and the person appointed should be called the 'County Officer'. He should receive a retaining fee of £40 a year. This, together with fees earned, should be sufficient to attract suitable men to whole-time posts.

Clerk of the Crown and Peace, Etc. (Ireland)

Vice-Regal Cttee. Rep. pp. iv, 31. 1920

1920 *Cmd.* 805, *xiii*, 177
apptd. Oct., 1919. *sgd. June*, 1920

J. Wakely (*Ch.*), Manders, Headlam, Wright, Marron, Brown, Warren.

'*To enquire into various matters connected with the Offices of Clerks of the Crown and Peace, County Court Registrars, and Local Registrars of Title in Ireland.*'

The principal officer of the Court of Quarter Sessions was the Clerk of the Peace, and the principal officer for the Assize Court was the Clerk of the Crown. The County Officers and Courts (Ireland) Act of 1877 made provision for the union of the two offices as vacancies occurred, and there is now one for each county, except Cork, where there is one for each Riding. The appointment to the office was placed in the hands of the Lord Lieutenant. Some witnesses asked that the Lord Chancellor, who has practical knowledge of candidate's qualifications, should make the appointment, but the Committee stated that as the Lord

Lieutenant consults the Lord Chancellor, his power to appoint should remain unchanged. The Report describes the work of the Clerk, and the growth of his duties and responsibilities are illustrated by his work in connection with Local Registration of Titles, arising out of the Land Purchase Acts. The recommendations outline a scheme for qualifications, duties, salaries and remuneration.

Royal Irish Constabulary

Cttee. Rep. pp. 33. 1902. Mins. of ev. 1902

1902 *Cd.* 1087, *xlii*, 279. *Mins. of ev.*, etc.; 1902 *Cd.* 1094, *xlii*, 313 *apptd. April, sgd. Oct.*, 1901

C. E. H. Vincent (*Ch.*), Holmes, Starkie.

'*To inquire into representations made by members of the Royal Irish Constabulary in certain Memorials which have recently been addressed to the Government.*'

The Memorials refer to increases of pay, lodging allowances for married men, pensions (including pensions for widows), etc. The claims were based on the lower scale of pay as compared with English forces, on the rise in the cost of living and of the standard of comfort since the rates were fixed in 1882, and the more dangerous work of the Irish police. The Committee rejected these claims. The figures suggested would place the Royal Irish Constabulary, largely a rural force, on a par with the police of the most populous and wealthy English towns; the price of provisions had not risen in the twenty years; although the basic pay was below that of artisans, if the value of pensions were added, it exceeded that of the majority of them; married men of all ranks should be able to live within their pay and allowances; and the work was not more dangerous than that of English police. Resignations were only 1 per cent as compared with 3½ per cent in London, and there were many applicants await-

ing appointment. The recommendations, some of which would require legislation, would require an increase on the vote of £33,000. They included an increased lodging allowance—the most substantial grievance—shortening of the incremental periods for constables, and increased pay for sergeants.

—— Report, *Dublin Metropolitan Police.* pp. 16. 1902. Mins. of ev., apps., index. 1902

1902 *Cd.* 1088, *xlii*, 209. *Mins. of ev.*, etc.; 1902 *Cd.* 1095, *xlii*, 227 *sgd. Oct.*, 1901

Whilst the Committee was considering the Memorials from the Royal Irish Constabulary, it was asked to consider similar ones from the Dublin Metropolitan Police. Detailed recommendations were made involving an additional expenditure of £2,400.

Royal Irish Constabulary and Dublin Metropolitan Police

Cttee. Rep. pp. 35. 1914. Mins. of ev., apps., index. 1914

1914 *Cd.* 7421, *xliv*, 247. *Mins. of ev.*, etc.; 1914-16 *Cd.* 7637, *xxxii*, 359 *apptd. Jan., sgd. May*, 1914

D. Harrel (*Ch.*), Headlam, Starkie.

'*To enquire into the questions raised in the Memorials presented through the Chief Commissioner of the Dublin Metropolitan Police, and the Inspector-General of Constabulary, and to report what improvements (if any) are required in the pay and allowances of the two Forces, and how far the cost of such improvements can be met by any practicable reforms in their organization.*'

The Memorials presented mainly referred to pay, good service, or merit pay, lodging allowance, subsistence and other allowances, pensions on retirement, and pensions for widows and children of deceased members of the Force. Constable E. Barrett stated, in evidence, that the settlement in 1882 and 1908 was 'no settlement at all' and had caused discontent ever since. For example, the senior men were given 2s. per week rise, whereas 1s. per week was stopped for the first time for men living in barracks—up to two-thirds of the whole. In addition, great changes in the standard of living had taken place since 1908 and whilst other incomes had been increased the incomes of the police had been left at a standstill (q. 4174). Though the Constabulary witnesses had over-estimated the changes in the cost of living since 1901, it had been substantial; there had also been a remarkable advance in the standard of living of the farming, artisan and labouring classes from which the Forces drew their recruits, while the number of resignations of constables who go to better paid Forces, e.g. to England, or to better paid work, is too high. In 1901 there were 791 first-class candidates for the Force on the waiting list, but in 1913 there were only 19 first-class candidates for 227 vacancies. While the increase of 25 per cent asked for was not justified, a substantial increase was, and the rates set out should be paid without delay. Parallel recommendations are made for the Dublin Metropolitan Police.

Headlam suggests various economies, including the amalgamation of the two Forces.

Re-organization and Pay of the Irish Police Forces

Vice-Regal Com. Rep. pp. 20. 1920

1920 *Cmd. 603, xxii*, 1125
apptd. Oct., sgd. Dec., 1919

J. Ross (*Ch.*), Taylor, Headlam, Smith, Wright, Murphy.

'*To inquire and report as to the re-organization of the two Irish Police Forces to be initiated concurrently with the grant to those Forces of the rates of pay prescribed by the Desborough Committee.*'

'By comparing the duties and conditions of Officers serving in both Police Forces here and those of the Officers serving in Great Britain we have endeavoured to recommend a scale that will harmonize with that appearing in the Desborough Report.' (See *Breviate 1917–39*, p. 527.) For constables this meant a scale of basic pay of 70s. per week rising to 95s. twenty-two years from appointment, other rates of pay being proportionate; pensions after twenty-five years' service at one-half pensionable pay at the date of retirement and at two-thirds pensionable pay after thirty years' service. Similar recommendations are made regarding the Dublin Metropolitan Police. Officers and men in this force should be entitled to a sworn inquiry where serious charges involving dismissal are brought against them.

Belfast Prison

Rep. pp. 10. 1919

1919 *Cmd. 83, xxvii*, 881
apptd. Dec., 1918. *sgd. Feb.*, 1919

W. H. Dodd.

'*Enquiring into and reporting upon certain Complaints as to the treatment of prisoners in Belfast Prison.*'

After complaints about prison food and ventilation, 95 prisoners sent to prison under the Defence of the Realm Act had caused disturbances by putting their heads out of the windows of their cells and shouting provocative remarks and singing rebel songs. After repeated attempts to persuade them to desist, the Governor ordered their removal to another part of the prison. The prisoners resisted, and much prison furniture was smashed. Force was used, including hose pipes and hand-cuffings. The food was under the control of the Food Controller, and cells were ventilated, but the prisoners caused the disturbance when windows had been blocked in an attempt to prevent the shouting and singing. Continuing the prisoners in restraint at Mass and at Communion was rendered necessary by the acts of the prisoners themselves, some of whom refused to give an undertaking. All the evidence proved that the Governor had discharged a delicate duty with considerateness and success.

Alleged Outrage at Drumdoe House, County Roscommon, 11th July, 1905

Enquiry. Rep. pp. 3. 1906

1906 (151) *xcviii*, 1

D. S. Henry, J. H. H. Swiney.

Explosion at Lord Ashtown's Lodge, Glenahiery, County Waterford

Reps. pp. 4. 1908. pp. 8. 1908

1908 *Cd.* 4010, *Cd.* 3977, *xii*, 163

I. R. B. Jennings, E. G. Preston, P. Rielly.

Reports of two outrages.

State of Galway East Riding, Oct. 1907

Rep. p. 1. 1908

1908 *Cd.* 3949, *xc*, 5

T. J. Smith.

The Riding is in an unsatisfactory and disturbed state, mainly owing to the agitation for the sale and division of grazing farms and estates. Athenry district is in a very unsettled state and requires a large force of police to keep down crime. There is no serious boycotting, though a good many people are boycotted to the extent of being unable to get labour locally, and some find it difficult to get goods, especially in the local shops. All contrive in some way to get what they want.

Dublin Disturbances

Vice-Regal Com. Rep. pp. iii, 15. 1914. Mins. of ev., apps. 1914

1914 *Cd.* 7269, *xviii*, 513. *Mins. of ev., etc.*; 1914 *Cd.* 7272, *xviii*, 533 *apptd. Dec.*, 1913. *sgd. Feb.*, 1914

D. S. Henry (*Ch.*), Brown.

'To inquire into certain disturbances and riots which took place in the City of Dublin *in the months of August and September*, 1913.'

From 31st August to 21st September, 1913, there were fifteen riots in Dublin due to industrial unrest. Between January and August there had been thirty strikes, many being accompanied by violence and intimidation, which had resulted in organized attacks on the police. The protection given to the Tramway Company by the police during the strike caused great resentment. Details of each riot are given, including the one in Sackville Street in which Larkin, of the Transport Workers' Union, was arrested while out on bail. Although some innocent people had been injured, the police were commended for discharging their duties with courage and patience. Only in one case, and that for the purpose of protecting two tramcars, was the assistance of the military called. During the riots 200 police had been injured, and there were forty-five cases of prosecutions and convictions.

Recent events in the Irish Command

Army. Correspondence. pp. 4. 1914. pp. 16. 1914

1914 *Cd.* 7318, *Cd.* 7329, *lii*, 1

Correspondence between the War Office and the military command in Ireland over the possibility that troops might be asked not only to undertake operations in Ulster to maintain order and preserve property, but to initiate active operations.

The papers begin with a memorandum of an interview between the Secretary of State for War, 13th Dec., 1913:—'The law clearly lays down that a soldier is entitled to obey an order to shoot only if that order is reasonable under the circumstances. No one, from General Officer to Private, is entitled to use more force than is required to maintain order and the safety of life and property. No soldier can shelter himself from the civil law behind an order given by a superior if that order is, in fact, unreasonable and outrageous. If, therefore, officers and men in the Army were led to believe that there was a possibility that they might be called upon to take some outrageous action, for instance, to massacre a demonstration of Orangemen who were causing no danger to the lives of their neighbours, bad as were the effects on discipline in the Army, nevertheless it was true that they were, in fact and in law, justified in contemplating refusal to obey. But there never had been, and was not now, any intention of giving outrageous and illegal orders to the troops. The law would be respected, and must be obeyed. What had now to be faced was the possibility of action being required by His Majesty's troops in supporting the civil power, in protecting life and property when the police were unable to hold their own. Attempts had been made to dissuade troops from obeying lawful orders given to them when acting in support of the civil power. This amounted to a claim that officers and men could pick and choose between lawful and reasonable orders, saying that they would obey in one case and not in another.' . . . 'If any officer should tender his resignation they would ask for his reasons, and if he indicated in his reply that he desired to choose which order to obey, I would at once submit to the King that the officer should be removed.'

Paget, 17th March, informed the War Office, in respect of an instruction to move troops to guard certain barracks, that in the present state of the country any such move would create intense excitement in Ulster and might possibly precipitate a crisis. He therefore did not feel justified in moving troops, but was keeping them in readiness. On the 20th March, Paget reported that officers in two brigades were either resigning or would prefer to accept dismissal if ordered north. He was informed that no resignations should be accepted and that officers should be relieved of their commands.

A Minute by Gough explained that the officers concerned felt that more information was needed before they were called on to make decisions so vitally affecting their careers, in particular as to the meaning of 'duty as ordered' and 'active operations' in Ulster, that if the duty was maintenance of order and preservation of property, all concerned would undertake it. If however, it meant the initiation of active military operations in Ulster, 64 officers would, under protest, prefer to be dismissed.

On 23rd March, 1914, the Secretary of State gave a memo. to Gough which stated:—'You are authorized . . . to inform the officers of the 3rd Cavalry Brigade that the Army Council are satisfied that the incident which has arisen in regard to their resignations has been due to a misunderstanding. It is the duty of all soldiers to obey lawful commands given to them through the proper channel by the Army Council, either for the protection of public property and the support of the civil power in the event of disturbances, or for the protection of the lives and property of the inhabitants. This is the only point it was intended to be put to the officers in the questions of the General Officer Commanding, and the Army Council have been glad to learn from you that there never has been and never will be in the Brigade any question of disobeying such lawful orders. His Majesty's Government must retain their right to use all the forces of the Crown in Ireland, or elsewhere, to maintain law and order and to support the civil power in the ordinary execution of its duty. But they have no intention whatever of taking advantage of this right to crush political opposition to the policy or principles of the Home Rule Bill.'

Landing of Arms at Howth on July 26th, 1914

R. Com. Rep. pp. 15. 1914. Mins. of ev., apps., index. 1914

1914–16 Cd. 7631, *xxiv*, 805. *Mins. of ev., etc.*; 1914–16 Cd. 7649, *xxiv*, 821 *apptd. Aug., sgd. Sept.*, 1914

Lord Shaw (*Ch.*), Andrews, Molony.

'To *enquire into and report upon the events connected with and ensuing upon the recent landing of arms at Howth, including the circumstances in which the Military were requisitioned to assist the civil power in the City of Dublin, and the origin and character of the disturbances which occurred.*'

The first part of the episode began on Sunday afternoon, 26th July, when a yacht entered the harbour of Howth. It was met by about 1,000 Irish Volunteers who quickly unloaded arms and ammunition. They prevented access to the neighbourhood of any person not connected with the enterprise and no disorder took place. When the cargo had been unloaded, they formed up and proceeded to Dublin in an orderly and well-controlled manner. They were met at Kilbarrack by a number of the Dublin Metropolitan Police Force and these were later assisted by 160 soldiers. While parleying was going on between the authorities and the front ranks of the volunteers, the rest of the volunteers, with the arms, completely disappeared (Sergeant Sullivan. Mins. of ev. p. 4). The episode thus ended with no more than a scuffle or two in which some bayonet wounds were inflicted. The second part of the episode occurred in Bachelors Walk when the soldiers were on their way back to the barracks; large crowds had provoked the soldiers, who had fired into the crowd on the understanding that orders had been given to do so. The police and the military had been called by Mr. Harrel, the Assistant Commissioner of the Dublin Metropolitan Police, to intercept the volunteers, after he had received a telephone call from Mr. Heard, the County Inspector at Howth, who had told him that he had only eleven constables at Howth. The Commissioners stated that their Report in all particulars and their conclusions were unanimous. Amongst the latter were

that the employment of the police and the military were not in accordance with the law, particularly Section 202 of the Customs Act, 1876. Apart from the fundamental illegality regarding the seizure of rifles, the events and circumstances did not warrant military intervention. Apart from the possession of contraband rifles, the gathering of the Irish Volunteers and their march towards Dublin did not constitute an unlawful assembly requiring dispersal by military aid; their presence and conduct produced no terror to the lieges and did not endanger life or property or the King's Peace. The calling in of military aid to suppress it as an unlawful assembly was unjustifiable. Between Fairview and Bachelors Walk the military were subjected to insults and assailed with missiles, but the danger did not justify the use of firearms. The promiscuous firing of rifles by twenty-one soldiers took place without orders, but the troops were under the impression that the order was given directly and passed from man to man.

The attention of the Lords of the Treasury is called to the fact that some of the victims were innocent of any connection with the hostile crowd.

Rebellion in Ireland

R. Com. Rep. pp. 14. 1916. Mins. of ev., apps. 1916

1916 Cd. 8279, *xi*, 171. *Mins. of ev., etc.*; 1916 Cd. 8311, *xi*, 185 *apptd. May, sgd. June*, 1916

L. Hardinge (*Ch.*), Shearman, Chalmers.

'To *enquire into the causes of the recent outbreak of rebellion in Ireland, and into the conduct and degree of responsibility of the civil and military executive in Ireland in connection therewith.*'

The Report begins with a description of the machinery of Irish Government, the powers of the Lord Lieutenant, the Chief Secretary, the police and the legal powers of the Irish executive. 'If the Irish system be regarded as a whole it is anomalous in quiet times, and almost unworkable in times of crisis.' The Report then reviews in detail the circumstances and critical incidents leading up to the final rising. These cannot be summarized succinctly, but the following are amongst the chief points made.

Mr. Birrell, the Chief Secretary, described the background of the rebellion in the following manner: 'The spirit of what to-day is "Sinn Feinism" (ourselves alone) is mainly composed of the old hatred and distrust of the British connection, always noticeable in all classes, and in all places, varying in degree, and finding different ways of expression, but always there as a background of Irish politics and character.'

In the winter of 1913, during industrial strikes, an armed force was created called the Citizen Army, composed of working men, and inspired by anarchist sentiments based on Irish discontent. Its leader was James Connolly, a man of energy and ability. In November of the same year twelve men came together in Dublin to discuss and form the *Irish National Volunteers*. These men included J. McNeill, B. Hobson, F. H. Pearse and T. O'Rahilly. Sixty-five thousand men had enrolled by June, 1914, when John Redmond got control of it. On the 25th September, when the Prime Minister was due to visit, Redmond spoke strongly in favour of recruiting, but by the 30th September six of the founders dissociated themselves from Redmond and recruited 13,000 men into a new force called the *Irish Volunteers*; eight thousand were known to be drilling and to possess 1,400 rifles (a large consignment of arms had been landed at Howth for the Irish National Volunteers in July, 1914). In spite of the breach of the Proclamation of 1913 prohibiting the import of arms, on the landing of arms at Howth as on earlier landings at Larne, the Government decided to take no action and to institute no prosecution; and on 5th Aug., 1914, the restriction on the import of arms was removed. By December 1915 the Redmondite or National Volunteers had sunk to insignificance. Between January 1916 and the outbreak of the insurrection in April, the Irish Volunteers steadily increased in numbers and discipline and were supplied with arms and explosives by theft or otherwise. (The German ship bringing arms was captured in April and Sir Roger Casement was arrested.) By March 1916 a campaign had begun and continued to the effect that any attempt to disarm the volunteers would be resisted. The Chief Commissioner had urged drastic action, and this report was seen by the Lord Lieutenant and Chief Secretary, but no answer was returned to the Royal Irish Constabulary. On 16th April a forged document was circulated which led members of the Irish Volunteers and Citizen Army to believe that they would shortly be disarmed. This was undoubtedly one of the proximate causes of the outbreak. Early in the morning of 24th April, the Chief Secretary concurred in the proposed arrest and internment of the ringleaders in England, but the carefully planned rebellion broke out before any effective steps could be taken, and by noon many portions of the city of Dublin had been occupied simultaneously by rebellious armed forces.

From 1914 onwards the Chief Secretary had been kept informed of the condition of Ireland through confidential reports from the Inspector General of the Royal Irish Constabulary, the Chief Commissioner and the Detective Department of the Dublin Metropolitan Police, and the Army Intelligence Department, but there was also plenty of other information such as seditious speeches, and articles and pamphlets which were published openly to intimidate the Government against repressive measures. Lord Middleton called attention in the House of Lords to the condition of Ireland and gave warnings at later periods. In a discussion in March 1915 the Lord Lieutenant had shown his anxiety to deal with the ringleaders, but he had also indicated that he was unable to move because of the general attitude of the Government towards Ireland; this it was impossible to disturb. In evidence Mr. Birrell stated that at a conference at the War Office on 20th March, 1916, he had asked that soldiers with fixed bayonets, etc., should be put in the streets of Dublin. He was told that 'we are very busy training men . . . and cannot spare them' (qq. 539, 540).

Amongst the general conclusions, the Commission stated 'that the main cause of the rebellion appears to be that lawlessness was allowed to grow up unchecked, and that Ireland for several years past has been administered on the principle that it was safer and more expedient to leave law in abeyance if collision with any faction of the Irish people could thereby be avoided. Such a policy is the negation of that cardinal rule of Government which demands that 'the enforcement of law and the preservation of order should always be independent of political expediency'. The importation of large quantities of arms, the toleration of the drilling and manoeuvring of armed forces, and the reluctance shown by the Irish Government to repress written and spoken seditious utterances was largely prompted by the pressure brought to bear by the Parliamentary representatives of the Irish people. It was not disputed that the seditious bodies were prepared to assist a German landing, and powers should have been invoked to suppress sedition under the Defence of the Realm Act. The Chief Secretary as the administrative head of His Majesty's Government was found to be 'primarily responsible for the situation that was allowed to arise, and the outbreak that occurred'. From various sources the Government had abundant information on which they could have acted many months before the leaders themselves contemplated any actual rising.

The evidence includes statements by Sir Matthew Nathan, Under Secretary (q. 1), and the Chief Secretary, Mr. Augustine Birrell (q. 520).

Arrest and Subsequent Treatment of Mr. Francis Sheehy Skeffington, Mr. Thomas Dickson, and Mr. Patrick James McIntyre

R. Com. Rep. pp. 12. 1916

1916 Cd. 8376, xi, 311
apptd. Aug., sgd. Sept., 1916

J. Simon (Ch.), Molony, Henry.

'To inquire into and report upon the facts and circumstances connected with the treatment of Mr. Francis Sheehy Skeffington, Mr. Thomas Dickson and Mr. Patrick J. McIntyre upon and after their arrest on the Twenty-fifth day of April last.'

The insurrection broke out on 24th April. On 25th April Mr. Sheehy Skeffington, a well-known figure in Dublin who had no connection with the Rebellion and was opposed to the use of physical force, was arrested. His arrest had no connection with that of Mr. Dickson and Mr. McIntyre, who were arrested three hours later; the only reason for arresting them was that they were in Alderman Kelly's shop, against whom there was no foundation for suspicion. Neither had any connection with the Sinn Fein movement. The Report details the incidents and circumstances in which Capt. Bowen Colthurst ordered them to be shot. Capt. Colthurst said that he thought he had the right to shoot. The proclamation of martial law does not confer on officers or soldiers any new powers, but is a warning that the Government, acting through the military, is taking such forcible and exceptional measures as are needed to restore order. The measures taken can be justified only by the practical circumstances of the case. The shooting of unarmed and unresisting civilians without trial constituted murder, whether martial law has been proclaimed or not. Failure to understand and apply this elementary principle seems to explain the free hand which Capt. Colthurst was not restrained from exercising. On 6th and 7th June Capt. Colthurst was tried for murder by Court Martial in Dublin, and found guilty but insane.

APPENDIX I

COMPLETE LIST OF PAPERS OF CERTAIN COMMISSIONS

THE papers of four Commissions are so voluminous or complicated in their arrangement that the references to them cannot be conveniently printed in the text. A complete list is given below, together with the Bound Sessional volume numbers and paper numbers (left hand columns). A list of memoranda issued by the Committee on the Health of Munition Workers is added.

It is important to note that the papers of each Commission were grouped into volumes and given their own volume numbers (right hand columns) which have no relation to the volume numbers of the Bound Sessional Sets. This sometimes gives rise to confusion, since the footnote and other references in a Commission's report may quote the Commission's volume number. But this is insufficient to enable the information to be found in the Sessional Sets, for which the Sessional volume number is necessary. Thus, the usefulness of the Poor Law Commission's *List of Oral and Non-Oral Witnesses* is limited by the fact that it gives only the volume number of the Commission's papers, and a second process is necessary to find the number of the paper and of the Sessional volume. In its report, the Commission uses over twenty different forms of reference. That of the Commission on *Congestion in Ireland* uniformly refers to the volume number of the Commission's papers. Both the Commission on *Local Taxation* and on *Canals and Inland Waterways* use the volume number of their papers, the former sometimes also giving the paper number. The searcher's work in following up such references can be reduced if he has by him the list below, which gives the two sets of volume numbers, and the extreme question numbers in each volume of the minutes of evidence. It will also enable him to use the standard form of reference in his own work:—Session/paper no./volume no./volume page no. See *Guide to Parliamentary Papers*, p. 45.

Local Taxation

1899	C.9141	xxxv	Local Taxation. R. Com. 1st Rep. Valuation for and Collection of Local Rates.
	C.9142	,,	—— 2nd Rep. Valuation and Rating in respect of Tithe Rentcharge.
1901	Cd.638	xxiv	—— Final Rep. England and Wales.
1902	Cd.1221	xxxix	—— —— App.
	Cd.973	,,	—— Valuation in Ireland. Rep.
	Cd.1068	,,	—— Final Rep. Ireland.
	Cd.1067	,,	—— Final Rep. Scotland.
1903	Cd.1480	xxiii	—— Index to Final Reps.
1898	C.8763	xli	—— Mins. of ev. Vol. I (England, Scotland, Ireland) (qq. 1–11773).
1898	C.8764	xlii	—— —— Apps. Pt. I (England, Scotland, Ireland).
	C.8765	,,	—— —— Apps. Pt. II (England).
1899	C.9150	xxxvi	—— Mins. of ev., apps. Vol. II (London. Tithe rentcharge, England and Wales) (qq. 11774–14245; 18139–20985).
	C.9319	,,	—— Mins. of ev., apps. Vol. III (Scotland) (qq. 14246–18138).
1900	Cd.201	xxxvi	—— Mins. of ev., apps. Vol. IV (Rating of site value, etc.) (qq. 20986–23381; 27539–27773).
	Cd.383	,,	—— Mins. of ev., apps. Vol. V (Ireland) (qq. 23382–27538).
1899	C.9528	xxxvi	—— Classification and Incidence of Imperial and Local Taxes. Memos.

Canals and Waterways

1906	Cd.3183	xxxii	Canals and Waterways. R. Com. 1st. Rep.	Vol. I. Pt. I.
	Cd.3184	,,	—— —— Mins. of ev. (qq. 1–11329)	Vol. I. Pt. II.
1907	Cd.3716	xxxiii, Pt.I	—— 2nd Rep.	Vol. II. Pt. I.
	Cd.3717	,,	—— —— Mins. of ev. (Ireland)*	Vol. II. Pt. II.
	Cd.3718	,,	—— —— Mins. of ev. (England, Wales, Scotland)*	Vol. III.
	Cd.3719	xxxiii, Pt.II	—— —— Returns. (History, capital, traffic, works, etc.)	Vol. IV.
1909	Cd.4839	xiii	—— 3rd Rep.	Vol. V. Pt. I.
	Cd.4840	,,	—— —— Mins. of ev. (England, Wales, Scotland) (qq. 32813–42673)	Vol. V. Pt. II.
	Cd.4841	,,	—— —— France, Belgium, Germany, Holland. W. H. Lindley. Reps., etc.	Vol. VI.
1910	Cd.4979	xii	—— 4th and Final Rep. England, Wales, Scotland	Vol. VII.
	Cd.5204	,,	—— —— Apps. (App. 16. United States. Mr. Lindsay. Rep.)	Vol. VIII.
	Cd.5083	,,	—— Cost of improving Canal Routes. J. W. Barry. Reps.	Vol. IX.
	Cd.5447	xiii	—— Water Supplies of Canal Routes. R. B. Dunwoody. Reps.	Vol. X.
1911	Cd.5626	xiii	—— Final Rep. Ireland	Vol. XI.
	Cd.5653	,,	—— —— Apps.	Vol. XII.

* In Cd.3717 and Cd.3718, the question numbers included are not
continuous:
    Cd.3717 (qq. 12056–17552; 20399–20474; 21077–21767; 25847–
            26370; 26931–27012; 32576–32812)
    Cd.3718 (qq. 11330–12055; 17553–20398; 20475–21076; 21768–
            25846; 26371–26930; 27013–32575)

Poor Laws and Relief of Distress

1909	Cd.4499	xxxvii	Poor Laws and Relief of Distress. R. Com. Rep.	
	Cd.4945	,,	—— Index	Vol. XXXV.
	Cd.4625	xxxix	—— Mins. of ev. Officers of L.G.B. (qq. 1–14880)	Vol. I.
	Cd.4626	,,	—— —— Apps.	Vol. IA.
	Cd.4627	,,	—— —— —— Index	Vol. IB.
	Cd.4684	xl	—— Mins. of ev., app. London witnesses (qq. 14881–24739)	Vol. II.
	Cd.4704	,,	—— —— Index	Vol. IIA.
	Cd.4755	,,	—— Mins. of ev., app. Poor Law and Charitable Assocs. (qq. 24740–35450)	Vol. III.
	Cd.4764	,,	—— —— Index	Vol. IIIA.
	Cd.4835	xli	—— Mins. of ev., app. B.M.A. and witnesses from Liverpool and Manchester, Yorkshire, Midlands (qq. 35451–48347)	Vol. IV.
	Cd.4836	,,	—— —— Index	Vol. IVA.
	Cd.4888	,,	—— Mins. of ev., app. Urban and N.E. counties. (qq. 48348–53067)	Vol. V.
	Cd.4889	,,	—— —— Index	Vol. VA.

1909	Cd.4850	xlii	—— Relief in the Dioceses. Special Reps.	Vol. XIII.
	Cd.4573	„	—— Medical Relief. J. C. McVail. Rep.	Vol. XIV.
	Cd.4593	„	—— Charities. A. C. Kay, H. V. Toynbee. Rep.	Vol. XV.
	Cd.4653	xliii	—— Industrial and Sanitary Conditions and Pauperism. Rep. Poor Law System. Memo. A. D. Steel-Maitland. Miss R. E. Squire.	Vol. XVI.
	Cd.4690	„	—— Outdoor Relief and Wages. Miss C. Williams. T. Jones. Rep.	Vol. XVII.
1910	Cd.5200	lv	—— —— Employment of Women Paupers	Vol. XXXVI.
1909	Cd.4795	xliv	—— Relieving Distress outside the Poor Law. C. Jackson. J. C. Pringle. Rep.	Vol. XIX.
	Cd.4632	„	—— Boy Labour. Rep. C. Jackson	Vol. XX.
	Cd.4631	xlv	—— Hospitals and Poor Law Medical Relief. Norah B. Roberts. Rep.	Vol. XXII.
	Cd.4944	„	—— Unemployed Workmen Act, 1905. Questions and Replies by Distress Cttees.	Vol. XXVII.
1910	Cd.5035	xlvii	—— Mins. of ev., app. Eng. (Rural Centres) National Conference of Friendly Societies (qq. 67566–77734)	Vol. VII.
	Cd.5036	„	—— —— Index	Vol. VIIA.
	Cd.5066	xlviii	—— Mins. of ev., app. 'Unemployment' (qq. 77735–88666)	Vol. VIII.
	Cd.5067	„	—— —— Index	Vol. VIIIA.
	Cd.5068	xlix	—— —— Further Mins. of ev. (qq. 89048–94628; 95324–99350; 100020–100590)	Vol. IX.
	Cd.5069	l	—— —— —— Index	Vol. IXA.
	Cd.5072	li	—— Miscellaneous Papers	Vol. XI.
	Cd.4983	„	—— History of Poor Law. Loch, Prof. Smart, Mrs. Webb, Booth. Memos.	Vol. XII.
	Cd.5037	lii	—— Children. Misses Williams, Longman and Phillips. Rep.	Vol. XVIII.
	Cd.5074	„	—— Cases of refusal of out-relief. Miss G. Harlock. Rep.	Vol. XXI.
	Cd.5076	„	—— Able-bodied Male Inmates. C. T. Parsons. Rep.	Vol. XXIV.
	Cd.5077	liii	—— Statistics	Vol. XXV.
	Cd.4974	liv	—— Visits by Commissioners. (Urban, Rural, etc.) Reps.	Vol. XXVIII.
	Cd.5078	„	—— Administration of Charities, etc. Documents	Vol. XXVI.
1909	Cd.4630	xxxviii	—— Rep. Ireland.	
	Cd.4890	xliv	—— Relieving distress outside the Poor Law. C. Jackson. Rep.	Vol. XIXB.
1910	Cd.5070	l	—— Mins. of ev., app. Ireland. (qq. 99351–100019; 100591–100928)	Vol. X.
	Cd.5071	„	—— —— Index	Vol. XA.
	Cd.5244	liv	—— Statistics. Ireland	Vol. XXXI.

1909	Cd.4922	xxxviii	—— Rep. Scotland.
1910	Cd.4978	xlvi	—— Mins. of ev., app. Scotland. Unemployment, see Cd.5068. (qq. 53068–67565; 88667–89046; 94629–95323) Vol. VI.
	Cd.4982	xlvii	—— —— Index Vol. VIA.
	Cd.5073	lii	—— Relieving distress outside the Poor Law in Scotland. J. C. Pringle. Rep. Vol. XIXA.
	Cd.5075	,,	—— Children. C. T. Parsons, Misses Longman and Phillips. Rep. Vol. XXIII.
	Cd.5243	liv	—— General Assembly's Cttee. Rep., app. Vol. XXIX.
	Cd.5440	,,	—— Statistics. Scotland Vol. XXX.
	Cd.5199	,,	—— Institutions in Holland, Belgium, Germany and Switzerland. Reps. Vol. XXXII.
	Cd.5441	lv	—— Foreign and Colonial Systems of Poor Relief Vol. XXXIII.
	Cd.5442	,,	—— Alphabetical Lists of Oral and Non-oral witnesses Vol. XXXIV.
	Cd.5443	lv, Pt.II	—— General Consolidated Index Vol.XXXVII.

Health of Munition Workers

Committee. Memoranda only

1914–16	Cd.8132	xxix	Sunday Labour. No. 1.
	Cd.8133	,,	Industrial Canteens. No. 3.
	Cd.8151	lv	Welfare Supervision. No. 2.
1916	Cd.8185	xxiii	Employment of Women. No. 4.
	Cd.8186	,,	Hours of Work. No. 5.
	Cd.8199	,,	Canteen Construction and Equipment. No. 6.
	Cd.8213	,,	Industrial Fatigue and its Causes. No. 7.
	Cd.8214	,,	Special Industrial Diseases. No. 8.
	Cd.8215	,,	Ventilation and Lighting of Munition Factories and Workshops. No. 9.
	Cd.8216	,,	Sickness and Injury. No. 10.
	Cd.8370	,,	Investigation of Workers' Food and Suggestions as to Dietary. No. 11.
	Cd.8344	,,	Output in relation to Hours of Work. No. 12.
	Cd.8362	,,	Juvenile Employment. No. 13.
	Cd.8387	,,	Washing Facilities and Baths. No. 14.
	Cd.8409	,,	Effect of Industrial Conditions upon Eyesight. No. 15.
1917–18	Cd.8522	xx	Medical Certificates for Munition Workers. No. 16.
			Health and Welfare of Munition Workers Outside the Factory (not published). No. 17.
	Cd.8628	,,	Output and Hours of Work and Sunday Labour. No. 18.
	Cd.8798	,,	Investigation of Workers' Food and Suggestions as to Dietary. No. 19.
	Cd.8801	,,	Weekly Hours of Employment. No. 20.
1918	Cd.9046	xv	Investigation of Industrial Accidents. No. 21.
	Non-Parl.		Health of the Munition Worker. A Handbook for Directors, Managers, Foremen and others in authority in Munition Works of all kinds.

Congestion in Ireland

Formal Reps. not cited

1906	Cd.3267	xxxii	Congestion in Ireland. R. Com. Mins. of ev., etc. Dublin (qq. 1–5229) I.

1907	Cd.3319	xxxv	—— —— Donegal (qq. 5230–12766)	II.
	Cd.3414	,,	—— —— London (qq. 12767–18507)	III.
	Cd.3509	xxxvi	—— —— London (qq. 18508–22081)	IV.
	Cd. 3630	,,	—— —— London (qq. 22082–27369)	V.
1908	Cd.3748	xxxix	—— —— Co. Sligo, Co. Leitrim (qq. 27370–34905)	VI.
	Cd.3785	xl	—— —— Co. Down, Co. Antrim, etc. (qq. 34906–42126)	VII.
	Cd.3786	,,	—— Statistics of Holdings, etc.	
	Cd.3839	xli	—— Mins. of ev., etc. Kerry, Cork (qq. 42127–46737)	VIII.
	Cd.3845	,,	—— —— Co. Mayo (qq. 46738–52012)	IX.
	Cd.4007	xlii	—— —— Co. Galway, Co. Roscommon (qq. 52013–59393)	X.
	Cd.4089	,,	—— —— London (qq. 59394–60386)	XI.
	Cd.4097	,,	—— Final Rep.	XII.
	Cd.4098	xliii	—— Index to mins. of ev.	
	Cd.4099	,,	—— Digest of mins. of ev.	

The minutes of evidence to the first eleven Reps. are referred to in the Final Rep. by the roman numeral corresponding to the number of the report in question. See Final Rep., p. v.

APPENDIX II

SPECIAL REPORTS ON EDUCATIONAL SUBJECTS
Edited by M. E. Sadler

1897	C.8447	xxv	Various countries including Reps. by R. L. Morant, M. E. Sadler	Vol. I.
1898	C.8943	xxiv	England, Wales, France, etc.	Vol. II.
	C.8988	xxv	Switzerland, Prussia, Sweden, etc.	Vol. III.
1900	Cd.416	xxi	Canada, Newfoundland, West Indies	Vol. IV.
	Cd.417	xxii, Pt. I	Cape Colony, Natal, Australia, New Zealand, Ceylon, Malta	Vol. V.
	Cd.418	xxii, Pt.II	Preparatory Schools for boys: their place in English Secondary education	Vol. VI.
1902	Cd.834	xxvi	Rural education in France	Vol. VII.
	Cd.835	,,	Scandinavia, Holland, Switzerland, etc.	Vol. VIII.
	Cd. 1157	xxvii	—— Netherlands	Supplement.
	Cd.836	,,	Germany	Vol. IX.
	Cd.837	xxviii	U.S.A., Pt. I.	Vol. X.
	Cd.1156	xxix	—— Pt. II.	Vol. XI.
1905	Cd.2377	xxv	West Indies, C. America, St. Helena, Cyprus, Gibraltar	Vol. XII.
	Cd.2378	xxvi	W. Africa, E. Africa, Uganda, Mauritius, etc.	Vol. XIII.
	Cd.2379	,,	Malay States, Hong Kong, Falkland Islands, etc.	Vol. XIV.
	Cd. 2498	,,	School training, home duties for women. Pt. I. U.S.A.	Vol. XV.
1906	Cd.2963	xxviii	—— Pt. II. Belgium, Sweden, Norway, etc.	Vol. XVI.
1907	Cd.3537	xxii	Schools public, private. N. Europe	Vol. XVII.
1908	Cd.3777	xxvi	The French primary school teacher	Vol. XVIII.
1908	Cd.3860	xxvii	School training, home duties for women. Pt. III. Germany and and Australia	Vol. XIX.

1910	Cd.4997	xxiii	Classics in secondary schools. Germany	Vol. XX.
1908	Cd.3866	xxvii	School excursions, Vacation schools	Vol. XXI.
1909	Cd.4477	xviii	Provisions for children under compulsory school age. Belgium, France, etc.	Vol. XXII.
1909	Cd.4812	xviii	Education in Russia	Vol. XXIII.
1911	Non-Parl.	Bd. of Ed.	Secondary and University education. France	Vol. XXIV.
1912	Non-Parl.	„	Universities. Dominions	Vol. XXV.
1912	Non-Parl.	„	Teaching of mathematics. U.K. Pt. I.	Vol. XXVI.
1912	Non-Parl.	„	—— Pt. II.	Vol. XXVII.
1914	Non-Parl.	„	School and employment. U.S.A.	Vol. XXVIII.

APPENDIX III

SELECT LIST OF ANNUAL REPORTS 1900–1939

THE annual reports of Departments and other statutory bodies, and the memoranda and statistics they contain, are invaluable sources of information, but their reference numbers are scattered through the sessional and general alphabetical indexes. The paper and volume numbers of some of the principal series are given below.

The list is confined to a selection of those reports bearing upon the major subjects covered by the *Breviate* which are most frequently required by researchers. As no such list was included in the *Breviate* for 1917–1939 it has been extended to include those years and thus together with a similar list in the *Select List of British Parliamentary Papers, 1833–1899*, provides the references for chief annual reports from 1834 to 1939.

The reports have been tabulated according to their substantial contents and not under the precise name of the issuing body, which may have changed during the period, e.g. Local Government Board to Ministry of Health.

The titles of the reports in each series are as follows:

1. Finance Accounts of the U.K.
2. Inland Revenue. Reps. of Commissioners.
3. Customs. Reps. of Commissioners. 1910: Customs and Excise.
4. Trade. Annual Statement of Trade of the U.K. with Foreign Countries and British Possessions. 1922: Non-Parl.

———

5. Navigation and Shipping of the U.K. Annual Statement. 1923: Non-Parl.
6. Railway and Canal. Reps. of Commissioners. (1933–34: 45th Rep. not printed.)
7. Factories and Workshops. Reps. of Chief Inspector.
8. Strikes and Lockouts. 1902: Strikes and Lockouts in U.K. and Conciliation and Arbitration Boards. 1914–16: last Rep.

———

9. Labour.—Abstract of Statistics. Published irregularly.
10. Labour.—Ministry of Labour.
11. Unemployment Assistance Board.
12. Local Government Board. 1920: Ministry of Health.

———

13. Local Government Board (Scotland). 1920: Scottish Board of Health. 1929–30: Scottish Department of Health.
14. Health.—Reps. of M.O. to L.G.B. 1922: State of Public Health. Reps. of Chief M.O., Ministry of Health. Non-Parl.
15. Education.—Reps. of Chief M.O. to Board of Education. 1922: Health of the School Child. Non-Parl.
16. Lunacy. Reps. of Commissioners. 1914–16 Lunacy and Mental Deficiency, Board of Control. 1922—1936-7 Non-Parl.

———

17. Lunacy (Scotland). Reps. of Commissioners. 1914–16: General Board of Control for Scotland.

18. Education. Board of Education.
19. Education (Scotland). Cttee. of Council.
20. Reformatory and Industrial Schools. Reps. of Inspectors. Continued in the Reps. of the Children's Branch of the Home Office, 1923, 1924, 1925, 1928, 1938. Non-Parl.

---

21. Judicial Statistics. Criminal and Civil (England and Wales).
22. Judicial Statistics (Scotland).
23. Prisons. Reps. of Commissioners and the Directors of Convict Prisons.
24. Prisons (Scotland). Reps. of Commissioners.

---

25. Registrar General. 1923: Statistical Review, England and Wales. 1922: Non-Parl.
26. Registrar General (Scotland). 1921: Non-Parl.
27. Registrar General (Scotland). Detailed Ann. Reps. 1914–16: Combines the information of the general and detailed reports. 1921: Non-Parl.
28. Statistical Abstract for the U.K.

IRELAND

1. Agricultural Statistics with Detailed Rep. on Agriculture.
2. Local Government Board.
3. Lunacy. Reps. of Inspectors. 1922: Non-Parl.
4. Education. Ann. Reps. of Commissioners.

---

5. Criminal and Judicial Statistics.
6. Prisons. Reps. of General Prisons Board.
7. Reformatory and Industrial Schools. Reps. of Chief Inspector.
8. Registrar General. Detailed Ann. Reps.

1—4

Session	Finance		Inland Revenue		Customs		Trade	
1900	(241)	xlvii	Cd.347	xviii	Cd.319	xviii	Cd.187	lxxxvi
1901	(238)	xxxvii	Cd.764	xviii	Cd.763	xviii	Cd.549	lxxvi
							Cd.664	lxxvi
1902	(234)	lv	Cd.1216	xxii	Cd.1226	xxii	Cd.1105	xcviii Pt. I
							Cd.1173	xcviii Pt.II
1903	(219)	xxxvi	Cd.1717	xix	Cd.1753	xix	Cd.1582	lxix
							Cd.1617	lxx
1904	(219)	xlix	Cd.2228	xviii	Cd.2227	xviii	Cd.2043	xc
							Cd.2081	xci
1905	(200)	xliv	Cd.2633	xxiv	Cd.2647	xxiii	Cd.2497	lxxix
							Cd.2626	lxxx
							Cd.2668	lxxxviii
1906	(208)	lxv	Cd.3110	xxvi	Cd.3079	xxvi	Cd.2928	cxvi
							Cd.3022	cxvii
							Cd.3282	cxiv
1907	(212)	xlvii	Cd.3686	xx	Cd.3701	xx	Cd.3466	lxxxii
							Cd.3529	lxxxiii
							Cd.3687	lxxxiii
1908	(192)	lxii	Cd.4226	xxiv	Cd.4232	xxiv	Cd.4100	cii
							Cd.4150	ciii
							Cd.4266	ciii
1909	(200)	l	Cd.4868	xxvii	Cd.4862	xvi	Cd.4687	lxxxii
							Cd.4784	lxxxiii
							Cd.4949	lxxxiii
1910	(201)	lix	Cd.5308	xxxvi	Cd.5302	xxii	Cd.5159	lxxxvii
							Cd.5298	lxxxvii
							Cd.5305	lxxxviii
1911	(201)	xlv	Cd.5833	xxix Pt. I	Cd.5827	xv	Cd.5699	lxxix
							Cd.5852	lxxx
							Cd.5853	lxxx

Session	Finance		Inland Revenue		Customs		Trade	
1912–3	(169)	xlix	Cd.6344	xxix	Cd.6462	xvii	Cd.6216	lxxxv
							Cd.6336	lxxxvi
							Cd.6491	lxxxvi
1913	(173)	xli	Cd.7000	xxviii	Cd.6993	xix	Cd.6810	lx
							Cd.6970	lxi
1914	(297)	l	Cd.7572	xxxvi	Cd.7574	xvii	Cd.7135	lxxxiii
							Cd.7401	lxxxii
							Cd.7585	lxxxiii
1914–6	(273)	xxxviii	Cd.8116	xxiv	Cd.7621	xiii	Cd.7754	lxv
							C.7968	lxiv
							Cd.8069	lxv
1916	(93)	xvii	Cd.8425	xi	Cd.8428	vi	Cd.8284	xxv
							Cd.8357	xxvi
1917–8	(102)	xix	Cd.8887	xv	Cd.8938	x	Cd.8632	xxviii
							Cd.8714	xxix
1918	(82)	xv	Cd.9151	x	Cd.9215	vii	Cd.9127	xxi
							Cd.9136	xxii
1919	(121)	xxxii	Cmd.502	xxiv	Cmd.503	xiii	Cmd.342	xliii
							Cmd.366	xliv
1920	(124)	xxvii	Cmd.1083	xviii	Cmd.1082	xiii	Cmd.945	xli
							Cmd.1093	xlii
1921	(146)	xix	Cmd.1436	xiv	Cmd.1435	x	Cmd.1503	xxxii
							Cmd.1504	xxxii
							Cmd.1505	xxxiii
							Cmd.1506	xxxiii
1922	(88)	xi						
1922 Sess. II			Cmd.1780	ii	Cmd.1776	ii	Continuing Non-Parl.	
1923	(89)	xiii	Cmd.1934	xii Pt. I	Cmd.1933	x		
1924	(103)	xiii	Cmd.2227	xi	Cmd.2226	viii		
1924–5	(116)	xvi	Cmd.2547	xiv	Cmd.2485	ix		
1926	(90)	xvi	Cmd.2783	xii	Cmd.2721	ix		
1927	(71)	xiii	Cmd.2989	x	Cmd. 2960	viii		
1928	(82)	xiii	Cmd.3176	x	Cmd.3172	vii		
1928–9								
1929–30	(1)	xviii	Cmd.3500	xv	Cmd.3435	ix		
	(138)	xviii			Cmd.3651	ix		
1930–1	(106)	xviii	Cmd.3802	xv	Cmd.3961	xi		
1931–2	(81)	xiv	Cmd.4027	xi	Cmd.4195	vii		
			Cmd.4196	xi				
1932–3	(123)	xvi	Cmd.4456	xiii	Cmd.4455	x		
1933–4	(91)	xvi	Cmd.4739	xiii	Cmd.4740	xi		
1934–5	(94)	xii	Cmd.5015	ix	Cmd.5014	vii		
1935–6	(112)	xv	Cmd.5297	xii	Cmd.5296	viii		
1936–7	(131)	xvi	Cmd.5574	xii	Cmd.5573	ix		
1937–8	(140)	xvi	Cmd.5865	xii	Cmd.5876	ix		
1938–9	(131)	xvi	Cmd.6099	xii	Cmd.6098	x		

5–8

Session	Navigation and Shipping		Railways and Canals		Factories and Workshops		Strikes and Lockouts	
1900	Cd.214	lxxxviii	Cd.78	xviii	Cd.27	xi	Cd.316	lxxxiii
					Cd.223	xi		
1901	Cd.604	lxxv	Cd.488	xviii	Cd.668	x	Cd.689	lxxiii
1902	Cd.1113	c	Cd.956	xxiii	Cd.841	xii	Cd.1236	xcvii
					Cd.1112	xii		
					Cd.1300	xii		
1903	Cd.1612	lxxi	Cd.1589	xx	Cd.1610	xii	Cd.1623	lxvi
1904	Cd.2122	xci	Cd.2073	xix	Cd.1816	x	Cd.2112	lxxxix
					Cd.1979	x		
					Cd.2139	x		
1905	Cd.2556	lxxx	Cd.2393	xxiv	Cd.2324	x	Cd.2631	lxxvi
					Cd.2569	x		
1906	Cd.3093	cxvii	Cd.2882	xxvii	Cd.2848	xv	Cd.3065	cxii
					Cd.3036	xv		
1907	Cd.3545	lxxxiv	Cd.3399	xxi	Cd.3323	x	Cd.3711	lxxx
					Cd.3586	x		
1908	Cd.4256	civ	Cd.4017	xxv	Cd.3986	xii	Cd.4254	xcviii
					Cd.4166	xii		
1909	Cd.4789	lxxxiv	Cd.4605	xlvi	Cd.4664	xxi	Cd.4680	xlix
1910	Cd.5292	lxxxvii	Cd.5049	lvii	Cd.5191	xxviii	Cd.5325	lviii

Session	Navigation and Shipping	Railways and Canals	Factories and Workshops	Strikes and Lockouts
1911	Cd.5840 lxxix	Cd.5529 lxx	Cd.5693 xxii	Cd.5850 xli
1912–3	Cd.6398 lxxxv	Cd.6086 xlv	Cd.6239 xxv	Cd.6472 xlvii
		Cd.6651 xlv		
1913	Cd.7021 lxi		Cd.6852 xxiii	
1914	Cd.7616 lxxxii	Cd.7385 xlvii	Cd.7491 xxix	Cd.7089 xlviii
1914–6		Cd.7847 xxxiv	Cd.8051 xxi	Cd.7658 xxxvi
1916		Cd.8255 xv	Cd.8276 ix	
1917–8		Cd.8584 xviii	Cd.8570 xiv	
1918		Cd.9007 xiii	Cd.9108 xi	
1919	Cmd.327 xliv	Cmd.177 xxviii	Cmd.340 xxii	
1920	Cmd.953 xlii	Cmd.717 xxiv	Cmd.941 xvi	
1921	Cmd.1419 xxxiv	Cmd.1440 xvii	Cmd.1403 xii	
	Cmd.1442 xxxiv			
1922	Continuing Non-Parl.		Cmd.1705 vii	
1922 Sess. II		Cmd.1743 ii		
1923			Cmd.1920 xi	
1924		Cmd.2006 xii	Cmd.2165 ix	
		Cmd.2197 xii		
1924–5		Cmd.2399 xv	Cmd.2437 xii	
1926		Cmd.2622 xv	Cmd.2714 x	
1927		Cmd.2840 xii	Cmd.2903 ix	
1928		Cmd.3043 xii	Cmd.3144 ix	
1928–9		Cmd.3298 ix		
1929–30		Cmd.3497 xvii	Cmd.3360 xiii	
			Cmd.3633 xiii	
1930–1		Cmd.3809 xvii	Cmd.3927 xiii	
1931–2		Cmd.4038 xiii	Cmd.4098 ix	
1932–3		Cmd.4283 xv	Cmd.4377 xii	
1933–4		Not printed	Cmd.4657 xi	
1934–5		Cmd.5003 xi	Cmd.4931 viii	
1935–6		Cmd.5154 xiv	Cmd.5230 x	
1936–7		Cmd.5439 xv	Cmd.5514 x	
1937–8		Cmd.5855 xv	Cmd.5802 x	
1938–9		Cmd.6012 xiv	Cmd.6081 xi	

9–12

Session	Abstract of Labour Statistics	Ministry of Labour	Unemployment Assistance Board	Local Government Board. Health
1900	Cd.119 lxxxiii			Cd.292 xxxiii
1901	Cd.495 lxxiii			Cd.746 xxv
1902	Cd.1124 xcvii			Cd.1231 xxxv
1903	Cd.1755 lxvii			Cd.1700 xxiv
1904				Cd.2214 xxv
1905	Cd.2491 lxxvi			Cd.2661 xxxi
1906				Cd.3105 xxxv
1907	Cd.3690 lxxx			Cd.3665 xxvi
1908	Cd.4413 xcviii			Cd.4347 xxx
1909				Cd.4786 xxviii
				Cd.4928 xxix
1910	Cd.5041 cx			Cd.5260 xxxviii
	Cd.5458 cx			Cd.5275 xxxviii
1911				Cd.5865 xxxi
				Cd.5978 xxxi
1912–3	Cd.6228 cvii			Cd.6327 xxxv
				Cd.6331 xxxv
1913				Cd.6980 xxxi
				Cd.6981 xxxi
				Cd.6982 xxxi
1914	Cd.7131 lxxx			Cd.7444 xxxviii
				Cd.7610 xxxviii
				Cd.7611 xxxviii
1914–6	Cd.7733 lxi			
1916				Cd.8195 xii
				Cd.8196 xii
				Cd.8197 xii
				Cd.8331 xiii
				Cd.8309 xiii
				Cd.8332 xiii
1917–8				Cd.8697 xvi

Session	Abstract of Labour Statistics	Ministry of Labour	Unemployment Assistance Board	Local Government Board. Health
1918				Cd.9157 xi
1919				Cmd.413 xxiv
1920				Cmd.923 xvii
				Cmd.917 xvii
				Cmd.932 xvii
				Cmd.913 xvii
1921				Cmd.1446 xiii
1922				Cmd.1713 viii
1923				Cmd.1944 xi
1924				Cmd.2218 ix
1924–5		Cmd.2481 xiv		Cmd.2450 xiii
1926	Cmd.2740 xxix	Cmd.2736 xiii		Cmd.2724 xi
1927		Cmd.2856 x		Cmd.2938 ix
1928	Cmd.3140 xxv	Cmd.3090 xi		
1928–9		Cmd.3333 vii		Cmd.3185 vi
1929–30		Cmd.3579 xv		Cmd.3362 xiv
1930–1	Cmd.3831 xxxii	Cmd.3859 xv		Cmd.3667 xiii
				Cmd.3937 xiv
1931–2		Cmd.4044 xi		Cmd.4113 x
1932–3		Cmd.4281 xiii		Cmd.4372 xii
1933–4	Cmd.4625 xxvi	Cmd.4543 xiii		Cmd.4664 xii
1934–5		Cmd.4861 x		Cmd.4978 ix
1935–6		Cmd.5145 xiii	Cmd.5177 xiii	Cmd.5287 x
1936–7	Cmd.5556 xxvi	Cmd.5431 xii	Cmd.5526 xii	Cmd.5516 x
1937–8		Cmd.5717 xii	Cmd.5752 xiii	Cmd.5801 xi
1938–9		Cmd.6016 xii	Cmd.6021 xii	Cmd.6089 xi

13–16

Session	L.G.B. Health (Scotland)	M.O. to L.G.B., Min. of Health	Chief M.O. to Bd. of Ed.	Lunacy	
1900	Cd.182 xxxvi	Cd.299 xxxiv		(246)	xxxvii
1901	Cd.701 xxvii	Cd.747 xxvi		(245)	xxviii
1902	Cd.1051 xxxviii	Cd.1344 xxxvi		(246)	xl
		Cd.1343 xxxvi			
1903	Cd.1521 xxvi	Cd.1714 xxv		(231)	xxvii
1904	Cd.2001 xxviii	Cd.2213 xxvi		(232)	xxix
1905	Cd.2514 xxxiv	Cd.2611 xxxii		(220)	xxxv
1906	Cd.2989 xxxvii	Cd.3100 xxxvi		(224)	xxxviii
1907	Cd.3470 xxix	Cd.3656 xxv		(225)	xxx
		Cd.3657 xxvii			
1908	Cd.4142 xxxii	Cd.4289 xxx		(200)	xxxiii
1909	Cd.4679 xxx	Cd.4634 xxviii		(213)	xxxi
		Cd.4935 xxix			
		Cd.4958 xxix			
1910	Cd.5228 xl	Cd.5263 xxxix	Cd.4986 xxiii	(204)	xli
		Cd.5312 xxxix	Cd.5426 xxiii		
		Cd.5313 xxxix			
1911	Cd.5620 xxxiii	Cd.5939 xxxii	Cd.5925 xvii	(207)	xxxiv
1912–3	Cd.6192 xxxvii	Cd.6341 xxxvi	Cd.6530 xxi	(185)	xxxix
		Cd.6342 xxxvi			
1913	Cd.6720 xxxiii	Cd.6909 xxxii		(182)	xxxiv
1914	Cd.7327 xl	Cd.7181 xxxvii	Cd.7184 xxv	(264)	xli
		Cd.7511 xxxix			
		Cd.7612 xxxix			
1914–6	Cd.8041 xxvi	Cd.8085 xxv	Cd.7730 xviii		
		Cd.8153 xxv	Cd.8055 xviii		
1916	Cd.8273 xiii	Cd.8423 xiii	Cd.8338 viii	(6)	xiii
1917–8	Cd.8517 xvi	Cd.8496 xvi	Cd.8746 xi	(25)	xvi
		Cd.8767 xvi		(143)	xvi
1918	Cd.9020 xi	Cd.9169 xi	Cd.9206 ix	(102)	xi
1919	Cmd.230 xxv	Cmd.462 xxiv	Cmd.420 xxi	(156)	xxv
1920	Cmd.824 xxi	Cmd.978 xvii	Cmd.995 xv	(193)	xxi
	Cmd.825 xvii				
	Cmd.992 xvii				
1921	Cmd.1319 xiii	Cmd.1397 xii	Cmd.1522 xi	(221)	xv
1922	Cmd.1697 viii				
1923	Cmd.1887 xi	Continuing Non-Parl.	Continuing Non-Parl.	1922—36–7 Non-Parl.	
1924	Cmd.2156 x				

Session	L.G.B. Health (Scotland)	M.O. to L.G.B., Min. of Health	Chief M.O. to Bd. of Ed.	Lunacy
1924-5	Cmd.2416 xiii	Continuing Non-Parl.	Continuing Non-Parl.	1922—36-7 Non-Parl.
1926	Cmd.2674 xi			
1927	Cmd.2881 x			
1928	Cmd.3112 x			
1928-9	Cmd.3304 vii			
1929-30	Cmd.3529 xiv			
1930-1	Cmd.3860 xiv			
1931-2	Cmd.4080 x			
1932-3	Cmd.4338 xii			
1933-4	Cmd.4599 xii			
1934-5	Cmd.4837 ix			
1935-6	Cmd.5123 xi			
1936-7	Cmd.5407 xi			
1937-8	Cmd.5713 xii			(174) xiii
1938-9	Cmd.5969 xi			(171) xii

17–20

Session	Lunacy (Scotland)	Education	Education (Scotland)	Reformatory and Industrial Schools
1900	Cd.368 xxxvii	Cd.328 xix / Cd.329 xix / Cd.330 xix	Cd.170 xxiv / Cd.171 xxiv	Cd.408 xliii
1901	Cd.755 xxviii	Cd.756 xix / Cd.757 xix / Cd.758 xx	Cd.585 xxii / Cd.586 xxii	Cd.511 xxxiii
1902	Cd.955 xli / Cd.1046 xli	Cd.1275 xxiv	Cd.1108 xxxiii / Cd.1109 xxxiii	Cd.840 xlvii / Cd.1106 xlviii / Cd.1310 xlviii
1903	Cd.1539 xxviii	Cd.1763 xx	Cd.1592 xxii / Cd.1593 xxii	Cd.1549 xxix
1904	Cd.2019 xxix		Cd.1973 xxi / Cd.1974 xxi	Cd.1828 xxxvi / Cd.2160 xxxvi
1905	Cd.2504 xxxvi	Cd.2271 xxv	Cd.2520 xxix / Cd.2521 xxix	Cd.2274 xxxviii / Cd.2508 xxxviii
1906	Cd.3021 xxxix	Cd.2783 xxviii / Cd.3270 xxviii	Cd.2942 xxx / Cd.2943 xxx	Cd.2731 liii / Cd.2935 liii / Cd.3170 liii
1907	Cd.3520 xxx		Cd.3521 xxiii / Cd.3522 xxiii	Cd.3438 xlii
1908	Cd.4131 xxxii	Cd.3862 xxvi	Cd.4084 xxviii / Cd.4085 xxviii	Cd.3759 liii / Cd.4052 liii / Cd.4341 liii
1909	Cd.4619 xxxii	Cd.4566 xviii	Cd.4779 xxi	Cd.4640 xlvi / Cd.4929 xlvi
1910	Cd.5315 xli	Cd.5130 xxii	Cd.5252 xxvi	Cd.5203 lvii / Cd.5406 lvii
1911	Cd.5720 xxxv	Cd.5616 xvi	Cd.5683 xxi	Cd.5753 xl / Cd.5949 xl
1912-3	Cd.6211 xxxix	Cd.6116 xxi	Cd.6242 xxiv	Cd.6296 xlvi / Cd.6502 xlvi
1913	Cd.6825 xxxiv	Cd.6707 xx	Cd.6726 xxii	Cd.7196 xlvii
1914	Cd.7404 xli	Cd.7341 xxv	Cd.7392 xxix	Cd.7776 xxxiv
1914-6	Cd.7944 xxvii	Cd.7934 xviii	Cd.7928 xx	Cd.8091 xxxiv
1916	Cd.8313 xiii	Cd.8274 viii	Cd.8278 viii	Cd.8367 xv
1917-8	Cd.8565 xvi	Cd.8594 xi	Cd. 8648 xi	
1918	Cd.9068 xi	Cd.9045 ix	Cd. 9091 ix	
1919	Cmd.143 xxv	Cmd.165 xxi	Cmd.264 xxi	
1920	Cmd.794 xxi	Cmd.722 xv	Cmd.782 xv	
1921	Cmd.1396 xv	Cmd.1451 xi	Cmd.1266 xi	
1922	Cmd.1723 viii	Cmd.1718 vii	Cmd.1666 vii	
1923	Cmd.1909 xii Pt.I	Cmd.1896 x	Cmd.1885 x	
1924	Cmd.2198 xi	Cmd.2179 ix	Cmd.2174 ix	
1924-5	Cmd.2487 xv	Cmd.2443 xii	Cmd.2433 xii	
1926	Cmd.2737 xiii	Cmd.2695 x	Cmd.2676 x	
1927	Cmd.2939 xi	Cmd.2866 viii	Cmd.2902 viii	
1928	Cmd.3160 xi	Cmd.3091 ix	Cmd.3111 ix	
1928-9		Cmd.3307 vi	Cmd.3312 vi	
1929-30	Cmd.3413 xv	Cmd.3545 xiii	Cmd.3565 xiii	
1930-1	Cmd.3654 xv	Cmd.3856 xii	Cmd.3867 xii	

Session	Lunacy (Scotland)	Education	Education (Scotland)	Reformatory and Industrial Schools
1931-2	Cmd.3976 xi	Cmd.4068 ix	Cmd.4033 ix	
	Cmd.4163 xi			
1932-3	Cmd.4431 xiv	Cmd.4364 xi	Cmd.4322 xi	
1933-4	Cmd.4712 xiii	Cmd.4631 xi	Cmd.4601 xi	
1934-5	Cmd.4838 x	Cmd.4968 viii	Cmd.4850 viii	
1935-6	Cmd.5124 xiii	Cmd.5290 ix	Cmd.5140 x	
1936-7	Cmd.5408 xiii	Cmd.5564 x	Cmd.5428 x	
1937-8	Cmd.5715 xiii	Cmd.5776 x	Cmd.5709 x	
1938-9	Cmd.5970 xii	Cmd.6013 x	Cmd.6007 x	

21-24

Session	Judicial Statistics (England and Wales)	Judicial Statistics (Scotland)	Prisons	Prisons (Scotland)
1900	Cd.123 ciii	Cd.28 ciii	Cd.380 xli	Cd.138 xlii
	Cd.181 ciii	Cd.407 ciii		
1901	Cd.659 lxxxix			Cd.565 xxxii
	Cd.705 lxxxix			
1902	Cd.953 cxvii	Cd.878 cxvii	Cd.804 xlv	Cd.1060 xlvii
	Cd.1115 cxvii	Cd.1317 cxvii	Cd.1278 xlvi	
1903	Cd.1441 lxxxiii			Cd.1540 xxix
	Cd.1588 lxxxiii			
1904	Cd.2010 cvii	Cd.1830 cvii	Cd.1800 xxxv	Cd.2013 xxxvi
	Cd.2040 cvii			
1905	Cd.2336 xcix	Cd.2317 xcix	Cd.2273 xxxvii	Cd.2468 xxxvii
	Cd.2403 xcix			
1906	Cd.2871 cxxxv	Cd.2755 cxxxv	Cd.2723 l	Cd.2924 li
	Cd.2945 cxxxv	Cd.3226 cxxxv	Cd.3169 l	
1907	Cd.3315 xcviii			Cd.3457 xxxi
	Cd.3477 xcviii			
1908	Cd.3929 cxxiii	Cd.3829 cxxiii	Cd.3738 lii	Cd.4044 lii
	Cd.4029 cxxiii	Cd.4395 cxxiii	Cd.4300 lii	
	Cd.4424 cxxiii		Cd.4300-I lii	
1909	Cd.4544 civ	Cd.4914 civ	Cd.4847 xlv	Cd.4604 xlv
			Cd.4848 xlv	
1910	Cd.5096 cxi	Cd.5417 cxi	Cd.5360 xlv	Cd.5164 xlv
	Cd.5097 cxi		Cd.5361 xlv	
1911	Cd.5473 cii	Cd.5981 cii	Cd.5891 xxxix	Cd.5672 xxxix
	Cd.5501 cii		Cd.5892 xxxix	
1912-3	Cd.6047 cx	Cd.6529 cx	Cd.6406 xliii	Cd.6190 xliii
	Cd.6071 cx		Cd.6407 xliii	
	Cd.6602 cx			
	Cd.6650 cx			
1913				Cd.6763 xxxviii
1914	Cd.7282 c	Cd.7164 c	Cd.7092 xlv	Cd.7403 xlv
	Cd.7267 c		Cd.7093 xlv	
			Cd.7601 xlv	
			Cd.7602 xlv	
1914-6	Cd.7767 lxxxii	Cd.7734 lxxxii	Cd.7837 xxxiii	Cd.7927 xxxiii
	Cd.7807 lxxxii	Cd.8126 lxxxii		
	Cd.8148 lxxxii			
1916	Non-Parl.	1916-1926 Non-Parl.	Cd.8342 xv	Cd.8265 xv
1917-8	Non-Parl.		Cd.8764 xviii	Cd.8578 xviii
1918	Non-Parl.		Cd.9174 xii	Cd.9064 xii
1919	Cmd.215 li		Cmd.374 xxvii	Cmd.78 xxvii
	Cmd.294 li			
1920	Cmd.684 l		Cmd.972 xxiii	Cmd.698 xxiii
	Cmd.831 l			
1921	Cmd.1424 xli		Cmd.1523 xvi	Cmd.1255 xvi
	Cmd.1362 xli			
1922 Sess. II	1922, 1923 Non. Parl.		Cmd.1761 ii	1921—1925 Non-Parl.
1923	Cmd.2001 xxiv		Cmd.2000 xii Pt.II	
1924	Cmd.2265 xxv			
1924-5	Cmd.2277 xxviii		Cmd.2307 xv	
	Cmd.2385 xxviii			
	Cmd.2494 xxviii			
1926	Cmd.2602 xxix		Cmd.2597 xv	Cmd.2689 xv
	Cmd.2717 xxix			

Session	Judicial Statistics (England and Wales)		Judicial Statistics (Scotland)		Prisons		Prisons (Scotland)	
1927	Cmd.2811	xxv	Cmd.2992	xxv	Cmd.2826	xii	Cmd.2873	xii
	Cmd.2971	xxv			Cmd.3003	xii		
1928	Cmd.3055	xxv	Cmd.3007	xxv			Cmd.3092	xii
	Cmd.3174	xxv	Cmd.3161	xxv				
			Cmd.3162	xxv				
1928–9	Cmd.3301	xxi	Cmd.3240	xxii	Cmd.3292	ix	Cmd.3309	ix
			Cmd.3241	xxii				
1929–30	Cmd.3426	xxx	Cmd.3414	xxx	Cmd.3607	xvii	Cmd.3553	xvii
	Cmd.3581	xxx	Cmd.3431	xxx				
	Cmd.3649	xxx						
1930–1	Cmd.3853	xxxii	Cmd.3684	xxxii	Cmd.3868	xvi	Cmd.3866	xvi
	Cmd.3962	xxxii	Cmd.3699	xxxii				
			Cmd.3956	xxxii				
1931–2	Cmd.4036	xxvi	Cmd.3963	xxvi	Cmd.4151	xii	Cmd.4063	xii
	Cmd.4187	xxvi	Cmd.4177	xxvi				
			Cmd.4186	xxvi				
1932–3	Cmd.4360	xxv	Cmd.4422	xxvi	Cmd.4295	xv	Cmd.4336	xv
	Cmd.4450	xxv	Cmd.4445	xxvi				
1933–4	Cmd.4608	xxvi	Cmd.4707	xxvi	Cmd.4553	xv	Cmd.4561	xv
	Cmd.4710	xxvi						
1934–5	Cmd.4977	xxii	Cmd.4757	xxii	Cmd.4872	xi	Cmd.4839	xi
	Cmd.4997	xxii						
1935–6	Cmd.5185	xxv	Cmd.5017	xxv	Cmd.5153	xiv	Cmd.5125	xiv
	Cmd.5277	xxv	Cmd.5018	xxv				
			Cmd.5210	xxv				
1936–7	Cmd.5520	xxvi	Cmd.5299	xxvi	Cmd.5430	xv	Cmd.5409	xv
	Cmd.5560	xxvi	Cmd.5547	xxvi				
1937–8	Cmd.5690	xxvii	Cmd.5583	xxviii	Cmd.5675	xiv	Cmd.5710	xiv
	Cmd.5859	xxvii	Cmd.5779	xxviii	Cmd.5868	xiv		
1938–9	Cmd.5878	xxv	Cmd.5877	xxv			Cmd.5967	xiv
	Cmd.6135	xxv	Cmd.6078	xxv				

25–28

Session	Registrar General		Registrar General (Scotland) Ann. Rep.		Registrar General (Scotland) Detailed Ann. Rep.		Statistical Abstract	
1900	Cd.323	xv	Cd.87	xvi	Cd.296	xvi	Cd.306	xcviii
1901	Cd.761	xv	Cd.507	xvi	Cd.777	xvi	Cd.750	lxxxvi
1902	Cd.1230	xviii	Cd.1035	xix	Cd.1258	xix	Cd.1239	cxii
1903			Cd.1517	xvi			Cd.1727	lxxx
1904	Cd.2003	xiv	Cd.2016	xv	Cd.1923	xv	Cd.2192	cii
	Cd.2197	xiv						
1905	Cd.2617	xvii	Cd.2456	xix	Cd.2316	xix	Cd.2622	xciv
	Cd.2618	xviii						
	Cd.2619	xviii						
1906	Cd.3279	xx	Cd.2870	xxii	Cd.2790	xxi	Cd.3092	cxxx
					Cd.2794	xxi		
					Cd.3200	xxii		
1907			Cd.3417	xvi	Cd.3650	xvi	Cd.3691	xciv
1908	Cd.3833	xvii	Cd.4015	xviii	Cd.4275	xviii	Cd.4258	cxviii
1909	Cd.4464	x	Cd.4597	xii	Cd.4808	xii	Cd.4805	c
	Cd.4961	xi						
1910			Cd.5108	xi	Cd.5251	x	Cd.5296	civ
1911	Cd.5485	x	Cd.5617	xii	Cd.5879	xii	Cd.5841	xcviii
	Cd.5988	xi						
1912–3	Cd.6578	xiii	Cd.6143	xiv	Cd.6380	xiv	Cd.6399	cii
1913	Cd.7028	xvii	Cd.6843	xvi			Cd.7022	lxxiv
1914	Cd.7512	xiv			Cd.7332	xiv		
1914–6	Cd.7780	ix	Cd.7893	x	Cd.7699	x	Cd.7636	lxxvi
	Cd.8002	viii	Cd.8160	xi			Cd.8128	lxxvi
1916	Cd.8206	v	Cd.8339	vi				
1917–8	Cd.8484	v					Cd.8448	xxxvi
	Cd.8869	vi						
1918			Cd.9014	vi			Cd.9137	xxiv
1919	Cmd.40	x	Cmd.282	x			Cmd.491	lii
			Cmd.287	x				
1920	Cmd.1010	x	Cmd.655	xii				
	Cmd.608	x	Cmd.980	xii				
	Cmd.700	x						
	Cmd.1017	xi						

Session	Registrar General	Registrar General (Scotland) Ann. Rep.	Registrar General (Scotland) Detailed Ann. Rep.	Statistical Abstract
1921				Cmd.1246 xl
1922	Continuing	Continuing		Cmd.1774 iv
Sess.II	Non-Parl.	Non-Parl.		
1923				
1924				Cmd.2207 xxiv
1924–5				
1926				Cmd.2620 xxviii
1927				Cmd.2849 xxiv
1928				Cmd.3084 xxiv
1928–9				Cmd.3253 xxi
1929–30				Cmd.3465 xxix
1930–1				Cmd.3767 xxix
1931–2				Cmd.3991 xxiv
1932–3				Cmd.4233 xxv
1933–4				Cmd.4489 xxvi
1934–5				Cmd.4801 xxii
1935–6				Cmd.5144 xxv
1936–7				Cmd.5353 xxvi
1937–8				Cmd.5627 xxvii
1938–9				Cmd.5903 xxv

IRISH

1–4

Session	Agricultural Statistics	L.G.B.	Lunacy	Education
1900	Cd.143 ci	Cd.338 xxxv	Cd.312 xxxvii	Cd.164 xxiii
1901	Cd.557 lxxxviii		Cd.760 xxviii	Cd.583 xxi
1902	Cd.1170 cxvi Pt.I.	Cd.1259 xxxvii	Cd.1265 xl	Cd.1224 xxix
1903	Cd.1614 lxxxii	Cd.1606 xxv	Cd.1762 xxvii	Cd.1576 xxi
1904	Cd.2196 cv	Cd.2012 xxvii		Cd.2078 xx
1905		Cd.2320 xxxii / Cd.2655 xxxiii	Cd.2262 xxxv	Cd.2502 xxviii
1906	Cd.2722 cxxxiii / Cd.3173 cxxxiii	Cd.3102 xxxvi	Cd.2771 xxxviii / Cd.3164 xxxix	Cd.2955 xxix
1907		Cd.3682 xxviii		Cd.3469 xxii
1908	Cd.3791 cxxi / Cd.4352 cxxi	Cd.4243 xxxi	Cd.3745 xxxiii / Cd.4302 xxxiii	Cd.4082 xxvii
1909	Cd.4940 cii	Cd.4810 xxx	Cd.4760 xxxii	Cd.4639 xx
1910	Cd.5382 cviii	Cd.5319 xl	Cd.5280 xli	Cd.5182 xxv
1911	Cd.5964 c	Cd.5847 xxxiii	Cd.5788 xxxv	Cd.5670 xxi
1912–3	Cd.6377 cvi	Cd.6339 xxxvii	Cd.6386 xxxix	Cd.6197 xxiv
1913	Cd.6987 lxxvi	Cd.6978 xxxii	Cd.6935 xxxiv	Cd.6769 xxii
1914	Cd.7429 xcviii	Cd.7561 xxxix	Cd.7527 xli	Cd.7410 xxvii
1914–6		Cd.8016 xxv	Cd.7990 xxvi	Cd.7913 xx
1916	Cd.8266 xxxii	Cd.8365 xiii		Cd.8258 viii
1917–8	Cd.8563 xxxvi	Cd.8765 xvi	Cd.8454 xvi / Cd.8940 xvi	Cd.8557 xi
1918				Cd.9088 ix
1919	Cmd.112 li	Cmd.65 xxv	Cmd.32 xxv	Cmd.179 xxi
1920		Cmd.578 xxi	Cmd.579 xxi	Cmd.884 xv
1921	Cmd.1316 xli	Cmd.1432 xiv	Cmd.1127 xv	Cmd.1507 xi

5–8

Session	Judicial Statistics	Prisons	Reformatory and Industrial Schools	Registrar General Detailed Ann. Rep.
1900	Cd.225 civ / Cd.313 civ / Cd.246 civ	Cd.293 xli	Cd.345 xliii	Cd.295 xv
1901	Cd.725 lxxxix / Cd.682 lxxxix	Cd.707 xxxii	Cd.731 xxxiii	Cd.697 xv
1902	Cd.1208 cxvii / Cd.1187 cxvii	Cd.1241 xlvii	Cd.1310 xlviii	Cd.1225 xviii
1903	Cd.1746 lxxxiii / Cd.1676 lxxxiii	Cd.1719 xxix		Cd.1711 xvi
1904	Cd.2218 cvii / Cd.2149 cvii	Cd.2194 xxxv	Cd.1799 xxxvi	Cd.2089 xiv / Cd.2222 xiv

Session	Judicial Statistics		Prisons		Reformatory and Industrial Schools		Registrar General Detailed Ann. Rep.	
1905	Cd.2632	xcix	Cd.2659	xxxvii	Cd.2257	xxxviii	Cd.2673	xvii
	Cd.2593	xcix						
1906	Cd.3112	cxxxv	Cd.3103	li	Cd.2707	liv	Cd.3123	xx
	Cd.3050	cxxxv			Cd.3146	liv		
1907	Cd.3654	xcviii	Cd.3698	xxxi	Cd.3623	xlii	Cd.3663	xvi
	Cd.3616	xcviii						
1908	Cd.4200	cxxiii	Cd.4253	lii	Cd.4272	liii	Cd.4233	xvii
	Cd.4151	cxxiii						
1909	Cd.4793	civ	Cd.4792	xlv	Cd.4852	xlvi	Cd.4769	xi
	Cd.4747	civ						
1910	Cd.5320	cxi	Cd.5286	xlv	Cd.5318	lviii	Cd.5265	x
	Cd.5264	cxi						
1911	Cd.5866	cii	Cd.5785	xxxix	Cd.5854	xl	Cd.5783	xi
	Cd.5848	cii						
1912–3	Cd.6419	cx	Cd.6365	xliii	Cd.6444	xlvi	Cd.6313	xiv
	Cd.6329	cx						
1913	Cd.6916	lxxvi	Cd.6996	xxxviii			Cd.6917	xvi
1914	Cd.7064	c	Cd.7469	xlv	Cd.7081	xlvii	Cd.7528	xv
	Cd.7536	c			Cd.7554	xlvii		
	Cd.7600	c						
1914–6	Cd.8077	lxxxii	Cd.8082	xxxiii	Cd.8092	xxxiv	Cd.7991	ix
	Cd.8006	lxxxii						
1916					Cd.8426	xv	Cd.8416	vi
1917–8	Cd.8636	xxxvii	Cd.8450	xviii	Cd.8680	xviii	Cd.8647	vi
1918	Cd.9066	xxv	Cd.8992	xii			Cd.9123	vi
1919	Cmd.43	li	Cmd.42	xxvii	Cmd.59	xxix	Cmd.450	x
	Cmd.438	li						
1920			Cmd.687	xxiii	Cmd.571	xxv	Cmd.997	xi
1921	Cmd.1431	xli	Cmd.1375	xvi	Cmd.1128	xvii	Cmd.1532	ix

ALPHABETICAL INDEX

This brief index is designed to assist readers to find individual documents in cases where their location is not sufficiently indicated by the Table of Contents. It is based on the key word or words of the title. Where this is identical with the subject heading, no separate entry has been made. Where there is a series of reports under the same title, the page number of the first only is given.

INDEX TO CHAIRMEN AND AUTHORS

This index is intended as a guide to finding documents by the name of the chairman or author as printed on the document. It does not necessarily identify persons, since there may be change of surname, elevation to the peerage under a different name, or change of individual's practice in signature respecting initials and hyphens. Sometimes individuals may be popularly known by both Christian and surname together: readers should then consult the index under both.